Science and Football VI

Science and Football VI showcases the very latest scientific research into the variety of sports known as football. These include the games of association football, the rugby codes (union and league) and the national codes (American, Australian and Gaelic). The book aims to bridge the gap between theory and practice in football studies and presents important new work in key areas such as:

- biomechanics
- sports medicine
- paediatric exercise science
- match analysis
- environmental physiology
- physiology of training
- fitness assessment
- psychology
- social sciences.

Sports scientists, trainers, coaches, physiotherapists, medical doctors, psychologists, educational officers and professionals working in the range of football codes will find this in-depth, comprehensive text an essential and up-to-date resource of scientific information for their respective fields.

Thomas Reilly is Director of the Research Institute for Sport and Exercise Sciences at Liverpool John Moores University. He is President of the World Commission of Science and Sports and Chair of the International Steering Group on Science and Football.

Feza Korkusuz is Director of the Medical Centre and Chair of the Department of Physical Education and Sports at Middle East Technical University, Ankara, Turkey. He is corresponding editor for *Clinical Orthopaedics and Related Research* and is on the International Education Board of *Technology and Health Care Journal*.

The papers contained within this volume were first presented at the Sixth World Congress on Science and Football, held in January 2007 in Antalya, Turkey.

Science and Football VI

The Proceedings of the Sixth World
Congress on Science and Football

Edited by
Thomas Reilly and
Feza Korkusuz

 Routledge
Taylor & Francis Group

LONDON AND NEW YORK

First published 2009
by Routledge
2 Park Square, Milton Park, Abingdon, Oxon OX14 4RN

Simultaneously published in the USA and Canada
by Routledge
711 Third Avenue, New York, NY 10017

Routledge is an imprint of the Taylor & Francis Group, an informa business

First issued in paperback 2011

Typeset in Goudy by
HWA Text and Data Management, London

British Library Cataloguing in Publication Data
A catalogue record for this book is available from the British Library

Library of Congress Cataloging-in-Publication Data
A catalog record for this book has been requested

ISBN10: 0–415–42909–9 (hbk)
ISBN10: 0–415–66616–3 (pbk)
ISBN10: 0–203–89368–9 (ebk)

ISBN13: 978–0–415–42909–2 (hbk)
ISBN13: 978–0–415–66616–9 (pbk)
ISBN13: 978–0–203–89368–5 (ebk)

Contents

PART V
Match analysis 159

Figures

Tables

Preface

The current volume represents the proceedings of the Sixth World Congress of Science and Football. The event was held in Antalya, Turkey from 15–20 January 2007, hosted by the School of Physical Education and Sports, Ankara University in collaboration with the School of Physical Education and Sports at Middle East Technical University. The Congress continued the line of previous conferences held under the aegis of the International Steering Group on Science and Football. The series of conferences was initiated at Liverpool in 1987, later followed by meetings at Eindhoven (1991), Cardiff (1995), Sydney (1999) and Lisbon (2003). The proceedings providing a scientific record of these events have been published by E&FN Spon or by the publishers of this volume – Routledge.

The Steering Group on Science and Football is one of a number affiliated to the World Commission of Science and Sports. This body is charged by the International Council for Sports Science and Physical Education (ICSSPE) with building bridges between theory and practice in specific sports. It does so by orchestrating regular conferences and a major World Congress on a four-yearly basis, co-ordinated by the relevant Steering Group and publishing the proceedings. This publication therefore is a compendium of research activities and findings which are both up to date and relevant to practice. Its usefulness is reflected in the large number of citations evident in peer-review publications within mainstream journals and the applied nature of the contents.

The International Steering Group on Science and Football operates not just to effect links between research and its applications but also to identify common threads between the various football codes. The Congress therefore provides a unique opportunity for cross-fertilization between the football games and the transfer of ideas across them. The end result is a strengthening of sport science support work by extending the knowledge base from which personnel working in applied settings can draw.

The Sixth World Congress benefited from the administrative help provided by the staff of Serenas Tourism Congress Organisation Services and from its supporting institutions, namely the Turkish Football Federation, the Turkish National Olympic Committee and the General Directorate of Youth and Sport. Ernin Ergen and Feza Korkusuz shouldered the bulk of the organisational work, ably supported by their academic colleagues and the Scientific Programme Committee. Without the support of their many colleagues from within the two universities and the highly efficient secretarial help from Biken Inanc, the Congress administration would have buckled under the enormous workload.

The Congress programme included keynote addresses, oral communications, posters, demonstrations, symposia and workshops. A special thanks goes to Surhat Müniroğlu for co-ordinating the link with the Turkish Football Federation and for setting up the workshops. Technical support at the formal sessions was ably implemented by the staff of Serenas.

The presentation of the Book of Abstracts for the Congress was facilitated by Hakim Gur, editor of the *Journal of Sports Science and Medicine*. These abstracts were published in a special supplement of the journal (Volume 6 No. 10, 2007). These are available at: http://www.fssn.org

An innovation at the closing ceremony of the Congress was the award of prizes in the open and poster categories prior to the passing of an Australian Rules football on to the organisers of the Seventh World Congress of Science and Football. The literal pass from podium to platform symbolised the inclusion of the different football codes at this gathering as well as the forward progression of the 'science and football' movement. The location of the next Congress was decided after formal presentations by candidates for host. The outcome was that Nagoya, Japan was selected as the site of the Seventh World Congress in 2011. The intervening years are likely to witness further burgeoning in research programmes to reach fruition for communication at this attractive forum for scientific exchanges.

Thomas Reilly
Chair, International Steering Group on Science and Football;
President of the World Commission of Science and Sports
(a service group of the International Council for
Sports Science and Physical Education)
July 2007

Introduction

This volume comprises the proceedings of the Sixth World Congress on Science and Football held in Antalya, Turkey in January 2007. It reflects the sustained research output in the different sciences applied to football in its various codes since the first of the series was published in 1988. A comparison of the content of the six volumes demonstrates how research programmes have paralleled developments within the games. All the football codes, international and national forms of football, are represented and the range of topics addressed testify to the fact that football is a fertile area for research investigation.

The contents represent a record of the subjects covered in the Sixth World Congress for those manuscripts having passed the peer review process. The ten parts of the book demonstrate similarities with previous volumes and illustrate a balance of work across these areas. Inevitably there is some overlap between different parts, for example injuries in young football players could find a place either in 'sports medicine' or 'paediatric exercise science'. Similarly, some of the contributions in the 'social sciences' section might have been included with 'paediatric exercise science'. The decision was based on attempts to provide a reasonable balance in the distribution of articles among the parts of the book.

Roughly one-quarter of the communications at the Congress were accepted for publication. The editors thank the authors for their careful preparation of manuscripts and also the referees for scrutinising the first drafts. A special note of thanks for coping with the nuances of the electronic submissions and revisions goes to Laura Ramsay and Zoe Miveld at the office of the Research Institute for Sport and Exercise Sciences at Liverpool John Moores University. Whilst the contents constitute but a fraction of the material presented and discussed at the Congress, they nevertheless provide a sizeable sample of activity at the event. They also identify for readers the areas of research into football that are currently attracting scientific investigation.

Thomas Reilly
Feza Korkusuz

Part I

Introductory keynote address

1 Science and football

An update

Thomas Reilly

Research Institute for Sports and Exercise Sciences, Liverpool John Moores University, UK

Introduction

This opening address provides an opportunity to place the Sixth World Congress in Science and Football in perspective. The event is held every four years, previous meeting having been organised in Liverpool (1987), Eindhoven (1991), Cardiff (1995), Sydney (1999) and Lisbon (2003). The meetings are held under the auspices of the World Commission of Science and Sports (WCSS). The WCSS has separate steering groups for football, swimming, skiing, racket sports and cricket, with a group dedicated to Science and Cycling recently formed.

The aims of the movement in science and football are to:

1 bring together scientists whose work is directly related to football and practitioners keen to obtain current information about its scientific aspects;
2 bridge the gap between research and practice so that scientific knowledge about football can be communicated and applied;
3 debate the common threads among the football codes, both in research and practice.

The scientific applications extend to all the football codes, including the two versions of rugby football and the various national football games. Indeed, there is some convergence between rugby union and rugby league and players, coaches and trainers move between these codes. There has also been a degree of mobility between Gaelic football and Australian Rules, with native players from Ireland transferring successfully to the Australian game.

The material communicated at the Science and Football congress is published as proceedings and contributes to the scientific knowledge base. All manuscripts are subject to peer review so there is strict quality control over what findings are reported in the public domain. Details of previous proceedings are listed in Table 1.1 and material from these sources is often cited in experimental reports.

A glance at previous contents illustrates the range of topics covered (Table 1.2). The most popular area of application is match analysis, irrespective of the code. All scientific disciplines are represented and frequently novel use of contemporary technologies are reported and discussed.

Table 1.1 Proceedings of the previous Congresses on Science and Football; the first three volumes were published by E& FN Spon, the last two by Routledge, London

Venue	Year	Title	Editors
Liverpool	1988	*Science and Football*	T. Reilly, A. Lees, K. Davids and W. J. Murphy
Eindhoven	1993	*Science and Football II*	T. Reilly, J. Clarys and A. Stibbe
Cardiff	1997	*Science and Football III*	T. Reilly, J. Bangsbo and M. Hughes
Sydney	2002	*Science and Football IV*	W. Spinks, T. Reilly and A. Murphy
Lisbon	2005	*Science and Football V*	T. Reilly, J. Cabri and D. Araujow

The Steering Group is also pivotal in supporting satellite meetings and facilitating links with relevant governing and professional bodies. For example, its workshop on 'talent identification and development' in Sydney (1999) was a platform for a special issue devoted to this topic in the *Journal of Sports Sciences* (see Williams and Reilly, 2000). The WCSS is formally linked to this journal which was recently the outlet for the FIFA/FMARC Consensus on Sports Nutrition, also published in book form (Maughan, 2007).

Development of science and football

The First World Congress of Science and Football was held in Liverpool in 1987. It was remarkable for a number of reasons, mainly for being the event at which representatives from all the football codes convened formally for the first time. Since then there have been noteworthy developments among each of the football games.

The increasing commercialisation of association football (soccer) has been linked to its massive television appeal. American football arguably has a global audience but without a worldwide attraction. Rugby union and rugby league have both professional high-performance levels, accentuated since the first Rugby World Cup was held in 1987. Practitioners in Australian Rules have embraced technology as much as have counterparts in any other game. Gaelic football provides a model for community engagement with its firm base in the local parish and inter-county systems. The hybrid game of International Rules played between

Table 1.2 Distribution of communications (excluding keynotes and workshops) to the first five World Congresses on Science and Football

Field	No of communications
Match analysis	51
Medicine and environmental aspects	41
Fitness testing	39
Physiology of training	30
Psychology	29
Management and coaching	27
Biomechanics	26
Paediatric exercise science	20
Nutrition and metabolism	16
Physiology of match-play	13
Sociology	4

Australia and Ireland is still striving to bring the two codes together satisfactorily in an international context.

There is now opportunity to study football from a range of scientific perspectives. Biomechanics and physiology are utilised to examine equipment, shoes and clothing, the immediate interface with players and the training and competitive environment, surfaces, facilities and climate; behavioural, social, economic and organisational issues are relevant topics in psychology and the social sciences. The football scenario is constantly changing, this state of flux posing new challenges with each change.

In all football codes there has been a growing acceptance of sports science support services. Support for coaches and practitioners is primarily in the form of expertise in performance analysis, nutrition, psychology, lifestyle counselling, physiology and strength and conditioning.

The emphasis on performance analysis is reflected in the adoption of multi-camera systems for analysis of activities in matches. These services are available to all the top European association football clubs, individual professional clubs and international rugby teams. This service has revolutionised the nature of the feedback given to players and coaches. This type of technology has been embraced less readily in assisting match officials, its main input being in the rugby codes.

Laboratory methods are still accessible to footballers, mainly when there is a link to university facilities. Assessments include maximal and submaximal responses in the case of maximal oxygen uptake and determination of lactate threshold, respectively. Sophisticated assessment of body composition may be undertaken using dual-energy x-ray absorptiometry (Egan *et al.*, 2006). Innovations in training technology are quickly trialled by football players, often before they are validated scientifically. These include strength training modalities for improving eccentric muscle actions. Deep-water running is more readily accepted in the scientific literature (Reilly *et al.*, 2003) as useful in recovery, during rehabilitation and as supplementary training to reduce injury risk. Vibration loading that causes damage in occupational contexts is employed in football contexts without strict guidelines for separating the training stimulus from risk to health.

In all the football codes there has been a growing acceptance of sports science support services. Support for coaches and practitioners is desired in the form of performance analysis, nutrition, physiology, strength and conditioning, psychology and life-style counselling.

Simulating different environments

The work rate associated with match play can be simulated in laboratory conditions using protocols that correspond closely to the activity patterns of competition. In this way training and nutritional interventions can be accommodated. When a non-motorised treadmill is used, the sprint portion of the protocol can be adopted as a measure of performance with power output being recorded from measurements of treadmill belt velocity and the force resisting forward motion.

Hypoxic normobaric chambers have rendered it possible to study altitude and provided an augmented training stimulus, especially during rehabilitation from injury. Heat chambers allow players to cope better with high ambient temperatures but pre-cooling the body has been explored as an alternative coping strategy. The mechanisms whereby pre-cooling the body assists performance in sports like football have been addressed but post-exercise cooling as a means of assisting recovery processes is still to be fully investigated.

The competitive environment is now a worldwide platform for participants in all the football codes. The Irish diaspora means that players can compete as far away as Australia and USA. There is a brawn drain of rugby union players from Argentina and soccer players from Brazil, mainly to the lucrative professional leagues in Europe. Similarly, Europe has benefited from the migration of rugby union players from South Africa and rugby union, rugby league players, coaches and sports scientists from Australia and New Zealand. Such movement entails travel fatigue, jet lag and climatic stress whose long-term consequences for health are unknown. Monitoring such effects places an emphasis on the application of scientific methods and the use of portable equipment suitable for field conditions (Reilly *et al.*, 2001).

Virtual reality environments provide simulations where the competitive context can be visualised and experienced subjectively. In this scenario it is possible to explore individual responses to a range of challenging stimuli. The utility of these facilities is yet to be examined in full, albeit useful in defined contexts such as penalty taking. Here the eye movements, reactions and forces can be registered to identify characteristics of successful performers.

The behavioural and social context

As a social phenomenon, the games are regulated by match officials with varying degrees of power and discretion. Referees and their assistants are treated with relative disrespect despite the fact that they are working physiologically as hard as the players. This level of strain is reflected in their mean heart rate.

The stress on referees is also manifest in the decision-making requirements of the game. The quality of mental performance is affected by physiological state and the concomitant exercise at high intensity. For example, cognitive performance is likely to be adversely affected at the work-rate levels observed in match officiating (Reilly and Smith, 1986; Reilly and Gregson, 2006).

Football in its different forms is also a great means of bringing communities together. Passion is expressed on the terraces and the stands. Fan behaviour is still a problem issue, whether it is friendly invasion of the pitch after an important victory or hooliganism at football stadia in Argentina. Although largely eliminated from its birthplace in the English leagues, crowd behaviour and control are persistent concerns for the game's regulators.

The political context

The political context of high-performance sport has changed enormously over the last two decades, since science and football became a recognised entity. The Berlin Wall entered was a symbol of separation between Eastern Europe and the western world. Eastern Europe, and East Germany in particular, provided the model of state-aided sports science support. This model was in sharp contrast to the funding of the United States Olympic Centre in Colorado Springs, for example. The Australian Institute of Sport in Canberra provided a more recent and more polished model, before its expansion to accommodate satellites in the Australian states with a central co-ordinating hub. Within Europe the Swedish Olympic Centre receives good reviews from its athletes. The Japan Institute of Sports Science (JISS) is technologically the most advanced, with laboratory facilities that are comprehensive and state of the art. Other ambitious programmes include the ASPIRE Centre in Doha, Qatar, focusing first on soccer, and track and field athletics, its aspirations in the former being realised in its victory in the 2006 Asian Games final.

Where the football codes are concerned, there has been a re-think about how best to identify and develop young talent. In soccer France has based its central system at Clairefontaine. The professional clubs in the Netherlands choose to have their own nurseries, a system adopted also in Spain, Portugal and Italy, for example. The Football Association in England has moved from a National Centre of Excellence to locate young talent among the professional clubs. What model fits best may depend on national and cultural circumstances. Around the world there is huge investment in talent development programmes. Thailand is due to follow the JISS model, albeit on a much smaller scale. In countries where soccer is not the top sport, a different model applies. The Irish Institute of Sport set up in 2006 caters chiefly for Olympic aspirants, yet Gaelic football, the other Gaelic games and rugby union dominate the competitive sports environment. The former games are based on the parish and county units whilst the provinces provide the key to success in rugby union. Basketball in Lithuania is the dominant sport so the new football academies in Kaunas and elsewhere have the task of changing attitudes of youngsters towards the game. With organisation and strategy being required for success at international level, those countries without systematic support are at a competitive disadvantage. This necessary support includes the input of well trained sports science personnel.

Overview

The acceptance of scientific applications to the football codes is no longer questioned. Scientific support systems have been promulgated hand in hand with the progressive professionalisation of the various codes of the game at their highest competitive level. These developments have been accompanied by the growth of sports science as a viable profession, most notably in its applied aspects.

The globalisation of the football games has helped to elevate the level of play in the domestic leagues that are most highly commercialised. The outcome is that the cosmopolitan nature of playing populations has made it more difficult to nurture the national teams in those countries, and in the nations whose best players migrate to participate in the really top leagues. The trend has, in turn, placed emphasis on the importance of national schemes for talent identification and development and the incorporation of scientific know-how alongside the craft knowledge of practitioners engaged in such schemes.

Participation in high-performance sport is the prerogative of a relatively small proportion of the active population. The football codes possess great spectator appeal, generate passion and emotions that sometimes spill over into problems of misbehaviour and crowd control. Their main attraction may lie in football as a healthy recreational activity and in an era of increasing morbidities associated with a sedentary lifestyle, as a health intervention. Arguably, compliance may be better for recreational football than for traditionally prescribed exercise regimens. The ultimate benefit of football in its various forms may lie in its ability to promote community commitment in its activities and their outcomes.

References

Egan, E., Wallace, J., Reilly, T., Chantler, P. and Lawlor, J., 2006, Body composition and bone mineral density changes during a Premier League season as measured by dual-energy X-ray absorptiometry. *International Journal of Body Composition Research*, 4, 61–6.

Maughan, R.J., 2007, *Nutrition and Football: The FIFA/FMARC Consensus on Sports Nutrition*. London: Routledge.

Reilly, T. and Gregson, W., 2006, Special populations: the referee and assistant referees. *Journal of Sports Sciences*, 24, 795–80.

Reilly, T. and Smith, D., 1986, Effect of work intensity on a psychomotor task during exercise. *Ergonomics*, 29, 601–6.

Reilly, T., Lees, A., Davids, K. and Murphy, W.J., 1988, *Science and Football*. (London: E& F. Spon).

Reilly, T., Clarys, J. and Stibbe, A., 1993, *Science and Football II*. (London: E&FN Spon).

Reilly, T., Bangsbo, J. and Hughes, M., 1997, *Science and Football III*. (London: E& FN Spon).

Reilly, T., Atkinson, G. and Budgett, R., 2001, Effect of low-dose temazepam on physiological variables and performance tests following a westerly flight across five time-zones. *International Journal of Sports Medicine*, 22, 166–74.

Reilly, T., Dowzer, C.N. and Cable, N.T., 2003, The physiology of deep-water running. *Journal of Sports Sciences*, 21, 959–72.

Reilly, T., Cabri, J. and Araujo, D., 2005, *Science and Football V*. (London: Routledge).

Spinks, W., Reilly, T. and Murphy, A., 2002, *Science and Football IV*. (London: Routledge).

Williams, A.M. and Reilly, T., 2000, Talent identification and development in soccer. *Journal of Sports Sciences*, 18, 657–67.

Part II
Biomechanics

2 The biomechanics of football skills

Adrian Lees

Research Institute for Sport and Exercise Sciences, Liverpool John Moores University, UK

Introduction

The worldwide popularity of soccer has led to an extensive interest in the scientific analysis of the skills of the game. The kick is the skill which defines soccer and although there are many variants of this skill, it is the maximal soccer instep kick of a stationary ball that has received most attention in the biomechanical literature. The soccer kick is three-dimensional (3D) in nature but it is only recently that 3D studies have been undertaken. Prior to that, the studies conducted used a two-dimensional (2D) analysis. Naturally, the information derived from these studies was limited, but nevertheless provided a good starting point for future investigations. Both 2D and 3D studies have concerned themselves with the kinematics and kinetics of the kicking skill. Most have been concerned with the characteristics of the kicking leg although more recently there has been an interest in the support leg and upper body actions.

Other football skills have received less attention. The soccer throw-in is one skill which has been the subject of contemporary interest as it is now recognised that a throw-in in the attacking third of the pitch can provide goal-scoring opportunities.

The purpose of this overview is to report recent developments in the application of biomechanics to selected football skills.

Analyses of the kicking skill: 2D and early 3D studies

Lees and Nolan (1998) have previously reviewed a number of 2D studies. This review has been useful for (a) defining the general characteristics of the kicking skill as it evolves from the young child to the mature adult; (b) providing values of maximal ball velocity (ranging between 20 to 30 m.s^{-1}); (c) establishing the nature of football interaction (ball velocity is approximately 1.2 times foot velocity); (d) reporting data on kicking leg linear kinematics (velocities of the ankle, knee and hip); (e) describing kicking leg angular kinematics (segmental interaction between the thigh which rotates more slowly and the shank which rotates more rapidly during the downswing); (f) reporting kicking leg angular kinetics (joint moments at the ankle, knee and hip), and (g) noting ground reaction forces acting on the support leg during kicking. Some of these issues are elaborated upon in Lees (2003).

The studies referred to above have been very useful for providing a basis of knowledge and understanding concerning the maximal instep kick, but one must remember that the analytical facilities available to these authors were limited. Typically information was collected using cine film analysis, often at relatively low frames rates (e.g. 64 Hz). Cine film by its very nature provides a 2D view of the skill and most authors had neither the equipment nor analytical skills to go beyond their 2D approach. The frame-rate limitation of 2D analysis was the easiest to overcome, and the availability of more sophisticated high-speed cameras (with frame rates up to and beyond 200 Hz) enabled appropriate recordings to be obtained. These cameras were expensive items of equipment and the development of video provided a cheaper alternative. The immediate disadvantage of video was its low frame rate (50 or 60 Hz) which is generally unsuitable for fast skills like kicking. High-speed video systems have been developed but these were as expensive as the high-speed cine film cameras and so provided little advantage.

The method for obtaining 3D reconstructions of a skill was developed by Adbel-Aziz and Karara (1971) but it was only in the early 1990s that this method began to have an impact on sports skills. This was due to the cost of multiple cameras and the development of suitable algorithms for implementing the method. The method required two or more 2D recordings from cine film (or video) and from the coordinates recorded from each view it was possible to reconstruct the 3D position of the joint marker. This was a time-consuming process which required the manual digitisation of many points in each frame of film over many frames and for a minimum of two camera views. Nevertheless, biomechanists were interested in applying these new analysis methods to sports skills in general, and the maximal instep kick in particular. Many reports using this method were incomplete and most have, in general, not managed to identify critical characteristics of the 3D nature of the kicking action, namely hip, trunk and shoulder rotations. Further comment on these limitations is provided by Lees and Nolan (2002).

Contemporary 3D studies of kicking

The increasing availability of suitable equipment for analysing 3D sports skills meant that by the end of the 1990s more detailed analyses were being reported in the literature. These studies in general are characterised by appropriate methodology, detailed presentation of data, including a focus on the 3D aspects of the skill and a sound discussion of results.

Kinematic analyses were the first to be reported in the literature. A kinematic description and a comparison of the kicking leg for the maximal instep and side-foot kicks have been reported by Levanon and Depena (1998) for skilled amateur players. They used a dual film camera configuration and a frame rate of 200 Hz. As well as reporting a comprehensive set of data for joint angles of the ankle, knee and hip in three planes (flexion/extension, abduction/adduction, internal/external rotation) for each kick, they also presented the only data in the literature to date on the orientation of the pelvis during the kick. Unsurprisingly, the authors found that the side-foot kick was slower with the foot and shank angled out more (to give a side foot impact with the ball). The value of this study, however, is that it reports comprehensive 3D data for kicking leg kinematics which had been rigorously obtained. It should therefore be considered as a landmark report in this area.

Nunome *et al.* (2002) also had an interest in the instep and side foot kicks but they also reported the kinetic characteristics of the joints of the kicking leg for skilled amateur players. The kinetic analysis of kicking has been surprisingly absent from the literature since the early 2D work reported in Lees and Nolan (1998). In Nunome and co-workers' study, the authors also used a dual film camera system operating at 200 Hz and reported data on joint moments at the ankle (about 35 Nm dorsiflexion, 15 Nm inversion) knee (about 100 Nm extension, 15 Nm external rotation) and hip (about 280 Nm extension, 40 Nm external rotation, 100 Nm adduction). Small differences were apparent between the instep kick and the side foot kick which related to the slower and more outwardly rotated foot in the side foot kick. The value of this study is that it was the first to provide comprehensive and rigorous 3D kinetic data on kicking.

Changes in the variables that characterise the kick as the speed of the kick increased were investigated in professional players by Lees and Nolan (2002). Ball speed was manipulated by using a speed–accuracy paradigm so as the accuracy demand increased the speed of kick reduced. This was thought to be a more appropriate manipulation of kicking speed than by asking subjects to make voluntary changes. They used a dual film camera system operating at 100 Hz and concluded that (1) the movement patterns demonstrated by players were consistent, but greater consistency was associated with the slower more precise action used in the accuracy condition and (2) the increases in ball speed were associated with increases in range of motion at the pelvis, hip and knee joints. The latter finding was related to a 'principle of movement' which implies that to increase performance, a greater range of motion at the joints is necessary.

Nunome *et al.* (2006) extended their previous research to investigate kinematic and kinetic characteristics of kicking with the preferred and non-preferred foot, again using a dual film camera system at 200 Hz and skilled amateur players. They found ball velocities of 32 and 27 m.s^{-1} with foot velocities of 22 and 20 m.s^{-1} for the preferred and non-preferred foot respectively. The difference in performance was attributed to the greater speed of the preferred foot, which in turn was related to the increased muscle moment at the knee. They concluded that the improved performance of the preferred foot was due to strength rather than co-ordination in their highly skilled players. Of course, the same may not be true for less skilled players.

All of the above studies focused exclusively on the kicking leg during a maximal kick. Kellis *et al.* (2004) investigated the influence of approach angle on the 3D kinematics of the support leg for skilled amateur players. They used a dual video camera system operating at 120 Hz. They also investigated ground reaction forces and the influence of approach angle. They reported that approach angle had no effect on ball speed, contrary to that reported by Isokawa and Lees (1988). They also reported higher medio-lateral ground reaction forces as the angle of approach increased and altered knee joint kinematics from which they argued that knee joint loading would be influenced by approach angle. This study is important as it represents the only study in the literature which has reported data on the support leg.

New methods for 3D data collection

The above studies have used some form of visual recording of data (cine film or video) and through a process of hand digitisation obtained the 3D co-ordinates of relevant landmarks representing the joints of the body. This is a time-consuming process and as a result has led to the use of small numbers of subjects. In another sports skill (the vertical jump), Redano and Squadrone (2002) have shown that 10 trials are required in order to establish a stable mean value for the representation of a range of kinematic and kinetic variables describing these movements. Recently, this has also been confirmed for kicking (Lees *et al.*, 2005b). Thus, a substantial number of subject-trial combinations is required in order to determine the defining characteristics of a skill and this is only possible using optoelectronic data collection systems.

Optoelectronic data collection systems rely on cameras based on video technology to detect the light reflected from spheres attached to the joints. Usually infra-red light is used so as to not interfere with subject performance, and six or eight cameras are used in order to ensure all of the target spheres are visible. Although based on video technology, the frame rates of the cameras are not limited. A typical sample rate is 240 Hz. In this system the target spheres are placed on the limb or joints and special procedures are required in the software to estimate the location of joint centres. (Note in the case of hand digitisation, the joint centres are estimated by the operator and can lead to large measurement errors).

As the use of optoelectronic data collection systems are new to the analysis of kicking, there is need to establish that the data collected from them are comparable to those obtained from conventional film or video systems. The aim of the study by Lees *et al.* (2004) was to quantify the 3D kinematic characteristics of the kicking leg, trunk and upper body during the maximal instep soccer kick using an optoelectronic motion analysis system and to evaluate the suitability of automatic motion analysis for the collection of data on kicking. They reported similar pelvis retraction angles as Levanon and Dapena (1998) on similar subjects, but greater than that reported for the professionals in the study of Lees and Nolan (2002). This in turn appeared to lead to hip and knee speeds which were greater than that shown by the professionals. However, the greater knee speed did not lead to greater foot speed, probably because of complex muscle actions and co-ordination limitations at the knee joint. With regard to the methodology, the authors reported that the optoelectronic method appeared to be robust and suitable for investigations of the kicking skill, with the exception of information around the kicking foot, where great care had to be taken to ensure all targets can be tracked unambiguously.

Shan and Westerhoff (2005) also recognised that the upper body had an important role to play in the performance of the kick. They used a full-body model and a 3D optoelectronic motion capture system to compute selected whole-body kinematic variables. Specifically they calculated the ranges of angular motion of the trunk segment and at the shoulder, elbow, hip, and knee and ankle joints. Their main finding was that in experienced kickers the shoulder joint of the arm on the non-kicking side went through a large range of motion in the flexion–extension and abduction–adduction axes. This implies the arm contra-lateral to the kicking leg has a role to play in influencing the efficiency of the kick. In fact this is a quantitative expression of the action-reaction principle which can be identified through qualitative analysis (Lees, 2002). Shan and Westerhoff also reported greater ranges of motion in the hip, knee and ankle for skilled players compared to novice players, and also remarked on the better coordination of the action in skilled players in a way which enables a whole body stretch–shorten cycle to take place. This was evident as the kicking leg and contra-lateral arm were withdrawn simultaneously enabling a 'stretch' to take place across the pelvis-shoulder region. This was followed by a 'shorten' as the kicking leg and contra-lateral arm reversed their direction of motion producing the action-reaction movement noted above. Thus two important movement principles are demonstrated in this action leading to a greater effectiveness in the skilled player.

The advent of rapid data collection using optoelectronic methods has enabled researchers to investigate specific issues regarding the kicking action. These have still been limited by low subject numbers or trials, and in some cases low sample rates. It was noted above that a quantitative representation of skills only stabilise after about the tenth trial. There is also no normative data for the kinematics and kinetics of the maximal instep soccer kick (which is quite normal in gait analysis for example) that would enable future researchers to make comparisons between levels of ability, age, gender or other factors of interest. Recently, Lees *et al.* (2008) have attempted to address these issues. Their study used 10 skilled players who each performed 10 trials with the 3D motion data collected at 240 Hz and ground reaction force data collected at 960 Hz. A complete lower body analysis was undertaken which provided kinematic and kinetic data for both the kicking and support legs, and pelvis. Methodological issues of 3D angular interpretation were addressed as were the interpretation of the data in an attempt to develop a greater understanding of the kicking skill. Although details of this study are too lengthy to report here, its comprehensive biomechanical coverage of the maximal instep kick would make it of interest to researchers in this field.

Other football skills: the throw-in

The basic nature of the throw-in skill was described by Lees (2003). Since then two further investigations into the throw-in have been reported in the literature, both investigating selected factors which can influence throw-in performance. It is well known from previous studies that the throw-in range achieved is enhanced by a run-up, but the basic mechanism for this has not been identified. Lees *et al.* (2005a) undertook a kinetic analysis of the standing and running throw-in and reported data on shoulder torque. They found that the retraction torque at the shoulder generated when the ball was taken behind the head was enhanced in the running throw-in. This in turn allowed a greater propulsive torque to be generated. More specifically the enhanced retraction torque was generated by the forward action of the trunk as the ball was held behind the head. This represents a stretch–shorten action as noted above for kicking, and the forward speed of the body appears to be sufficient to create the 'stretch' required to enhance performance. In fact there was a very good correlation between retraction torque and propulsive torque confirming that this stretch-shorten action enabled by the run approach was indeed a key feature in performance enhancement.

The role of strength was further investigated by De Carnys and Lees (2007). The role of practice was also investigated in this study. Both male and female subjects took part in a six-week programme of (a) strength conditioning of the shoulder and upper body (b) repeated practice and (c) no intervention as a control group. Both standing and running throw-ins were investigated. The control group showed no performance improvement over the six weeks while the two intervention groups did. The strength conditioned group showed a 7 per cent improvement in the running throw performance which came from an improved release speed. The practice group showed a 6 and 9 per cent improvement in standing and running throw respectively. The improvement in the standing throw came from an improved release angle while in the running throw the speed of release was the influencing factor, possibly suggesting some neuro-muscular improvement of the stretch-shorten action as noted above. The authors speculated that a combination of strength training and practice might be the most effective training regimen.

Conclusion

This overview has attempted to track through the developments of biomechanics as it has applied to two selected skills in soccer. The introduction of fast automatic data capture systems based on optoelectronic motion analysis has meant that high-speed and reliable data collection for kicking and other skills can be undertaken. It is therefore likely that in the near future many more studies reporting the kinematics and kinetic of soccer skills will be reported.

References

Abdel-Aziz, Y.I. and Karara, H.M., 1971, Direct linear transformation from comparator co-ordinates into space co-ordinates in close range photogrammetry. In *Proceedings of the Symposium on Close Range Photogrammetry*, (Falls Church: American Society of Photogrammetry), pp. 1–18.

De Carnys, G. and Lees, A., 2007, The effects of strength training and practice on soccer throw-in performance. Communication to the Sixth World Congress of Science and Football, Antalya, Turkey, January 16–20.

Isokawa, M. and Lees, A., 1988, A biomechanical analysis of the instep kick motion in soccer. In *Science and Football*, edited by Reilly, T., Lees, A., Davids, K. and Murphy, W.J. (London: E& FN Spon), pp. 449–55.

Kellis, E., Katis, A. and Gissis, I., 2004, Knee biomechanics of the support leg in soccer kicks from three angles of approach. *Medicine and Science in Sports and Exercise*, 36, 1017–28.

Lees, A., 2002, Technique analysis in sports: a critical review. *Journal of Sports Sciences*, 20, 813–28.

Lees, A., 2003, Biomechanics applied to soccer skills. In *Science and Soccer* (2nd edition), edited by Reilly, T., (London: E&FN.Spon), pp. 123–34.

Lees, A. and Nolan, L. 1998, Biomechanics of soccer : a review. *Journal of Sports Sciences*, 16, 211–34.

Lees, A and Nolan, L., 2002, Three dimensional kinematic analysis of the instep kick under speed and accuracy conditions. In *Science and Football IV*, edited by Spinks, W., Reilly, T. and Murphy, A., (London: Routledge), pp. 16–21.

Lees, A., Kershaw, L. and Moura, F. 2004, The three-dimensional nature of the maximal instep kick in soccer. *Journal of Sports Sciences*, 22, 493–4.

Lees, A., Kemp, M. and Moura, F., 2005a, A biomechanical analysis of the soccer throw-in with a particular focus on the upper limb motion. In *Science and Football V l*, edited by Reilly, T., Cabri, J. and Araujo, D., (London, Routledge), pp. 89–94.

Lees, A., Rahnama, N. and Barton J.G., 2005b, The stability and between-day reliability of kinetic data for the maximal soccer instep kick. *Journal of Sports Sciences*, 23, 110–11.

Lees, A., Steward, I., Rahnama, N. and Barton, G., 2008, Understanding lower limb function in the performance of the maximal instep kick in soccer. *Journal of Sports Sciences*, (in press)

Levanon, J. and Dapena, J. 1998, Comparison of the kinematics of the full-instep and pass kicks in soccer. *Medicine and Science in Sports and Exercise*, 30, 917–27.

Nunome, H., Asai, T., Ikegami, Y. and Sakurai, S., 2002, Three-dimensional kinetic analysis of side-foot and instep kicks. *Medicine and Science in Sports and Exercise*, 34, 2028–36.

Nunome, H., Ikegami, Y., Kozakai, R., Apriantono, T. and Sano, S., 2006, Segmental dynamics of soccer instep kick with the preferred and non-preferred leg. *Journal of Sports Sciences*, 24, 529–41.

Shan, G. and Westerhoff, P., 2005, Full-body characteristics of the maximal instep kick by male soccer players and parameters related to kick quality. *Sports Biomechanics*, 4, 59–72.

3 Body segment orientations for curved running in soccer players

Paul Brice,[1] *Neal Smith*[2] *and Rosemary Dyson*[2]

[1]English Institute of Sport, UK; [2]University of Chichester, UK

Introduction

Research into locomotion has tended to focus on linear motion, such as straight treadmill or overground running, with only limited data on non-linear motion that would be used in soccer play (Hamill *et al.*, 1987; Smith *et al.*, 1997). Due to the open skilled nature of soccer performance, these non-linear actions are situation specific and rarely replicated, in terms of speed, distance, severity or intensity. Thus, standardisation is difficult and problematic for appropriate investigation. Smith *et al.* (1997) highlighted non-linear motion in the form of curvilinear running (motion along a constant grade of curvature), at a range of radii of 5 m to 15 m during soccer play. The ability to perform and maintain curved motion and perform overlapping runs or channelled runs along the defensive line to remain onside are essential components of the game. With the performance of non-linear motion so inherent in the game of soccer, biomechanical analysis of non-linear motion would aid further understanding of the mechanisms involved in performance of these movements.

The generation of centripetal force, directed towards the centre of the curvature is a fundamental requirement in curved motion. This can be observed in the differing body lean angles exhibited by the two performers in Figure 3.1. The inward body lean serves to counteract a rotating moment, thus facilitating continuation of the curved path. Smith *et al.* (1997) documented that a greater amount of lower-extremity muscular work occurred in the outside limb of the curve, yet it was not clear how the individual body segments contributed to the maintenance of 'body lean'. Three-dimensional kinematics allow measurement of these individual body segment movements in space. As the sagittal plane is constantly changing during curved motion, there is a requirement to have local reference axes, on which any identified lean may be quantified. Once researchers understand how these curved motions are sustained, coaches can identify and improve the technique, and subsequent performance of soccer players in a game situation. The aim of the study was to quantify body lean at the lower extremities and torso, to identify segmental contribution to the maintenance of curved running patterns in soccer.

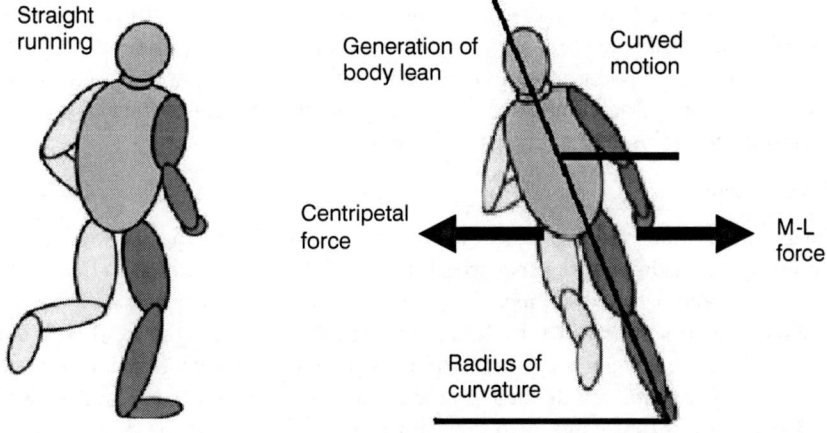

Figure 3.1 Factors affecting curved motion (dark = outside, light = inside limb)

Methods

Subjects

Eight male soccer players (age 21.7 ± 2.3 years, mass 72.3 ± 6.4 kg) volunteered for the study. All subjects were of similar ability (university 1st XI) and reported no injuries or health issues prior to testing. All subjects wore appropriate soccer apparel. Soccer footwear was standardised for all subjects (Mizuno pro model). Informed consent was obtained and subjects were free to withdraw from the study without prejudice at any time. The study had received ethical clearance from the University of Chichester.

Procedure

A pilot notational analysis study, observing 24 English Premier League players, revealed the presence of curved motion to range from 3.5 m to 11 m radius of a curve during soccer play, and also velocities that would be representative of game-related movement. Upon arrival at the test venue, all subjects were given sufficient time to warm up and familiarise themselves with the curved paths (0 m, 3.5 m) and criterion velocities (5.4 m.s^{-1}, 4.5 m.s^{-1} and 3.5 m.s^{-1}). Cone markers were placed on the turf surface to identify the appropriate curved path. In order to avoid a side-stepping cutting manoeuvre during the tightest radii (< 3.5 m) and speeds >5.4 m.s^{-1}, the running velocity was capped at 5.4 m.s^{-1}.

All subjects performed 12 individual trials on natural turf. Motion was monitored by two sets of infrared timing light gates (Cla-Win timer, University of Chichester, UK) situated 2 m apart at greater trochanter height, within the calibration capacity. Subject motion was monitored during each trial by two video cameras (Panasonic VHS), which sampled at 50 Hz using the genlock facility and with the optical axis positioned approximately 120 degrees apart, with a shutter speed of 1/500. Subjects were required to produce the correct criterion velocity

(±5%), with a trial only successful if a full stride cycle of right heel strike (RHS1) to right heel strike (RHS2) was performed within the calibration space. Prior to each trial a 25-point three-dimensional calibration frame was placed in the movement volume and aligned with its axis along the tangent of the curve (Peak Performance Technologies, Englewood, USA).

Data analysis

Image digitisation and analysis were performed using Motus 32 software (Peak Performance Technologies, Englewood, USA). All trials were digitised at 50 Hz using a 16-point whole-body model, with each view digitised sequentially. Five key events of right heel strike (RHS1), right toe off (RTO), left heel strike (LHS), left toe off (LTO) and right heel strike (RHS2) signified one complete stride cycle. A local reference frame was defined from left and right hip joint centres, and left and right shoulder co-ordinates, with the third axis calculated from the cross-product. Data were smoothed with a Butterworth filter using a cut-off frequency of 4 Hz derived from residual analysis. To assess differences in whole-body movements at each segment (neck to vertical (N2V), outside upper leg to vertical (RU2V), outside lower leg to vertical (RL2V), inside upper leg to vertical (LU2V), inside lower leg to vertical (LU2V) and spine to vertical (S2V)) between curvilinear and straight running during an entire stride cycle, data were compared statistically adopting a two-way ANOVA with repeated measures (curve × speed). Differences were reported at the $P < 0.05$ significance level.

Results

The general pattern of a greater range of movement (ROM) was evident during curved compared to straight running as indicated in Table 3.1. Although all computational angles of S2V, N2V, RU2V and LU2V revealed a greater ROM during curved compared to straight running, this was due to differing combinations of maximal and minimal values. Using the LU2V angle as an example, although ROM values between straight and curved were similar (9.84° in curved section, 7.89° in straight section), these were achieved by different maximum and minimum combinations. The lower minima represent a greater amount of body lean.

Table 3.1 Mean angular ranges of motion values of computed lean angles for straight (0 m) and curved (3.5 m) at 5.4 m.s^{-1}; all values are in degrees

Angle	Curved			Straight		
	Range	Max	Min	Range	Max	Min
S2V	13.68	165.28	151.59	5.04	182.69	177.64
N2V	36.02	169.72	139.52	16.30	188.83	171.55
RU2V	12.32	161.20	148.87	10.13	184.69	174.55
LU2V	9.84	152.69	142.85	7.89	173.16	165.27

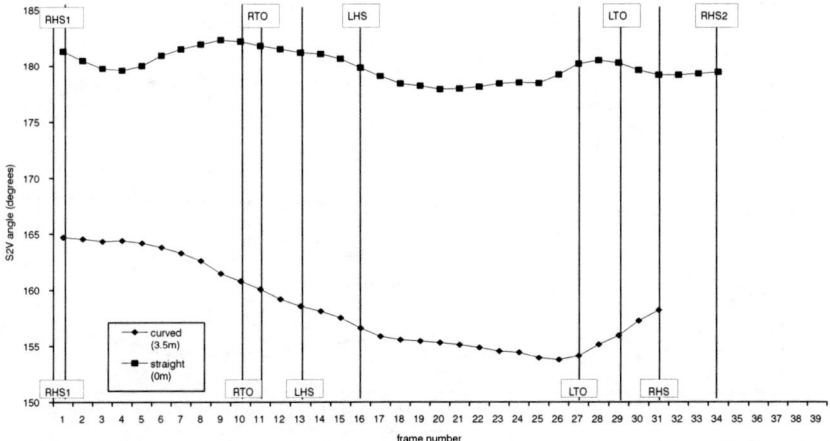

Figure 3.2 Representative trace of the computational spine to vertical (S2V) angle during straight and curved running at 5.4 m.s⁻¹ beginning with right (outer) leg heel strike

Figure 3.2 shows the adaptation of torso lean at the tightest curvature, depicted by the S2V angle. Straight motion is shown by square data points, which oscillate up to 10 degrees around 180 (vertical). Values obtained for angular displacement of spine to vertical (S2V) were computed from the creation of virtual markers of the body between mid-hip (half way between outside hip and inside hip) and mid-shoulder (half way between inside shoulder and outside shoulder), which were projected onto a frontal reference plane to ascertain the spine's orientation or amount of lean throughout the stride cycle. For torso lean angles, significant differences occurred at RHS1, RTO, LTO and RHS2 for curve effect (P < 0.05) and RHS1, LHS, LTO for speed effect (P < 0.05). It should also be noted that the stride time became shorter as the curve severity increased.

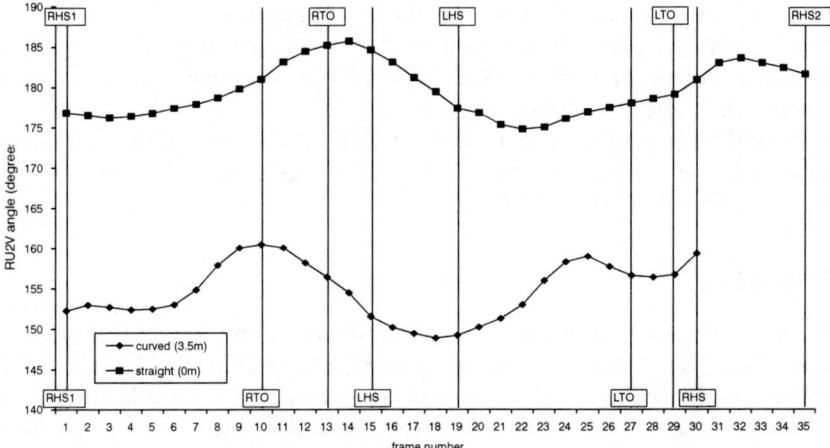

Figure 3.3 Representative trace of the computational outside upper leg to vertical (RU2V) angle during straight and curved running at 5.4 m.s⁻¹

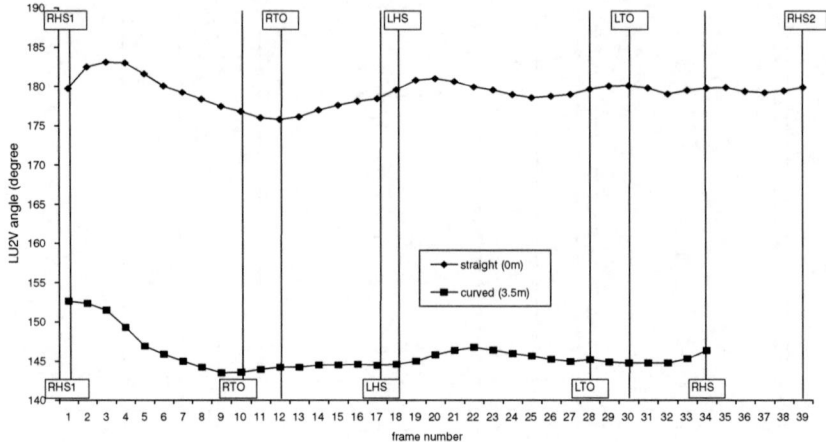

Figure 3.4 Representative trace of the computational inside upper leg to vertical (LU2V) angle during straight and curved running at 5.4 m.s⁻¹

The three main areas of adaptation to curved running were at the torso, and the inside and outside leg. Figure 3.3 highlights the adaptative differences between the outer thigh angle with respect to vertical.

The pattern of oscillation is mirrored between straight and curved conditions, yet the amount of lean is significantly different at all key events for curve ($P < 0.05$), and all key events except for RTO for speed. Mean values were altered from approximately 180° to approximately 155° during the curved condition. During the curved running mid-stance phase of the stride cycle (RHS1 to RTO), the outside right limb showed the greatest adaptive RU2V lean.

Figure 3.4 shows that the thigh segment of the inside leg displayed even greater adaptation to curved motion with LU2V much smaller as the leg maintained adduction, and would represent an adducted position through the stride cycle. The variation in the inside thigh angle was also less, suggesting that this leg followed a more consistent path. In comparison, the outside leg showed a progressive abduction during the stance phase, and a relative adduction during the swing phase of the curved running cycle (Figure 3.2).

For inside leg, outside leg, and torso, angular lean values displayed fundamental adaptive movement patterns which highlighted the different contribution of each segment to maintenance of body lean.

Discussion

Results showed that curved running produced significantly greater amounts of whole-body lean compared to straight running. The S2V angle highlighted the important contribution of the lean generated from the spinal column, due to the mass of torso as the largest segment. Notable differences occurred between straight and curved running of typically 25° greater amount of S2V lean at the 3.5 m radius of curvature.

The outer leg RU2V angle demonstrated approximately 155° throughout the stride cycle; however, the inner leg LU2V angle was approximately 10° lower at 145° throughout the stride cycle. This asymmetry provides insight into the differing roles of the inside and outside limbs, as previously shown by Smith *et al.* (1997). This may highlight the importance of the inside limb to provide a lowered position of the body, which will also alter the position and orientation of the centre of mass of the body during curved running performance. The outside limb can then use strong gluteal muscles to create mediolateral force and centripetal acceleration for maintenance of the curved path. Such mechanisms combined with an eccentric force from the heaviest torso segment provide the three key adaptations required for successful curved running in soccer. Therefore, coaches are recommended to prescribe abductor, adductor, quadriceps, and core stability strengthening programmes to maximise non-linear curved running performance.

References

Hamill, J., Murphy, M. and Sussman, D., 1987, The effects of track turns on lower extremity function. *International Journal of Sports Biomechanics*, 3, 276–86.

Smith, N.A., Dyson, R.J. and Hale, T., 1997, Lower extremity muscular adaptations to curvilinear motion in soccer. *Journal of Human Movement Studies*, 33, 139–53

4 Player perceptions of soccer ball performance

Jonathan Roberts, Paul Neilson, Andrew Harland and Roy Jones

Sports Technology Research Group, Loughborough University, UK

Introduction

The launch of a new soccer ball, especially for a major tournament, often instigates debate about the suitability and performance characteristics of modern balls. The soccer balls are typically criticised for being 'too light' or for 'moving too much in the air' yet these opinions are based on the subjective perceptions of the players, which often do not correlate with objective, scientific tests.

A set of procedures has been produced by FIFA to assess the quality of a football and only those balls that meet the minimum requirements can be used in competitive games. Balls are designated as International Match Ball Standard, FIFA Inspected or FIFA Approved depending on the set of requirements that the ball has met, with the FIFA Approved standard being the most stringent. A wide range of materials and construction methods can still be used, however, to produce FIFA Approved balls, and this can result in a variety of footballs with different playing characteristics.

The aim of this study was to develop experimental methods to elicit, analyse and understand players' perceptions of soccer balls. The objective was to use these methods to compare the playability and performance characteristics of a prototype ball with approved match balls. In future, these techniques may be used to assess ball attributes earlier in the design process

Methods

Four ball types (A–D) were selected for inclusion in the testing – three of the ball types were match balls used at professional level and one was a prototype ball. Five balls of each type were used throughout the testing so that the test was not delayed whilst balls were retrieved.

Thirty-eight male players from four professional clubs in the English leagues participated in the tests. Three of the players were full internationals, whilst twelve were under-19 internationals. Nineteen of the players were defenders, eleven were midfielders and eight were strikers; their ages ranged from 16 to 33 years (mean 19 years, standard deviation 3 years).

The test procedure was outlined to the players at the start of each test. Demographic details were collected from the players and they were asked to sign a participation consent form, a requirement of the university's Ethical Advisory Committee who cleared the test procedure in advance. The players were then asked to complete four skill tests using the different ball types. These were:

- Passing: short and long range passes of 10 m and 40 m.
- Ball control: close control exercises such as dribbling and juggling the ball.
- Heading: a short game of head tennis followed by heading crosses.
- Shooting: straight and curved power shots to a target 20 m away.

The players were requested to perform each of the skills with one ball type at a time. After performing a particular skill, the players were requested to give their opinion on different characteristics of each ball most relevant to the skill performed. Scaled response questions were used to quantify the players' subjective perceptions. For each characteristic, a 1 to 7 scale was constructed with descriptors at each end to give the scale orientation. The questions were printed onto A2 sized hardboard so that the players could quickly and easily refer to them when giving their responses. On completion of the four skill tests, the players were asked to rank the balls in order of overall preference for match-play.

The questions were developed from the results of a previous study (McFarlane, 2004), where players were interviewed to obtain their perceptions of different ball types whilst performing similar skill tests. Ball characteristics of importance to the players and the vocabulary they used emerged from an analysis of the interview transcripts following a procedure outlined by Roberts *et al.* (2001). These characteristics and descriptors formed the basis of the questions, which were then discussed with an elite football coach to minimise ambiguity.

The tests were conducted both indoors and outdoors, on natural and 3G artificial pitches, in both wet and dry conditions. The total duration of the test was less than one hour.

Data analysis and results

Parametric statistics were considered inappropriate for analysing the players' responses as they are only valid for use with interval data that are normally distributed. Although scale values were obtained during the testing, the players were inexperienced in conducting perception tests using rating scales. It is unlikely, therefore, that the players used the scales in such a way that the differences between scale values represented an equal change in sensation, a requirement for interval data. As a result, the scale values obtained from each player were first transformed into a ball ranking for each question and these ordinal data were analysed using non-parametric statistics.

Rank sums were calculated for the four ball types for each question and these were then used to identify perceived differences between the balls. The Friedman two-way analysis of variance by ranks was used to determine if there were any

Table 4.1 Friedman's T values for the questions asked during the passing and shooting tests

Skill	Question	T value
Passing	Ball roll	9.5
	Flight stability	11.6
	Surface pace	22.8
Shooting	Ball speed	17.7
	Lateral movement	22.6
	Swerve	23.0
	Overall preference	26.8

significant differences and Fisher's least significant difference (LSD) was calculated to identify where the differences lay (Meilgaard et al., 1999).

The Friedman's test statistic, T, for each question asked during the passing and shooting tests is listed in Table 4.1. At the 0.05 level of significance, the critical value for T is 7.8; values greater than this indicate that the players perceived differences between the balls.

It can be seen from Table 4.1 that, for all questions asked during the passing and shooting tests and also for the overall preference ranking, the players consistently identified significant differences between the ball types.

To identify which balls were perceived to differ, the rank sum was used to position each ball on a scale for each characteristic, as illustrated in Figure 4.1. Two balls were considered to be significantly different if their rank sums differed by more than Fisher's LSD (Meilgaard et al., 1999). In Figure 4.1, the bars represent the magnitude of Fisher's LSD; if the bars do not overlap, then the balls can be considered to be significantly different at the 0.05 level.

The three characteristics, ball roll, flight stability and surface pace, were studied during the passing test. It can be seen from Figure 4.1 that the players perceived ball B to have a significantly more consistent roll along the ground than balls C and D, a more stable ball flight than balls A and D, whilst ball C was perceived to have the slowest bounce off the surface.

When shooting at goal, balls B and D were perceived to travel significantly faster through the air than balls A and C. The flight of the ball was also considered in terms of lateral movement (when a straight shot was hit with little spin) and in terms of swerve (when sidespin was imparted on the ball to bend the ball flight). The players perceived that ball D moved laterally during the flight more than any of the other balls and could also be made to swerve more than balls A and C.

Finally the players were asked to rank the ball in terms of overall preference for match-play. The results, shown on the last scale in Figure 4.1, indicate that the players preferred balls B and D compared to balls A and C. Further analysis of the data revealed another trend. Twenty of the players used ball C on a regular basis and when their data were considered separately, they rated ball C as being as suitable for match-play as balls B and D. This observation suggests that players' preferences are influenced by the type of ball that they are accustomed to using. Ball A, however, was consistently disliked by the majority of players.

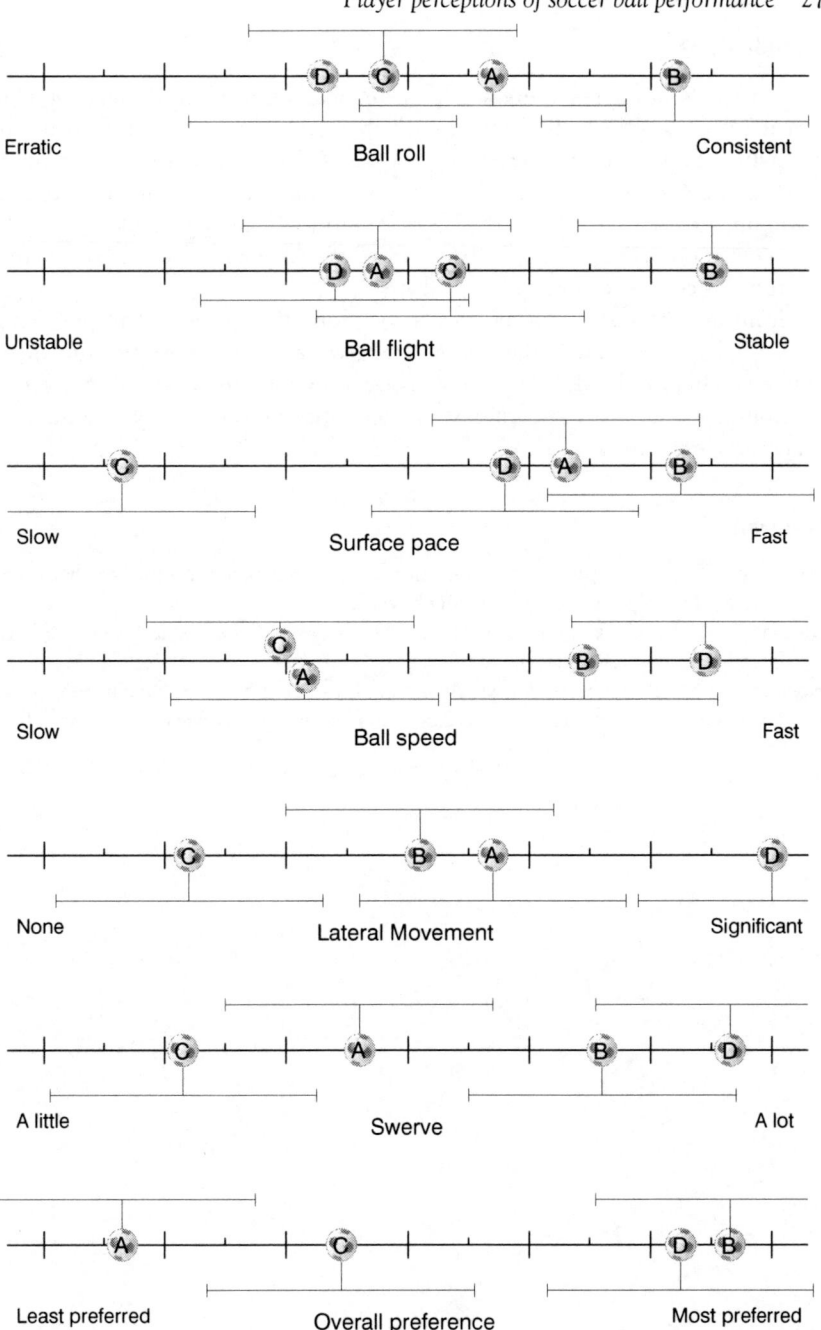

Figure 4.1 Rank sums ± ½ Fisher's LSD for each question asked during the heading and shooting tests

Conclusions

The methods developed were successful in measuring players' perceptions of soccer balls. Significant differences in ball characteristics were identified and the suitability of a prototype soccer ball was evaluated against tournament standard balls. Difficulties were experienced in conducting the tests in a consistent environment as the weather in the UK was notoriously unpredictable. This had a direct effect on the surface the test was carried out on and also influenced whether the test was conducted indoors or outdoors.

In future, the tests could be used to identify differences in ball preference between goalkeepers and outfield players or between players from different football cultures. They could also be used to assess a football in a variety of different environments, such as comparing ball performance in wet and dry conditions or on natural and artificial turf.

References

McFarlane, T., 2004, Psychological assessment of player perception of soccer balls. BSc Undergraduate Thesis, Loughborough University.

Meilgaard, M., Civille, G.V. and Carr, B.T., 1999, *Sensory Evaluation Techniques*, 3rd edn (Boca Raton, FL: CRC Press).

Roberts, J., Jones, R., Harwood, C., Mitchell, S. and Rothberg, S., 2001, Human perceptions of sports equipment under playing conditions. *Journal of Sports Sciences*, 19, 485–97.

5 Development of a mechanical kicking simulator

C. E. Holmes, R. Jones, A. Harland and D. Ward

Sports Technology Research Group, Loughborough University, UK

Introduction

Background

Impacting machines or 'robots' have been utilised for experimental verification of prototypes and computer models of equipment for ball sports. In the case of soccer, kicking machines are used during ball development as they provide repeatable impact conditions unobtainable during human testing procedures. The study aimed to develop a kicking machine to allow the accurate and repeatable simulation of the impact between foot and ball that occurs within the various kicks in games of soccer and rugby.

The design of the kicking machine was based on a rigid A-frame, using an asynchronous servo-motor, capable of accelerating the kicking leg to a maximum velocity of $40 \, rad.s^{-1}$. The various kicks that occur within a game of soccer and rugby can be produced in an accurate and repeatable manner, using an adjustable teeing mechanism and interchangeable end effectors. Previous player studies have stated maximum ball launch velocities of $38.1 \, m.s^{-1}$ and $37.0 \, m.s^{-1}$ for rugby and soccer respectively. High-speed video of soccer and rugby ball impacts at $10,000 \, Hz$, enabled detailed analysis of launch conditions and ball deformation to be conducted. A maximum ball speed of $50 \, m.s^{-1}$ was achieved, with the repeatability of the leg speed calculated to $0.016 \, m.s^{-1}$ (1SD).

Mechanical simulators

Athletes have been extensively used by manufacturers during the development and testing of sporting equipment. However, athletes will tire during testing and therefore provide inconsistent performance. During the human evaluation of golf club performance it was found that 'this evaluation technique requires many trials because weather conditions and physical condition of the golfer at the time of testing greatly affect the distance of the hit ball' (Suzuki and Ozaki, 2002). Mechanical simulators have been developed to overcome the issue arising from athlete fatigue. 'Smart structures have been used increasingly over the last four decades to recreate consistent athlete/sports motions which offer increased repeatability' (Harper, 2006). Mechanical simulators are now used by manufacturers, governing bodies and academic institutes to provide accurate and repeatable simulations.

Mechanical simulators are designed to replicate either an athlete's motion or the launch conditions of the projectile. Mechanical simulators developed by Hatze (1992) and Schempf (1995) aimed to replicate an athlete's motion during the game of tennis and football respectively. Hatze developed a device capable of replicating the human forehand tennis stroke, dubbed the 'manusimulator' (Figure 5.1), which aimed to exhibit all degrees of freedom in the shoulder, elbow and wrist joints, and used adjustable spring dampening combinations to account for the muscular actions at impact. The device was used to analyse tennis racket performance objectively, but was unable to achieve the racket impact speeds measured during game-related studies.

Schempf (1995) developed the kicking robot ('roboleg') as a tool to evaluate existing and future soccer balls and boot designs, whilst removing 'the statistical variance associated with human testing' (Figure 5.1). The complex design was manufactured at a significant cost and was designed 'to approximate, as closely as possible, the human kinematics and dynamics during the action of kicking a soccer ball'. Spring-loaded actuators were used to replicate the thigh rotation and swing of the shank, whilst linear actuators were used to simulate the Achilles tendon. This allowed for a toe-up and toe-down motion, whilst a small gearing system allowed for toe rotation. During the replicated motion, the individual joints are sequentially actuated using user-defined delays. These delays are determined through analysis of human motions. During preliminary testing the roboleg achieved ball velocities of $40\,\mathrm{m.s^{-1}}$, with good repeatability, which was comparable to that of a human kick. However, due to the complex nature of the simulator, the roboleg experienced multiple problems including gear mesh failure and over-heating. As a result this machine is no longer used.

The main issue concerned with mechanical simulators is their increased complexity, as they try to recreate the human structure using mechanical parts. In order to reduce the complexity of the machine, a number of mechanical simulators aim to reproduce the launch characteristics of the projectile's motion. Kotze (2002) in conjunction with the International Tennis Federation developed a high-speed tennis serve device (Figure 5.2). The device consists of a drive arm, which rotates the constrained racket through the throat. The servo-driven arm accelerates the racket to the correct service speed, where it makes contact with a dropped ball at the desired impact location. The device is capable of producing impact velocities of up to $60\,\mathrm{m.s^{-1}}$.

A simplified mechanical simulator was used to test extensively the +Teamgeist™ soccer ball used in the 2006 World Cup, (Figure 5.2). 'The adidas football laboratory in Scheinfeld features a high-tech robotic leg which is used for a variety of ball tests. The machine is able to repeat an identical kick in the exact same angle and with exactly the same speed and power, time and time again' (adidas 2006). The device consists of a pneumatically driven kicking leg which operates as a mechanical pendulum. The pendulum is attached to a simple pinion and

Figure 5.1 Athlete motion simulators; 'manusimulator' (Hatze, 1992) and 'roboleg' (Schempf, 1995)

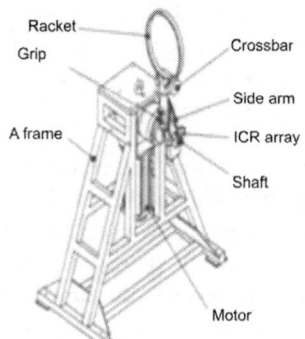
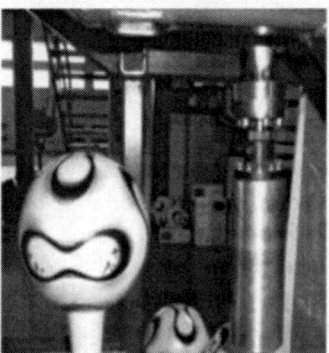

Figure 5.2 Launch characteristics simulators; high speed tennis serve device (Kotze, 2002) and kicking robot (adidas, 2006)

rack system. 'Two pistons are attached to either side of the rack, such that the push–pull arrangement is formed which generates the required linear motion of the pinion to drive the leg (Price, 2006). The kicking robot is only capable of achieving 25 m.s^{-1} ball velocity, which is lower than those measured during player testing studies. This along with the inconsistency of air pressure, associated with pneumatically driven machines, are its main limitations.

Player testing

There have been a number of studies examining ball velocities achieved during the kicking of a soccer ball. Neilson (2003) carried out a comprehensive study of 25 professional players, at five senior English football clubs. A high-speed camera operating at 500 frames per second with a shutter speed set to 1/1000 s captured the initial trajectory of the ball after impact. A maximum-recorded velocity of

$33.1\,\mathrm{m.s^{-1}}$ was stated for a full power kick, with a maximum ball spin of 833 rev. $\mathrm{min^{-1}}$ achieved during an instep and outstep swerve kick. The velocities stated by Neilson (2003) were similar to the maximum measured during a study by Asami and Notle (1983), $34.0\,\mathrm{m.s^{-1}}$.

There is little literature detailing the initial launch characteristics of a rugby ball during various types of kick. Holmes (2006) carried out a study to determine the launch characteristics of a place kick, drop kick and spiral kick (kick to touch). Fourteen elite kickers were evaluated; all players were established kickers and had international representative honours, including four full internationals.

The subjects were asked to perform the different kicks on a specially marked rugby ball at a distance of 60 m from the posts. Each skill was performed until they had achieved five 'good' strikes. The initial movement of the ball after impact was captured using a high-speed camera (NAC 500) operating at 500 frames per second with a shutter speed of 1/1000 s. The maximum velocity of $38.1\,\mathrm{m.s^{-1}}$ was achieved during a drop goal and tumble and spiral spins of 810 rev.min^{-1} and 681 rev.min^{-1} were measured during a drop goal and spiral kick respectively.

Design and development

Design of mechanical simulator

Athlete motion simulators have generally been proven unreliable due to their complex nature. In order to produce ball impact conditions accurately and reliably, the simulator was designed around a simple leg rotation device. Current research suggests that players are capable of producing launch velocities of $38 = \mathrm{m.s^{-1}}$. In order to allow for future gains in athletic performance, the simulator must be capable of producing ball velocities of $45\,\mathrm{m.s^{-1}}$, with a repeatability of 1 per cent.

The mechanical simulator was designed around a rigid A-frame design, manufactured from $50\times 50\,\mathrm{mm}$ steel box section. The tee cage at the front of the welded structure provides a substantial frame on which to base the adjustable teeing system, capable of manipulation about three axes. The velocity of the end effector was calculated using Equation 2.1 defined by Plagenhoef (1971). The mass of the foot was calculated as 3.489 kg, based on the 50th percentile male (Hay, 1993), with the coefficient of restitution defined as 0.5 (Lees and Nolan, 1998), and the mass of the ball 0.453 kg (FIFA, 2006).

$$V_{\mathrm{Ball}} = V_{\mathrm{Foot}}\left(\frac{M(1+e)}{M+m}\right) \tag{5.1}$$

V_{Ball}	= Ball velocity after impact
V_{Foot}	= Foot velocity prior to impact
M	= Relative mass of foot
m	= Mass of ball
e	= Coefficient of restitution

   The drive system uses a Lenze 6.9 kW asynchronous geared servo-motor to rotate the kicking leg, and is capable of accelerating to a maximum velocity of 40 rad.s^{-1} in 270°. The machine's software allows the length and rate of acceleration and deceleration to be specified, allowing different impact conditions to be achieved.

   The counterbalanced kicking leg consists of two aerospace grade aluminium plates, connected by a number of cross members. This achieved the desired strength-to-weight ratio, whilst maintaining a safety factor of 5.4 under impact loading conditions at 45 m.s^{-1}. In order to achieve the variety of different impact conditions, the kicking leg is designed with an interchangeable end effector.

Preliminary testing

The leg motion software was defined to achieve a constant velocity throughout impact. During the total movement (1080°), the leg accelerates for 270° and decelerates for 720°. This creates a smooth profile and minimises stress within the leg. High-speed video of soccer and rugby ball impacts at 10,000 Hz, enabled a detailed analysis of launch conditions and ball deformation to be performed. A maximum ball speed of 50 m.s^{-1} was achieved, with the repeatability of the leg velocity calculated to ±0.032 m.s^{-1} (95 per cent confidence).

Rugby place kick

In order to validate the design, the place kick was first simulated. Player testing data have provided the launch conditions to be achieved whilst performing the place kick. The key variables are the launch angle (30.22°), spin rate (476 rev.min^{-1}) and ball velocity (33.6 m.s^{-1}). The variables to be optimised are ball placement angle, ball position with respect to machine centre of rotation, impact position with respect to ball centre and impact velocity. The launch angle was manipulated by adjusting the position of impact using the teeing mechanism, whilst the ball velocity was achieved by varying the leg velocity during the impact (21.5 rad.s^{-1}). The flight of the ball was captured using high-speed video (10,000 Hz), the footage digitised using Image Pro Plus software, and the ball velocity, spin rate and launch angle numerically calculated. The software allows the displacement of the centre of the ball to be calculated over a given time interval.

Conclusion

The mechanical kicking simulator developed is capable of reproducing the launch conditions experienced during rugby and soccer game related impacts in an accurate and repeatable manner (Figure 5.3). A maximum velocity of 50 m.s^{-1} was achieved, with the repeatability of the leg velocity calculated to ±0.032 m.s^{-1} (95 per cent confidence). This velocity is currently greater than those measured during player testing. The adjustable teeing mechanism and velocity profile software allows for the initial launch angle and ball velocity of a rugby place kick to be accurately replicated. The tumble axis spin produced during simulation is lower

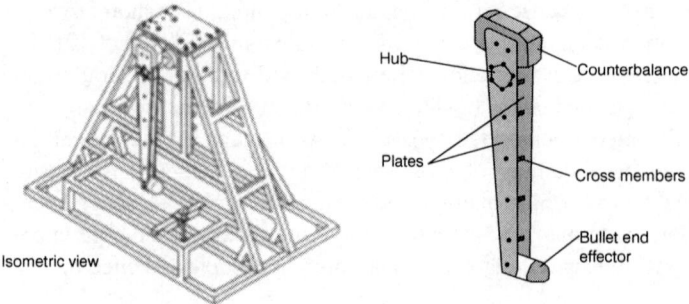

Figure 5.3 CAD images depicting the completed kicking robot and kicking leg

than that recorded experimentally. This is possibly due to the current differences between the end effector and the leg motion of the simulator in comparison to the players kicking action. The development of this mechanical kicking simulator allows manufacturers to create and evaluate new products in an accurate and repeatable manner.

Acknowledgements

The authors would like to thank Steve Carr, Andrew Hallam and Neville Carpenter for their manufacturing, design and electrical support. They would also like to thank their collaborators, adidas.

References

adidas, 2006, 'Testing and development of the adidas +Teamgeist'. http://www.press.adidas.com(Accessed 01/09/06).

Asami, T. and Nolte, V., 1983, Analysis of powerful ball kicking. In: *Biomechanics VIII*, edited by Matsui, H. and Kobayashi, K. (Baltimore, MD: University Park Press), pp. 695–700.

FIFA., 2006, *Laws of the game: the ball*. http://www.fifa.com. (Accessed 01/09/06).

Harper, T., 2006, Robotic simulation of golf swings. PhD Thesis (unpublished). Loughborough University, UK.

Hatze, H., 1992, The effectiveness of grip bands in reducing racket vibration transfer and slipping. *Medicine and Science in Sports and Exercise*, 24, 226–330.

Hay, J., 1993, *The Biomechanics of Sports Techniques*. (Englewood Cliffs, NJ: Prentice Hall).

Holmes, C., 2006, Ball launch characteristics of elite rugby union players. *Engineering of Sport*, 6, 211–16.

Kotze, J., 2002, A tennis serve impact simulation machine. *Engineering of Sport*, 4, 477–83.

Lees, A. and Nolan, L., 1998, The biomechanics of soccer: a review. *Journal of Sports Sciences*, 16, 221–34.

Neilson, P., 2003, Dynamic soccer ball performance measurement. 5th World Congress of Science and Football. 11–15 April, Lisbon, Portugal.

Plagenhoef, S., 1971, *Patterns of Human Movement*. (Englewood Cliffs, NJ. Prentice Hall).

Price, D., 2006, 'Advanced modelling of soccer balls'. PhD Thesis (restricted access). Loughborough University, UK.

Schempf, H., 1995, Roboleg: a robotic soccer-ball kicking leg. *IEEE International Conference on Robotics and Automation.* Nagoya, Japan: IEEE, pp. 1314–19.

Suzuki, M. and Ozaki, Y. 2002, Three dimensional analysis of a new golf swing robot emulating skilful golfers. *Engineering of Sport*, 4, 450–5.

6 Foot interaction during kicking in Australian Rules football

Kevin Ball

Centre for Ageing, Rehabilitation, Exercise and Sport, Victoria University, Australia

Introduction

Kicking is the most important skill in Australian Rules football (ARF). A major technical factor and coaching cue in coaching kicking is the nature of contact with the ball (Ball, 2006). While the nature of impact has been a focus of research in soccer (e.g. Tsaousidis and Zatsiorsky, 1996; Bull Andersen et al., 1999; Nunome et al., 2006), there are no reports in the scientific literature for ARF. Importantly, Tsaousidis and Zatsiorsky (1996) reported that work could be done on a soccer ball during impact due to the relatively long contact times and distance the ball moved while in contact with the foot. This information has important implications for conditioning and coaching cues. On a more general level, no ARF data exist in the scientific literature for impact characteristics during kicking of an ARF ball.

The aims of this study were to provide basic information on impact during an ARF kick, to determine if work could be performed on the ball during an ARF kick, and to examine if differences in impact characteristics existed for different length kicks.

Methods

Eight elite level Australian Football League (AFL, age 23.3 ± 2.5 years, height 1.83 ± 0.31 m, mass 91 ± 10 kg) footballers kicked an Australian Rules football over distances of 30 m and 50 m using the drop punt technique. All kicks were performed using Sherrin ARF footballs (Sherrin Australia – used in AFL competition, mass = 450 g) which were inflated to AFL specified pressure range of 62–76 kPa and were monitored for pressure changes during testing. The venue was the regular training ground for the team.

For each kick, players performed their preferred run-up approach and kicked from a line indicated by two markers. Another player was positioned at a distance of 30 m from the kick line for a short kick and at 50 m for a long kick. Trials were conducted until a good kick was obtained. A good kick was defined as one that was accurate (the player being targeted could catch – termed mark in ARF – the ball at the specified distance without having to move more than one step in any direction) and typical of the player's technique (based on the kicker and the kicking coach's subjective opinion).

Video records were captured for each kick using a Redlake Motionscope PCI 1000 high-speed video camera (Redlake, San Diego) sampling at 1000 Hz with good kicks stored to disk.

From high-speed video footage, two frames were identified: these were at initial contact of foot and ball (contact) and the frame immediately before the foot and ball separated after impact (release). Four points (head of the fibula, lateral malleolus, top point of ball, bottom point of ball) were digitised using Silicon Coach analysis tools. All points were digitized twice with the average of the two points used in further analysis. Coordinates (XY) for the four points at contact and release were transferred to Microsoft Excel for further analysis. The XY coordinates of the head of the fibula and the lateral malleolus were used to define the shank angle. The shank was defined as the angle between the horizontal axis and the line between the ankle of the kicking foot and the head of the fibula. The change in shank angle was the difference between the shank angle at contact and the shank angle at release. The XY coordinates for the top and bottom of the ball were used to approximate the centre of the ball. Distance the ball moved while in contact with the ball was defined as the distance between the centre of the ball at impact and the centre of the ball at release.

To calculate change in ball velocity, the five frames immediately before contact (initial velocity) and five frames immediately after release (final velocity) were used. For initial ball velocity, the top and bottom of the ball were digitized and averaged to approximate the centre of the ball. This procedure was performed for all five frames and the velocity between each frame (i.e. change in displacement divided by 0.001 s) was calculated. Initial ball velocity was then calculated from ball displacement as the average of frame-to-frame velocities between the five frames. Change in ball velocity was calculated by determining the difference between initial and final ball velocity in the horizontal and vertical direction and then summing the two components.

Work performed on the ball (mass × acceleration × distance) was approximated using the mass of the ball (450 g), the time the ball was in contact with the foot and the change in ball velocity data to calculate acceleration and the distance the ball moved while in contact with the foot. Time in contact between the foot and the ball was defined as the difference in time between contact and release. This time was calculated using the timer function supplied by Silicon Coach.

To compare long and short kicks, t-tests were conducted. Effect sizes of large (d > 1.2) medium (d > 0.6) and small (d > 0.2) as defined by Cohen (1988) were used to provide more information for each analysis. An alpha level of $P = 0.05$ was set for significance.

Results

Table 6.1 reports mean and standard deviation values for measured variables as well as the results of the t-tests comparing long and short kicks.

Table 6.1 Mean and standard deviation of measured parameters and statistical comparison of long and short kicks

		Distance the ball moved (m)	Change in shank angle (degrees)	Time in contact (ms)	Change in ball velocity (m.s⁻¹)	Work (J)
Long kick (50 m)	Mean	0.24	18	10.0	25.0	271
	SD	0.06	3	1.1	1.1	36
Short kick (30 m)	Mean	0.19	14	9.8	22.1	198
	SD	0.02	2	1.2	1.8	43
t-test (P-value)		0.068	0.048	0.79	0.027	0.001
Effect size (*d*)		0.046	0.049	0.005	0.063	0.115
		Small effect	Small effect	–	Medium effect	Medium effect

The mean 'time in contact' between the foot and ball was 10 ms with a maximum of 13 ms recorded for one of the long kicks. The mean 'distance the ball moved' during contact was 0.24 m and the mean 'change in shank angle' was 18 degrees. Work done on the ball for the long kick was 271 J and 198 J for the short kick.

Short and long kicks differed significantly for 'change in ball velocity', 'change in shank angle' and 'work done' on the ball. In all cases, longer kicks produced the greater values. A small non-significant effect size existed between short and long kicks for 'distance the ball moved' while in contact with the foot. A medium effect existed for change in 'Bball velocity'. No difference existed between kicks for 'time in contact' between foot and ball.

Discussion

The mean time in contact between the foot and the ball of 9.8 ms for the short kick and 10 ms for the long kick lay between values reported for soccer kicking (16 ms, Tsaousidis and Zatsiorsky 1996: 9 ms, Asai *et al.*, 1995). The mean distance the ball moved while in contact with the foot (0.19 m for short kicks and 0.24 m for long kicks) also lay between values reported for soccer (0.26 m, Tsaousidis and Zatsiorsky, 1996: 0.15 m, Asai *et al.*, 1995). Work done on the ARF ball was less than the 290–310 J calculated from data reported by Tsaousidis and Zatsiorsky (1996) for the soccer kick. Given the ARF ball is kicked while it is moving and differs in shape from the soccer ball, differences in these values might be expected. As well, the kicks performed in this study were not maximal, compared to maximal kicks studied by Tsaousidis and Zatsiorsky (1996). No comparative data exist for change in shank angle or change in ball velocity.

Work is done on the ball during the kick in ARF. The duration of impact and distance the ball moved during time in contact with the foot were both considerable. Similar to the conclusions of Tsaousidis and Zatsiorsky (1996) for soccer kicking, as work can be done on the ball during impact, it is not appropriate to use momentum equations for ARF kicking.

Differences existed between short and long kicks at ball contact. The shank moved through a greater range for long kicks compared to short kicks (18° compared to 14°). More work was done on the ball for the long kick. As well, a small non-significant effect existed for the distance the ball moved while in contact with the boot, with the long kick moving the ball 0.05 m further than the short kick (P = 0.068 only). However, no difference existed for contact times. This indicated greater power existed for longer kicks, as might be expected

The change in shank angle, the work done on the ball and distance the ball moves during the time it is in contact with the foot have implications for training of kicking skills. Given the large changes that existed for these parameters, muscular force generated at the hip and/or knee can be applied to the ball during ball contact. Conversely, a lack of force applied at impact will lead to reduced work on the ball and hence lower resultant ball speeds and kicking distances. Post-hoc evaluation of the knee angle during impact indicated that between 8° and 20° of knee extension was produced, confirming that the quadriceps has the potential to apply force to the ball during ball contact. As the camera image was maximized to examine ball contact, hip angles and pelvic motion could not be evaluated. However, there might also be hip flexion and pelvic tilt during impact and these movements might also allow for development (or absorption) of force. The examination of pelvic motion during ball impact is an important direction for this work.

Conclusions

This study has provided basic data describing the ball-to-foot contact during an ARF kick and has highlighted a number of important points. During an ARF kick, the ball remains in contact with the foot and moves enough distance for work to be performed. This has important implications for training and conditioning the kicking skill. Significant differences existed between short and long kicks for amount of work done and change in shank angle while the ball was in contact with the boot.

References

Asai, T., Akatsuka, T. and Kaga, M., 1995, Impact process in kicking in football. In: *Book of Abstracts. XVth Congress of the International Society of Biomechanics*, edited by Hakkinen, K., Keskinen, K.L., Komi, P.V. and Mero, A., (Jyvaskyla, Finland: Gummeras Printing), pp. 74–5.

Ball, K., 2006, Kicking and injury. In *AFL 2006 National Coaching Conference notes*. Australian Football Association.

Bull Andersen, T., Dorge, H.C. and Thomsen, F.I., 1999, Collisions in soccer kicking. *Sports Engineering*, 2, 121–5.

Cohen, J., 1988, *Statistical Power Analysis for the Behavioural Sciences,* 2nd edn, (Hillsdale, NJ: Lawrence Erlbaum Associates).

Nunome, H., Lake, M., Georgakis, A. and Stergioulas, L.K., 2006, Impact phase kinematics of instep kicking in soccer. *Journal of Sports Sciences,* 24, 11–22.

Tsaousidis. N. and Zatsiorsky, V., 1996, Two types of ball-effector interaction and their relative contribution to soccer kicking. *Human Movement Science,* 15, 861–76.

7 Ball–foot interaction in impact phase of instep soccer kicking

Hironari Shinkai,[1] *Hiroyuki Nunome,*[1]
Yasuo Ikegami[1] *and Masanori Isokawa*[2]

[1] Research Centre of Health, Physical Fitness and Sports, Nagoya University,
Japan; [2] Department of Health Promotion Sciences, Tokyo Metropolitan
University, Japan

Introduction

There are various collisions in many sports activities. In soccer, the most typical collision is impact on the ball during kicking. To date, several papers have focused on the ball-impact phase of soccer kicking (Asami and Nolte, 1983; Asai *et al.*, 1995, 2002; Tsaousidis and Zatsiorsky, 1996; Tol *et al.*, 2002; Nunome *et al.*, 2006). However, in soccer instep kicking, as the contact time between the ball and foot lasts approximately 10 ms, only a few studies have adequately captured this phase using an sufficiently high-speed sampling rate (Asai *et al.*, 1995, 2002; Tol *et al.*, 2002; Nunome *et al.*, 2006).

Previous authors who have analysed foot angular kinematics during ball contact reported only on its plantar flexion motion (Asami and Nolte, 1983; Asai *et al.*, 1995, 2002; Tol *et al.*, 2002; Nunome *et al.*, 2006). However, in instep kicking, soccer players usually strike the ball with the medial side of the instep not with the centre of instep (Tol *et al.*, 2002). In these cases, the foot moves three-dimensionally and includes abduction/adduction and inversion/eversion motions.

From a dynamics viewpoint, it is reasonable to suppose that the passive motion of the foot during ball contact, as in plantar flexion, is due to the reaction force acting from the ball. Tol *et al.* (2002) reported that the impact force (preferably peak force) that repeatedly occurs during ball contact is related to anterior ankle impingement syndrome. Thus, understanding the nature of this force during ball contact is very important, not only for performance enhancement, but also for prevention of injury. However, there is only one study illustrating the interaction between the foot and ball using an unusual toe-kicking technique (Tsaousidis and Zatsiorsky, 1996). Moreover, there are only two studies in which the peak magnitude of the ball reaction force was estimated (Asai *et al.*, 2002; Tol *et al.*, 2002). In the present study, an attempt is made to illustrate the nature of ball–foot interaction and to quantify the peak passive force on the foot more adequately using ultra-high speed cameras.

The present study, therefore, has three aims related to the impact phase of instep soccer kicking: (1) to illustrate the three-dimensional motion of the foot (plantar/dorsal flexion, abduction/adduction, inversion/eversion), (2) to quantify the ball deformation and displacement of its centre of gravity and (3) to estimate the peak magnitude of the ball reaction force acting on the foot.

Methods

Eleven experienced male soccer players (age $= 21.5 \pm 2.0$ years; height $= 1.75 \pm 0.06$ m; mass $= 67.6 \pm 6.3$ kg) participated in this study after providing informed written consent. All participants had palyed for more than ten years and preferred to kick the ball using their right leg. After adequate warm-up, they were instructed to perform ten consecutive maximal instep kicks to the centre of a goal net 11 m away. The target was the centre region of the net (1 m square). Two successful shots that hit the target and had minimal ball spin were selected for each subject. A FIFA-approved Size 5 soccer ball (mass $= 0.43$ kg) was used and its inflation was maintained throughout the trials at 900 hPa. All subjects wore the same type of shoes to minimize the effect of shoe type on the ball–foot interaction. Two electrically synchronized ultra-high-speed video cameras (MEMRECAM fx-6000, NAC Inc., Tokyo, Japan) located to the lateral side and behind were used. The sampling rate of 5000 Hz was used to adequately analyse the foot and ball behaviour during ball impact.

Hemisphere markers were fixed securely onto several body landmarks on the lateral side of the kicking limb, including the middle of the thigh, lateral epicondyle, head of fibula, lateral malleolus, lateral side of calcaneus, fifth metatarsal base and fifth metatarsal head (see Figure 7.1a). The direct linear transformation (DLT) method was used to obtain the three-dimensional coordinates of each marker. As shown in Figure 7.1a, the segments of thigh, shank and foot were defined as vectors (S_{Thigh}, S_{Shank} and $S_{Foot,}$ respectively). The foot plantar/dorsal flexion angle was defined as the angle between S_{Shank} and S_{Foot} on the plane perpendicular to the vector (V_{FS}) made by the cross-product of S_{Foot} and S_{Shank}. The abduction/adduction angle was defined as the angle between the vectors (V_{ST}) made by the cross-product of S_{Shank} and S_{Thigh} and V_{FS} on the plane perpendicular to S_{Shank}. The inversion/eversion angle was defined as the angle between S_{Shank} and the vector (V_{F}) defined by the cross-product of S_{Foot} and vector pointing from the lateral side of the calcaneus toward the lateral malleolus on the plane perpendicular to vector (V_{S-SF}) defined by the cross-product of S_{Shank} and V_{FS}.

The displacement of the centre of gravity of the ball (CGB) was acquired using the following procedure from the lateral side image. First, from five points on the right half circumference of the ball (the opposite side of the foot-contacting face), the geometric centre of the ball was obtained (CB). Next, the distance between the marker on the fifth metatarsal base and the CB was measured in each frame. The change in distance between the marker and the CB from the instant of foot contact was defined as ball deformation. Third, the ball was divided into three parts: a) right half of the ball (assumed no deformation), b) left half of the ball being deformed and c) the part actually in contact with the foot which was assumed to be a flat plane perpendicular to the CGB trajectory (see Figure 7.1b). Each part was transposed to three-dimensional hemisphere and circular

(a)

(b)

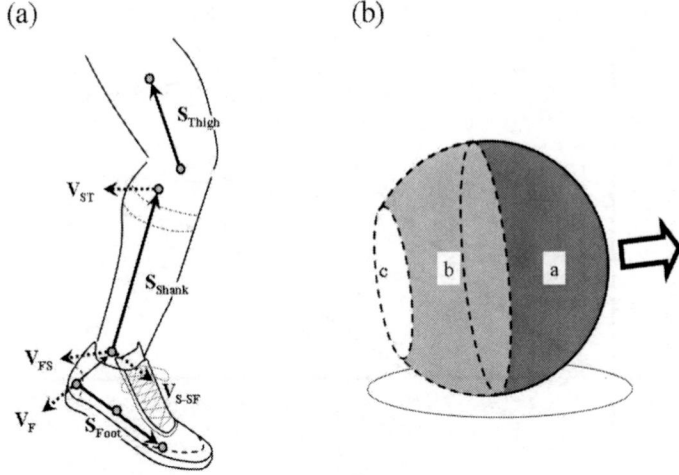

Figure 7.1 (a) Definition of marker location and vector for calculation of 3-D foot angular motion; (b) 3-D hemisphere model of the deformed ball divided into three parts

disc model and its centre of the gravity was computed. Finally, the displacement of the CGB was computed using the centre of gravity of each part.

The contact time of the foot with the ball was obtained from the number of frames in which contact between them was observed from the lateral side image. Foot velocity was calculated from displacement of the fifth metatarsal base which was assumed to approximately reflect the position of the foot's centre of gravity. The CGB velocity was calculated and the velocity of the point of right edge of the ball was also calculated for comparison. The initial ball velocity was computed as the average of the 3 ms just after impact.

The ball deformation and CGB velocity were smoothed using a Butterworth digital low-pass filter with a cut-off frequency at 300 Hz. The filtered ball deformation change was used to measure the peak deformation and its time of occurrence. The filtered CGB velocity change was also used for estimation of the peak magnitude of the force acting from the ball. It was expected that the peak ball reaction force occurs when the ball is maximally deformed. The peak acceleration of the CGB was computed as the slope of linear regression lines fitted to its velocity change between 1 ms before and after the time of peak deformation. Subsequently the peak ball reaction force was calculated by multiplying the peak acceleration and the mass of the ball.

It can be seen that the unsmoothed changes of the foot angular motion had sufficient quality to describe precisely its nature during ball impact. Thus, they were demonstrated as raw changes.

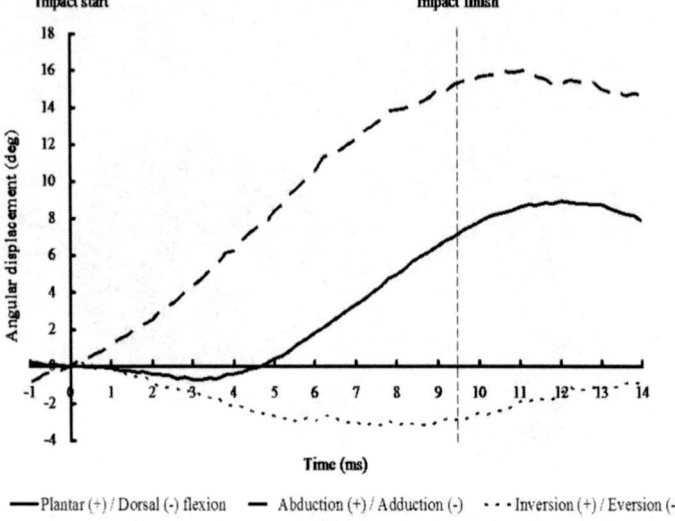

Figure 7.2 Three-dimensional angular displacement of the foot during ball impact phase; the baseline was defined as the position of the foot at initial ball contact

Results

Figure 7.2 shows the average angular displacement of the foot during ball impact. The average contact time between the foot and ball during kicking was 9.5 $\pm$ 0.5 ms. The foot was distinctively plantarflexed (7.1 $\pm$ 6.2°), abducted (15.3 $\pm$ 5.9°) and everted (2.9 $\pm$ 1.9°) during contact with the ball. As shown, the foot began to be abducted and everted just after the moment of ball contact. In contrast, the foot was dorsiflexed slightly at the beginning of the impact, and then began to plantarflex after the middle of the impact.

The average foot velocity just before impact was 20.6 $\pm$ 1.0 m.s^{-1}, the average initial ball velocity was 28.8 $\pm$ 1.7 m.s^{-1} and the average ball–foot velocity ratio was 1.40 $\pm$ 0.07. The changes of the CGB, ball right edge, foot velocity and the ball deformation are shown in Figure 7.3. There was an apparent time lag (2.2 $\pm$ 0.2 ms) for the onset of the CGB and ball right edge velocity. The peak deformation of the ball was 6.8 $\pm$ 0.6 cm and its time of occurrence was 4.3 $\pm$ 0.3 ms after ball contact. It can be seen that the CGB velocity exceeded that of the foot after the peak ball deformation (see Figure 7.3). The maximum ball reaction force calculated from the CGB velocity slope was 2847 $\pm$ 538 N.

Discussion

The first purpose of this study is to describe the three-dimensional motion of the foot during ball impact. The results of the present study succeeded in establishing a new, complicated feature of foot motion during ball impact. Prior to the known

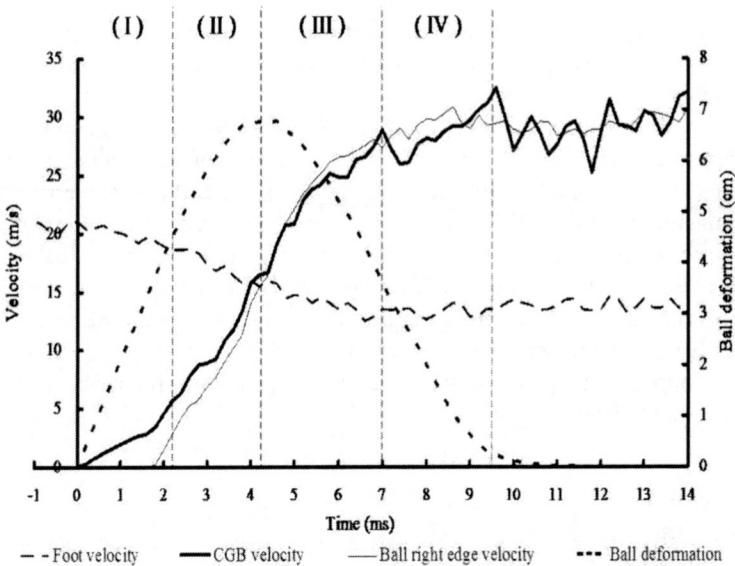

Figure 7.3 The aspect of ball-foot interaction during ball impact phase

foot plantarflexion motion (Asami and Nolte, 1983; Asai *et al.*, 1995, 2002; Tol *et al.*, 2002; Nunome *et al.*, 2006), a slight dorsiflexion motion was clearly detected during the first half of ball impact. Moreover, the foot was passively moved in other directions i.e. abduction and eversion. Plural and synchronized use of ultra high-speed (5000 Hz) cameras had a distinct advantage in illustrating these multi-axial motions of the foot. Experienced players are typically impacting the ball with the medial side of the instep (a hybrid position between the instep and side-foot kicking). This is likely to be responsible for this complicated foot motion.

Another characteristic of the present study is that ball deformation and behaviour of CGB during ball impact were quantified in detail by ultra high-speed cinematography. In consequence, the period of impact, though it lasts only less than 10 ms, can be divided into four phases. At the beginning of ball impact, although the opposite edge of the ball showed no movement, the centre of gravity of the ball (the CGB) began to move together with the ball deformation of the kicked side (Phase I). Then, it seems that the ball began to move as whole while continuing to deform (Phase II). In this phase, it is assumed that the foot propels the ball until ball deformation reached its maximum. At the maximal ball deformation, the CGB velocity exceeds that of the foot (Phase III). It is logical to assume that the recoil of the ball is a major contributor to increased ball velocity and the foot is no longer positively propelling the ball in this phase. Finally, when the ball has nearly reached launching velocity at the end of foot–ball impact, there is little force interaction between the ball and foot although the foot still seems to have contact with the ball (Phase IV).

From these results, it is considered that the effective duration to increase ball velocity during ball impact is about two-thirds of the visual contact time between ball and foot.

The peak ball reaction force, estimated from the velocity slope of the CGB, was approximately 2800 N, which is rather larger than the values previously reported (Asai *et al.*, 2002; Tol *et al.*, 2002). This study is the first to estimate the peak magnitude of the ball reaction force directly, in contrast to several indirect procedures used in most previous studies. This may account for the higher value of the present study. Tol *et al.* (2002) suggested that repetition of this large force involves the risk of anterior ankle impingement syndrome. From the results of the present study, as the estimated impact force of instep kicking was even higher, cautions about medical risks, especially to growing children and players with ankle injuries, should be expressed.

Conclusion

Representative impact phase kinematics and kinetics of instep kicking were revealed in the detailed time-series data of the present study. Ultra high-speed sampling images (5000 Hz) clarified that the three-dimensional motion of the foot includes not only dorsi/plantarflexion but also abduction and eversion during ball contact. The peak ball reaction force reached nearly 2800 N. Moreover, the impact period can be divided into four phases according to the state of ball–foot interaction. It is considered that the optimum duration to increase ball velocity during ball impact is about two thirds of visually-determined contact time between ball and foot.

References

Asai, T., Akatsuka, T. and Kaga, M., 1995, Impact process of kicking in football. In *Proceedings of the XVth Congress of the International Society of Biomechanics*, edited by Hakkinen, K., Keskinen, K.L., Komi, P.V. and Mero, A. (Jyvaskyla: Gummerus Printing), pp. 74–5.

Asai, T., Carré, M. J., Akatsuka, T. and Haake, S. J., 2002, The curve kick of a football I: impact with the foot. *Sports Engineering*, 5, 183–92.

Asami, T. and Nolte, V., 1983, Analysis of powerful ball kicking. In *Biomechanics VIII-B*, edited by Matsui, H. and Kobayashi, K. (Champaign, IL: Human Kinetics Publishers), pp. 695–700.

Nunome, H., Lake, M., Georgakis, A. and Stergioulas, L.K., 2006, Impact phase kinematics of instep kicking in soccer. *Journal of Sports Sciences*, 24, 11–22.

Tsaousidis, N. and Zatsiorsky, V., 1996, Two types of ball–effector interaction and their relative contribution to soccer kicking. *Human Movement Science*, 15, 861–76.

Tol, J. L., Slim, E., Soest, A. J. and Dijk, C. N., 2002, The relationship of the kicking action in soccer and anterior ankle impingement syndrome. *American Journal of Sports Medicine*, 30, 45–50.

8 Effect of approach velocity in soccer kicking

Lars Bo Kristensen[1] and Thomas Bull Andersen[2]

[1] No affiliation; [2] University of Aarhus, Denmark

Introduction

The soccer kick exhibits a proximal-to-distal movement pattern, in which the aim is for the most distal segment (shank–foot) to achieve the highest possible speed at impact (Lees and Nolan, 1998). Usually, this movement pattern is only analysed for two segments (thigh and shank–foot). However, the pelvic movement obviously influences the movement of the whole leg. Accordingly, acceleration of the hip will influence the movement of the whole leg. Hence, the approach velocity is thought to affect kicking velocity due to a change in acceleration of the hip as described above – this effect having direct application to the game of soccer. The speed of approach is normally implicit in the standard inverse dynamics equations or the motion-dependent equations (Putnam, 1991) used to analyse the kicking action, but the relationship between the speed of approach and the release speed of the ball has not yet been studied and reported explicitly.

Knowledge about the influence of speed of approach on the maximal speed of the ball is needed (i) in order to evaluate results from laboratory studies involving standardisation of the speed and (ii) in real game situations in order to verify if an instant change of normal selected speed of approach can result in higher speed of the ball using the instep place kick to a stationary ball with a running approach. This study was set up to determine if these relations are evident.

It has been shown that a running approach results in a higher speed of the ball than a stationary kick (Opavsky, 1988). The authors did not report the speed of approach of the kicker, nor did the study reveal the influence of different speeds of approach on the maximal speed of the ball.

A simulation study (Sørensen *et al.*, 2000) showed that the speed of approach and take-off angle are important in long jump, but an increase of the preferred speed of approach will not instantly lead to a longer jump, indicating an optimal subject-specific speed of approach related to the current anthropometric and performance profile of the subject. We hypothesise that a similar optimal subject-specific speed of approach is present in soccer kicking.

In the present study we aim to investigate the effect of different approach velocities on ball velocity in maximal instep soccer kicks. Furthermore, we plan to describe the parameters that are important for this effect.

Materials and methods

Six male sub-elite subjects performed the experiments. Before the experiments ten markers were placed on the left and right leg to enable a two-dimensional analysis to be carried out. Furthermore, three markers were placed on the ball to determine the position of the balls centre. The marker coordinates throughout the movement were recorded at 240 Hz using Qualisys Track Manager (Qualisys, Gothenburg, Sweden).

To control the approach velocity during the experiment, two photocells were placed 2.5 m and 1 m before the ball. The maximal running velocity was measured before the kicking trials. The subjects started their approach 13 m before the ball and first used a self-selected approach velocity. The subjects were then guided to perform trials in which the approach velocity was approximately 33, 50 and over 90 per cent of the maximal running velocity. In the end, the subjects performed a further series of kicks at a self-selected approach velocity. Only trials in which a target area of 1×1 m was hit were used in the analyses. At each approach velocity the experiment continued until three trials were within the target area. The trial with the highest ball velocity was selected for further analysis.

For each trial the ball velocity, approach velocity just before the support leg came in contact with the ground, and foot velocity at impact were calculated. A movement-dependant inverse dynamics analysis according to Putnam (1991) was performed and the work from each moment in the shank was calculated. The ball velocity was calculated as the mean velocity of the centre of the ball between five and ten frames after impact.

Results

The results showed that the maximal ball velocity was reached at the self-selected approach velocity. The maximal ball velocity was 29.07 (SD 0.93) m.s^{-1} and the self-selected approach velocity was 73.53 per cent (SD 4.70) of the maximal running velocity. Figure 8.1 shows the relation between the approach velocity and the ball velocity. Table 8.1 shows a collection of results including the work performed on the shank from the different movement dependent moments.

Table 8.1 Approach and ball velocities (in percent and m.s^{-1}) and work performed on the shank originating from the different movement dependant torques (in percent)

Trial	$V_{approach}$ (%)	V_{ball} (m.s^{-1})	W_{muscle} (%)	$W_{omega\ thigh}$ (%)	$W_{alpha\ thigh}$ (%)	$W_{hip\ acc}$ (%)	$W_{gravity}$ (%)
Self selected 1	73.5	29.1	52.9	20.5	0.8	8.4	7.4
Low	42.0	25.2	54.7*	18.1**	−0.2*	20.6	6.9
Medium	56.1	26.1	52.3	21.0**	−1.1	20.7	7.2
High	92.7	25.0	51.2*	18.6**	2.1*	21.1	7.0
Self selected 2	76.0	29.0	52.7	20.6	−0.5	19.1	8.1

Note: * indicates a significant difference between low and high approach velocity and ** indicates a significant difference between medium and low or high approach velocity. For the ball velocity, there is a significant difference between both self-selected approach velocities and all other approach velocities.

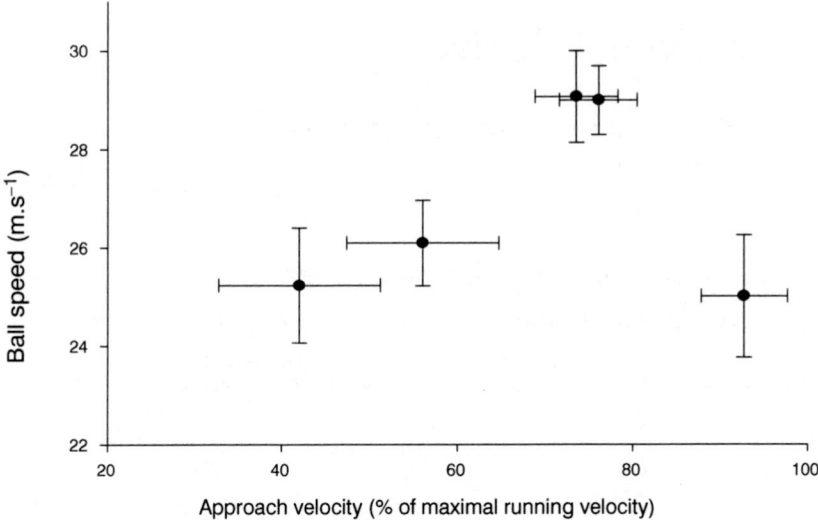

Figure 8. 1 Approach velocities and ball speed

Discussion and conclusion

The study revealed that the approach velocity influences the ball velocity. An approach velocity below or above the self-selected approach velocity will contribute to a lower ball velocity. This information can be used by a defending player in forcing an attacking opponent to perform his/her shot on goal at odd approach velocities – instead of committing a crucial penalty or free kick. The present results indicate that the effect is mainly caused by less work being produced by the knee extensor muscles and not by factors related to the acceleration of the hip.

References

Lees, A. and Nolan, L., 1998, The biomechanics of soccer: a review. *Journal of Sports Sciences*, 16, 211–34.

Opavsky, P., 1988, An investigation of linear and angular kinematics of the leg in two types of soccer kick. In *Science and Football*, edited by Reilly, T., Lees, A., Davids, K. and Murphy, W., (London: E & FN Spon), pp. 460–7.

Putnam, C.A., 1991, A segment interaction analysis of proximal-to-distal sequential motion patterns. *Medicine and Science in Sports and Exercise*, 23, 130-144.

Sørensen, H., Simonsen, E., and van den Bogert, A., 2000, Influence of approach velocity on long jump performance. In *International Society of Biomechanics XVIIth Congress – Book of Abstracts*, edited by Herzog, W. and Jinha, A. (Calgary: Calgary University), p. 166.

9   Kicking velocity

Barefoot kicking superior to shod kicking?

Thorsten Sterzing[1], Janina Kroiher[2] and Ewald M. Hennig[2]

[1] Department of Human Locomotion, Chemnitz University of Technology, Germany; [2] Biomechanics Laboratory, University of Duisburg-Essen, Germany

Introduction

The kicking motion is the most typical sport-specific technique in soccer. The most important game-related parameters of a good kick are kicking accuracy and kicking velocity. Players who are able to kick the ball more accurately and faster than others have a clear advantage in certain situations of the game. More accurate kicking skills of one team compared to another allow the team to control the game more easily and offers a wider range of tactical opportunities. With respect to maximum ball velocity a few, but potentially decisive, situations have to be considered. For instance, a faster moving ball reduces the goal-keeper's reaction time to a kick on goal. Therefore, it might make the difference between winning or losing a match. So naturally, kicking in soccer has received attention also in biomechanical research (Lees, 1996; Barfield, 1998). Among the various kicking techniques, the full instep kick is the technique that enables players to achieve the fastest ball velocity (Levanon and Dapena, 1998).

For analytical purposes, the kicking motion may be divided into four phases: the approach phase; the swing phase; the collision phase; and the follow-through. The duration of the core phase, the collision phase, is rather short as it takes only about 8 to 15 ms according to various studies listed by Asami and Nolte (1983). Thus, within the collision phase the player is not able to influence the kicking motion and its outcome once this phase has started. This means that the success of the kick is already determined immediately before the functional unit of foot and shoe hits the ball. In order to analyse the collision phase of the kicking motion the pure application of classical theories according to Newton's mechanics are not sufficient as the soccer kick cannot be seen as a purely elastic impact. Generally, accelerations of objects in sports may be classified as throwing-like or impact-like situations. However, kicking incorporates aspects of both of these types of ball and effector interaction, as during the collision phase the ball is displaced while being in contact with the foot (Tsaousidis and Zatsiorsky, 1996). Therefore, it is of interest whether the biomechanical interaction of the kicking limb with the ball changes when kicking with or without a shoe.

The shoe, as the most critical piece of equipment for the individual soccer player, is an important input variable for maximum ball velocity. Astonishingly, the literature offers just a few contributions concerning at the influence of soccer shoes on shooting velocity. Different soccer shoes evoke significantly different ball velocities when used for a full instep kick (Hennig and Zulbeck, 1999). Velocity differences up to $2.7 \mathrm{km.h^{-1}}$ could be shown between different shoe models. However, attempts to explain the reason for these differences have failed so far. This is not surprising as the soccer shoe consists of multiple functional and interactive elements which have to be regarded as a system. For example, weight was found not to be a decisive factor for achieving different ball velocities. It was shown that a lighter shoe worn on the kicking leg increases foot velocity while keeping the achieved ball velocity constant (Amos and Morag, 2002).

It is commonly believed that players wearing appropriate soccer shoes are able to kick the ball harder than players not wearing shoes. Questioning this assumption takes the topic to its original roots as the basic consideration that a shoe is first of all an artificial interface between foot and ball during kicking has been neglected so far. The biomechanical behaviour of shod compared to barefoot kicking may differ. Shod kicking has been reported to be inferior to barefoot kicking in a case study of one subject, although a valid scientific study design was missing (Plagenhoef, 1971).

The purpose of this study was to examine the general influence of the shoe on the kicking procedure with respect to ball velocity. It is necessary to know whether a soccer shoe acts as an enhancing, reducing or neutral piece of equipment in fast kicking. Features like mechanical support and protection of the foot must be taken into consideration as both factors can change the velocity of the full instep kick.

Materials and methods

Nineteen experienced soccer players participated in this study (age: 24.7 ± 3.1 years, height: 1.77 ± 0.05 m, mass: 73.9 ± 5.4 kg). All were fully capable of performing a good soccer style full instep kick. There were five different kicking conditions to be investigated: Brand A (AAA), Brand B (BBB), each subject's own shoe (OSC), sock without shoe (SOC) and barefoot (BAR). The selection of these kicking conditions was based on the following notions. Brand A and Brand B models represented premium products of two globally leading soccer footwear companies. The subject's own shoe reflected the most familiar shoe condition of the individual subjects. The sock and barefoot conditions were chosen as they do not exhibit any mechanical influence on the kicking procedure during the collision phase. However, the sock reduces pain in the superficial anatomical foot structures, e.g. the skin. The ball that was used in this study was an Alex Athletics indoor soccer ball. In contrast to the official outdoor soccer balls, this type of ball has a felt surface which reduces impact pain during unshod kicking. During the study the ball circumference was 73.4 cm and ball mass was 418.6 g. Ball pressure was kept constantly at 1 bar. Only the circumference of the ball was slightly bigger than stated in the official FIFA *Laws of the Game*.

The study was designed as a laboratory experiment. Kicking took place on artificial turf (DD – Soccer Grass HPF CROWN/ DIN 18035 T 7 120μ, 8800 dtex, density 30000/m^2). Measurements of peak ball velocity were taken by means of a radar gun (Stalker Pro, Applied Concepts Inc., Plano, TX). Ground reaction forces of the final stance leg step were obtained by using a Kistler force plate 9281 (size: 40×120 cm). The resultant shear force parameters serve as an indicator for the similarity of the approach process in the different kicking conditions.

Subjects had to perform six maximum full instep kicks of a stationary ball in each kicking condition. The approach, being another decisive factor for fast kicking, was standardized for all subjects. A three-step approach was required as it reflects a usual approach condition. In order to minimize the influence of fatigue a mandatory rest period of one minute was required between single kicks. The order of kicking conditions was randomized for each subject.

To avoid the influence of different traction properties of the stance leg on kicking velocity (Anjos and Adrian, 1986), subjects had to wear a neutral shoe model at the stance leg all throughout the test. All subjects wore the same shoe at the stance leg, a shoe model that was not used as a kicking condition for the kicking foot. Different approach conditions could not be avoided in this study with regard to the kicking leg and therefore have to be considered during data analysis.

Subjects were required to give a pain rating on an anchored nine-point perception scale (1 – very low; 9 – very high) after each single kick. They also had to give a velocity ranking according to perceived ball velocity (1 – highest speed; 5 – lowest speed) for the five kicking conditions at the end of data collection. In addition, subjects were invited to comment on potentially self-observed modifications of kicking technique due to the different kicking conditions. Variation of kicking technique was also monitored qualitatively by the study coordinator, a soccer expert.

Results

For data evaluation in this study, only 13 out of the 19 subjects could be used. Before the data were analysed, 6 subjects had to be excluded due to their severe and obvious modification of their kicking techniques when performing in the sock and/or barefoot condition. The modification was observed and judged either by the assessor and/or the subjects themselves. It turned out that the required task to perform a maximum full instep kick in the sock and/or the barefoot condition could not be fulfilled by about one third of the subjects. Impact pain between the foot and the ball was simply too high. Therefore, in order to examine the biomechanical support mechanisms of shod versus unshod kicking, only subjects who were able to perform the kicks with maximum power could be considered for the evaluation process.

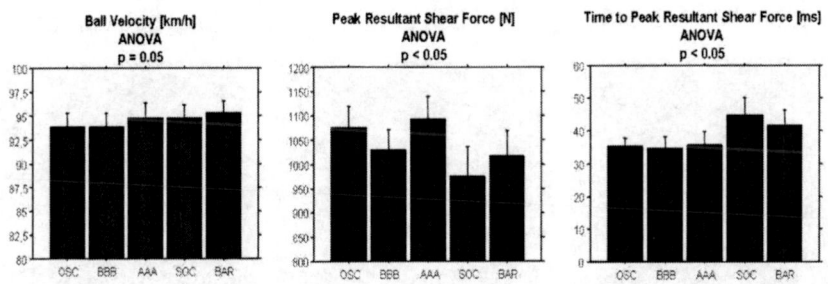

Figure 9.1 Means and standard errors for ball velocity and GRF parameters (stance leg)

For the remaining group of subjects (n = 13), a repeated measures ANOVA revealed a strong trend (P = 0.05) towards higher ball velocity in the barefoot condition (Figure 9.1). Ball velocity for the five kicking conditions ranged from to 93.8 to 95.3 kmh⁻¹.

All shod conditions showed a trend towards inferior performance compared to the barefoot condition. These findings are remarkable, especially as peak resultant shear force and time to peak resultant shear force values of the stance leg indicate a more cautious approach to the kick in the barefoot and in the sock condition. Data show significantly lower peak resultant shear forces for the unshod kicking conditions. Also, significantly higher values for time-to-peak resultant shear forces could be observed (Figure 9.1). However, a more cautious approach would suggest rather lower kicking velocity due to reduction of momentum according to kinetic chain theories. Potential reasons for a more cautious approach in the sock and barefoot conditions are worse traction properties during the three-step approach, uneven leg height in the unshod conditions and maybe also a generally uncomfortable feeling in these unfamiliar kicking conditions.

With regard to ball velocity the more cautious approach was overcompensated most likely by superior collision biomechanics during the impact phase. Theoretically, the effective striking mass of the unshod kicking conditions should be lower compared to the shod conditions as wearing soccer shoes constitutes additional weight of about 200 to 330g. It was shown that lower shoe weight resulted in higher foot speed during full instep kicking, two factors that finally even out the resulting ball velocity to remain constant (Amos and Morag, 2002). So regardless of the weight of the functional unit of foot and shoe, pure anatomical foot structures seem to perform better in full instep situations than does the functional unit of foot and shoe. A higher degree of plantarflexion angle in the barefoot condition at the ankle joint at initial ball contact is an adequate explanation for this, as high-speed video pictures suggest in a case study. In the shod kicking conditions, there seems to be more 'give' in the system of foot and shoe during the collision phase. The plantarflexion angle at final ball contact is increased compared to initial ball contact for the shod conditions, whereas it remains unchanged in the barefoot condition. Potentially, the sole plate or the heel counter of the shoe limits the amount of the plantarflexion angle at initial

initial ball contact   **full ball contact**   **final ball contact**

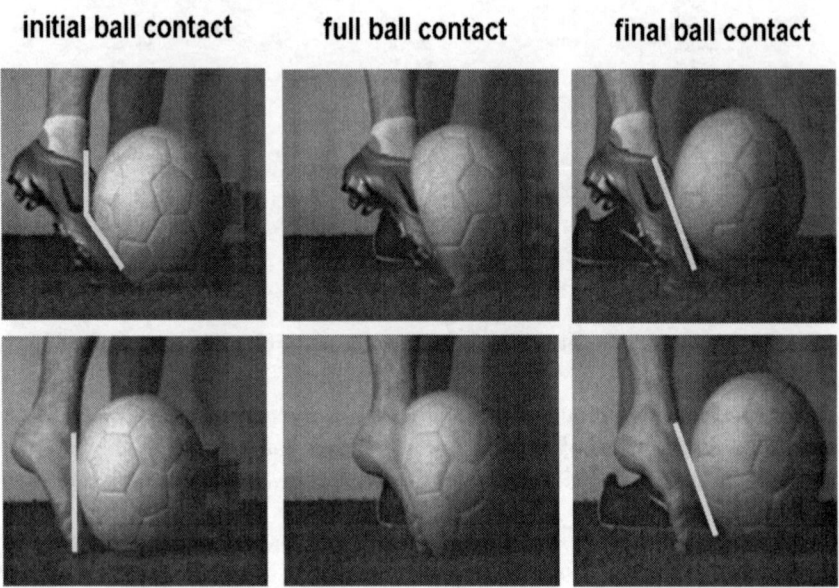

Figure 9.2 Plantarflexion angle during collision phase

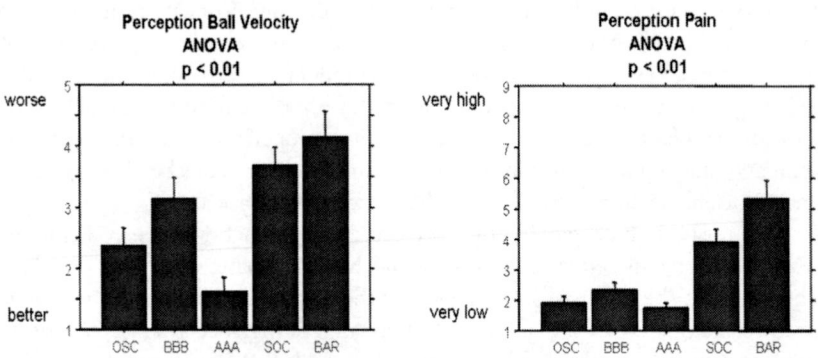

Figure 9.3 Means and standard errors for perception parameters

ball contact in the shod conditions. This might lead to lower foot rigidity and more 'give' during the collision phase of the kick which in turn results in more energy dissipation, energy being ineffective with regard to the propulsion of the ball (Figure 9.2).

Perception data showed highly significant differences between the kicking conditions for the velocity ranking and for the pain rating (Figure 9.3). With regard to ball velocity, the shod conditions were ranked superior (P<0.01) compared to the unshod conditions. This finding is in contrast to the actual measured velocities. As expected, the barefoot and the sock conditions were perceived to be clearly

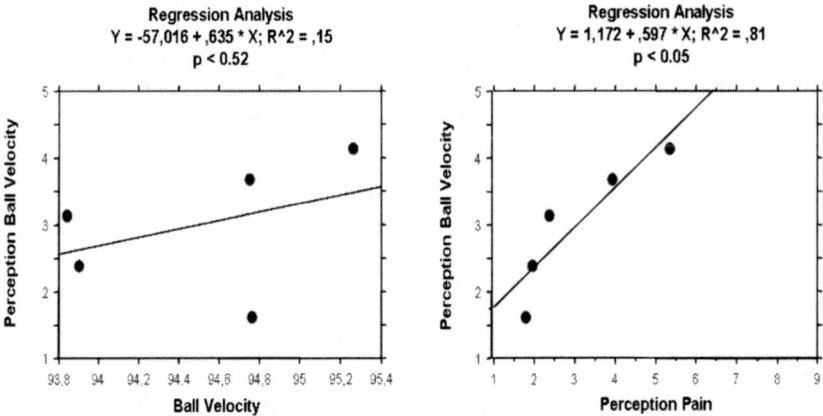

Figure 9.4 Regression analyses for perception parameters

most painful (P<0.01). The sock condition in fact reduced the pain compared to the barefoot condition but was still perceived to be seriously more painful than the shod conditions.

Despite perceiving the highest amount of pain in the barefoot condition, subjects were able to kick faster in this condition compared to shod conditions. Interestingly, the ranking values of ball velocity do not coincide with the actual ball velocity values. The ranking follows the pattern of pain perception, as regression analyses showed (Figure 9.4). The more painful a kicking condition was perceived, the lower the kicking condition was ranked with regard to perceived ball velocity. In this study therefore, pain perception has to be regarded as the determining aspect for the ball-velocity ranking.

Discussion and conclusion

It is known that in test situations of short duration certain subjects are able to neglect even strong feelings of discomfort or even pain. This aspect has to be considered during the evaluation of the data presented.

Nevertheless, it became more than obvious that soccer shoes have an important protective function for the foot during full instep kicking. Regardless of the issue of foot protection, the present study offers valuable insight into the purely biomechanical influence of soccer shoes during full instep kicking. It shows that barefoot kicking enabled the subjects to perform faster full instep kicks compared to shod kicking. Therefore, it could be shown that soccer shoes do not generally provide beneficial mechanical support for the enhancement of the resulting ball velocity. For most soccer shoe properties, footwear enhances athletic performance, e.g. by providing excellent traction and high stability during the player's interaction of foot and ground. With regard to kicking velocity the general assumption that a shoe provides beneficial support for the player needs to be reconsidered according to this study.

From a design perspective the enhancement of kicking velocity requires work on soccer shoe constructions that allows the active use of the full amount of the foot's plantarflexion right at the beginning of initial ball contact. Shoe models that are currently used do not allow active use of the full amplitude and thus they reduce foot rigidity during the collision phase.

Acknowledgement

This study was supported by Nike Inc., USA.

References

Amos, M. and Morag, E., 2002, Effect of shoe mass on soccer kicking velocity. 4th World Congress of Biomechanics, Calgary, Alberta, Canada.

Anjos dos, L. A. and Adrian, M. J., 1986, Ground reaction forces during kicks performed by skilled and unskilled subjects, *Revista Brasileira De Ciencias Do Esporte*, 8(1), 129–33.

Asami, T. and Nolte, V., 1983, Analysis of powerful ball kicking, In *Biomechanics VIII-B*, edited by Matsui, H. and Kobayashi, K. (Champaign, IL, Human Kinetics), pp. 695–700.

Barfield, W. (1998) The biomechanics of kicking in soccer, *Clinics in Sport Medicine*, 17, 711–28.

Hennig, E. and Zulbeck, O., 1999, The influence of soccer boot construction on ball velocity and shock to the body, 4th Symposium on Footwear Biomechanics, Canmore, Alberta, Canada.

Lees, A., 1996, Biomechanics applied to soccer skills. In *Science and Soccer*, edited by Reilly, T. (London: E & FN Spon), pp. 123–33.

Levanon, J. and Dapena, J., 1998, Comparison of the kinematics of the full-instep and pass kicks in soccer. *Medicine and Science in Sports and Exercise*, 30, 917–927.

Plagenhoef, S., 1971, *Patterns of Human Motion*, (Englewood Cliffs, NJ, Prentice Hall).

Tsaousidis, N. and Zatsiorsky, V., 1996, Two types of ball–effector interaction and their relative contribution to soccer kicking, *Human Movement Science*, 15, 861–76.

10 Kinematic analysis of high-performance rugby props during scrum training

Mark Sayers

Centre for Healthy Activities, Sport and Exercise, University of the Sunshine Coast, Australia

Introduction

There are approximately 19 scrums per game in rugby union (rugby) (International Rugby Board, 2003a), with many teams using the scrum as a means to establish both dominance over the opposition and initiate attack. An indication of the importance of the scrum to the game is reflected by International Rugby Board statistics from the 2003 Rugby World Cup which indicated that 29 per cent of tries originated from a scrum (International Rugby Board, 2003b). Although the scrum is a key aspect of the game, it has been the subject of considerable comment from the medical community for many years (Quarrie *et al.*, 2002). Some practitioners have called for significant changes to scrum laws, such as banning pushing in the scrum, in an endeavour to reduce the potential for injury (Bourke, 2006). The arguments against such a radical change are extensive (Cameron, 2006; Standfield, 2006; Wilson, 2006) and so extreme changes to scrummaging laws are not likely to occur in the near future.

Despite the importance of the scrum to the game and the undoubted issues that surround scrummaging and injury, there is limited research on the biomechanics of scrummaging (Milburn, 1986, 1990, 1993; Quarrie and Wilson, 2000). In addition, these studies have focused on measuring scrum kinetics with no scientific publications reporting the kinematics of scrummaging in elite rugby players. Clearly there is a need for more research on the techniques adopted by high performance competitors.

The use of scrummaging machines for training in rugby is common. Typically, international rugby teams use scrummaging machines for approximately 20 to 80 per cent of their total scrum training (unpublished data based on over 15 years of coaching and sports science involvement with international teams from Australia, New Zealand, Italy, and Wales). During a typical scrum training session, scrummaging machines are used for a variety of purposes ranging from strength and conditioning, to timing and teamwork development and advanced technical enhancement. Despite the popularity of this training device, little is known about the efficacy of using a scrummaging machine as a training tool to prepare for live (game-based) scrums. The purpose of this study was to examine the sagittal plane kinematics of several international rugby props during a combination of both training and game-based scrummaging drills with the aim of developing a greater understanding of the techniques involved.

Methods

Materials

This study was based on kinematic analyses of props (n = 5) from an international rugby team during machine-based scrum training. In each case the near-side of the prop closest to the camera was examined due to difficulties in identifying far-side body landmarks (e.g. the far side of the prop is hidden, by the hooker and lock making it very difficult to digitise far side landmarks). Analyses were also limited to two dimensions due to the ease of data capture, and to minimise interference with training. Twelve body landmarks and one point on the machine were marked with reflective tape prior to videoing (see Figure 10.1). In cases where the landmark was concealed by part of the subject's uniform, all efforts were made to ensure that the anatomical landmark was visible through the material.

High-speed video recordings were collected over 30 trials (6 per subject) at 500 Hz (TroubleShooter HR, Fastec Imaging, San Diego, USA) during, three-man (front row), five-man (front row and the two locks) and eight-man (full) scrums against a standard scrummaging machine (Powa Scrum, Powa Products, New Zealand). Following data capture, all landmarked points were digitised for every fifth frame from first movement of the prop (Start) through to 0.2 s after the engagement (End) using standard software (SiliconCoach Digitiser, Silicon Coach Ltd, New Zealand). Scaled data were smoothed via a digital low-pass filter with a 10 Hz cut-off frequency. To allow for potential end-points errors, 10 additional frames were digitised either side of the Start and End with these data being deleted after the smoothing process.

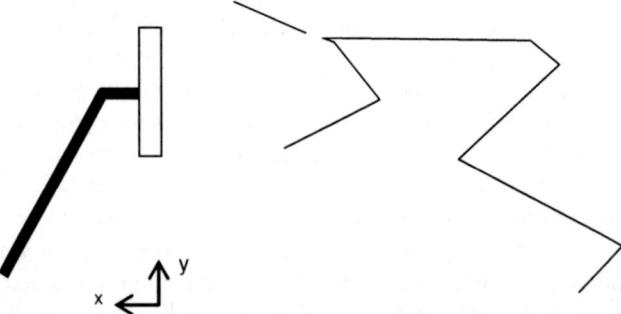

Figure 10.1 Representation of the stick figure created by linking the 12 landmarks; the diagram also illustrates the orientation of the planes of motion (NB: the direction of the x-axis was reversed so that movements towards the scrummaging machine were allocated positive values)

Linear and joint kinematics

Sagittal plane angular kinematic data were calculated for each joint segment together with linear kinematic data for the movements of the centre of mass (CoM) with respect to the horizontal (CoM_x) and vertical (CoM_y) axes using specifically written spreadsheet routines (Microsoft Excel 2002, Microsoft Corporation, USA). Absolute joint angular displacement data were calculated for the ankle, knee, hip, pelvis and spine (180° in full extension). Relative trunk angles were calculated with respect to the horizontal. The standard convention of labelling joint extension as a positive angular velocity (recorded as deg.s^{-1}) was used throughout analyses of angular kinematic data.

Statistics

A series of one-way analysis of variance (ANOVA) were used to test for differences in scrum technique between the machine and live scrummaging. Scheffe's post-hoc procedures were used when required. All statistical analyses were performed using SPSS for Windows (version 14.0). A significance level of $P<0.05$ was used for all analyses and data are presented as means ± SD unless stated otherwise.

Results

Results indicated many differences in linear kinematics across scrum types. Not surprisingly, peak CoM_x velocities differed significantly between scrums ($F_{2,42} = 64.31$, $P<0.001$), with post-hoc analyses showing greater CoM_x velocities for eight-man (2.43 m.s^{-1} [±0.24]) than both the three-man (2.26 m.s^{-1} [±0.08]) and five-man scrums (1.82 m.s^{-1} [±0.04]). The trend towards adopting different set-up positions for each scrum type was also evident in the analysis of the CoM_x values from the Start to engagement ($F_{2,42} = 444.11$, $P<0.001$). Analysis showed greater CoM_x values for the three-man (0.68 m [±0.08]) than both the five-man (0.58 m [±0.05]) and eight-man scrums (0.58 m [±0.07]) although the latter two were similar.

There were clear differences in the lower limb kinematics during each of the three types of scrums studied. For example, peak hip extension angular velocities were significantly different across each scrum type ($F_{2,42} = 2183.68$, $P<0.001$). Post-hoc analyses showed that hip extension angular velocities were greater for five-man (121 deg.s^{-1} [±2.5]) than both the three-man (6 deg.s^{-1} [±1.4]) and eight-man scrums (88 deg.s^{-1} [±3.0]), with the values for the eight-man scrum being greater than those for the three-man. Similarly, peak knee extension angular velocities were significantly different across each scrum type ($F_{2,42} = 7187.74$, $P<0.001$), although post-hoc analyses showed that hip extension angular velocities were greater for three-man (81 deg.s^{-1} [±1.8]) than both the five-man (17 deg.s^{-1} [±0.4]) and eight-man scrums (51 deg.s^{-1} [±1.7]), with the values for the eight-man scrums being greater than those for the five-man.

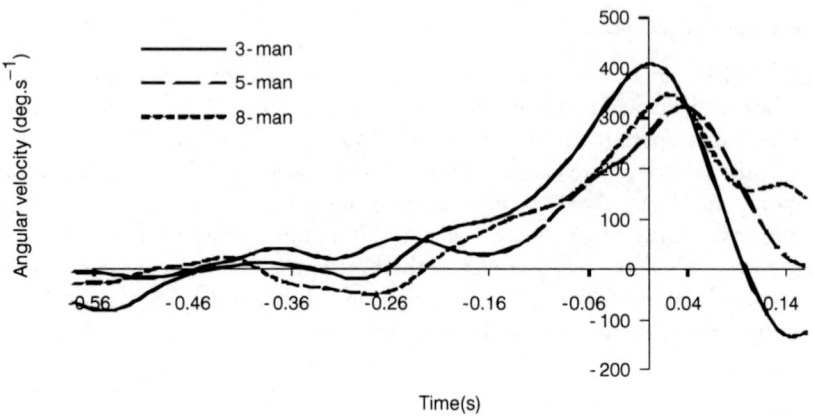

Figure 10.2 Knee angular velocity versus time data for each scrum type for one of the subjects (NB: each line represents the mean of the six trials for that scrum type).

Analyses of the timing and coordination of the movements also indicated considerable differences in the actions occurring at each joint for every scrum type. Figure 10.2 shows the knee angular velocity versus time data for Subject 2 across each scrum type. These data are typical of those reported for other subjects, with the peak in leg extension velocities occurring after engagement for both the five-man and eight-man scrums. Conversely, in the majority of cases for the three-man scrums, peak leg extension velocities occurred at the point of engagement. Figure 10.3 shows the ankle, knee, and hip angular velocity versus time data for Subject 2 during the five-man scrums. These data are again typical for this scrum type, showing peak hip extension occurring prior to peak knee extension, with peak angle extension velocity occurring later, well after engagement.

Notably, subjects also frequently recorded different set-up positions (i.e. body position) at the start of each scrum, with values such as absolute ankle angle varying significantly across scrum type ($F_{2,42} = 100.57$, $P = 0.011$). Post-hoc testing showed that absolute ankle angles were smaller for three-man (101 deg [±2.3]) than both the five-man (115 deg [±2.4]) and eight-man scrums (113 deg [±3.9]) although the latter two were similar. However, at engagement there were no significant differences in the ankle ($F_{2,42} = 0.027$, $P = 0.973$), knee ($F_{2,42} = 0.007$, $P = 0.993$), or hip ($F_{2,42} = 0.024$, $P = 0.977$) angles for any of the scrum types. Similarly, each prop adopted similar knee ($F_{2,42} = 0.163$, $P = 0.449$) and hip ($F_{2,42} = 0.813$, $P = .450$) positions at the End of the scrum, with angles for both joints approximating 120 deg (knee = 125 deg [±3], hip = 123 deg [±2]). However, subjects did record significantly different trunk angles at engagement ($F_{2,42} = 36.99$, $P < 0.001$), with the trunk angles being smaller for three-man (0 deg [±2.3]) than both the five-man (6 deg [±2.6]) and eight-man scrums (5 deg [±2.2]) although the latter two were similar.

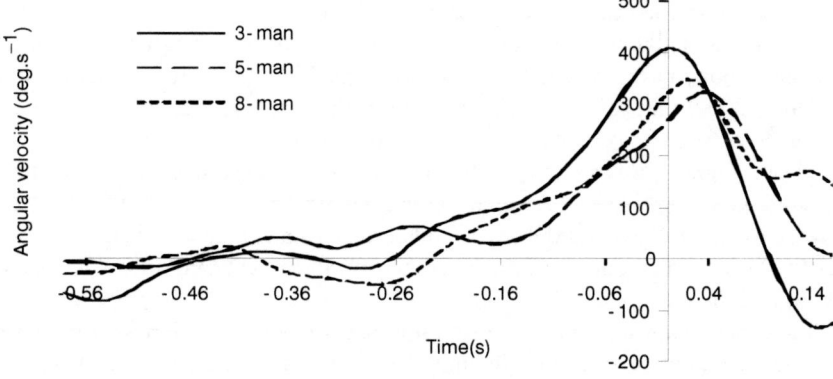

Figure 10.3 Ankle, knee, and hip angular velocity versus time data for one of the subjects during the five-man scrums (NB: each line represents the mean of the six trials)

Discussion

The fact that the eight-man scrum recorded the most rapid CoM_x engagement velocities was expected, but the high values noted during the three-man scrums were surprising (three-man scrum CoM_x engagement velocities were greater than those recorded for the five-man scrum). The results from this research appear to contradict the previous research by Milburn (1990; 1993) who showed a sequential increase in force in a scrum with the addition of extra players (e.g. three-man, to five-man, to eight-man). A possible explanation for the high three-man CoM_x engagement velocities exhibited by subjects in the current study is linked to the different set-up positions, with the greatest values for CoM_x recorded for the three-man scrums. That is, the props setting up consistently further from the machine for the three-man scrums resulted in a greater distance to accelerate the CoM, and hence greater impact velocities were achieved. This possible "over reaching" was probably the cause of the slightly lower trunk angles recorded at engagement for the three-man scrums and highlights the importance of ensuring consistency in training practices, particularly with regard to set-up positions.

The considerable differences that were evident in the angular kinematic data between scrum types raises real concern about the validity of using of three-man and five-man scrum training in the preparation for eight-man scrummaging. The majority of data showed significant differences in start, engagement, and/or end positions across all scrum types. Of interest was the fact that the highest peak knee and hip extension velocities occurred during three-man and five-man scrummaging, and not for the eight-man scrums (the scrum that recorded the greatest CoM_x engagement velocities). This indicated that props actually reduced the rate of leg extension during the engagement process when assisted by a lock and/or flanker. While this phenomenon might be expected in lower-level players (as some sort of mechanism to reduce impact force at engagement), it was completely unexpected in these international level competitors. It was anticipated that there would be consistency in the body positions adopted by all players, across all scrum types at engagement. Previous measurements of impact forces during machine-based scrum training have exceeded 1000 kg (Milburn, 1986, 1990, 1993; Quarrie and Wilson, 2000) and so it was not surprising that these high-performance players all adopted similar positions during this high impact (and potentially dangerous) part of training. It was also not surprising that these highly proficient players were able to adopt leg angles approximating the optimal "pushing position" suggested by Quarrie and Wilson (2000) at the end of the scrum engagement (these authors have shown maximum isometric scrummaging force occurring with 120 degree knee and hip angles).

The lack of any clear proximal to distal sequencing for any of the scrum types tested, represents a surprising finding. Clearly more research is needed on the interaction between the various members of the scrum, and how the props act as conduits for the transfer of force from the entire scrum into the machine (or other team). It could also be assumed that the issues concerning the validity of three-man and five-man scrum training (and machine-based scrummaging in general) mean that even experienced players such as those tested here find it difficult to coordinate the transfer of force effectively during some of these drills.

The absence of previous research on the kinematics of scrum training means that comparison with published data on scrummaging is not possible. It is anticipated that the high-performance athletes used in this project can be used as models for future comparisons. The high level of scrummaging proficiency exhibited by these subjects was evident by the small standard deviations for each of the kinematic variables tested (highly reproducible techniques), indicating each subject had achieved a high degree of technique mastery. Despite the subjects' technical proficiency, this study has been able to show that high performance props vary their scrummaging techniques during different machine-based training drills. More surprisingly, no clear pattern existed that would explain the nature of these changes (e.g. relatively random changes in technique). Although more investigation is warranted, the findings of this research place considerable doubt on the efficacy of three-man and five-man machine based scrummaging training as a means to improve eight-man scrummaging performance.

Conclusion

It was concluded that clear differences exist in the sagittal plane kinematics of props during different types of scrummaging training. The implications of these findings are considerable, as these data suggest that the excessive use of scrummaging machines, plus some scrum training drills (e.g. three-man and five-man) may have a negative training effect for eight-man machine scrum-training and potentially other live scrummaging situations.

References

Bourke, J. B., 2006, Rugby union should ban contested scrums. *British Medical Journal*, 332 (7552), 1281.

Cameron, M., 2006, Rugby union should ban contested scrums – Reality check is needed. *British Medical Journal*, 332 (7554), 1391.

International Rugby Board, 2003a, Review of the Game 2003. Retrieved 5 January, 2006, from http://www.irb.com/playing/game_analysis/pdfs/game_2003.pdf

International Rugby Board, 2003b, RWC 2003 – Statistical Review and Match Analysis. Retrieved 5 January, 2006, from http://www.irb.com/NR/rdonlyres/98062213-C48B-4837-BC0A-26A22F81C38D/0/RWC_2003.pdf

Milburn, P. D., 1986, A *Biomechanical Analysis of the Efficiency and Safety of Various Rugby Union Scrummaging Techniques*. Technical Report for the National Sports Research Program. (Belconnen, ACT: Australian Sports Commission).

Milburn, P. D., 1990, The kinetics of rugby union scrummaging. *Journal of Sports Sciences*, 8, 47–60.

Milburn, P. D., 1993, Biomechanics of rugby union scrummaging: Technical and safety issues. *Sports Medicine*, 16, 168-179.

Quarrie, K. L., Cantu, R. C. and Chalmers, D. J., 2002, Rugby Union injuries to the cervical spine and spinal cord. *Sports Medicine*, 32, 633–53.

Quarrie, K. L. and Wilson, B. D., 2000, Force production in the rugby union scrum. *Journal of Sports Sciences*, 18, 237–46.

Standfield, R. W., 2006, Rugby union should ban contested scrums - Technique is important. *British Medical Journal*, 332 (7554), 1391.

Wilson, D. M., 2006, Rugby union should ban contested scrums - Scrums are contested in junior rugby. *British Medical Journal*, 332 (7554), 1391.

11 A study of the knuckle effect in football

Takeshi Asai,[1] *Kazuya Seo,*[2] *Osamu Kobayashi*[3] *and Hiroyuki Nunome*[4]

[1] Tsukuba University, Japan; [2] Yamagata University, Japan; [3] Tokai University, Japan; [4] Nagoya University, Japan

Introduction

To date, miniature soccer balls (Carré *et al.*, 2004; Carré and Asai, 2004) and standard-size soccer balls (Asai *et al.*, 2006) have been studied in terms of their basic aerodynamic properties, and observed for surrounding flow using both wind tunnel experiments and computer-simulated computational fluid dynamics (CFD) (Asai *et al.*, 2000; Barber *et al.*, 2006). However, all of these studies have focused on stationary analyses; to understand the knuckle effect, which is fundamentally a non-stationary phenomenon, it is essential to use a non-stationary analysis that incorporates a time component. In the present study, we therefore analyzed the dynamics of the wake of non-rotating soccer balls by non-stationary CFD using a combination of large eddy simulation (LES) and a fluid visualization method using titanium tetrachloride. We also examined the fundamental mechanism of the knuckle effect.

Methods

Computer fluid dynamics (CFD)

Analyzing meshes were prepared using MSC.Patran (MSC.Software Inc.) and GAMBIT (Fluent Inc.) from computer-aided design model for a soccer ball (32-ball panel type). The unstructured analyzing meshes used a triangular tetrahedral element and comprised approximately one million units. The cylindrical space (2.44m radius $\times$ 4.88m length) was used for the analyzing meshes. The initial flow velocity was set at four conditions for this analysis: 15, 20, 25 and 30m.s^{-1} (Asai *et al.*, 2002). This analysis defined the velocity inlet and the pressure outlet. An incompressible unsteady analysis was performed by digitizing a Navier–Stokes equation using the finite volume method based on fully unstructured meshes with a commercial CFD code (FLUENT6.2, Fluent Inc.). The turbulent model of this study was the large eddy simulation (LES) model.

Visualization experiment

A visualization experiment using titanium tetrachloride (Asai *et al.*, 2006) was also conducted in order to visualize the flow around the soccer ball during flight. A soccer ball was placed directly in front of a soccer goal 15 m away and the subject performed a straight kick that involved virtually no rotation and a side-spinning curve kick. Both kicks were placement kicks delivered at the same velocity, as would occur in a real game. A high-speed VTR camera (Photron Ultima; Photron Limited) was set up at a midpoint between where the ball was placed and the soccer goal, and photographs were taken at 4,500 Hz.

The experimental procedure was as follows: each soccer ball was brush-painted with titanium tetrachloride, placed on a designated spot and then kicked towards a goal; as the ball flew towards the goal, the air flow around it was revealed by white smoke produced by the titanium tetrachloride; photographs were taken using a high-speed video camera; finally, the ball was collected and cleaned.

Results and discussion

CFD

Observation of time-series data of drag coefficient and lateral force coefficient revealed an unstable early period that tended to stabilize thereafter. Although the momentum involved fine vibrations, the value was low and within a range that could be mostly ignored. In the present study, therefore, the mean drag coefficient value in the 0.2 s period from 0.2 s to 0.4 s after the start of calculations was defined as the drag coefficient for that case.

The drag coefficient for CFD in the present study was about 0.19 for all cases at 15–30 m/s, and about 0.15 for 32-panel balls in the wind tunnel experiment (Figure 11.1). It was therefore slightly greater in the present study than was recorded in the wind tunnel experiment. Similar to the variation seen in the wind tunnel experiment of 32-panel balls, the CFD drag coefficient varied little in response to the change in the Reynolds number. Examination of the distribution of flow velocity around the ball at a supracritical CFD range revealed that the boundary

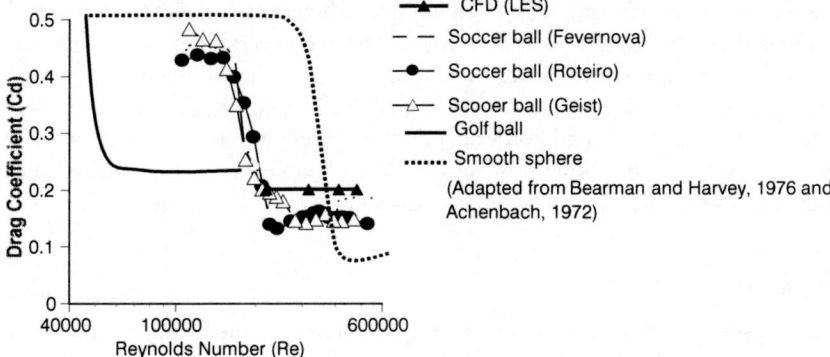

Figure 11.1 Drag coefficient of wind tunnel tests (Asai *et al.*, 2006) and CFD

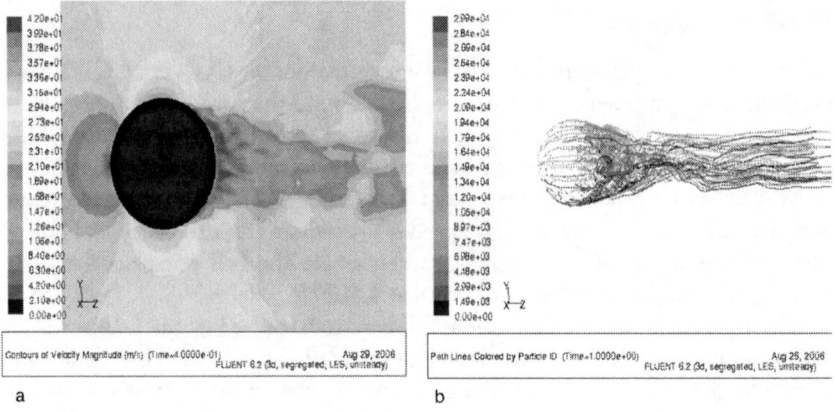

Figure 11.2 Contours of velocity magnitude (a) and path lines of the ball (b) on CFD

layer separation point receded to about 120 degrees from the front stagnation point (Figures 11.2(a) and 11.2b). This was a similar result to that obtained from visualization experiment images.

Examination of the CFD lateral force coefficient revealed irregular changes reaching a maximum of about 0.1, from about 0.1s when the drag coefficient value began to stabilize. This trend was seen in all cases and, although the details remain unclear, it is thought that this was related to the trailing vortex structure. When the trailing vortex in CFD was displayed in terms of peripheral ball vorticity, a decrease in the wake region similar to that seen in the visualization experiment images was evident. Although the overall impression was one of similarity, it cannot be determined whether or not the small-scale vortexes were similar. When the flow from the ball to a point a short distance away was examined using a pass line display, a near wake was observed, but the slightly separated far wake was reduced. Images from actual visualization experiments revealed many instances of non-symmetrical structures that incorporated a vortex loop, suggesting that for the CFD in the present study the vortex in the early stage was scattered. The precise cause of this is unclear, but it is possible that the inability of the LES model used in the present study to express retrograde transport (inverse cascade) of energy was a contributing factor. Therefore, although it is possible to use LES analysis to predict roughly the drag coefficient and separation point, predicting the trailing vortex structure, especially far wake, is more difficult. In future, attempts must be made to improve mesh quality and quantity, turbulence models, schematic calculations, and border conditions. Improving the hardware will also be important for enhancing the accuracy of calculations. For high-precision CFD, increased calculation resources will be required.

Visualization experiment

The images from the visualization experiment were examined based on the angle of the boundary layer separation point from the front stagnation point (that is,

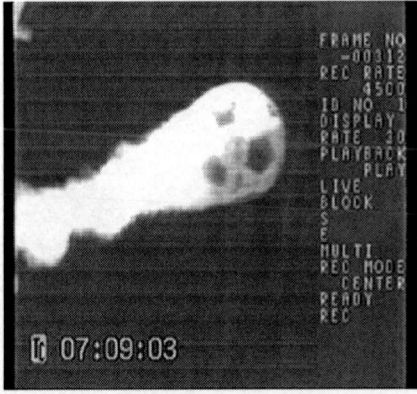

Figure 11.3 Flow visualization of non-spinning soccer ball

Figure 11.4 Flow visualization of a non-spinning soccer ball from side view (ball velocity: 24 m.s⁻¹) (flow is from right to left)

the tip of ball). During the high-velocity kick, the separation point receded to ~120° from the front stagnation point and the vortex region shrank (Figure 11.3). Reportedly, the Re_{crit} during the transition to turbulence of a non-spinning smooth ball is ~3.5 × 10⁵, and separation below the Re_{crit} occurs at ~75° from the front stagnation point, while that above the Re_{crit} occurs at ~135° from the front stagnation point (Taneda, 1978). For the soccer ball, the difference in values before and after transition was smaller, although it reached ~30° and was accompanied by a difference in the vortex region.

Examination of a high-speed VTR camera image of a non-rotating soccer ball while in flight revealed a slightly irregular vortex blob in the path of the ball (Figure 11.4). From an image having a broad angle of view, the number of these blobs was counted per unit of time and the Strouhal number (St) was calculated (Equation 11.1).

$$St = nd / U \qquad (11.1)$$

Figure 11.5 Flow visualization of the large-scale fluctuations of the vortex trail (flow is from right to left)

Here, n is the frequency, d is the ball diameter, and U is the flow velocity.

By calculating the number of vortex blobs from this broad angle view, the St (broad angle view) was estimated to be about 0.5. However, when vortex blobs seemingly with a vortex ring directly behind the ball were calculated from an image taken from a panned, narrower angle view, the frequency increased and the St (narrow angle view) was estimated to be about 1.0. One of the reasons the number of vortex blobs differed depending on the measured view angle was because directly after they occur, vortex blobs tend to coalesce with time, causing the measured frequency to change. Further detailed examination is required to determine which method is the most valid for identifying the St. If the frequency is calculated from a vortex blob, such as a vortex ring, directly after it occurs and the St is then estimated, the likely outcome would be a high mode value of about 1.0. This would be close to a smooth ball Reynolds number of 4×10^5. After balls undergoing a knuckle effect were airborne, large-scale fluctuations of the vortex trail were observed when the St was between 0.1 and 0.01 (Figure 11.5). The precise mechanism behind the vortex fluctuation observed in the present study was unclear, but the St low-mode association will need to be investigated further. Also, it is highly possible that the amount of movement generating this fluctuation is related to the knuckle effect of the soccer ball.

Conclusions

The purpose of this study was to analyze the dynamics of the wake of non-rotating soccer balls by non-stationary CFD using a combination of large eddy simulation (LES) and a fluid visualization method using titanium tetrachloride. We also examined the fundamental mechanism of the knuckle effect. The results may be summarized as follows.

1   CFD range revealed that the boundary layer separation point receded to about 120 degrees from the front stagnation point. This was a similar result to that obtained from visualization experiment images.
2   When the flow from the ball to a point a short distance away was examined using a pass line display, a near wake was observed, but the slightly separated far wake was reduced.
3   If the frequency is calculated from a vortex blob, such as a vortex ring, directly after it occurs and the St is then estimated, the likely outcome would be a high mode value of about 1.0.
4   After balls undergoing a knuckle effect were airborne, large scale fluctuations of the vortex trail were observed when the St was between 0.1 and 0.01. Also, it is likely that the amount of movement generating this fluctuation is related to the knuckle effect of the soccer ball

References

Asai, T., Masubuchi, M., Nunome, H., Akatsuka, T. and Ohshima, Y., 2000, A numerical study of magnus force on a spinning soccer ball. In *International Research in Sports Biomechanics*, edited by Hong, Y. (London: Routledge), pp. 216–23.

Asai, T., Carré, M.J., Akatsuka, T. and Haake, S.J., 2002, The curve kick of a football, I: impact with the ball. *Sports Engineering*, 5, 183–92.

Asai, T., Seo, K., Kobayashi, O. and Sakashita, R., 2006, Flow visualization on a real flight non-spinning and spinning soccer all. In: *The Engineering of Sport 6*, Vol. 1, edited by Moritz, E.F. and Haake, S.J. (Sheffield: International Sports Engineering Association) pp. 327–32.

Barber, S., Haake, S.J. and Carré, M.J., 2006, Using CFD to understand the effects of seam geometry on soccer ball aerodynamics. In: *The Engineering of Sport 6*, Vol. 2, edited by Moritz, E.F. and Haake, S.J., (Sheffield: The International Sports Engineering Association), pp. 127–32.

Carré, M.J. and Asai, T., 2004, Biomechanics and aerodynamics in soccer. In: *Biomedical Engineering Principles in Sports*, edited by Hung, G.K. and Pallis, J.M. (New York: Kluwer Academic Plenum Publishers), pp. 333–64.

Carré, M.J., Goodwill, S.R., Haake, S.J., Hanna, R.K. and Wilms, J., 2004, Understanding the aerodynamics of a spinning soccer ball. In: *The Engineering of Sport 5*, Vol. 1, edited by Hubbard, M., Mehta, R.D. and Pallis, J.M (Sheffield: The International Sports Engineering Association), pp. 70–6.

Taneda, S., 1978, Visual observations of the flow past a sphere at Reynolds numbers between 10^4 and 10^6. *Journal of Fluid Mechanics*, 85, 187.

12 Ground reaction force of a drop jump on different kinds of artificial turf

Rudy Verhelst, Philippe Malcolm, Patricia Verleysen, Joris Degrieck, Dirk De Clercq and Renaat Philippaerts

Ghent University, Belgium

Introduction

Artificial turf has started to find acceptance in soccer, especially with the development of the so-called 'third generation' turf, which consists of a sand- and rubber-infilled structure. Several types of infill have been developed, aimed at minimising injury rates and enhancing performance. An important property that has been related to injuries on sport surfaces is the shock reduction of that surface. This applies to running in general (Scot and Winter, 1990), and soccer-specific actions like jumping-landing sequences in heading and goal-keeping actions.

There are several ways to test the effect of the impact of a player on a surface. In the past, playing surfaces were mostly tested by means of mechanical tests, which have the advantage that they show a high repeatability. For artificial soccer pitches, FIFA uses the Artificial Athlete for shock absorption, simulating the impact of a person during a vertical jump. It consists of a mass falling onto a spring that rests, via a load cell and test foot on the surface. The force is recorded and compared to the maximum force measured on a concrete surface. This ratio is known as the 'force reduction' and is used as a measure for the shock absorption of the surface (Fédération Internationale de Football Association, 2006). Currently biomechanical tests with actual players have become more popular because they provide better external validity and are a valuable addition to the current test procedure (Meijer *et al.*, 2006), provided test-retest repeatability is acceptable. Durá *et al.* (1999) have described a standardised biomechanical test procedure to assess the effect of shock absorbing sports surfaces in jumping by means of a drop jump.

The aim of the present study was therefore to analyse the vertical ground reaction force (VGRF) pattern during a typical land–jump–land sequence on different types of natural turf, to evaluate test–retest reproducibility and to compare the effect of the different surfaces on the external forces when performing a drop jump. A test rig that could be equipped with different surfaces was developed.

Figure 12.1 Drop-jump movement

Materials and methods

Seven male recreational football players (mass 71.9±6.7 kg, height 1.79±0.16 m, age 26.0±1.8 years) performed five drop jumps on two artificial turf surfaces (Desso DLW Sports Systems DD Challenge Pro), one with 3 cm SBR rubber infill, and one with 3 cm TPE infill. Although these types of artificial turf normally have a mixed sand-rubber infill, no sand was added because the aim was to compare the effect of the SBR and the TPE. The drop-jump movement consisted in falling from a 50 cm platform immediately followed by a maximal vertical jump and a second landing (Figure 12.1). This movement is somewhat similar to jumping for a header and the landing afterwards in the actual soccer game. As in the study by Durá *et al.* (1999), the subjects were asked to keep their arms crossed on their chest to reduce the variability of movement performance, since arm movement could help to obtain more or less height by movement synchronisation. They could perform several jumps to get familiar with the movement before the actual measurements were done. All subjects wore the same soccer boots (14 permanent studs, shoe size EUR 44), so the footwear design could not have an interfering influence on the measurements.

Vertical ground reaction force was recorded with a Kistler force plate at 1000 Hz, placed under the artificial turf (Figure 12.2). The tests were filmed with a high-speed camera (Redlake Motion Pro) at 100 Hz. Markers were attached to toe (articulatio metatarsophalangealis 5), ankle (malleolus lateralis), knee (epicondylus lateralis) and hip (trochanter major) in order to allow a 2-D kinematic analysis to be prepared.

Results

Figure 12.3 shows the typical VGRF pattern of a drop jump with a first peak for the first impact, a period where the person is in contact with the surface (GRF>0), then a period where the person is in the air after take-off (GRF = 0) and finally a second impact peak. From the force data, several parameters were obtained.

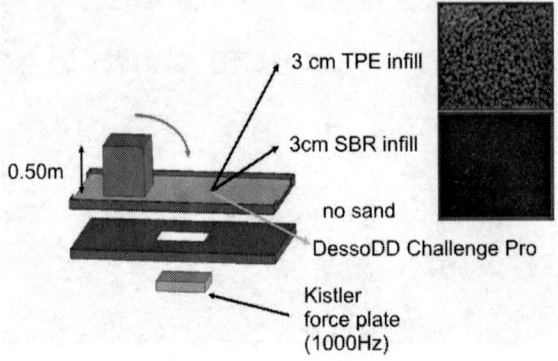

Figure 12.2 Experimental setup

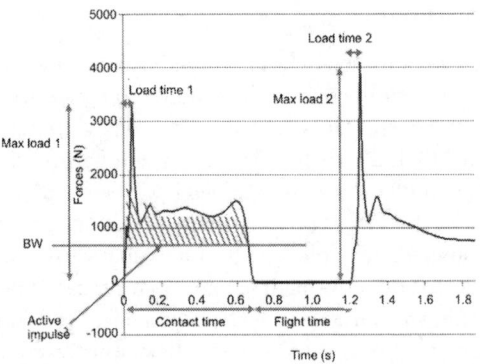

Figure 12.3 Analysed parameters of the vertical ground reaction force

Statistical analysis on these parameters was done with SPSS 12.0. The result of this analysis is presented in Table 12.1.

The variables that were analysed are: flight time, load time of peak 1 and 2, contact time, maximum load of peak 1 and 2, maximum and average load rate (LR) of peak 1 and 2 and the active impulse. Table 12.1 shows the average and standard deviation of the measured variables on TPE infill and SBR infill.

Discussion

In order to analyse the inter-trial variability of the different variables, the average measures intra-class correlation was calculated for each variable on each substrate. The lower limit above which trials could be averaged for further variance analysis was chosen at 0.70 (see Table 12.2 for an overview of the correlation coefficients). Most parameters showed good repeatability: only the load time of peak 1 and the active impulse on TPE had an ICC smaller than 0.70. The variability on the flight

Table 12.1 Analysed parameters for the drop jump on artificial turf with TPE and SBR infill

	TPE infill			SBR infill		
	Average		Standard deviation	Average		Standard deviation
Flight time [s]	0.497	±	0.032	0.499	±	0.037
Load time 1 [s]	0.056	±	0.007	0.054	±	0.011
Load time 2 [s]	0.058	±	0.010	0.062	±	0.007
Contact time [s]	0.484	±	0.187	0.500	±	0.169
Maximum load 1 [N]	2873.0	±	887.0	2724.0	±	628.0
Maximum load 2 [N]	4067.0	±	1186.0	3976.0	±	1216.0
Maximum LR Fz peak 1 [kN.s−1]	166.1	±	85.2	121.9	±	29.7
Average LR Fz peak 1 [kN.s−1]	59.3	±	25.1	54.1	±	15.9
Maximum LR Fz peak 2 [kN.s−1]	319.2	±	145.7	271.6	±	127.3
Average LR Fz peak 2 [kN.s−1]	80.2	±	33.7	70.3	±	24.8
Average active impulse Fz [Ns]	351.0	±	20.0	359.0	±	32.0

time and contact time was very low, as ICC values were higher than 0.95. The average measured values for flight time and contact time were almost the same on both surfaces (see Table 12.1), suggesting that the landing-jump movement was not affected by the difference in surfaces.

Non-parametric Wilcoxon tests revealed no significant differences between the surfaces for any of the parameters as all of the P values were above 0.05. However, the maximum and average load rates in the force peak of the second impact had a P value of 0.091, suggesting a trend towards significant differences between the TPE and the SBR. The comparison of the average values (see Table 12.1) revealed that the maximum load rate on the TPE infill (319.2 kN.s^{-1}) was higher than on the SBR infill (271.6 kN.s^{-1}). The average load rate on TPE (80.2 kN.s^{-1}) was also higher than on SBR (70.3 kN.s^{-1}). This difference in load rate can probably be attributed to the intrinsic material differences, as well as differences in the shape of the infill particles.

A similar conclusion can be drawn for the load rate of the first impact: the maximum load rate on TPE (166.1 kN.s^{-1}) was higher than on SBR (121.9 kN.s^{-1}), and the average load rate on TPE (59.3 kN.s^{-1}) was also higher than on SBR (54.1 kN.s^{-1}), yet with higher P value (0.237 and 0.398 respectively) than in the second impact. The reason for this can probably be found in the more uniform way of landing during the second impact, whereas the subjects have different ways to step of the platform, which causes more variation in the first impact.

Table 12.2 The ICC Cronbach alpha value (correlation r) and Wilcoxon signed ranks test (P value)

	Correlation r (ICC)		
	TPE infill	SBR infill	P value
Flight time [s]	0.955	0.954	1.000
Load time 1 [s]	0.858	0.798	0.735
Load time 2 [s]	0.686	0.733	0.128
Contact time [s]	0.992	0.990	0.310
Maximum load 1 [N]	0.857	0.756	0.866
Maximum load 2 [N]	0.771	0.903	0.398
Maximum LR Fz peak 1 [N.s^{-1}]	0.807	0.797	0.237
Average LR Fz peak 1 [N.s^{-1}]	0.991	0.731	0.398
Maximum LR Fz peak 2 [N.s^{-1}]	0.716	0.775	0.091
Average LR Fz peak 2 [N.s^{-1}]	0.734	0.859	0.091
Active impulse Fz [Ns]	0.636	0.969	0.612

As for the pathophysiological relevance of this difference in load rate, it could be suggested that a repetitive exposure to higher load rates might lead to musculoskeletal overuse injuries, as proposed by Nigg et al. (2000).

Material tests with the Artificial Athlete for shock absorption (Fédération Internationale de Football Association, 2006) on TPE confirmed the above findings. The force reduction on the 3 cm TPE infill (0.53) was lower than on the 3 cm SBR infill (0.58).

As the Wilcoxon test suggests that the load rate has a higher potential to discriminate between two surfaces than the maximum load, it would be interesting to use the comparison of load rates, rather than of the maximum forces, for the Artificial Athlete for shock absorption. This might improve the discriminative power of the test.

Conclusions

The high repeatability shows that the experimental setup was a good alternative for material tests. No significant differences were found for the analysed variables between the TPE and the SBR infill. However, a tendency towards significance was found for the maximum and average load rate of the second impact. On average, the load rate on the TPE was higher than on the SBR infill. These results were confirmed with material tests.

It needs to be stressed however, that no significant differences were found. Therefore, further tests with more subjects and probably also other soccer-specific movements are required in order to examine whether TPE infill really might present a higher risk for overload injuries or not.

In the future, it might be relevant to analyse the kinematics of the drop-jump movement. This might reveal differences in movement, as the subjects might adapt their movement (knee and ankle flexion) to the difference in characteristics of the playing surfaces. It would also enable the performance (e.g. the jump height) on the surfaces studied to be compared.

Acknowledgements

This study was funded by the Flemish Institute for the Promotion of the Scientific and Technological Research in Industry (IWT). The authors would like to acknowledge the assistance of Desso DLW Sport Systems.

References

Durá, J.V., Hoyos, J.V., Lozano, L. and Martinez, A., 1999, The effect of shock absorbing sports surfaces in jumping. *Sports Engineering*, 2 (2), 103–8.
Fédération Internationale de Football Association, 2006, FIFA *Quality Concept: Handbook of Test Methods for Football Turf*. http://www.fifa.com
Meijer, K., Dethmers, J., Savelberg, H., Willems, P. and Wijers, B., 2006, Biomechanical analysis of running on third generation artificial soccer turf. In: *The Engineering of Sport*, edited by Moritz, E. and Haake, S. (Berlin: Springer).
Nigg, B.M., Macintosh, B.R. and Mester, J., 2000, Forces acting on and in the human body. In *Biomechanics and Biology of Movement* 3rd edn, (Champaign, IL: Human Kinetics).
Scot, S.H. and Winter, D.A., 1990, Internal forces at chronic running injury sites. *Medicine and Science in Sports and Exercise*, 22, 357–69.

13 Development of a sliding tester

Rudy Verhelst, Patricia Verleysen, Joris Degrieck, Stijn Rambour and Gustaaf Schoukens

Ghent University, Belgium

Introduction

Today, artificial turf is becoming more and more used for soccer, especially with the development of the so-called 'third generation' turf, which consists of a sand and rubber-infilled structure. The most inherent problem of artificial turf is injury due to sliding. A statistical survey by ISA Sport (Joosten, 2003) has revealed that 62 per cent of the football players considered that artificial turf is unsuitable for making sliding tackles and that there is a need for the development of a method of measurement in order to define a sliding tackle. The existing testing devices for sliding, used by FIFA and UEFA (Boisnard, 1999; FIFA, 2006), focus on the coefficient of friction (COF) between a silicon artificial skin and the turf, as well as the abrasion caused to the skin. However, a crucial variable in the process of skin burning, the temperature, cannot be measured. The aim of this study was therefore to develop a new test device that can assess how well different types of turf are fit for sliding on them. This sliding tester, consisting of a ramp and a sledge with an artificial skin, provides a very realistic approximation of sliding in soccer, considering realistic values for player speed and mass which can be varied. The increased temperature during sliding as well as the friction is measured, in order to assess the risk of burn wounds.

Materials and methods

The new test device consists of a ramp, from which a sledge is launched onto the field (Figure 13.1). The mass of the sledge can be varied between 14.8 and 30.8 kg by means of extra weights. Combined with a contact surface of about 0.01 m^2, this leads to a very realistic contact pressure. The speed at which the sledge enters the field is variable up to 6 m.s^{-1}, depending on the release height. This is again a very realistic value, considering that the maximum speed of a football player during sprinting is no more than 10 m.s^{-1} and that real sliding will never be done at maximum speed. At the bottom of the sledge, thermocouples in a newly developed artificial skin measure the temperature during the sliding action.

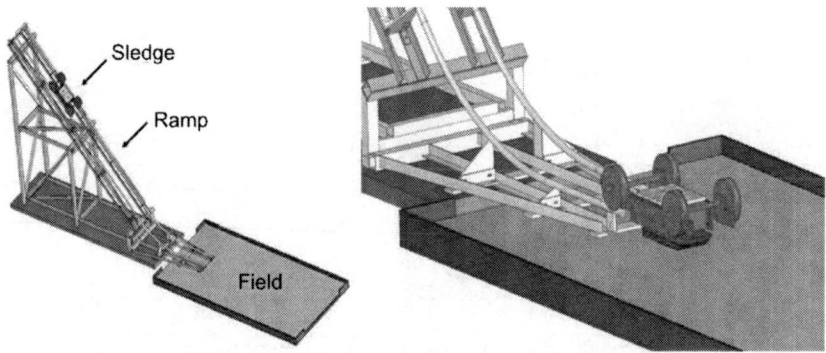

Figure 13.1 Experimental setup

Results

The typical form of a temperature curve, measured at 1000 Hz, is illustrated in Figure 13.2. As soon as the sledge makes contact with the field, the contact temperature rises dramatically until the sledge comes to a standstill, after which the temperature gradually goes down again.

Experiments were conducted in the laboratory on three different surfaces: natural turf and two types of artificial turf. The first one was a one-year-old Desso DLW Sports Systems Challenge Pro, the second one a Challenge Pro² with a different fibre compound, both with SBR rubber infill. On each of the surfaces, five sliding tests were done with measurement of the temperature history and the sliding distance.

Temperature rise

As depicted in Figure 13.3, the rise in temperature was significantly smaller on natural than on artificial turf. However, there was a clear difference between different types of artificial turf: the rise in temperature on Challenge Pro² was smaller than on the one-year-old Challenge Pro ($5.3 \pm 0.5°C$ resp. $9.7 \pm 0.9°C$).

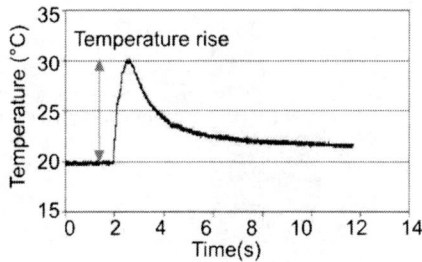

Figure 13.2 Typical curve of temperature measurement

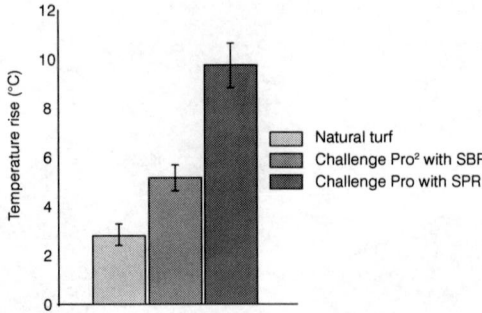

Figure 13.3 Comparison of temperature rise on different surfaces

Sliding distance

The sliding distance differed on the three surfaces as well. On natural turf the sledge stopped after 1.6 ±0.1 m, on the Challenge Pro^2 after 1.1 ±0.1 m and on the one-year-old Challenge Pro after 1.9 ±0.2 m (see Figure 13.4).

Coefficient of friction

The coefficient of friction (COF) can be calculated with the formula:

$$\text{COF} = c\left(\frac{h}{l}\right) \tag{13.1}$$

with h the initial launching height of the sledge, L the sliding distance and c a constant, depending on the energy loss during the launch. Figure 13.5 shows the calculated COF for each of the surfaces. The natural turf and the one-year-old Challenge Pro had a COF between 0.4 and 0.5, whereas the Challenge Pro^2 has a COF of about 0.65.

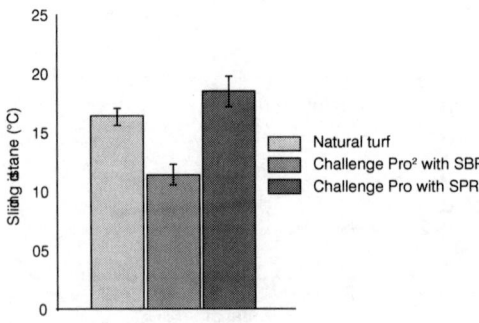

Figure 13.4 Comparison of sliding distance on different surfaces

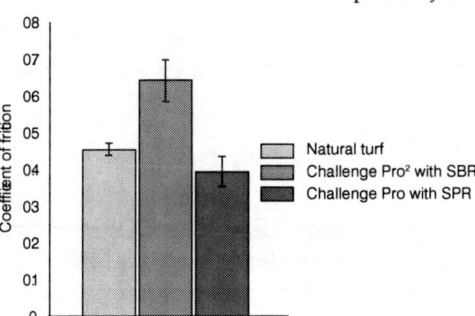

Figure 13.5 Comparison of COF on different surfaces

Influence of mass and velocity

Further experiments were conducted on artificial turf to assess the influence of variables like the initial velocity and the mass of the sledge. Table 13.1 shows the influence of the velocity and mass on the temperature rise on a certain type of artificial turf. As the initial velocity is varied from 2.4 m.s⁻¹ up to 4.2 m.s⁻¹, with a constant mass of 14.8 kg, the temperature rise increases from 4.1 ±0.4°C to 8.4 ±0.6°C. As the mass is varied from 14.8 kg up to 30.8 kg, with a constant velocity of 3.7 m.s⁻¹, the temperature rise increases rather linearly from 8.0 ±0.2°C to 14.0 ±1.0°C.

Discussion

Temperature rise

Comparing the rise in temperature between different conditions allows the classification of different kinds of surfaces. It is clear that, in order to reduce the risk of potential burning wounds, the rise in temperature should be as low as possible. Figure 13.3 shows that the risk for burn wounds is smaller on natural turf

Table 13.1 Measured rise in temperature (average and standard deviation) as a function of mass and speed of the sledge

Mass [kg]	Speed [m.s⁻¹]	Average rise in temperature [°C]	Standard deviation rise in temperature [°C]
14.8	2.4	4.1	0.4
14.8	3.1	5.6	0.4
14.8	3.7	8.0	0.2
14.8	4.2	8.4	0.6
18.8	3.7	9.5	0.6
22.8	3.7	11.2	0.8
26.8	3.7	12.6	1.3
30.8	3.7	14.0	1.0

than on artificial turf, confirming the findings of Joosten (2003). It also proves that the test can discriminate between different types of artificial turf.

Sliding distance and COF

There does not seem to be a clear correlation between the sliding distance or the COF and the rise in temperature. The COF of natural turf, which is the safest surface for sliding, was not clearly lower (or higher) than both the artificial surfaces. This suggests that a classification of surfaces based on their COF is not correct.

Influence of mass and velocity

As expected, the temperature rise increased linearly with the mass, since the kinetic energy – and thus the energy that has to be dissipated – is proportional to the mass. Theoretically, it would be expected that the velocity has a quadratic influence on the rise in temperature as the kinetic energy is proportional to the square of the velocity. However, the results in Table 13.1 suggest quite a linear trend. This can probably be explained by the fact that the sliding distance increased with the initial velocity. This means that with higher initial velocity, the sledge comes into contact with a larger part of the surface, which has a cooling effect on the skin.

Conclusions

In this study a new testing device has been developed to simulate sliding in soccer. Unlike previous test methods, this device takes into account the conditions of real sliding in terms of load, speed and type of movement. Measurements have proved that this apparatus can discriminate between different types of surfaces. Whereas previous methods classified surfaces based on their COF, this study has demonstrated that the measurement of the rise in temperature is essential and more accurate.

The test device can also be used for more fundamental research on the sliding phenomenon, as extensive sliding tests with soccer players are not (ethically) possible due to the risk of burn injuries. Measurements with the device allow studies of the influence of different variables such as the load or the initial speed of the player to be conducted.

This study was primarily concerned with the temperature effects that arise during sliding. An injury provoked by sliding will be caused by a combination of two effects: a rise in temperature that leads to skin burning and an abrasion effect that damages the upper layer of the human skin. The abrasion can be assessed by a method like the Securisport device, as explained above. Moreover, the measurements in this study have been carried out on sport surfaces in normal conditions. Obviously, the sliding tester needs further evaluation in other conditions like on frozen fields or outdoor fields in the rain, and a maximum value for the rise in temperature should be set, in order to standardise the testing unit and introduce it as a possible test device for FIFA and UEFA.

Acknowledgements

This study was funded by the Flemish Institute for the Promotion of the Scientific and Technological Research in Industry (IWT). The authors would like to acknowledge the assistance of Desso DLW Sport Systems.

References

Boisnard, D., 1999, The securitest: apparatus to measure the interaction between foot and sport surface. In *ISSS Technical Forum*, Mallorca. http://www.isss.de

FIFA, 2006, *FIFA Quality Concept: Handbook of Test Methods for Football Turf.* http://www.fifa.com

Joosten, T., 2003, Players' experiences of artificial turf. In *ISSS Stadia Turf Summit*, Amsterdam. http://www.isss.de

Part III

Sports medicine

14 Acute and chronic spinal injuries in soccer

Ömür Serdal Altinsöz, Yaşar Salci
and Feza Korkusuz

Department of Physical Education and Sports, Middle East Technical University, Turkey

Introduction

Cervical and/or lumbar acute and/or chronic spinal injuries in soccer are more common than expected. Brooks and Fuller (2006) reported 12.3 per cent head and neck injuries during football training and at matches. Delaney and Al-Kashmiri (2005) presented high rates of neck injuries in the United States for soccer and American football players presenting to emergency departments from 1990 to 1999. The cumulative number of neck fractures and dislocations, and total neck contusions, sprains and strains during this time period were 214 and 17,927, respectively (Delaney and Al-Kashmiri, 2005). Total neck injury and fracture/ dislocation rates in soccer when compared to American football were 17 per cent and 13 per cent, respectively. Rates of fractures/dislocations, and contusions, sprains and strains presenting to emergency departments in the United States from 1993 to 1999 for every 10,000 participants ranged from 0 to 0.064 and from 1.14 to 2.31, respectively.

Injuries to the cervical spine in American football players (Torg *et al.*, 2002) and Irish rugby players (Shelly *et al.*, 2006) are well recognized. Recognition of the problems led to a series of studies released to the epidemiology, mechanics and prevention of injuries to the cervical spine and the spinal cord.

In soccer, however, acute and chronic recurrent low-energy trauma to the cervical and/or lumbar spine is less recognized. In a cross-sectional descriptive study, Kartal *et al.* (2004) assessed early degenerative changes in active amateur and veteran soccer players using biomechanical, radiological, and magnetic resonance measurements. More recently, Altunsoz *et al.* (2007) concentrated on the degeneration of the lumbar spine due to playing soccer. It was concluded that playing soccer may cause spinal degeneration at the cervical and lumbar spine.

The aim of this study is to review chronic recurrent low-energy trauma to the cervical and/or lumbar spine that may lead to degenerative changes in soccer players.

Methods

Design of the study

A descriptive cross-sectional study was designed. Dependent variables and independent variables were participants (active and veteran soccer players and their age-matched controls), and trunk muscle strength, flexibility and radiological assessment of lumbar spine degeneration, respectively.

Participants

Fifteen active (age range 20 to 25 years) and 14 veteran (age range 30 to 35 years) soccer players participated in the study. Active participants had been playing soccer for at least 5 years in the first and second division amateur teams whereas the veterans had played soccer for first and second division amateur teams for at least 10 years. The period between the veterans' cessation of playing to measurement time was in the range of 3 months to 2 years. Age-matched subjects (active group's age-matched control, Control 1 and veteran group's age-matched control, Control 2), who did not participate in regular sports and their weekly physical activity levels were less than $45 \, min.day^{-1}$ and $3 \, days.week^{-1}$, formed the control groups. The aim of the study and possible side effects of measurements were explained to each participant and written permission was obtained. Body height and mass were measured and the body mass index (BMI), defined as the ratio of body mass in kilograms to the square of the standing body height in metres ($kg.m^2$), was calculated.

Trunk muscle strength

Isokinetic trunk muscle strength was measured using the Biodex Pro-3 System (Biobex Medical Inc, Shirly, NY). Peak torque to body weight parameter was recorded. Participants warmed up on a cycle ergometer for 5 min before the tests. After warm-up, participants were placed in a semi-standing (hips and knees flexed at 15 to 30 degrees) position on the seat of the instrument (Figure 14.1). The axis of rotation of the dynamometers' resistance adaptor was adjusted in line with the anterior superior iliac spine. Torso straps were firmly applied for maximum restraint and comfort. The pelvis and thighs were stabilized with straps designed to minimize extraneous body movements. After stabilization, participants performed 2 to 3 movements for formalization, and finally performed the test.

Subjects performed trunk flexion and extension for five repetitions at $1.05 \, rad.s^{-1}$ and 10 repetitions at $2.09 \, rad.s^{-1}$ with a 10–second rest interval between the test speeds. The reliability of trunk flexion and extension isokinetic strength testing had been previously established with intra-class correlation coefficients and were reported as 0.89–0.95 for the peak torque of trunk flexion and 0.80–0.92 for the peak torque of trunk extension at the speed of $1.57 \, rad.s^{-1}$.

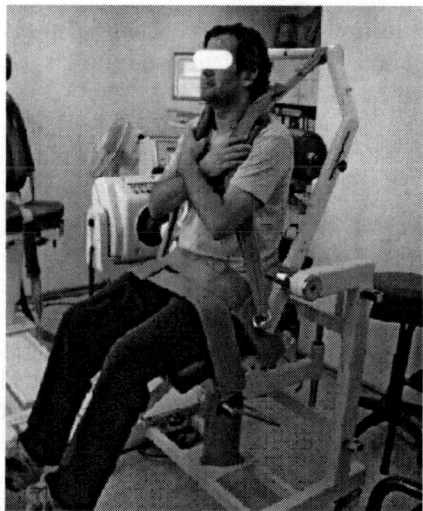

Figure 14.1 Trunk muscle strength measurements

Spinal flexibility

A modified Schober test was used to measure lumbar flexion flexibility. The test method required a plastic tape measure and pen to mark the skin overlaying the lumbosacral spine. With the subject standing erect, the first mark was placed at the lumbosacral junction. A second mark was placed 5 cm below the lumbosacral junction, and the third mark 10 cm above the junction. The subject was than asked to bend forward as far as possible, as though to touch the toes and the new distance between marks two and three was measured. Lumbar flexion was expressed as the difference between this measurement and the initial distance of 15 cm.

Radiological assessment of degeneration

Anterior-posterior and lateral radiographs of the lumbar spine were obtained on Agfa Crurix films using the Siemens Multix C x-ray machine. The distance of the x-ray source to the participants was 100 cm and the tube current was 6.4 mA per second; 72 Kwp-energy was used to obtain the images. Degenerative changes were scored according to Kellgren and Lawrence (1958).

Data collection and analyses

Data were collected in-season from September 2005 to June 2006 for first and second division amateur teams of Ankara with permission of team managers and technical directors. A multivariate analysis of variance (MANOVA) analysis was performed to compare groups. Post-hoc Bonferroni tests were used to identify statistically significant differences. The Statistical Package for Social Sciences

(SPSS) was used for statistical analyses. Correlation between dependent variables, lumbar spine degeneration, spinal flexibility, and trunk strength, was assessed by Pearson's coefficient calculations.

Results

The groups were comparable in terms of age, mass, height, experience and BMI values. Descriptive demographic data for participants are presented in Table 14.1.

A multivariate analysis of variance (MANOVA) was conducted to determine the effect of playing soccer on the back strength and degeneration variables. Significant differences were found between the soccer and control groups on dependent measures, Wilks' $\Lambda = 0.42$, ($F_{15,135} = 3.27$, $P < 0.001$). Analyses of variances (ANOVA) on each dependent variable were conducted as follow-up tests to the MANOVA. Using the Bonferroni method, each ANOVA was tested at the 0.05 level. A significant difference was found between veteran soccer players and active soccer players in terms of lumbar disc degeneration ($F_{3,53} = 4.18$, $P < 0.01$ $\eta^2 = 0.19$). Veteran soccer players displayed greater lumbar spine degeneration (Table 2) than active players.

The active soccer players showed greater trunk extension strength (Table 14.3) at 1.05 ml.s^{-1} than the other groups in the study, ($F_{3,53} = 7.33$, $P < 0.001$, $\eta^2 = 0.29$). They also demonstrated greater trunk flexion in both speeds than veteran players ($F_{3,53} = 5.41$, $P < 0.003$, $\eta^2 = 0.23$ and ($F_{3,53} = 4.76$, $P < 0.005$, $\eta^2 = 0.21$ There was no significant difference between soccer groups and the age-matched control groups in terms of their spinal flexion, ($F_{3,53} = 0.03$, $P < 0.80$, $\eta^2 = 0.02$).

Discussion

Playing soccer can cause acute and chronic injuries that may lead to lumbar spine degeneration. Axial loading during spear tackles in American football is the main mechanisms of acute cervical spine injuries (Torg et al., 2002). Chronic injuries to the cervical spine in soccer are less frequently evaluated. Recently, Kartal et al. (2004) reported cervical spinal degeneration due to playing soccer. It was assumed

Table 14.1 Physiological details of participants

	N	Age (years)	Mass (kg)	Height (m)	BMI (kg/ m^2)	Experience (years)
Active soccer players	15	21.5 ± 1.6	73.3 ± 6.1	1.75 ± 0.052	23.8 ± 1.5	7.7 ± 1.9
Control group 1	15	22.6 ± 1.5	70.5 ± 11.7	1.75 ± 0.078	23 ± 2.9	
Veteran soccer players	14	31.9 ± 2.4	76.0 ± 12.3	1.74 ± 0.041	24.9 ± 3.6	15.2 ± 3.7
Control group 2	13	31.0 ± 1.7	77.3 ± 13.2	1.76 ± 0.058	24.7 ± 3.4	

Table 14.2 Lumbar disc degeneration differences between groups (neans ± SD)

	N	Lumbar disc degeneration (Kellgren and Lawrence 1958)	Spinal flexibility (cm)
Active soccer players	15	0.40 ± 0.5*	22.1 ± 1.5
Control group 1	15	0.33 ± 0.4	21.6 ± 1.2
Veteran soccer players	14	1.21 ± 0.8*	21.8 ± 1.0
Control Group 2	13	0.84 ± 1.1	22.1 ± 1.2

* Demonstrates the significant difference between active soccer players and veterans

Table 14.3 Comparisons of the four groups' (20–25 soccer, 20–25 control, 30–35 soccer, and 30–35 control) trunk extension/flexion strengths (Nm) at two speeds (1.05 and 2.09 rad.s^{-1}) (means ± SD)

	N	Trunk flexion at 1.05 (%)	Trunk extension at 1.05 (%)	Trunk flexion at 2.09 (%)	Trunk extension at 2.09 (%)
Active soccer players	15	279.2 ± 47.2*	497.5 ± 54*[†]	247.4 ± 36.3*	462.4 ± 65.5
Control group 1	15	251.7 ± 27.6	415.7 ± 62.4[†]	212.9 ± 34.1	411.7 ± 53.5
Veteran soccer players	14	233.9 ± 42.5*	428.2 ± 81*	198.1 ± 22.9*	418.5 ± 90.2
Control group 2	13	222.0 ± 41.6	391.6 ± 53.6	206.7 ± 53.2	389.8 ± 67.8

* Demonstrates the significant difference between active soccer players and veterans [†] demonstrates the significant difference between active soccer players and their controls

that similar mechanisms that cause cervical spinal degeneration may lead to lumbar spinal degeneration in soccer players.

There was a significant difference between soccer playing groups; veteran soccer players displayed significant signs of lumbar spine degeneration when compared to the active group. Lumbar spine degeneration may occur without low-back symptoms. Results were consistent with other studies. Videman *et al.* (1995) demonstrated lumbar spine degeneration increased in former elite athletes, especially in former weight-lifters, when compared to age-matched controls. Similarly, Sohal and Allen (1978) discovered lower lumbar spinal degeneration and free radical formation in connection with strenuous exercise. Reilly *et al.* (2000) declared that many activities in soccer were forceful and explosive and power output during such activities is related to the strength of the muscles engaged. Leatt *et al.* (1986) found height reduction in the spine induced by circuit training with weights and distance running, implicating spinal loading. Troup *et al.* (1987) highlighted that the nucleus of the disc and epiphyseal plates of the spine were especially vulnerable to injury without pain.

Lumbar flexibility of soccer players was similar to age-matched controls in this study. Some previous authors (Biering-Sorensen, 1984; Mayer *et al.*, 1984) noted a general decrease in spinal mobility associated with low-back pain in sports, and Howes and Isdale (1972) also showed a decrease in spinal mobility in their subjects. The lack of a significant difference between active soccer players and age-matched sedentary controls in the present study is at odds with these findings. The degeneration of the lumbar spine in the veteran soccer players compared with the other groups may be explained by the active soccer players' greater trunk extension strength at 1.05 rad.s⁻¹. Having abnormal trunk extension strength may cause lumbar spine degeneration in later years. Furthermore, a negative correlation was found between trunk flexion strength at 2.09 rad.s⁻¹ and lumbar spine degeneration. This result suggests that possessing high trunk flexion strength prevented degeneration of the lumbar spine. It is recommended that technical directors should take trunk flexion strength and spinal flexibility into consideration in their training programmes in order to prevent degeneration of the lumbar spine.

These investigations provide some support for the idea that playing and training for soccer at high intensity over a long period of time may cause degeneration in the lumbar spine without symptoms of pain. Degeneration of the lumbar spine can be observed in soccer players in later years. Trunk extension strength may be a reason for the lumbar spine degeneration. A small sample and the cross-sectional nature of the current study make it difficult to draw inferences for an entire population of soccer players.

References

Altunsoz, O.S., Salci, Y. and Korkusuz, F., 2007, Effects of long term playing soccer on lumbar spine degeneration. *Journal of Sports Science and Medicine*, 6 (Suppl. 10), 23–4.

Biering-Sorensen, F., 1984, Physical measurements as risk indicators for low-back trouble over a one-year period. *Spine*, 9, 106–19.

Brooks, J.H.M. and Fuller, C.W., 2006, The influence of methodological issues on the results and conclusions from epidemiological studies of sports injuries. *Sports Medicine*, 36, 459–72.

Delaney, S.J. and Al-Kashmiri, A., 2005, Neck injuries presenting to emergency departments in the United States from 1990 to 1999 for ice hockey, soccer and American football. *British Journal of Sports Medicine*, 39, 21–6.

Howes, R.G. and Isdale, I.C., 1972, The loose back: an unrecognized syndrome. *Rheumatology and Physical Medicine*, 11, 72–7.

Kartal, A., Yildiran, I., Senkoylu, A. and Korkusuz, F., 2004, Soccer causes degenerative changes in the cervical spine. *European Spine Journal*, 13, 76–82.

Kellgren, J.H. and Lawrence, J.S., 1958, Osteoarthrosis and disk degeneration in an urban population. *Annals of the Rheumatic Diseases*, 17, 388–97.

Leatt, P., Reilly, T. and Troup, J.G., 1986, Spinal loading during circuit weight-training and running. *British Journal of Sports Medicine*, 20, 119–24.

Mayer, T.G., Gatchel, R.J., Kishino, N., Keeley, J., Capra, P., Mayer, H., Barnett, J. and Mooney, V., 1984, Objective assessment of spine function following industrial injury: a prospective study with comparison group and one-year follow-up. *Spine*, 10, 482–93.

Reilly, T., Bangsbo, J. and Franks, A., 2000, Anthropometric and physiological predispositions for elite soccer. *Journal of Sports Sciences*, 18, 669–83.

Shelly, M.J., Butler, J.S., Timlin, M., Walsh, M.G., Poynton, A.R. and O'Byrne, J.M., 2006, Spinal injuries in Irish rugby. *Journal of Bone and Joint Surgery*, 88–B, 771–5.

Sohal, R.S. and Allen R.G., 1978, Oxidative stress as a causal factor in differentiation and aging: a unifying hypothesis. *Experimental Gerontology*, 25, 499–522.

Torg, J.S., Guille, J.T. and Jaffe, S., 2002, Injuries to the cervical spine in American football players. *Journal of Bone and Joint Surgery*, 84–A, 112–22.

Troup, J.D., Foreman, T.K., Baxter, C.E. and Brown, D., 1987, Volvo Award in Clinical Sciences: the perception of back pain and the role of psychophysical tests of lifting capacity. *Spine*, 12, 645–57.

Videman, T., Sarna, S., Battie, M.C., Koskinen, S., Gill, K., Paananen, H. and Gibbons, L., 1995, The long-term effects of physical loading and exercise lifestyles on back-related symptoms, disability, and spinal pathology among men. *Spine*, 20, 699–709.

15 Enthesis pain and height growth velocity curve in junior high school soccer players

Rie Nakazawa,[1] *Masaaki Sakamoto,*[1]
Takehiko Yamaji,[1] *Kazumasa Nakagawa,*[1]
Nobuaki Inomata,[1] *Shin-ichi Sakurai*[1] *and*
Yoichi Kusama[2]

[1] Gunma University Graduate School of Medicine, Japan; [2] Maebashi Kise Junior High School, Japan

Introduction

In soccer, the period from 9 to 13 years of age is commonly called the golden age. This period is considered most important for training soccer players because the efficiency of acquiring techniques is high, but the period overlaps with the adolescent growth spurt, increasing the risk of incurring injuries. An imbalance in physical growth occurs during the growth period and extension stresses on muscle and tendon may be very likely to injure musculoskeletal junctions. Sports injuries during the growth period have been associated with the increase in height per year, which suggests that this height increase is involved in the occurrence of enthesis pain that characterizes the growth period.

The purpose of this study was to examine the relationship between the height growth velocity curve and enthesis pain of the lower extremities among the junior high school soccer players.

Methods

Subjects

The subjects were 107 male students belonging to soccer clubs of three junior high schools (47, 23, and 37 students, respectively) in Gunma Prefecture. The purpose of this study was explained to the school presidents, instructors, parents, and subjects, and informed consent was obtained. This study was approved by the Ethical Review Board of the Japanese Society of Physical Fitness and Sports Medicine.

Study items

To confirm enthesis pain, pain of motion and tenderness, the musculoskeletal junctions were examined by palpation, and the onset time was established by interview. The subjects' heights that were measured yearly during periodic school health check-ups from the first grade of elementary school to the grade at the time of this study were utilised.

Height growth velocity curve

The height growth per year was calculated, and the height growth velocity curves were prepared using the cubic spline curve of SPSS. The phases were determined according to Murata's (1996) classification (Figure 15.1).

The relationship between each phase and enthesis pain was investigated by means of the chi-square test. In addition, the phase at time of enthesis pain onset was investigated.

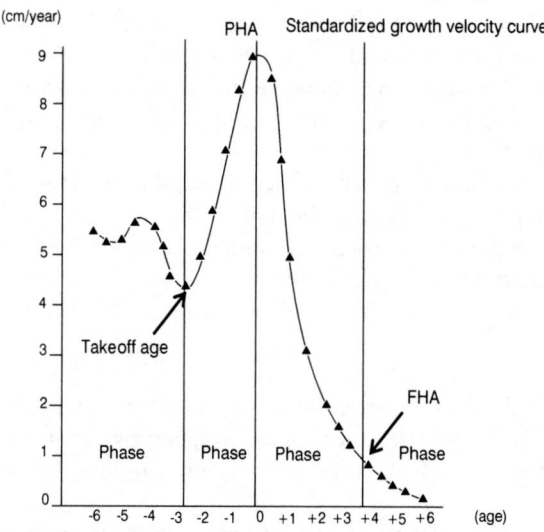

Phase : To take off age
Phase : From take off age to PHA (age of peak height velocity)
Phase : From PHA to FHA * (age of final height)
Phase : From FHA
*FHA: At this age, the height increase for one year became 1 cm or less.

Figure 15.1 The phase of the height growth velocity curve

Table 15.1 The location of enthesis pain

Location	Number
Anterior inferior iliac spine	3
Patella superior	1
Patella inferior	3
Patella tendon	7
Tuberositas tibias	18
Achilles tendon	5
Plantaris muscle	4

Table 15.2 Enthesis pain and height growth velocity curve phase

	Phase I	Phase II	Phase III	Total
Enthesis pain group	2	19	11	32
Non enthesis pain group	6	29	37	72
Total	8	48	48	104

Results

Height growth velocity curves were calculated for 104 subjects, excluding 3 subjects whose height measurements in elementary schools were missing (1 second grader and 2 first graders). At the time of measurement, 8 subjects were in phase I, 48 were in phase II, and 48 were in phase III.

There were 32 subjects who suffered from enthesis pain (31, Table 15.1): 2 were in phase I; 19 were in phase II; and 11 were in phase III. The relationship between the height growth velocity curve phase and the presence or absence of enthesis pain was investigated by means of the chi-square test; there was no significant association (Table 15.2).

The onset time of enthesis pain could be confirmed in 29 of the 32 subjects who reported enthesis pain. The phase at the time of onset was I in 5 subjects, II in 19, and III in 5, showing that enthesis pain most frequently occurred in phase II.

The chi-square test was not significant.

Conclusion

There are large individual variations in growth and development from the upper grades of elementary school to junior high school. Setting a training level without considering individual growth rates causes sports injuries during the growth period.

To understand how growth and development vary among individuals, it is useful to evaluate individual developmental age using the height growth velocity curve. Sekiguchi *et al.* (1993) investigated the relationship between the age of peak height velocity (PHA) of the height growth velocity curve and the onset time of Osgood-Schlatter disease; they found that the onset time was consistent with phase II. Koga *et al.* (2000) reported that the occurrence of Osgood-Schlatter's disease was concentrated at about the secondary height growth peak. Similarly, in the present study, the onset time of enthesis pain most frequently corresponded to phase II. Since height increased rapidly and the growth of bones and muscles/ tendons were imbalanced in phase II, close attention should be paid to careful training during this period of growth.

In Japan, the height growth velocity curve can be prepared using heights measured in April–June every grade by the method specified by the School Health Law, and easily evaluated in sporting fields. Promotion of the evaluation of development age using the height growth velocity curve in sporting fields, and calling attention to the possible occurrence of enthesis pain and adjustment of the training level, particularly for players in phase II, are important for preventing sports injuries during the growth period.

Acknowledgments

The authors wish to express their profound gratitude to the presidents, teachers, and soccer club members of each junior high school who cooperated in this study. We would also like to thank the physical therapists for their cooperation in obtaining the measurements.

References

Koga, Y., Omori, G., Tanabe, Y. and Terashima, K., 2000, Sports disorders in growth period. *Orthopaedic Surgery and Traumatology*, 43, 1181–7.

Murata, M., 1996, Height velocity curve in childhood and adolescence. *Obstetrical and Gynecological Therapy*, 72, 401–6.

Sekiguchi, H., Koga, Y., Ushiyama, Y., Sugimoto, H., Kawasaki, M. and Yoguchi, A., 1993, Growth evaluation to estimate strength of sports activities. *Japanese Journal of Orthopaedic Sports Medicine*, 12, 513–15.

16 Sports injuries in female soccer players

Hiroyuki Horino

School of Sport Sciences, Waseda University, Japan

Introduction

In recent years as female soccer players have been increasing in number, several researchers have investigated sports injuries amongst them (Brynhildsen *et al.*, 1990; Engström *et al.*, 1991). They reported that the ratio of injuries to the leg joint and knee joint were higher than the other regions. Moreover, compared with male footballers, it was reported that the rates of anterior cruciate ligament damage and compression fracture were notable (Lindenfeld *et al.*, 1994; Arendt and Dick, 1995; Mandelbaum and Putukian, 1999; Wojtys *et al.*, 2003).

In order to prevent sports injuries, it is important to clarify the relation between the players' growing process and sports injuries. Moreover, it is most important for coaches and players to understand effective prevention strategies and proper treatment for sports injuries and to practise them when a player is injured. In particular, there is little research on sports injuries in female footballers who placecontinuously.

The purpose of this study was to clarify the characteristics of sports injuries in female soccer players. A further objective was to discuss prevention of the sports injuries in woman footballers, regard to their knowledge and their experience of receiving first aid.

Methods

Altogether 365 university female soccer players (20.2±1.25 years) participated in this study. After explanation and voluntary consent, subjects completed a questionnaire to investigate their experience of injuries throughout their career, such as sites of injury, situation, age, and subjective cause. They reported all sports injuries which had interrupted their training in the past. Their knowledge and practice of first aid ("rest", "ice", "compression", and "elevation" – "RICE") were also investigated.

Results

The sites of injury and participants' age are indicated in Table 16.1. The incidence of leg injury was remarkably high compared with other regions. In particular, the percentages of the injuries to leg and knee joints were notably high. As Table 16.2 shows, non-contact injuries were significantly higher than contact injuries ($\chi^2(1) = 44.46$, $P<0.001$). The injury rate increased remarkably at 16 years (during high school).

About half of the players had received first aid treatment ("RICE") since they reached 18 years. Table 16.3 shows experience of receiving first aid. Although their knowledge and practice of "Rest" and "Ice" were at a high level, "Compression" and "Elevation" were not as well-known or practised.

Discussion

The results indicated that for these female soccer players many of the injuries occurred on the lower extremity and were non-contact injuries. Our data support several research reports that the ratio of injuries at the leg joint and the knee joint were remarkably high in female footballers.

Wojtys *et al.* (1996) argued that female soccer players had some problems with anterior cruciate ligament damage. They pointed out two problems in women athletes, such as shortage and imbalanced timing in exerting muscular power in hamstrings and quadriceps femoris. According to Heidt *et al.* (2000), combined training aimed at improvements in capabilities of speed and agility can decrease sports injuries. That is, it is considered that the physiological characteristics of the female player can be improved by suitable training to increase her abilities. Therefore, in order to complement the female physiological characteristics, it

Table 16.1 Injury site and age

	Less than 12	13–15	16–18	19–24	Total	(%)
Head, face, neck	1	3	7	8	19	(2.9)
Arm/forearm	0	1	1	3	5	(0.8)
Shoulder, clavicle	1	1	2	5	9	(1.4)
Elbow	0	1	1	3	5	(0.8)
Hand	4	0	9	19	32	(4.9)
Trunk	0	8	9	21	38	(5.8)
Hip	0	0	1	6	7	(1.1)
Thigh	0	4	18	37	59	(9.0)
Knee	4	3	37	69	113	(17.3)
Leg	1	5	16	15	37	(5.6)
Ankle	3	17	104	187	311	(47.5)
Foot	1	2	6	11	20	(3.1)
Total	15	45	211	384	655	
(χ^2)	(2.3)	(6.9)	(32.2)	(43.5)		(100.0)

Table 16.2 Injury occurence

	Number	(%)
Contact	255	39
Non-contact	400	61

Table 16.3 Experience of using first aid ("RICE")

	Age	Adequate experience	Inadequate experience	No experience	Uninformed
Rest	Less than 12	61.5	7.7	7.7	23.1
	13–15	66.7	23.1	2.6	7.7
	16–18	56.6	26.9	12.1	4.4
	19 or older	55.2	28.2	15.1	1.5
Ice	Less than 12	23.1	15.4	46.2	15.4
	13–15	64.1	12.8	12.8	10.3
	16–18	64.0	16.9	11.1	7.9
	19 or older	71.9	12.8	12.8	2.6
Compression	Less than 12	14.3	7.1	71.4	7.1
	13–15	36.8	13.2	39.5	10.5
	16–18	31.5	11.0	45.3	12.2
	19 or older	47.2	14.3	33.5	4.5
Elevation	Less than 12	8.3	8.3	66.7	16.7
	13–15	18.3	21.1	39.5	21.2
	16–18	28.3	15.6	47.8	8.3
	19 or older	42.3	13.7	40.5	3.6

is important for coaches and players to recognize and to establish appropriate training programmes.

It became clear that sports injuries increased at high school when the females' performance level and training load increased. However, our results indicated that university players were not knowledgeable about first aid methods. Inadequate treatment for injuries can worsen the damage and cause delay in recovery from the injury.

Our data also indicated that most of the females were not adequately informed about first aid for sports injuries. In order to improve the playing environment for female footballers, it is important to spread both knowledge and adequate practice of first aid from a young age.

Conclusion

Serious injuries increased from high school age. Therefore, coaches and players of female soccer teams should have appropriate knowledge and positive awareness about sports injuries so as to facilitate proper prevention and treatment.

References

Arendt, E. and Dick, R., 1995, Knee injury patterns among men and women in collegiate basketball and soccer. *American Journal of Sports Medicine*, 23, 694–701.

Brynhildsen, J., Ekstrand, J., Jeppsson, A. and Tropp, H., 1990, Previous injuries and persisting symptoms in female soccer players. *International Journal Sports Medicine*, 11, 489–92.

Engström, B., Johansson, C. and Tömkvist, H., 1991, Soccer injuries among elite female players. *American Journal of Sports Medicine*, 19, 372–5.

Heidt, R. S. Jr. Sweeterman, L. M., Carlonas, R. L., Traub, J. A. and Tekulve, F. X., 2000, Avoidance of Soccer injuries with preseason conditioning. *American Journal of Sports Medicine*, 28, 341–3.

Lindenfeld, T. N., Schmitt, D. J., Hendy, M. P., Mangine, R. E. and Noyes, F. R., 1994, Incidence of injury in indoor soccer. *American Journal of Sports Medicine*, 22, 364–71.

Mandelbaum, B. R. and Putukian, M., 1999, Medical concerns and specificities in female soccer players. *Science and Sports*, 14, 254–60.

Wojtys, E.M., Kothari, S.U. and Huston, L.J., 1996, Anterior cruciate ligament functional brace in sports. American Journal of Sports Medicine, 24, 539–46.

Wojtys, E.M., Huston, L.J., Schock, H.J., Boylan, J.P. and Ashton-Miller, J.A. (2003). Gender differences in muscular protection of the knee in torsion in size-matched athletes. *Journal of Bone and Joint Surgery*, 85, A(5), 782–9.

17 A comparison of injury in professional and non-professional male graduate youth soccer players

Franck Le Gall,[1] *Christopher Carling*[2] *and Thomas Reilly*[3]

[1] Institut National du Football, France; [2] Lille Football Club, France; [3] Research Institute for Sport and Exercise Sciences, Liverpool John Moores University, UK

Introduction

Youth soccer academies are paramount in producing players capable of playing at professional level and eventually representing their country. The Clairefontaine National Institute of Football (Institut National du Football – INF)., France, is widely respected for its approach to the development and care of future professional players. However, there is a limited amount of information on injury in elite male youth players hoping to become professional players (Le Gall *et al.*, 2006). At elite levels, the impact of injury has to be considered from the point of view of player development and skill acquisition. An audit of injury in elite English youth players showed that a significant proportion of development time can be missed through injury (Price *et al.*, 2004). An elite player who is frequently or severely injured may struggle to achieve maximal levels of skill if training and competition are missed. A player's potential to succeed may therefore in part be determined by his susceptibility to injury (Singer and Janelle 1999).

The aim of the present study therefore was to investigate in elite French youth soccer players, whether incidence, severity and patterns of injury differed in graduate players who did not acquire a professional contract compared to those who succeeded in signing a contract as a full-time professional.

Materials and methods

In this prospective observational study, injuries were investigated in elite youth players at the Clairefontaine Institut National du Football. The INF has a three-year residency policy and segregates its players into three age groups: INF 1st year (under 14 years old), INF 2nd year (under 15 years old) and INF 3rd year (under 16 years old). In the present study, epidemiological data were collected on a total of 192 players who completed the three-year residency cycle. Graduate players were divided into two cohorts for comparison: those that succeeded in signing a contract as a full-time professional (professional graduates) and those who did not acquire a professional contract (non-professional graduates). Data were captured over a period of ten seasons from August 1994 to June 2004. Consent forms were completed for each subject by a parent or guardian as the players were under the legal age of consent. Ethics approval for the study was obtained from the Fédération Française de Football.

A recordable injury was defined as one received during training or competition and which prevented the injured party from participating in normal training or competition for more than 48 hours, not including the day of the injury (Price *et al.*, 2004). Re-injuries were defined as the same type of injury to the same side and location within two months after the final rehabilitation day of the previous injury (Hagglund *et al.*, 2005). The type, location and severity of the injury were recorded, the latter depending upon the time the player was absent from training or competition. Injury severity was classed into four sub-divisions; as major (more than 4 weeks), moderate (1–4 weeks), mild (4–7 days) and minor (2–3 days) respectively (Le Gall *et al.*, 2006). Finally, the precise date of each injury was recorded in order to examine monthly variations in the data over the entire playing season.

Data were analysed using frequencies and cross-tabulation procedures, and statistical comparisons within the data set were investigated using the non-parametric Mann-Whitney U-test (SPSS Science Inc, Chicago, IL). The level of accepted statistical significance was set at $P<0.05$.

Results

Altogether, 192 graduate players were assessed over the 10-year study period with 49 (25.5%) classed as professionals and 143 (74.5%) as non-professionals. Injuries documented across all age groups totalled 1152 with an overall injury acquisition per player of 4.4 per 1000 playing hours (Table 17.1). No significant difference in overall incidence of injury was reported between groups.

There was no significant difference in the incidence of training injuries between graduate groups. A higher incidence of match injury was reported in professional graduates, a result approaching significance (13.9 v 9.1, $P = 0.064$). Professional players reported a significantly greater incidence of match injury for the U16 category compared to non-professionals (17.8 v 10.0, $P = 0.039$).

Table 17.2 illustrates injuries according to severity. Professionals sustained a significantly higher incidence of minor injuries compared to non-professionals (2.2 v 1.1, $P = 0.020$). When moderate and major injuries were combined (injuries

Table 17.1 Injuries according to training and competition

Competition	Injuries professionals			Injuries non-professionals			Injuries all groups		
	N	%	Per 1000 hours exp	N	%	Per 1000 hours exp	Total	%	Per 1000 hours exp
Training	226	64.8	3.9	570	71.0	3.4	796	69.1	3.5
Match	123	35.2	13.9	233	29.0	9.1	356	30.9	10.3
Total	349	100.0	5.3	803	100.0	4.2	1152	100.0	4.4

Table 17.2 Severity of injuries

Severity	Injuries professionals			Injuries non-professionals			Injuries all groups		
	No.	%	Per 1000 hours exp	No.	%	Per 1000 hours exp	No.	%	Per 1000 hours exp
Minor (1–3 days)	147	42.1	2.2	205	25.5	1.1	352	30.6	1.4
Mild (4–7 days)	94	26.9	1.4	243	30.3	1.3	337	29.3	1.3
Moderate (1–4 weeks)	82	23.5	1.2	262	32.6	1.4	344	29.9	1.3
Major (1 month+)	26	7.4	0.4	93	11.6	0.5	119	10.3	0.5

lasting more than one week), a significantly higher percentage was reported in non-professionals (44.2% v 30.9%, $P = 0.027$). Players were absent from training and competition for an average of 33.5 and 36.2 days per year for professionals and non-professionals respectively. Both groups were most often absent from training and competition in the U14 group (professionals = 36.7 days and non-professionals = 44.7 days).

No significant differences were reported in injury types between graduate groups. The majority of injuries in both groups were contusions, sprains and strains. The only result approaching significance was the higher incidence of contusions/haematomae in professionals (1.9 v 1.2, $P = 0.064$). No significant differences were reported between groups for any particular injury location. Both professionals and non-professionals incurred the majority of their injuries to the ankle and thigh regions. A significant difference was reported in the incidence of lower extremity injuries in professionals compared to non-professionals (3.9 v 2.8, $P = 0.037$). For match injuries, professional graduates reported a significantly greater incidence of injuries to the lower leg (1.7 v 0.5, $P = 0.020$) and foot (1.3 v 0.6, $P = 0.037$).

No significant differences were found between groups in overall injury patterns and injury patterns in training. In professionals, there was a significantly higher incidence of contusions to the lower leg ($P = 0.031$) in matches. Professionals reported a significantly higher incidence of re-injury compared to non-professionals (0.14 v 0.06, $P = 0.039$).

No significant differences between groups were found in percentage of total injury according to month. A significantly greater percentage of match injuries was reported in non-professionals versus professionals in September (19.3% v 9.7%, $P = 0.012$).

Discussion

The present study is the first to identify and compare injury profiles – incidence, severity and patterns – in elite non-professional and professional graduate youth soccer players. No significant difference was found in the overall incidence of injury and training and match injury between professional and non-professional graduates. This result suggests that general injury incidence was not a deciding factor in whether the players progressed to professional status or not.

The significantly higher incidence of match injury reported in professionals in their final year at the centre may be linked to an increase in playing intensity. The majority of professional contracts are signed in the final year and the professional graduates were perhaps more determined and aggressive in trying to catch the eye of watching talent scouts, consequently increasing the risk of injury.

The impact of an injury in soccer can be considered in relation to its severity and the ability of players to recover both mentally and physically from injury determines the standard of achievement over time (Williams and Reilly, 2000). In the present study, a significantly higher incidence of injuries classed as minor (layoff duration of 1–3 days) was sustained in professional graduates whereas a significantly higher percentage of injuries lasting more than one week (moderate and major injuries combined) was reported in non-professionals. Injuries of longer duration impact negatively on player development time and skill acquisition. When development time lost to injury was compared within the different age categories, non-professional graduates lost close to five per cent more of their development time during their first year spent at the centre. This first year spent at the centre is extremely important in terms of skill acquisition and tactical development and the greater development time lost could have been a contributing factor in non-professionals eventually not signing a professional contract.

In the present study, it seemed that reoccurrence of injury is not a factor affecting the chances of elite youth players turning professional, as successful graduates reported a significantly higher incidence of re-injury than the unsuccessful players. The reasons for this higher incidence of re-injury in professional graduates are unclear although premature return to play may be a valid explanation (Walden *et al.*, 2005). Whilst the INF physician had the final word on when the players could return to play, many different factors contribute to this decision such as the importance of a game or practice, pain tolerance, motivation, and personality factors (Emery *et al.*, 2005).

The most frequent types (contusions, sprains, strains) and locations (ankle and thigh) of injury across both groups were similar, suggesting a common feature of playing soccer at elite youth levels (Le Gall *et al.*, 2006). However, significantly more injuries to the lower extremities and contusions to the lower leg in matches were reported in professional graduates. A major limitation of the present study is the lack of detailed information on the mechanism of injury: therefore, it is difficult to draw conclusions from these results. We can surmise that professional graduates may have played a more aggressive game or were targeted by other players due to their outstanding talent, factors which would lead to greater physical contact and increase the likelihood of injury to the lower regions of the body.

A significantly greater percentage of match injury was reported in September (the first month of matches) in non-professionals. It is difficult to suggest reasons for this discrepancy between groups as all the players followed the same pre-season August training programme. In early season, some youth players may not yet have reached an appropriate level of fitness and were therefore not in optimal physiological condition to withstand the stresses associated with the intensity of elite competition. Further investigation is warranted into identifying reasons for this disparity in early-season match injury.

Conclusion

In elite French youth players, there is no certainty whether injury played a part in whether players progressed or not to professional level. More complex factors such as game intelligence, anticipation and decision-making skills may better determine players' employability as professionals (Reilly *et al.*, 2000; Williams and Reilly, 2000). Nevertheless, injuries of a longer duration and subsequent development time lost were identified as more likely contributors to the failure of players who did not turn professional than were general injury incidence, patterns, seasonal disposition and re-injury.

References

Emery, C.A., Meeuwisse, W.H. and Hartmann, S.E., 2005, Evaluation of risk factors for injury in adolescent soccer: implementation and validation of an injury surveillance system. *American Journal of Sports Medicine*, 33, 1882–91.

Hagglund, M., Walden, M., Bahr, R. and Ekstrand, J., 2005, Methods for epidemiological study of injuries to professional football players: developing the UEFA model. *British Journal of Sports Medicine*, 39, 340–6.

Le Gall, F., Carling, C., Reilly, T., Vandewalle, H., Church, J. and Rochcongar, P., 2006, Incidence of injuries in elite French youth soccer players: a ten-season study. *American Journal Sports Medicine*, 34, 928–38.

Price, R.J., Hawkins, R.D., Hulse, M.A, and Hodson, A., 2004, The Football Association medical research programme: an audit of injuries in academy youth football. *British Journal of Sports Medicine*, 38, 466–71.

Reilly, T., Williams, A.M., Nevill, A. and Franks, A., 2000, A multidisciplinary approach to talent identification in soccer. *Journal of Sports Sciences*, 18, 695–702.

Singer, R.N. and Janelle, C.M., 1999, Determining sport expertise: from genes to supremes. *International Journal of Sports Psychology*, 30, 117–50.

Walden, M., Hagglund, M. and Ekstrand, J., 2005, Injuries in Swedish elite football: a prospective study on injury definitions, risk for injury and injury pattern during 2001. *Scandinavian Journal of Medicine and Science in Sports*, 15, 118–25.

Williams, A.M. and Reilly, T., 2000, Talent identification and development in soccer. *Journal of Sports Sciences*, 18, 657–67.

18 The effect of a succession of matches on the activity profiles of professional soccer players

Kunle Odetoyinbo,[1] *Blake Wooster*[2] *and Andy Lane*[3]

[1] Wolverhampton Wanderers Football Club, Medical Sports Science Department, UK; [2] ProZone Group Ltd, UK; [3] University of Wolverhampton, Department of Sport Sciences, UK

Introduction

In modern day soccer, as in many sports, the capacity to recover from intense training, competition and matches is often considered an important determinant of subsequent performance. Incomplete recovery may be a regular occurrence in soccer where players are required to compete repeatedly within a short time frame. Given that insufficient recovery may have implications with regards to fatigue, overreaching and injury (Naessens et al., 2000; Junge and Dvorak, 2004), enormous time and resources are invested into recovery practices, including diet (Burke and Loucks, 2006), hydration (Maughan et al., 2005), cold water immersion (Rubley et al., 2003), compression garments (Kraemer and Bush, 1998) and cool downs (Reilly and Rigby, 2002).

Professional UK-based soccer players competing in the Premiership and Championship leagues are often required to play competitive matches with only 1–2 days recovery and during the Christmas period these players may be required to play up to four matches in 7–8 days. This problem has been the subject of much debate, with many high-profile managers calling for this fixture congestion to be alleviated through the introduction of a mid-season break, as is the case in many European leagues. The potential for residual fatigue in these matches is high with possible implications in terms of the movement behaviours of players competing in successive matches.

With research to date limited to the influence of fatigue within matches (Di Salvo et al., 2006b) and over different phases of the season (Mohr et al., 2003), the aim of this study was to investigate recovery via analysis of activity profiles in professional UK-based soccer players over an intense period of matches.

Methods

This study incorporated time–motion analysis data captured via the computerised ProZone3 system (ProZone Group Ltd, UK). The video capture was performed at a variety of Premiership and Championship football stadia, where eight colour cameras were installed (ProZone®) at all four corners of the stadia. The camera's parameters (position, orientation, zoom and field of vision) were determined and fixed when installed (Vicon Surveyor 23x cameras dome/SVFT-W23). The eight cameras were positioned in order to produce a whole vision of the field. Furthermore every area of the field was covered by at least two cameras for accuracy, occlusion, resolution and resilience.

All cameras were cabled back to a central point and connected within a video distribution box. The distribution box splits the information gathered three ways: 1) to the primary capture equipment, 2) to the backup capture equipment and 3) to a telemetry unit. The primary capture equipment consisted of a high-specification server running Microsoft Windows Server 2000 (Microsoft®) and ProZone's proprietary capture software, PZ Stadium Manager ®. This system has been independently validated to verify the capture process and subsequent accuracy of data (Di Salvo *et al.*, 2006a).

Initially 14 teams from the Premiership and 8 teams from the Championship were assessed during an 8–day day fixture period (26 December 2005 to 3 January 2006). For the purpose of this study only those players who played 3 matches within 5 days (with 2 days in between Matches 1 and 2, plus 3 days between Matches 2 and 3) and completed 3 full matches (minimum 90 minutes) whilst playing in the same tactical position, were analysed.

This research model provided 16 players from 4 teams in a variety of outfield positions (3 full backs, 7 central defenders, 3 central midfielders, 1 wide midfielder and 2 attackers).

Activity profiles were constructed for each player's contribution based on ProZone's generic categories and thresholds:

- Sprint ($7.0\,\text{m.s}^{-1}$ and above)
- High-speed run ($5.5 – 6.9\,\text{m.s}^{-1}$)
- Run ($4.0–5.4\,\text{m.s}^{-1}$)
- Jog ($2.0–3.9\,\text{m.s}^{-1}$)
- Walk ($0.2–1.9\,\text{m.s}^{-1}$)
- Stand ($0–0.1\,\text{m.s}^{-1}$)

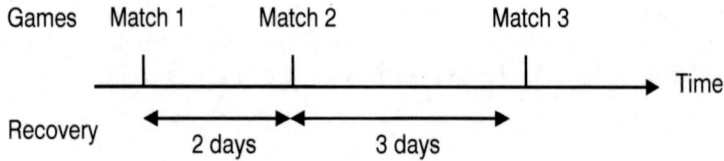

Figure 18.1 Research model

(A speed value was assigned to 'standing' in order to record the time spent performing this activity profile).

The distance covered, frequency and time spent for all of the above activity profiles were analysed, together with:

- High-intensity (HI) distance when the player's own team is in possession (m)
- HI distance when player's own team is without possession (m)
- HI distance when the ball is out of play (m)
- Recovery time (average time in between HI activity (s)
- Distance covered per minute of match (m)
- Average speed $(m.s^{-1})$
- Top speed $(m.s^{-1})$
- Relative Intensity (number of high intensity activities/time)

(HI includes all activity profiles above 5.5 $m.s^{-1}$).

A one-way ANOVA test was employed to determine the effect of successive matches using an SPSS statistical package. Post hoc analysis by paired t-test was undertaken to examine where differences between matches occurred.

Results and discussion

Recent computerised time–motion analysis describing distances covered by elite outfield soccer players in a single match ranged between 10.5–12.5 km (Bangsbo and Michalsik, 2002; Di Salvo *et al.*, 2006b) which are in the region of those reported in this study (10493 ± 1002 m to 10790 ± 809 m). Overall observation of the data suggests that the activity profiles were influenced by the short recovery periods between matches.

A difference was found (376.8 ± 259.2 v 273.6 ± 211 m, $P < 0.05$) in the amount of 'high intensity' (HI) distance covered with possession of the ball. Keeping possession of the ball is an important aspect of soccer match-play (Hughes and Franks, 2005) and the physical cost of work with the ball can place greater physical demands on players than movement without the ball (Reilly and Ball, 1984). In this study less work with the ball was completed by the third match, which might reflect aspects of fatigue that manifest across successive games. This result is supported by the finding that players performed less HI work when the ball was out of play (82.2 ± 40.9 v 53.1 ± 38.1 m, $P < 0.05$ for Matches 1 and 3 respectively). In these instances there is an opportunity for players to slow down in their movement and use the break in play to recover. Optimum performance often requires HI movement during this period, with coaches emphasising the need for players to move into positions early before 'effective' playing time restarts. These data suggest that players have difficulty in maintaining these aspects of HI performance when required to compete with very short recovery periods between matches.

Table 18.1 Mean values (±SD) for each variable for Matches 1–3 over 5 days

	Distance (m)		
	Match 1	Match 2	Match 3
Total distance	10695.9±882.5	10789.9±809.2	10492.6±1001.9
HI distance	889.2±263	858.5±300.8	768.8±260.8
Sprint distance	233.3±89.6	214.6±115.2	190.6±76
High speed run	655.9±186.1	643.9±197.2	578.3±206.8
Run distance	1639.7±311.1	1652.1±335.4	1613.6±367.2
Jog distance	4237.3±531.6	4415.8±497.8	4301.7±587.9
Walk distance	3902.8±195.2**	3839.1±194.7	3785.1±297.6**
HI with possession	376.8±259.2*	299.1±234.9	273.6±211*
HI without possession	430.3±134.6	500.4±171.7	442.1±145.8
HI distance ball out of play	82.2±40.9*	59±33.6	53.1±38.1*
	Frequency (number)		
	Match 1	Match 2	Match 3
Total number HI activities	113.6±26.6	114.1±36.4	99.1±35.9
Sprints	34±12.3	34.1±15.9	27.1±12.1
High speed run	126.5±28.9	126±40.8	111.1±38
Runs	364.9±59.2	378.8±83.2	352.8±85.2
Jogs	962.5±111.5	1002.6±133.7	956.2±146.6
	Duration (seconds)		
	Match 1	Match 2	Match 3
Sprinting	30.2±11.7	27.9±14.8	24.6±9.8
High speed run	107.3±30.3	105.3±32.1	94.5±33.7
Running	355.9±67	358.8±72.1	351±79.7
Jogging	1500.9±182.9	1563.6±167.4	1521.4±200.5
Walking	3491.4±241.9**	3426.7±217.9	3362.1±311.8**
	Other		
	Match 1	Match 2	Match 3
Recovery (s)	52.1±13.6	57.1±33.6	62.3±22.6
Relative intensity	1.2±0.3	1.2±0.4	1.1±0.4
Distance per minute	110.8±9.8	112.8±8.4	111.9±9
Top Speed (m/s)	9.1±0.3	9.0±0.5	9.0±0.3

* Denotes significant difference $P<0.05$ ** denotes significant difference $P<0.01$

With players generally performing less HI activity across the three matches, it may have followed that the walking profile demonstrated an inverse relationship. This was not the case with players also walking less across successive matches ($3902±195.2$ m v $3785.1±297.6$ m and $3491.4+241.9$ s v $3362.1±311.8$ s, $P<0.01$, in Matches 1 and 3 respectively). In fact, the only activity profiles not to demonstrate an obvious decline across games were the 'jogging' and 'running' profiles ($2.0–5.4$ m.s^{-1}), with the mean jogging distance covered actually increasing across games ($4237.3±531.6$ m v $4301.7±587.9$ m in Matches 1 and 3). This may suggest that HI intermittent activity behaviours, synonymous with modern-day soccer, could not be maintained during this intense fixture schedule and instead, players increasingly showed tendencies to cruise through matches.

Some of the results from this study, although not displaying statistical changes, may still have a bearing on match situations. For example, in Matches 1 and 3, the

HI distance covered (which encompasses sprint and high speed run distance), was 889.2 ± 263 v 768.8 ± 260.8 m respectively, which equates to approximately 114 ± 27 v 99 ± 36 HI activities performed for Matches 1 and 3. Given that margins for physical performance in elite level sports are so small, these observations cannot be ignored. The average recovery (time in between each discrete HI activity) increased across the course of Matches 1 to 3 by approximately 10 seconds (52.1 ± 13.6 v 57.1 ± 33.6 v 62.3 ± 22.6 s, respectively). A similar finding was observed in hockey players who played three games in four days (Spencer *et al.*, 2005). This alludes to the possibility that players may seek increased recovery times through slower activity profiles and that this is more likely when required to play matches in quick succession. It could be that in elite circles the more experienced players adapt their movement behaviour in the knowledge that they will be required to play successive matches with short rest periods between games.

Differences in activity profiles for individual players were also found within groups (total distance, HI distance, and high-intensity distance in possession, $P < 0.05$). Much of this can be explained by the hugely varying positional demands in football, which differentiate the workload and therefore recovery requirements of players with differing tactical roles. This was a limitation of the study, as was the potential impact of home and away influence and the relative demands imposed by differing opposition over the three matches.

The overall distance covered by players was quite similar between Matches 1 to 3 and this suggests a possible limitation of using distance covered as an indicator of match demands. It may be more pertinent to focus on the HI aspects of play, which constitute the more critical elements of soccer as indicative of this study.

Conclusion

In this study the activity profiles of UK-based professional soccer players were considered when three matches were played in five days. Overall, results suggest that players were able to recover when the total distance is considered over three matches. The data, however, also indicate that some residual fatigue may be apparent that affects certain high-intensity aspects of play.

The current findings provide a detailed description of the physical demands placed on elite soccer players during short recovery periods, which will influence the way teams approach training and preparation during intense playing schedules. The results might also be considered by governing bodies when designing fixture programmes. Other factors such as positional demands, home versus away fixtures, the varying approach of opposing teams and the nature of the matches previously played in, warrant further investigation.

References

Bangsbo, J. and Micholski, L., 2002, Assessment of the physiological capacity of elite soccer players. In *Science and Football IV*, edited by Spinks, W., Reilly, T. and Murphy, A. (London: Routledge), pp. 53–62.

Burke, L.M. and Loucks, A.B., 2006, Energy and carbohydrate for training and recovery. *Journal of Sports Sciences*, 24, 675–85.

Di Salvo, V., Collins, A., McNeill, B. and Cardinale, M., 2006a, Validation of Prozone®: a new video-based performance analysis system. *International Journal of Performance Analysis in Sport*, 6, 108–19.

Di Salvo, V., Baron, R., Tschan, H., Calderon Montero, F.J., Bachl, N. and Pigozzi, F., 2006b, Time–motion analysis performed in elite level soccer to quantify physical demands depending on positional role. *International Journal of Sport Medicine*, 27, 1–6.

Hughes, M. and Franks, I., 2005, Analysis of passing sequences, shots and goals in soccer. *Journal of Sports Sciences*, 23, 509–14.

Junge, A. and Dvorak, J., 2004, Soccer injuries. *Sports Medicine*, 34, 929–38.

Kraemer, W.J., and Bush, J.A., 1998, Compression garments: influence on muscle fatigue. *The Journal of Strength and Conditioning Research*, 12, 211–15.

Maughan, R.J., Shirreffs, S.M., Merson, S.J. and Horswill, C.A., 2005, Fluid and electrolyte balance in elite male football. *Journal of Sports Sciences*, 23, 73–9.

Mohr, M., Krustrup, P. and Bangsbo, J., 2003, Match performance of high-standard soccer players with special reference to development of fatigue. *Journal of Sports Sciences*, 23, 521–28.

Naessens, G., Chandler, T.J., Kibler, W.B. and Driessens, M., 2000, Clinical usefulness of nocturnal urinary noradrenaline excretion patterns in the follow up of training processes in high level soccer players. *Journal of Strength and Conditioning Research*, 14, 125–31.

Rubley, M.D., Holcomb, W.R. and Guadagnoli, M.A., 2003, Habituation following repeated ice bath immersion of the ankle. *Journal of Sport Rehabilitation*, 12, 323–32.

Reilly, T. and Ball, D., 1984, The net physiological cost of dribbling a ball. *Research Quarterly for Exercise and Sport*, 55, 49–50.

Reilly, T. and Rigby, M., 2002, Effect of an active warm-down following competitive soccer. In *Science and Football IV*, edited by Spinks, W., Reilly, T. and Murphy, A. (London: Routledge), pp. 226–9.

Spencer, M., Rechichi, C., Lawrence, S., Dawson, B., Bishop, D. and Goodman, C., 2005, Time–motion analysis of elite field hockey during several games in succession: a tournament scenario. *Journal of Sports Medicine and Science*, 8, 382–91.

19 Effects of whole-body vibration and PNF stretching on the flexibility and range of movement in elite Australian Rules football players

Ben Hinton,[1] *John Quinn,*[2] *Michael Newton*[1] *and Michael McGuigan*[1]

[1] Edith Cowan University, Australia; [2] Essendon Football Club, Australia

Introduction

The ability to collect the ball effectively from beneath the knees is a major skill in Australian Rules football (ARF), and flexibility in the lower limbs is a contributing factor in its success. It has been proposed that insufficient joint range of movement (ROM) caused by poor muscle flexibility is a probable cause of muscle injury (Shellock and Prentice, 1985; Jonhagen et al., 1994). A large number of hamstring injuries results every year from playing ARF with tightness of the hamstring musculature being cited for its regular occurrence (Orchard and Seward, 2002).

Whole-body vibration (WBV) training was originally used with Russian gymnasts in the 1970s and with cosmonauts to prepare their bodies for space travel (Issurin, 2005; Luo et al., 2005), and has been used in recent years as an exercise intervention (Cardinale and Bosco, 2003; Vella, 2005). Recent investigations focusing on WBV have reported positive results for its use in increasing jump height (Bosco et al., 1998; Torvinen et al., 2002; Cochrane and Stannard, 2005), bone density (Verschueren et al., 2004), localised blood flow (Mark et al., 2003), ROM and flexibility (Issurin, Liebermann and Tenenbaum, 1994; Issurin and Tenenbaum, 1999; Cochrane and Stannard, 2005; Sands et al., 2006; van den Tillaar, 2006).

Proprioceptive neuromuscular facilitation (PNF) stretching has been found to result in increased joint ROM and has been shown to be more effective than other forms of stretching such as static or ballistic stretching (Feland et al., 2001; Ross, 1999; Spernoga et al., 2001; van den Tillaar, 2006). Whole-body vibration influences similar mechanisms to that of PNF stretching, suggesting that WBV may confer a positive effect on muscle flexibility and the joint ROM. Issurin et al. (1994) and Sands et al. (2006) reported that joint ROM increased when vibratory stimulation (VS) was used in conjunction with static stretching. Both of these studies applied the VS treatment whilst the subjects performed the stretching exercises.

The purpose of this study was to determine whether WBV training conferred a positive effect on hamstring flexibility when incorporated with PNF stretching. It is hypothesised that the flexibility of the hamstring muscles is greater with WBV training and PNF stretching than PNF stretching alone.

Methods

Subjects

Twenty elite ARF players who participated in the 2006 Australian Football League (AFL) season agreed to take part in the study. Before participation, the subjects were fully informed about the protocol, and informed consent was obtained from all subjects prior to commencement. Ethical clearance was obtained from the Human Research Ethics Committee at Edith Cowan University. During the study, two subjects were forced to withdraw from the study due to injury which was not caused by the training protocol, leaving eighteen subjects (10 from the WBV group and 8 from the control group) (height 1.868 ± 0.061 m; mass 83.9 ± 8.0 kg; age 20 ± 3 years) to complete the study.

Test procedure

On the test days, all subjects performed a general five-minute warm up as instructed by fitness personnel at the football club. This protocol was the same for the duration of the study. Immediately following the warm up, subjects lay supine on a bench with the leg to be tested actively raised by the subject with the knee fully extended. The assessor used an extendable goniometer (Model 01135, Lafayette Instrument Company Inc, Indiana) and recorded active ROM as the angle (in degrees) between the mid-axilla and the epicondyle of the femur using the greater trochanter as the point of rotation. Each leg was tested three times and the average of these results used for analysis. The opposite leg remained extended on the bench. The same assessor performed all measurements during all test sessions to maintain a high reliability ($r = 0.95$). The assessor did not know which group the subjects belonged to when the subjects were tested to maintain non-bias during the study.

Training procedure

After the pre-test, subjects were randomly assigned to either a whole-body vibration group (WBV) or a control group (PNF only). Each subject was instructed at the familiarisation session how to complete the flexibility training. The training protocol was conducted after a general five-minute warm-up as instructed by fitness personnel at the football club. This protocol was the same for the duration of the study. At completion of the warm up, the control group performed ten dynamic squats moving through the full ROM. Each squat took approximately 4–5 s to complete. The WBV group performed ten dynamic squats moving through the full ROM whilst exposed to a vibration treatment on the VibroGym Professional vibration platform (VibroGym, Haarlem) for 45 s at a frequency of 40 Hz and amplitude of 2 mm. Each squat was also completed in 4–5 s.

The flexibility training involved both groups (WBV and control). After performing the dynamic squats, each group participated in PNF stretching of the hamstring muscles two times for each leg. Each subject stretched passively assisted by a partner. The subject lay supine on a mat on the floor and extended the leg to be stretched with the knee fully extended while the opposite leg remained lying in a straightened position on the floor. The partner stretched the subject's raised leg until either the subject indicated that he wished the stretching to stop, or the leg being stretched began to shake. This position was held for 30 s. The subject then performed a 5 s isometric contraction of the stretched leg by pushing the heel into the resisted hand of the partner. The hamstring muscles were then stretched again for a further 30 s. During stretching, the pelvis remained parallel to the ground. Each leg was stretched twice per training session in an alternating fashion at a frequency of three times per week for the six-week duration of the study.

Statistical analyses

Statistical analyses were performed using SPSS for Windows v14. Differences in ROM of the hamstrings of the left and right legs were tested by a 1×4 analysis of variance (ANOVA). The average increases in ROM from pre-test to post-test were tested using an independent samples t-test. Statistical significance was set at $P < 0.05$.

Results

Due to logistical issues, only three out of the four test sessions were completed. No significant differences in the initial ROM measurements were found between both groups.

After calculating the average increase per group from pre-test to post-test, it was found that the WBV group had a significantly larger average increase ($P < 0.05$) in hamstring flexibility (19.8%) when compared to that of the control group (9.2%). There was a significant difference in ROM found on the right leg from pre-test to post-test between the two groups (Figure 19.1).

Discussion/conclusion

The use of PNF stretching had a positive effect on the ROM of the hamstring muscles. However, when combined with WBV, the ROM increased to a greater extent (Figure 19.1). The superior result of the WBV group on hamstring ROM compared to the control group could be explained by two possible mechanisms.

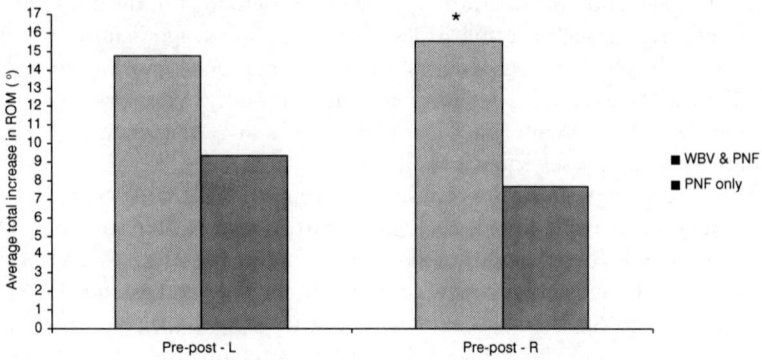

Figure 19.1 Average total increases in ROM for both groups from pre-test to post-test

* Significant difference in ROM between the two groups (*P*<0.05)

The first is the enhanced localised blood flow following WBV treatment (Bovenzi *et al.*, 2000; Rittweger *et al.*, 2000; Kerschan-Schindl *et al.*, 2001). Kerschan-Schindl *et al.* (2001) found an increase in blood flow after a WBV treatment of 9 min. The elevated blood flow increases muscle temperature which improves elasticity and facilitates a possible increase in ROM when stretching.

The second possible mechanism may be the activation of the tonic vibration reflex (TVR) (Eklund and Hagbarth, 1966; van den Tillaar, 2006). Whole-body vibration causes the soft tissues to deform which is capable of activating muscle spindles and may enhance the stretch-reflex loop (Eklund and Hagbarth, 1966; Wakeling *et al.*, 2002; Cardinale and Bosco, 2003). Cardinale and Bosco (2003) suggested that WBV exposure inhibits activation of the antagonist muscles through Ia-inhibitory neurons. Therefore activating the quadriceps would allow for a greater stretch of the hamstrings, allowing for an increase in ROM (van den Tillaar, 2006).

These two mechanisms could not be substantiated in the current study due to the lack of specific measurement equipment. The results from this study showed that combining WBV and PNF produces a greater increase in flexibility than PNF stretching alone. Further research should be directed at clarifying the mechanisms behind this finding.

References

Bosco, C., Cardinale, M., Tsarpela, O., Colli, R., Tihanyi, J., von Duvillard, S. P. *et al.*, 1998, The influence of whole body vibration on jumping performance. *Biology of Sport*, 15 (3), 157–64.

Bovenzi, M., Lindsell, C. J. and Griffin, M. J., 2000, Acute vascular responses to the frequency of vibration transmitted to the hand. *Occupational and Environmental Medicine*, 57, 422–30.

Cardinale, M. and Bosco, C., 2003, The use of vibration as an exercise intervention. *Exercise and Sports Sciences Reviews*, 31(1), 3–7.

Cochrane, D. J. and Stannard, S. R., 2005, Acute whole body vibration training increases vertical jump and flexibility performance in elite female field hockey players. *British Journal of Sports Medicine*, 39, 860–5.

Eklund, G. and Hagbarth, K. E., 1966, Normal variability of tonic vibration reflexes in man. *Experimental Neurology*, 16, 80–92.

Feland, J. B., Myrer, J. W. and Merrill, R. M., 2001, Acute changes in hamstring flexibility: PNF versus static stretch in senior athletes. *Physical Therapy in Sport*, 2(3), 186–93.

Issurin, V. B., 2005, Vibrations and their applications in sport: a review. *Journal of Sports Medicine and Physical Fitness*, 45, 324–36.

Issurin, V. B., Liebermann, D. G. and Tenenbaum, G., 1994, Effect of vibratory stimulation training on maximal force and flexibility. *Journal of Sports Sciences*, 12, 561–6.

Issurin, V. B. and Tenenbaum, G., 1999, Acute and residual effects of vibratory stimulation on explosive strength in elite and amateur athletes. *Journal of Sports Sciences*, 17, 177–82.

Jonhagen, S., Nemeth, G. and Eriksson, E., 1994, Hamstring injuries in sprinters: the role of concentric and eccentric hamstring muscle strength and flexibility. *American Journal of Sports Medicine*, 22, 262–6.

Kerschan-Schindl, K., Grampp, S., Henk, C., Resch, H., Preisinger, E., Fialka-Moser, V. *et al.*, 2001, Whole-body vibration exercise leads to alterations in muscle blood volume. *Clinical Physiology*, 21, 377–82.

Luo, J., McNamara, B. and Moran, K., 2005, The use of vibration training to enhance muscle strength and power. *Sports Medicine*, 35, 23–41.

Mark, A., MacDonald, M., Rabowchuck, M., Gordon, C. and Blimkie, C., 2003, Cardiovascular and metabolic responses during whole-body vibration exercise: a pilot study. *Canadian Journal of Applied Physiology*, 28 (Suppl.), S81.

Orchard, J. and Seward, H., 2002, Epidemiology of injuries in the Australian Football League: seasons 1997–2000. *British Journal of Sports Medicine*, 36, 39–45.

Rittweger, J., Beller, G. and Felsenberg, D., 2000, Acute physiological effects of exhaustive whole-body vibration exercise in man. *Clinical Physiology*, 20, 134–42.

Ross, M., 1999, Effect of lower-extremitiy position and stretching on hamstring muscle flexibility. *Journal of Strength and Conditioning Research*, 13(2), 124–9.

Sands, W. A., McNeal, J. R., Stone, M. H., Russell, E. M. and Jemni, M., 2006, Flexibility enhancement with vibration: acute and long-term. *Medicine and Science in Sports and Exercise*, 38, 720–5.

Shellock, F. G. and Prentice, W. E., 1985, Warming up and stretching for improved physical performance and prevention of sports-related injuries. *Sports Medicine*, 2, 267–78.

Spernoga, S. G., Uhl, T. L., Arnold, B. L. and Gansneder, B. M., 2001, Duration of maintained hamstring flexibility after a one-time, modified hold-relax stretching protocol. *Journal of Athletic Training*, 36(1), 44–8.

Torvinen, S., Kannus, P., Sievanen, H., Jarvinen, T. A. H., Pasanen, M., Kontulainen, S., Nenonen, A., Jarvinen, T.L., Packala, T., Jarvinen, M. and Vuori, I., 2002, Effect of four-month vertical whole body vibration on performance and balance. *Medicine and Science in Sports and Exercise*, 34, 1523–8.

van den Tillaar, R., 2006, Will whole-body vibration training help increase the range of motion of the hamstrings? *Journal of Strength and Conditioning Research*, 20 (1), 192–6.

Vella, C. A., 2005, Whole-body vibration training: shake up clients' workouts with this low-impact training method. *IDEA Fitness Journal*, 2(1), 23–5.

Verschueren, S. M. P., Roelants, M., Delecluse, C., Swinnen, S., Vanderschueren, D. and Boonen, S., 2004, Effect of 6–month whole body vibration training on hip density, muscle strength, and postural control in postmenopausal women: a randomised controlled pilot study. *Journal of Bone and Mineral Research*, 19, 352–9.

Wakeling, J. M., Nigg, B. M. and Rozitis, A. I., 2002, Muscle activity damps the soft tissue resonance that occurs in response to pulsed and continuous vibrations. *Journal of Applied Physiology*, 93, 1093–103.

Part IV
Paediatric exercise science

20 Heart rate and Match analysis of Finnish junior football players

Tomi Vanttinen,[1] *Minna Blomqvist,*[1] *Henri Lehto*[1] *and Keijo Hakkinen*[2]

[1] Research Institute for Olympic Sports; [2] Department of Biology of Physical Activity, University of Jyvaskyla, Finland

Introduction

The fatigue caused by association football (soccer) and the resulting decrease in physiological performance have been well documented (Mohr et al., 2005). Exercise intensity during a soccer game has been reported to be around 75 per cent of the $\dot{V}o_{2max}$ estimated from the heart rate monitoring (Reilly, 1997). Most of the research concerning Match analysis (Luhtanen, 1993) and the intensity of the game (Reilly, 2005) has been done with elite male players and less information is available on junior players, although it has been shown that the heart rates of children in a small-sided game are compatible with the corresponding 11-per-side adult game (Drust and Reilly, 1997). The purpose of this study was to analyze game events and examine exercise intensity of junior players at 10, 12 and 14 years of age in a 90–minute, 11–per-side football game on a full-sized field.

Methods

The subjects of this study were 10-year-old (height 1.43 ±0.05 m, mass 32.5 ±3.5 kg, body fat 9.2 ±3.4%, n = 5 defenders + 5 midfields + 3 forwards = 13), 12-year-old (1.54 ±0.10 m, 41.6 ±7.6 kg, 10.1 ±4.2%, n = 6 def + 7 mid + 3 for = 16) and 14-year-old (1.68 0.09 m, 54.5 ±7.7 kg, 8.3 ±5.5%, n = 5 def + 6 mid + 3 for = 14) Finnish sub-elite male football players. All analysed players in each age group played a 2×45 min (11 v 11) game on a full-sized indoor football field (92×54 m) wearing Suunto T6 heart rate monitors (Suunto Oy, Finland). The teams were organized in a tactical formation known as a 4–4–2, which consisted of 4 defenders, 4 midfielders, and 2 forwards. Goalkeepers were not analysed. The game events were analysed with Dartfish Team Pro software using a method introduced by Luhtanen et al. (1998). In the Match analysis data, the total number of offensive actions (receiving + dribbling + passing = Off) as well as the percent of success (Off%) was counted for each player and age group. Due to the small number of defensive actions (interceptions + tackles + aerial duels + ground duels = Def) only the total number of defensive actions was counted. The results are expressed as an average/player. Previously analysed Match and heart rate values of adult (A) Finnish national team and highest level club team were used as reference. The heart rate (HR) data of the games were analysed using Suunto and Firstbeat Pro software. The subjects' maximal oxygen uptake and maximal heart rate were measured on a treadmill in order to examine exercise intensity of the game.

One-way ANOVA with Tukey's post hoc test was applied to detect differences between the age groups and playing positions. When the effects of playing positions were statistically analysed, all players were combined as one group due to small number of players within one age group. The differences between the two halves in each age group were analysed using a t-test. Pearson's correlation coefficient was applied to evaluate the relationships between HR and Match analysis data. The level of significance was set at $P<0.05$.

Results

As shown in Table 20.1 no differences were found between the age groups in the number of offensive and defensive actions. Group A succeeded significantly better in offensive actions than groups 10y and 14y. Comparison between the two halves revealed a significant increase in success of offensive actions ($P<0.05$) from first to second half in the 12y and 14y groups. When examining the effects of playing positions on the total number of actions, it was found that midfield players (95.0 ±30.8) differed significantly ($P<0.05$) from defenders (81.9 ±21.8) and forwards (70.6 ±25.1).

Maximal oxygen uptake ($\dot{V}O_{2\,max}$) of different age groups measured in laboratory were 48.8 ± 5.2 ml.kg^{-1}.min^{-1} in 10y, 49.4 ± 4.3 ml.kg^{-1}.min^{-1} in 12y and 50.5 ± 5.9 ml.kg^{-1}.min^{-1} in 14y which were significantly lower ($P<0.01$) than adult reference value measured from highest level Finnish club team (58.6 ± 4.4 ml. kg^{-1}.min^{-1}). The average exercise intensity of the game and corresponding energy expenditure in different age groups are presented in Table 20.2. The average heart rate in the game increased from 76.5% (157 beats.min^{-1}) to 82.5 % (171 beats. min^{-1}) of maximal heart rate (HRmax) and oxygen uptake ($\dot{V}O_2$) from 62.3 % (30.4 ml.kg^{-1}.min^{-1}) to 72.8% $\dot{V}O_{2\,max}$ (37.4 ml.kg^{-1}.min^{-1}) from 10y to 14y. Total energy expenditure (MJ) in the game increased with increasing age mainly due to increasing body mass but also because of increased exercise intensity which can be observed from the body mass adjusted energy expenditure values (kJ.kg^{-1}).

Exercise intensity during the game, expressed as proportion of playing time under 50%, between 50–75% or over 75% of $\dot{V}O_{2\,max}$ (Table 20.3.) and excess post-exercise oxygen consumption (EPOC) estimated from HR (Rusko et al., 2003), increased with increasing age but as seen in Figure 20.1 the age effect was lower in forwards than defenders or midfielders. The proportion of playing time over 75% of $\dot{V}O_{2\,max}$ was significantly lower in group 10y and 12y when compared to adults.

When comparing the EPOC values between first and second half in each age group a significant difference was found in 10y ($P<0.05$), 14y ($P<0.01$) and A ($P<0.01$) groups. In addition a significant difference in EPOC was found between defenders and midfielders ($P<0.01$) in the first half, and in the second half between defenders and midfielders ($P<0.05$) and defenders and forwards ($P<0.05$). There

Table 20.1 Number of defensive and offensive actions and the percent of successful offensive actions

	Entire Game				First half			Second half		
	Total	Def	Off	Off%	Def	Off	Off%	Def	Off	Off%
10y	85.6 (18.8)	18.8 (4.5)	66.8 (19.2)	73.3 (9.1)	11.1 (3.9)	36.9 (13.5)	73.8 (7.7)	7.6 (3.0)	30.7 (10.8)	72.2 (12.0)
	ns.	ns.	ns.	**A	ns.	ns.	*14y	ns.	ns.	ns.
12y	91.4 (41.5)	20.1 (12.7)	71.3 (34.2)	75.5 (5.5)	10.5 (6.2)	37.3 (14.0)	72.9 (7.2)	8.3 (6.5)	34.9 (23.5)	79.2 (8.4)
	ns.	ns.	ns.	ns.	ns.	ns.	ns.	ns.	ns.	ns.
14y	85.4 (33.1)	20.1 (7.4)	65.3 (30.6)	70.8 (4.2)	11.5 (5.3)	32.8 (17.5)	66.1 (8.2)	8.6 (4.1)	32.1 (15.0)	74.8 (7.3)
	ns.	ns.	ns.	***A	x	x	x	x	x	x
A	84.5 (17.2)	20.1 (6.3)	64.4 (17.5)	81.5 (7.7)	x	x	hx	x	x	x

Standard deviation (SD) shown in brackets; ns, not significant; * P<00.5; ** P<0.01; *** P<0.0001

Table 20.2 Average heart rate (beats.min^{-1}), oxygen uptake (ml.kg^{-1}.min^{-1}) and energy expenditure (MJ) of the game in different age groups

	HRavg	%HRmax	$\dot{V}O_{2\,max}$ avg	% $\dot{V}O_{2\,max}$	MJ	kJ.kg^{-1}
10y	157 (14)	76.5 (6.3)	30.4 (5.1)	62.3 (9.7)	1.98 (0.34)	62.6 (14.8)
	*14y	*14y *A	**14y ***A	**14y **A	***14y ***A	***A
12y	158 (11)	79.0 (6.3)	31.8 (4.1)	65.9 (8.9)	2.40 (0.32)	58.5 (7.2)
	ns.	ns.	*14y ***A	*A	***14y ***A	***A
14y	171 (12)	82.5 (4.0)	37.4 (6.2)	72.8 (5.9)	3.62 (0.67)	66.4 (10.8)
	ns.	ns.	*A	ns.	***A	*A
A	162 (8)	85.0 (4.3)	44.0 (4.6)	75.0 (6.0)	6.03 (0.75)	80.7 (8.5)

Standard deviation (SD) shown in brackets; ns, not significant; * $P<00.5$; ** $P<0.01$; *** $P<0.0001$

Table 20.3 Proportion of playing time under 50%, between 50–75% and over 75% of $\dot{V}O_{2\,max}$ in different age groups

	Entire game			First half			Second half		
	<50%	50–75%	>75%	<50%	50–75%	>75%	<50%	50–75%	>75%
10 y	24.5	43.3	32.1	19.2	43.3	37.4	30.1	43.3	26.5
	(18.1)	(11.4)	(18.7)	(17.3)	(14.1)	(21.4)	(19.8)	(10.8)	(18.2)
	**14y	*A	**14y	*A	*A	**14y	**14y	ns.	*14y
	**A		**A			**A	**A		**A
12 y	18.7	42.8	38.5	18.1	38.7	43.2	19.3	46.7	33.9
	(15.8)	(16.2)	(22.7)	(17.0)	(14.4)	(22.1)	(17.5)	(19.3)	(27.2)
	ns.	*A	**A	ns.	ns.	*A	ns.	*A	*A
14 y	7.2	33.6	59.2	5.9	28.7	65.3	8.6	38.7	52.9
	(8.1)	(15.0)	(20.6)	(7.1)	(17.1)	(22.1)	(9.2)	(14.0)	(20.1)
	ns.	ns.	ns.	ns.	ns.	ns.	ns.	ns.	ns.
A	6.7	25.4	67.8	4.6	23.5	71.1	8.6	28.3	62.7
	(4.7)	(14.3)	(18.3)	(4.4)	(15.0)	(17.4)	(6.4)	(14.7)	(20.0)

Standard deviation (SD) shown in brackets; ns, not significant; * $P<00.5$; ** $P<0.01$; *** $P<0.0001$

was also a weak correlation ($r = 0.34$, $P<0.05$) between the changes in EPOC and changes in total number of actions from first to second half.

Discussion

The primary findings of this study were:

- Total number of game events did not differ between age groups.
- Exercise intensity of the game increased with increasing age.
- Exercise intensity and total number of game events varied according to playing positions.

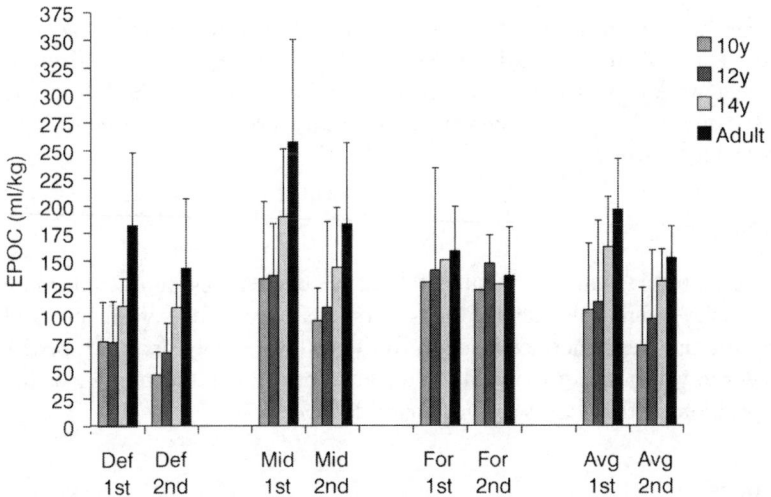

Figure 20.1 Exercise intensity of the game in different playing positions and age groups (Def = defenders, Mid = midfielders, For = forwards, Avg = average)

The Match analysis revealed no differences between the age groups in the number of offensive or defensive actions. Both offensive and defensive actions declined in the second half compared to the first. The midfield players did approximately 20 per cent more actions in the game than defenders or forwards. The success of offensive actions in the 12 y and 14 y groups increased from first to the second half. One reason for improved success could be a related weakening of defence to fatigue, which was also in the reported decreased number of defensive actions.

When applied to same exercise type, EPOC can be used to compare the demand of exercise. The EPOC values of 14y indicated that they were able to sustain a HR close to adult values in both halves when compared to 10y and 12y. Similarly the proportion of playing time over 75 per cent of maximal oxygen uptake gradually increased with increasing age. Thus it seems that children utilize more aerobic energy production during soccer games than youth and adult players, which could be due to the limited capacity for anaerobic energy production before puberty (Eriksson *et al.*, 1971).

Intensity of the game was decreased by 15 to 30 per cent when comparing the EPOC of two halves. Corresponding decreases have been reported previously and the main reason has been proposed to be a depletion of muscle glycogen (Bangsbo, 1994). It is also noteworthy that the intensity demands of different playing positions varied greatly. The relationship between the changes in EPOC and changes in total number of actions from first to second half implies that the reduction in physical effort is reflected also in the total number of actions i.e. less effort, less actions.

Furthermore it is important to keep in mind that there are several limitations to be considered. First, the Match and heart rate data of junior players were collected only from one game with limited number of subjects. Second, in general the methodological errors related to subjects and measurements are more likely to appear when working with children. Third, various heart rate analysis of this study were based on sophisticated mathematical models (reported error between 5 to10 per cent) which have been validated only with adults.

Conclusion

It seems that before puberty, children rely on aerobic energy production more than adult players and that the playing position has an influence on the physical load and the number of actions made in the game. These are important aspects to consider in youth soccer to avoid discrepancy (or overload) in training as the playing positions of the players are not finally defined.

References

Bangsbo, J., 1994, The physiology of soccer – with special reference to intense intermittent exercise. *Acta Physiologica Scandinavica*, 15, 1–155.

Drust, B. and Reilly, T., 1997, Heart rate responses of children during soccer play. In *Science and Football III*, edited by Reilly, T., Bangsbo, J. and Hughes, M. (London: E and FN Spon), pp. 196–200.

Eriksson, B.O., Karlsson, J. and Saltin, B., 1971, Muscle metabolites during exercise in pubertal boys. *Acta Paediatrica Scandinavica*, 217, 154–7.

Luhtanen, P., 1993, A statistical evaluation of offensive actions in soccer at World Cup level in Italy 1990. In *Science and Football II*, edited by Reilly, T., Clarys, J. and Stibble, A. (London: E and FN Spon), 215–20.

Luhtanen, P., Valovirta, E., Blomqvist, M. and Brown, E. (1998). Game understanding and game performance in soccer and modified soccer in finnish youth players. In *Abstracts: IV World Congress of Notational Analysis of Sport*, edited by Tavares, F. (University of Porto: Portugal), p. 71.

Mohr, M., Krusturp, P. and Bangsbo, J., 2005, Fatigue in soccer: a brief review. *Journal of Sports Sciences*, 23, 593–9.

Reilly, T., 1997, Energetics of high-intensity exercise (soccer) with particular reference to fatigue. *Journal of Sport Sciences*, 15, 257–63.

Reilly, T., 2005, An ergonomics model of the soccer training process. *Journal of Sport Sciences*, 23, 561–72.

Rusko, H.K., Pulkkinen, A., Saalasti, S., Hynynen, E. and Kettunen, J., 2003, Pre-prediction of EPOC: a tool for monitoring fatigue accumulation during exercise? ACSM Congress, San Francisco, 28–31 May. Abstract: *Medicine and Science in Sports and Exercise*, 35(5) Suppl. 183.

21 Influence of age, maturity and body dimensions on selection of under-17 Algerian soccer players

Samir Chibane, [1,2] *Christophe Hautier,* [1]
Claudio Gaudino, [1] *Raphaël Massarelli* [1] *and*
Nabila Mimouni [2]

[1]Centre of Research and Innovation on Sport, University Claude Bernard –
Lyon I, France; [2]Institute Superior of Sciences and Technology of Sport, Algeria

Introduction

That soccer is unarguably the world's most popular sport can be judged from the estimated 352.6 million television audience of the 2006 FIFA World Cup Matches. Many authors have shown the importance for clubs and national teams of detecting and recruiting talented players in order to develop their full potential. Identifying talents at an early age is far from being a mechanistic process (Reilly et al., 2000), as the selection of young elite soccer players requires the analysis of several factors (Maguire and Pearton, 2000). Strong inter-individual variations of these parameters are observed in childhood and adolescence. However, sports governing bodies neglect this significant point and generally gather together youngsters of a chronological age within the same 12-month period.

Within the same category, there are differences between youths born shortly after the cut-off date relative to those born almost one year after the cut-off date. Dividing the population under study in four quarters relative to the month of birth, these authors observed that individuals who are born at the beginning of the year are more likely to be selected, since they are physically stronger and more experienced than those who are born late (Helsen et al., 2005; Vincent and Glamser, 2006). The authors concluded that relative age has an important implication for selection of youth players. Additionally, at the same chronological age, individual differences in maturity status are associated with variations in the functional capacities of the youth player and may influence his selection (Malina et al., 2004). Adolescence is characterized by rapid changes in size proportions, body composition and physical performance. Timing and tempo of the adolescent growth spurts and sexual maturation vary among subjects, hence children of the same chronological age vary considerably in biological maturity status. Within the same age group boys who are advanced in maturity for their chronological age are taller, heavier, stronger, more powerful and have a greater aerobic power and a larget fat-free mass than boys whose maturity is delayed (Malina *et al.*, 2004). Consequently, in sports in which these characteristics are advantageous, early maturing adolescents, within the same age group, are likely to be selected over the majority of male athletes who are late maturing (Vaeyens *et al.*, 2005). For these reasons, evaluation and detection of young players should always be done considering their physiological age and maturity status. Previous studies have proposed several techniques to evaluate or measure the maturity of the children.

Traditionally, biological age in children has been determined by the use of standardized hand-wrist radiographs for assessment of bone age or by determining Tanner's stages of maturity by physical examination of secondary sex characteristics. For a number of reasons, however, these methods may not be suitable or feasible for research studies of healthy children. Radiographs can be costly, and they involve irradiation, which may not be acceptable to parents of healthy children in the absence of a clinical necessity. Tanner staging also has several drawbacks in a research setting. It is invasive to the extent that it involves undressing and, therefore, may be regarded as an invasion of privacy for many children.

In contrast, there are noninvasive methods to determine physical maturity which can be used without ethical problems. Mirwald *et al.*, (2002), established a maturity offset according to regression equations based on anthropometric measurements to predict the age at peak height velocity (PHV). This maturity offset, computed from age, standing height, sitting height, weight and leg length, gives the number of years before or after the predicted age at PHV. Malina *et al.* (2005) proposed a classification of youths into late, average or advanced in maturation from the percentage of predict adult stature.

In this study, we chose the more suitable method of Mirwald *et al.* (2002) as it was very difficult to assess parent stature necessary for the application of Malina and co-workers' (2005) method, because of the sociocultural parameters of our specific population.

The aim of the present study was to compare age, anthropometric measures and maturity status (years from PHV) among young adolescent male Algerian soccer players. The first hypothesis at the base of the study was that players with a greater relative age (chronological age) are more likely to be identified as 'talented' and consequently selected; the second hypothesis was that early maturing adolescents are more represented in the national team. The confirmation of the two (or either) hypotheses may lead to the conclusion that elite players should be characterized by greater body dimensions partly responsible for their selection in the Algerian national team.

Methods

The subjects of the study were 91 (28 elite and 63 sub-elite) young male Algerian soccer players (mean age = 16.6 years). Elite players were selected to play in the national youth soccer teams. Sub-elite participants played in regional selections.

Anthropometric measurements and the determination of body composition were made according to classical methods. The players and their parents gave informed written consent to participate to the study, approved by the Algerian ethics committee.

Subjects were grouped according their month of birth. The first month of the selection year was 'month 1' (September), while 'month 12' represents the last month of the selection period (August). The subjects were subsequently placed within 4 quarters (first quarter from September to November, second quarter from December to February … etc) according to the literature which specifies that it is necessary to begin cutting off with the month which corresponds to the beginning of the sporting season (Helsen *et al.*, 2005; Philippaerts *et al.*, 2006).

The evaluation of biological maturity was performed on the basis of age at PHV calculated as shown in the following equation (21.1) (Mirwald *et al.*, 2002):

$$MO = -9.236 + 0.0002708LLSHI - 0.001663ALLI + 0.007216ASHI + 0.02292WHR. \qquad (21.1)$$

MO maturity offset
LLSHI leg length/sitting height interaction
ALLI age/leg length interaction
ASHI age/sitting height interaction
WHR weight/height ratio

Thus a maturity offset of −1.0, 0 or +1.0 indicate respectively that the subject was measured 1 year before maturity (before PHV), at the time of maturity or 1 year after maturity (Beunen *et al.*, 2002).

Results were expressed as mean ± standard deviation (SD). All data sets were checked for normality of distribution. Student's t-test was used to assess the significance of the differences for anthropometric, PHV, and total lean mass data. χ^2 test was used to assess differences between the observed birth-dates distribution in regional and national groups. Significance level was set at $P<0.05$.

Results

The two groups (elite and sub-elite) were of broadly similar chronological age (Table 21.1) and chi-square tests demonstrated no difference between the observed birth date distributions in regional or national groups. Accordingly, no difference was observed concerning the quarter distribution between national and regional selection ($P = 0.64$) (Figure 21.1).

After calculation of the PHV, the subjects selected in the national team were significantly more mature than the players in the regional selection ($P < 0.01$) (Figure 21.2). All subjects of the national selection reached or exceeded the peak of maturity (Figure 21.3), 42.9% of the subjects ranged between 0 and 1, 53.57% between 1 and 2 and 3.57% at the top of 2, whereas the regional selection showed

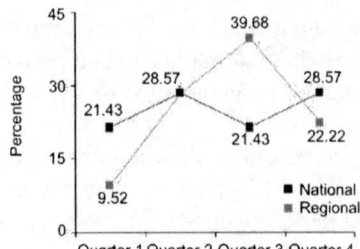

Figure 21.1 Quarter distribution of under-17 Algerian soccer players

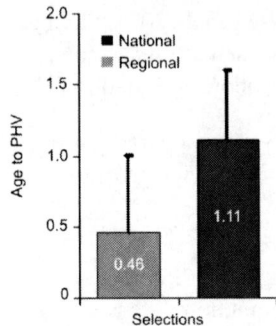

Figure 21.2 Mean age to PHV of under-17 Algerian soccer players

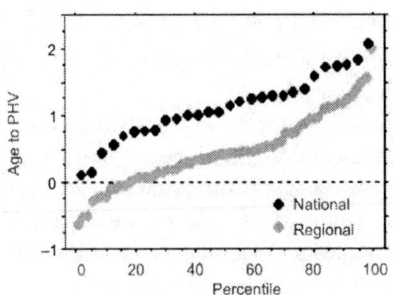

Figure 21.3 Percentile distribution of under-17 Algerian soccer players

that 32% of the subjects were below the peak of maturity, namely 57.62% between 0 and 1 and 10.16% between 1 and 2.

Body weight and height were significantly higher in national athletes ($P<0.001$) who also presented significantly higher lean body mass ($P<0.01$) compared to the regional players. Additionally, the national soccer players presented a significantly higher thigh circumference ($P<0.001$) compared to regional players (Table 21.1).

Table 21.1 Mean and standard deviation of age, weight, height, body fat, lean body mass and thigh circumference of regional and national under-17 Algerian players

	Regional selection		National selection	
	Mean	SD	Mean	SD
Age (years)	16.60	0.27	16.59	0.28
Height (m)	1.72	0.054	1.75	0.069
Mass (kg)	61.45	7.71	69.23***	7.77
Lean body mass (kg)	49.74	7.22	53.99**	7.32
Thigh circumference (cm)	53.03	3.59	55.87***	3.56

** $P<0.01$; *** $P<0.0001$

Discussion

In the present study, mean ages of regional and national selections (16.6 years) were not significantly different and indicated that subjects are grouped in a unique category. National players have been selected one year earlier among regional selections and continue to train in their respective clubs. They were, however, grouped during brief punctual seminars organized before important competitions. Thus, all these players performed a similar training volume and contests in the national Algerian championship. As all were born in Algeria, it can be considered that socio-cultural, economic and nutritional factors are similar among subjects.

The main result shows that birthdate distribution is not significantly different between regional and national teams. This is in opposition with the conclusions of Helsen and co-workers (2005), who showed a clear relative age effect in European national youth selection indicating an over-representation of players born in the first months of the selection year. Helsen *et al.* (2000) had previously observed that players born early in the selection year were more likely to be identified as talented and to be exposed to higher levels of coaching. More generally, soccer is characterized by a significant over-representation of players born in the early part of the selection year among youth and senior professional players (Helsen *et al.*, 2005). A similar relative age effect should be observed in our population. However, even when subjects were grouped in four quarters, no relative age effect was observed. This finding may be attributed to the specificity of the population i.e. regional selection is the result of a first detection process which may obscure the relative age effect. However, no significant difference was observed in each selection group between representation of subjects born early and late in the sport season.

It may be suggested that a relative age effect was not observed in the present study because players were in a very sensitive period of growth which may hide birth date differences to the benefit of body development differences in relation to maturation stages. In the population studied, time to PHV was so variable among subjects that chronological age seems to have no further effect on selection. For this reason, influence of maturation status should be greater in this study than relative age.

A comparison of the PHV showed a highly significant difference between the national selection and the regional selection. Players of the national selection presented an age to PHV (1.11 ±0.49) much higher than that of the regional players (0.46 ±0.54; $P<0.001$). All subjects of the national selection reached or exceeded the peak of maturity whereas 32% of the subjects in the regional selection were below the peak of maturity (Figure 21.3). This observation confirms our hypothesis that more players having crossed the peak of maturity are present in national rather than in regional selections.

Reasons for this discrepancy may be:

1   The youngsters who are advanced in maturity tend to perform better in tasks requiring strength, power, and speed compared with average and late maturing boys of the same age (Malina *et al.*, 2000, 2005). Philippaerts *et al.* (2006) showed that speed of limb movement, trunk strength, upper-body muscular endurance, explosive strength, agility, cardiorespiratory endurance and anaerobic capacity showed peak development at PHV.
2   Mature young players present larger body dimensions that give them a better physical performance. These results are in accordance with results of different authors, who confirmed that boys and girls advanced in maturity (age at PHV) are, on the average, taller, heavier and presented a more important muscular volume than peers who are either in the medium values or late in the biological maturation of their body (Malina *et al.*, 1986; Mirwald *et al.*, 2002; Malina *et al.*, 2005). The present results are in accordance with these findings. In soccer, where advanced physical development is a clear advantage (Helsen *et al.*, 2000), early morphological development appears to be an important characteristic that coaches eagerly search when they scout for 'talents'.

It is difficult to determine which of the two factors, anthropometric and/or physical characteristics, influence the selection of early under-17 soccer players of the Algerian national team. In fact, physical performance and body dimensions are strongly related in young subjects. Martin *et al.* (2004) reported leg volume and lean leg volume to be predictive of anaerobic performance (maximal power, optimal velocity and optimal torque) in boys and girls aged between 7 and 16 years. In the same way, differences in body size induce differences in $\dot{V}O_{2\,max}$ (Malina *et al.*, 2004) and partly explain differences in endurance performance and sprint repetition capacity.

References

Beunen, G., Baxter-Jones, A. D., Mirwald, R.L., Thomis, M., Lefevre, J., Malina, R.M. and Bailey, D.A., 2002, Intra-individual allometric development of aerobic power in 8- to 16-year-old boys. *Medicine and Science in Sports and Exercise*, 34, 503–510.

Helsen, W. F., Hodges N. J., Van Winckel, J. and Starkes, J.L., 2000, The roles of talent, physical precocity and practice in the development of soccer expertise. *Journal of Sports Sciences*, 18, 727–36.

Helsen, W. F., Van Winckel J. and Williams, A.M., 2005, The relative age effect in youth soccer across Europe. *Journal of Sports Science*, 23, 629–36.

Maguire, J. and Pearton R., 2000, The impact of elite labour migration on the identification, selection and development of European soccer players. *Journal of Sports Sciences*, 18, 759–69.

Malina, R. M., Beunen G., Wellens, R. and Claessens, A., 1986, Skeletal maturity and body size of teenage Belgian track and field athletes. *Analysis of Human Biology*, 13, 331–9.

Malina, R. M., Pena Reyes, M. E., Eisenmann, J.C., Horta, L., Rodrigues, J. and Miller, R., 2000, Height, mass and skeletal maturity of elite Portuguese soccer players aged 11–16 years. *Journal of Sports Sciences*, 18, 685–93.

Malina, R. M., Bouchard, C. and Bar-Or, O., 2004, *Growth, Maturation and Physical Activity*, (Champaign, IL: Human Kinetics).

Malina, R. M., Cumming S. P., Morano, P.J., Barron, M. and Miller, S.J., 2005, Maturity status of youth football players: a noninvasive estimate. *Medicine and Science in Sports and Exercise*, 37, 1044–52.

Martin , R. J., Dore, E.,Twisk, J., Van Praagh, E., Hunter, C.A. and Bedu, M., 2004b, Longitudinal changes of maximal short-term peak power in girls and boys during growth. *Medicine and Science in Sports and Exercise*, 36, 498–503.

Mirwald, R. L., Baxter-Jones, A. D., Bailey, D.A. and Barnes, G.P., 2002, An assessment of maturity from anthropometric measurements. *Medicine and Science in Sports and Exercise*, 34, 689–94.

Philippaerts, R. M., Vaeyens, R., *et al.*, 2006, The relationship between peak height velocity and physical performance in youth soccer players. *Journal of Sports Sciences*, 24, 221–30.

Reilly, T., Williams, A. M.,Nevill, A. and Franks, A., 2000, A multidisciplinary approach to talent identification in soccer. *Journal of Sports Sciences*, 18, 695–702.

Vaeyens, R., Philippaerts, R. M. and Malina, R.M., 2005, The relative age effect in soccer: a Match-related perspective. *Journal of Sports Sciences*, 23, 747–56.

Vincent J. and Glamser F. D., 2006, Gender differences in the relative age effect among US Olympic development program youth soccer players. *Journal of Sports Sciences*, 24, 405–13.

22 Chronological versus skeletal bone age in schoolboy footballers

Amanda Johnson,[1] *Patrick Doherty*[2] *and Anthony Freemont*[3]

[1] Manchester United Football Club, UK; [2] York St John University, UK;
[3] University of Manchester, UK

Introduction

Youth footballers, in training and competition, are normally categorised according to their chronological age that is based on the birth date, rather than the maturity stage reached. It has been documented (Malina and Eisenmann, 2004) that boys born on the same day mature at different rates. This study was planned to establish if any significant differences existed between chronological age and biological age in schoolboy footballers.

The pressure to produce elite athletes for club and country is becoming more apparent as is the financial rewards and obligations for the individuals and clubs. This has become critical in professional soccer for teams competing in the Union of European Football Associations (UEFA) Champions League competition. To ensure that professional clubs were encouraging youth development, UEFA has changed the regulations and now each squad of 25 has to contain four 'locally' trained players who have been involved with the Academy for a minimum of three years between the ages 15 and 21 years. For the 2007–8 season this number was increased to six, and to eight for the following season. This change has consequently led to an increase in the amount of training that has to be undertaken by immature athletes to ensure that they attain the highest levels of achievement when they reach adulthood. The amount of training required to reach the elite level of any sport has been researched in a number of studies (Bloomfield, 1992; Ericsson *et al.*, 1993), the general consensus being that it takes a period of ten years of directed and organised coaching. It is essential to optimise the windows of opportunity of specific developmental periods in young developing athletes to maximise their potential (Bloomfield, 1992; Ericsson *et al.*, 1993). The question of how to identify the correct periods of development and what criterion is used is constantly being sought from science. Club coaching and medical staff are duty bound to seek the safest, most successful methods to develop players to perform at the highest level.

In youth sport chronological age is the traditional method of dividing children into competitive groups but it has been documented that chronological age can differ by as much as four years from biological age; biological age may be a more accurate method of identifying critical periods of development (Leite *et al.*, 1987). To some extent the differences between chronological age and biological age in youth players has been previously explored (Malina *et al.*, 2000; Le Gall *et al.*, 2006) albeit over a limited period of time. Biological age can differ by at least one year from chronological age and still be considered normal in a healthy immature athlete. The ranking of biological age over chronological age by one year means that children are classified as being early developers and the inverse situation means that they are classified as late developers (Malina *et al.*, 2004). Various methods are used to assess the radiographs but all compare biological age to chronological age (Van Lenthe *et al.*, 1998). When biological age is assessed, maturity indicators in the long and short (or round) bones in the hand and wrist are compared with standard radiographs of normal children at various stages of maturation and chronological age (Leite *et al.*, 1987).

Biological age, determined using either non-invasive or invasive measures, can give the coach and medical staff an accurate indication of the stage of maturity an athlete has reached and indicate if the athlete is an early or late developer. This information can be a significant factor when determining long term development plans (Balyi, 2004).

The most common method to determine biological age traditionally uses a plain x-ray of the left hand and wrist (Rucci *et al.*, 1995; Malina *et al.*, 2004). Other joints such as the hip, knee, ankle and foot have previously been used (Castriota-Scanderbeg and De Micheli, 1995; Aicardi *et al.*, 2000; Malina *et al.*, 2004). X-rays are used most commonly for the assessment of biological age of children with growth disorders (Rucci *et al.*, 1995; Gilli, 1996; Mora *et al.*, 2001) although they are being used more frequently to assess development of normal growth in athletic children (Malina *et al.*, 2000.) There is some debate about the best x-ray approach to biological age measurement in clinical research (Gilli, 1996) but nevertheless x-ray remains one of the best approaches to determine maturity. The alternatives, such as Tanner staging approach (Tanner, 1962) albeit non-invasive, is considered less preferable for a number of reasons including reliability and child protection issues. Even though the amount of x-ray exposure is regarded as minimal ($1 \pm 2\,mrad$) (Carpenter and Lester, 1993) the cost and ethical issues of invasive measures need to be considered in non-clinical situations particularly if a long-term study on a large number of subjects is planned.

The main study aim was to investigate the differences and interrelationships between chronological age and biological age in Academy footballers over a longer period of time than previous studies and across a greater range of age groups. A secondary aim was to investigate differences between two approaches to measurement of biological age.

Methods

All the participants involved were volunteers from Manchester United Football Club Academy. The study period was five years from 2001–2006. Consent forms were completed by both the boys and parents' or guardians. Ethical approval was granted by Manchester University. All participants were male, aged between 8 and 16 years. The specific chronological ages for each year of measurement are shown in Table 22.1.

All the boys lived at home and attended local schools. Academy regulations stipulate that the boys must live within an hour's drive from the training ground for the 9–11-year-old boys and within 1.5 hours for the 12–16-year-old boys. All boys were recruited to the club via a scouting network.

A longitudinal cross-sectional design enabled data to be collected on injury, skeletal age and exposure for every Academy boy that consented to the study. Once accepted into the club, a basic medical screening was carried out and all boys underwent a basic radiograph of the left wrist which was repeated at the start of every season. The medical screening was used to identify any predisposing factors which may have prevented full involvement in the training and games programme. The x-ray was carried out by a university hospital department and both biological age assessment methods were analysed by specifically trained personnel.

The RUSBA approach (radius ulna and short bone; part of the Tanner–Whitehouse method) is a frequently used method to assess biological age. The original approach used a reference population of children from the UK in the 1950s. (Tanner, 1962). This database has recently been revised with a more updated reference population that reflects social and race classifications (Tanner et al., 2001). The x-rays of the left wrist and hand are compared with plates and descriptives of individual bones from the reference population and a score is allocated which can be converted into biological age (Van Lenthe et al., 1998). The FELs method uses a reference population from the USA. It uses a bone-by-bone comparison but also ratios between epiphyses and diaphyses (Malina et al., 2004). The most commonly used alternative is the Greulich Pyle method which although carried out on Academy boys (Le Gall et al., 2006), is considered less accurate than the RUSBA method (Cole et al., 1988; Stanitski, 1989, Castriota-Scanderbeg, 1996).

The biological age scores were classified into three categories: early, normal or late maturers. If biological age was more than a year older or younger than chronological age the players were classified as early or late maturers respectively. Normal maturers were classified as such if the biological age was within one year of the chronological age. This classification has been used in a number of studies involving biological age and athletes. (Malina et al., 2000, 2004; Le Gall et al., 2006).

Results

Descriptively there were differences in the means and in all cases the FELs approach gave the higher mean. Analysis of variance (ANOVA) comparison, with post hoc follow up between approaches, for each year found that all three approaches differed significantly from each other ($P > 0.05$) with the exception

Table 22.1 Year-on-year age data for each measurement approach

	Measure	N	Mean	SD	Min	Max
Year 1	Chronological age	75	12.57	2.43	8.04	16.10
	FELs	75	13.20	3.03	6.59	18.00
	RUSBA	75	12.16	2.93	5.90	16.50
Year 2	Chronological age	103	11.66	2.50	8.21	17.07
	FELs	103	12.07	2.96	6.80	18.00
	RUSBA	103	11.28	2.76	7.00	16.50
Year 3	Chronological age	115	11.85	2.34	8.63	16.15
	FELs	115	12.36	3.05	7.77	18.00
	RUSBA	115	11.66	2.86	7.40	16.50
Year 4	Chronological age	113	11.65	2.27	8.19	16.06
	FELs	113	11.96	3.01	6.50	18.00
	RUSBA	113	10.96	2.96	6.10	16.50
Year 5	Chronological age	110	11.60	2.22	8.09	16.10
	FELs	110	11.62	2.91	6.35	17.66
	RUSBA	110	10.60	2.77	5.70	16.50

of year 3 where the chronological age and RUSBA method ages were similar and year 5 where the chronological age and FELs ages were similar.

Repeated measures 5×3 ANOVA for bone age with a between subjects factor of age-group found significant mean differences for all age groups between all three approaches ($F = 211$, $P < 0.001$). A significant interaction effect was found between measurement approach across all years of measurement ($F = 9.64$, $P < 0.001$). The percentage of estimates of early normal and late developers was 32.5 %, 56.4%, 11.1% and 10.7%, 54.6%, 34.7% for FELs and RUSBA, respectively.

Discussion

Variation in the biological age measures, albeit not anticipated, is understandable. The full maturity status has a potential for a ceiling effect, in the RUSBA approach, due to differences between the reference markers used to estimate biological age. When considering bone age the FELs method includes all the short and carpal bones and lower end of the radius and ulna. Objective measurements are also taken of the epiphyseal plates of the radius and ulna and the first, third and fifth short bones of the hand (Malina *et al.*, 2004). The RUSBA is dependent on a subjective analysis only of the radius and ulna and the first, third and fifth bones of the hand and carpal bones are not included. The RUSBA status is limited to 16.5 years and in the context the actual study age range was 8 to 16 years of age (Van Lenthe *et al.*, 1998). These absolute limits within the RUSBA score do not allow for variation above the mean which correspondingly led to a ceiling effect when compared to FELs.

The literature suggests that training should be appropriately targeted to the developmental stage of the individual (Bloomfield, 1992; Ericsson *et al.*, 1993, Balyi, 2004), yet our findings suggest that the identification of these stages, by chronological age, is questionable. The wide spread of data in biological age and variation in development stages reached by individual players, within an age group, makes it very difficult to plan a training session or to have confidence in biological age parity within competitive age group categories. Some boys may have passed a specific development stage and others could be well short of it which makes a targeted session only beneficial to 60 per cent of the group.

Although previous work had found up to a four-year difference in biological age or the stage of maturity, reached by an individual, none of these studies matched the actual study age groups to the age group categories used in youth football (Malina *et al.*, 2004; Le Gall *et al.*, 2006). A further limitation was that they only measured adolescent boys. Our study yielded similar differences to those above, but across a much wider age range and over a five-year time period. Our findings are highly applicable to coaches and clinicians working in Academy football.

Conclusion

The study complements the existing literature by adding support, via a longitudinal study, to the importance of knowing biological age. The significant interaction effects and differences between age groups for all three expressions of age cast doubt on the use of any one method. Importantly, it questions the sole use of chronological age to categorise children into competitive groups. Although variation exists between RUSBA and FELs, what is clear is that both confirm that chronological age is inaccurate to the extent that at least 40 per cent of cases differ significantly from biological age. The FELs method led to more cases being rated as early developers whereas RUSBA rated more cases as late developers.

An important consideration in longitudinal studies in Academy football is that only a very few boys continue year on year. In terms of statistical analysis and statistical power, this creates difficulties when applying valid case analysis.

References

Aicardi, G., Vignolo, M., Milani, S., Naselli, A., Magliano, P. and Garzia, P., 2000 Assessment of skeletal maturity of the hand-wrist and knee: a comparison among methods. *American Journal of Human Biology,* 12, 610–15.

Balyi, I., 2004, Diving. *LTAD Workshops.* (London: Crystal Palace NSC).

Bloomfield, J., 1992, Talent identification and profiling. In *Textbook: Science and Medicine In Sport,* edited by Bloomfield, J., Fricker, P.A. and Fitch, K. D. (Oxford: Blackwell Scientific Publications), pp. 187–98.

Carpenter, C. and Lester, E.L., 1993, Skeletal age determination in young children-analysis of the three regions of the hand/wrist film. *Journal of Pediatrics Orthopometry,* 13, 76–9.

Castriota-Scanderbeg, A., 1996 *Untrasound and skeletal maturation,* 25, 142.

Castriota-Scanderbeg, A. and De Micheli, V., 1995, Ultrasound of femoral head cartilage: a new method of assessing bone age. *Skeletal Radiology,* 24, 197–200.

Cole, A.J., Webb, L. and Cole, T.J., 1988, Bone age estimation: a comparison of methods. *British Journal of Radiology*, 61, 683–6.

Ericsson, K.A., Krampe R.T. and Heizmann, S., 1993, Can we create gifted people? Ciba Foundation Symposium, 178, 222–31; discussion 32–49.

Gilli, G., 1996, The assessment of skeletal maturation. *Hormonal Research*, 45 Supplement 2, 49–52.

Le Gall, F., Carling, C., and Reilly, T., 2006, Biological maturity and injury in elite youth football. *Scandinavian Journal of Medicine Science and Sports*, 17, 564–72.

Leite, H. R., O'Reilly, M. T. and Close, J. M., 1987, Skeletal age assessment using the first, second, and third fingers of the hand. *American Journal of Orthodentistry Dentofacial Orthopometry*, 92, 492–8.

Malina, R. M. and Eisenmann, J. C., 2004, Maturity-associated variation in the growth and functional capacities of youth football (soccer) players 13–15 years. *European Journal of Applied Physiology*, 91, 555–62.

Malina, R. M., Pena Reyes, M. E., Eisenmann, J. C., Horta, L., Rodrigues, J. and Miller, R., 2000, Height, mass and skeletal maturity of elite Portuguese soccer players aged 11–16 years. *Journal of Sports Sciences*, 18, 685–93.

Malina, R. M., Bouchard, C., and Bar-Or, O., 2004, *Growth, Maturation and Physical Activity.* (Leeds: Human Kinetics).

Mora, S., Boechat, M. I., Pietka, E., Huang, H. K. and Gilsanz, V., 2001, Skeletal age determinations in children of European and African descent: applicability of the Greulich and Pyle standards. *Pediatric Research*, 50, 624–8.

Rucci, M., Coppini, G., Nicoletti, I., Cheli, D. and Valli, G., 1995, Automatic analysis of hand radiographs for the assessment of skeletal age: a subsymbolic approach. *Computer Biomedical Research*, 28, 239–56.

Stanitski, C. L., 1989, Common injuries in preadolescent and adolescent athletes: recommendations for prevention. *Sports Medicine*, 7, 32–41.

Tanner, J.M., 1962, *Growth at Adolescence*, 2nd edn. (Oxford: Blackwell Scientific Publications).

Tanner, J. M., Healy, M.J.R., Goldstein, H. and Cameron, N., 2001, *Assessment of Skeletal Maturity and the Prediction of Adult Height (TW3 method)*, (London: Harcourt Publishers).

Van Lenthe, F.J., Kemper, H.C. and Van Mechelen, W., 1998, Skeletal maturation in adolescence: a comparison between the Tanner-Whitehouse II and the Fels method, *European Journal of Paediatrics*, 157, 798–801.

23 A cross-cultural comparison of the participation histories of English and French elite youth soccer players

Paul R. Ford,[1] *Franck Le Gall,*[2] *Christopher Carling*[3] *and A. Mark Williams*[1]

[1] Research Institute for Sport and Exercise Sciences, Liverpool John Moores University, UK; [2] Institut National du Football, France; [3] Lille Football Club, France

Introduction

The development of skill and expertise in young soccer players is the main goal of youth academies and national development programmes around the world. Expert athletes involved in sports other than soccer in countries such as Canada have been shown to progress from participating in play activities early in their development to more structured practice activities later on (Côté , 1999). Three stages of youth development have been proposed by these researchers. These stages are sampling (6–12 years), specialising (13–15 years) and investment (16+ years) (Côté *et al.*, 2003). During the sampling years athletes are expected to participate in a large amount of play activity across a number of sports, but a low amount of structured practice. During the specialising years the prediction is that they should participate in similar amounts of play and structured practice in one or two sports. During the investment years they are expected to participate in a large amount of structured practice in their primary sport, but a low amount of play activity.

Researchers have tested Côté's (1999) model in soccer by examining the participation histories of elite players. In Brazil, the participation histories of professional players revealed their sampling years lasted from 6–15 years old. During this period they participated in large amounts of soccer-specific play only, with no participation in coach-led practice or other sports (Salmela and Moraes, 2003). In England, there has been no clear support for Côté's (1999) model. Time spent in coach-led practice differentiated elite from recreational players (Ward *et al.*, 2004), but the extra time that some of these elite youth players who subsequently progressed to professional status spent in play activity differentiated them from elite players who did not progress to this status (Ford *et al.*, 2006). These studies show that the amount and type of soccer activity that young players participate in during their development (and therefore the eventual level of expertise attained) are partly dependent on the culture and country that they live in (Salmela and Moraes, 2003). Certain countries are subjectively 'renowned' for developing expert soccer players and teams, for example, France, who between 1996 and 2006 has won six European and two World national team titles from U17 to adult level. Although many factors can affect the outcome of national team tournaments, this profile of success suggests that the level of soccer expertise is greater in France compared with many other nations. It is therefore valuable to examine whether the amount and type of soccer activity that young players participate in during their development in France differ from that exhibited in less successful nations in international competition such as England.

The objective of this study is to compare the participation histories of elite youth French players living at the Clairefontaine Academy in Paris, France to those of elite youth English soccer players based at a Premier League club in London, England.

Materials and methods

Participants were elite under-14 (U14) youth soccer players selected at random from the Clairefontaine Academy in Paris, France ($n = 23$) and an English Premier League Youth Academy ($n = 16$) in London, England. They completed a retrospective questionnaire recording the amount of time spent between the ages of 6 and 14 years in different types of soccer-specific activities. To explore for differences across variables a 2–group (French, English) × 9 ages (6–14 years) × 5 activities (match play, coach-led practice, individual practice, play, indirect involvement) mixed-design ANOVA with repeated measures on the last two factors was conducted. Descriptive statistics were calculated for the milestones data and for the number of other sports in which the players participated.

Results

Milestones

There were no differences between French and English players in the average age at which they started playing soccer (5 years), the age they began participating in supervised training by an adult (7 years), or the age they began participating in an organised league (8 years). French players began participating at the Clairefontaine Academy later (13 years) than the English players began their involvement at their Academy (11 years).

Soccer activity

The French players spent more hours per week compared to English players in soccer-specific play activity at the U7 to U10 age groups (see Figure 23.1), in coach-led practice at U13 and U14 age groups (see Figure 23.2), and in the total amount of participation time at U8. The English players spent more time

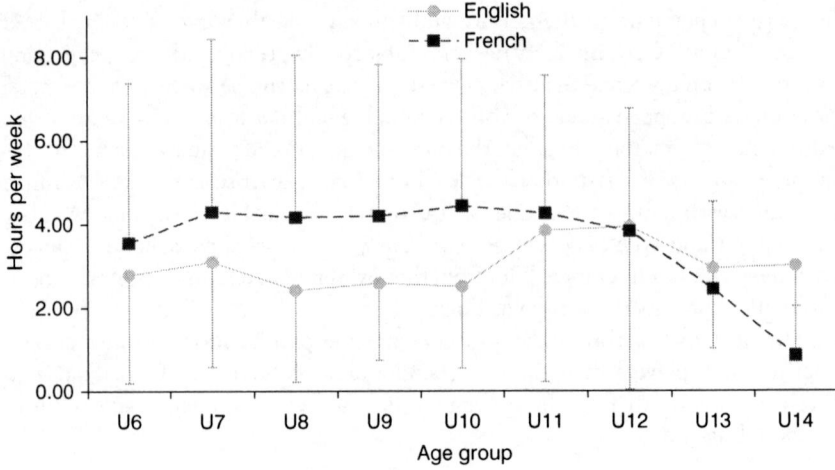

Figure 23.1 Mean (and s.d.) hours per week spent in play activity as a function of age group

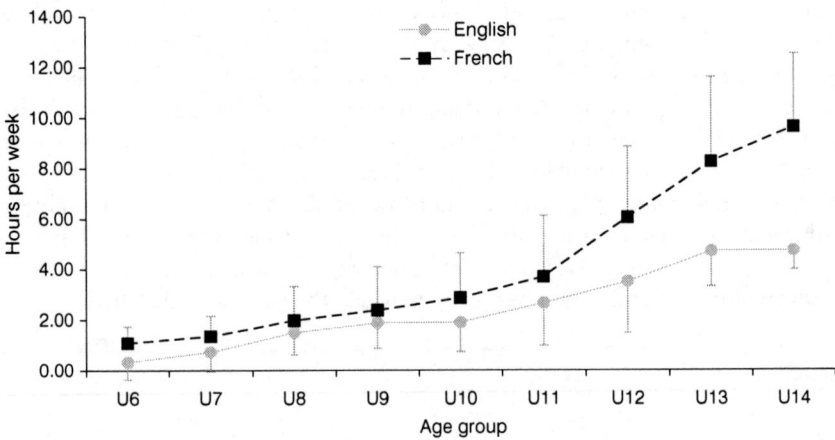

Figure 23.2 Mean (and s.d.) hours per week spent in coach-led practice as a function of age group

in soccer-specific play activity compared to French players at the U14 age group only. There were no differences between groups across age groups for time spent in match-play, individual practice, and indirect involvement.

The French players spent more time in soccer-specific play compared to coach-led practice at the U7 age group. At the U13 and U14 age groups, they spent more time in coach-led practice compared to soccer-specific play. For the English players there were no significant differences between time spent in play and coach-led practice across age groups.

Other sport activity

The English elite youth soccer players were shown to participate in five or six other sports during their development (range = 2 to 11 sports, median = 5). They began participating in these other sports at 10 years of age (range = 5 to 14 years, median = 10). They finished participating in these other sports at 12 years of age (range = 8 years to 'still participating', median = 13). They spent an average of two hours per week (range = 1 to 7 hours, median = 2) participating in these other sports. They participated in these other sports at school (outside of physical education classes), clubs, and in play activity.

The majority (n = 14) of the French elite youth soccer players did not participate in any other sports. The nine players who did participate in other sports were shown to participate in two other sports (range = 1 to 6 sports, median = 2 sports). They began participating in these other sports at 8 years of age (range = 5 to 12 years, two hours per week (range = 1 to 4 hours, median = 2) participating in these other sports. They mainly participated in these other sports at clubs, although some participated at school and in play activity.

Discussion

The French elite youth soccer players were shown to engage in more soccer-specific play activity early (U7 to U10) in their participation histories, and more soccer-specific coach-led practice later at U13 and U14 compared to their English counterparts. The data for the French players support models of skill acquisition predicting that expert athletes progress from participating in play activities early in their development to more structured practice activities later on (Côté , 1999). However, contrary to Côté 's (1999) model, between the ages of 6–12 years old (i.e., sampling years) the French players participated solely in soccer-specific play activity and not in play activity in other sports. The small number of French players who did participate in other sports did so between the ages of 6 and 12 years, as per Côté 's (1999) model. Also, contrary to Côté (1999), at the age of 13 and 14 years (i.e., specialising years) the French players participated in 10 hours per week of soccer-specific coach-led practice only. At this stage they did not participate in any hours of play activity or in any other sports as would be predicted by the model.

The data for the English elite youth soccer players did not fit the model proposed by Côté (1999). In each year of their development the English players spent two to four hours in soccer-specific play activity. They spent a maximum of four hours per week in the other soccer activities. The English players participated in a relatively large number of other sports (n = 5 to 6). They did so mainly between the ages of 6 and 12 years, as per Côté 's (1999) model. Five English players were still participating in three or more other sports at the age of 14 years. The model of Côté (1999) predicts that expert athletes would be participating in two sports at this stage in their development. At 15 years (i.e., one year's time) the players would be predicted to be solely participating in soccer-specific structured practice and competition if still based at the Academy.

There are several advantages to young players participating in soccer-specific play activities early in their development rather than more structured practice activities. Play activity promotes guided discovery and discovery learning. Skills learnt under discovery conditions are less prone to being forgotten over time and to psychological stress compared to skills learnt under more traditional prescriptive methods. Under discovery learning conditions, players must find their own solutions to problems. At these early ages, the role of the coach is to create practice opportunities for players to learn on their own. This 'hands-off' approach to coaching may develop 'smart' learners who are able to apply their skills in a variety of situations. To this end, coaches can manipulate the constraints of the game such that the desired skills emerge during the practice. Important constraints that can be manipulated are the rules and laws of the game, as well as any conditions or equipment changes imposed by the coach (Williams and Hodges, 2005).

References

Côté , J., 1999, The influence of the family in the development of talent in sport. *The Sport Psychologist*, 13, 395–417.

Côté , J., Baker, J. and Abernethy, B., 2003, From play to practice: a developmental framework for the acquisition of expertise in team sports. In *Expert Performance in Sports: Advances in Research on Sport Expertise*, edited by Starkes, J.L. and Ericsson, K.A, (Champaign IL.: Human Kinetics Publishing), pp. 89–114.

Ford, P.R., Ward, P., Hodges, N.J., and Williams, A.M., 2006, Antecedents of selection into professional soccer: the roles of play and practice in progression and regression. *Journal of Sport and Exercise Psychology*, 28, S68.

Salmela, J.H. and Moraes, L.C., 2003, Development of expertise: the role of coaching, families, and cultural contexts. In *Expert Performance in Sports: Advances in Research on Sport Expertise*, edited by Starkes J.L. and Ericsson, K.A. (Champaign IL.: Human Kinetics Publishing), pp. 275–94.

Ward, P., Hodges, N.J., Williams, A.M. and Starkes, J.L., 2004. Deliberate practice and expert performance: defining the path to excellence. In *Skill Acquisition in Sport: Research, Theory and Practice*, edited by Williams, A.M. and Hodges, N.J. (London: Routledge), pp. 231–58.

Williams, A.M. and Hodges, N.J., 2005, Practice, instruction and skill acquisition in soccer: challenging tradition. *Journal of Sports Sciences*, 23, 637–50.

24 Physical loading, stress and recovery in a youth soccer tournament

P. Luhtanen,[1] *A. Nummela*[1] *and*
K. Lipponen[2]

[1] Research Institute for Olympic Sports, Finland; [2] Football Association of
Finland, Finland

Introduction

Variations in the RR interval in the electrocardiogram provide important information, which can be used for monitoring physiological loading (training and match conditions in soccer) and the stress-recovery process between training and playing days among players. Heart rate and heart rate variability (HRV) have been employed to asses training effect indirectly by using the EPOC (excess post-exercise oxygen consumption ($ml.kg^{-1}$)) prediction method (Rusko et al., 2003).

A higher level of physical fitness has been connected to higher values of HRV, especially HFP (e.g. De Meersman, 1993), even though some studies have not found that effect of physical training on HRV (Loimaala et al., 2000). Improved physical fitness leads to increased resources of the ANS (autonomic nervous system) at rest; i.e. increased parasympathetic and decreased sympathetic modulation (e.g. De Meersman, 1993). On the other hand, hard training with insufficient recovery can lead to decreased physical fitness and decreased parasympathetic and increased sympathetic modulation (Uusitalo et al., 2000). Physical exercise is known to decrease HRV acutely, and the recovery of the initial HRV takes from a few minutes up to 24 hours, depending on the intensity of the exercise (Furlan et al., 1993). Indices of the HRV are field-capable variables to reflect stress-recovery processes to avoid overtraining during periods of intensive training. These methods have been used in endurance sports (Hynynen et al., 2006a, 2006b) but not in soccer. In this study the effects of training on nocturnal cardiac autonomic modulation of international level young soccer players were investigated with HRV analysis. A new method of HRV analysis was employed to evaluate athletic training and recovery. The purposes of the research were to compare 1) physical loading of young international level soccer players in training and match conditions and 2) investigate stress and recovery states of young soccer players during an international soccer tournament as indicated by HRV measurements.

Methods

Study design

To test the effects of match-play on autonomic modulation, nocturnal HRV after a match day and an easy training day were compared.

Data collection

In order to determine individual cardiorespiratory fitness profiles, the subjects ($n = 10$, age 16.9 ± 0.2 years) performed a standardized five-minute warm-up and a progressive $\dot{V}O_{2\,max}$ test on a treadmill declined one degree starting at a speed of $9\,km.h^{-1}$ and increasing speed by $1\,km.h^{-1}$ after every three minutes. The test lasted until the individual reached his subjective maximum. Lactate was analysed from fingertip blood samples taken after each speed and 1, 4 and 10 minutes after exhaustion. Heart rate and oxygen consumption were measured breath-by-breath during the whole test (Oxycon Mobile, Jaeger, Germany). From this test, $\dot{V}O_{2\,max}$, HR max, aerobic threshold and anaerobic threshold were determined (Nummela, 2004). Every night during the training camp of the Finnish youth soccer team between 25 February and 3 March 2006, RRI indices were recorded. The RRI recordings were done with a Suunto t6 wristop computer (Suunto Ltd, Vantaa, Finland) that detects the time between RR peaks with an accuracy of 1 s and allows the storage of 100,00 RIs. Also RRI data during all training sessions and matches during the tournament were collected. The players rated their perceived exertion after each match and training session as well as their state of recovery every morning using RPE-scale from 0 to 10 (modified from Borg, 1982).

Data analysis

Nocturnal HRV was analysed as a continuous four-hour period between midnight and 0400 hours. All the RRIs recorded during the training sessions and matches were analyzed. Autonomic modulation was analyzed with traditional and new (Kettunen and Saalasti, 2004) HRV indices with Firstbeat PRO software version 1.4.1 (Firstbeat Technologies Ltd, Jyväskylä, Finland). The personal input parameters were age, weight, height, gender, smoking habits, activity class, resting and maximal HR, and maximal aerobic capacity (in metabolic equivalents/ METs). During night recordings electrode gel was used on the electrode belt to increase conductivity. In Firstbeat PRO software, the recorded RRI-data are first scanned through an artefact detection filter to perform an initial correction of falsely detected, missed and premature heart beats. The consecutive artefact-corrected RRIs are then resampled at a rate of 5 Hz by using linear interpolation to obtain equidistantly sampled time series (for more detailed information, see Saalasti, 2003). The analysis of stress and recovery is based on the detection of sympathovagal reactivity that exceeds momentary metabolic requirements for the autonomic nervous system (ANS). The program calculates HRV indices second-by-second using the short-time Fourier Transform method, and HR- and HRV-derived variables that describe respiration rate and oxygen consumption ($\dot{V}_{O_2}$) using neural network modelling of data (Saalasti, 2003; Kettunen and Saalasti, 2004, 2005; Firstbeat Technologies, 2005). The calculation of $\dot{V}_{O_2}$ takes into account the respiration rate and on/off dynamics, and the estimated $\dot{V}_{O_2}$ has been found to be more accurate than methods based only on HR, especially during the start of exercise and recovery from exercise (Pulkkinen *et al.*, 2004). Also excess post-exercise oxygen consumption (EPOC) during exercise is estimated based on the RRI-data (Saalasti, 2003). The software also calculates second-by-second indices of stress and relaxation, reflecting activity of the sympathetic (stress index) and parasympathetic (recovery index) nervous system. Stress index is calculated from HR, high-frequency power (HFP), low-frequency power (LFP) and HRV-derived respiratory variables. Stress index is high when heart rate is elevated, HRV is reduced and there are inconsistencies in the frequency distribution of HRV due to changes in respiratory period. Recovery index is calculated from HR and HFP and it is high when HR is close to the basal resting level and HRV is great and regular. For non-exercise data segments, continuous indices of stress and relaxation are used to identify the time when the body is in a stress state, a relaxation state or an unrecognized state. These states are further used in calculation of 'relaxation–stress balance', i.e. the accumulation or decrease of resources during the recording period. For more details, see Kettunen and Saalasti (2004) and the Firstbeat PRO Software User Manual (www.firstbeat.fi). In the present study, all the exercise related variables (HR, $\dot{V}_{O_2}$, EPOC, time in three different intensity zones; I < AerT, AertT < II < AnT and III > AnT) were calculated individually from the RRI data collected during training sessions and matches. Nocturnal HRV variables included the traditional variables, HR, LFP and HFP, and the new variables, stress index and recovery index.

Statistics

The results (absolute values) are presented in mean ± standard deviation (SD). Natural logarithm of the traditional HRV indices and heart rate (HR) as well as the new Firstbeat PRO software derived HR- and HRV-based stress and recovery indices were used in statistical analysis with Students *t*-test for paired samples.

Results

Mean $\dot{V}_{O_{2max}}$ was 53.5 $\pm$3.3 ml.kg.$^{-1}$min.$^{-1}$, HRmax 198 $\pm$5 beats.min.$^{-1}$, AerT 38.0 $\pm$2.2 ml.kg.$^{-1}$min^{-1} and AnT 46.3 $\pm$3.0 ml.kg.$^{-1}$min.$^{-1}$. The mean EPOC values in light and heavy training sessions were 18 $\pm$4 ml.kg^{-1} and 72 $\pm$ 10 ml.kg^{-1} ($P<0.001$), respectively. In three matches, the mean EPOC values were 213 $\pm$15 ml.kg^{-1}, 150 $\pm$12 ml.kg^{-1} and 136 $\pm$9 ml.kg^{-1} ($P<0.01$). In matches, heart rate was on average 37 % (range 7–76%) under AerT, 43% (range 20–67%) between AerT and AnT and 20% (range 4–36%) over AnT. In the most exacting (first) match the perceived exertion on Borg's scale was 7.0 and average heart

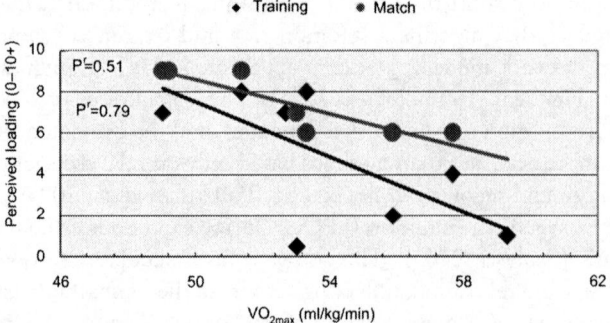

Figure 24.1 Relationships between the perceived exertion of players and $\dot{V}O_{2max}$ in training sessions (square dots) and matches (round dots)

rate 166 beats.min^{-1}. Significant relationships were found between the perceived exertion of physical loading in the training sessions and in matches with $\dot{V}O_{2max}$ (Figure 24.1).

Average nocturnal heart rates (HR) after each match were 53 ± 3, 50 ± 4 and 51 ± 4 beats.min^{-1} (ns). The nocturnal HRV stress index was 0.061 ± 0.002, 0.053 ± 0.001 and 0.064 ± 0.002 (ns), and relaxation index 98 ± 2, 103 ± 3 and 98 ± 3 (ns), respectively. The relative HRV stress and relaxation indices of the tournament days are shown in Figures 24.2 and 24.3. The indices have been related to the lowest stress index and relaxation index during tournament. In comparison of easy training day (1.3) and match day (26.2), a significant difference was observed in resting heart rate, 50 ± 5 beats.min^{-1} v 53 ± 5 ($P<0.05$), and in relaxation index, 102 ± 4 v 98 ± 7 ($P < 0.05$), respectively.

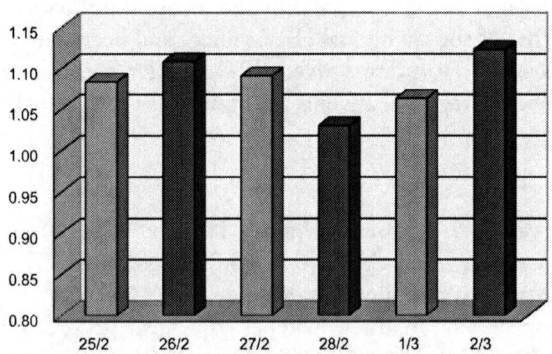

Figure 24.2 The relative stress indices of the consecutive tournament days.; 1st, 3rd and 5th bars are training days and 2nd, 4th and 6th bars are match days

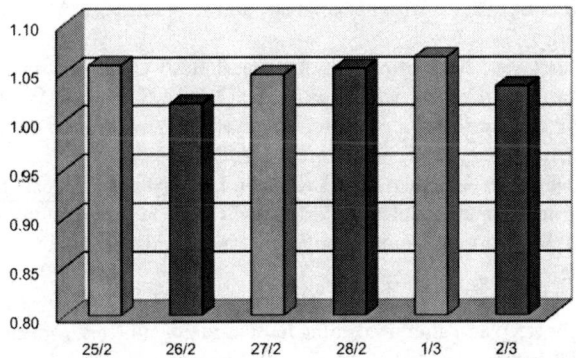

Figure 24.3 The relative relaxation indices of the consecutive tournament days; 1st, 3rd and 5th bars are training days and 2nd, 4th and 6th bars are match days

Discussion

Average HR and the new HRV-based recovery index (Kettunen and Saalasti, 2004) differentiated nocturnal autonomic modulation after easy training days and match days. Therefore, the new methods of HRV analysis seem to enhance the ability to measure changes in cardiac autonomic modulation after hard matches. The reduced HRV after physical exercise is known to recover to initial levels in less than 24 hours (Furlan *et al.*, 1993), but players typically train one or two times per day or train once and play a match, and the recovery is not always perfect. Maximal oxygen uptake showed a significant relationship to the perceived exertion in training sessions and matches and the loading of the whole tournament. The players having $\dot{V}O_{2\,max}$ on average 50 ml.kg^{-1}.min^{-1} rated training sessions, matches and the tournament physically very strenuous. However, the player with $\dot{V}O_{2max}$ of 60 ml.kg^{-1}.min^{-1} evaluated the same training sessions and matches as slightly strenuous or strenuous. According to the HRV stress and recovery indices the stress level was at its highest after the first and last matches and lowest after the second match and after a single training day's session. This trend was seen also in the mean nocturnal heart rate.

Conclusion

In conclusion, the results have shown that the heart rate variability measurements according to the Firstbeat PRO software analysis can be applied to evaluate players' physical loading and recovery in soccer.

References

Borg, G.A.V., 1982, Psychological bases of perceived exertion. *Medicine and Science in Sports and Exercise*, 14, 377–81.

De Meersman, R.E., 1993, Heart rate variability and aerobic fitness. *American Heart Journal*, 125, 726–31.

Firstbeat Technologies, 2005, http://www.firstbeat.fi/files/VO2_Estimation.pdf.

Furlan, R., Piazza, S., Dell'Orto, S., Gentile, E., Cerutti, S., Pagani, M. and Malliani, A. 1993. Early and late effects of exercise and athletic training on neural mechanisms controlling heart rate. *Cardiovascular Research*, 27, 482–8.

Hynynen E., Nummela A., Rusko H., Hämäläinen I. and Jylhä R., 2006a, Effects of training on cardiac autonomic modulation during night sleep in cross country skiers. *Congress Proceedings*. International Congress on Science and Nordic Skiing. 18–20 June, Vuokatti, Finland, 35.

Hynynen, E., Uusitalo, A., Konttinen, N. and Rusko, H., 2006b, Heart rate variability during night sleep and after awakening in overtrained athletes. *Medicine and Science in Sports and Exercise*, 38, 313–17.

Kettunen, J. and Saalasti, S., 2004, Procedure for detection of stress by segmentation and analyzing heart beat signal. United States Patent Application 20050256414, WO 2004/016172 A1.

Kettunen, J. and Saalasti, S. 2005. Procedure for deriving reliable information on respiratory activity from heart period measurement. United States Patent Application 20050209521.

Loimaala, A., Huikuri, H., Oja, P., Pasanen, M. and Vuori, I., 2000, Controlled 5–month aerobic training improves heart rate but not heart rate variability or baroreflex sensitivity. *Journal of Applied Physiology*, 89, 1825–9.

Nummela, A., 2004, Kestävyysominaisuuksien mittaaminen. In: *Kuntotestauksen käsikirja*. edited by Keskinen, K., Häkkinen, K. and Kallinen, M., (Helsinki: Liikuntatieteellinen Seura), pp. 51–78.

Pulkkinen, A., Kettunen, J., Martinmäki, K., Saalasti, S. and Rusko, H. K., 2004, On- and off-dynamics and respiration rate enhance the accuracy of heart rate based $\dot{V}O_2$ estimation. *Medicine and Science in Sports and Exercise*, 36, Supplement 253.

Rusko, H., Pulkkinen A., Saalasti, S., Hynynen, E. and Kettunen, J., 2003, Pre-prediction of EPOC: a tool monitoring fatigue accumulation during exercise? San Francisco 28–31 May 2003. Abstract: *Medicine and Science in Sports and Exercise*, 35 (5), Suppl. S183.

Saalasti, S. 2003. *Neural networks for heart rate time series analysis*. Ph.D. Dissertation. Department of Mathematical Information Technology, University of Jyväskylä, Finland. Jyväskylä Studies in Computing, 33, Jyväskylä: University of Jyväskylä

Uusitalo, A.L.T., Uusitalo, A. and Rusko, H., 2000, Heart rate and blood pressure variability during heavy endurance training and overtraining in the female athlete. *International Journal of Sports Medicine*, 21, 45–53.

25 Differences in muscularity of psoas major and thigh muscles in relation to sprint and vertical jump performances between elite young and professional soccer players

Y. Hoshikawa,[1] *J.M. Campeiz,*[2]
K. Shibukawa,[2] *K. Chuman,*[2] *T. Iida,*[1]
M. Muramatsu[1] *and Y. Nakajima*[1]

[1] Sports Photonics Laboratory, Hamamatsu Photonics K.K, Japan; [2] Yamaha
Football Club Co.Ltd, Japan

Introduction

Sprinting and jumping are the most essential abilities in attaining high-level soccer playing standards. Many efforts have been made in identifying anthropometric, biomechanical and physiological factors in order to establish a more efficient training method for improving the requisite abilities. In particular, the influence of muscular strength on these abilities has been extensively studied, but previous findings remain controversial (Dowson *et al.*, 1998, Kukolj *et al.*, 1999).

Muscular strength was basically determined by muscle cross-sectional area (CSA). Recently we reported that CSA of psoas major and thigh muscles correlated with the best 100-metre record in junior sprinters (Hoshikawa *et al.*, 2006). The aim of the study was to compare high-level youth and professional soccer players in sprinting and vertical jumping with regard to muscularity of these muscle groups.

Methods

Thirty first-team professional soccer players aged 23.8 ±5.2 years (PRO) and 24 youth team academy players aged 17.0 ±0.7 years (YNG) from one of the most successful clubs in Japan participated in the study. All subjects were outfield players and goalkeepers were not used. Height and body mass of PRO and YNG were 1.773 ±0.045 m, 72.1 ±5.5 kg and 1.720 ±0.006 m, 63.7 ±5.5 kg respectively. Whole body composition was measured using the BOD POD system (LMI, Inc.). Cross-sectional magnetic resonance images (0.2–T Signa Profile, GE) were taken in the 70 per cent (upper), 50 per cent (middle), and 30 per cent (lower) of femur length in both thighs, and midway between the fourth and fifth lumbar vertebrae to determine CSA of the quadriceps femoris (QF), the hamstrings (HAM) and the adductors (ADD) in the thigh at each cross-sectional level and the psoas major (PM). Sprinting times (s) were measured on a grassed field using infrared photocell sensors placed at 5, 10, 15, and 20 metre distances. Every gating signal was confirmed carefully to detect the runner's trunk and converted into average velocities (m.s^{-1}) within each distance. Vertical height of squat jump (SJ) and counter-jump (CJ) were measured by filming with height calibration. The top of the head was digitized to measure the vertical jump height for each performance.

Effect size (ES) was calculated for each variable to examine the difference between PRO and YNG. The statistical software SPSS ver. 11.5 was used to perform single and multiple regression analyses on the relationship between the sprint and vertical jump performances and the variables of anthropometry, body composition and muscle CSA. Since a significant difference was found in height between PRO and YNG, the values relative to height were used for fat-free mass and muscle CSA in the regression analyses. Statistical significance was set at $P<0.05$.

Results

Table 25.1 shows the differences in performances, body composition and muscle CSA between PRO and YNG. Effect sizes were less than -1.0 in the sprint and more than 1.0 in the vertical jump performances as well as muscle CSA. The largest ES was found in PM (ES $= 1.9$) followed by the sprint time for 20 m (ES $= -1.8$) and ADD$_{up}$ (ES $= 1.6$). Only small and non-significant correlation coefficients were found between performances and variables of body composition and muscle CSA when the correlations were calculated separately for PRO and YNG (Table 25.2). However, when all the data were pooled, modest but significant correlation coefficients (0.38–0.58) were found in fat-free mass and all of the muscle CSA except HAM for sprint performances.

Stepwise multiple regression analyses on the pooled data produced standard partial regression coefficients (beta weights) in the prediction model for sprint velocities and vertical jump heights as follows:

Average velocity
5–m: $0.495 \times$ ADD$_{mid}$/ht $+ 0.289 \times$ PM/ADD with adjusted $r^2 = 0.212$
10–m: $0.371 \times$ PM/ht $+ 0.313 \times$ ADD$_{mid}$/ht with adjusted $r^2 = 0.299$
15–m: $0.449 \times$ PM/ht $+ 0.256 \times$ ADD$_{mid}$/ht $+ 0.233 \times$ QF$_{up}$/QF$_{mid}$ with adjusted $r^2 = 0.356$ (Figure 1A)
20 m: $0.562 \times$ PM/ht $+ 0.282 \times$ QF$_{up}$/QF$_{mid}$ with adjusted $r^2 = 0.332$

Vertical jump height
SJ: $0.575 \times$ QF$_{up}$/ht $+ 0.290 \times$ PM/QF with adjusted $r^2 = 0.342$
CJ: $0.616 \times$ QF$_{up}$/ht $+ 0.273 \times$ PM/QF with adjusted $r^2 = 0.382$ (Figure 25.1b)
(where ht is height in m, ADD$_{mid}$ is CSA of adductors at the mid-thigh in cm^2,

Table 25.1 Differences between PRO and YNG

	Sprint (sec)				Vertical jump (cm)		Body composition		Muscle cross-sectional area (cm^2)			
	5m	10m	15m	20m	SJ	Cj	Fat (%)	FFM (kg)	QF$_{mid}$	HAM$_{lo}$	ADD$_{up}$	PM
PRO	0.99 (−0.02)	1.72 (−0.04)	2.36 (−0.05)	2.96 (−0.06)	42.8 (−3.8)	57.1 (−4.0)	7.7 (−2.3)	66.5 (−5.50)	83.4 (−6.9)	42.8 (−5.3)	66.2 (−5.9)	19.8 (−1.8)
YNG	1.02 (−0.04)	1.78 (−0.04)	2.45 (−0.05)	3.08 (−0.07)	38.4 (−3.7)	50.6 (−4.1)	8.8 (−2.5)	58 (−4.6)	74.5 (−7.3)	36.5 (−4.5)	57.8 (−4.3)	16.5 (−1.7)
Difference	−0.03	−0.06	−0.09	−0.12	4.4	6.5	−1.1	8.5	8.9	6.3	8.4	3.4
ES	−1.1	−1.6	−1.7	−1.8	1.1	1.6	−0.5	1.6	1.2	1.2	1.6	1.9

Mean (s.d), FFM fat-free mass, QF$_{mid}$ quadriceps femoris at middle of thigh, HAM$_{lo}$ hamstrings at lower thigh, ADD$_{up}$ adductors at upper thigh

Table 25.2 Simple correlation coefficients

| | Sprint (m/s) | | | | | | | | | Vertical jump (cm) | | | | | |
| | 5m | | | 15m | | | 10–20m | | | SJ | | | CJ | | |
	YNG	PRO	Total	YNG	PRO	Total	YNG	PRO	Total	YNG	PRO	Total	YNG	PRO	Total
Weight (kg)	–	–	–	–	–	–	–	–	–	–	–	0.36*	–	–	0.31**
Body composition	–	–	–	–	–	0.38*	–	–	0.36*	–	–	0.46*	–	–	0.49*
Fat (%)	–	–	–	–	–	–	–	–	–	–	–	–	–	–	–
FFM/ht (kg/m)	–	–	0.33	–	–	0.45*	–	–	0.45*	–	–	0.46*	–	–	0.54*
CSA relative to height (cm²/m)															
QF up	–	–	–	–	–	0.38*	–0.44	–	0.49*	–	0.41	0.53*	0.44	–	0.58*
QF mid	–	–	–	–	–	0.27	–	–	0.35*	–	–	0.41*	–	–	0.49*
QF lo	–	–	–	–	–	–	–	–	–	–	–	–	–	–	–
HAM up	–	–	–	–	–	–	–	–	0.30	–	–	0.38*	0.45	–	0.37*
HAM mid	–	–0.39	–	–	–0.36	–	–	–	–	–	–	–	–	–	0.30
HAM lo	–	–	–	–	–	0.31	–	–	0.30	–	–	0.37*	–	–	0.448
ADD up	–	–	0.33	–	–	0.45*	–	–	0.46*	–	–	–0.49*	–	–	0.51*
ADD lo	–	–	0.41*	–	–	0.45*	–	–	0.32	–	–	0.36*	–	–	0.35*
PM	–	–	0.32	–	–	0.52*	–	–	0.53*	–	–	0.48*	–	–	0.52*

$p < 0.01$ indicating the correlation coefficient is not significant

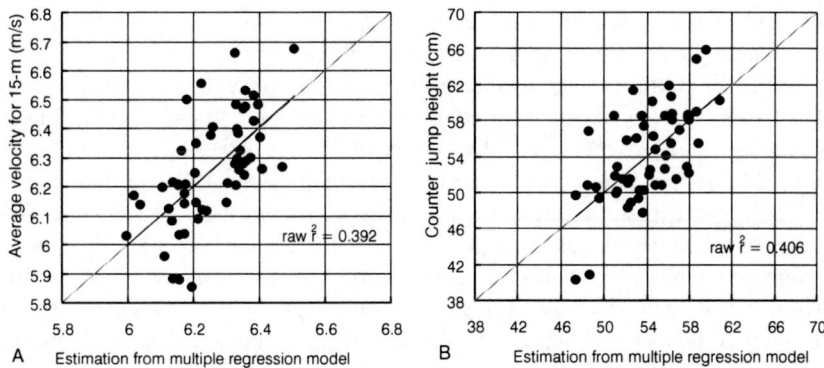

Figure 25.1 Relationship between the multiple regression model and 15m sprint velocity (a) and CJ (b)

PM is CSA of psoas major in cm², PM/ADD is ratio of CSA of psoas major and the average of ADD at the upper, middle and lower thigh. QF_{up}/QF_{mid} is ratio of CSA of quadriceps femurs at the upper and middle thigh. PM/QF is ratio of CSA of psoas major and the average of QF at the upper, middle and lower thigh.)

Discussion

Although the absolute difference in the average was smaller by less than 0.12 seconds in 20 m sprint time between PRO and YNG, values of ES larger than 1.0 were found in the sprint and vertical jump performances. In addition, large ES values were also found in all the muscle CSA measures between PRO and YNG. The differences in CSA were still significant even in terms of the values relative to height.

The subject groups appeared to be homogeneous in their sprinting ability. The range of sprint times for 20 m was within only 0.4 s (2.84 to 3.24 s). However, psoas major, which showed the largest ES, was found to be the first significant contributor in the stepwise regression model to predict the sprint velocity at a distance longer than 10 m. Previously we reported that psoas major expressed as the ratio to QF at the mid-thigh range was the first explanatory contributor in the model to predict best 100 m records in junior sprinters (Hoshikawa *et al.*, 2006). The results in this study were in line with the previous study and indicated that psoas major might be important rather in the initial phase of sprint running.

In addition, ADD at the mid-thigh and the ratio of QF at the upper and mid-thigh range were also selected as significant explanatory variables in distances shorter and longer than 15 m respectively, indicating that the critical muscle group for the initial phase of sprint running was dependent on sprint distance. The hip and knee extensors are the main accelerators in the initial phase of sprinting (Delecluse, 1997). However, psoas major, ADD, and QF at upper thigh range may all act as hip flexors and fixators during sprinting. Since a larger hip flexor torque is needed to reverse angular momentum of the hip extension in accelerating the leg forward within a short period of the air-phase of sprinting, the development of the muscle groups can be an advantage to enhance sprint performance. On the other hand, HAM was not significantly correlated at any distance in this study. The hamstrings have been reported as contributing most to produce the highest level of speed (Mero *et al.*, 1992, Delecluse, 1997). It is possible that the influence of HAM on sprint performance might be evident at distances longer than 20 m.

For vertical jump performance, QF at upper thigh range and ratio of psoas major to QF were selected as significant contributors for both SJ and CJ. Knee extension strength determines vertical velocity at the take-off of vertical jumping. Thus, it was reasonable that QF as an agonist muscle for knee extension was selected as the first explanatory variable for vertical jump performance. However, the finding that the ratio of psoas major to QF was selected as a second contributor seems to be conflicting as the larger QF makes the ratio lower. Although we can not address the reason clearly, this result suggests that development of QF accompanied by development of psoas major is required for better performance in vertical jumping.

In conclusion, the data presented indicate that the predominant development of specific muscle groups influenced, in part, short sprint and vertical jump performances of soccer players. Therefore the training of these muscles is essential in order for younger soccer players to enhance their playing abilities.

References

Delecluse, C., 1997, Influence of strength training on sprint running performance. *Sports Medicine*, 24, 147–56.

Dowson, M. N., Nevill, M. E., Lakomy, H. K. A., Nevill, A. M. and Hazeldine, R. J., 1998, Modelling the relationship between isokinetic muscle strength and sprint running performance. *Journal of Sports Sciences*, 16, 257–65.

Hoshikawa, Y., Muramatsu M., Iida, T., Uchiyama, A., Nakajima, Y., Kanehisa, H. and Fukunaga, T., 2006, Influences of the muscularity of the psoas major and thigh muscles on 100m race performance in junior sprinters, *Medicine and Sciences in Sports and Exercises*, 38, 2138–43.

Kukolj, M., Ropret, R., Ugarkovic, D. and Jaric, S., 1999, Anthropometric, strength, and power predictors of sprinting performance. *Journal of Sports Medicine and Physical Fitness*, 39, 120–2.

Mero, A., Komi, P. V. and Gregor, R. J., 1992, Biomechanics of sprint running. *Sports Medicine*, 13, 376–92.

26 Relationship between the ability to repeat sprints and maximal aerobic power in young soccer players

Carlo Castagna,[1,2] *Stefano D'Ottavio,*[1,2]
Manzi Vincenzo[1] *and José Carlos Barbero Álvarez*[3]

[1] Corso di Laurea in Scienze Motorie, Università di Roma Tor Vergata, Italy;
[2] Federazione Italiana Giuoco Calcio, Italy; [3] Universidad de Granada, Spain

Introduction

Maximal aerobic power ($\dot{V}O_{2max}$) and repeated sprint ability (RSA) are considered important sport-specific fitness components for high-level youth soccer players (Reilly *et al.*, 2000). Research carried out with adult team-sport participants the possible relationships between $\dot{V}O_{2\,max}$ and RSA has produced conflicting results (Spencer *et al.*, 2005). Furthermore, at present there have been no studies of the possible relationship between RSA and $\dot{V}O_{2\,max}$ in youth soccer-players. Due to this, appropriate testing and training strategies for developing the soccer-specific fitness of talented players are not yet clear. Consequently the aim of this study was to investigate the possible relationships between $\dot{V}O_{2\,max}$ and RSA in a group of young soccer players. As a working hypothesis we assumed significant effects of $\dot{V}O_{2\,max}$ on sprint decrement during RSA.

Methods

Subjects

Nineteen subjects (see Table 26.1) were randomly drawn from a population of regional-level youth soccer players, to participate in this study.

Fitness assessment

Maximal aerobic power was assessed using a sport-specific multistage shuttle-run test to exhaustion (Yo-Yo endurance test). Gas analysis was performed using a portable lightweight breath-by breath gas analyser (K4b2, COSMED, Rome, Italy). Repeated sprint activity (RSA) was assessed according to Reilly *et al.* (2000) where the soccer players completed $7 \times 30\,m$ line sprints with 20s active

Table 26.1 Players' characteristics and physiological responses

Age (years)	16.5 ± 1.2
Height (m)	175.2±0.063
Body Mass (kg)	66.9±8.3
$\dot{V}O_{2\,max}$ (ml.kg.$^{-1}$.min^{-1})	56.0±4.7
HRmax (beats.min^{-1})	201.0±6
Fatigue index (%)	5.8±2.3
Total sprint time (s)	33.2±1.3
RSA: peak blood lactate (mmol.l^{-1})	13.4±2.7

recovery between bouts. Sprint times were assessed using photocell beams (Muscle Lab, Bosco System, Rome, Italy). Fatigue index (FIX) during the RSA test was calculated according to Fitzsimons *et al.* (1993). Blood lactate (BLa) analyses were performed before (Pre), and 3 min (3 min) after the RSA protocol (Lactate Pro, Akray, Tokyo, Japan) using finger tip sampling.

Statistical analyses

Data are reported as mean ± standard deviation. Pearson's correlation coefficient was used to assess the relationship between aerobic fitness parameters and RSA variables. Significance was assumed at 5% ($P \le 0.05$) a priori.

Results

Pre-exercise, and 3 min BLa concentrations were 2.1±0.4 and 13.4±2.7 mmol.l^{-1}, respectively ($P < 0.0001$). Mean total sprint (TT) and Total Ideal sprint times (TI) were 33.2±1.3 and 31.4±1.2 s, respectively. The $\dot{V}O_{2\,max}$ was not significantly correlated to FIX (r = -0.40, P = 0.12), TT (r = -029, P = 0.26) and TI (r = 0.06, p = 0.80). However using the median split technique ($\dot{V}O_{2\,max}$ median = 56.2 ml. kg.$^{-1}$min^{-1}) a significant correlation was found between $\dot{V}O_{2\,max}$ and FIX (r = -0.77, P = 0.02) in the players possessing a low $\dot{V}O_{2\,max}$ (n = 9, 52.3±3.4 ml. kg.$^{-1}$ min^{-1}).

Discussion and conclusions

The results of the present study partly confirmed our working hypothesis that $\dot{V}O_{2\,max}$ and FIX during RSA are not related in youth soccer players. However, closer analysis of our data revealed a moderate ($r^2 = -0.60, P < 0.02$) and significant correlation between $\dot{V}O_{2\,max}$ and FIX in players possessing below median $\dot{V}O_{2\,max}$ levels (n = 9, 56.2±3.4 ml. kg.$^{-1}$min^{-1}). These results suggest a mutual influence between $\dot{V}O_{2\,max}$ and RSA in youth soccer players with lower level of fitness (<56.2 ml.kg.$^{-1}$.min^{-1}) and that RSA may be developed independent of aerobic fitness once a threshold level of aerobic capacity is achieved (i.e. 56 ml.kg^{-1}.min^{-1}). Our results are in agreement with previous research suggesting $\dot{V}O_{2\,max}$ levels of at least 60 ml. kg.$^{-1}$.min^{-1} are desirable for high-level youth soccer players (Reilly *et al.*, 2000). Additionally, it appears that RSA should be regarded as specific for soccer once the $\dot{V}_{O_2\,max}$ threshold is exceeded. The present data also highlight the importance of testing both $\dot{V}_{O_2\,max}$ and RSA performance separately in youth soccer players.

References

Fitzsimons, M., Dawson, B., Ward, D. and Wilkinson, A., 1993, Cycling and running tests of repeated sprint ability. *The Australian Journal of Science and Medicine in Sport*, 25, 82–7.

Reilly, T., Bangsbo, J. and Franks, A., 2000, Anthropometric and physiological predispositions for elite soccer. *Journal of Sports Sciences*, 18, 669–83.

Spencer, M., Bishop, D., Dawson, B. and Goodman, C., 2005, Physiological and metabolic responses of repeated-sprint activities specific to field-based team sport. *Sports Medicine*, 35, 1025–44.

Part V

Match analysis

27 Team kinematics of small-sided soccer games

A systematic approach

W.G.P. Frencken and K.A.P.M. Lemmink

Center for Human Movement Sciences, University Medical Center Groningen, University of Groningen, Netherlands

Introduction

Background

In recent years, the growing need and interest in performance analysis have led to new forms of match analysis techniques. Modern-day techniques include video-based statistical analysis systems, video-based tracking systems and electronic tracking systems. For an overview, see *Handbook of Soccer Match Analysis* (Carling *et al.*, 2005).

Despite the ongoing development of these innovative technologies, they are most frequently used for the more traditional notational analysis and 'time–motion' analysis. Notational analysis refers to the process of recording all events during a match. It accurately reflects what happened during a match. This kind of analysis mainly focuses on activities of the player holding the ball. 'Time–motion' analysis refers to the type and intensity of the player's movement. Thus, it is an analysis to measure physical/physiological load. In most of these analyses, a distinction is made between player positions and player quality. Also, differences between successful teams and unsuccessful teams are investigated. This is reasonable, because the differences eventually account for winning or losing.

It can be argued that the aforementioned methods account for technical and physical aspects of the game. However, another important factor that can make the difference in competitive play is the tactics employed. Analyses from a tactical perspective are scarce but would be beneficial to performance analysis. Often, analyses of team performance are the sum of individual player performances. However, we argue that studying the team as a whole has added value. Thus, what is lacking in performance analysis is an analysis of the team as a whole. This means that the team is more than the sum of all players. However, in order to study tactics, an adequate tool must be used. In this review, we introduce a way to study team kinematics and team tactics from a systematic perspective. This approach is demonstrated with preliminary data on small-sided soccer games. In this study, we investigated team kinematics of goal-scoring opportunities.

Systematic approach in soccer

Before soccer may be described as a complex system, the general characteristics of a systematic approach have to be outlined. Such a system must be: 1) an 'open' system (reciprocal relation with the environment), 2) it must be composed of interacting subsystems and 3) it must be subject to changes over time. The result of these characteristics is that the system possesses a high degree of flexibility and adaptability (McGarry *et al.*, 2002).

The gross behaviour of the system is the result of the interactions between the subsystems. However, the behaviour of the system is constrained (Newell, 1986). Organismic, environmental and task constraints determine the eventual behaviour. These constraints respectively refer to constraints from within the person (i.e. strength, height), from the environment (i.e. gravity, temperature) and to the characteristics of the task (i.e. instructions, rules).

Such a systematic approach has proved to be useful for the analysis of several sports, i.e. tennis (Palut and Zanone, 2005) and squash (McGarry *et al.*, 1999). However, there are major differences between tennis and squash on the one hand and soccer on the other. In the first place, possession alternates equally in the former whereas possession is not equally distributed in the latter. In the second place, the number of players is far greater in soccer. Finally, in tennis and squash, players stay on their own part of the court, whereas in soccer, players of different teams interfere with each other. Therefore, when describing soccer from a systematic perspective, it must be clear what the actual system is.

Twenty-two soccer players take part in a soccer match, equally divided over two teams. Although these teams have the same aim (to score a goal), there is a conflict (to score a goal at the different ends of the pitch). According to Gréhaigne *et al.* (1997), the essence of the game can be described as follows: 'a team must coordinate its actions to recapture, conserve and move the ball so as to bring it within the scoring zone and to score a goal'. This means that, in terms of a systematic approach, on the level 'match' two complex dynamical systems exist these are two conflicting, interacting complex dynamical systems (Lebed, 2006). The subsystems in both systems are the individual players. The interaction of the subsystems results in behaviour that is constrained by all three categories. Among the imposed constraints are match rules, individual skill, field dimensions and number of players. During a match there is an equilibrium; both teams seek to disturb the equilibrium to create goal-scoring opportunities. In other words, attempts are made to perturb the stability of the other system. Hughes *et al.* (1998) have defined a perturbation in soccer as 'an incident that changes the rhythmic flow of attacking and defending, leading to a shooting opportunity', i.e. individual skill or a penetrating pass. If a perturbation leads to a shooting opportunity, the perturbation is referred to as a 'critical incident'. Hughes *et al.* (1998) showed that these perturbations could be reliably identified in soccer. This ensures that the third criterion is met.

Mathematically, the behaviour of a dynamical system can be described with a dependent variable. The value of this variable is the state the system is in. The independent variables are infinite. These may include the states of the subsystems, interactions, constraints, and so on. This approach allows scientists to study the spatial-temporal aspects of a complex dynamical system. The power of this approach is that simple variables reflect the complex behaviour of a complex dynamical system. In the next section, we will introduce some variables that reflect team kinematics and may serve as dependent variable.

Variables

The two variables that we propose are based on common knowledge of the soccer game. The variables are 1) the centre of a team and 2) surface area of a team and are explained below.

In order to score a goal, it is fundamental to advance on the pitch. Similarly, citing Gréhaigne *et al.* (1997) '...bring the ball in the scoring zone'. As a result, the overall forward or backward movement of a team on the pitch can be represented by the centre of team. This is the mean (X,Y) of all players of one team. It is important to remember that in this approach, two systems exist at the level 'match'. Therefore, there are two centres of teams. This concept represents 'pressure'. Thus, the shorter the distance between the two centres, the higher the pressure. As a result, the likelihood of player mistakes increases. Therefore, also the number of perturbations and critical incidents is likely to increase.

However, the centre of team does not give information on player distribution on the field. Players can either be very close or far way from the centre. The surface area therefore represents overall team 'position'. It is the total field coverage of one team. In a goal-scoring example, the attacking team plays wide and deep in order to create free space. By doing so, the possibility for perturbations and critical incidents increases. On the other hand, the defensive team becomes compact. Distances between players are kept short. This is the basis of the defending strategy. The implications for surface area are clear. Surface area is larger for the attacking team when compared to the defending team. It can be argued that, based on surface area, it can be determined which team has possession. A pilot study was conducted to test the aforementioned variables.

Methods

Materials

We used an innovative electronic player tracking system, called Local Positioning Measurement (LPM, Abatec Electronic GmbH, Austria) for data collection. Players were equipped with a vest that contained a transponder. Beacons surrounding the field, recorded signals of all players at 50 Hz. Measurements took place at the artificial turf field at PSV Eindhoven's youth facility in the Netherlands.

Subjects and set-up

Ten male, elite youth soccer players (aged 16-18) participated in the study, including two goalkeepers and eight outfield players. Two four-a-side games of four minutes were played. Goalkeepers were only allowed to defend the goal. No additional instructions were given with respect to game playing.

Operationalization and data analysis

Small-sided games were used to reduce the number of players because of the complexity. The rationale for this is that it is thought that small-sided games represent 11 v 11 from a physiological perspective. In addition, small-sided games are also used for tactical training and development, according to several Dutch coaches.

Only attacks that resulted in goal-scoring opportunities, following a critical incident, were included in the analysis. Shots from distance were excluded. Goal attempts had to be performed after seven or less passes after recovery of possession because in regular competitive playing, most goals are scored when this criterion is met (Hughes and Franks, 2005). In total, nine attacks were included in the analysis and data on the position of the centre of teams were only analysed lengthwise.

Results

Seven out of nine attacks displayed similar results. Figure 27.1 shows a representative example. The position of the centre of team shows an 'in-phase' relation (Figure 27.1a). The expected 'anti-phase' relation or the surface area is less clear (Figure 27.1b).

In seven out of nine goal-scoring opportunities, the distance between the centres of teams was almost zero. On two occasions, the centres changed positions (Figure 27.1c). On five occasions, this was accompanied by a sudden increase in surface area for the attacking team (Figure 27.1d) or a decrease in surface area of the defensive team.

Discussion

Performance and match analysis are gaining more and more attention. This leads to the use of innovative technologies. However, these technologies are rarely used for match analysis from a tactical perspective. Here, the need for and benefit of such analyses is stated. First, a powerful framework must be developed that contains the right variables and the right approach.

In this report, such a framework is outlined. Although a lot of work still needs to be done, this seems a promising approach. Results of the experiment show that there is an 'in-phase' relationship between the centres of teams. This represents the natural 'rhythmic flow of attacking and defending', as described by Hughes *et al.* (1998). The system is stable over time. However, moments of instability are

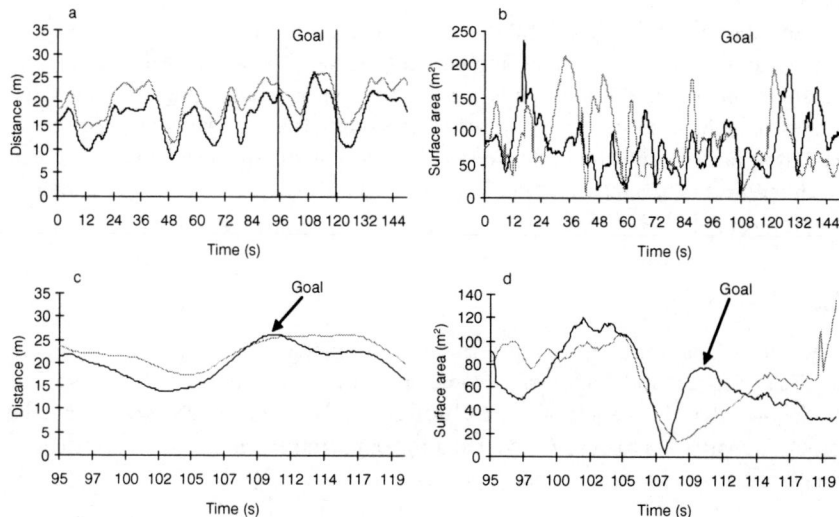

Figure 27.1 a) Centres of the team during a small-sided game; b) surface area during a small-sided game; c) centres of team when a goal is scored; d) surface area when a goal is scored

also noted. The instable moments are the result of perturbations. Unnecessary loss of possession (lack of skill, bad pass) accounts for most perturbations. After a perturbation, the distance between the centres decreases. On several occasions, centres overlap (distance is zero) or change position. This means that the centre of the attacking team is between the goal of the opponent and the centre of the opponent. The defensive team is overrun. It must be taken into account that the effects of lateral motion of the centre of team should be investigated. Possibly, perturbations affect stability in this direction as well. Especially in possession football this could be the case, as it is the aim to play the ball from side to side in order to find an 'opening'. This 'opening' could be described by a large distance between the centres of the teams.

The expectation for the surface area was that an anti-phase relation could be detected. However, surface area did not show a clear anti-phase relation. This is probably caused by the small number of players. Besides, four-a-side games are very dynamic. In order to free up space, players run all over the field and do not stick to fixed positions. Therefore, surface area alone might not be a useful dependent variable to use for small-sided games. In the set-up of the experiment, the maximal number of passes for an attack was seven. The rationale for this choice was that most successful attacks have seven or less passes (Hughes and Franks, 2005). The analysis showed that the success of the attacks depended not only on the number of passes. Also, the ability of a team to shift quickly from defense to attack and vice versa is critical. Especially if there is a discrepancy between the attacking and defending team, goal-scoring opportunities arise. Therefore, the 'rate of change' of both variables can also be a variable that describes game play. This suggestion requires further investigation.

Although this framework and these results are promising, it remains to be seen if the variables in this analysis apply to regular football games with 22 players. Furthermore, the question is if it is possible to translate the findings of small-sided games to regular soccer games. This is important from a coaching perspective. Finally, it must be the aim in future research to objectify the instability, which can be different for each team. It depends on the quality of the players and the tactics employed (4–4–2, 4–3–3, etc.).

Conclusions

The aim of this study was to stress the need for a systematic approach for match analysis in soccer and demonstrate some preliminary data from small-sided games. It is shown that the 'centre of teams', 'surface area' and 'rate of change' seem to be promising variables to describe goal-scoring opportunities in soccer. Nevertheless, analyses have to be refined and extended.

References

Carling, C., Williams, A.M. and Reilly, T., 2005, *Handbook of Soccer Match Analysis: A Systematic Approach to Improving Performance*. (London: Routledge).

Gréhaigne, J.F., Bouthier, D. and David, B., 1997, Dynamic-system analysis of opponent relationships in collective actions in soccer. *Journal of Sports Sciences*, 15, 137–49.

Hughes, M. and Franks, I., 2005, Analysis of passing sequences, shots and goals in soccer. *Journal of Sports Sciences*, 23, 509-14.

Hughes, M., Dawkins, N., David, R. and Mills, J., 1998, The perturbation effect and goal opportunities in soccer. *Journal of Sports Sciences*, 16, 20.

Lebed, F., 2006, System approach to games and competitive playing. *European Journal of Sport Science*, 6, 33–42.

McGarry, T., Khan, M.A. and Franks, I.M., 1999, On the presence and absence of behavioural traits in sport: an example from championship squash match-play. *Journal of Sports Sciences*, 17, 297–311.

McGarry, T., Anderson, D.I., Wallace, S.A., Hughes, M. and Franks, I.M., 2002, Sport competition as a dynamical self-organizing system. *Journal of Sports Sciences*, 20, 771–81.

Newell, K.M., 1986, Emergence of movement coordination. In *Visual Perception and Action in Sport*, edited by Williams, A.M., Davids, K. and Williams, J.G. (London: E&FN Spon), pp. 313-18.

Palut, Y. and Zanone, P.G., 2005, A dynamical analysis of tennis: concepts and data. *Journal of Sports Sciences*, 23, 1021–32.

28 Has soccer changed in the last three World Cups?

Julen Castellano Paulis,[1] *Abigail Perea Rodríguez*[1] *and Ángel Blanco-Villaseñor*[2]

[1] University of Basque Country, Spain; [2] University of Barcelona, Spain

Introduction

A common characteristic of observational methodology is that we can only observe the behaviour partially. That is why we need to know if the observed variance is related to the individual, the measuring tools, the place or other facets.

This study continues this line of investigation opened a few years ago (Blanco-Villaseñor *et al.*, 2000; Castellano *et al.*, 2000; Castellano and Blanco-Villaseñor 2003, 2004a, 2004b, 2006; Perea *et al.*, 2005, 2006), but focusing on the soccer World Cups. Matches of the last three World Cups (France 1998, Korea–Japan 2002 and Germany 2006) were observed, registered and analysed.

In total, 56 matches were used in this investigation to perform a variance analysis of four facets (World Cup, area, result and interaction contexts) and using different techniques to estimate variance components (Wright and Piersel, 1992; Marcoulides, 1996; Weiming and Fang, 2001; Kane, 2002). Through this analysis, we can define which facets that provide more information for the taxonomic tool which was used in the observation and determine which facets of the tool should be optimized.

Methods

The matches used for this investigation were recorded in VHS video format, and digitalized in MPG format. Specific software developed for the observation of game actions in soccer, SOCCAF v2.2 video (Perea *et al.*, 2006) was used to register the multi-event sequential data. An analysis of the data quality was performed using SDIS-GSEQ v4.1.2 (Bakeman and Quera, 1996). The variance component analysis of four facets was performed using SAS (Schlotzhauer and Littlell 1997; SAS Institute Inc, 1999) and GT (Ysewijn, 1996). The facets analysed were: World Cup (3 levels), result (7 levels), area (5 levels) and interaction contexts (48 levels). Altogether, 56 competition matches were observed, codified and registered in this investigation: 24 of them were played in France 1998, 20 in Korea–Japan 2002 and 12 in Germany 2006. In total, more than 150,000 events were registered.

Results

The results of the analysis are summarized in Table 28.1, showing the degrees of freedom (DF), significance and variance components in percentages for each facet of the model (taxonomic tool) and its interactions (significant for Pr > FType < 0.001). The generalizability absolute and relative coefficients for the design of the model Result × Area × Interaction Contexts/World Cup (RAI/W) appear in the last row. The variance assumed by the World Cup facet is 1 per cent.

Discussion

Using the variance components and generalizability studies, we can obtain more information than just a description of 'here' and 'now'. Variance analysis models give us information about the variance of each chosen facet.

In the model, the 'Interaction context' (I) facet shows the highest per cent of variability of the model (13 per cent). The 'Result' (R) facet, analyzed independently, represents the second level of the variability of the model (5 per cent). We can interpret this result as a difference in the way the teams play, depending on the actual result of the match (losing, winning or drawing). The 'Area' (A) facet contributes 1 per cent of the variability of the model, but when it interacts with

Table 28.1 Results obtained in the variance and generalizability analysis

Word Championship × Result × Area × Interaction Context			
		$r^2 = 0.999$	
Facets	DF	Pr > FType IIISS	% variance
World Cup (W)	2	<0.0001	1
Result (R)	6	<0.0001	5
World Cup × Result	12	<0.0001	2
Area (A)	4	<0.0001	1
World Cup × Area	8	0.0043	0
Result × Area	24	0.0002	1
World Cup × Result × Area	48	0.5147	1
Interaction Context (I)	47	<0.0001	13
World Cup × Interaction Context	94	0.0019	1
Result × Interaction Context	281	<0.0001	9
World Cup × Result × Interaction Context	562	0.2339	5
Area × Interaction Context	188	<0.0001	27
World Cup × Area × Interaction Context	376	0.1176	5
Result × Area × Interaction Context	1124	0.0158	19
World Cup × Result × Area × Interaction Context	2248	0.9968	11
R A I / W		$\rho2 = 0.899$	
		$\phi = 0.895$	

the other variables, it has 53 per cent of the total variability. When the 'Area' (A) facet is combined with the 'Interaction context' (I) facet, we obtain a relevant variability value, 27 per cent, which indicates that the interaction contexts are related to the area where they are more likely to appear. We also observe that most facets and their interactions are significant.

The 'World Cup' (W) facet shows how the play has evolved over the years. When we analyze it individually, the variability percent is very low at only 1 per cent and it is significant; this means that over the three last championships, the teams have played almost the same way. When this figure is combined with the other facets, the percent reaches only 14 per cent.

The residual error of the model ($W \times R \times A \times I$) is 11 per cent. That is, we still do not have all the facets to explain completely the variability of the model.

The generalizability study analyzed the design RAI/W. The results showed that the data were generalizable to a universe score close to 1 (0.89).

In conclusion, the results were satisfactory. It is necessary to analyze more World Cups in future to confirm our theory that the teams play this championship in the same way.

Acknowledgements

We gratefully acknowledge the support of the Spanish government project 'Análisis de la conducta interactiva en deportes de equipo: innovaciones metodológicas y tecnológicas en el proceso de la comunicación y acción de juego' (Dirección General de Investigación, Ministerio de Ciencia y Tecnología, Plan Nacional I+D+I) [Grant number SEJ2005–01961/PSIC].

References

Bakeman, R. and Quera, V., 1996, *Análisis de la interacción: Análisis secuencial con SDIS y GSEQ*. (Madrid: RA-MA).

Blanco-Villaseñor, A., Castellano, J. and Hernández Mendo, A., 2000. Generalizabilidad de las observaciones de la acción del juego en el fútbol. *Psicothema*, 12, Suplemento 2, 81–6.

Castellano, J., Hernández Mendo, A., Gómez de Segura, P., Fontetxa, E. and Bueno, I., 2000, Sistema de codificación y análisis de la calidad del dato en el fútbol de rendimiento. *Psicothema*, 12(4), 635–41.

Castellano, J. and Blanco-Villaseñor, A., 2003, El marcador como elemento orientador del comportamiento estratégico de los equipos de fútbol: Estimación y análisis de la variabilidad. VIII Congreso de Metodología de las Ciencias Sociales y de la Salud, Valencia.

Castellano, J. and Blanco-Villaseñor, A., 2004a. El soporte de marca en el fútbol y la variabilidad del comportamiento estratégico de los equipos. In *Investigación en Ciencias del Deporte*, edited by González y E. Requena, (Universidad del País Vasco), pp. 57 – 66.

Castellano, J. and Blanco-Villaseñor, A., 2004b, A time vs frequency model for the estimation and analysis of variability in soccer. VII Congreso Europeo de Evaluación Psicológica, Málaga.

Castellano, J. and Blanco-Villaseñor, A., 2006, Estrategia y rendimiento en fútbol: análisis de la variabiliad, en Socialización y deporte: revisión crítica. In *Diputación Foral de Álava*, edited by Castellano Paulis, J., Sautu Apellaniz, L. M., Blanco-Villaseñor, A., Hernández Mendo, A., Goñi Grandmontagne, A. and Martínez de Ilarduya, F., pp. 181 – 188.

Kane, M., 2002, Inferences about variance components and reliability-generalizability coefficients in the absence of random sampling. *Journal of Educational Measurement*, 39, 165–81.

Marcoulides, G. A., 1996, Estimating variance components in generalizability theory: The covariance structure analysis approach. *Structural Equation Modeling*, 3, 290–9.

Perea, A. E., Alday, L. and Castellano, J. 2006. Aplicación informática específica para la observación de la acción de juego en fútbol. In *Evaluación e intervención en el ámbito deportivo*, edited by Castellano Paulis, J., Sautu Apellaniz, L. M., Blanco-Villaseñor, A., Hernández Mendo, A., Goñi Grandmontagne, A. and Martínez de Ilarduya, F. Diputación Foral de Álava, pp. 285 – 294.

Perea, A. E., Castellano Paulis, J., Hernandez Mendo, A., Álvarez Pastor, D. and Luis Pérez Castellano, E., 2005, Pautas para el análisis de la calidad del dato en la observación de los deportes colectivos: una aplicación en el fútbol. I Congreso Virtual de Investigación en la Actividad Física y el Deporte, IVEF-SHEE de Vitoria-Gasteiz, September.

SAS Institute Inc., 1999, SAS/STAT *User's Guide, Version 7–1*, (Cary, NC: SAS Institute Inc).

Schlotzhauer, S. D. and Littell, R. C., 1997, *SAS System for Elementary Statistical Analysis*, second edition, (Cary, NC: SAS Institute Inc).

Weiming, L. and Fang, Y., 2001, Model selections, variance component explanations and index comparisons in the application of generalizability theory: Comments on Ziu and Zhang (1998, 1999). *Acta Psychologica Sinica*, 33, 467–70.

Wright, D. and Piersel, W. C., 1992, Components of variance in behavior ratings from parents and teachers. *Journal of Psychoeducational Assessment*, 10, 310-18.

Ysewijn, P., 1996, GT: Software for Generalizability Studies. Mimeograph.

29 Influence of playing in the European Champions League on performance in the Spanish Football League

Carlos Lago-Peñas and
Joaquín Lago-Ballesteros
HI-20 Research Group, University of Vigo, Spain

Introduction

In modern football, the number of matches played by teams during a season has been notably increased. Top teams are involved in several competitions and play most of the weeks at least two matches, one of the European Champions League and the other in their domestic national league at the weekend. However, the impact of playing a European Champions League match for a given team on its result in the national football league in the same week has not been analysed (Thiess, 1994).

This research had two goals. The first aim was to study the impact of playing in the Champions League on performance in the Spanish League. The second was to analyse whether being a beginner team in the Champions League is a relevant variable to explain the impact of playing in the Champions League on performance in the Spanish League.

Methods

The sample consisted of the 184 matches of the Spanish Football League in the seasons 2003–2004, 2004–2005 and 2005–2006 of those teams playing the European Champions League. The dependent variable was the result obtained by teams (win, defeat or draw), in the 184 matches of the Spanish Football League Seasons 2003–2004, 2004–2005 and 2005–2006 analysed.

Five independent variables were included in the study. The first independent variable (Champions League, CL) is binary: 1 means that the team in question played a match in the Champions League during the week analysed and 0 otherwise.

The second variable is also binary: 1 means that the team in question is making a debut (DEB) in the European competition, 0 otherwise.

The third variable is playing at home or away (PH): 1 means that the team in question plays at home and 0 means that it is a visitor (Pollard, 1986).

For the aims of this study, a variable, LEV, was created to measure the difference in the level among teams in each match of the Spanish Football League. This difference among teams was calculated according to Equation (29.1), where P_A is the position of the team observed in the previous day of the Spanish Football League and P_B is the position of the opponent.

$$LEV = P_A - P_B \qquad (29.1)$$

Finally, DEB × CL is the interaction between the variables Champions League and teams that are making their debut in the European competition. Two logit multinomial regression models were used in order to analyze the impact of playing a Champions League match for a given team on its result in the Spanish Football League in the same week. When interpreting the regressions, positive or negative coefficients for the variables indicate a positive or negative influence on the values of the dependent variable respectively (Long, 1997; Atkinson and Nevill, 2001; Nevill *et al.*, 2002).

The models used in the estimation are as shown in the Equations (29.2) and (29.3).

$$RE_i = \beta_1 + \beta_2 \cdot CL_i + \beta_3 \cdot PH_i + \beta_4 \cdot LEV_i + \varepsilon_i \qquad (29.2)$$

$$RE_i = \beta_1 + \beta_2 \cdot CL_i + \beta_3 \cdot DEB_i + \beta_4 \cdot PH_i + \beta_5 \cdot LEV_i + \beta_6 \cdot (DEB_i \cdot CL_i) + \varepsilon_i \qquad (29.3)$$

where: RE = result
i = random disturbance
β = coefficients of the variable

Results and discussion

As can be seen in Table 29.1, according to the estimation of a multinomial logit model, playing in the European Champions League had no statistically significant impact on the probability of winning a given match in the Spanish Soccer League. That is, playing in the Champions League does not reduce the probability of winning in the national championship. The variables playing at home and level were statistically significant and had the expected coefficient. Playing at home

Table 29.1 The results of teams in the Spanish Football League: the influence of playing the European Champions League

Independent variable	Defeat vs win
Level (LEV)	0.07 (0.03)**
Playing at home (PH)	0.95 (0.40)**
Champions League (CL)	0.46 (0.40)
Intercept	−0.30 (0.34)

Note: Estimation is by maximum likelihood; robust standard errors in parenthesis; *$P<0.01$ **$P<0.05$; intercept = the probability of win vs defeat or draw when all independent variables = 0

Table 29.2 The results of teams in the Spanish Football League: the influence of playing the European Champions League for teams making their debut in the competition

Independent variable	Defeat vs win
Playing at home (PH)	1.07 (0.41)**
Level (LEV)	0.03 (0.03)
Champions League (CL)	−0.28(0.56)
Debut (DEB)	−2.12 (0.64)**
DEB × CL	2.31 (0.93)**

Notes: Number of observations 172; LR χ^2 (10) = 37.90**, pseudo R^2 =0.10; estimation is by maximum likelihood; robust standard errors in parenthesis; *P<0.01 **P<0.05

increased the probability of winning in comparison with playing away and the higher the difference between teams, the higher the probability of winning in a match.

According to the results shown in Table 29.2, playing in the European Champions League does not reduce the probability of winning in the Spanish Football League for teams making their debut in the competition. Contrary to conventional wisdom, it had a positive effect. The variable playing at home was statistically significant. However, for teams making their debut in the competition the variable level was not statistically significant (P>0.05).

Conclusions

The main findings from this empirical analysis are the following:

- Playing in the European Champions League does not reduce the probability of winning in the Spanish Football League.
- Contrary to conventional wisdom, playing in the European Champions League does not reduce the probability of winning in the Spanish Soccer League for teams making their debut in the competition: it has a positive effect.
- The higher the difference between teams, the higher the probability of winning in a match.

References

Atkinson, G. and Nevill, A., 2001, Selected issues in the design and analysis of sport performance research, *Journal of Sports Sciences*, 19, 811–27.

Long, S., 1997, *Regression Models for Categoricals and Limited Dependent Variables*. Advanced Quantitative Techniques in the Social Sciences 7. (Beverly Hills, CA: Sage Publications).

Nevill, A., Atkinson, G., Hughes, M. and Cooper, S.M., 2002, Statistical methods for analysing discrete and categorical data recorded in performance analysis. *Journal of Sports Sciences*, 20, 829–44.

Pollard, R., 1986, Home advantage in soccer: a retrospective analysis. *Journal of Sports Sciences*, 4, 237–46.

Thiess, G., 1994, La necesitá di una teoria de la gara. *SDS, Revista di Cultura Sportiva*. Ano XIII, 30, 13–19.

30 Deceleration and turning movements performed during FA Premier League soccer matches

Jonathan Bloomfield,[1] *Remco Polman*[2] *and Peter O'Donoghue*[3]

[1] Sports Institute for Northern Ireland, UK; [2] Department of Sport Science, The University of Hull, UK; [3] School of Sport, University of Wales Institute Cardiff, UK

Introduction

Time–motion analysis studies have provided a breakdown of match time between different locomotive movements for men's soccer (e.g. O'Donoghue *et al.*, 2001). The movement of soccer players has been expressed as distance covered (e.g. Reilly and Thomas, 1976; Ohashi *et al.*, 1988) and the frequency and duration of high-intensity bursts and recovery periods (O'Donoghue *et al.*, 2005). Such information has yet to indicate the patterns of movement in soccer as well as the deceleration and turning movements. These aspects provide important information concerning the agility demands of soccer. Sprinting has often been selected as a mode of motion for analysis and relates to acceleration and speed. However, following every sprint there must also be a phase of deceleration which has not been included in previous time–motion analyses and as a consequence, this detail is lacking or otherwise incorporated as a separate category such as running or jogging. Furthermore, due to the need to change direction, cut, spin or twist acutely and rapidly, players are required to perform braking movements which can have a high eccentric stress (Woods *et al.*, 2004). Turning ability has previously been related with the velocity of movement in soccer (Grehaigne *et al.*, 1997). Players who are travelling at $\leq 2\,\mathrm{m.s^{-1}}$ appear to be able to turn in a sector $\leq 240°$ during movement with respect to the direction they are moving in. However, the scope for direction change decreases as velocity increases with players restricted to a sector of $\leq 80°$ of potential movement when moving at speeds $\geq 5\,\mathrm{m.s^{-1}}$. This method was used to analyse the pre-goal phases of the 1992 European Nations Cup final between Denmark and Germany (Grehaigne *et al.*, 1997). Players attempting to turn acutely at high velocities risk losing balance. Also players who are aware of opponents' manoeuvrability based on current velocity can play the ball in a way that does not cross any turning sector of coverage.

Bloomfield *et al.* (2004) provided a detailed time–motion analysis technique that includes details of turning performed by players. The classification system has been used to investigate the physical demands of FA Premier League soccer for different positions (Bloomfield *et al.*, 2007) as well as injury risk. A strength of the method is that it includes deceleration, braking, and turning movements associated with ankle and knee injuries, which have been counted during competitive netball performances (Williams and O'Donoghue, 2005). Bloomfield *et al.* (2007) used the approach to describe the movement performed by English FA Premier League soccer players in terms of frequency, duration and percentage time for different locomotive movements, movement in different directions and movement of different intensities. While the movement, direction and intensity attributes of activities were described in isolation as well as in combination, it has been recognised that the temporal patterns that occur within movement sequences are critically important to understanding the agility requirements of the game (Bloomfield *et al.*, 2005). Indeed, with agility conditioning programmes being undertaken by professional players, a full understanding of the agility requirements of soccer match-play is needed to inform the process of developing such programmes. Agility requirements of soccer can be enlightened by the volume and type of deceleration and turning movements performed during competitive matches. The movements within or between which turns are performed can be analysed by exploring temporal relationships between movements performed before and after turns. Therefore, the purpose of the current investigation was to characterise the nature of deceleration and turning performed during elite soccer competition.

Methods

The on-field activity of 55 FA Premier League soccer players was recorded from Sky Television's PlayerCam facility for approximately 15 minutes each. The 15 minutes recorded was reduced to approximately 5 minutes per player by only including video sequences where the player was in possession of the ball, competing for the ball, evading opponents in order to become available to receive the ball, supporting team mates in possession of the ball, tracking and channelling opponents who are in possession or might receive the ball as well as technical and tactical positioning movements. In this study, all these movements were grouped together and labelled as 'purposeful'. There was a good inter-observer agreement for identifying purposeful movements ($\kappa = 0.9227$). The video sequences were analysed using the Observer Pro system Version 5.1 (Noldus Information Technology, The Netherlands). The method accounted for both timed movements (performed over a period of measurable time) and non-timed actions (instantaneous events) such as turns and on-the-ball skills to be recorded. The timed movements were characterised by:

- the locomotive movement type being performed by the player;
- the direction in which the movement was performed with respect to the position the player's torso was facing when the movement commenced;

• the perceived intensity of the movement which was classified as low, moderate, high or very high.

One of the timed classifications was deceleration. It was classified by the perceived start of diminished effort from a rapid acceleration, high-intensity run or sprint and ended when the player was perceived to enter a new mode of motion. Two of the categories not timed were braking and turning. Braking was classified when the player observed took a single step in order to stop the entire body from travelling in a particular direction and transferred body weight from one foot to the other. The turns were classified by the direction turned (to the left or right) as well as by a category angle of the turn (<90°, 90° to 180°, 180° to 270°, or >270°). The video sequences were initially viewed at normal speed and replayed at slower speeds during data entry using the review and scroll functions of the video control that performed a video replay. The method of Bloomfield *et al.*, (2004) is labour intensive and so a reliability evaluation study is essential. There was a good inter-observer agreement for movement type ($\kappa = 0.7277$), direction of movement ($\kappa = 0.6968$), intensity of movement ($\kappa = 0.7062$) and game-related activity ($\kappa = 0.7891$) with a moderate strength of agreement being achieved for turning ($\kappa = 0.5639$) (Bloomfield *et al.*, 2006).

Altogether, 26,613 movements were recorded for the 55 players and 5,115 of these were turning events. A Microsoft Excel spreadsheet was programmed to extract details of turning movements performed together with the locomotive movements performed immediately before and immediately after each deceleration, brake and turn.

The frequency of movements performed before and after decelerating and braking events was cross-tabulated. Where 20 per cent or more of the expected frequencies in a cross tabulation were ≥ 5, the chi-squared test of independence was applied to determine whether movement preceding the deceleration or braking had an influence on the movement that followed it. As the data were taken from 15 minutes of recorded match activity for 55 players, the frequencies could be scaled by 6/55 to determine an average frequency for a player's performance in a match. In addition, the mean duration of deceleration movements performed was determined and a Mann Whitney U test was used to compare the duration of deceleration movements that followed runs with the duration of those that followed sprints. For the turns, a chi squared test of independence was applied to the angle (<90° or $\geq 90°$) and direction of turn (to the left or to the right) and movement performed before each turn to determine if the nature of movement was influenced by the angle of turn. None of the expected frequencies within the cross-tabulation of these two variables had an expected count of less than 5. A further chi-squared test of independence was applied to the angle and direction of turn and movement performed after each turn to determine if the nature of movement was influenced by the angle of turn. Four of the 36 cells in the cross-tabulation of these two variables had frequencies of less than 5. This value is less than 20 per cent of the cells and, therefore, the application of the chi-squared test of independence was valid. In the current study, $P<0.05$ indicated a significant influence of movements performed before and after decelerating and braking events as well as of angle and direction of turn on movement performed before or after turns.

Results

Table 30.1 shows the total frequency of deceleration movements related to the movements that preceded them and followed them. Players performed the equivalent of 54.1 decelerations during a match. There was no significant difference in the profile of activity that followed decelerations after the runs and decelerations that followed sprints ($\chi^2_6 = 9.9$, $P = 0.131$). The mean ±SD duration of deceleration movements was 0.76 ± 0.58 s. The duration of those decelerations that followed running movements of 0.80 ± 0.55 s was not significantly greater than those that followed sprints of 0.74 ± 0.59 s ($z = 1.4$, $P = 0.160$). The 'other' activities shown in Table 30.1 include slides, jumps and landings.

Table 30.2 shows the frequency of instantaneous braking movements arranged in terms of the activities that preceded them and that followed them. There was

Table 30.1 Frequency of activities preceding and following deceleration movements

Pre-activity	Post-activity		
	Run	*Sprint*	*Total*
Stand	5	5	10
Walk	17	31	48
Jog	26	79	105
Run	7	33	40
Sprint	3	14	17
Skip	17	42	59
Shuffle	42	150	192
Other	8	17	25
Total	125	371	496

Table 30.2 Frequency of movements that preceded and followed instantaneous braking movements

Pre-activity	Post-Activity								
	Stand	*Walk*	*Jog*	*Run*	*Sprint*	*Skip*	*Shuffle*	*Other*	*Total*
Stand	1	1	10	4	2	5	18		41
Walk	2	3	11	5		3	11	1	36
Jog	3	3	12	9	2	5	6	2	42
Run		1		2	1	3	13		20
Sprint	3		4	2	1	5	15		30
Skip	4	6	3	7	2	3	14		39
Shuffle	8	3	9	15	4	15	30	2	86
Other				1	2		4		7
Total	21	17	49	45	14	39	111	5	301

Table 30.3 Frequency of locomotive movements performed immediately before and after turning movements during purposeful movement within 13 minutes and 45 minutes of soccer match play

Before turn	After turn									
	Jog	Run	Shuffle	Skip	Decel.	Sprint	Stand	Brake	Walk	Total
Jog	391	107	140	307	0	45	49	10	170	1219
Run	81	75	61	57	18	36	3	8	8	347
Shuffle	176	128	178	173	1	113	62	30	102	963
Skip	322	91	82	263	0	44	39	5	231	1077
Decel.	35	11	33	31	0	7	7	2	28	154
Sprint	3	8	15	1	33	21	0	2	0	83
Stand	79	32	45	42	0	17	0	1	147	363
Brake	20	15	28	22	1	21	7	1	13	128
Walk	241	59	76	178	0	23	51	3	150	781
Total	1348	526	658	1074	53	327	218	62	849	5115

Table 30.4 Frequency of locomotive movements performed immediately before and after turning movements of different angles in different directions

Before turn	After turn									
	Jog	Run	Shuffle	Skip	Decel.	Sprint	Stand	Brake	Walk	Total
Before										
<90° left	556	161	371	490	64	31	150	38	321	2182
<90° right	549	149	376	494	55	46	157	46	354	2226
≥90° left	58	16	103	53	15	3	34	27	55	364
≥90° right	56	21	113	40	20	3	22	17	51	343
After										
<90° left	617	222	264	440	16	137	90	23	373	2182
<90° right	529	216	323	437	33	146	86	28	365	2226
≥90° left	70	47	41	100	1	25	19	3	58	364
≥90° right	69	41	30	97	3	19	23	8	53	343

the equivalent of 32.8 braking movements per match. The 'other' activities shown in Table 30.2 include slides, jumps and landings.

Table 30.3 shows the locomotive movement performed immediately before and immediately after each turn. There were 21 per cent of the turns performed within the same locomotive movement and 79 per cent of turns performed during a transition between one locomotive movement and another. Table 30.4 shows the different movements performed before and after turns in different directions and over different angles of turn. The frequency profile of movements performed before ($\chi^2_{24} = 185.0$, $P<0.001$) and after ($\chi^2_{24} = 69.6$, $P<0.001$) turns were significantly influenced by the angle of turn with more turns of <90° before or after jogging and shuffling movements and more turns of ≥90° during skipping, braking and deceleration movements.

Discussion

The purpose of the current investigation was to characterise the nature of deceleration, braking and turning movements performed during elite soccer competition. The current results provide useful knowledge for those developing speed and agility conditioning exercises and testing procedures specifically for elite soccer players. The purpose of the current investigation was to characterise the nature of deceleration and braking movements performed during elite soccer competition. The results suggest that that there were more deceleration ($n = 496$) than braking movements ($n = 301$) and that much more decelerations occur following sprinting than after high-intensity running. This difference is perhaps due to the scope of a high-intensity run becoming a sprint following further acceleration but also suggests that deceleration from high-intensity running may be dissipated through lower intensity running or jogging rather than through an obvious deceleration phase. In contrast, the deceleration phase of a sprint appears much more identifiable and prevalent. Furthermore, 40.4 per cent of decelerations post-sprinting are followed by shuffling movements. This holds significance for the severity of the eccentric stresses placed on muscles. It has also been suggested that the rapid change of eccentric to concentric function is where muscles are most vulnerable to injury, in particular the hamstring group (Verrall *et al.*, 2001). In addition, 12.6 per cent of sprints involved a deceleration phase followed by immediately sprinting or running again. It is therefore important to account for these factors when conditioning the players and for preventing injury. The importance of this factor is highlighted when considering the high occurrence of hamstring injuries in soccer (Woods *et al.*, 2004). In this respect, a 10–week conditioning period of the Nordic hamstring exercise (a partner exercise focusing on the eccentric phase) can develop maximal eccentric hamstring strength in well-trained soccer players and may be beneficial to prepare for elite soccer match-play (Mjolsnes *et al.*, 2004).

A braking step also precedes and follows many different types of movement in different directions and intensities. However, these mostly occur when the player is shuffling with 28.5 per cent pre-shuffling and 36.8 per cent post-shuffling, including 27.0 per cent of shuffles incorporating a braking step within the shuffling movement. Also, 41.8 per cent of braking steps occurred following standing, walking, jogging and other unorthodox movements. This would suggest that players need to be explosive from standing or slow-moving motion in order to perform high-intensity activities. Also, on approximately 5 to 6 occurrences during a match, players were required to run or sprint, perform a braking step and continue to run or sprint. These events entail a rapid change of eccentric to concentric muscle function associated with injury risk. This would suggest that the players require a high level of leg strength, speed and agility and an extensive movement repertoire.

In terms or turning, the current data challenge the assumptions of Grehaigne *et al.* (1997) for soccer players to have the ability to turn acutely during running and sprinting and this has been demonstrated in the FA Premier League. In this respect 6 per cent of turns ≥90° were performed following running or sprinting. It is therefore important for players to have this ability in their movement repertoire to succeed at an elite level. Players with such levels of agility will be able to cover greater sectors of the pitch and react to balls being played to different locations relative to their position on the pitch and current direction of movement.

The highest frequency of turns surrounded movements at low intensity with standing, walking, jogging and skipping accounting for 67.3 per cent of movements before a turn and 68.2 per cent of movements that occur after a turn. Of these, 69.7 per cent and 68.1 per cent occurred before and after a turn of <90° respectively and 51.1 per cent and 69.2 per cent occurred before and after a turn of ≥90° respectively. This would suggest that higher-intensity activity is performed with less turning within the movements. This may also reflect upon a need to create space using less overall movement. Furthermore, almost 80 per cent of turns were performed in the transition of one locomotive movement to another. This would suggest that a player often turns and changes pace but performs running and sprinting in more linear directions. In fact, while sprinting there were only 21 occasions when players turned and continued sprinting. These all occurred at an angle <90°. These are important findings when considering the strength and conditioning of the players. Young *et al.* (2001) reported that straight speed and agility training methods are specific and produce limited transfer to the other. Furthermore, reactive strength of the leg extensor muscles has been shown to have importance in change-of-direction performance but other technical and perceptual factors that influence agility performance also should be considered (Young *et al.*, 2002). Therefore, a combined programme of soccer-specific speed and agility exercises, maximum strength training and plyometrics should have a positive effect on performance (e.g. Polman *et al.*, 2004; Wisløff *et al.*, 2004).

There was also a similar number of turns that occurred in both directions and therefore when designing agility programmes, it is important to balance the volume of turns to the left and right. However, the complexity of the movement patterns that occur in soccer are highlighted in this analysis. There appear to be very few repeated patterns and there were no combination of angle of turn or direction of turn where any movement combination accounted for more than 10 per cent of turns.

This study has highlighted the volume and pattern of deceleration, braking and turning movements performed in match-play. This information should be considered by those developing conditioning programmes and testing procedures for soccer players.

References

Bloomfield, J., Polman, R. and O'Donoghue, P.G., 2004, The 'Bloomfield Movement Classification': notion analysis of individual players in dynamic movement sports, *International Journal of Performance Analysis of Sport*, 4(2), 20–31.

Bloomfield, J., Jonsson, G.K., Polman, R.C.J., Houlahan, K. and O'Donoghue, P.G., 2005, Temporal pattern analysis and its applicability in soccer. In *The Hidden Structure of*

Social Interaction: From Genomics to Cultural Patterns, edited by Anolli, L., Duncan, S., Magnusson, M. and Riva, G. (Amsterdam: IOS Press B.V). pp. 237–51.

Bloomfield, J., Polman, R. and O'Donoghue, P.G. (2006), Reliability of the Bloomfield Movement Classification, *Performance Analysis of Sport 7*, edited by Dancs, H., Hughes, M. and O'Donoghue, P.G., 23–26 August 2006, Szombathely, Hungary, (Cardiff: CPA UWIC Press), pp. 197–204.

Bloomfield, J., Polman, R.C.J. and O'Donoghue, P.G., 2007, Physical demands of different positions in English FA Premier League soccer. *Journal of Sports Science and Medicine*, 6, 63–70.

Grehaigne, J.F., Bouthier, D. and David, B., 1997, A method to analyse attacking moves in soccer, In *Science and Football III*, edited by Reilly, T., Bangsbo, J. and Hughes, M. (London: E&FN Spon), pp. 258–64.

Mjolsnes, R., Arnason, A., Osthagen, T., Raastad, T. and Bahr, R., 2004, A 10–week randomized trial comparing eccentric vs. concentric hamstring strength training in well-trained soccer players. *Scandinavian Journal of Medicine and Science in Sports*. 14(5), 311–17.

O'Donoghue, P.G., Boyd, M., Lawlor, J. and Bleakley, E.W., 2001, Time-motion analysis of elite, semi-professional and amateur soccer competition, *Journal of Human Movement Studies*, 41, 1–12.

O'Donoghue, P.G., Rudkin, S., Bloomfield, J., Powell, S., Cairns, G., Dunkerley, A., Davey, P., Probert, G. and Bowater, J., 2005, Repeated work activity in English FA Premier League soccer, *International Journal of Performance Analysis of Sport (e)*, 5(2), 46–57.

Ohashi, J., Togari, H., Isokawa, M. and Suzuki, S., 1988, Measuring movement speeds and distances covered during soccer match play. In *Science and Football*, edited by Reilly, T., Lees, A., Davids, K. and Murphy, W.J. (London: E & FN Spon), pp. 329–33.

Polman, R.C.J., Walsh, D., Bloomfield, J. and Nesti, M., 2004, Effective conditioning of female soccer players. *Journal of Sports Sciences*. 22, 191–203.

Reilly, T. and Thomas V., 1976, A motion analysis of work-rate in different positional roles in professional football match-play. *Journal of Human Movement Studies*, 2, 87–9.

Verrall, G.M., Slavotinek, J.P., Barnes, P.G. Fon, G.T. and Spriggins A.J., 2001, Clinical risk factors for hamstring muscle strain injury: a prospective study with correlation of injury by magnetic resonance imaging. *British Journal of Sports Medicine*, 35, 435–39.

Williams, R. and O'Donoghue, P., 2005, Lower limb injury risk in netball: a time-motion analysis investigation, *Journal of Human Movement Studies*, 49, 315–31.

Wisløff, U., Castagna, C., Helgerud, J., Jones, R. and Hoff, J., 2004, Strong correlation of maximal squat strength with sprint performance and vertical jump height in elite soccer players. *British Journal of Sports Medicine*. 38, 285–8.

Woods, C., Hawkins, R.D., Maltby, S., Hulse, M., Thomas, A. and Hodson, A., 2004, The Football Association Medical Research Programme: an audit of injuries in professional football: analysis of hamstring injuries. *British Journal of Sports Medicine*. 38, 36–41.

Young, W. B., McDowell, M.H. and Scarlett, B.J., 2001, Specificity of sprint and agility training methods. *Journal of Strength and Conditioning Research*, 15(3), 315–19.

Young, W.B., James, R. and Montgomery, J.I., 2002, Is muscle power related to running speed with changes of direction? *Journal of Sports Medicine and Physical Fitness*, 42, 282–8.

31 Comparative analysis of the high-intensity activity of soccer players in top-level competition

A. Zubillaga,[1] G. Gorospe,[1] A. Hernández-Mendo[2] and A. Blanco-Villaseñor[3]

[1] Universidad del País Vasco, Spain; [2] Universidad de Málaga, Spain; [3] Universidad de Barcelona, Spain

Introduction

The analysis of the physical activity that a football player completes during competition is a basic reference point when establishing the means and loads in the planning of training. Volume and intensity of the player's activity during the match are essential measures in the rating of effort. Several authors have highlighted the importance of the activity that the player does at a high intensity, as a key to distinguish the player's strain level (Bangsbo et al., 1991; Möhr et al., 2003),

The diversity of the applied methodologies, as well as the characteristics and size of the samples analysed, diminishes the reference value of the results. Therefore some authors classify players in three (Bangsbo et al., 1991; Drust et al., 1998) or four different positions (Reilly and Thomas, 1976).

This research project presents as original features: 1) a sample formed by a total of 6112 recordings of players activity, obtained in a high competition level; 2) the tool used, the AMISCO® system, which records activity of players during the match, with very high levels of accuracy, reliability and validity (Zubillaga, 2006); and 3) the classification of players in seven different positions.

The objectives of this research were to describe and compare the physical activity at high intensity of top-level players during competition, taking into account their playing position.

Methods

The AMISCO® system has been used to register players' activity. This system allows us to record and analyse the activity of each soccer player during competition. In order to apply the system, eight cameras and several computers were installed in the different stadia. The match was recorded and digitized, and sent to the production centre via ADSL where a double register process was started. On one hand, each player's position and movements were registered with a frequency of 25 recordings per second. Also the players' actions with the ball are registered. After the process was complete, all the data were mixed and the matches were subject to data quality control. The reliability, validity and accuracy were calculated, obtaining results that show the high quality of the registered data (Zubillaga, 2006).

The analysis can be developed from three perspectives: 1) the match reproduction in a two-dimensional view; 2) technical data analysis; and 3) the physical data analysis for each player.

From the recording of 194 matches at the highest competitive level (Spanish League and Spanish Cups, UEFA Cup and Champions League) in the 2003–04 season, we have considered a sample of 6112 entries that correspond to the players' activity during each half of the match. A selection criterion was that each subject played the whole game.

Although in each record more than thirty variables have been considered, in this research, we have only taken into account those that refer to the high-intensity activity of players. From the average of the movement coordinates, players have been classified in seven playing positions. The defined positions and their frequency are: wide fullback ($N = 1326$), centre fullback ($N = 1388$), pivot ($N = 1187$), centre midfield ($N = 215$), wide midfield ($N = 1032$), centre forward ($N = 275$), striker ($N = 689$).

The analytical approach that we have used characterises the activity of the player at two levels according to movement speed: from $14\,km.h^{-1}$ to $21\,km.h^{-1}$, and a higher speed of $21\,km.h^{-1}$. We considered also the players' activity at more than $21\,km.h^{-1}$. Moreover, the total distance run by the players in each half was shown.

We used SPSS program (V13.0) for statistical analysis. An ANOVA test on one factor was calculated, using as factor the playing position. As 'post hoc' analysis, minimum significant differences and the Tamhane's T2 test were implemented.

Results

The descriptive analysis of the results shows the values obtained (average and standard deviation) for each of the defined positions in each half. The average of the total distance covered by the players was 5.598 km, with a standard deviation of 0.481 km. The confidence interval of 95 per cent for the average was between 5586 and 5610 km. The results for each position are shown in Table 31.1 and Figure 31.1.

In all the variables analysed, significant differences ($P < 0.05$ or $P < 0.01$) were obtained, among several defined positions, as shown for example, in Figure 1 for the activity done at a speed higher than $14\,km.h^{-1}$.

Discussion

The differences in players' activity according to position have been analysed by several authors (Reilly and Thomas, 1976; Bangsbo *et al.*, 1991). The variety

Table 31.1 Distances covered in various positional roles according to types of activities for each half of the match (average and standard deviation in km)

Distances	Total (km)	14–21 km.h⁻¹	>14 km.h⁻¹	>21 km.h⁻¹
Wide fullback	5.557 ± 0.375	0.958 ± 0.198	1.299 ± 0.271	0.341 ± 0.126
Centre fullback	5.205 ± 0.325	0.736 ± 0.166	0.932 ± 0.207	0.196 ± 0.082
Pivot	5.929 ± 0.366	1.193 ± 0.255	1.431 ± 0.299	0.238 ± 0.099
Centre midfield	5.925 ± 0.465	1.175 ± 0.304	1.463 ± 0.344	0.287 ± 0.104
Wide midfield	5.835 ± 0.417	1.112 ± 0.245	1.514 ± 0.302	0.402 ± 0.135
Centre forward	5.750 ± 0.426	1.080 ± 0.239	1.420 ± 0.313	0.339 ± 0.128
Striker	5.383 ± 0.516	0.859 ± 0.222	1.213 ± 0.302	0.353 ± 0.135
Total	5.598 ± 0.481	0.981 ± 0.279	1.279 ± 0.348	0.298 ± 0.137

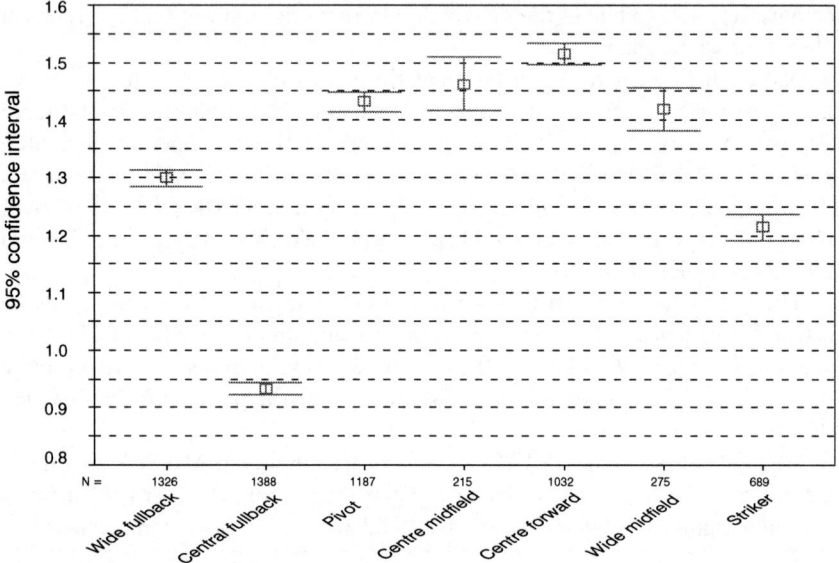

Figure 31.1 Confidence interval for the average distance run over by the players in each half of the game at a higher speed than 14 km.h⁻¹ depending on their position

of methods and reference values used to characterise the activity show a great variation which makes the comparison of results difficult.

The total distances obtained in this research were higher than shown by Bangsbo *et al.* (1991), Reilly and Thomas (1976), Drust *et al.* (1998), Pirnay *et al.*, (1993) or Mohr *et al.* (2003).

In relation to the high-intensity activity, the different values used to establish those levels permit comparison with only a few authors. The values obtained are lower than those recorded by Van Gool *et al.* (1988) and Mohr *et al.* (2003).

Conclusions

The originality, accuracy and reliability of this method, and the size and characteristics of this updated sample, as well as the diversity of seven defined positions, characterise the present research.

The playing position determines activity on the field. This means that the search for individualisation in training systems of players at high competition levels, should consider the player's position as a key factor, although the current criteria of training organisation do not help to apply it. Conclusions are applicable to the recovery of injured players and enlarge the criteria to select players, as the competitive features from the different soccer positions have been determined.

References

Bangsbo, J., Nörregaard, L. and Thorsoe, F., 1991, Activity profile of competition soccer. *Canadian Journal of Sport Sciences*, 16, 110–16.

Drust, B., Reilly, T. and Rienzi, E., 1998, Análisis de la prestación física y de la performance en futbolistas sudamericanos de élite. In *Futbolista Sudamericano de élite: morfología, análisis del juego y performance*, edited by Rienzi, E., Mazza, J.C., Reilly, T. and Carter, J.E.L. (Buenos Aires: Biosystem Servicio Educativo), pp. 89–101.

Mohr, M., Krustrup, P. and Bangsbo, J., 2003, Match performance of high-standard soccer players with special reference to development of fatigue. *Journal of Sports Sciences*, 21, 519–28.

Pirnay, F., Geurde, P. and Marechal, R., 1993, Necesidades fisiológicas de un partido de fútbol. *Revista de Entrenamiento Deportivo*, 7(2), 44–52.

Reilly, T. and Thomas, V., 1976, A motion analysis of work-rate in different positional roles in professional football match-play. *Journal of Human Movement Studies*, 2, 87–97.

Van Gool, D. ,Van Gerven, D. and Boutmans J., 1988, The physiological load imposed on soccer players during real match play. In *Science and Football*, edited by Reilly, T., Lees, A., Davids, K. and Murphy, W. (London: E. and F.N. Spon), pp. 51–9.

Zubillaga, A., 2006, La actividad del jugador de fútbol en alta competición: análisis de variabilidad. Doctoral thesis, University of Málaga.

32 An intelligent system for analysis of tactics in soccer

Mikhail Shestakov,[1] *Andrey Talalaev,*[2]
Nadegda Kosilova,[1] *Nina Zasenko,*[1] *Anna*
Zubkova,[1] *Andrey Leksakov,*[1] *Alexey*
Averkin[3] *and Anton Gusev*[4]

[1] Russian State University of Physical Education, Russia; [2] Russian Football
Union, Russia; [3] Dorodnicyn Computer Center, Russia; [4] International University
of Dubna, Russia

Introduction

One of the main problems in soccer is to coordinate in real time the collective
behaviour of team members, who solve a common task by solving individual
tasks. The specificity of the problem lies in the fact that soccer players with their
collective and individual skills, individual behaviour, incomplete knowledge of the
environment and limited resources should succeed in reaching the common goal
in a dynamically changing game. Soccer players act in time and space inside an
unpredictable environment that often complicates team work. When organizing
a team's play, the main task is to coordinate the actions of players, all trying to
realize their individual actions. Thus, the behaviour of soccer players as a team
is a more complex phenomenon than coordinated individual actions of separate
athletes.

We have developed a digitized soccer match-analysis tool recognizing situation
patterns in a real soccer match. Our research started from interviewing soccer
coaches in order to understand their interpretation of detailed spatial situations.
So we determined a set of descriptions, fuzzy linguistic variables and defined formal
description of a spatial situation.

The objective of this study was to create an intelligent system for tactical
analysis (ISTA) in a group of interacting players in game situations and during
tactical training exercises.

Methods

To create ISTA, we used multi-agent technologies elaborated by specialists in the
field of artificial intelligence. According to the adopted terminology we use the
word 'agent' instead of 'soccer player'.

When analysing team work of a multi-agent system, one should take into
account that it is organized with the help of the group (team) plan of actions of
the agents. This plan has the following peculiarities:

1   The group plan requires the consent of the group of agents to follow some instructions in the group actions.

2   The agents should take responsibilities in respect of their individual actions and the activity of the group as a whole (individual intentions about how to act).

3   At the same time, the agent should take responsibility in respect of the actions of the other agents (coordinated intention).

4   The plan of the group activity may include plans of individual agents for the assigned actions and plans of the subgroups.

The experimental connection of size and distance was defined in the work of Kandrashina (1989). Corrected matrix of object size and distance is shown in Table 32.1. For example, two small objects with distance between them, where another small object can be put, are near to each other.

This kind of spatial-situation description was used in deriving spatial knowledge from the text and then modified while investigating soccer team behaviour. This formal spatial-situation description is static, so it produces a motionless world view. In order to move and score on the soccer field, not only distance and directions, but also the speed of the players and some other movement characteristics should be considered.

Spatial situation on a soccer field is described by the determining of spatial relations between players, ball and goal. We might not calculate dimensions of these objects, but accept that a soccer player is <middle-sized>, the goal is <big> and the ball is <small>. Determination of static spatial relations (e.g. relations of directions and distance) is shown on the drawing below (Figure 32.1; the same approach as used by Musto, 1999.

Then the speed of each player and the ball are added. Possible speeds are <standing> (0 m.s^{-1}), <walking> (<2 m.s^{-1}), <jogging> (from 2 to 4 m.s^{-1}), <running> (from 4 to 5.8 m.s^{-1}), <high speed running> (from 5.8 to 7 m.s^{-1}) and <sprinting> (>7 m.s^{-1}). This information is taken from previous work (while building a spatial situation description, current and previous coordinates of the players and the ball are needed).

There are many typical spatial situations on a soccer field. Formal spatial-situation description defines a 'pattern' abstracted from objects' coordinates using qualitative spatial data. We are trying to recognize 'local' situation double-pass etc., and predict movements of each player during realization of this game pattern (Figure 32.2). Two players can play together having determined the same spatial situation pattern, without sending any messages (as players in real soccer). So if a

Table 32.1 Connection of object size and distance

	Small and small	Middle-sized and middle-sized	Big and big
Small	Near	Near	Near
Middle-sized	Not far	Near	Near
Big	Far	Not far	Near

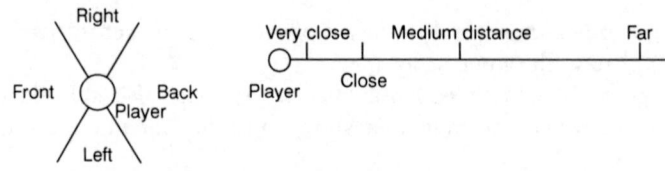

Figure 32.1 Spatial relations (distance, directions)

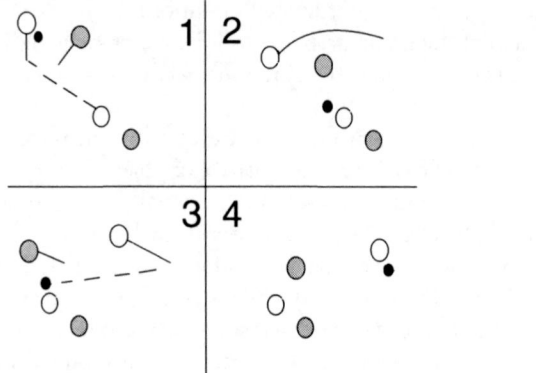

Figure 32.2 Spatial situation pattern of double-pass

player 'knows' that his role is 'assistance' in double-pass pattern, he will pass back to the first player after catching the ball. In other cases he will ignore his partner. Example of a rule: check cross (–1,P2,P3,P4,2):-result ('cross'), close (–1,P3), close (P2,P4), approach (–1,P2), assert (result ('ste–1'), result); check cross (–1,P2,P3,P4,1):-result ('nothing'), close (–1,P4), close (P2,P3), so far (–1,P2), with ball (–1), assert (result ('cross'), result).

Nowadays, coaches of real soccer teams often have at their disposal digitized records of matches, involving coordinates of every footballer and the ball at any time of the game. Having built formal spatial-situation description for every second of a match, we can compare it with the pattern database. At first the patterns must be defined. The pattern can be 'emergency situation' or 'defender error'. Different patterns (maybe 'emergency situation' and 'defender error', or 'fighting for the ball' can appear concurrently).

Thus, a coach can make automatic analysis of all digitized games for some spatial-situation patterns. It is an irreplaceable instrument in getting data for visually teaching his team during theoretical sessions.

Our training support tool prototype recognizes very few situation patterns. We are building formal situation description for each 0.1 second of a soccer match (digitized record of a real human match). Then we use qualitative spatial reasoning to determine the game pattern, which exists on the field at the moment. Higher level functions are PROLOG knowledge database. It is important not only to find situation patterns but also to predict movements of players. Once found, the situation is divided into steps: 'double-pass step 1', 'double-pass step 2' etc: if 'double pass step 3' is not followed by 'step 4', then an error has occurred.

The system ISTA was adapted in order to work with the Qualisys motion capture camera with high-speed video 'Oqus' (Qualisys AB, Sweden), that permitted the creation of a database of game combinations for learning a sample of the artificial neural network. To complete the computer training support tool, which deals with the digitized match-record database and automatically recognizes pre-defined situation patterns, we use a fully-defined description of the spatial situation, while human players do spatial reasoning with reference to some dominant objects. We aim to provide an algorithm to cut unnecessary spatial relations and objects from agent spatial-situation description.

Using this approach for processing video records of matches played by teams of different levels to identify some patterns in tactical actions of the teams used in a match. We analysed four games of the leading European club teams (group A), five games of the Russian national youth team (16 years) in the European championship of 2006 (group B), and five games of Second Division teams participating in the regular Russian championship (group C).

The hierarchy of tactical group actions in soccer consists of tactical variant, tactical scheme, and tactical combination. We recognized the following combinations: in attack – wall pass, pass to a third player, scissor movement; in defence – counteraction to wall pass, counteraction to the combination 'pass to a third player', covering. Tactical schemes consisting of several tactical combinations were registered: in attack – run and centre, run through the centre, flank run with pass to the other flank; in defence – man-to-man marking, zonal marking, horizontal and vertical displacement.

Results

Our study revealed some specific features of tactics organization in teams of different qualifications during official games. Data presented in Table 32.2 demonstrated that teams of group A used less diverse tactical schemes ($P<0.05$), but repeated the same scheme more often ($P<0.01$) in a game, than teams of groups B and C. Teamwork in defence was more often used in group A, than in the other two groups ($P<0.05$). The reliability of team actions in defence was considerably lower in groups B and C, than in group A.

The data displayed in Table 32.3 revealed the formation of tactical schemes in attack and distribution of tactical combinations by four zones of the field.

Zone 1 – the quarter of the field around the penalty area of attacking team; zone 4 – the quarter of the field around the penalty area of defending team; zones 2 and 3 – in the centre of the soccer field on the sides of corresponding attacking and defending teams. Players of group A used more combinations during the realization of a single scheme ($P<0.05$) than players of lower qualification (groups B and C). It was found that teams of higher qualification improved interactions in immediate proximity of the opposing goal (group A – 40 per cent in zone 4), while less-qualified teams organized most of their collective actions in their own half of the field (group B – 40 per cent in zone 2; group C – 50 per cent in zone 2). The lack of technical preparedness of players of groups B and C must have prevented

Table 32.2 Group tactical actions of teams of different qualification in a game

	Tactical variants in attack			Tactical variants in defence		
	No. of schemes	No. of repetitions	% success	No. of schemes	No. of repetitions	% success
Group A	6±1.1	31±3.5	20	4±0.2	20±3.1	80
Group B	9±2.1	18±2.1	40	3±0.2	15±4.3	60
Group C	8±3.1	12±1.3	50	3±0.7	12±2.4	50

Table 32.3 Number of group combinations in a single scheme of attack and their distribution by field zones, %.

	Number of combinations	Zone 1	Zone 2	Zone 3	Zone 4
Group A	15±5.2	5	25	30	40
Group B	7±2.8	10	40	35	15
Group C	4±1.2	30	50	20	10

them from reliable performance in the opposing half of the field in the face of active defence of the opponent.

Conclusions

Digitized data of football matches can easily be used for automatic situation recognition. Error detection block can become an irreplaceable human coach assistant.

The intelligent system of tactics analysis (ISTA) in a group of players was realized as a hybrid system with the use of the expert system (programming language – Prolog Visual), fuzzy controllers, and an artificial neural network. The game was analysed on video and during real training sessions.

Results of our study with the use of ISTA demonstrate that top-class European club teams create significantly more group combinations in the opponent's penalty area (40 per cent) than the teams of lower qualification, who organize most of their group combinations in their own half of the field (50 to 80 per cent).

Significant difference was found in the number and diversity of tactical actions used by teams of different qualification. On average, top players performed twice as many group tactical actions as players of lower qualification. However, less qualified teams demonstrated greater diversity in tactics ($P < 0.05$).

References

Kandrashina, E., 1989, *Spatial and Temporal Knowledge Representation in Artificial Intelligence*, (Moscow: Svjaz).

Musto, A., 1999, On spatial reference frames in qualitative motion representation, *FKI-Bericht*, FKI-230–99, Munich: Technische Universität.

33 Activity profile, heart rate and blood lactate of futsal referees during competitive games

António Rebelo,[1] *António Ascenção,*[1] *José Magalhães*[1] *and Peter Krustrup*[2]

[1] Universidade do Porto, Spain; [2] Department of Human Physiology, University of Copenhagen, Denmark

Introduction

Several recent studies have evaluated the locomotor activities and physiological demands of football referees and assistant referees (Bragada, 2001; Krustrup and Bangsbo, 2001; Krustrup *et al.*, 2002; Helsen and Bultynck, 2004; Castagna *et al.*, 2005; Reilly and Gregson, 2006). Such studies have provided important information about match specific physical testing and training of football match officials. Futsal, the FIFA-regulated indoor football, has become a popular indoor alternative to football, with millions of players and fans worldwide. However, the scientific knowledge regarding the physical demands of futsal playing is rather limited and so far, no studies have investigated the activity profile and physiological demands of futsal refereeing. Despite some similarities with football refereeing, several futsal-specific features, including pitch size, number of players, game rules and position of the referees may impose distinct activity profiles and physiological demands. Thus, the aims of the present study were to describe the activity profile of futsal referees during competitive games, including number of activity changes, total distance covered (TD), high-intensity running (HIR), sprinting (SPR) and sideways running (SR) and to examine the physiological demands by measuring heart rate and blood lactate. In addition, intermittent exercise performance of futsal referees was determined by the Yo-Yo Intermittent Endurance Test, level 2 (Yo-YoIE2).

Methods

Participants

Twelve high-level Portuguese futsal referees (33.0 ±5.0 years; 1.73 ±0.05 m; 73.2 ±8.4 kg and 15.7 ±5.4% fat mass) participated in this study. The Yo-Yo intermittent endurance level 2 test performance was 975 ±237 (range: 760–1240 m). All the participants had at least more than five years of experience in the top Portuguese futsal league.

Activity profile analysis

Six referees were filmed during matches of the 2005–2006 Portuguese top league season to determine their locomotor activity. For this purpose, two VHS movie cameras (NV-M50, Panasonic, Germany) placed at the side of the pitch (level with the half-way line, at a height of about 15 m and at an approximate distance of 15 m of the touch line) were used. Each camera obtained close up images from each referee. The videotapes were later replayed for computerized time–motion analyses (Krustrup and Bangsbo, 2001). The locomotor pattern categories included standing (0 km.h^{-1}), walking (6 km.h^{-1}), jogging (8 km.h^{-1}), low-speed running (12 km.h^{-1}), moderate-speed running (15 km.h^{-1}), high-speed running (18 km.h^{-1}), sprinting (25 km.h^{-1}), sideways (10 km.h^{-1}) and backwards (10 km.h^{-1}) running. The match activities were later divided into total distance covered, high-intensity running (HIR > 15 km.h^{-1}), sprinting (SPR) and sideways running (SR).

Heart rate and blood lactate

Heart rate (HR) was recorded at 5 s intervals throughout each game using a Polar Vantage NV heart rate monitor (Polar, Kempele, Finland). Blood samples were collected from the ear lobe at rest and 1–2 min after the end of the game, and were immediately analysed to determine blood lactate concentration using a YSI 1500 S (Yellow Spring Instruments, Yellow Springs, OH, USA).

Statistics

The data are presented as means and standard deviations. Difference in heart rate during the first and second half was tested for significance using a paired *t*-test. Changes in match activities and heart rate within each 10 min period of the game were evaluated by one-way analysis of variance (ANOVA) with repeated measures. The level of significance was set at 5 per cent.

Results

Activity profile

As can be depicted from Table 33.1, the number of activity changes was as high as 1771 ±314 (±SD) over ~80 min, which corresponds to a change in activity each 2.7 s. Total distance covered was 5.61 ±0.82 km of which high-intensity running, sprinting and sideways running accounted for 0.93 ±0.18, 0.18 ±0.07 and 1.00 ±0.46 km, respectively. The number of HIR and SPR bouts was 137 ±21 and 19 ±8, with a mean duration of ~1.3 s.

Table 33.1 Activity profile of futsal referees during competitive games, data are means ±SD (n = 6)

		Standing	Walking	Jogging	Low speed	Moderate speed	High speed	Sprint	Sideways	Backwards	Total
Percentage of total time	Mean	49.3	29.7	4.9	3.7	2.2	1.3	0.5	7.4	1.1	100.0
	SD	6.9	2.1	1.1	1.0	0.4.	0.4	0.2	3.5	1.0	0.0
Number of repetitions	Mean	396	549	182	116	69	49	19	166	27	1572
	SD	12	32	43	23	10	13	8	73	23	153
Distance covered (m)	Mean	0	2411	532	594	438	311	181	1000	143	5610
	SD	0	259	113	146	60	89	77	459	131	474
Duration (s)	Mean	6.1	2.6	1.3	1.5	1.5	1.3	1.3	2.4	1.7	
	SD	0.9	0.2	0.0	0.1	0.1	0.0	0.1	0.5	0.5	

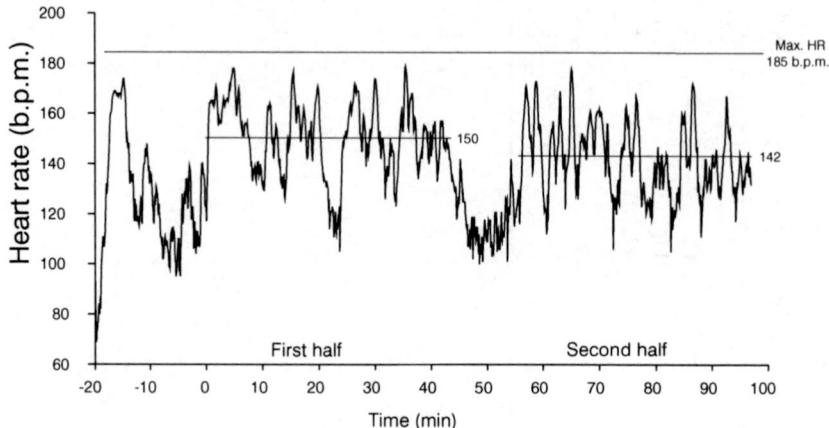

Figure 33.1 An example of the heart rate response of a futsal referee during a competitive game, with mean heart rates during the first and second half of 150 and 142 beats.min⁻¹ respectively; the heart rate profile clearly reflects the intermittent feature of the futsal game

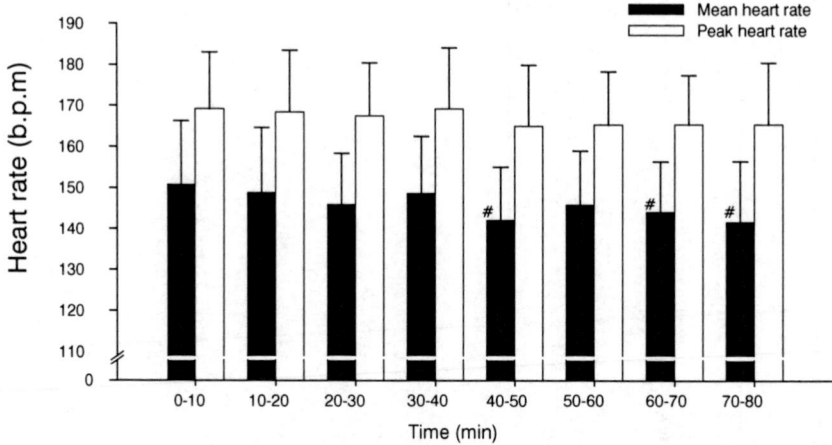

Figure 33.2 Mean heart rate (filled bars) and peak heart rate (open bars) for referees in 10-min intervals during competitive futsal games; data are means ±SD (n = 12); # denotes significant difference from 0–10 min

Heart rate

An example of a futsal referees' heart rate response is given in Figure 33.1. Mean heart rate during a match was 146 ± 1 beats.min⁻¹ corresponding to $78 \pm 6\%$ of maximal heart rate (HRmax 191 ± 9 beats.min⁻¹).

The mean heart rate was lower ($P<0.05$) in the second half compared to the first half (143 ± 13 vs 149 ± 14 beats.min⁻¹). The mean heart rate was lower ($P<0.05$) in the first, third and fourth 10-min period of the second half compared to the first 10-min period of the first half (Figure 33.1). Peak heart rate during a match was 176 ±14 beats.min^{-1} or 92 ±7% of maximal heart rate. Heart rate was observed to be in the range of 70–80%, 80–90% and 90–100% of HRmax for 37 ±4, 41 ±6 and 9 ±3 of total time, respectively.

Blood lactate

Blood lactate was 1.5 ±0.5 (0.9–2.8) mmol.l^{-1} after the game. This value was higher ($P<0.05$) than at rest (1.0 ±0.3 (0.8–1.5) mmol.l^{-1}).

Discussion and conclusion

Futsal is becoming a popular indoor alternative to soccer, with specific rules and millions of players and fans worldwide. Given the growing competitive level of the game observed in the last decade, increasing physiological demands have been imposed upon futsal referees. However, in contrast to soccer, and to the best of our knowledge, this is the first study that analysed the activity profile of futsal referees during competitive matches as well as the physiological demands imposed by the game. Time–motion analysis showed that Futsal referees covered a lower total distance (5.6 km) than both top level soccer referees (10.3 km) and assistant referees (7.3 km) (Krustrup and Bangsbo, 2001; Krustrup *et al.*, 2002). However, the futsal referees performed a higher number of sprints and sideways running bouts than football referees, with values corresponding to those of assistant referees. Like football match officiating, futsal refereeing is highly intermittent, with a tremendously high number of activity changes. Actually, the high-intensity running bouts are even shorter than for referees and assistant referees with average sprint distances of less than 10 m. The heart rate data recorded in the present study show that the aerobic loading is moderate-to-high for futsal referees during a game. Thus, average heart rates were ~145 beats.min^{-1} which is higher than for assistant referees but lower than for referees. Unexpectedly, the blood lactate values were only slightly higher than resting values after the game (1.5 vs 1.0 mM). This does not mean that blood lactate values are not high for some futsal referees after the most intense periods of a game, but it clearly stresses that the lactacid anaerobic energy turnover is of less importance for futsal referees than football referees and assistant referees having average values of around 5 mM after games (Krustrup and Bangsbo, 2001; Krustrup *et al.*, 2002). These findings may well be related to the duration of the high-intensity actions, which are shorter for futsal referees (1.3 s) than for football match officials (~2 s).

In conclusion, futsal refereeing is generally characterized as intermittent exercise with numerous very brief bouts of fast speed and sideways running interspersed by long low intensity recovery periods. Heart rate was moderate-to-high. Interestingly, blood lactate was low suggesting that a majority of the anaerobic energy turnover was provided by breakdown of adenosine triphosphate and creatine phosphate. These data reinforce the importance of sprint performance and the ability to recover between intense exercise periods for futsal referees. Therefore, the ability to perform repeated brief sprints and to perform intermittent match-specific movements including sideways running, should be incorporated in training and testing strategies for futsal referees.

References

Bragada, J., 2001, Avaliação da intensidade dos exercícios de treino. *Treino Desportivo*, 14(3):18–26.

Castagna, C., Abt, G. and D'Ottavio, S., 2005, Competitive-level differences in Yo-Yo intermittent recovery and twelve minute run test performance in soccer referees. *Journal Strength Conditioning Research*, 19(4): 805–9.

Helsen, W. and Bultynck, J.B., 2004, Physical and perceptual-cognitive demands of top class refereeing in association football. *Journal of Sports Sciences*, 22: 179–89.

Krustrup, P. and Bangsbo, J., 2001, Physiological demands of top-class soccer refereeing in relation to physical capacity: effect of intense intermittent exercise training. *Journal of Sports Sciences*, 19: 881–91.

Krustrup, P., Mohr M. and Bangsbo, J., 2002, Activity profile and physiological demands of topclass soccer assistant refereeing in relation to training status. *Journal of Sports Sciences*, 20: 861–71.

Reilly, T. and Gregson, W., 2006, Special populations: the referee and assistant referee. *Journal of Sports Sciences*, 24: 795–801.

34 Analysis of actions ending with shots at goal in the Women's European Football Championship (England 2005)

Józef Bergier,[1] *Andrzej Soroka*[2] *and Tomasz Buraczewski*[1]

[1] The Józef Piłsudski University of Physical Education, Poland; [2] State Higher Vocational School, Poland

Introduction

Women's football is a young sports discipline and thus it needs to be examined and constantly observed. More and more scientific research in Poland is concentrated on women's football (Bergier 1997, 2005; Bergier and Buraczewski 2005; Bergier and Soroka 2005a, 2005b, 2006). Sports events of the highest rank such as the European Championship provide opportunities to observe changes and trends among the top teams in women's football. Quantitative and qualitative data derived from the observation of players' actions during the game contributes to the rationalization of training programmes for these players.

Offensive actions resulting in a shot on goal and scoring are becoming more and more important in football. Their detailed identification will enable coaches to choose appropriate means in the training process.

The main aim of the study is to analyse offensive actions from their start to the moment of a shot on goal. The specific aims consider the structure of offensive actions as well as the topography of characteristic actions with the ball.

Methods

The sample for the study consisted of 15 games of the 2005 Women's European Football Championship in England. Altogether, 353 offensive actions resulting in a shot on goal, 50 of which were successful ones (i.e. ending with a goal), were analysed.

The course of the actions resulting in a shot on goal was coded from the video recording with the use of the authors' observation sheets. The place where the action started, its duration, the number of passes and players taking part in the action were taken into consideration in the analysis. With regards to final passes in offensive actions, their distance, direction, plane, the way and place (topography) of their appearance were taken into account (Jin 2002).

To analyse the shots, five pitch zones and eight goal sectors were mapped out. The accuracy and effectiveness of the shots were taken into consideration as well (Bergier 1996).

Results

The main aim in football games is to score goals. The start of the action, especially the first pass that poses a threat to the opponent's goal is becoming more and more important. In female football the offensive actions resulting in a shot on goal (Figure 34.1) took place mainly in the offensive (41.6%) as well as in the central zones (41.2%), with 17.2% of actions happening in the defensive area of the attacking team.

The results of the study indicate that short actions that lasted up to 5 seconds were dominant in the footballers' play – 56.9%. Actions performed after an individual attack amounted to 30.3%, with one player 24.6%, and with two players, 18.4%.

Altogether, 30.9% of actions with no passes were observed which is undoubtedly the result of a great number of individual attacks. There were 22.1% of actions with one pass and 15.9% with two passes. The footballers rarely played multi-pass actions which would end with a shot on goal.

The first pass in the offensive action resulting in a shot on goal was typically in the bottom plane – 53.0%, the pass at the average distance from 10 to 25 metres

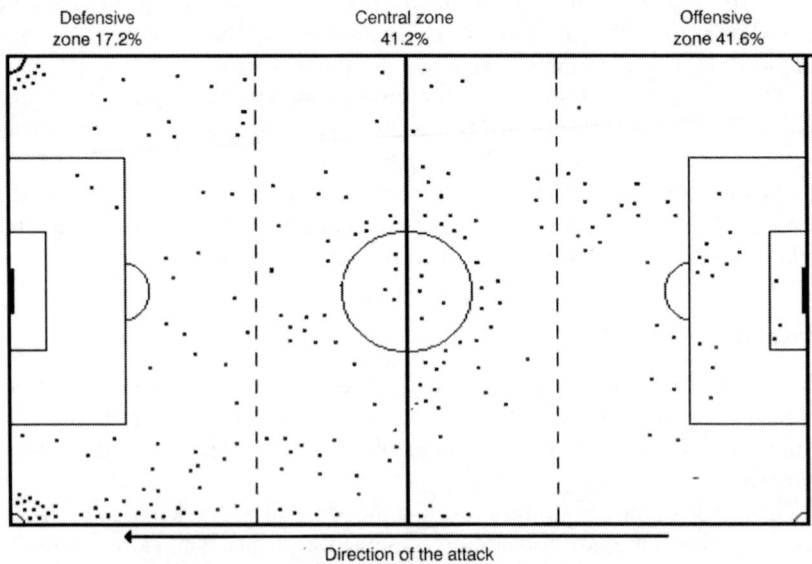

Figure 34.1. The topography of the passes which start actions ended with a shot on goal

– 40.4%, and the short pass up to 10 metres – 32.6%. The preferred type was the crosswise pass – 40.0% and the perpendicular pass – 31.7%, the play after a set piece 42.2% was the dominant tactic. Less preferred were passes without holding on to the ball i.e. one touch – 19.6%.

For final passes in the movements resulting in a shot on goal, preferences of pass planes were observed. These turned out to be bottom passes – 48.3%. With respect to the length of passes, they were usually played at medium distance – 46.5%, similar to the first passes.

No significant differences in the method of passes were observed (without receiving the ball i.e. one touch – 30.1%, with receiving the ball – 27.9%, after dribbling – 23.2% and after a set piece 21.8%). There were no dominant passes among these types (crosswise and perpendicular – 34.4% each, diagonal – 24.3%, backward passes constituted 6.8%).

Final passes in the actions resulting in a shot on goal were definitely located (in contrast to the first passes) in the offensive zone – 64.4% and into the central zone – 34.7%. This trend was even more visible in final passes ending with an accurate shot (offensive zone – 64.4%, central zone – 34.7%, defensive zone – 0.9%) and especially in actions ending with a goal (offensive zone – 77.7%, central zone – 32.3% and there was a lack of passes from the defensive zone).

Shots on goal were mainly performed from inside the penalty area – 60.1% and from its extension – 34.6%. Of the shots ending with a goal, 84.0% were from inside the penalty area and 16.0% were from outside the area.

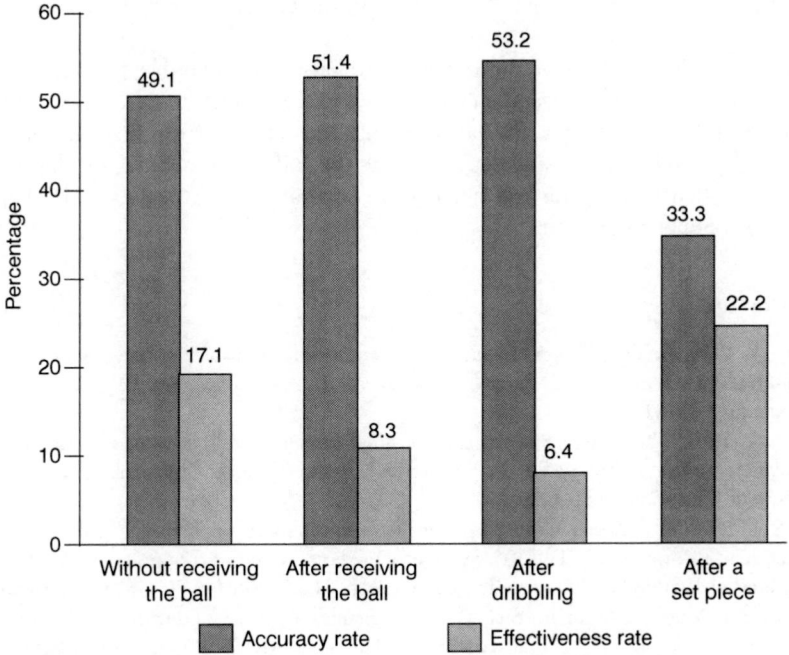

Figure 34.2 Accuracy and effectiveness of shots on goal according to the type of performance

In the tournament, shots were mainly performed in the upper plane – 37.7%, in the bottom plane – 33.7%, from medium distances – 45.3% and from short distances up to 10 metres – 36.8%. The most frequent way of performing a shot on goal was a kick without controlling the ball on touch – 61.2%, which also had one of the highest rates of effectiveness – 17.1% (Figure 34.2).

Analysing the sectors of the goal into which goals were scored, the predominance of the bottom sectors was observed with an effectiveness of 70.0%. The majority of the goals were scored after shots into the bottom left-hand sector – 22.0% and into the bottom right-hand sector – 20.0%. Shots into the upper sectors accounted for 30.0% of the goals.

Conclusion

The main observations on performance at the Women's European Championships were:

1   Places from where the first and especially final passes in movements resulting in a shot on goal started were mainly inside the offensive and central zones of the pitch.
2   If the action was longer, the number of passes was more than three and if there were more than three players, it was more difficult to score a goal.
3   Shots on goal, mainly those resulting in a goal, were performed by the players from inside the penalty area and the preferred way was a shot without holding onto the ball after hitting it 'first-time' into the bottom sectors of the goal.

After detailed analysis of the offensive actions, it is advisable to take into consideration the pitch zones, the places which enable players to perform actions ending with a shot on goal, the planes, types and length of the first and final passes. The results of the study suggest that the individual abilities of players, especially when playing the ball quickly in cooperation with one or two other players, should be improved.

References

Bergier, J., 1996, Analiza działań ofensywnych I defensywnych piłkarzy nożnych w turnieju olimpijskim – Barcelona 92. *Rocznik Naukowy* Vol. II, AWF Warszawa: IWFiS w Białej Podlaskiej, 27–41.

Bergier, J., 1997, The structure of the game in final football match of women during the Olympic games – Atlanta'96. In *Woman and Sport*. (Gdansk: University School of Physical Education), 121–129.

Bergier, J., 2005, Piłka nożna kobiet jako nowe wydarzenie sportowe, *Trener*, 2, 2–3.

Bergier, J. and Buraczewski, T., 2005, Symmetry of shots as an indication of coordinating abilities at World Cup; in female football U-19. In J.Sadowski (ed.) *Coordination Motor Abilities in Scientific Research*. (Biala Podlaska: Faculty of Physical Education), 150–156.

Bergier, J. and Soroka, A., 2005a, Analiza działań ofensywnych w meczu finałowym II Mistrzostw Świata kobiet do lat 19 Tajlandia – 2004 (Niemcy – Chiny). *Trener* 2, 3–8.

Bergier, J. and Soroka, A., 2005b, Analiza akcji bramkowych w II Mistrzostwach Świata kobiet do lat 19 Tajlandia – 2004. In S. Żak, M. Spieszny and T. Klocek (eds) *Gry zespołowe w wychowaniu fizycznym i sporcie*. Studia i Monografie 33 (Krakow: AWF w Krakowie), 197–203.

Bergier, J. and Soroka, A., 2006, Zróżnicowanie gry bramkarek na II Mistrzostwach Świata kobiet do lat 19 Tajlandia – 2004, 2, 22–28.

Jin, C. J., 2002, Research on goals in during European Football Championship in 2000. *Journal of Beijing University of Physical Education*, 25, 281–3.

35 Game characteristics of Asian women's rugby

Jun Kuroiwa,[4] *Iwao Kameyama,*[1] *Masahiro Kurosu,*[1] *Takeshi Itoh,*[1] *Mutsuo Yamada,*[2] *Kayoko Komatsu,*[1] *Tetsuya Tsubakihara,*[3] *Ichiro Watanabe*[4] *and Yuichi Ueno*[4]

[1] Ryutsu Keizai University, Japan; [2] Saitama Medical University, Japan; [3] Musashi Institute of Technology, Japan; [4] Japan Rugby Football Union, Japan

Introduction

The development of women's rugby contributes not only directly but also indirectly to the development of rugby itself as a global sport. Recently women's rugby in Japan has developed more broadly and the national team took part in competitions from the first Women's Rugby World Cup (WRCW) held in 1991 through to the fourth WRWC.

The purpose of this study was to clarify the characteristics of Asian women's rugby in comparison to the women's rugby worldwide as well as with the level of men's rugby worldwide.

Materials and methods

The games of the top four teams in the Asian Qualifying Tournament (AQT) for the 2006 Women's Rugby World Cup 2006 (2006 WRWC) held in Thailand and the games of the top four teams of 2006 WRWC held in Canada were analysed. The top four games of the AQT were recorded using a digital video camera. The recorded data were captured into a computer, converted to MPG file and then analysed using 'Power Analysis' (Smile Works Co). The results of the 2006 WRWC were derived from the data from the International Rugby Board (IRB). The number of tries, penalty goals, line-outs, scrums, maul/rucks, passes, length of in-play time and kicking were adopted as measures for game assessment. These variables were determined based on the report of the 2003 Rugby World Cup (2003 RWC).

Results and discussion

Based on the game results in the Asian qualifiers, there was a significant difference in team performance between the finalists and the other teams. With regard to

Table 35.1 Game results of top four games of Asian Qualifying Tournament of 2006 WRWC and Women's Rugby World Cup 2006

Asian Qualifying Tournament of 2006 WRWC			
Semi-finals	Japan	78–0	Hong Kong
	Kazakhstan	67–0	Thailand
Final	Kazakhstan	19–3	Japan
Women's Rugby World Cup 2006			
Semi-final	New Zealand	40–10	France
	England	20–14	Canada
Final	New Zealand	25–17	England

Table 35.2 Scoring profiles in the Asian Qualifying Tournament of 2006 WRWC and Women's Rugby World Cup 2006

	AQT 2006 WRWC		2006 WRWC	
Scores (points)	167		126	
Tries (points/number)	135	27	95	19
Conversions (points/number)	26	13	16	8
Penalties (points/number)	6	2	15	5
Drop Goals (points/number)	0	0	0	0
Try:conversion:penalty	81:15.5:3.5		75:13:12	

the results of the 2006 WRWC, the scores of the teams except New Zealand and France were not significantly different, as shown in Table 35.1.

As shown in the scoring profiles of the game, the total scores of the AQT were higher than those of the 2006 WRWC games. This result was not directly related to the offensive performance of the AQT teams, but was due to the difference in the total scores in the semi-final games. The success rates of conversion kicks after a try were less than 50 per cent in both AQT and 2006 WRWC, which were much lower than the 67 per cent success rates of the conversion kicks after a try shown in the match report of the 2003 RWC.

Compared to the 2003 IRB WRC game report, ball possessions at line-outs and scrums, in-play time, the number of maul/rucks in Asian women's rugby were significantly lower than observed in men's rugby. The numbers of penalty goals and kicks were lower than in men's rugby as a result. Though the superiority of physical fitness in men is obvious, the skill levels of men were also superior to those of the women. The reason for the lower levels of ball possession and ball continuity was identified with the lack of individual and team skills.

Conclusion

The game characteristics of the Asian Qualifying Tournament of 2006 WRWC were as follows:

Table 35.3 Mode of play of Asian Qualifying Tournament of 2006 WRWC and World Cup 2003

	AQT 2006 WRWC	2003 RWC
Scores	55.7	59.0
Number of tries	9.0	6.9
Number of penalty goals	0.7	4.3
Number of line-outs	25.7	33.0
Possession retained of line-outs	67%	80%
Number of scrums	20.3	21.0
Possession retained of scrums	78%	91%
Number of penalties	25.0	24.0
Ball in play time	0:27:02	0:33:17
Number of ruck/mauls	114.7	136.0
Number of passes	229.3	241.0
Number of kicks	25.7	52.0

- The differences in performance among the top four teams were significant in AQT, but the differences between teams were not significant in the 2006 WRWC.
- As regards game performance, the ratio of scoring tries was much higher than other types of scoring in AQT. Lower ratios of scoring by penalty goals were observed in comparison to the ratio of scoring penalty goals in the 2006 WRWC and the 2003 RWC.
- The success rates for ball possession in scrums and line-outs of the AQT teams were much lower than those of the 2003 RWC.
- Ball continuity in AQT was inferior to that in the 2003 RWC.
- The numbers of kicks (penalty goal-kicking and general field play kicking) were much lower in AQT 2006 and 2006 WRWC than those in the 2003 RWC.

References

International Rugby Board, 2003, *RWC 2003 Statistical Review and Match Analysis*. (Cardiff: International Rugby Board).

36 Match activities and fatigue development of elite female soccer players at different levels of competition

Peter Krustrup,[1] *Helena Andersson,*[2] *Magni Mohr,*[1] *Morten Bredsgaard Randers,*[1] *Jack Majgaard Jensen,*[1] *Mette Zebis,*[3] *Donald Kirkendal*[4] *and Jens Bangsbo*[1]

[1] Department of Exercise and Sport Sciences, University of Copenhagen, Denmark; [2] Department of Health Sciences, Örebro University, Sweden; [3] Institute of Sports Medicine Copenhagen, University of Copenhagen, Denmark; [4] University of North Carolina, USA

Introduction

The physical aspects of high-level male soccer have been studied extensively (Withers *et al.*, 1982; Ohashi *et al.*, 1988; Van Gool *et al.*, 1988; Bangsbo *et al.*, 1991; Reilly, 1997; Helgerud *et al.*, 2000; Krustrup *et al.*, 2005, 2006; Mohr *et al.*, 2003). Less information exists about the physical demands in female soccer (Tumilty and Derby, 1992; Davis and Brewer, 1993; Brewer and Davis, 1994; Shephard, 2000; Todd *et al.*, 2002; Polman *et al.*, 2004; Krustrup *et al.* 2005). Body dimensions (Jensen and Larsson, 1993, Rico-Sanz, 1998) and maximum aerobic power (Rhodes and Mosher, 1992; Davis and Brewer, 1992; Jensen and Larsson, 1993; Tamer *et al.*, 1997; Krustrup *et al.* 2005) of female players have been determined. In addition, some studies have examined the activity profile and heart rate during match play (Reilly, 1997; Shephard, 2000; Krustrup *et al.* 2005). However, the main focus has been on total distance covered, which is believed to be a poor indicator of physical match performance, since the majority of the ground is covered by low-intensity activities such as walking and jogging, which hardly can be considered physically demanding (Mohr *et al.*, 2003).

Mohr *et al.* (2003) studied work profiles of elite male soccer players and the development of fatigue during a soccer game. They found that the amount of high-intensity running was lowered after intense exercise periods as well as at the end of the game. Additionally, it was demonstrated that international top-class players exercise at a higher intensity during a game than professional players at a moderate competition level (Mohr *et al.*, 2003). In a follow-up study it was shown that 30 m sprint performance was unaltered at half-time, but lowered after the game as well as after an intense exercise period in the first half (Krustrup *et al.*, 2006), findings which confirm that fatigue occurs both temporarily during and towards the end of a game. Recently, Krustrup *et al.* (2005) showed that high-intensity running and sprinting are lowered in females towards the end of a soccer game and that the amount of high-intensity running in a game was related to training status, but it has not been examined whether the work-rate profile of female soccer players is dependent on the standard of play. Likewise, it is yet to be investigated whether jumping and sprinting performance deteriorates during elite female soccer games. Thus, the aims of the present study were to determine the activity profile of elite female soccer players at different levels of competition during a soccer match and to examine the development of fatigue during a game.

Methods

Subjects

A total of 58 elite female soccer players participated in the study; i.e. 16 central defenders, 23 midfield players and 19 attackers. In the first part of the study, top-class players (n = 19) were observed in international matches or the US top league, whilst high-level players (n = 15) were investigated in Danish or Swedish Premier League matches. In the second part of the study, Scandinavian national team players were studied in domestic games as well as international games (n = 12). Twelve of the Danish Premier League players were tested for sprint and jumping performance before and after domestic games. The players were fully informed of all experimental procedures before giving their informed consent to participate.

Match analyses

The players were video-filmed individually close-up during the entire match by VHS movie cameras (NV-M50, Panasonic, Germany). The video tapes were later replayed on a monitor for computerized coding of the activity pattern. The following locomotor categories were used: standing ($0 km·h^{-1}$), walking ($6 km·h^{-1}$), jogging ($8 km·h^{-1}$), low-speed running ($12 km·h^{-1}$), moderate-speed running ($15 km·h^{-1}$), high-speed running ($18 km·h^{-1}$), sprinting ($25 km·h^{-1}$) and backward running ($10 km·h^{-1}$). Jogging, low-speed running and backward running was categorized as low-intensity running; whereas moderate-speed running, high-speed running and sprinting was categorized as high-intensity running. The locomotor categories were chosen in accordance with Krustrup *et al.* (2005).

Sprint and jump tests

Twelve players performed a repeated sprint test before and immediately after the game, consisting of three 30 m sprints, separated by a 25 s period of active recovery, during which the players jogged back to the starting line. Thus, the test lasted ~1 min. The sprint times were recorded by infra-red light sensors, having a precision of 0.01 s (Time It, Eleiko Sport, Halmstad, Sweden). On another occasion, the same players performed a counter movement jump test before and after the game. The jump test consisted of three counter-movement jumps with the hands fixed on the hips and was performed on a jumping mat (Time It, Eleiko Sport, Halmstad, Sweden). The jumps were interspersed with 30 s rest periods and the best jump was used as the test result.

Statistical analysis

Differences between match performance in domestic and international games were tested by a two-way (time × level) ANOVA for repeated measures. Differences in sprint performance were also tested by a two-way ANOVA (no. of sprint × time). Jump performance was tested by a one-way ANOVA for repeated measures. A Tukey post-hoc test was used to identify the points of difference. Significance level was set as $P<0.05$. Differences between top-class and moderate-level elite players were tested by Student's unpaired t-test. Significance level was set as $P<0.05$. Values are presented as means ±SEM.

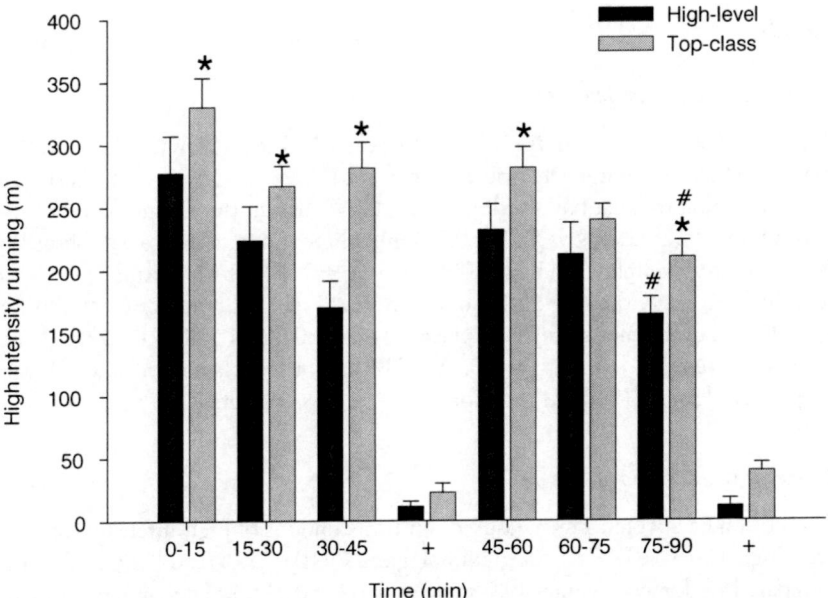

Figure 36.1 High-intensity running in 15 min periods by top-class (gray bars) and high-level (black bars) female players during a soccer game; * denotes significant difference ($P<0.05$) between top-class and high-level elite players. # denotes significant difference ($P<0.05$) between the first and last 15 min period

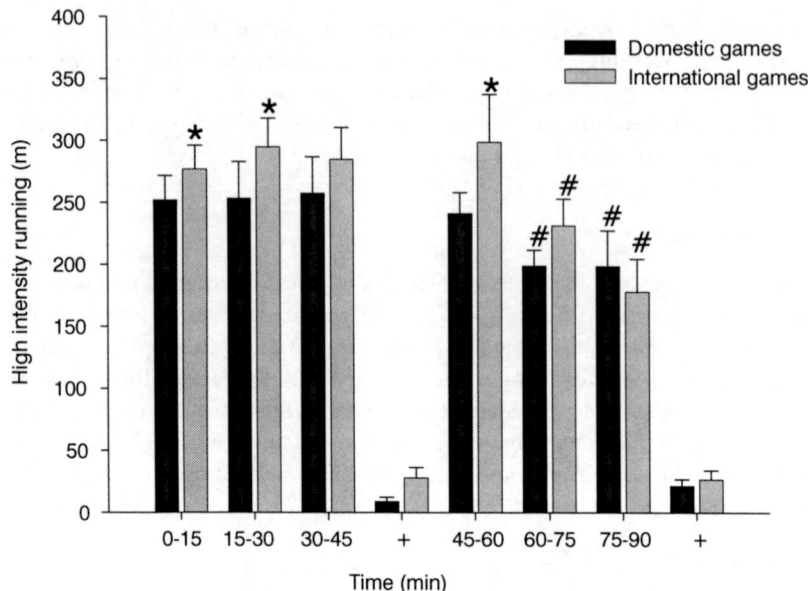

Figure 36.2 High-intensity running in 15 min periods by elite female soccer players during domestic (black bars) and international games (gray bars); * denotes significant difference (P<0.05) between domestic and international games. # denotes significant difference (P<0.05) from the first 15 min period

Results

High-level vs top-class players

The total distance covered during a match was 10.33 ±0.15 km for the top-class players, which was similar to the elite players (10.44 ±0.15 km). The distance covered during the first half was longer (P<0.05) than in the second half for top-class players (5.28 ±0.09 vs 5.05 ±0.08 km), whereas no difference was observed for moderate-level players (5.22 ±0.09 vs 5.21 ±0.08 km). The distance covered with high-intensity running during a match was 28 per cent greater (P<0.05) for top-class than for moderate-level players (1.68 ±0.09 vs 1.30 ±0.10 km). The distance covered by sprinting was 0.46 ±0.02 km for top-class players, which was 24 per cent longer (P<0.05) than for moderate-level players (0.38 ±0.05 km).

Domestic vs international games

Total distance covered was measured and the amount of high-intensity running was higher (P<0.05) in international games (10.0 ±0.5 and 1.6 ±0.4 km) compared to domestic games (9.7 ±0.6 and 1.4 ±0.4 km). The amount of high-intensity running was 18 per cent lower (P<0.05) in the last compared to the first 15 min interval of the second half of domestic games, with a tendency for a greater decline in international games (40 per cent; Figure 36.2).

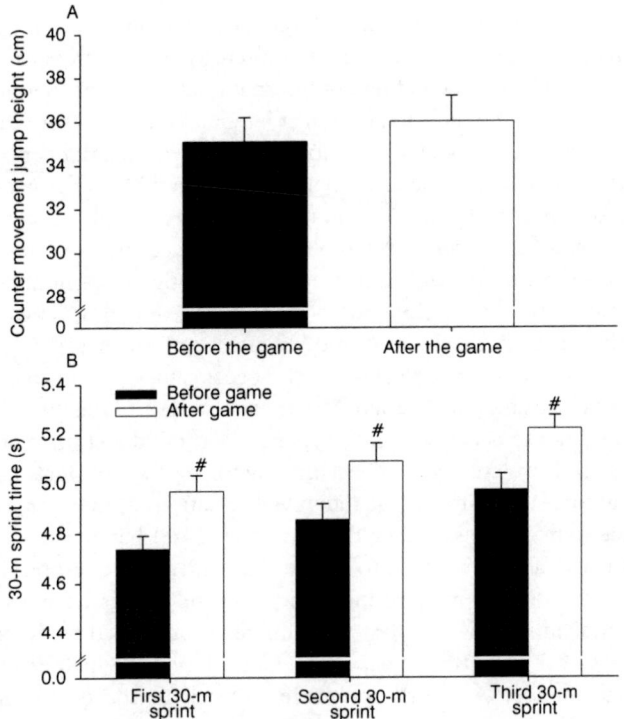

Figure 36.3 Counter-movement jump height (a) and repeated sprint-performance (b) before (filled bar) and after (open bar) elite female soccer games; values are means ±SEM. # denotes significant difference (P<0.05) compared to before game

Jump and sprint performance before and after an elite game

The jump height was 36 ±1 cm (range: 31–43 cm) after the game, which was not different from before the game (35 ±1 cm; 30–41 cm) (Figure 36.3a). The average sprint time for three 30 m sprints was 5.09 ±0.06 s, which was slower (P<0.05) than before the game (4.86 ±0.06 s). The first, second and third sprint performed after the game was slower (P<0.05) than before the game (Figure 36.3b).

Discussion and conclusion

The present study shows that the work-rate profile is dependent on the standard of play. Thus, top-class female players ran significantly longer at high intensities and sprinted more than the other group of elite female players at a lower standard. For players at both competitive levels the amount of high-intensity running and sprinting decreased during the game, indicating development of fatigue. Another interesting finding of the present study was that national team players covered a slightly higher total distance and ran much more at high-intensity during international than during domestic games. This finding suggests that the top-class players are not always utilizing their physical capacity in domestic games. The observation of a 40 per cent decline in high-intensity running from the first to the last 15 min period of the second half of international games, furthermore suggest that some players were unable to perform at a required intensity for 90 min during a top-class game. For example, two national team players did not perform a single sprint for the last 10 min of decisive matches in Euro 2005, although their team needed another goal to qualify for the next round. Although these findings are clear indications of a deteriorated ability to perform high-intensity running, time–motion analyses cannot provide direct evidence of fatigue. Sprint and jump tests were therefore carried out before and after competitive high-level games. These tests revealed that maximal sprint and repeated performance but not jumping ability deteriorated at the end of elite female soccer games. The average decline in sprint performance amounted to about 5 per cent for each of the three 30 m sprint, which corresponds to 1.5 m during 30 m sprints. Without doubt these performance decrements are large enough to affect the outcome of sprint duals and perhaps even the outcome of a game. Large individual variations in the decrease in sprint performance were observed among the players (1–13%) but all the tested players performed worse after compared to before the game. The question, however, is what causes the decline in sprinting ability. Recent studies have shown that a number of individual slow- and fast-twitch fibres are depleted of glycogen during male soccer games (Krustrup *et al.*, 2006). Considering the high aerobic loading and the high number of intense actions in elite female soccer this may well be the case also for female players. In support of this notion, average blood lactate was observed to decline from around 5 mM at half time to around 2.5 mM after competitive elite female games (Krustrup *et al.* unpublished data). Speculativly, glycogen depletion of individual fibres would affect sprint performance but not jumping performance, which is solely dependent on alactacid anaerobic energy turnover. However, further investigations are required to establish the potential mechanism of the development of fatigue in elite female soccer games.

In summary, the present findings underline that elite female soccer is physically demanding and that fatigue occurs towards the end of games. It can furthermore be concluded that the physical demands of elite soccer is dependent on the level of competition and suggest that the training status of some players is not high enough to cope with the demands in international games over 90 min.

References

Bangsbo, J., Nørregaard, L. and Thorsøe, F., 1991, Activity profile of competition soccer. *Canadian Journal of Sports Science*, 16 (2); 110–16.

Brewer, J. and Davies, J. A., 1994, The female player. In *Football (Soccer)*, edited by Ekblom, B. (Oxford: Blackwell), pp. 95–99.

Davis, J.A. and Brewer, J. 1992, Physiological characteristics of an international female squad. *Journal of Sports Sciences*, 10, 142–3.

Davis, J. A. and Brewer, J., 1993, Applied physiology of female soccer players. *Sports Medicine*, 16, 180–9.

Helgerud, J, Engen L.C., Wisloff, U. and Hoff, J., 2001, Aerobic endurance training improves soccer performance. *Medicine and Science in Sports and Exercise*, 33, 1925–31.

Jensen, K. and Larsson, B., 1992, Variations in physical capacity among the Danish national soccer team for women during a period of supplemental training. *Journal of Sports Sciences*, 10, 144–5.

Jensen, K. and Larsson, B, 1993, Variations in physical capacity in a period including supplemental training of the national Danish soccer team for women. In : *Science and Football II*, edited by Reilly, T., Clarys, J. and Stibbe A. (London: E&FN. Spon)

Krustrup, P., Mohr, M., Ellingsgaard, H. and Bangsbo, J., 2005, Physical demands during an elite female soccer game: importance of training status. *Medicine and Science in Sports and Exercise*, 37, 1242–8.

Krustrup, P., Mohr, M., Nielsen, J.J., Nybo, L. and Bangsbo, J., 2006, Muscle and blood metabolites during a soccer game: implications for sprint performance. *Medicine and Science in Sports and Exercise*, 38, 1165–74.

Mohr, M., Krustrup, P. and Bangsbo, J., 2003, Match performance of high-standard soccer players with special reference to development of fatigue. *Journal of Sports Sciences*, 21, 439–49.

Ohashi, J., Togari, H., Isokawa, M. and Sukuzi, S., 1988, Measuring movement speeds and distance covered during soccer match-play. In *Science and Football*, edited by Reilly, T., Lees, A., Davids, K. and Murphy, W.J. (London/ New York; E&FN Spon), pp. 434–40.

Polman, R., Walsh, D., Bloomfield, J. and Nesti, M., 2004, Effective conditioning of female soccer players. *Journal of Sports Sciences*, 22, 191–203.

Reilly, T., 1997, Energetics of high-intensity exercise (soccer) with particular reference to fatigue. *Journal of Sports Sciences*, 15, 257–63.

Rhodes, E. C. and Mosher, R. E., 1992, Aerobic and anaerobic characteristics of elite female university players. *Journal of Sports Sciences*, 10, 143–4.

Rico-Sanz, J., 1998, Body composition and nutritional assessments in soccer. *International Journal of Sport Nutrition*, 8 (2), 113–23.

Shephard, R. J., 2000, Exercise and training in women: Part I: Influence of gender on exercise and training responses. *Canadian Journal of Applied Physiology*, 25 (1), 19–34.

Tamer, K., Gunay, M., Tiryaki, G., Cicioolu, I. and Erol, E., 1997, Physiological characteristics of Turkish female soccer players. In *Science and Football III*, edited by Reilly, T., Bangsbo, J. and Hughes, M, (London: E&FN Spon), pp. 37–9.

Todd, M. K., Scott, D. and Chisnall, P. J., 2002, Fitness characteristics of English female soccer players: an analysis by position and playing standard. In *Science and Football IV*, edited by Spinks, W., Reilly, T. and Murphy, A, (London: Routledge) pp. 374–81.

Tumilty, D.McA. and Darby, S., 1992, Physiological characteristics of Australian female soccer players. *Journal of Sports Sciences*, 10, 145.

Van Gool, D., Van Gerven, D. and Boutmans, J., 1988, The physiological load imposed on soccer players during real match-play. In *Science and Football*, edited by Reilly, T., Lees, A., Davids, K. and Murphy, W.J., (London/New York; E&FN Spon), pp 51–9.

Withers, R.T., Maricic, Z., Wasilewski, S. and Kelly, L., 1982, Match analysis of Australian professional soccer players. *Journal of Human Movement Studies*, 8, 159–76.

37 Diachronic analysis of interaction contexts in the 2006 World Cup

Julen Castellano Paulis,[1] *Abigail Perea Rodríguez*[1] *and Antonio Hernández Mendo*[2]

[1] University of Basque Country, Spain; [2] University of Malaga, Spain

Introduction

Observing how interaction occurs in a concurrent and competitive situation helps to design better training methods. From this point of view, information about the physiological aspects of the game is incomplete in terms of coaching whereas knowledge about the interaction processes generated by the relations with team-mates and against opponents is relevant.

Soccer is a fluid game, with mobility as one of the principles of play (Nicholls *et al.*, 1993: 190). Within this framework of social uncertainty, to perform a rigorous observation of the game is a task which gets more and more difficult the more the investigation extends to some interaction aspects (Suzuki and Nishijima, 2005). The flow of behaviour in soccer probably has an order (Lanhan, 1993) which we need to investigate for a better understanding of the game dynamics (Gréhaigne *et al.*, 1997). Twelve matches played during the 2006 World Cup have been codified and registered with this objective, taking the time into account and adapting Gréhaigne's (1988) proposal.

The lag technique for sequential analysis has been employed to investigate if the behaviours observed during the game have a certain cadence. Through this analysis, it can be determined if the presence or absence of these behaviours occurred by chance or followed some transitions which are repeated throughout the game and can be defined as a behavioural pattern (Yamanaka *et al.*, 1993; Olsen and Larsen, 1997; Yamanaka *et al.*, 1997; Yamanaka *et al.*, 2002).

Methods

Matches

The matches used for this investigation were recorded in VHS video format and digitalized in MPG format. A specific software developed for the observation of game action in soccer, SOCCAF v2.2 video (Perea, *Alday and Castellano*, 2006) was used to register the multi-event sequential data. An analysis of the data quality was performed using SPSS 13.0, GT (Ysewijn, 1996) and SAS (SAS Inc. Institute,

Table 37.1 Interaction contexts proposed in the observational tool SOCCAF (Castellano, 2000)

Code	Description
RM	The ball is located between the backward area of the observed team and the medium area of the other team.
RA	The ball is located between the backward area of the observed team and the forward area of the other team.
MR	The ball is located between the medium area of the observed team and the backward area of the other team.
MM	The ball is located between the medium area of the observed team and the medium area of the other team.
MA	The ball is located between the medium area of the observed team and the forward area of the other team.
AR	The ball is located between the forward area of the observed team and the medium area of the other team.
AM	The ball is located between the forward area of the observed team and the medium area of the other team.
AO	The ball is located between the forward area of the observed team and the empty area of the other team.
OA	The ball is located between the empty area of the observed team and the forward area of the other team.

1999). Finally, the lag technique (Sackett, 1987) was employed for the sequential analysis using SDIS-GSEQ v4.1.2 (Bakeman and Quera, 1996).

Twelve competition matches were observed, codified and registered in this investigation. The matches were played during the final phase of the 2006 World Cup.

Taxonomic system

The taxonomic system SOCCAF (Castellano, 2000), which was also employed in previous research, was used in this investigation. Using SOCCAF, the behaviour of the 22 players is observed as a whole, that is, every behaviour observed during the game, can be interpreted as a context of the interaction between the players.

Data quality

Prior to registering the data, a data-quality analysis (Blanco-Villaseñor, 1998; Blanco-Villaseñor and Angera Argilaga, 2000) was performed obtaining satisfactory results (Blanco-Villaseñor *et al.*, 2000; Perea *et al.*, 2005). The data-quality analysis included a variance components analysis and a generalizability study.

The sequential order as a time characteristic was used to describe the evolution of events during the match. Twelve matches of the second phase of the 2006 World Cup were registered continuously, without time gaps, to obtain a set of data which could be used for lag sequential analysis. This analysis was carried out using SDIS-GSEQ v4.1.2 (Bakeman and Quera, 1996) and the highest data quality were ensured (Kappa–Cohen association index over 0.85).

Table 37.2 Matching behaviours for the prospective and retrospective perspectives

Code	Description
Prospective perspective	
REC1	The observed team recovers the ball in its backward area
REC2	The ball was recovered in the medium area
REC3	The ball was recovered in the forward area of the observed team
RM, RA, MR, MM, MA, AR, AM	Interaction contexts (see Table 37.1)
INT	The observed team intercepted the ball but could not recover it
IRF	Foul for the observed team
IRC	Foul against the observed team
Retrospective perspective	
PER1	The observed team lost the possession of the ball in the backward area
PER2	The ball was lost in the medium area
PER3	The ball was lost in the forward area of the observed team
RM, RA, MR, MM, MA, AR, AM	Interaction contexts (see Table 37.1)
INT	The observed team intercepted the ball but could not recover it
TIR	The observed team shouted at goal
IRF	Foul for the observed team
IRC	Foul against the observed team

Results

Results showed more than 70 playing patterns. The relationship between the criterion behaviours and the matching behaviours was estimated through the hypergeometric Z scores.

Table 37.2 summarizes the nine behavioural patterns obtained using the interaction contexts as criterion behaviours. The interaction contexts used as criterion behaviours were: RM, RA, MR, MM, MA, AR, AM and AO. The matching behaviours used in the analysis are shown in Table 37.3.

Discussion

The succession of interaction contexts did not occur by chance but according to an internal logic, which could be explained by certain offensive contexts that appeared to be closer to scoring opportunities, and by other more propitious to ball recovering situations. Like other investigations which used observational methodology, we propose new guides to describe, and, if possible, to predict the networks of endogenous interactions.

The results obtained in the lag sequential analysis are close to the results observed as this analysis was carried out with data sets of other World Cups (Castellano 2000, 2005; Castellano and Hernández Mendo, 1999, 2002; Castellano and Blanco-Villaseñor, 2006). The interaction contexts define patterns where the transitions between contexts follow the proximity concept, that is, interaction contexts with

Table 37.3 Obtained adjusted residuals, Pearson's χ^2, degrees of freedom and approximate P-value, Germany 2006

	Retrospective perspective			Criterion behaviour	Prospective perspective		
	R–3	R–2	R–1		R1	R2	R3
			–	RM	MM (8.45)	MM (2.11)	MM (2.80)
		IRF (2.42)	RA (7.98) IRF (2.03)	RA	RA (13.10) MM (4.15)	MM (3.91)	MM (2.75)
		MM (2.22)	MM (7.90)	MR	AR (8.78)		
			–	MM	AR (2.97)	MM (2.93) AR (2.52)	AR (3.04)
	RA (3.10) MM (4.37)	RA (2.33) MM (2.46)	RA (9.09) MM (5.35)	MA	RA (9.25) MM (3.41)		
			–	AR	–		
				AM	–		
				AO			
χ^2	2810.3	5284.7	23480.1		23111.4	7571.6	2847.1
Degrees of freedom	84	91	91		98	98	98
P-value	0.001	0.001	0.001		0.001	0.001	0.001

a strong defensive component are more likely to be followed by similar defensive contexts. This also occurs with the offensive and medium interaction contexts; they are more likely to be followed by repetitions of themselves.

These results can be interpreted in terms of an existent intrinsic logic during the game, whereby teams must follow certain paths to score a goal (Bishovets *et al.*, 1993; Lanham, 2005).

Acknowledgements

We gratefully acknowledge the support of the Spanish government project 'Innovaciones en la evaluación de contextos naturales: Aplicaciones al ámbito del deporte' (Dirección General de Investigación, Ministerio de Ciencia y Tecnología) [Grant number BSO2001–3368].

References

Bakeman, R. and Quera, V., 1996, *Análisis de la interacción: Análisis secuencial con SDIS y GSEQ.* (Madrid: RA-MA).

Bishovets, A., Gadjiev, G. and Godik, M., 1993, Computer analysis of the effectiveness of collective technical and tactical moves of footballers in the matches of 1988 Olympics and 1990 World Cup. In *Science and Football II*, edited by Reilly, T., Clarys, J. and Stibbe, A., (London: E&FN Spon), pp. 232–8.

Blanco-Villaseñor, A., 1998, Evaluación predictiva de la variabilidad y generalización de conductas de juego en tenis. Paper presented at V Congreso de Evaluación Psicológica (Symposium 'Aplicaciones de la observación sistemática en la evaluación de actividades físico-deportivas'). Benalmádena Costa, Málaga. (30 April–13 May1998).

Blanco-Villaseñor, A. and Anguera Argilaga, M. T., 2000, Evaluación de la calidad en el registro del comportamiento: Aplicación a deportes de equipo. In *Métodos Numéricos en Ciencias Sociales*, edited by Oñate, E.,, García, F., Sicilia, L. and Ramallo, (Barcelona: CIMNE), pp. 30–48.

Blanco-Villaseñor, A., Castellano, J. and Hernández Mendo, A., 2000, Generalizabilidad de las observaciones de la acción del juego en el fútbol. *Psicothema*, 12, Suppl. 2, 81–6.

Castellano, J., 2000, Observación y análisis de la acción de juego en fútbol. Doctoral thesis. San Sebastián: Universidad del País Vasco.

Castellano, J., 2005, La secuencialidad de los contextos de interacción en el fútbol. Congreso Internacional "Actividad Física y Deporte en la Sociedad del Siglo XXI". Universidad Europea de Madrid (UEM).

Castellano, J. and Blanco-Villaseñor, A., 2006, Análisis del comportamiento estratégico de los equipos de fútbol. In *Socialización y Deporte: Revisión Crítica. Diputación Foral del Álava*, edited by Castellano Paulis, J., Sautu Apellaniz, L.M., Hernández Mendo, A., Blanco-Villaseñor, A., Goñi Grandmontagne A., and Martínez de Ilarduya, F.

Castellano, J. and Hernández Mendo, A., 1999, Análisis secuencial en el fútbol de rendimiento. *Psicothema*, 12, Suppl. 2, 117–121.

Castellano, J. and Hernández Mendo, A., 2002, Análisis diacrónico de la acción de juego en fútbol. *Revista Digital de Educación Física y Deportes*, 49 [www.efdeportes.com].

Gréhaigne, J. -F., 1988, Game systems in soccer from the point of view of coverage of space. In *Science and Football I*, edited by Reilly, T., Lees, A., Davids, K. and Murphy, W.J., (London: E&FN Spon), pp. 316–21.

Gréhaigne, J. -F., Bouthier, D. and David, B., 1997, A method to analyse attacking moves in soccer. In *Science and Football III*, edited by Reilly, T., Bangsbo, J. and Hughes, M., (London: E&FN Spon), pp. 258–66.

Lanham, N., 1993, Figures do not cease to exist because they are not counted. In *Science and Football II*, edited by Reilly, T., Clarys, J. and Stibbe, A., (London: E&FN Spon) pp.180–5.

Lanham, N., 2005, The goal complete: the winning difference. In *Science and Football V*, edited by Reilly, T., Cabri, J. and Araújo, D., (London and New York: Routledge), pp. 194–200.

Nicholls, G., McMorris, T., White, A. and Carr, C., 1993, An investigation into the validity of the use of centrality as a criterion for stacking studies in soccer. In *Science and Football II*, edited by Reilly, T., Clarys J. and Stibbe, A., (London: E&FN Spon), pp. 190–3.

Olsen, E. and Larsen, O., 1997, Use of match analysis by coaches. In *Science and Football III*, edited by Reilly, T., Bangsbo, J. and Hughes, M., (London: E&FN Spon), pp. 209–20.

Perea, A. E., Alday Ezpeleta, L. and Castellano Paulis, J., 2006, Aplicación informática específica para la observación de la acción de juego en fútbol, In *Evaluación e Intervención en el Ámbito Deportivo* edited by Castellano Paulis, J., Sautu Apellaniz, L. M., Blanco-Villaseñor, A., Hernández Mendo, A., Goñi Grandmontagne and A. y Martínez de Ilarduya, F. Diputación Foral de Álava, pp. 285–94.

Perea, A. E., Castellano Paulis, J., Hernandez Mendo, A., Álvarez Pastor, D. and Luis Pérez Castellano, E., 2005, Pautas para el análisis de la calidad del dato en la observación de los deportes colectivos: una aplicación en el fútbol. Paper presented at I Congreso Virtual de Investigación en la Actividad Física y el Deporte, celebrado en el IVEF-SHEE de Vitoria-Gasteiz, September.

Sackett, G. P., 1987, Analysis of sequential social interaction data: some issues. Recent developments, and a causal inference model. In *Handbook of Infant Development*, edited by Osofsky, J.D. (New York: Wiley), pp. 855–78.

SAS Institute Inc., 1999, *SAS/STAT User's Guide, Version 7–1*, Cary, NC: SAS Institute Inc.

Suzuki, K. and Nishijima, T., 2005, Measurement of a soccer defending skill using game performances. In *Science and Football V*, edited by Reilly, T., Cabri, J. and Araújo, D. , (London and New York: Routledge), pp. 253–261.

Yamanaka, K., Hughes, M. and Lott, M., 1993, An analysis of playing patterns in the 1990 World Cup for association football. In *Science and Football II*, edited by Reilly, T., Clarys, J. and Stibbe, A., (London: E&FN Spon), pp. 206–14.

Yamanaka, K., Liang, D.Y. and Hughes, M., 1997, An analysis of the playing patterns of the Japan national team in the 1994 World Cup qualifying match for Asia. In *Science and Football III*, edited by Reilly, T., Bangsbo, J. and Hughes, M. (London: E&FN Spon), pp. 221–8.

Yamanaka, K., Nishikawa, T., Yamanaka, T. and Hughes, M.D., 2002, An analysis of the playing patterns of the Japan national team in the 1998 world cup for soccer. In *Science and Football IV*, edited by Spinks, W., Reilly, T. and Murphy, A. (London and New York: Routledge), pp. 101–105.

Ysewijn, P., 1996, GT: Software for Generalizability Studies. City Mimeografía.

38 The impact of individualism on the outcome of penalty shoot-outs in international football tournaments

Jon Billsberry,[1] Patrick Nelson[1] and Gareth Edwards[2]

[1] The Open University, UK; [2] The Leadership Trust Foundation, UK

Introduction

International football tournaments such as the World Cup and the European Championship attract enormous worldwide attention (Hoffman *et al.*, 2002). Arguably, they are becoming the world's largest festivals with houses, cars and bodies around the world being festooned with national symbols and television audiences twice the size of the next largest sporting event, the opening ceremony of the Olympics (Reuters, 2006). Television audiences for the games in the knockout stages of competitions are enormous: 284 million people watched the 2006 World Cup final between Italy and France live and an estimated 5.9 billion people watched at least one World Cup match (Reuters, 2006). When games are deadlocked and go to penalty shoot-outs all of this attention is focused on the individual taking his penalty kick. Quite literally, the fate of his nation rests with him; he knows that his every movement is being observed by millions of passionate supporters. For example, 23.9 million people in Italy and 22.1 million people in France are reported to have watched the penalty shoot-out in the 2006 World Cup final (Reuters, 2006). Some players have reported the immense psychological stress (e.g. Pearce, 2000; Owen, 2005) this places on the individual player making them almost incapable of standing-up.

Despite the focus of world attention on penalty shoot-outs, very little research has been published on the spectacle (Jordet *et al.*, 2007). To date, just one empirical, one experiment, and two computer modelling reports have been published on the penalty shoot-out. However, policy-makers have begun to explore the suitability of the penalty shoot-out with particular focus being given to the individualistic nature of the tie-breaker. Speaking in September 2006, FIFA President, Sepp Blatter, talking about the use of penalty shoot-outs to determine the results of drawn games in the knock-out stages of international football tournaments said:

When it comes to the World Cup final, it is passion, and when it goes to extra time it is a drama. But when it comes to penalty kicks, it is a tragedy. ... Football is a team sport and penalties are not for a team, it is the individual.

(Szczepanik, 2006)

Blatter's quote can be interpreted in several ways. On an aesthetic level, there is ugliness in settling the results of team games with a competition of individuals acting independently of the team. From a care perspective, Blatter's observation might be seen to question whether it is right to place individuals in a situation where their actions determine the results of games. From a fairness issue, this quote from the most senior football policy-maker hints that people from individualistic nations might have an advantage in penalty shoot-outs that they do not have in the team game. Consequently, we decided to explore whether the individual nature of the penalty shoot-out has an impact on the outcome. Specifically, we asked: 'Does the national culture dimension of individualism/collectivism influence the results of penalty shoot-outs in international football tournaments?'

Methods

To explore the impact of national culture on the success rate of penalty shoot-outs in international football tournaments, two datasets were needed: (1) information on the national culture dimension of individualism/collectivism, and (2) the results of penalty shoot-outs in international football tournaments.

National culture data

Data on the individualism/collectivism of national cultures came from Hofstede's (1980, 1983, 2006) seminal studies of national cultures. Hofstede began gathering data in 1968. Initially, 116,000 employees of IBM around the world completed his questionnaire allowing him to control for corporate culture and to describe the national culture characteristics of 40 countries.

Data were retrieved from Hofstede's own website (Hofstede, 2006). Unfortunately, some regions of the world, especially in Africa, are less well represented in his data and he has composite scores for the countries in the Arab world, east Africa, west Africa and southern Africa. The relevant composite scores have been used for assigning cultural values to Egypt and Nigeria.

Penalty shoot-out data

Our original intention was to limit our analysis to just the World Cup, the Olympics and the four major continental tournaments as previous research has explored the high-stress nature of penalty shoot-outs in these competitions (Jordet *et al.*, 2007). Unfortunately, there have only been 82 shoot-outs in these competitions, which are insufficient for our analysis, especially as there is only matching culture data for 56 of these shoot-outs (see Table 38.1).

Table 38.1 Summary statistics for the major tournaments

	N (qualifiers)	+ Hofstede data	Collectivist wins	Individualist wins	Same culture scores
World Cup	20 + (1)	20	11	8	1
European Championships	11	11	9	2	–
African Cup of Nations	19	2	2	0	–
Copa América	14	10	4	6	–
Asian Nations Cup	12 + (1)	10	6	3	1
Olympics	4	3	2	1	–
Totals	80 + (2)	56	34 (61%)	20 (36%)	2 (3%)

Consequently, we were forced to expand our data collecting to include every shoot-out that has been taken in a competitive international football tournament since the first one in the Asian Cup in 1972. The total number of shootouts is 182 up to, and including, the 2006 World Cup.

The tournaments in this dataset are the premier global competition, the World Cup, the four major continental competitions, the European Championship (known as the European Nations Cup until 1976), the African Cup of Nations, the Copa América, and the Asian Nations Cup, and the following minor tournaments: African Games, Afro-Asian Cup of Nations, Asian Games, Confederation of Southern African Football Associations Cup (COSAFA), Cecafa Senior Challenge Cup (CECAFA; also known as Al Amoudi Senior Challenge Cup), Confederación Centroamericana y del Caribe de Fútbol (CCCF and CONCACAF) tournaments, FIFA/Confederations Cup, Gold Cup, Intercontinental Championship, Olympic Games, Panamerican Games, South Asian Gold Cup, South Asian Football Federation Cup, South East Asian Games, Tiger Cup, West Asian Games, and the West Asian Championship.

Although all of these minor tournaments are competitive, most are of less importance to players and spectators than the major global and continental tournaments. In such circumstances, the levels of stress and anxiety in penalty shoot-outs will be lessened and are less likely to exhibit the effect predicted in the major tournaments. To limit the dilution of the effect, we set a criterion that to be included in the dataset a country must have participated in at least two penalty shoot-outs in global or major continental tournaments. A second criterion was needed to provide some reliability to the data. As the results of a penalty shoot-out are win (100%) or lose (0%), we decided that to provide sufficient sensitivity in the data, nations had to compete in at least five penalty shoot-outs and have taken at least twenty spot-kicks. This filtering eliminated all but sixteen countries.

Table 38.2 Summary statistics for the sixteen nations

Nation	No. of shoot-outs	Wins	Losses	Win/loss %	Individualism
South Korea	8	6	2	75.0	18
Argentina	11	8	3	72.7	46
Germany[1]	7	5	2	71.4	67
Nigeria	6	4	2	66.7	20
Brazil	11	7	4	63.6	38
Colombia	5	3	2	60.0	13
Thailand	11	6	5	54.5	20
France	6	3	3	50.0	71
Egypt	7	4	3	50.0	38
Iran	11	5	6	45.5	41
Uruguay	7	3	4	42.9	36
Mexico	11	4	7	36.4	30
Spain	6	2	4	33.3	51
Italy	6	2	4	33.3	76
Netherlands	5	1	4	20.0	80
England[2]	6	1	5	16.7	89

Notes:
[1] The penalty shoot-out records of West Germany and Germany have been added together.
[2] Culture data for the United Kingdom has been assigned to England.

Results

To explore the relationship between individualism/collectivism, a regression analysis was run with win/loss percentage as the dependent variable and the culture dimension of individualism entered as the independent variable. Table 38.3 and Figure 38.1 show the results of the regression analyses. Using ANOVA, the results show that the model has an R of 0.629, an R^2 of 0.395 and an adjusted R^2 of 0.352. The difference between the R^2 and the adjusted R^2 is caused by the limited number of countries (i.e. 16) used in the model. Nevertheless, the adjusted of 0.352 means that the national culture dimension of individualism/collectivism accounts for 35.2% of the variance in the results of penalty shoot-outs. In other words, for one standard deviation movement along the Y axis (individualism/collectivism score; i.e. 24.1), there is a 35.2% shift in the Y axis (the win/loss percentage in penalty shoot-outs).

Before moving on to discuss the nature of these results, it is important for us to acknowledge an important limitation of our analysis; it is built on correlation data and therefore it is not possible to attribute causality to the relationship. However, the natural relationship between these factors is that individualism, being a national culture dimension, will underlie and influence the performance variable.

Table 38.3 Analysis of variance for individualism and penalty shoot-out outcomes

Variables	β	SE	t	Sig.
(Constant)		8.697	8.455	0.000
Individualism	−0.629	0.169	−3.025	0.009*

* Significant at the 0.01 level
[1] $R^2 = 0.395$; Model Adjusted $R^2 = 0.352$; B = 73.535

Discussion

These results demonstrate a strong national culture bias in favour of collectivist nations. Intuitively, this might appear strange. Surely, being an individualist undertaking an individualist task would be beneficial. Our explanation for this phenomenon is that this logic misunderstands the psychology of individualist nations. In individualistic societies, there are weaker ties between people and less 'community feel'. As a consequence, there is less binding people together and less cohesiveness (Hofstede, 1980; Smith et al., 2002). In such societies, there is an individualization of news coverage with a greater focus on the actions of individuals. In such societies, for example the UK and the US, news coverage often singles out individuals for particular scrutiny. For example, the coverage of the manager of the England football team is so extreme, fickle and aggressive that it put off some candidates for the post when it was last vacant. In such societies, people taking penalty kicks during shoot-outs will expect to be publicly lambasted for the exit of their team from the competition if they miss their attempt. Hence, such players may feel both more pressure from the individualized attention and may inwardly focus on the fear of missing rather than the benefits of scoring.

The 'double whammy' of being from an individualistic national culture is that the criticism that players receive means more to them. People in these cultures focus more on individual achievement, reputation and self-image; self-esteem comes from individual achievement rather than group achievement. Hence, penalty-takers from countries with individualistic cultures are not only likely to be more fearful of missing due to the greatly likelihood of individualized blame being directed towards them, but the individualized blame is likely to be more hurtful to them as it challenges their self-image. When the pressure is at its greatest, the additional fear that players from individualized cultures feel may influence their ability to take a penalty kick. As we know from other research, greater pressure means that penalty kick takers are more likely to miss (Jordet et al., 2007).

Conclusion

This report has shown that there is a clear underlying bias that influences the results of penalty shoot-outs in international football tournaments. The effect of this bias its pronounced. The fact that an underlying factor can be found to have an influence on the results of football matches is not new or something that automatically makes the use of penalty shoot-outs invalid. It is well-known that money exerts influence over football results, especially at club level, that access to facilities and coaches has restricted the performance of many nations, and that there are national characteristics, such as GNP, industrial development and climate that are all associated with performance (Hoffman *et al.*, 2002). We would argue that the relationship between individualism and the outcome of penalty shoot-outs falls into a different category. Whereas links between money, GNP, climate and the like do influence football matches, these are factors that the football authorities can do little to offset; they are the realities of the world that will influence the results of football matches no matter how the game is played or decided. Penalty shoot-outs, on the other hand, are just one option amongst many that the football authorities can use to determine the results of deadlocked games in international football tournaments. In such circumstances, the authorities have a responsibility to choose methods that are as fair to all participating nations as possible with no underlying bias favouring any particular nations unless it is based on skill. Our analysis suggests that the use of penalty shoot-outs in international football tournaments does have an underlying bias that exerts a considerable impact on the results of penalty shoot-outs. Accordingly, we find ourselves drawn to the conclusion that FIFA should consider replacing them.

References

Hoffmann, R., Ging, L.C. and Ramasamy, B., 2002, The socioeconomic determinants of international soccer performance. *Journal of Applied Economics*, 5, 253–72.

Hofstede, G., 1980, *Culture's Consequences: International Differences in Work-Related Values*. (London: Sage).

Hofstede, G., 1983, The cultural relativity of organizational practices and theories. *Journal of International Business Studies*, Fall, 75–89.

Hofstede, G., 2006, Geert Hofstede™ Cultural Dimensions (available at: http://www.geert-hofstede.com/hofstede_dimensions.php; accessed 15 September 2006).

Jordet, G., Hartman, E., Visscher, C. and Lemmink, K.A.P.M., 2007, Kicks from the penalty mark in soccer: the roles of stress, skill, and fatigue for kick outcomes. *Journal of Sports Sciences*, 25, 121–9.

Owen, M., 2005, *Off the Record: My Autobiography*. (London: Collins Willow).

Pearce, S., 2000, *Psycho: The Autobiography* (with Bob Harris). (London: Headline Book Publishing).

Reuters, 2006, World Cup scores TV equivalent of 64 Super Bowls (available at: http://today.reuters.com/news/articleinvesting.aspx?view = CN&storyI = 2006–07–25T110753Z_01_L25114158_RTRIDST_0_MEDIA-WORLDCUP-TV.XML&rpc = 66&type = qcna; accessed 28 September 2006).

Smith, P.B., Peterson, M.F. and Schwartz, S.H., 2002, Cultural values, sources of guidance, and their relevance to managerial behavior: A 47–nation study. *Journal of Cross-Cultural Psychology*, 33, 188–208.

Szczepanik, N., 2006, Shoot-outs face sudden death under Blatter plan. *The Times*, 28 September 2006, p. 82.

39 Match analyses of Australian international female soccer players using an athlete tracking device

Adam Hewitt,[1,2] *Robert Withers*[1] *and Keith Lyons*[2]

[1] Flinders University, Australia; [2] Australian Institute of Sport, Australia

Introduction

The physiological characteristics of women soccer players have been reported previously (Jensen and Larsson, 1992; Rhodes and Mosher, 1992; Davis and Brewer, 1993; Tumilty, 1993; Tamer *et al.*, 1997; Todd *et al.*, 2002; Krustrup *et al.*, 2005). These studies show that maximal aerobic power, sprinting ability and intermittent exercise performance of elite players are critical determinants of fitness (Jensen and Larsson, 1992; Rhodes and Mosher, 1992; Davis and Brewer, 1993; Tumilty, 1993; Tamer *et al.*, 1997; Todd *et al.*, 2002; Krustrup *et al.*, 2005). Only Krustrup *et al.* (2005) have reported the activity profile of elite international female soccer players during match play. They studied 14 players from the Danish Division 1 during competitive matches using video based time–motion analysis and they reported the total distance covered during a game to be 10300 m (range: 9700–11300 m).

Over the past thirty years, video tracking has generally been considered the most accurate and accessible method for estimating movement distances in time-motion studies (Edgecomb and Norton, 2006). However, video systems do not function in real time, may be subject to errors due to gait changes during game movements and are extremely labour intensive (Edgecomb and Norton, 2006).

Until recently, the testing of sport performance and more specifically team sport performance, has been restricted to laboratory-based or simulated field tests. Multiple factors that are hard to control for, plus the need for extremely labour-intensive, expensive equipment and unacceptable error rates have limited the use of sport-specific field testing (Larsson, 2003). The global positioning system (GPS) is a navigation system which was originally developed for military use but it has recently been applied to aviation, marine and outdoor recreational activities. The GPS system utilises 27 operational satellites which are in orbit around the earth. Each satellite is equipped with an atomic clock. The satellites constantly send information (at the speed of light) about exact time to the GPS receiver. By comparing the time given by a satellite and the time within the GPS receiver, the signal travel time is calculated. The distance to the satellite is then determined by multiplying the signal travel time by the speed of light. Up until 1999 the US Department of Defense included a deliberate error into the GPS system, designed to reduce the risk of hostile forces using the GPS system against the US (Larsson, 2003). The advent of GPS technology miniaturisation has meant that the GPS packaging is now small enough to be worn unobtrusively by players during training and competition.

The athlete tracking devices were developed by the Collaborative Research Centre for Microtechnology which is an Australian government initiative. In addition to the GPS module, the athlete tracking devices are equipped with triaxial accelerometers, triaxial gyroscopes and triaxial magnetometers. The aim of this study was to utilise this emerging technology to measure the activity profiles and physical demands of Australian international female soccer players.

Methods

Subjects

Fifteen Australian national female soccer players participated in the study. Their age, height and mass were: 23.5 ± 2.5 (±SD) years, 1.70 ± 0.05 m and 64.88 ± 4.6 kg, respectively. The average number of international appearances for each player was 46.

The playing positions were: defenders (N = 6, 24.3 ±1.0 years, 1.69 ±0.02 m and 63.2 ±0.8 kg), midfielders (N = 5, 23.4 ±3.75 years, 1.70 ±0.03 m and 63.1 ±2.7 kg) and attackers (N = 4, 22.9 ±0.8 years, 1.71 ±0.08 m and 71.1 ±1.7 kg).

The players were competing in the 2006 Asian Football Confederation (AFC) Women's Asian Cup held in Australia which also doubled as the AFC qualification path for the 2007 FIFA Women's World Cup. The four matches analysed involved three nations ranked higher than Australia (15): Japan (13), Korea DPR (7) and China PR (8) and one nation ranked below Australia, Korean Republic (23).

Match analysis

Players were fitted with the athlete tracking device via a Lycra sleeveless garment which was equipped with a pocket to house the device. The athlete tracking device was located above the midpoint of the shoulder blades. Many players are wearing similar garments under playing attire and none of them reported any discomfort. Locomotor activity was categorised as: strolling (0–5 km.h^{-1}), walking (5–8 km.h^{-1}), low-speed running (8–12 km.h^{-1}), moderate-speed running (12–16 km.h^{-1}), high-speed running (16–20 km.h^{-1}) and sprinting (>20 km.h^{-1}).

Table 39.1 Whole-game locomotor activity profile of Australian international female soccer players

Speed (km.h^{-1})	Locomotor description	Distance (m)		
		Mean	SD	%
0–5	Slow walking	2400	120	26
5–8	Walking	2100	110	23
8–12	Low-speed running	2330	190	26
12–16	Moderate-speed running	1410	160	15
16–20	High-speed running	620	110	7
20+	Sprinting	280	80	3
Total		9140	1030	

Table 39.2 Results of 2006 Women's Asian Cup, playing formations and total average distance covered by Australian players per match

	Opponent	Final score	Formations	Distance (m)
Round 1	Korea Republic	4–0	4–3–3 vs 3–4–4	9060± 760
Round 3	DPR Korea	0–0	4–3–3 vs 5–3–2	9230±770
Semi-final	Japan	2–0	4–4–2 vs 4–5–1	9670±810
Final	China	2–2*	4–4–2 vs 4–4–2	8900±760#

Source: AFC Women's Asian Cup website   (http://www.the-afc.com/english/competitions/WomenAsianCup2006/fixtures/default.asp)
* = China won the match 4–2 on penalties after extra time.
# = Total distance covered at completion of normal match time.

Results

Locomotor activity patterns are presented in Table 39.1. The total distance covered during a game was 9140 m, 2310 ± 580 m of which comprised moderate speed to sprint running (≥12 km.h^{-1}). Average distances covered were: defenders 9010 (7200–9760) m; midfielders 9640 (7620–10960) m; and attackers 8510 (8490–9440) m.

Discussion

The results of this study showed that Australian international female soccer players covered an average of 9140 m during a full game. This value is less than the 10300 m reported by Krustrup *et al.* (2005). Possible reasons for these differences are the: 1) styles of play, 2) methods of analysis, 3) styles of play of the opposition, and 4) physical capacities of the players.

The styles of play of both teams will influence the physical requirements of the game. The impact of changing the style of play, formation of the team or emphasis of the match all affect the amount and type of running required. The style of play and the result of the match have not been reported or acknowledged during previous research on the activity profiles on male and female soccer players. Variation in the distances covered and the running profiles for each game in this study are probably largely influenced by the different playing styles and formations. Even within a playing formation written out on paper, the different instructions to individual players and team rules will influence the amount of running required by the players in those positions. The technical and tactical abilities of the players will also influence the running requirements. For example, a team in control of the ball for long periods of the game and maintaining possession may not need to cover as much ground as the team without the ball. Applications of GPS technology to team sport are relatively new. No research has been conducted which compares the traditional video-based time–motion analysis methods with GPS-based values. However, the relative ease of collecting information on multiple players during a single session will allow more data during matches to be collected.

Krustrup *et al.* (2005) reported a $\dot{V}O_{2\,max}$ of 49.4 ml.kg^{-1}.min^{-1} (43.4–56.8) for their Danish Division 1 players who were tested using an incremental treadmill test. Routine fitness testing, using the Multi-stage Shuttle Test (Léger and Lambert, 1982) and conducted at the AIS prior to the Australian women's soccer team competing for the 2006 AFC Women's Asian Cup, resulted in $\dot{V}O_{2\,max}$ values of 54.8 ± 3.5 (48.0–59.0) ml.kg^{-1}.min^{-1}. Although the Australian female soccer players covered less distance in a match than the Danish Division 1 players, the difference was not due to their lower maximal aerobic power. These findings support those of Krustrup *et al.* (2003) which showed that maximal oxygen consumption was not correlated with the total distance covered by male youth soccer players. Conversely, Helgerud *et al.* (2001) demonstrated a significant increase in the total distance covered, number of sprints and involvements with the ball when players are subjected to additional training which is designed to increase $\dot{V}O_{2\,max}$.

In summary, our findings expand on the limited data in the literature on the running requirements of women's football. We were able to demonstrate that GPS is an emerging technology that can be further utilised in applied research on team sports. The ability to collect data on numerous players in the same game or training session will allow researchers access to unprecedented information.

References

AFC Asian Women's Cup 2006– Schedule/results, Asian Football Confederation, Malaysia, viewed 5 January 2007, <http://www.the-afc.com/english/competitions/WomenAsianCup2006/fixtures/default.asp>.

Davis, J. A. and Brewer, J., 1993, Applied physiology of female soccer players. *Sports Medicine*, 16, 180–9.

Edgecomb, S. J. and Norton, K. I., 2006, Comparison of global positioning and computer-based tracking systems for measuring player movement distance during Australian Football. *Journal of Science and Medicine in Sport*, 9, 25–32.

Helgreud, J., Engen, L, C., Wisloff, U. and Hoff, J., 2001, Aerobic endurance training improves soccer performance. *Medicine and Science in Sports and Exercise*, 33, 1925–31.

Jensen, K. and Larsson, B., 1992, Variations in physical capacity among the Danish national soccer team for women during a period of supplemental training. *Journal of Sports Sciences*, 10, 144–5.

Krustrup, P., Mohr, M., Amstrup, T., Rysgaard, T., Johansen, J., Steensberg, A., Pedeersen, P. and Bangsbo, J., 2003, The Yo-Yo intermittent recovery test: physiological response, reliability, and validity. *Medicine and Science in Sports and Exercise*, 33, 697–705.

Krustrup, P., Mohr, M., Ellingsgaard, H. and Bangsbo, J., ,2005, Physical demands during an elite female soccer game: importance of training status. *Medicine and Science in Sports and Exercise*, 37, 1242–8.

Larsson, P., 2003, Global Positioning System and sport-specific testing. *Sports Medicine*, 33, 1093–101.

Leger, L. A., and Lambert, J., 1982, A maximal multistage 20–m shuttle run test to predict $\dot{V}O_{2\,max.}$ *European Journal of Applied Physiology and Occupational Physiology* 49, 1–12.

Rhodes, E. C. and Mosher, R. E., 1992, Aerobic and anaerobic characteristics of elite female university players. *Journal of Sports Sciences*, 10, 143–4.

Tamer, K., Gunay, M., Tiryaki, G., Cicioolu, I. and Erol, E., 1997, Physiological characteristics of Turkish female soccer players. In: *Science and Football III*, edited by Reilly, T., Bangsbo, J. and Hughes, M., (London, E&FN Spon), pp. 37–9.

Todd, M. K., Scott, D. and Chisnall, P. J., 2002, Fitness characteristics of English female soccer players: an analysis by position and playing standard. In: *Science and Football IV*, edited by Spinks, W. Reilly, T. and Murphy, A. (London: Routledge), pp. 374–81.

Tumility, D., 1993, Physiological characteristics of elite soccer players. *Sports Medicine*, 16, 80–96.

40 Performance profiles of soccer players in the 2006 UEFA Champions League and the 2006 FIFA World Cup tournaments

Marc Rowlinson and Peter O'Donoghue

School of Sport, University of Wales Institute Cardiff, UK

Introduction

Until 1998–99, only one team per country qualified for the European Cup except for the country where the previous year's winners came from. This meant that a maximum of five teams from Europe's four major soccer leagues could participate with many teams reaching the last 16 round being weaker than teams from Europe's four major soccer leagues who had not qualified. Since 1998–99, more than one club from countries with strong national soccer leagues have been allowed to compete in the UEFA Champions League. This regulation has allowed as many as four clubs from each of the English FA Premier League, Italian Serie A, Spain's La Liga and Germany's Bundesliga to reach the last 16 in the 2006–2007 Champions League. Top international players from countries inside and outside Europe play for teams in the four major European soccer leagues (Bloomfield *et al.*, 2004a, 2004b, 2005). There has been much speculation in recent years that the UEFA Champions League tournament is a higher quality competition than the FIFA World Cup:

> I think the European Champions Cup is now bigger than the World Cup. All the best players are in Europe now.
>
> (Sir Alex Ferguson, 2003)

Clubs are able to recruit players from different nationalities in a way that national squads are unable to. Vaeyens *et al.* (2005) have described some restrictions on the make up of club squads in Belgium, but these are still much less restrictive than eligibility criteria for national sides.

The quality of different competitions can be compared by examining the relevant fitness characteristics of players who participate in those competitions (Dunbar and Power, 1997). Performance analysis is an academic discipline within sports science that permits the strategy (James *et al.*, 2002) and quality of play (Gerisch and Reicheldt, 1993) in different tournaments to be investigated in an objective and reliable manner. The analysis of positive and negative applications of different offensive and defensive skills is a promising way of analysing quality of play. There are two alternative approaches to analysing positive and negative play that have been used in soccer research (Gerisch and Reichelt, 1993; Olsen and Larsen, 1997). Gerisch and Reichelt's (1993) method involved analysing all of the one-on-one situations that each individual player was involved in during the course of a match. This allowed the percentage of different types of one-on-one situations performed successfully by a player to be determined. The main criticism of Gerisch and Reichelt's (1993) method is that for each one-on-one situation, one player is deemed to have successfully achieved his objective while the other is deemed to have been unsuccessful. This is the case no matter how well or how poorly the players cope with the situation. Olsen and Larsen (1997) analysed the performances of Norwegian international players over a four-year period using positive to negative ratios for each individual as well as for the whole team. The method allows positive and negative events involving players under consideration to be recorded based on the absolute quality of play rather than relating a player's performance to the current opponent.

Therefore, the aim of the current research was to describe the positive and negative play of a set of players in UEFA Champions League matches and in the FIFA World Cup. Research in tennis has demonstrated that relying on individual performances for each player in a study can lead to unrepresentative results (Wells et al., 2004). Therefore, the purpose of the current investigation was to compare play in the two tournaments using performance profiles based on three UEFA Champions League matches and three FIFA World Cup played in 2006 by each player.

Methods

The subjects chosen for this study were eight high-profile professional soccer players: three defenders, three midfielders and two forwards. These eight soccer players had played for the full match duration in at least three matches of the knockout stages of the 2005–2006 UEFA Champions League and in at least three matches of the 2006 FIFA World Cup. A shortlist of 13 eligible players was considered for the current investigation with the eight players chosen to reflect, a mixture of different positions, nationalities and club sides. No club or nation was represented by more than two players within the sample of eight players. The three matches chosen for each player in each tournament were selected in a way that attempted to use a range of strengths of opposition.

A manual notational analysis system was developed to record tallies of positive and negative applications of a set of five defensive and six offensive skills used in soccer. A positive action was classified as an instance of a skill being performed by a player that would lead to the most beneficial outcome for his team under the circumstances in which the skill was performed. The first five of the events identified below are classed as defensive events with the other six being classed as offensive events:

1   *Tackle* is when the player attempted to dispossess the opponent of the ball through a physical challenge or defensive pressure.
2   *Block* is when the player attempts to prevent a ball played by an opponent from reaching its intended target by contacting the ball without keeping possession of the ball.
3   *Clearance* is when the player attempts to kick the ball away from an area where the team which the opponent make an attempt on goal.
4   *Headed clearance* is when the player attempts to head the ball away from an area where the opponent team makes an attempt on goal.
5   *Interception* is when the player attempts to prevent a ball played by an opponent from reaching its intended target by contacting the ball and keeping his own team in possession of the ball.
6   *Pass* is when the player is in possession of the ball and attempts to play the ball to one of his own team with any part of the body except the head.
7   *Cross* is when the player is in possession of the ball and attempts to play it into the opponent's penalty area from a wide area with the aim of creating a goal-scoring opportunity.
8   *Shot* is when the player is in possession of the ball and makes an attempt to score a goal for his team with any part of the body except the head.
9   *Headed pass* is when the player is in possession of the ball and attempts to play the ball with his head to one of his own team mates.
10 *Headed shot* is when the player is in possession of the ball and makes an attempt with his head to score a goal for his team.
11 *Dribble* is when the player is in possession of the ball and attempts to travel with the ball, maintaining possession of the ball while doing so.

Television coverage of the matches used was recorded onto VHS video cassette or DVD from the satellite and terrestrial channels that showed the matches. The matches were then played back using the pause facilities provided by video and DVD players where necessary during the analysis of the activity of the players selected for the study. Positive and negative instances of the 11 events performed by the players were tallied using a specifically designed data collection form.

An intra-operator reliability test was conducted by the primary author notating a single player performance twice, with two weeks between each observation. This revealed a total percentage error of 3.2 per cent using the method of Hughes *et al.* (2004). This value was deemed acceptable as it was lower than the 5 per cent error.

The data that were recorded were entered into a Microsoft Excel spreadsheet so as the mean frequencies for positive and negative applications of each event could be determined for each player for UEFA Champions League matches and for FIFA World Cup matches. The mean values of eight players in the UEFA Champions League matches and the FIFA World Cup matches were entered into SPSS version 12.0 (SPSS In., Chicago, IL.) where Wilcoxon signed ranks tests were used to compare the percentage of defensive, offensive and all events that were performed in a positive manner by the players between the FIFA World Cup and the UEFA Champions League. Any P value of less 0.05 was deemed to be significant.

Results

Table 40.1 shows that players executed each type of event in a positive manner more than in a negative manner within both tournaments. All eight players, including the three defenders, performed more offensive events than defensive events during each tournament. There was no significant difference in the percentage of defensive events performed positively between the FIFA World Cup and the UEFA Champions League (77.7 $\pm$16.5% v 82.4 $\pm$7.9%, $z = 0.3$, $P = 0.799$). Similarly, there was no significant difference in the percentage of offensive events performed positively between the FIFA World Cup and the UEFA Champions League (88.3 $\pm$3.6% v 88.2 $\pm$2.1%, $z = 0.1$, $P = 0.889$). The 88.0 $\pm$2.7% of all events performed positively in the UEFA Champions League was not significantly greater than the 86.6 $\pm$3.5% performed in the FIFA World Cup ($z = 0.8$, $P = 0.401$).

Discussion and conclusions

Previous studies of players of different levels have used independent samples (Dunbar and Power, 1997). The current study has used two samples related to the same group of eight players to investigate the quality of play at two different levels of soccer. If international soccer was more demanding than elite club soccer then one would have expected the players to have performed a significantly lower percentage of positive events during international matches. The explanation for the similarity of technical effectiveness comes from the restrictions imposed on national sides. When a national side may have weaker players in certain positions, these players cannot be replaced by better players. Club teams, on the other hand, can recruit players through the transfer market that will strengthen their squads. Bloomfield *et al.* (2005) reported that 38.5% of players in Europe's top four soccer leagues in the 2002–2003 season were foreign players. This ability to sign players from any country in the world means that the top club sides in Europe are comparable with the top national teams in terms of the quality of players.

Team cohesion (Carron, 1982) affects the performance of each individual on the team. A greater level of team cohesion is possible for club sides than for international sides where players train together less frequently. There are alternative indicators of quality of play that could have been used in the current investigation, for example mastery of the ball (Luhtanen *et al.*, 1997), work-rate of players (Bangsbo *et al.*, 1991) and strategy used (James *et al.*, 2002). Mastery of the ball has been investigated for teams rather than individual players (Luhtanen *et al.*, 1997). However, Ali (1988) found that a team that makes attacks with a higher number of passes has a far greater chance of success than those who do so with a lower number of passes. The current investigation offers support for the findings of Hughes *et al.* (1988) that successful soccer teams had more

Table 40.1 Frequency of events performed by players within matches

Indicator	FIFA World Cup		UEFA Champions League	
	Positive	Negative	Positive	Negative
Defence				
Tackle	4.5+3.1	1.8+0.7	5.0+2.4	2.0+1.2
Block	0.0+0.8	0.0+0.1	1.0+1.0	0.0+0.0
Clearance	1.0+1.4	0.2+0.3	1.5+1.9	0.2+0.2
Headed clearance	2.4+4.5	0.2+0.5	2.1+1.8	0.3+0.5
Interception	3.1+2.1	0.0+0.1	3.8+2.5	0.0+0.1
All defence	11.9+8.9	2.2+1.0	13.5+8.6	2.5+1.6
Offence				
Pass	32.1+14.3	3.8+2.2	32.9+15.5	3.6+1.5
Cross	2.0+2.1	0.0+0.1	1.9+2.5	0.0+0.1
Shot	0.9+0.8	0.2+0.2	1.5+1.9	0.2+0.4
Headed pass	2.0+1.2	0.2+0.2	2.3+1.6	0.3+0.4
Headed shot	0.3+0.4	0.0+0.0	0.3+0.4	0.0+0.0
Dribble	6.5+3.3	2.0+1.3	7.7+6.2	1.6+1.2
All offence	43.7+15.6	6.1+3.2	46.5+19.2	5.7+2.5
All events	55.6+17.5	8.3+2.4	60.0+16.8	8.2+2.9

touches of the ball than the unsuccessful teams. Work-rate has been found to be similar between different levels of soccer (O'Donoghue *et al.*, 2001). A more serious reason for not investigating work-rate is that television coverage does not follow individual players during FIFA World Cup and UEFA Champions League matches. Few differences have been found between the strategy adopted by a team when playing in domestic and European club competition (James *et al.*, 2002). Furthermore, a strategy that involves whole teams and their analysis does not lend itself to the comparison of individual player performances in two different tournaments.

The results from this study support the findings of Olsen and Larsen (1997) that the average player performs more attacking actions during the course of a match than defensive ones. This finding could have methodological limitations as important off-the-ball defensive actions are not recorded. Examples of such off-the-ball defensive actions include tracking players, pressurising players, using offside traps and marking opposing players the ball could be passed to. Other limitations of the current investigation are that only eight players were analysed for three matches each in each of the two tournaments. A direct comparison between the winners in the two tournaments is not possible as Italy and Barcelona will not play each other in a competitive match.

In conclusion, it was found that the percentage of events performed positively by a set of eight players was not significantly different between the knockout stages of the UEFA Champions League and the FIFA World Cup. Further research should be undertaken to compare domestic, continental and international soccer performances using a greater number of players represented by a greater number of performances each.

234   Rowlinson and O'Donoghue

References

Ali, A. H., 1988, A statistical analysis of tactical movement patterns in soccer. In *Science and Football I*, edited by Reilly, T., Lees, A., Davids, K. and Murphy, W.J. (London: E&FN Spon), pp. 302–9.

Bangsbo, J., Norregaard, L. and Thorso, F., 1991, Activity profile of professional soccer. *Canadian Journal of Sports Science*, 16, 110–16.

Bloomfield, J.R.. Polman, R.C.J. and O'Donoghue, P.C., 2004a, A statistical comparison of the 2002–03 league tables for Europe's four major soccer leagues. *Journal of Sports Sciences*, 23, 193–4.

Bloomfield, J., Polman, R. and O'Donoghue, P.G., 2004b, Analysis of nationality and international experience of elite players from 4 major European leagues. *Journal of Sports Sciences*, 22, 501–2.

Bloomfield, J., Polman, R. C. J. , Butterly, R. and O'Donoghue P.G., 2005, An analysis of quality and body composition of four European soccer leagues. *Journal of Sports Medicine and Physical Fitness*, 45, 58–67.

Carron, A.V., 1982, Cohesiveness in sport groups: interpretations and considerations. *Journal of Sport Psychology*, 4, 123–38.

Dunbar, G. M. J. and Power, K., 1997, Fitness profiles of English professional and semi-professional soccer players using a battery of field tests. In *Science and Football III*, edited by Reilly, T., Bangsbo, J. and Hughes, M. (London: E&FN Spon), pp. 27–32.

Gerisch, G. and Reichelt, M., 1993, Computer and video aided analysis of football games. In *Science and Football II*, edited by Reilly, T., Clarys, J. and Stibbe, A. (London: E&FN Spon), pp. 167–74.

Hughes, M.D., Robertson, K. and Nicholson, A., 1988, An analysis of the 1986 World Cup of association football. In *Science and Football I*, edited by Reilly, T., Lees, A., Davids, K. and Murphy, W.J. (London: E&FN Spon), pp. 363–7.

Hughes, M., Cooper, S.M. and Nevill, A., 2004, Analysis of notation data: reliability, In *Notational Analysis of Sport*, 2nd edn, edited by Hughes, M. and Franks, I.M., (London: Routledge), pp. 189–204.

James, N., Mellalieu, S. D. and Hollely, C., 2002, Analysis of strategies in soccer as a function of European and domestic competition. *International Journal of Performance Analysis of Sport*, 2(1), 85–103.

Luhtanen, P. H., Korhonen, V.and Ilkka, A., 1997, A new notational analysis system with special reference to the comparison of Brazil and its opponents in the World Cup 1994. In *Science and Football III*, edited by Reilly, T., Bangsbo, J. and Hughes, M. (London: E&FN Spon), pp. 229–33.

O'Donoghue, P.G., Boyd, M., Lawlor, J. and Bleakley, E.W., 2001, Time-motion analysis of elite, semi-professional and amateur soccer competition. *Journal of Human Movement Studies*, 41, 1–12.

Olsen, E. and Larsen, O., 1997, Use of match analysis by coaches. In *Science and Football III*, edited by Reilly, T., Bangsbo, J. and Hughes, M. (London: E&FN Spon), pp. 209–20.

Vaeyens, R. Coutts, A. and Philippaerts, R.M., 2005, Evaluation of the under 21 soccer rule: do young adult soccer players benefit? *Journal of Sports Sciences*, 23, 1003–12.

Wells, J., O'Donoghue, P. G. and Hughes, M., 2004, The need to use representative player data from multiple matches in performance analysis, In *Performance Analysis of Sport VI*, edited by O'Donoghue, P.G. and Hughes, M. (Cardiff: CPA Press, UWIC), pp. 241–4.

41 Analysis of goals scored in the 2006 World Cup

M.F. Acar,[1] B.Yapicioglu,[1] N.Arikan,[2]
S.Yalcin,[1] N. Ates[1] and M. Ergun[1]

[1] School of Physical Education and Sports, Ege University of Izmir, Turkey;
[2] Notational Analysis of Vestel Manisaspor F.C. Manisa, Turkey

Introduction

Football is a branch of sports watched by a wide range of spectators today'. The rapid advance of technological and scientific studies, and the sport reaching a wide range of locations means a large number of people have an interest in this area (Yapicioglu, 2002). Soccer is not only a game, but a professional sport, the object of scientific research, an exciting spectacle and a commercial activity (Ali, 1988).

Football is the world's favourite sport, played by over 240 million players in 1.4 million teams and in 300,000 clubs across the world. Every four years, the spotlight of world attention is on the month-long FIFA World Cup, when billions of people in more than 200 countries around the world tune in to watch arguably the biggest show on earth. The World Cup is the greatest prize in association football. The soccer World Cup provides an opportunity to examine the best teams and players in the world. In addition to the physiological, psychological and anthropometric research of recent years, the analysis of the performance of football players in the field in terms of techniques and tactics has become popular.

Notational analysis is utilized in many sports and is viewed as an important process which allows coaches to collect objective information to provide feedback on performance (Franks, 1997). Day-by-day, the importance of analysis in football is increasingly recognized. During a match approximately 1000 changes of activity take place – a change of activity every 5.65s (Reilly, 1996). One of the most important aspects of the coaching process is the analysis of individual and team performance (Ali, 1988) and match analysis provides a means of quantifying some performance variables.

The purpose of this research is to analyze the goals scored in the World Cup in Germany in 2006. Another aim is to compare observations with previous World Cup results.

Methods

Altogether there were 64 matches in the 2006 FIFA World Cup. All of these matches were recorded through the medium of a DVD recorder. Whilst the teams scored goals in 57 matches, 7 of these matches ended without any score. The analysis of the goals scored and their download onto a computer were achieved using the Muna Match Analysis program. All goals were analysed using DVD players which had stop, slow and fast-forward functions and use of a special computer program. The results were interpreted by taking the mathematical averages of the data acquired and comparing these with the averages from the previous World Cups.

The following criteria were taken into consideration during the analysis of the goals:

1   which part of the body was used to score the goal score;
2   from which position the goal was scored;
3   the area in which the goal was scored (inside/outside the penalty area);
4   when the goals were scored;
5   the distribution of the goals during the ;
6   the number of passes before the goal;
7   the period of the goal attacks (how long the goal attacks lasted);
8   the distribution of the players scoring goals according to the parts of the pitch.

Results

In all, 147 goals were scored in all of the 64 matches in 2006 FIFA World Cup. Only in 7 of these matches were no goals scored. The goal average per match was 2.29.

While 80 per cent of the goals were scored using the foot, 20 per cent were headed (Figure 41.11). In all, 72 per cent of the goals scored by kicking were from right-foot kicks (85); 28 per cent of them were from left-foot (33) kicks.

Of the 147 goals (92), 63 per cent were from open play. Altogether, 37 per cent (55) of goals were scored after a set play, mainly following free kicks (Figure 41.2).

Of 134 goals scored, 79 per cent were from kicks made within the penalty area.

When the goals scored were analysed according to time in the game, the period in which most goals were scored in 76th–90th minutes of play (see Table 41.1). This figure accounts for 24 per cent (35) for all goals scored.

Of the 136 goals scored, 93 per cent were within the normal period of the match. Only 7 per cent (11 goals) of goals were recorded in extra time (Figure 41.4).

When the number of passes completed prior to a goal were analysed, 54 per cent (79 goals) of the goals were after one to four passes and 29 per cent (42

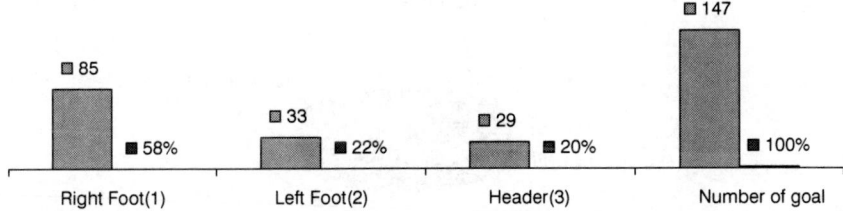

Figure 41.1 Goals scored using different parts of the body

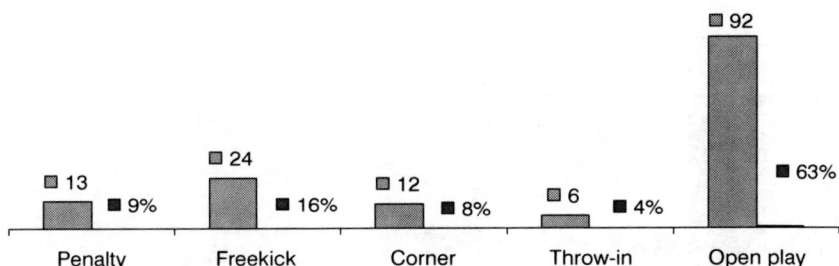

Figure 41.2 Phases of play leading to a goal

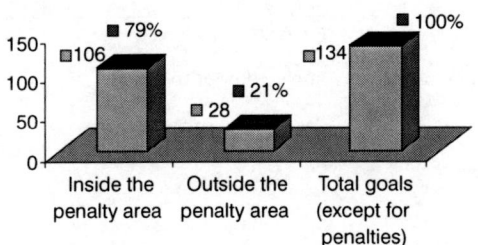

Figure 41.3 Place from what the goal was scored (except for the penalty)

Table 41.1 Match distribution of goals by 15 min periods

Time	Number	%
0–15 min.	23	16
16–30 min.	24	16
31–45 min.	20	14
46–60 min.	22	15
61–75 min.	12	8
76–90 min.	35	24
91+	11	7
Total	147	100

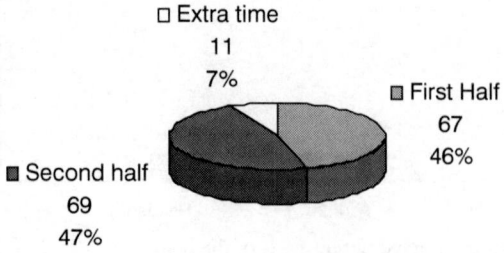

Figure 41.4 Distribution of the periods of play in which goals were scored

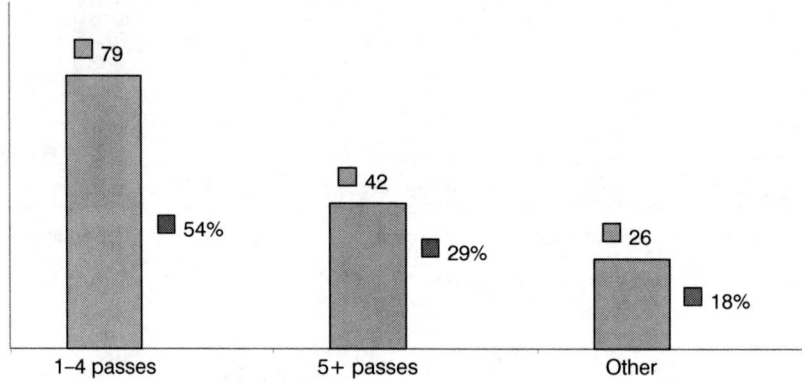

Figure 41.5 The number of passes completed prior to a goal

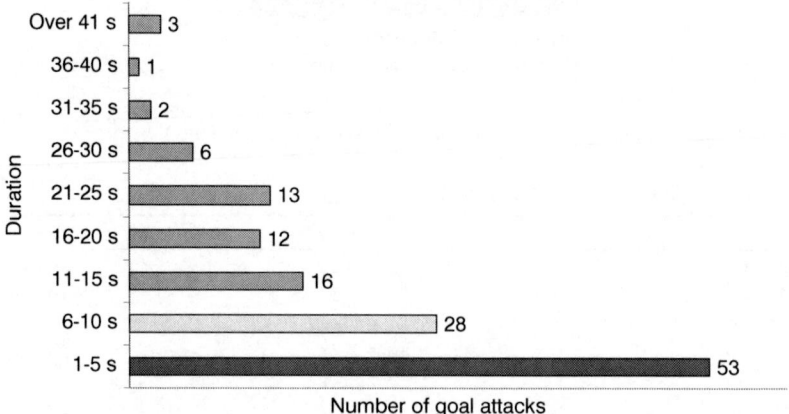

Figure 41.6 The duration of goal attacks

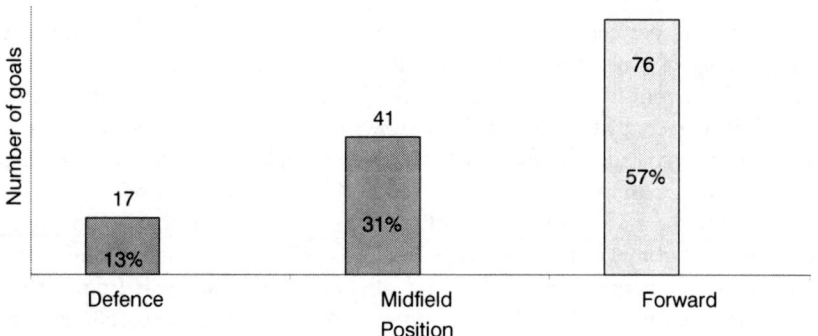

Figure 41.7 The distribution of the players scoring goals according to playing position

goals) were after five passes or more. The part 'other' in Figure 41.5, includes free kicks, penalties, passes from an opponent and own goals.

When the goals scored from the penalty are excluded, 61 per cent (81 goals) of 134 goals were scored within 10 seconds (Figure 41.6).

With regard to the position of the players and goals scored except for penalty kicks, 57 per cent of 134 goals (76 goals) were scored by forward players (Figure 41.7).

Discussion

In the 2006 FIFA World Cup in Germany 64 matches were played. While spectators watched goals being scored in 57 of these matches, 7 were completed without a goal. The average number of goals per match was 2.29. When compared with the previous World Cups – in 2002 Korea–Japan, this percentage was 2.52; in France '98 it was 2.67; in the USA '94 it was 2.71. This World Cup had the lowest value, except for Italy'90.

Altogether, 80 per cent (118 goals) of 148 goals were kicked, 72 per cent (85 goals) were scored with the right foot; 28 per cent (33 goals) were scored by left foot. In the previous studies, the average of goals achieved by the right foot in the 2002 World Cup was 44.1 per cent. Again in the previous World Cups, for instance, in Italy '90, 87 of 115 goals were scored kicked (75.6 per cent), 28 (24.3 per cent) headed. In Mexico '86, 113 of 132 goals (85.6 per cent) were kicked and 19 of them (14.4 per cent) were scored with headers.

In view of this information, more goals were scored by means of the foot than the head in the 2006 World Cup. The fact that the goals scored by headers (29 goals) remained at a percentage of 20 per cent may be due to the the midfield players not coming from the sides (wings), the awkwardness of the forward players or good defenders and the superior air-dominance of the goal-keepers.

When having a look at the development of goals, it was noted that 92 goals (63 per cent) were the result of mature attacks – in open play. The percentage of the goals as a consequence of set play such as corner, penalty, free-kick and throw-in was 37 per cent (55 goals). Data on the previous World Cups indicate the percentage of goals occurring as a result of set plays was 29 per cent in Korea–Japan, 24.6 per cent in France, 32.2 per cent in Italy '90, 27.3 per cent in Mexico '86, and 26 per cent in Spain '82. This shows that in previous tournaments, a majority of the goals in the form of back-up were realized as a result of mature attacks, however, an increase was observed in the scores from set plays.

Except for the 13 penalties, the other 79 per cent of 134 goals (106 goals) was completed from within the penalty area, 21 per cent (28 goals) of goals were from outside the penalty area. While the percentage of kicks made from within the penalty area in the 2002 World Cup was 87 per cent, this percentage was 99.6 per cent in France '98. In this World Cup, contrary to the others, goals from outside the penalty area were found to have increased.

When the distribution of the goals according to the halves was analysed, the numbers of goals scored in the 1st and 2nd halves of the match are close to each other. The teams scored 46 per cent (67 goals) of the goals in the first half and 47 per cent (69 goals) in the second half. The goal percentage in extra time, was 7 per cent (11 goals). In the 2002 World Cup, the teams scored more goals (55.4 per cent; 89 goals) in the second half of the match.

Considering the matches in 15 minute periods intervals, just as in the other World Cups, the last 15 minutes of matches were the period in which most goals are scored. A majority of the goals recorded (24 per cent, 35 goals) during the 75th–90th minutes can be considered as being due to factors such as lack of concentration and differences in conditioning levels.

Another criterion analysed was the number of passes prior to the kick at goal. Of the goals scored, 54 per cent (79 goals) were after one to four passes. This finding has been confirmed by several others analysing the games of different FIFA World Cup finals (Hughes *et al.*, 1988; Franks *et al.*, 1990). The percentage of goals after 5 passes or more was 29 per cent (42 goals).

Penalty goals, pass from an opponent and own goals are grouped as 'other' and accounted for 18 per cent (26 goals) of the goals. The percentage of goals after one to four passes in the previous World Cups are: 44 per cent in 2002, 29.8 per cent in France '98, 80 per cent in the USA '94, 84 per cent in Italy '90, 61.7 per cent in Mexico '86 and 79 per cent in Spain '82.

Hughes (1990) showed that 87 per cent of the goals recorded in 109 top level matches were scored after 5 passes or fewer. Reep and Benjamin (1968) also reported that 80 per cent of the goals scored in 3213 matches that were played between 1953–1968 were after three passes or fewer. Olsen (1988) reported goal-scoring strategies in the World Cup in Mexico 1986. He found that when penalties were ignored, only about 20 per cent of the goals were preceded by 5 or more passes, most of the goals being scored after two passes or less.

When the attack periods resulting in goals are analyzed, 61 per cent of 134 goals (81 goals) were scored within 1–10 s (except for the penalty). Playing fast and being well organized in attacking positions yields more scoring opportunities. Guia *et al.* (2003) showed the importance of a decreased number of contacts with the ball, increased space, decreasing the number of players needed in game play and increased execution time. The outcome that can be predicted from the 2006 World Cup's number of passes prior to goals and the periods of goal attacks examined above is that teams using fewer passes and getting organized more quickly scored more goals.

When looking at the scoring players' position on the pitch, except for penalty kicks, 57 per cent (76 goals) of 134 goals were scored by forward players, 31 per cent (41 goals) by mid-field players and 13 per cent (17 goals) by defenders. The efficiency of the mid-field and defenders, forwards close to the goal, and improving final kicking skills are requirements of contemporary soccer. The following conclusions about 2006 FIFA World Cup can be drawn from this study:

- 80 per cent of goals were kicked; 85 per cent of these goals by the right foot.
- 63 per cent of goals were from open play.
- 79 per cent of the goals (except for penalty kicks) were from inside the penalty area.
- 24 per cent were scored in the 76th–90th minutes.
- 93 per cent were scored done within 90 minutes i.e. during normal time.
- 54 per cent of goals were after up to 4 passes.
- 61 per cent of 134 goals, except for penalties, were scored within up to 10 seconds.
- Except for penalties and goals scored by forwards, 31 per cent of the goals were scored by midfield players and 13 per cent were by defenders.

References

Ali, A. H., 1988, A statistical analysis of tactical movement patterns in soccer. In; *Science and Football*, edited by Reilly, T., Lees, A., Davids, K. and Murphy, W.J., (London: E&FN Spon), pp. 302–8.

Franks, I.M., 1997, Use of feedback by coaches and players. In *Science and Football III*, edited by Reilly, T., Bangsbo, J. and Hughes, M. (London. E&FN Spon), pp. 267–8.

Franks, I.M., Partridge, D. and Nagelkerke, P., 1990, *World Cup 90: A Computer Assisted Technical Analysis of Team Performance*, Technical Report for the Canadian Soccer Association, (Vancouver: University of British Columbia).

Guia, N., Ferreira, N. and Peixoto, C., 2003, The efficiency of football offensive process. Increase technical performance. In *5th World Congress Book Of Abstracts*, (Madrid: Editorial Gymnos), pp. 50– 1.

Hughes, C., 1990, *The Winning Formula*, (London: Collins).

Hughes, M., Robertson, K. and Nicholson, A., 1988, Comparison of patterns of play of successful and unsuccessful teams in the 1986 World Cup soccer. In *Science and Football*, edited by Reilly, T. Lees, A., Davids, K. and Murphy, W.J. (London: E&FN Spon), pp. 363–7

Olsen, E., 1988, An analysis of goal scoring strategies in the World Championship in Mexico, 1986. In *Science and Football*, edited by Reilly, T., Lees, A., Davids K. and Murphy, W.J. (London: E&FN Spon), pp. 373–6.

Reep, C. and Benjamin, B., 1968, Skill and chance in association football, *Journal of the Royal Statistical Society*, Series A, 131, 581–5

Reilly, T., 1996, *Science and Soccer*. (London: E&FN Spon).

Yapicioglu, B., 2002, Examination of the Latin and European Schools with the help of computerized match analysis programmes in the FIFA World Cup. Ege University BESYO Master's thesis, Izmir, Turkey.

Part VI
Environmental physiology

42 Thermoregulatory response to base-layer garments during intermittent treadmill exercise

Bryan C. Roberts, Tom Waller and Mike P. Caine

Wolfson School of Mechanical and Manufacturing Engineering, Loughborough University, UK

Introduction

The use of base-layer garments in team sports has become widespread in recent years. Different types of garments purport to afford distinct functional properties to the wearer. However, to date the thermoregulatory effects and moisture management properties have yet to be systematically studied. The thermoregulatory response to a 'base-layer hot' and 'base-layer cold' garment was assessed using an intermittent treadmill protocol and compared to wearing a cotton T-shirt and when bare-chested. The base-layer hot garment purports to keep the wearer comfortably cool during exercise and is typically used in hot conditions, whereas the base-layer cold garment aims to keep the wearer comfortably warm during exercise, and is typically used in cold conditions. Both garments claim to reduce moisture retention as a result of good wicking properties. The aim of the study was to characterise the thermophysical differences between garments typically worn on the field of play under controlled repeatable conditions.

Methods

Four physically active males participated (age 26 years ±2, height 1.86 m±0.06, and mass 85 kg ±10.7; mean ±SD). The participants visited the laboratory on four occasions separated by 48 hours. An overnight fast was initiated prior to the test, furthermore caffeine and alcohol were avoided for at least 12 hours prior to exercise. Participants were instructed to drink 500 ml of water before retiring to bed and 500 ml following the first urination on waking. No further fluids were consumed until after testing had taken place. Participants refrained from using antiperspirants and were recently showered. Participants refrained from strenuous exercise for at least 12 hours prior to the tests. All testing was completed at the same time of day. During testing participants wore either a 100% cotton T-shirt (Canterbury of NZ), a base-layer hot garment (Canterbury of NZ; 85% polyester, 15% elastane), a base-layer cold garment (Canterbury of NZ; 65% nylon, 21%

polyester, 14% lycra) or exercised bare-chested. Garments were chosen according to the manufacturer's sizing charts and the order of testing was randomised. Mean skin temperatures were recorded pre-acclimatisation (PrA), post-acclimatisation (PoA), mid-exercise (ME), and at the end of exercise (EE) for the unclothed torso (back and front,) using an infra-red imaging camera (FLIR Systems, Thermovision Series A20). A fan was used to create a fixed airflow (circa $3 \, m \cdot s^{-1}$) across the front of the torso during active portions of the trial only i.e. no airflow was present during the infra-red image capture. Ambient humidity and temperature were recorded every 5 minutes using a humidity and temperature meter (Vaisala HMI 31). A rectal probe was inserted 10 cm beyond the anal sphincter as indicated by a gauze bung (Meir et al., 1994) and rectal temperature logged, as an indicator of core temperature, every 30 seconds (Grant Squirrel Logger). The mass of the trial garment, towel, shoes, shorts, and underwear was established before and immediately after testing using precision scales (Mettler Toledo SB8001) to quantify garment fluid retention during exercise.

After a 10-minute preparation period (putting on kit and inserting probe) in the laboratory, the participant assumed a standing position upon the rails of a treadmill, and the first infra-red image was recorded (image PoA). The participant then donned one of the three garments (or remained without a garment in the bare-chested trial) and stood motionless, in the absence of airflow, for a further 10-minute acclimatisation period. At the end of this period a second infra-red image was taken (image PrA). A treadmill protocol based on Drust et al. (2000) was then administered for a total period of 47 minutes 10 seconds, depicted in Figure 42.1. The protocol of Drust et al. (2000) was designed to be consistent with the aerobic demands of soccer and thus included walking, jogging and cruising phases at 6, 12 and 15 km·h⁻¹ respectively.

At the end of the first 23-minute exercise period a 70-second rest was implemented followed by a second bout of identical exercise. Two further infra-red images were taken, one 30 seconds into the 70-second rest period (image ME) and another at the end of exercise (image EE). In total four images were obtained, in all cases moisture was removed from the skin using a towel, immediately prior to the recording of the images. All image data were transferred to infra-red imaging software (ThermaCAM Researcher Pro 2.8) for analysis. Each infra-red image was analysed using a constant area polygon positioned over the torso/back area equivalent to the area covered by the garment. The mean, maximum and minimum temperatures of this area were recorded for each capture. Data are presented as mean ±SD unless otherwise stated. Analysis was by repeated-measures t-test. Differences between and within trials were considered significant where $P < 0.05$.

Results

Testing was completed in 20.5°C ±0.1 (ambient temperature) and 52.7% ±2.1 (ambient humidity). Results in Table 42.1 show that mean skin temperature values across all garment trials are similar post-acclimatisation. At both the mid- and end-exercise points mean skin temperature values were lowest when bare-chested

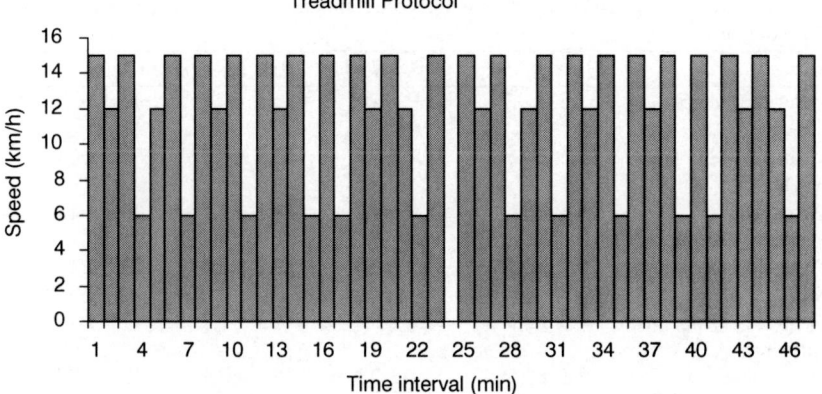

Figure 42.1 Graphical representation of the treadmill protocol

and highest when wearing cotton. Mean skin temperature values when wearing the base-layer hot garment fell between that of the bare-chested and base-layer cold trials at both the mid- and end-exercise points. However, when wearing the base-layer cold garment, mean skin temperature values were between that of the base-layer hot and cotton trial at the mid-exercise point but were similar to cotton at the end-exercise point.

The mean, maximum and minimum mean skin temperatures for front and back images recorded at the end-exercise point (EE) are shown in Table 42.2 for all trials. Both the front and back mean skin temperature values showed a similar trend to the overall torso values in Table 42.1. The bare-chested trial showed the lowest values followed by the base-layer hot trial and both the base-layer cold and cotton trials showed similar results. Maximum skin temperature values were lowest when bare-chested but similar when wearing any of the garments. Minimum skin temperature values were similar on the front of the torso but increased from (starting from the lowest and moving to the highest) bare-chested, base-layer hot, base-layer cold to cotton on the back of the torso.

For the front of torso images, the bare-chested trial demonstrated the greatest temperature reduction during exercise at $-3.4 \pm 1.0°C$. The temperature reductions across the other garment trials were $-2.9 \pm 0.7°C$, $-2.4 \pm 1.5°C$, $-2.3 \pm 1.4°C$ for base-layer hot, base-layer cold, and cotton trials, respectively. Similarly for the back of torso images, the bare-chested trial again demonstrated the greatest temperature reduction during exercise at $-2.7 \pm 0.7°C$. The temperature reductions across the other garment trials were $-1.8 \pm 0.7°C$, $-1.3 \pm 0.9°C$, $-1.5 \pm 1.1°C$ for base-layer hot, base-layer cold, and cotton trials, respectively.

Mean core temperature values increased significantly due to exercise (bare-chested $P<0.005$; wearing a garment $P<0.001$). However mean, maximum and minimum core temperature values did not vary significantly between trials. Kit (including garment) mass increased in all trials due to moisture retention. Garment

Table 42.1 Mean (°C) ±SD skin (torso) and core temperatures for each garment; mean of all participants

	Bare-chested	Base-layer hot	Base-layer cold	Cotton
Mean skin temperature (PrA)	31.5 ±0.7	31.0 ±0.2	31.1 ±1.0	30.9 ±0.9
Mean skin temperature (PoA)	31.5 ±0.6	31.4 ±0.7	31.5 ±0.7	31.5 ±0.6
Mean skin temptemperature (ME)	28.6 ±0.8	28.9 ±1.0	29.1 ±1.1	29.4 ±1.2
Mean skin temperature (EE)	28.7 ±0.7	29.3 ±0.3	29.7 ±1.0	29.7 ±1.0
Mean skin temperature difference (EE-PoA)	−2.8 ±0.5	−2.1 ±0.4	−1.8 ±1.2	−1.9 ±1.2
Maximum skin temperature (EE)	32.1 ±0.5	33.1 ±0.3	33.2 ±0.4	32.7 ±0.8
Minimum skin temperature (EE)	22.8 ±2.3	23.4 ±2.0	23.7 ±2.0	25.0 ±3.6
Mean core temperature (PoA to EE)	37.7 ±0.1	37.7 ±0.1	37.8 ±0.1	37.9 ±0.3
Mean core temperature difference (Max-Min)	1.5 ±0.3	1.5 ±0.2	1.4 ±0.2	1.5 ±0.1

mass gain due to moisture retention post-exercise was 0.029 kg ±0.021 kg, 0.042 ±0.026 kg, and 0.052 ±0.037 kg for base-layer hot, base-layer cold, and cotton trials respectively. Total mean kit (including garment) moisture uptake was 0.042 kg ±0.015 kg, 0.061 ±0.029 kg, 0.076 ±0.026 kg, and 0.082 ±0.049 kg for bare-chested, base-layer hot, base-layer cold and cotton trials, respectively.

Discussion

The infra-red data suggest that the functionality of the various garments differs, with the bare-chested and base-layer hot garment demonstrating lower mean skin temperatures than the base-layer cold and cotton garments. Mean maximum skin temperature values were lowest when bare-chested, but similar between the garment trials post-exercise. Mean minimum skin temperature values were lowest when bare-chested, followed by the base-layer hot trial, then the base-layer cold trial and highest when wearing cotton. This base temperature increase may explain the overall increase in mean skin temperature values shown across all trials in Table 42.1. Differences in skin temperatures due to air-flow can be seen between front and back images in Table 42.2. Front torso skin temperature values were lower than back torso images since forced convection by air flow is known to increase the removal of heat from the body to the atmosphere (Houdas and Ring, 1982).

A low mean skin temperature suggests a higher rate of total heat transfer from the core to the shell (skin) providing the surface area of heat transfer and core-to-skin transfer coefficient remains constant (Houdas and Ring, 1982). A higher rate of heat transfer allows for a more efficient thermoregulatory mechanism. Should

Table 42.2 Maximum and minimum (°C) ±SD skin temperature for each garment at the end-exercise point (EE); mean of all participants.

	Bare-chested	Base-layer hot	Base-layer cold	Cotton
Mean front skin temperature	28.2 ±1.6	28.7 ±0.6	29.2 ±1.4	29.4 ±1.2
Mean back skin temperature	28.7 ±0.8	29.6 ±0.2	30.2 ±0.7	30.0 ±0.9
Maximum front skin temperature	32.1 ±0.5	33.0 ±0.3	33.0 ±0.7	33.0 ±0.8
Maximum back skin temperature	32.0 ±1.1	33.3 ±0.3	33.3 ±0.5	32.7 ±0.9
Minimum front skin temperature	23.0 ±2.8	23.1 ±1.8	22.9 ±2.2	23.7 ±1.8
Minimum back skin temperature	22.8 ±2.0	23.4 ±1.8	23.7 ±1.2	24.5 ±2.2

the rate of heat transfer decrease it is likely that core temperature would increase more rapidly. Mean, maximum and minimum core temperature values did not vary significantly between trials during exercise. Meir *et al.* (1994) found no significant differences between peak core temperatures when comparing three different rugby league garments and bare-chested.

Pre-acclimatisation mean skin temperature values vary due to ambient conditions and clothing worn outside the laboratory. A 10-minute 'acclimatisation' period is essential in order to stabilise mean skin temperature prior to exercise (Houdas and Ring, 1982). During exercise the bare-chested condition is most effective at maintaining the lowest skin temperatures. This reflects the fact that there are no added layers of insulation or any barriers to the evaporation of moisture. Ideally a 'cooling' garment should offer little resistance to heat evaporation and in addition should disperse moisture over its entire surface to improve the efficiency of moisture evaporation. A fabric with high wicking capabilities will help in this respect by moving the moisture to its outer surface and dispersing it over the surface area of the garment. The base-layer hot garment performs closest to that of exposed skin and therefore is successful in maintaining a relatively low skin temperature. This may be due in part to its being a more lightweight garment, the inclusion of high wicking fabric and more interstices (gaps between yarns) due to a smaller fibre diameter. The base-layer cold and cotton garments performed similarly in that a higher skin temperature was maintained throughout the trials; however, the base-layer cold garment retained less moisture than the cotton garment. This result is unsurprising given that the base-layer cold garment is constructed from a high wicking fabric, whilst cotton has a higher absorbency and moisture regain compared to polyester and nylon. Cotton fibres are also known to swell when wet, reducing moisture vapour transfer.

The mean garment moisture uptake values recorded, including kit weight, show that cotton retained the most moisture, the base-layer hot garment retained least moisture but the difference between pre-trial and post-trial kit mass was least whilst running bare-chested. The difference in moisture retention of 0.02 kg observed here between garments has the potential to reduce performance as a result of increased energy expenditure during exercise.

Conclusions

This study has provided insight in to the subtle differences afforded by alternative fabric options on base-layer garments. The base-layer hot product successfully permits the body to remain cool during the exercise period to a level close to bare-chested. The base-layer cold product successfully maintains a higher skin temperature whilst permitting moisture transfer and evaporation. Further trials are necessary to identify the performance of these garments at different ambient temperatures. Further studies ought to consider factors such as participant's sweat rate and perceived comfort. A larger study population is necessary if elicitation of more subtle differences between the garments is sought.

In conclusion, mean skin temperature is affected by a person's choice of garment during intermittent exercise. Synthetic base-layer garments are more effective than cotton garments at actively reducing moisture retention, whilst maintaining desired skin temperature values.

Acknowledgements

The authors wish to acknowledge the financial support of Canterbury of New Zealand, the manufacturers of the garments used in this study.

References

Drust, B., Reilly, T. and Cable, N.T., 2000, Physiological responses to laboratory-based soccer-specific intermittent and continuous exercise. *Journal of Sports Sciences*, 18, 885–92.

Houdas, Y. and Ring, E.F.J., 1982, *Human Body Temperature: Its Measurement and Regulation.* (New York: Plenum Press).

Meir, R.A., Lowdon, B.J. and Davie, A.J., 1994, The effect of jersey type on thermoregulatory responses during exercise in a warm humid environment. *The Australian Journal of Science and Medicine in Sport*, 26(1/2), 25–31.

43 The impact of pre-cooling on soccer-specific exercise performed in the heat

N.D. Clarke, B. Drust, D.P.M. MacLaren and T. Reilly

Research Institute for Sport and Exercise Sciences, Liverpool John Moores University, UK

Introduction

A likely cause of fatigue when soccer is played in hot conditions is hyperthermia, when core temperature reaches a critical value (Nielsen *et al.*, 1993). Various strategies have been implemented to reduce thermoregulatory strain during exercise. The principle of pre-cooling is that the reduction in core body temperature prior to performing exercise increases the margin for metabolic heat production and the time before reaching a critical limiting temperature when a given exercise intensity can no longer be maintained (Reilly *et al.*, 2006). Pre-cooling can improve endurance exercise (Arngrimsson *et al.*, 2004) but there is limited research using high-intensity exercise (Marsh and Sleivert, 1999; Sleivert *et al.*, 2001). Pre-cooling has also been used as a technique prior to performing soccer-specific exercise (Drust *et al.*, 2000a), although pre-cooling was only performed under 'normal' laboratory conditions (20.5°C, 68.3% relative humidity). Therefore, pre-cooling may be of benefit during 90 min of soccer-specific exercise in the heat when core temperature would be expected to rise at a faster rate and reach a higher value. The present aim was to examine the effect of pre-cooling on the metabolic responses to soccer-specific exercise and on a measure of performance.

Methods

Twelve male university soccer players (mean age: 25 ±0.7 years; mass: 73.75 ±2.6 kg; height: 1.80 ±0.02 m; $\dot{V}O_{2max}$: 61.3 ±1.4 ml·kg^{-1}·min^{-1}) performed a soccer-specific protocol, which was a modified version of the one designed by Drust *et al.* (2000b) on two occasions in an environmental chamber (30.5°C and 42.2% r.h.). During the sessions 224 ±7 ml of flavoured water was consumed at 0, 15, 30, 45, 60 and 75 min of exercise. On one occasion the subjects underwent a period of pre-cooling, which involved the subject wearing a cooling vest (Cool Vest, Jackson Technical Solutions Ltd, Kent, UK) for 60 min prior to exercise, and again during the half-time interval. All of the trials were performed in a counter-balanced fashion.

During the soccer-specific protocol core temperature and heart rate were measured continuously using a heat-sensitive telemetry pill (CorTemp, HQ Inc., Florida, USA) and short-range radio telemetry (Polar S610i, Polar Electro, Kempele, Finland), respectively. The soccer-specific protocol was followed by a test of exercise capacity (Cunningham and Faulkner, 1969). Analysis of data was conducted using one-way ANOVAs with repeated measures except for performance, which was analysed using a Wilcoxon test. All results are reported as the mean ± the standard error of the mean (SEM) and a level of $P<0.05$ was considered statistically significant.

Results

There was a significant trial effect on core temperature ($F_{1,11} = 4.98$; $P<0.05$, Figure 43.1). Pre-cooling significantly reduced core temperature from 37.2 ±0.1°C to 36.6 ±0.1°C which as a consequence was significantly lower prior to the start of exercise compared to no pre-cooling. This trend remained during the first 15 min of exercise and during block 3 (31–45 min) core temperature was significantly lowered when pre-cooling was employed. There were no differences in the second half ($P>0.05$) although mean core temperature was lower during the pre-cooling trial (with pre-cooling: 38.2 ±0.1°C, without pre-cooling: 38.4 ±0.1°C; $P = 0.047$). A significant effect of time was observed ($F_{2,18} = 151.93$; $P<0.05$); core temperature increased significantly with each 15-min block of the soccer-specific protocol and decreased significantly during half-time ($P<0.05$).

Heart rate (Table 43.1) was significantly lower following pre-cooling during the first 15 min of each half. In addition, mean heart rate throughout the protocol was significantly lowered as a result of pre-cooling (with and without pre-cooling: 158 ±3 and 164 ±3 beats·min^{-1} respectively; $P = 0.030$). Heart rate increased significantly ($F_{3,31} = 517.66$; $P<0.05$) between each 15–min block of the soccer-specific protocol and decreased significantly during the half-time interval.

Following the soccer-specific protocol, there was a significant treatment effect on exercise capacity during the Cunningham and Faulkner test. Run time to exhaustion was significantly longer following pre-cooling (70.1 ±7.7 s) compared to the reference trial (57.1 ±5.3 s) ($P<0.05$).

Discussion

In the present study, a 60-min period of pre-cooling significantly reduced core temperature and heart rate and significantly improved exercise capacity following 90 min of soccer-specific exercise in the heat. Pre-cooling prior to soccer-specific exercise significantly reduced core temperature and heart rate and significantly enhanced exercise capacity measured by a high-intensity run to exhaustion.

Pre-cooling has previously been shown not to impact on muscle metabolism (Booth et al., 2001). Therefore it is unlikely that the increased exercise capacity observed in the present study and exercise performance in previous studies (Booth et al., 1997) can be explained on the basis of altered muscle metabolism.

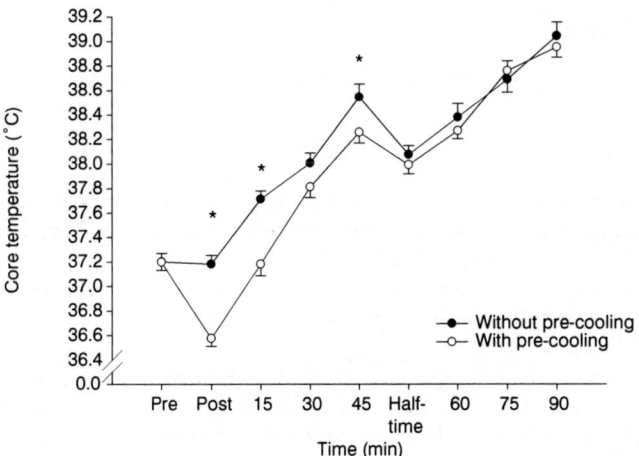

Figure 43.1 Core temperature during the soccer-specific protocol with and without pre-cooling; Pre: before pre-cooling; Post: after pre-cooling; * P<0.05

Table 43.1 Heart rate during the soccer-specific protocol with and without pre-cooling; *P<0.05

	Heart rate (beats.min⁻¹)					
	1–15 min	*16–30 min*	*31–45 min*	*46–60 min*	*61–75 min*	*76–90 min*
Without pre-cooling	152±3	162±3	166±3	163±2	168±3	172±3
With pre-cooling	144±2*	157±3	160±3	157±3*	163±3	168±3

Thus far the metabolic responses to exercise after pre-cooling have not been extensively investigated. It has been proposed that pre-cooling may enhance exercise performance by reducing the metabolic perturbation often observed with increased core and muscle temperatures (Marino, 2002). However, the reduced core temperature associated with pre-cooling allows for a greater heat storage before core temperature reaches a level high enough to stimulate heat dissipation (Drust *et al.*, 2000a), thereby reducing the physiological strain. This effect is highlighted in the present study in the lowered mean heart rate during the protocol following pre-cooling.

In conclusion a period of pre-cooling prior to soccer-specific exercise significantly reduced core temperature and heart rate during exercise. In addition, pre-cooling significantly enhanced exercise performance as indicated by a longer time to exhaustion during the high-intensity running test completed following the soccer-specific exercise. The mechanism for this improvement remains to be identified.

Acknowledgements

GlaxoSmithKline is acknowledged for its contribution to this study.

References

Arngrimsson, S. A., Petitt, D. S., Stueck, M. G., Jorgensen, D. K. and Cureton, K. J., 2004, Cooling vest worn during active warm-up improves 5-km run performance in the heat. *Journal of Applied Physiology*, 96, 1867–74.

Booth, J., Marino, F. and Ward, J. J., 1997, Improved running performance in hot humid conditions following whole body precooling. *Medicine and Science in Sports and Exercise*, 29, 943–9.

Booth, J., Wilsmore, B. R., Macdonald, A. D., Zeyl, A., McGhee, S., Calvert, D., Marino, F. E., Storlien, L. H. and Taylor, N. A. S., 2001, Whole-body pre-cooling does not alter human muscle metabolism during sub-maximal exercise in the heat. *European Journal of Applied Physiology*, 84, 587–90.

Cunningham, D. A. and Faulkner, J. A., 1969, The effect of training on aerobic and anaerobic metabolism during a short exhaustive run. *Medicine and Science in Sports*, 1, 65–9.

Drust, B., Cable, N. T. and Reilly, T., 2000a, Investigation of the effects of pre-cooling on the physiological responses to soccer-specific intermittent exercise. *European Journal of Applied Physiology*, 81, 11–17.

Drust, B., Reilly, T. and Cable, N. T., 2000b, Physiological responses to laboratory-based soccer-specific intermittent and continuous exercise. *Journal of Sports Sciences*, 18, 885–92.

Marino, F. E., 2002, Methods, advantages, and limitations of body cooling for exercise performance. *British Journal of Sports Medicine*, 36, 89–94.

Marsh, D. and Sleivert, G., 1999, Effect of precooling on high intensity cycling performance. *British Journal of Sports Medicine*, 33, 393–7.

Nielsen, B., Hales, J., Strange, S., Christensen, N., Warberg, J. and Saltin, B., 1993, Human circulatory and thermoregulatory adaptations with heat acclimation and exercise in a hot, dry environment. *Journal of Physiology*, 460, 467–85.

Reilly, T., Drust, B. and Gregson, W., 2006, Thermoregulation in elite athletes. *Current Opinion in Clinical Nutrition and Metabolic Care*, 10, 667–71.

Sleivert, G. G., Cotter, J. D., Roberts, W. S. and Febbraio, M. A., 2001, The influence of whole-body vs. torso pre-cooling on physiological strain and performance of high-intensity exercise in the heat. *Comparative Biochemistry and Physiology a-Molecular and Integrative Physiology*, 128, 657–66.

44 Effect of leg cooling at half-time breaks on performance of soccer-simulated exercise in a hot environment

Mikinobu Yasumatsu,[1] Osamu Miyagi,[2] Jiro Ohashi,[2] Haruhiko Togari,[3] Seidai Nishikawa,[3] Hiroshi Hasegawa,[4] Satoshi Ishizaki[5] and Tamae Yoda[6]

[1] Rikkyo University, Japan; [2] Daito Bunka University, Japan; [3] Heisei International University, Japan; [4] Hiroshima University, Japan; [5] Oyama National College of Technology, Japan; [6] Dokkyo University, Japan

Introduction

Physical performance can be impaired by elevations in core temperature in a hot environment (Kozlowski et al., 1985). It is well known that pre-cooling improves exercise performance due to the reduced physiological strain in hot environment (Quod et al., 2006). Although it has been reported that pre-cooling is of no significant benefit for intermittent exercise (Drust et al., 2000), it is not clear whether performance of intermittent exercise in the second half is affected by body cooling at half-time breaks. One of the reasons for the lack of information on the physiological and metabolic responses of players in soccer is the practical difficulty associated with conducting field studies.

We attempted to design an exercise protocol to simulate the physical demands faced by soccer players during a game (Yasumatsu et al., 2003). The aim of this study was to examine the effect of leg cooling at the middle of half-time breaks for soccer-related performance in a hot environment.

Methods

The soccer-simulated exercise protocol consisted of 90-min activity that incorporated the different exercise intensities observed during game-play (e.g. walking, jogging, sprints, jump, shoot, pass, 1-on-1 plays: Figure 44.1).

This 90-min period was divided into two identical 45 min blocks, separated by a 15-min intermission. Five college soccer players completed two trials on separate days, involving leg cooling by water immersion in about 25°C for 5 min (LC) or no leg cooling (NC) at half-time breaks.

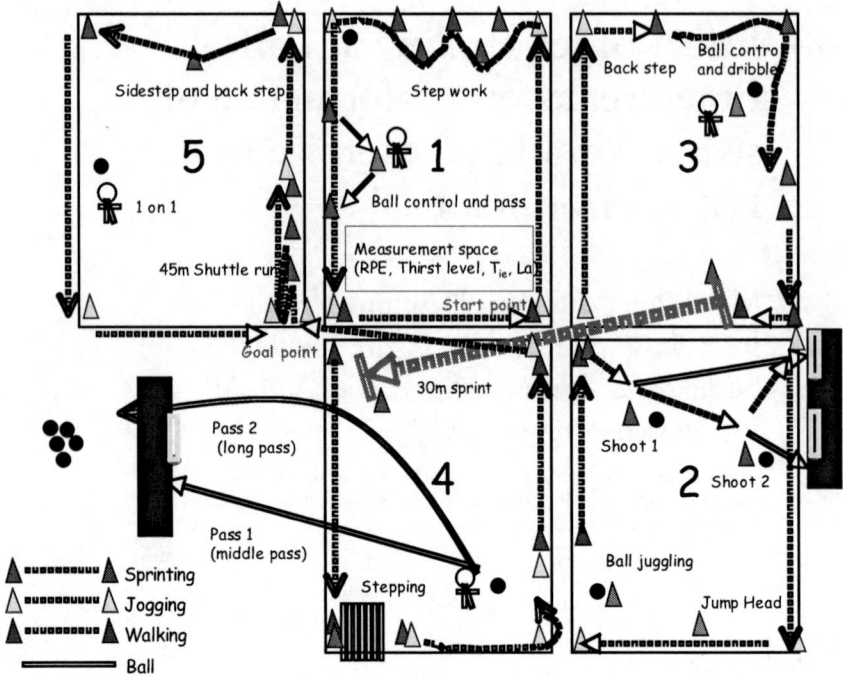

Figure 44.1 Schema of the soccer-simulated exercise

Heart rate was monitored continuously throughout exercise (5 s average). Concentration of blood lactate (La), intra-ear temperature (Tie), ratings of perceived exertion (RPE) and thirst level were measured every 5 minutes. Body water loss was calculated from measurements of body weight pre-exercise and post-exercise. Sweat rate was calculated from body weight loss and volume of water intake.

Performance tests consisted of soccer-simulated exercise protocol every 5 minutes. Exercise performance was evaluated from two shooting skills, two passing skills and ball juggling in 30 s, as technical performance. Furthermore, the times for 30 m sprints and 45 m shuttle runs were recorded as physical performance. The time for the 30 m sprint was measured with infra-red photoelectric cells. The time for shuttle running was measured with a hand stopwatch.

The results are presented as mean ±SE. The results of shooting and passing tests were expressed as the success rate. The results of ball juggling in 30 s were expressed as the number of times. For standardizing physical level, mean values of these first three bouts were taken as the base level. The results for 30 m sprints and shuttle running were expressed as the difference from base level. Statistically significant differences between LC and NC were assessed by two-way ANOVA for repeated measures and localised by a Fisher's Protected LSD post-hoc test.

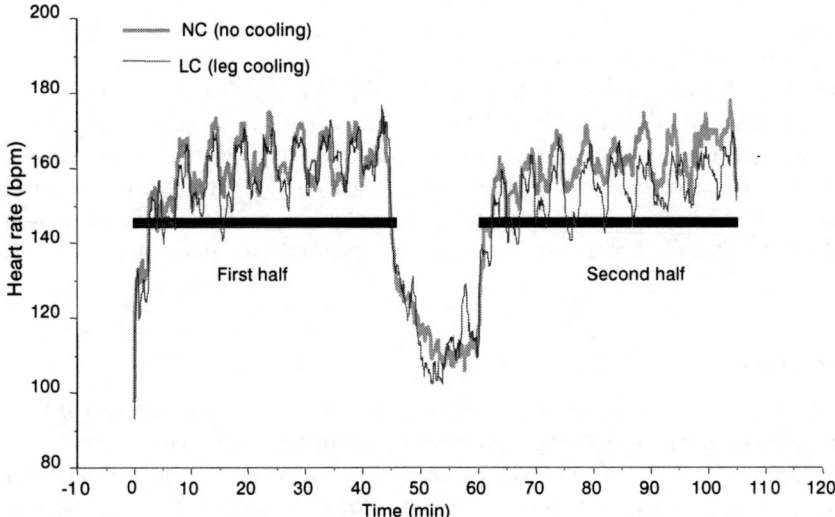

Figure 44.2 Heart rate during soccer-simulated exercise with cooling (LC) and without cooling (NC) during half time

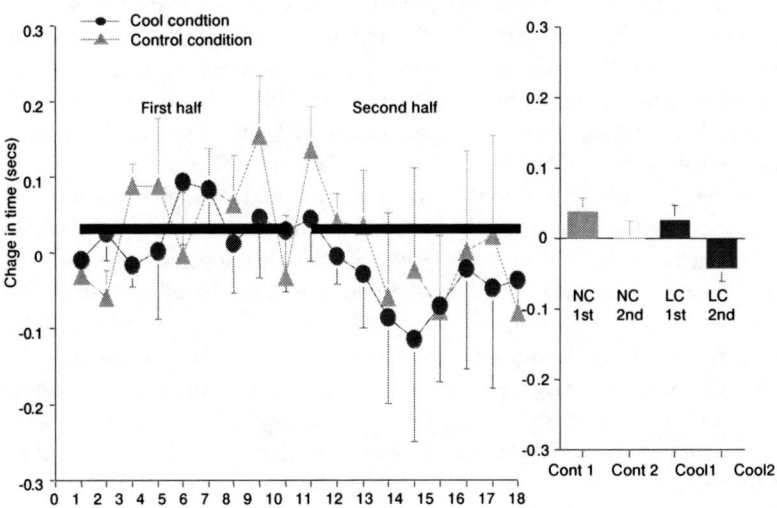

Figure 44.3 Change in seconds on 30 m sprint during soccer-simulated exercise with cooling (LC) and without cooling (NC) during half time.

Results

Environmental conditions were: $32.11 \pm 0.41°C$ wet-bulb globe temperature (WBGT), $37.77 \pm 0.86°C$ air temperature and $40.40 \pm 2.25\%$ relative humidity.

Lactate concentration, Tie, RPE, thirst level, sweat rate and body weight loss were not different between the two trials. Heart rate in the second half was significantly lower in the LC compared with the NC condition (Figure 44.2).

There was no difference in technical performances (shooting, passing and ball juggling) between the two trials. No significant difference was observed between the two trials for time of shuttle running (Figure 44.3). Although performance in the 30 m sprint in the second half (min ±SD) was significantly faster than in the first half (min ±SD) in the LC, there was no significant difference in the NC trial.

Discussion

The main finding of the present study suggests that leg cooling for 5 min at half-time breaks improved sprint performance in severe hot conditions.

Drust *et al.* (2000) concluded that pre-cooling is of no overall significant benefit for intermittent exercise, such as soccer. However, cooling between exercise sessions at half-time breaks in games has not been evaluated. In the LC trial, 30 m sprint performance in the second half was better than in the first half. This result suggests that cooling at half-time breaks is beneficial for intermittent exercise.

In physiological responses, we did not detect significant difference between LC and NC, except for heart rate. Several studies have shown that exercise heart rate for a given workload is reduced following pre-cooling. In the present study, skin temperature on the thigh fell by about 5.0ºC due to water immersion (data not shown). When skin temperature is reduced, it is likely that less blood flow is required for heat dissipation, resulting in an increased central volume for a given exercise intensity after a cooling manoeuvre (Quod *et al.*, 2006).

It has been recently suggested that the ability to produce high rates of power output and to sprint at high velocity is essential to performance in soccer (Cometti *et al.*, 2001). The results of our study suggest that muscle temperature level during half-time breaks is associated with performance in the second half of soccer games.

The physical demands during soccer-simulated exercise, including sprint distance, total distance, HR and La, were in agreement with several previous data related to soccer games (Ekblom, 1986; Ohashi *et al.*, 1988; Bangsbo, 1994). Therefore, it was demonstrated that this soccer-simulated exercise was useful for soccer-related experiments.

Conclusion

The results of this study suggest that leg cooling for only 5 min at half-time breaks reduced cardiorespiratory strain and improved sprint performance in the second half. Therefore, it is recommended that leg cooling should be encouraged at half-time breaks.

References

Bangsbo, J., 1994, *Fitness Training in Football: A Scientific Approach*. (Bagsvaerd: HO+Storm).

Cometti, G., Maffiuletti, N.A., Pousson, M., Chatard, J.-C., Maffulli, N., 2001, Isokinetic strength and anaerobic power of elite, subelite and amateur French soccer players, *International Journal of Sports Medicine*, 22, 45–51.

Drust B., Cable N.T., Reilly, T., 2000, Investigation of the effects of the pre-cooling on the physiological responses to soccer-specific intermittent exercise. *European Journal of Applied Physiology*, 81, 11–17.

Ekblom, B., 1986, Applied physiology of soccer, *Sports Medicine*, 3, 50–60.

Kozlowski, S., Brzezinska, Z. and Kruk, B., 1985, Exercise hyperthermia as a factor limiting physical performance: temperature effect on muscle metabolism. *Journal of Applied Physiology*, 59, 766–73.

Ohashi, J., Togari, H., Isokawa, M. and Suzuki, S., 1988, Measuring movement speeds and distances covered during soccer match-play, In *Science and Football*, edited by Reilly, T., Lees, A., Davids, K. and Murphy, W.J. (London, E&FN Spon), pp. 329–33.

Quod M.J., Martin D.T., Laursen P.B., 2006, Cooling athletes before competition in the heat. *Sports Medicine*, 36, 671–82.

Yasumatsu M., Miyagi O., Ohashi J., Togari H., Nishikawa S., Hasegawa H., Ishizaki S. and Yoda, T., 2003, The effect of water intake during games on the performance of soccer-simulated exercise in the hot environment. In *Book of Abstracts, World Congress on Science and Football 5*, (Madrid: Gymnos Editional Deportiva), pp. 306.

45 The relationships between pre-match hydration status, match performance, injury and body mass changes in elite Australian footballers

John Quinn,[1,2] *Caroline Finch*[2] *and*
Aaron J. Coutts[1,3]

[1] Essendon Football Club, Australia; [2] University of New South Wales, Australia;
[3] University of Technology Sydney, Australia

Introduction

It has been shown that hypohydration occurs during both training and competition in soccer, rugby league, gridiron and Australian Rules football (ARF) (Burke and Hawley, 1997; Meir *et al.*, 2003; Al-Jaser and Hasan, 2006). Hypohydration has been associated with reductions in endurance performance, intermittent sprint performance, muscular strength, perceptive discrimination and decision-making ability (Burke and Hawley, 1997; McGregor *et al.*, 1999; Cian *et al.*, 2001; Schoffstall *et al.*, 2001). Each of these factors is important for performance in ARF.

All ARF matches are more than two hours in duration and demand high-intensity, intermittent exercise. Depending on position, top-level players have been reported to cover between 10.7–20.1 km in a match (Dawson *et al.*, 2004). Although ARF is a winter sport, matches are quite often played in warm climates, particularly in the northern states of Australia. Combined, these factors mean that players may be at risk of high levels of dehydration and suggest that monitoring fluid status changes in players may be important.

To minimize deleterious effects of hypohydration on match performance, many top-level ARF teams now monitor hydration status with urine specific gravity (U_{sg}) and changes in body mass (DBM) during matches. To date, no research group has examined the practical usefulness of these measures in an elite football team environment. Therefore the purpose of this study was to determine if relationships exist between pre-match U_{sg}, match DBM and skill performance and injuries in elite ARF players.

Methods

Subjects

Thirty-four elite ARF players participated in this study (age: 22.8 ±3.7 years; BM: 89.4 ±8.6 kg; height: 1.88 ±0.06 m).

Hydration measures

The hydration status of each selected player for each match (n = 22) was determined by U_{sg} (n = 471), as well as changes in DBM for an entire season (n = 415). The U_{sg}, BM and DBM results were then compared to match-related skill and injury data.

Body mass measures

All players were required to record their BM approximately 15 min prior to and immediately following each match using calibrated digital platform scales accurate to 0.05 kg accurate (Model UC-321; A&D Co. Ltd., Australia). For the logistical reason of dealing with professional ARF players in a match environment, BM was taken with players in football clothing (and boots). To account for the trapped sweat in this clothing, the mass of this attire was measured pre-match and post-match. The DBM during each match was then calculated by subtracting the corrected BM_{post} from the BM_{pre}. No measures of fluid intake were taken.

Urine specific gravity measures

Each player provided a urine sample 2 hours prior to each match for determination of U_{sg}. The U_{sg} was measured from a 2 ml urine sample using a calibrated handheld refractometer (Model URC-NE, Atago Inc, Japan). The hydration test results were made available to players and staff 60 min prior to each match. Staff members responsible for fluid distribution during the match were notified of any player with an $U_{sg} > 1.020$ mg.l^{-1}. Staff members were then required to offer the identified player(s) the opportunity to drink more both prior to, and during the match.

Match statistics

Match statistics were determined using the official league statistics (Champion Data, Melbourne, Australia) and used to indicate player performance. Only players who spent more than 75 per cent of total match time on the field were included in this analysis. The key performance indicators used to demonstrate each player's skill involvement in each match were: *Effective possessions* – the number of kicks or handpasses that reached the intended target; and, *Ineffective possessions* – the number of kicks or handpasses that did not reach the intended target.

Match injuries

The match injury outcomes were determined using the medical reports from trained medical staff. Injuries were classified according to the number of matches missed as a result of that injury according to the methods of Orchard (2002).

Statistical analyses

Pearson's correlations and independent sample t-tests were used to assess the relationships between each of the variables. The statistical analysis used in the study was completed using SPSS Version 12.1. Significance was set at 0.05.

Results

Pre-match U_{sg} were 1.005 ±0.004 mg.l^{-1} (median: 1.004 mg.l^{-1}, range: 1.001–1.023 mg.l^{-1}). The BM was 90.8±8.1 kg pre-match and 89.6±8.0 kg post-match. The DBM for the players who played more than 75% of match time (N = 415) was 1.0 ±0.8 kg (1.13 ±0.68% BM), with wide individual player variability (range: 0.0–3.6% BM). There was a low incidence (8/471) of players with DBM >3%.

There were 21 match-related injuries that caused players to miss subsequent matches. The severity of injury ranged from one to seven matches missed (mean: 2.7±1.8 matches). There were no differences in the U_{sg} measures of the injured (N = 21) vs. the non-injured players (N = 463). There was no relationship between pre-match U_{sg} and injury incidence or severity when the U_{sg} was <1.020 mg.l^{-1} (P>0.05).

The players averaged 13.7±6.4 effective possessions and 2.7±2.7 ineffective possessions each match. There was only a significant relationship between DBM and total effective possessions when DBM exceeded 3% (r = 0.60, P<0.05). No other significant relationships were between any of the measured variables.

Discussion and conclusions

This study is the first investigation of relationships between pre-match U_{sg}, DBM, and match-related skill and injury measures. The present results demonstrated that ARF players only incur a mild fluid deficit during the course of each match. These results agree with most prior research on other football codes (Burke and Hawley, 1997; Meir *et al.*, 2003). For example, Meir *et al.* (2003) reported mean BM losses of 0.94±0.94 kg across four rugby league matches, with only two players experiencing DBM in excess of 3%.

Since DBM measures may not be a good independent marker of hydration status (Armstrong, 2005)d], U_{sg} was also used to monitor hydration status. Normal range for U_{sg} is 1.013–1.029 mg.l^{-1} and a U_{sg} >1.030 mg.l^{-1} indicates hypohydration (Armstrong, 2005). In this study, all the pre-match U_{sg} were within the normal range. Moreover, since U_{sg} values of 1.001–1.012 mg.l^{-1} suggest excess body water

(Armstrong, 2005), the present results indicate that most players from this team may have started each match in a hyperhydrated state.

In this study there were few relationships between U_{sg}, DBM and skill-involvement measures during the match or incidence and severity of injuries. A possible explanation for the lack of relationships is that the hydration strategies adopted by this team were effective in ensuring good hydration. Additionally, the fluid losses may not have been great enough to elicit large performance changes. For example, most studies suggest that fluid losses >1.8% BM are required to show significant decreases in physical and mental performance (Burke and Hawley, 1997). This may explain why only DBM of >3% in this study was associated with decreased skill involvement.

In summary, the U_{sg} results demonstrated that all players were well-hydrated prior to each match and that most commonly, only mild levels of DBM occur in ARF. However, the high variability in match DBM in this study suggests that monitoring of DBM and U_{sg} should be done on an individual basis. These results can be used to guide future hydration monitoring strategies for elite ARF players.

References

Al-Jaser, T.A. and Hasan, A.A., 2006, Fluid loss and body composition of elite Kuwaiti soccer players during a soccer match. *Journal of Sports Medicine and Physical Fitness*, 46, 281–5.

Armstrong, L.E., 2005, Hydration assessment techniques. *Nutrition Reviews*, 63, S40–54.

Burke, L.M. and Hawley, J.A., 1997, Fluid balance in team sports: Guidelines for optimal practices. *Sports Medicine*, 24, 38–54.

Cian, C., Barraud, P.A., Melin, B. and Raphel, C., 2001, Effects of fluid ingestion on cognitive function after heat stress or exercise-induced dehydration. *International Journal of Psychophysiology*, 42, 243–51.

Dawson, B., Hopkinson, R., Appleby, B., Stewart, G. and Roberts, C., 2004, Player movement patterns and game activities in the Australian Football League. *Journal of Science and Medicine in Sport*, 7, 278–91.

McGregor, S.J., Nicholas, C.W., Lakomy, H.K. and Williams, C., 1999, The influence of intermittent high-intensity shuttle running and fluid ingestion on the performance of a soccer skill. *Journal of Sports Sciences*, 17, 895–903.

Meir, R., Brooks, L. and Shield, T., 2003, Body weight and tympanic temperature change in professional rugby league players during night and day games: a study in the field. *Journal of Strength and Conditioning Research*, 17, 566–72.

Orchard, J., 2002, Understanding some of the risks for soft tissue injury--a Malcolm Blight legacy? *Journal of Science and Medicine in Sport*, 5, v-vii.

Schoffstall, J.E., Branch, J.D., Leutholtz, B.C. and Swain, D.E., 2001, Effects of dehydration and rehydration on the one-repetition maximum bench press of weight-trained males. *Journal of Strength and Conditioning Research*, 15, 102–8.

Part VII

Physiology of training

46 Heart rate recording optimization in soccer

Raul Martínez-Santos,[1] *Angel Blanco,*[2]
Fernando J. Sánchez[3] *and Asier Los Arcos*[4]

[1] University of the Basque Country, Spain; [2] University of Barcelona, Spain;
[3] University of Vigo, Spain; [4] Club Atletico Osasuna, Spain

Introduction

Heart rate monitoring (HRM) is a good example of empirical control of coaching practice. Peak performance and the formation of top-level players are now both professionalized and very technological intervention domains. Achten and Jeukendrup (2003), in their review about HR monitoring, denoted attention to physiological aspects of training and uses of HR in other coaching contexts.

Even though coaching is not a science but an intervention practice, both activities share the foundations of decision making on an empirical basis. Both coaches and scientists try to make statements based on facts and evidence rather than beliefs and hopes, and this is why HRM is more and more implemented in sports domains since it was first reported in 1983 (Laukkanen and Virtanen, 1998).

It is often thought that the more information we have the better, without taking into account the costs in time and storage it may have. For example, we can use a database like MS Access for storing records from a whole season with no limitations and make as many queries as we like; but if we want to use pivot-table reports of MS Excel, much faster and easier to understand, there is a limit of 15,000 rows per sheet. Furthermore, if we want to get our coaches to reflect on their own practice, we must provide them with understandable theoretical models and practical analytical procedures that allow them to make the most of their time.

The aim of this research was to assess if longer than 5 s recording intervals (time interval between two consecutive heart beats) affect the variability of data due to its own facets, due to the circumstances present when the HR value was recorded taking into account that this kind of assessment is far from the needs that medical contexts may demand (Ruha *et al.*, 1997).

Methods

Heart rate monitoring

Polar devices for HR monitoring have been validated several times in comparison with clinical electrocardiogram techniques (Goodie *et al.*, 2000; Kingsley *et al.*,

2005; Gamelin *et al*, 2006). The Polar Team System is used on a regular basis for recording HR during practice sessions in 1st and 2nd-B teams of the Club Atlético Osasuna (Pamplona, Spain). After every session HR files are downloaded to the computer with the latest available version of Polar Precision Performance SW and revised to remove non-activity periods and amending noisy records.

For this study we used data from 18 players in eight pre-season training sessions (2006–2007 season). All players were informed at the beginning of the season about this possibility according to international regulations.

HRM files compilation

Heart Rate Data Compiler Osasuna 1.0 (Martínez-Santos *et al.*, 2006) was designed and written for the compilation of HR files. Roughly speaking, this application allows the coach to put together as many HRM files from Polar as one may like, getting as output just one statistically computable file.

One of the features of this application is the possibility of filtering data *a posteriori* by selecting HR values every 10, 15 or more seconds. By doing that, in order to test our hypothesis we made six record sets with the same structure of variables (Table 46.1). Five of these were subsets of the original, one having a grand total of 177,377 records.

From a logical point of view, data subsets are contained incrementally: HR30 is contained in all the rest, HR25 in all the rest except HR30, and so on. In this way we got five samples of the same population whose statistical properties can be tested.

Statistical analysis

We have made an analysis of components of variance. The procedures employed were VARCOMP and GLM for testing the adjustment of the data to the general lineal model and homoscedasticity, all of them run on SAS 9.1.3 package. In addition, an analysis of generalizability was done (Ysewjin, 1996).

Table 46.1 Record sets and variables defined for data compilation

Recordsets	Players×	Sessions×	Drills×	Interval×	HR records
HR5	18	8	56	5 s	72,504
HR10	18	8	56	10 s	36,174
HR15	18	8	56	15 s	24,104
HR20	18	8	56	20 s	18,075
HR25	18	8	56	25 s	14,497
HR30	18	8	56	30 s	12,023

×: actual variables along with the numeric one: HR value

Results and discussion

Tables 46.2 and 46.3 show the results of the three analyses where three pertinent variables for soccer coaching control (different players' practice of different drills on different sessions) and a methodological one (HR recording interval) are crossed with each other in order to find out how much of the variance of the

Table 46.2 VARCOMP analysis results for (Players × Sessions × Drills × Intervals) model having HR values as dependent variable

Variance components	DF	Sum of squares	Mean square	Type 1 estimates
Players	17	12021479	707146	43.63009
Sessions	7	42449244	6064178	177.59528
Players × sessions	53	9669973	182452	23.28003
Drills	12	44977629	3748136	257.04348
Players × drills	195	11095109	56898	13.11967
Sessions × drills	36	17680546	491126	255.65160
Players × sessions × drills	228	10548027	46263	190.90176
Intervals	5	135.15	27.03	0.0058226
Players × intervals	85	672.74	7.91	−0.04601
Sessions × intervals	35	529.26	15.12	−0.03591
Player × sessions × intervals	265	1613.08	6.08	1.29513
Drills × intervals	60	1952.31	32.53	0.04425
Player × drills × intervals	975	7581.05	7.77	0.45279
Sessions × drills × intervals	180	4071.55	22.61	−0.03936
Play × sessions × drills × intervals	1140	9518.03	8.34	−6.67163
Error	174083	43860429	251.95	251.95

Table 46.3 GLM analysis results for (Players × Sessions × Drills × Intervals) model having HR as dependent variable and generalizability analysis for percentages of variance explain by every facet

Variance components	DF	GLM		GT variance explained
		F value	Pr > F	
Players	17	2806.68	<.0001	7%
Sessions	7	24068.90	<.0001	29%
Players × sessions	53	724.16	<.0001	7%
Drills	12	14876.40	<.0001	29%
Dlayers × drills	195	225.83	<.0001	7%
Sessions × drills	36	1949.29	<.0001	13%
Players × sessions × drills	228	183.62	<.0001	9%
Intervals	5	0.11	0.9907	.
Players × intervals	85	0.03	1.0000	.
Sessions × intervals	35	0.06	1.0000	.
Players × sessions × intervals	265	0.02	1.0000	.
Drills × intervals	60	0.13	1.0000	.
Players × drills × intervals	975	0.03	1.0000	.
Sessions × drills × intervals	180	0.09	1.0000	.
Players × sessions × drills × intervals	1140	0.03	1.0000	.

Note: $P < 0.0001$; $r^2 = 0.772$

dependent variable (exercise intensity measured upon HR values) is explained by each of them. In this particular case, we hoped not to find differences due to the presence of the factor [interval] which stood for the main characteristic of the six samples.The results clearly show that there are no differences at all between the variance that HR values shown because of the recording interval: every time that this variable is included, F values are close to zero (GLM) and no variance is explained (GT). In this sense, it is very interesting that all the other variables assume part of HR variance (top half of the tables) whereas none appears on the bottom half.

As far as the other variables are concerned, it is surprising that different practice drills or exercises have different or similar energetic demands which can help in finding training activities similar to the game itself for instance (Hoff, *et al.*, 2002; Chamari *et al.*, 2005; Reilly and White, 2005; Sassi *et al.*, 2005; Tessitore *et al.*, 2006). This point is confirmed by the fact that 58 per cent of the variance is explained by [sessions] and [drills].

The variable [players] is itself involved in 7 per cent of variability only which can be interpreted as a symptom of the power that the internal logic of the activities has on the players (Parlebas, 1999). This could be shown as well for three different training situations (Martínez-Santos *et al.*, 2006b).

Conclusion

According to our results, variance of HR record sets is not affected if the quantity of data is reduced, that is if only one value every 30 s is retained for analysis. This conclusion is valid for different players, in different sessions and different drills even though it should be reconsidered when more variables/facets are integrated in the analysis.

These results allow us to address coaching control and research in a more efficient way, as fewer resources should be employed for recording and storing data for the long term. In addition, other applications rather than more sophisticated database clients can be used by any kind of coaches.

References

Achten, J. and Jeukendrup, A. E., 2003, Heart rate monitoring: applications and limitations. *Sports Medicine*, 33, 517–38.

Chamari, K., Hachana, Y., Kaouech, F., Jeddi, R., Moussa-Chamari, I. and Wisloff, U., 2005, Endurance training and testing with the ball in young elite soccer players. *British Journal of Sports Medicine*, 39, 24–8.

Gamelin, F. X., Berthoin, S. and Bosquet, L., 2006, Validity of the polar S810 heart rate monitor to measure R-R intervals at rest. *Medicine and Science in Sports and Exercise*, 38, 887–93.

Goodie, J. L., Larkin, K. T. and Schauss, S., 2000, Validation of the Polar heart rate monitor for assessing heart rate during physical and mental stress. *Journal of Psychophysiology*, 14(3), 159–64.

Hoff, J., Wisloff, U., Engen, L. C., Kemi, O. J. and Helgerud, J., 2002, Soccer specific aerobic endurance training. *British Journal of Sports Medicine*, 36, 218–21.

Kingsley, M., Lewis, M. J. and Marson, R. E., 2005, Comparison of Polar 810 s and an ambulatory ECG system for RR interval measurement during progressive exercise. *International Journal of Sports Medicine*, 26, 39–44.

Laukkanen, R. M. T., and Virtanen, P. K., 1998, Heart rate monitors: state of the art. *Journal of Sports Sciences*, 16, S3–S7.

Martínez-Santos, R., Los-Arcos, A. Blanco, Á., and Sánchez, F. J., 2006a, Lógica interna de las tareas y demanda energética en el entrenamiento del fútbol. In *Investigaciones en praxiología motriz*, edited by Martínez, de Santos, R. and Etxebeste, J., (Vitoria-Gasteiz AVAFIEP y Dpto. de Educación Física de la UPV-EHU), pp. 173–86.

Martínez-Santos, R., Sánchez, F. J. and Los-Arcos, A., 2006b, *Heart rate data files compiling for coaching control and research: HRDC Osasuna 1.0* Paper presented at the VI World Congress of Science and Football, Antalya (Turkey).

Parlebas, P., 1999, *Jeux, Sports et Sociétés: Lexique de Praxéologie Motrice.* (Paris: INSEP-Publications).

Reilly, T. and White, C., 2005, Small-sided games as a alternative to interval-training for soccer players. In *Science and Football V*, edited by Reilly, T., Cabri, J. and Araújo, D. (London: Routledge), pp. 344–7.

Ruha, A., Sallinen, S. and Nissila, S., 1997, A real-time microprocessor QRS detector system with a 1 ms timing accuracy for the measurement of ambulatory HRV. *IEEE Transactions on Biomedical Engineering*, 44(3), 159–67.

Sassi, R., Reilly, T. and Impellizzeri, F. M., 2005, A comparison of small-sided games and interval training in elite porfessional soccer players. In *Science and football V*, edited by Reilly, T., Cabri, J. and Araújo, D. (London: Routledge), pp. 341–3.

Tessitore, A., Meeusen, R., Piacentini, M. F., Demarie, S. and Capranica, L., 2006, Physiological and technical aspects of '6–a-side' soccer drills. *Journal of Sports Medicine and Physical Fitness*, 46, 36–43.

Ysewjin, P., 1996, *Software for Generalizability Studies*: Mimeograph.

47 Monitoring training loads in professional rugby league

Aaron J. Coutts,[1] *Anita C. Sirotic,*[1,2]
Craig Catterick[2] *and Hayden Knowles*[2]

[1] University of Technology, Australia; [2] Parramatta Eels Football Club, Australia

Introduction

The training process must be carefully monitored if a physical performance is to be optimised (Impellizzeri *et al.*, 2005). Indeed, appropriate periodisation of the stress applied to athletes during training is important to obtain best results (Norris and Smith, 2002). Unfortunately, there have been few detailed reports of how training stress is periodised for team sports (Coutts *et al.*, 2003). A possible reason for the limited information available on this topic is that there have been few practical methods that can be used to monitor the training stress experienced by participants in team sports.

Some of the techniques used to quantify training loads in team sports require heart rate (HR) monitors and/or global positioning satellite (GPS) units. Whilst these methods can provide very detailed information on the training stress experienced by athletes, they have several limiting factors which can prohibit them from wide use in football clubs. In particular, these devices can be expensive, require a high level of technical expertise to operate, and data analysis can be time-consuming. Additionally, these methods cannot be easily used to compare the training stress imposed by various forms of training that are common in team sports (e.g. aerobic training vs power training). Combined, these factors limit the practical usefulness of these techniques for monitoring the periodisation of training load in teams.

The session-RPE method has been developed for quantifying training loads (Foster *et al.*, 1995). The session-RPE training load is determined by multiplying a rating of perceived exertion (RPE) relevant to the whole training session using Borg's Category Ratio-10 (CR-10) (Borg *et al.*, 1987) scale by the session duration (in minutes) (Foster *et al.*, 1995). This method has been shown to be a simple and valid technique for quantifying training intensity for the whole session in steady-state aerobic (Foster *et al.*, 1995; Foster *et al.*, 2001), intermittent-aerobic (Foster *et al.*, 2001; Impellizzeri *et al.*, 2004) and strength training (Day *et al.*, 2004; Sweet *et al.*, 2004). As it is a valid measure of training load in various types of training, session-RPE is now widely used by many top level football teams.

To our best knowledge, there have been no studies on periodisation strategies used in any football code. A few studies have reported on the in-season planning of training loads in soccer (Impellizzeri *et al.*, 2004; Impellizzeri *et al.*, 2005) and also described the general training loads during a season in semi-professional rugby league (Coutts *et al.*, 2003; Coutts *et al.*, 2007). Therefore, the purpose of this study was to use the session-RPE method to describe the training periodisation of an elite rugby league club during a training year.

Methods

Subjects

Twenty-five professional rugby league players (age: 23.8 ±3.2 years, body mass: 97.9 ± 8.1 kg, height: 1.84 ± 0.04 m) from the same National Rugby League (NRL) club participated in this study. The test procedures were approved by a research ethics committee and written informed consent was obtained from each subject.

Quantification of training load

Training loads were measured using the session-RPE method for every training session during the entire season. Session-RPE was revealed by asking each player 'How intense was your session?' according to Borg's CR-10 (1987) scale ~30 min after each training session. Players were asked to ensure that their RPE referred to the intensity of the whole session rather than the most recent exercise intensity. All players had been anchored with this scale for RPE before commencing the study. The data from each session were entered into a specialised on-line database that allows for fast analysis of training loads (www.trainingload.com, Acceleration Australia, Brisbane). The subjective training loads for each session during the season were described by the indices of intensity (i.e. RPE), training load (session-RPE), monotony and strain (Foster *et al.*, 2001).

Training and game duration were revealed for each session during each of the distinct training macrocycles: general preparation 6 weeks (November–December); specific preparation 5 weeks (January–February); match practice 4 weeks (February–March); and competition 26 weeks (March–August). The training loads during each of these macrocycles were analysed according to the various types of training completed. These were skill, conditioning, skills/conditioning, matches, and other (recovery, speed, wrestling and miscellaneous) training.

To examine any relationships between match performance, RPE or training load, comparison was made with standard match statistics collected by the club. Only statistics that related to physical work-rate such as tackles completed, hit ups, metres gained, scrums and line breaks were included in the correlation analysis.

Statistical analysis

A one-way ANOVA was used to determine any significant changes during each of the various types of training and training macrocycles. Pearson's correlation was used to assess relationships between subjective training load data and match statistics. All data are presented as mean ± SD. Statistical significance was set at $P<0.05$.

Results

Table 47.1 shows the mean weekly training loads for each of the types of training during the various macrocycles.

Table 47.2 shows the mean daily training loads completed between each match. Interestingly, the match loads did not significantly change during the competition period (499 ± 38 AU). However, the players did perceive the matches won to be of a significantly lower load than matches that were lost (win = 479 ± 32 vs loss = 520 ± 33, $P<0.05$). The match load was related to the number of tackles completed by the team during each match ($r = 0.54$, $P<0.05$).

Figure 47.1 shows training load, strain and monotony during each of the various training macrocycles.

Discussion

This study is the first to describe the periodisation of training loads for a professional rugby league team during a complete training year. As expected, higher training loads were completed in the preparatory macrocycles of training. It is likely that these higher loads were implemented in an attempt to increase strength, power and aerobic fitness prior to the competition season. In contrast, the training loads for conditioning and strength training were reduced during competition. These findings suggest the training for this team was periodised by increasing the emphasis on general conditioning/strength training in the preparatory macrocycles

Table 47.1 Mean (±SD) training loads (AU) for each of the types of training during training macrocycles

	General preparation	Specific preparation	Match practice	Competition
Conditioning	1452 ± 214^{bcd}	1036 ± 354^{acd}	699 ± 188^{a}	380 ± 342^{ab}
Strength	519 ± 263	815 ± 302^{cd}	494 ± 127^{b}	379 ± 136^{b}
Skills	453 ± 101^{bc}	790 ± 192^{a}	698 ± 120^{a}	613 ± 209
Other	201 ± 161^{b}	489 ± 89^{ad}	348 ± 172^{d}	150 ± 89^{bc}
Match			371 ± 70	499 ± 38^{c}

Notes: a – significant difference to general preparation; b – significant difference to specific preparation; c – significant difference to match practice; d – significant difference to competition; all $P<0.05$; AU – arbitrary units; every player did not complete each session.

Table 47.2 Mean (±SD) daily training loads (AU) completed between each match during the in-season

	5 days	6 days	7 days	8 days	9 days
Daily	239 ± 19	283 ± 35^{a}	278 ± 26^{a}	262 ± 23^{a}	295 ± 26^{a}

Notes: a – significant difference from 5 day recovery; $P<0.05$.

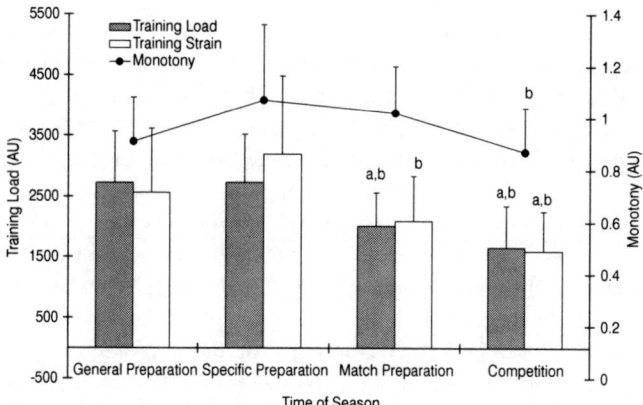

Figure 47.1 Periodisation of the various types of training through the different macrocycles (n = 37); a) significant difference from general preparation and specific preparation; b) significant difference from specific preparation

and reducing training loads to optimise recovery during competition. It is believed that this approach to periodisation will allow for fitness gains to be maximised in the pre-season peroid and allow for transient fatigue to be diminished during the competition phase (Banister, 1991).

The training loads experienced by the team in this study were generally greater than those previously reported in semi-professional rugby league players (Coutts *et al.*, 2003), but less than high-level endurance athletes (Foster and Lehmann, 1997). Moreover, the training loads of rugby league players in this study were typically less than the suggested load threshold for overreaching in semi-professional rugby league players (~3300 AU) (Coutts *et al.*, 2007). However, there were several occasions during the general preparation and specific preparation macrocycles when the weekly training loads for individual players exceeded this threshold zone for overreaching. Indeed, some players tolerated these loads whilst other players presented with general fatigue and muscle soreness. On these occasions the coaching staff of this team periodised reduced training loads in an attempt to minimise the risks of overreaching or injury.

Previous research has shown that soccer players who entered a competition season with symptoms of overreaching experienced performance reductions in sprint velocity, vertical jump height and leg strength throughout the course of an 11-week soccer season (Kraemer *et al.*, 2004). Therefore in a further attempt to ensure that the team was adequately recovered prior to the competition phase, the training loads in the match preparation macrocycle were reduced. This pre-season 'taper' was achieved by a reduction in conditioning and strength training.

The monotony values reported in this study demonstrate that there was greater variation in training with increased recovery days during the match preparation and competition periods. The training monotony levels ranged between 0.44 and 1.65 with higher values being observed during the general preparation macrocycle. These values are much lower than those observed in an underperforming marathon runner (>2.0) (Foster and Lehmann, 1997) and suggest that there is good variation in the distribution of training loads in top level rugby league.

Finally, descriptive analysis demonstrated that the mean daily training loads within the training week during the in-season were similar, with the exception of the short preparation week when there were only five days between matches. There was no relationship between match training loads, match outcome, or match statistics. However, there was a significant relationship between the team's match training load and the number of tackles completed by the team. This finding shows that the match training loads in rugby league may be related to skill involvement within the match.

These results show a periodised training structure in professional rugby league and strongly support the use of the session-RPE method as a practical device for guiding periodising and monitoring training loads for team members. These findings also show that training loads can be effectively periodised in team sports. We suggest that future studies examine optimal training load periodisation strategies in both the preparation and in-season training phases in football.

References

Banister, E.W., 1991, Modeling elite athletic performance. In *Physiological Testing of Elite Athletes*. edited by Green, H.J., McDougal, J.D. and Wenger, H.A. (Champaign, IL: Human Kinetics), pp. 403–24.

Borg, G., Hassmén, P. and Lagerstrom, M., 1987. Perceived exertion related to heart rate and blood lactate during arm and leg exercise. *European Journal of Applied Physiology and Occupational Physiology*, 56, 679–85.

Coutts, A.J., Reaburn, P.R.J., Murphy, A.J., Watsford, M.L. and Spurrs, R.W., 2003, Changes in physiological and performance characteristics of semi-professional rugby league players in relation to training load: a case study. *Journal of Science and Medicine in Sport*, 6, 37.

Coutts, A.J., Reaburn, P., Piva, T.J. and Murphy, A., 2007, Changes in selected biochemical, muscular strength, power, and endurance measures during deliberate overreaching and tapering in rugby league players. *International Journal of Sports Medicine*, 28, 116–24.

Day, M., McGuigan, M.R., Brice, G. and Foster, C., 2004, Monitoring exercise intensity during resistance training using the session-RPE scale. *Journal of Strength and Conditioning Research*, 18, 353–8.

Foster, C. and Lehmann, M., 1997, Overtraining syndrome. In *Running Injuries*, edited by Gnuten, N., (Philadelphia, PA: W.B. Saunders), pp. 173–88.

Foster, C., Florhaug, J.A., Franklin, J., Gottschall, L., Hrovatin, L.A., Parker, S., Doleshal, P. and Dodge, C., 2001, A new approach to monitoring exercise training. *Journal of Strength and Conditioning Research*, 15, 109–15.

Foster, C., Hector, L.L., Welsh, R., Schrager, M., Green, M.A. and Snyder, A.C., 1995, Effects of specific versus cross-training on running performance. *European Journal of Applied Physiology*, 70, 367–72.

Impellizzeri, F.M., Rampinini, E., Coutts, A.J., Sassi, A. and Marcora, S.M., 2004. The use of RPE-based training load in soccer. *Medicine and Science in Sports and Exercise*, 36, 1042–7.

Impellizzeri, F.M., Rampinini, E. and Marcora, S.M., 2005. Physiological assessment of aerobic training in soccer. *Journal of Sports Sciences*, 23, 583–92.

Kraemer, W.J., French, D.N., Paxton, N.J., Häkkinen, K., Volek, J.S., Sebastianelli, W.J., Putukian, M., Newton, R.U., Rubin, M.R., Gómez, A.L., Vescovi, J.D., Ratamess, N.A., Fleck, S.J., Lynch, J.M. and Knuttgen, H.G. 2004, Changes in exercise performance and hormonal concentrations over a big ten soccer season in starters and nonstarters. *Journal of Strength and Conditioning Research*, 18, 121–8.

Norris, S.R. and Smith, D.J., 2002, Planning, periodization, and sequencing of training and competition: the rationale for a competently planned, optimally executed training and competition program, supported by a multidisciplinary team. In *Enhancing Recovery: Preventing Underperformance in Athletes*, edited by Kellmann, M. (Champaign, IL: Human Kinetics), pp. 121–41.

Sweet, T.W., Foster, C., McGuigan, M.R. and Brice, G, 2004, Quantitation of resistance training using the session-RPE method. *Journal of Strength and Conditioning Research*, 18, 796–802.

48 Development of an offensive evasion model for the training of high-performance rugby players

Mark Sayers

Centre for Healthy Activities, Sport and Exercise, University of the Sunshine Coast, Australia

Introduction

Improvements in the defensive technique and tactical awareness of rugby union (rugby) players over the past eight years have made it increasingly difficult for the offence to penetrate the defensive line. For example, International Rugby Board statistics show that 50 per cent of all tries scored in international rugby in recent years have three or less passes preceding them (International Rugby Board, 2003). This figure suggests that the effectiveness of each ball carry has a considerable impact on try scoring ability. Not surprisingly evasion training has become increasingly important for modern rugby players, with many high-performance teams focusing much of their offensive training on this aspect of the game. However, there is a surprising lack of literature on the specific evasive techniques adopted by international-level players.

This research presents the sum of multiple studies, which have been conducted as both research projects and during the biomechanical servicing of high-performance teams undertaken over a ten-year period between 1996 and 2006. The evasion model developed as a result of these studies has been integrated into the training of national and international level rugby players from Australia and New Zealand and the creation of several coaching resources (Sayers, 1999, 2005, 2006). However, the research underpinning this model has not been reported previously in scientific publications. The purpose of this research was to develop a clear performance model of the evasion techniques utilised by elite rugby players. To ensure both internal and external validity, this model was based on a combination of qualitative assessment, performance analysis research, and advanced three-dimensional kinematic analyses.

Recent research on the 2003 Super 12 Rugby Competition (Sayers and Washington-King, 2005) indicated that evasive technique has a considerable impact on the outcome of each ball carry. This project added considerably to the body of knowledge in this area as previous research on rugby has dealt with subject areas peripheral to ball-carry effectiveness such as, time–motion analysis (e.g.

player tracking), game analysis, sprinting technique, and physical characteristics (McKenzie *et al.*, 1989; McLean, 1992; Deutsch *et al.*, 1998; Sayers, 1999; Deutsch *et al.*, 2002; Sasaki *et al.*, 2002; Duthie *et al.*, 2005). While analysis into each of these areas has provided insights into performance and success in rugby, none has addressed the specifics of the skills and characteristics associated with effective ball carries. Accordingly, this quantitative and qualitative investigation of ball carries in rugby was undertaken with a view to increasing the understanding of this important aspect of the game.

Methods

Three different types of data were collected to help develop this model. First, to examine the relationships between horizontal running velocity and evasion technique, a series of three-dimensional (3D) kinematic analyses were undertaking on high-performance rugby players ($n = 22$). Subjects were asked to complete a simple evasion task that required them to catch a pass while jogging, accelerate 6 m towards a target (nominal *defender*), perform a 45° change in direction, straighten, then reaccelerate and run another 5 m (Figure 48.1). This task was designed to duplicate the running paths used frequently in normal offensive play in the game and was based on drills familiar to the players.

Data were recorded during the direction change using two JVC digital camcorders (GR-DV900, Yokohama, Japan) operating at 50 Hz. Eighteen body landmarks were digitised and 3D kinematic variables developed using APAS (Ariel Dynamics Inc. USA) video-based motion analysis software incorporating standard DLT procedures. Transformed three-dimensional data were smoothed using a digital low-pass filter with a 7 Hz cut-off frequency.

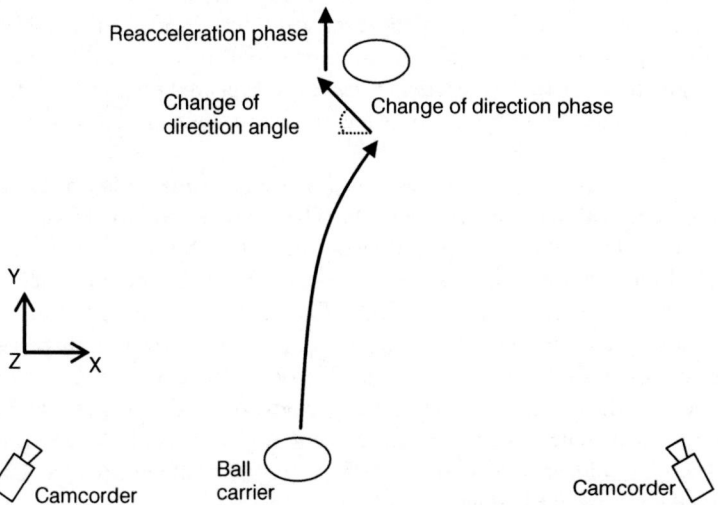

Figure 48.1 Diagram of the rugby-based agility test as viewed from above, showing positioning of the MiniDV camcorders, phases, and orientation of the planes of motion

Statistical analyses were undertaken to examine for significant correlations (Pearson's Product Moment) between biomechanical data and test performance. Of particular interest were the relationships between spatiotemporal stride and step parameters, and the subject's ability to maintain horizontal velocity of the centre of mass (CoM) during the change in direction (i.e. minimise the deceleration).

The second stage in the development of the evasion model involved the collection of performance analysis data via the systemic analysis of offensive play in approximately 60 international rugby matches using standard game analysis software (AnalyRugby and Try Maker Pro, Analy Sports, New Zealand). The purpose of this analysis was to examine whether the results from the initial biomechanical analyses were transferable to match settings. Quantitative analyses were undertaken on both individual skills and the combination of skills involved in each ball carry. Each offensive run was described in terms of the running line (at the defender – all runs where the attacker ran directly at the centre of the chest of a defender; oblique running patterns – runs towards the defensive line towards the shoulder of a defender; and, angled running patterns – all runs not directly towards the defensive line involving situations where an attacker tries to run around the defence using speed), reception speed (subjective measure), and the evasion techniques used (swerve – evasive movements initiated from the inside leg; the forward step – evasive movement involving stepping motions originated from the outside leg and involving predominantly forward motion; and, the lateral step – evasive movement involving a predominately sideways stepping motion). The outcome of each attacking run was then described subjectively based on the result of the impact with the defender (e.g. tackler outcome) and the orientation of the attacker in relation to the gameline.

Chi-squared (χ^2) analyses were conducted to determine which of the categories were associated with effective performance. Standard residual (R) testing was used to assess the magnitude by which the observed figure in the cell was above or below the expected value. A value of ≥ 2.0 or ≤ -2.0 represented a value either substantially more or less (respectively) than the expected for that cell (Grimm, 1993). The results of this analysis were used to create a series of offensive performance indicators (PIs).

The final part of this project was aimed at validating the PIs against several seasons of international-level competition. This involved the use of video-based qualitative analyses of evasive play (SiliconCoach Pro, Silicon Coach Ltd, New Zealand). Research was conducted over four years on 66 high-performance players during both game play and training drills. This analysis was designed to test the significant correlates from the first two parts of this project over far more subjects and against game performance. The outcome of this process was the refining of the model and the creation of evasion key performance indicators (KPIs).

All statistical analyses were performed using SPSS for Windows (versions 12.0 and 14.0). A significance level of $P<0.05$ was used for all analyses and data are presented as means ± SD unless stated otherwise.

Table 48.1 Significant correlates (P<0.05) between various spatiotemporal stride variables during the direction changing task, and the linear velocity of the CoM

Variables	r value
Horizontal velocity of the CoM (CoM$_y$) during change of direction phase	
Distance (Y axis) of the change of direction foot plant from the CoM (m)	−0.82
Distance (X axis) of the change of direction foot plant from the CoM (m)	−0.63
Change of direction angle (deg)	−0.69
Length of the change of direct step (m)	−0.71
Horizontal velocity of the CoM (CoM$_y$) during reacceleration phase	
Distance (Y axis) of the reacceleration foot plant from the CoM (m)	−0.57
Lateral velocity of the CoM (CoM$_x$) during the change of direction phase	
Distance (Y axis) of the change of direction foot plant from the CoM (m)	0.59
Distance (X axis) of the change of direction foot plant from the CoM (m)	0.62
Change of direction angle (deg)	0.69
Length of the change of direct step (m)	0.66

Results

Results for Part 1 of this research showed several of the spatiotemporal variables correlating significantly with linear translation of the CoM (see Table 48.1). The negative correlations between the horizontal velocity of the CoM (CoM$_y$) and the landing distance of foot plant (from the CoM) indicate that large landing distances are associated with significant reductions in CoM$_y$. The nature of these relationships was reversed for the lateral velocity of the CoM (CoM$_x$), indicating that larger landing distances resulted in greater CoM$_x$. Similarly the negative relationships between CoM$_y$ and the change of direction angle and step length indicate that the length and direction of the change of direction step had a significant effect on CoM$_y$.

Results from the second part of this project showed that several subjective measures were significantly related to effective offensive performance. First, positive phase outcomes were associated with receiving the ball at 'cruising' or sprinting, then accelerating into the contact zone, while negative phase outcomes were associated with receiving the ball jogging or walking, and then failing to accelerate into the contact zone ($\chi^2(4) = 88.41$, $P<0.001$). Next, offensive runs directly at the defender had substantially less positive phase outcomes and more negative phase outcomes than expected by chance, while oblique running patterns had substantially less negative phase outcomes ($\chi^2(3) = 81.52$, $P<0.001$). Results for the analysis of evasion technique and phase outcome showed a significant relationship between the two variables ($\chi^2(3) = 67.77$, $P<0.001$). Data showed that players using a forward step were substantially more likely to have a positive phase outcome, while being substantially less likely to have a negative phase outcome than expected by chance. This relationship reversed when a lateral stepping pattern was used (see Figure 48.2).

These studies resulted in the creation of a model of effective evasive performance as expressed by two simple PIs; 1) players must accelerate after receiving the ball, striving to maintain CoM$_y$ in the contact zone, and 2) players must avoid running

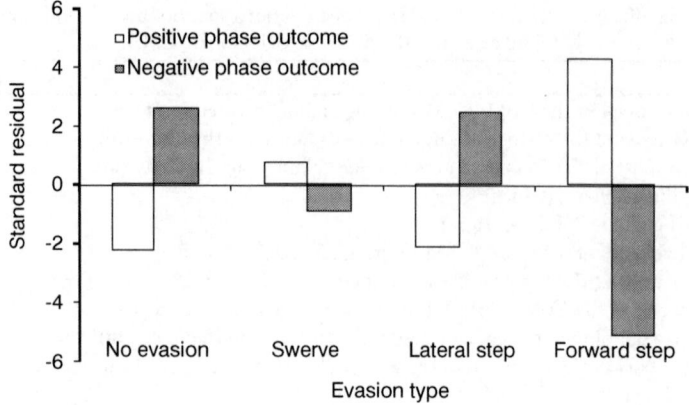

Figure 48.2 Standard residuals for χ^2 analysis on overall phase outcome and evasion pattern used

directly at defenders, and use an evasion technique that maintains CoM$_y$ (related to point 1). The systematic recording of impact skills of high-performance players in the final part of this study resulted in the addition of three more factors and the creation of five KPIs. In order of importance these were:

1   Players must accelerate into and through the contact zone.
2   Players must use positive stepping patterns to avoid both direct contact with the defender and maintain running velocity during the evasion (related to point 1).
3   Players should strive to offload the ball either prior to contact, or in contact (82 per cent of linebreaks were the result of offloads).
4   Players should avoid going to ground unnecessarily. This highly subjective measure related to the need to provide ideal 'attacking ball'. Analysis showed that 89 per cent of all poor attacking ball resulted from the ball carrier submitting in the tackle and going to ground too early, thereby minimising forward momentum.
5   Players should strive for deception by disguising their intentions. This other highly subjective measure resulted from the fact that despite some players showing good attacking skills (i.e. following the four KPIs listed above) they were still tackled heavily and achieved poor phase outcomes. Analysis of the video showed that these players tended to telegraph their intentions in attack, while more capable players appear very adapt at disguising the direction they were heading.

Discussion

The three studies conducted here all identify acceleration ability, and the ability to maintain CoM$_y$ during direction changes as key determinants of effective offensive skill. In the current study players who accelerated into the contact zone from 'cruising' velocities had the most positive phase outcomes. More importantly, players who failed to accelerate into the contact zone were likely to record negative phase outcomes. These findings indicate that acceleration ability is probably the most important KPI for effective ball-carrying performance in rugby, and appears to take precedence over all other factors in determining the outcome of a ball carry. This concurs with previous research that has identified a short acceleration phase as a vital component for successful running in field sports (Benton, 2001; Duthie *et al.*, 2003, 2005; Sayers, 1999, 2000; Sayers and Washington-King, 2005).

Another important outcome of these projects concerned the interaction that occurs between acceleration and direction changing ability in game play situations. For example, the first study highlighted that players must make a compromise between the need to change directions (to avoid contact with a defender) and their desire to maintain CoM_y with greater change of direction angles resulting in significant reductions in CoM_y. This finding highlights the potential problems with other forms of agility testing where timing gates are used to measure performance. That is, some agility tests such as the T-test require players to perform tasks that are not associated with effective rugby performance (e.g. lateral stepping patterns). This issue is reinforced with the results of the second project that showed that forward stepping patterns (not lateral) were associated with positive phase outcomes in the contact zone. This reinforces the notion that forward momentum must be maintained during changes in direction in the proximity of defenders (McKenzie *et al.*, 1989). It is also important to note that running straight into defenders resulted in predominantly negative outcomes. This outdated form of attack should be discouraged completely from the game, as even slight changes in direction (e.g. oblique runs) increased the chances of recording a positive phase outcome significantly. For this reason the evasion model presented here outlines the importance of stepping technique to avoid contact by listing evasion as the second most important KPI. The additional three KPIs that resulted from the highly subjective qualitative analyses used in the final part of this project have added greatly to the practical validity of the model. The third and fourth KPIs (relating to the importance of offloading in the tackle and avoiding going to ground unnecessarily) are linked to the need to maintain forward momentum (related to the first KPI). The final KPI relates to the highly subjective issue of deception. While these latter KPIs have not been developed based on the same scientific techniques as the first two KPIs, they are also crucial in determining the effectiveness of an offensive run. More importantly these KPIs have provided coaches with simple, yet effective coaching cues that are also readily identifiable by players. The marriage of subjective and objective scientific methods used in these projects have resulted in a far more robust model than that which could be developed using merely qualitative analyses alone.

Conclusion

A simple yet effective model for evasion technique was developed, based on ten years of research. Acceleration ability into the contact zone was identified as the most important determinant of effective performance. However, it was also critical that ball carriers developed an effective evasion technique based on lateral movements to minimise the reduction in forward momentum. The multifaceted approach adopted in this research has enabled a robust model to be developed – one that is in common use by international and provincial rugby teams today.

References

Benton, D., 2001, Sprint running needs of field sport athletes: a new perspective. *Sports Coach*, 24(2), 12–14.

Deutsch, M. U., Kearney, G. A. and Rehrer, N. J., 2002, A comparison of competition work rates in elite club and Super 12 rugby. In *Science and Football IV*, edited by Spinks, W., Reilly, T. and Murphy, A. (London: Routledge), pp. 160–6.

Deutsch, M. U., Maw, G. J., Jenkins, D. and Reaburn, P., 1998, Heart rate, blood lactate and kinematic data of elite colts (under-19) rugby union players during competition. *Journal of Sports Sciences*, 16, 561–70.

Duthie, G., Pyne, D. and Hooper, S., 2003, Applied physiology and game analysis of rugby union. *Sports Medicine*, 33, 973–91.

Duthie, G., Pyne, D. and Hooper, S., 2005, Time motion analysis of 2001 and 2002 Super 12 rugby. *Journal of Sports Sciences*, 23, 523–30.

Grimm, L. G. 1993, *Statistical Applications for the Behavioral Sciences*, (Singapore: John Wiley & Sons, Inc.).

International Rugby Board, 2003, Review of the Game 2003. Retrieved 5th January, 2006, from http://www.irb.com/playing/game_analysis/pdfs/game_2003.pdf

McKenzie, A. D., Holmyard, D. J. and Docherty, D., 1989. Quantitative analysis of rugby: factors associated with success in contact. *Journal of Human Movement Studies*, 17, 101–13.

McLean, D. A., 1992, Analysis of the physical demands of international rugby union. *Journal of Sports Sciences*, 10, 285–96.

Sasaki, K., Murakami, J., Shimozono, H., Furukawa, T., Katuta, T. and Kono, L., 2002, Contributing factors to successive attacks in rugby football. In *Science and Football IV*, edited by Spinks, W., Reilly, T. and Murphy. A. (London: Routledge), pp.167–70.

Sayers, M., 1999, Running techniques for running rugby. *The New Zealand Coach*, 7(3), 20–3.

Sayers, M., 2000, Running techniques for field sport players. *Sports Coach*, 23(1), 26–7.

Sayers, M., 2005, Dominating the contact zone. *Gameplan Rugby*, 13, 28–9.

Sayers, M., 2006, Contact zone training. *Gameplan Rugby*, 14, 30–3.

Sayers, M. and Washington-King, J., 2005, Characteristics of effective ball carries in Super 12 rugby. *International Journal of Performance Analysis in Sport*, 5(3), 92–106.

49 Use of weighted balls for improving kicking for distance

Biomechanics Unit, Centre for Ageing, Rehabilitation, Exercise and Sport,
Victoria University, Australia

Introduction

Australian Rules football (ARF) is one of the most popular sports in Australia. Integral to ARF is kicking and a desired element of any player's skill set is the ability to kick the ball long distances. Players who possess the ability to kick the ball longer distances are able to shoot further from the goal and can perform longer passes, increasing the difficulty of defending a particular kick as more options are available. The advantage of longer kicking has game-based statistical support, with Champion data analysis (official statisticians for the AFL) reporting that the number of effective long kicks during a game was the major predictor of score difference between AFL teams (Forbes, 2003).

In spite of the importance of distance kicking in ARF, there has been no study of interventions to increase a player's maximum kick distance. Only one group has examined important technical aspects associated with distance kicking, finding a number of technical differences between short and long kicking groups in elite junior ARF players (Baker and Ball, 1996). The link between strength qualities and kicking performance in ARF has also been examined in only one study but no correlations were found between isokinetic strength of the lower limb and ball speed immediately after ball contact in a maximal kick (Saliba and Hrysomalis, 2001). Kick performance has been improved with structured interventions in soccer (e.g. Manopolous et al., 2006), although not all studies have reported improvements (e.g. Trolle et al., 1993). Interventions to improve kicking performance remain somewhat equivocal on a general level and with no study specific to ARF, there is a need to examine training of kicking performance in ARF.

Weighted implements have been used in training to increase both baseball throwing speed and bat swing speed (Escamilla et al., 2000). In a meta-analysis of 10 studies using over- and under-weight implements in baseball throwing training, Escamilla et al. (2000) reported nine studies showed improvements in throwing speed in the baseball pitch. The only study not to show improvement used a weight-training device to provide resistance to the throwing motion rather than throwing an over- or under-weight ball. Weighted implements have not been used in any research into kicking but given the strong results for improvement in baseball, this intervention should be examined for kicking.

The aim of this study was to examine if specific distance training with regulation and weighted ARF balls could increase kicking distance of elite players.

Methods

Twenty-seven elite footballers (age 23.5 ± 4.5 years, height 1.81 ± 0.41 m, mass 89 ± 11 kg) contracted to an AFL football club at the time of testing participated in this study. After a standard warm-up, each player kicked an ARF ball for maximal distance. Kicks were performed using new Sherrin ARF footballs (Sherrin, Australia; used in AFL competition) inflated within the AFL specified pressure range of 62–76 kPa. Two markers were placed on the ground side by side to define the kick line from which players kicked the ball. In the region where the ball would land after the kick, marker pairs were placed 10 m apart and at 1 m intervals starting at 40 m and continuing to 75 m. An assessor was placed near this area to mark the point of contact with the ball on the ground and to measure the distance kicked. The distance was measured to the nearest marker. The same assessor also measured wind velocity at ground level using a wind meter. As there is no indication in the literature as to what constitutes a 'wind advantage', a threshold of 2 m.s^{-1} was set as the cut-off for 'legal' kicks. To confirm the threshold's appropriateness, the opinions of three AFL coaches were sought (when wind conditions reached 2 m.s^{-1}) and all considered it to be insignificant to distance. Importantly, the wind did not pass this threshold in either test session. For each player, the longest kick (out of five kicks) was chosen to indicate maximum kick distance.

Players were then divided into three groups. Group 1 (regulation) performed maximal kicks for the four-week intervention period using a regulation weight ball. Group 2 (weighted) performed maximal kicks using both regulation and weighted balls. Kick distance was monitored in each session and distances were fed back to each player to ensure maximal kicks were being produced. Group 3 (control) performed no specific kicking but performed at least the same amount of kicks as Group 1 and Group 2. The intervention strategy is reported in Table 49.1. The uneven N was due to player dropout during the intervention period.

To increase the mass of balls, each was soaked in water for a period of time to increase mass from the regulation 450 g up to 500 g. The choice of this mass was based on throwing studies indicating that the most effective mass increases occurred within 20 per cent of the regulation mass of the implement (Vasilev, 1983, as reported by Escamilla *et al.*, 2000). The ratio of weighted ball kicks to

Table 49.1 Number of kicks for Group 1 (regulation ARF balls) and Group 2 (combination of regulation and weighted ARF balls)

Week		1		2		3		4	
Session		1	2	1	2	1	2	1	2
Group 1 (regulation)	Regulation balls	4	5	6	6	7	7	8	8
Group 2 (weighted)	Weighted balls	2	2	2	2	2	2	3	3
	Regulation balls	2	3	4	4	5	5	5	5

regulation ball kicks of 2:1 was based on the finding that this was optimal for baseball throwing improvement (De Renne *et al.*, 1994). This combination is thought to provide the overload effect due to the weighted implement but not alter technique substantially.

The venue for both test sessions was the regular training ground for the team. All players performed a strength training programme as part of their pre-season training during the time that the kicking intervention was performed. For all players, the strength programmes were similar.

Two-way repeated measures ANOVA was used to compare the three groups for maximal distance and to compare pre- and post-intervention kicking distances. Tukey post-hoc tests were applied to examine significant differences between pairs of means. A one-way ANOVA was used to determine if the change in distance was significantly different between groups. Level of significance was set at $P<0.05$.

Results

The mean maximum kick distance for each group is displayed in Table 49.2. Significant main effects existed for the two-way ANOVA. Tukey's post-hoc analysis indicated Group 1 and Group 2 were significantly different from Group 3 for post-test distance values. No statistical difference existed between groups in the pre-test, or between Group 1 and Group 2 in the post-test The change from the pre-test to the post-test was also significant for both Group 1 and Group 2 but not for Group 3.

Discussion

The range of mean kick distances in this study (55–63 m) was larger than the 42–48 m distances reported by Baker and Ball (1996). This difference might be expected given that Baker and Ball (1996) tested elite junior (16 years and under) players compared with senior elite players in this study. As no previous study has examined kicking distance interventions in ARF, no comparison data exist for the changes in kick distance.

Kicking for distance performed over four weeks improved maximal kick distance in ARF players. The mean increases in kick distance between the pre-test and post-test of 4.8 m for Group 1 and 5.6 m for Group 2 were both significant.

Table 49.2 Mean kick distances and change in distance for Group 1 (regulation balls), Group 2 (weighted balls) and Group 3 (control) before and after a four-week distance kicking intervention

		Group 1 (N = 10)	Group 2 (N = 10)	Group 3 (N = 7)
Pre-test	Mean	58.7	56.2	55.5
	SD	5.0	4.2	2.5
Post-test	Mean	63.4	61.8	56.4
	SD	4.2	3.6	3.6
Change	Mean	4.8	5.6	0.9
	SD	2.5	2.7	2.6

Importantly, no difference existed for the control group between pre-test and post-test. This result indicated that to improve maximal distance, specific kick distance training is appropriate.

There was no advantage in using weighted balls compared with regulation balls for improving maximum kick distance. There was no significant difference between groups using regular balls or weighted balls and both groups improved by approximately 5 m. Given the mode of training with regulation balls, training was more easily administered, and that wetting ARF balls repeatedly reduces their useful lifespan, the use of regulation balls would be the most appropriate in an applied setting. However, the intervention period of four weeks was shorter than most of the weighted implement studies reported by Escamilla et al. (2000) and might have been too short for an adaptation to occur. The 'weighted ball group' did produce a larger increase than the regulation group (5.6 m compared to 4.8 m). Future work needs to increase the time period used for the intervention.

An important part of this research was the use of a control group. Escamilla et al. (2000) reported the lack of a control group to be a limitation of previous studies into the use of weighted implements in training. Given this study was performed in pre-season, increases in kick distance might be expected due to the combination of strength and football training rather than specific to the intervention. This point was supported by the control group increasing kick distance by 0.9 m. However, as the intervention groups both improved significantly while the control group did not, the positive results of this study are supported. It is essential in this type of study to use a control group.

Future work needs to combine both strength and skill-based conditioning aspects to determine if the combination of conditioning elements might further increase kicking distance. Multiple baselines would be appropriate (i.e. intervening with players at different times during the season rather than only during pre-season as was performed in this study). However, this type of testing is extremely unlikely to occur in a professional sports team due to the different nature of training during the season compared with the pre-season and the perception of injury risk. The use of different ball weights and different ratios of kicks with weighted and regulation balls are also areas worth exploring.

Conclusions

Specific kick distance training can improve maximal distance in ARF. The use of regulation balls or weighted balls can both improve distance. While there was no difference in improvement using either weighted or regulation balls, future testing needs to increase the intervention time to examine further the effects of weighted balls on kick distance training.

References

Baker, J. and Ball, K., 1996, Biomechanical considerations of the drop punt, *Technical Report for the Australian Institute of Sport AFL Football Development Squad,* (Canberra: Australian Institute of Sport).

De Renne, C., Buxton, B.P., Heltzer, R.K. and Ho, K.W., 1994, The effects of under and overweighted implement training on pitching velocity, *Journal of Strength Conditioning Research,* 8, 247–50.

Escamilla, R.F., Speer, K., Fleisig, G.S., Barrentine, S.W. and Andrews, J., 2000, Effects of throwing overweight and underweight baseballs on throwing velocity and accuracy. *Sports Medicine,* 29, 259–72.

Forbes, D., 2003, *Characteristics of Match Statistics in the AFL.* (Melbourne, Australia: Swinburne University/Champion Data Research).

Manopolous, E., Papadopolous, C. and Kellis, E., 2006, Effects of a combined strength and kick coordination training on soccer kick biomechanics in amateur players, *Scandanavian Journal of Medicine and Science in Sports,* 16, 102–10.

Saliba, L. and Hrysomalis, C., 2001, Isokinetic strength related to jumping but not kick performance of Australian footballers. *Journal of Science and Medicine in Sport,* 4, 336–47.

Trolle, M., Aagaard, P., Simonsen, J., Bangsbo, J. and Klaysen, K., 1993, Effects of strength training on kicking performance in soccer. In *Science and Soccer II,* edited by Reilly, T., Clarys, J. and Stibbe, A. (London: E&FN Spon), pp. 95–8.

Vasilev, L.A., 1983, Use of different weight to develop specialized speed-strength, *Soviet Sports Review,* 18, 49–52.

50 Effects of hypertrophy and a maximal strength training programme on speed, force and power of soccer players

Gregory Bogdanis,[1] *Aggeliki Papaspyrou,*[1]
Athanasios Souglis,[2] *Apostolos Theos,*[1]
Aristomenis Sotiropoulos[2] *and Maria
Maridaki*[1]

[1] Department of Sports, Medicine and Biology of Physical Activity, University of Athens, Greece; [2] Department of Team Sports, University of Athens, Greece.

Introduction

Muscle hypertrophy and neural adaptations are the mechanisms explaining increased muscle strength (Osteras *et al.*, 2002, Gabriel *et al.*, 2006). According to Osteras *et al.* (2002) a high-resistance training programme (>85% of one repetition maximum; RM) resulted not only in an increase in power output, but also in a shift of the force–power and force–velocity relationships. Similar training programmes have also resulted in increased maximal strength (Hoff *et al.*, 1999). The improvement of maximal strength in this type of training is explained by neural adaptations (Behm and Sale, 1993), while maximum benefit is gained when maximal mobilization during the concentric phase is emphasized (Almasbakk and Hoff, 1996).

Maximal strength and explosive power of the legs are important for soccer performance (Hoff and Helgerud, 2004). Wisloff *et al.* (2004) have shown that maximal strength in half squats determines sprint performance and jumping ability in high-level soccer players. Therefore, it has been suggested that resistance training for soccer players should include a low-repetition, high-resistance programme. This type of strength training has been effective in further improving sprinting velocity and jumping height in elite soccer players with small or no change in body mass (Hoff and Helgerud, 2004).

Although resistance training programmes are an integral part of soccer training, many coaches use lower loads (around 10 RM) that result in increases in strength mainly by inducing muscle hypertrophy (Campos *et al.*, 2002). However, there is no study comparing the effectiveness of this type of training with the high-load programme proposed by Hoff and Helgerud (2004). Therefore, the purpose of the present study was to examine the effects of two different resistance training programmes on force–velocity characteristics, maximal strength and soccer-specific performance.

Methods

Eighteen male soccer players (age: 22.9 ± 1.1 years, height: 1.80 ± 0.02 m, body mass: 75.4 ± 2.1 kg, body fat: $8.5 \pm 0.6\%$) gave their informed consent and took part in the present study which had ethical committee approval. Participants were divided in two equal groups matched for pre-training cycling power output. Testing was performed before (pre-training) and after (post-training) a six-week pre-season training period and included anthropometric measurements and lean leg volume (LLV) determination, force-velocity measurements on a modified cycle ergometer, vertical jumping, half squat strength, as well as soccer-specific field tests. All tests were performed within one week.

A modified friction-loaded cycle ergometer (Monark, model 864) equipped with a photocell was used to record (200 Hz) instantaneous flywheel velocity and acceleration continuously. Instantaneous values of power, total force (frictional and inertial) and pedal speed were averaged over each pedal down-stroke (Arsac *et al.*, 1996). A restraining harness, passed around the waist, was used to stabilize the participant on the saddle and limit the exercise to the lower limbs.

The individual force-pedal speed and power-pedal speed relationships were derived from the combined force, power and pedal speed data during the acceleration phase of four 6 s maximal sprints against resistive loads ranging from 2.5% to 10% of body mass (Arsac *et al.*, 1996). The force-pedal speed data were fitted using linear least squares regression, while a quadratic polynomial fitted the power-pedal speed data. These equations were used to calculate the individual theoretical maximal force generated at zero pedal speed (F_o), the maximal cycling speed (V_o) corresponding to zero load and the speed where the highest value of power is achieved (V_{opt}).

Vertical jump height was determined as the best of three counter-movement jump trials on a contact mat (Muscle Lab 4000). Half-squat strength (90° knee angle) was determined using a standard Olympic bar and free weights. The players were familiar with half squats as part of their regular strength training programmes. Maximal strength (1 RM) was reached gradually within four to six sets.

Field tests were used to assess sprint acceleration (10 m sprint time), short sprint performance: 40 m sprint time, speed-agility: cone T test time, Illinois test time, 10 × 10-m Zig-Zag test time (45° changes in direction of running). These tests were performed over three days, with two to three trials and full recovery for each test. The best time was recorded for analysis.

Following the pre-training tests, players were divided in two equal groups ($n = 9$). The training programme followed by both groups is summarized in Table 50.1. Each training week included four to six double sessions (two sessions per day) and one rest day. Resistance training was performed three times per week and included 8–12 upper and lower-body exercises. The only difference in training between the two groups was in the half-squat exercise performed during the

Table 50.1 Mean duration of each training item per session during the six weeks of pre-season training; values in parentheses denote the number of sessions for each item per week

	Week number					
Training item	1	2	3	4	5	6
Warm-up (min)	22.5(11)	18.4(12)	19.3(10)	21.0(12)	20.8(10)	20.4(10)
Continuous running (min)	15.7(6)	12.5(4)	10.0(2)	–	–	–
Variable intensity running (min)	18.5(6)	12.0(5)	10.0(2)	–	–	–
Interval training (min)	–	12.0(6)	12.0(6)	10.0(4)	10.0(2)	20.0(1)
Resistance training (min)	60.0(3)	60.0(3)	60.0(3)	60.0(3)	60.0(3)	60.0(3)
Speed training (m)	–	–	–	480.0(2)	440.0(3)	460.0(3)
Small group play (min)	20.0(1)	20.0(3)	20.0(2)	18.0(3)	16.0(3)	16.0(3)
Tactical skills (min)	10.0(3)	18.3(2)	16.1(3)	17.5(3)	22.5(4)	20.1(4)
Friendly game (min)	–	90.0(1)	90.0(1)	90.0(1)	90.0(1)	90.0(1)
Warm-down (min)	9.4(11)	8.9(12)	9.0(10)	9.9(12)	9.6(10)	8.9(10)

resistance training. One group performed four sets of five repetitions of half-squat aiming to increase maximal strength (S group). The load was equal to 90% 1 RM and sets were separated by 3 min rest intervals. Emphasis was put on maximal mobilization during the concentric action. The other group performed four sets of 12 repetitions of half squat against a resistance equal to 70% 1 RM, emphasizing both the eccentric and concentric action with controlled movement speed and an interval of 1.5 min between sets. This scheme was expected to induce greater muscle hypertrophy (H group) as well as strength increases. In order to maintain an optimum training stimulus, the load was re-adjusted at the end of three weeks of training, for both groups.

Changes in force–velocity and power characteristics as well as field test results were analysed using two-way analysis of variance (group × time) for repeated measures on one factor (time: pre- and post-training). When significant effects were found ($P<0.05$) differences were located using a Tukey post-hoc test. Relationships between variables were examined using Pearson's correlation coefficient (r). Results are presented as mean ± SE.

Results

Maximal squat strength was similar in both groups before training (H: 140 ± 10, S: 152 ± 11 kg), but increased almost twice as much in the S compared with the H group (H: 154 ± 11 vs S: 179 ± 13 kg, $P<0.01$). Lean leg volume (LLV) was increased only in the H group (from 7.78 ± 0.43 to 8.11 ± 0.45 l, $P<0.01$), but was unchanged in the S group (pre: 7.59 ± 0.37, post: 7.66 ± 0.30 l). Due to the increase of LLV only in the H group, the improvement in 1 RM strength per LLV was three times higher in the S compared to the H group (Figure 50.1).

The results of the force–velocity test showed an increase in F_o only in the S group, while maximal cycling speed (V_o) and optimum pedal speed (V_{opt}) remained unchanged. Peak power output increased more in the S compared to the H group

Table 50.2 Changes in force–velocity and power–velocity parameters and peak power output (PPO)

	V_{opt} (rev.min^{-1})		F_o (kg)		V_o (rev.min^{-1})		PPO (W)	
	H	S	H	S	H	S	H	S
Pre-training	125 ± 2	128 ± 2	19.4 ± 0.5	18.8 ± 0.8	247 ± 4	255 ± 3	1160 ± 42	1159 ± 39
Post-training	124 ± 2	126 ± 2	19.9 ± 0.5	19.9 ± 1.0*	245 ± 4	250 ± 4	1207 ± 42*	1231 ± 34**

Notes: * $P<0.05$, ** $P<0.01$ from before training

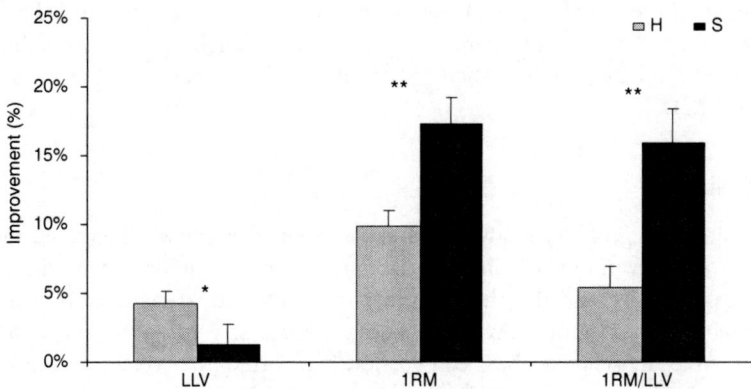

Figure 50.1 Percent changes in lean leg volume (LLV), maximal half-squat strength (1RM) and relative half-squat strength (1RM/LLV)

Notes:* $P<0.05$, ** $P<0.01$ between S and H.

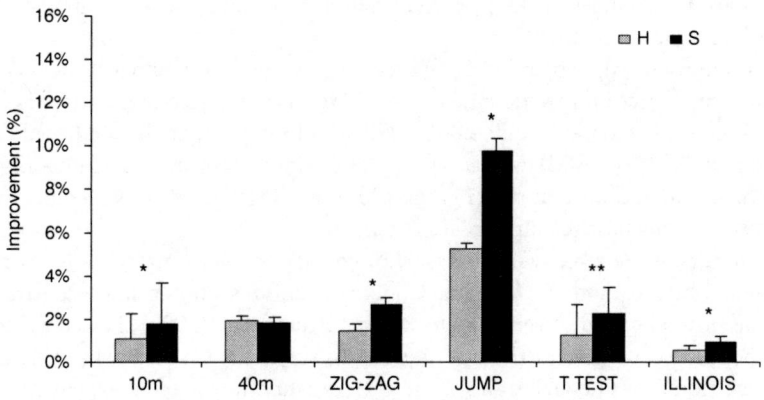

Figure 50.2 Percentage improvement in short sprint time (10 m and 40 m), 10 × 10 m zig-zag test, vertical jump, cone T test time and Illinois test time

Notes: * $P<0.05$, ** $P<0.01$ between S and H.

(Table 50.2). Improvement in squat strength was correlated with improvement in 10 m sprint time ($r = 0.67$, $P<0.01$), cone T-test ($r = 0.69$, $P<0.01$) and vertical jump ($r = 0.63$, $P<0.01$).

Sprint performance (10 m and 40 m sprints) was similar before training (10 m: 1.88 ± 0.02 s; 40 m: 6.11 ± 0.07 s, combined group times) and increased significantly ($P<0.01$) after training in both groups. However, the increase in 10 m sprint time was greater in the S compared to the H group (Figure 50.2). Similarly, the improvements in zig-zag test (pre-test combined groups: 21.70 ± 0.21 s), cone T test (pre-test combined groups: 10.53 ± 0.05 s) and Illinois test (pre-test combined groups: 14.88 ± 0.13 s) were greater in the S compared to the H group (Figure 50.2). The improvement in vertical jump height (pre-test combined groups: 49.2 ± 1.2 cm) was twoice greater in the S compared to the H group (Figure 50.2).

Discussion

The main finding of this study was that maximal strength was increased more in the S group without any increase in muscle mass, as indicated by the lack of increase in LLV and the threefold higher increase in strength in 1 RM/LLV, compared to the H group. An increase in maximal strength with only a small increase in leg muscle mass has been previously reported by Loveless *et al.* (2005), using a training programme similar to that of the S group. However, the present study is the first that compared two different types of resistance training. The H group also improved maximal strength, but this may be explained more by muscle hypertrophy, since LLV was significantly increased (Figure 50.1). The increase in strength without an increase in LLV in the S group may be attributed to neural adaptations, i.e. changes in the pattern of motor unit recruitment and increased rate coding (Gabriel *et al.*, 2006).

In most muscles, the upper limit of motor unit recruitment is about 85 per cent of the maximal force and an increase in force beyond that is accomplished entirely by rate coding (Duchateau *et al.*, 2006). This would imply that the load used by the S group (90% of 1 RM) was an appropriate stimulus for neural adaptations, while the lower resistance in the H group (70% of 1 RM) was effective mainly for increasing muscle mass (Campos *et al.*, 2002).

The results of the force–velocity test showed that only maximal force (F_o) was increased, while V_o and V_{opt} remained unchanged. This finding indicated that there was no shift of the power–velocity curve. Osteras *et al.* (2002) showed a shift of the power–force curve of the arm muscles in skiers after nine weeks of high-resistance training. The lack of a shift in the present study may be explained by differences in the duration of the training (6 vs 9 weeks).

Performance in the field tests was increased more in the S group, mainly when the test involved sprinting with changes in direction and explosive power (Figure 50.2). Wisloff *et al.* (2004) reported that maximal half-squat strength was highly correlated with 10 m sprint time and vertical jump height in elite soccer players.

In the present study, improvement in half-squat strength was correlated with improvement in field tests requiring explosive strength.

In summary, this study has shown that resistance training using high loads may be superior to a lower load (12 RM) programme, not only because it increases strength without a change in muscle mass but also because it results in a greater improvement in soccer-specific field tests.

References

Almasbakk, B. and Hoff, J., 1996, Coordination, the determinant of velocity specificity? *Journal of Applied Physiology*, 81, 2046–52.

Arsac, L., Belli, A. and Lacour, J-R., 1996, Muscle function during brief maximal exercise: accurate measurements on a friction-loaded cycle ergometer. *European Journal of Applied Physiology*, 74, 100–6.

Behm, D.G. and Sale, D.G., 1993, Velocity specificity of resistance training. *Sports Medicine*, 15, 374–88.

Campos, G.E.R., Luecke, T.J., Wendeln, H.K., Toma, K., Hagerman, F.C., Murray, T.F., Ragg, K.E., Ratamess, N.A., Kraemer, W.J. and Staron, R.S., 2002, Muscular adaptations in response to three different resistance-training regimens: specificity of repetition maximum training zones. *European Journal of Applied Physiology*, 88, 50–60.

Duchateau, J., Semmler, J.G. and Enoka, R.M., 2006, Training adaptations in the behavior of human motor units. *Journal of Applied Physiology*, 101, 1766–75.

Gabriel, D.A., Kamen, G. and Frost, G., 2006, Neural adaptations to resistive exercise: mechanisms and recommendations for training practices. *Sports Medicine*, 36, 133–49.

Hoff, J. and Helgerud, J., 2004, Endurance and strength training for soccer players: physiological considerations. *Sports Medicine*, 34, 165–80.

Hoff, J., Helgerud, J. and Wisloff, U., 1999, Maximal strength training improves work economy in trained female cross-country skiers. *Medicine and Science in Sports and Exercice*, 31, 870–7.

Loveless, D.J., Weber, C.L., Haseler, L.J. and Schneider, D.A., 2005, Maximal leg-strength training improves cycling economy in previously untrained men. *Medicine and Science in Sports and Exercice*, 37, 1231–6.

Osteras, H., Helgerud, J. and Hoff, J., 2002, Maximal strength-training effects on force-velocity and force-power relationships explain increases in aerobic performance in humans. *European Journal of Applied Physiology*, 88, 255–63.

Wisloff, U., Castagna, C., Helgerud, J., Jones, R. and Hoff, J., 2004, Strong correlation of maximal squat strength with sprint performance and vertical jump height in elite soccer players. *British Journal of Sports Medicine*, 38, 285–8.

51 Intermittent high-intensity drills improve in-seasonal performance of elite soccer players

Jack Majgaard Jensen, Morten Bredsgaard Randers, Peter Krustrup and Jens Bangsbo

Institute of Exercise and Sport Sciences, Department of Human Physiology, University of Copenhagen, Denmark

Introduction

Significant knowledge exists about the effect of aerobic and anaerobic training on muscular adaptation and performance (Reilly and Bangsbo, 1998). A number of studies have focused on aerobic high-intensity interval training of soccer players. For example, McMillan *et al.* (2005) examined the impact of 10 weeks of interval training on the performance of Scottish youth soccer players. The training consisted of 4×4 min dribbling separated be a 3 min active recovery period twice a week. Maximal oxygen uptake ($\dot{V}O_{2\,max}$) increased by 9 per cent. However, these players were at a moderate level and the training was performed in the pre-season. In addition, Chamari *et al.* (2005) examined the impact of eight weeks of interval training twice a week on 14-year-old soccer players in the competitive season. One of the training sessions consisted of small-sided games and the other session consisted of 4 min work 4 times at a heart rate above 90 per cent of HR_{max} separated by 3 min active recovery. The $\dot{V}O_{2\,max}$ increased by 12 per cent. Impellizzeri *et al.* (2006) used the same protocol for junior players during a 12-week training period, of which the first four weeks were in the pre-season preparation phase. One group of players carried out small-sided games, whereas the other group performed intermittent running. Both groups had significant improvements in aerobic fitness and match performance over the first four weeks, whereas no further significant improvements were observed during the following eight weeks. However, the effects of in-season intermittent high-intensity training for adult players are yet to be investigated.

Thus, the purpose of the present study was to examine the effect of a weekly 30 min session of intermittent high-intensity drills on physical performance of high-level soccer players in the competitive season.

Methods

Subjects

Nineteen professional soccer players in a Scandinavian under 20-elite soccer team took part in the study. The mean age, body mass and height were 17.7 (range: 17.2–19.9) years, 73.1 (62.5–84.5) kg and 1.80 (1.66–1.94) m, respectively. All players were informed of any risks and discomfort associated with the experiment before giving their written consent to participate.

Training and testing

The players were training 3.7 ± 0.1 times per week and with a total duration of 273 ± 7 min. They played 1.8 ± 0.1 matches or 119 ± 11 min per week. In a 12-week period during the season the players carried out 30 min of intermittent high-intensity drills with high aerobic and anaerobic demands (Bangsbo et al., 2006) 0.9 ± 0.1 times a week (IH-period). The IH-period took place in the last 12 weeks of the competitive season. The training consisted of small-sided games with the ratio between exercise and recovery being 2:1, e.g. 3 min play and 1.5 min recovery. Heart rate was recorded during each training session and an example is given in Figure 51.1.

Before and after the IH-period the players performed the following tests:

1   A repeated sprint test consisting of five 30 m sprints separated by 25 s of recovery. Fastest sprint time and the difference between fastest and slowest sprint time (fatigue time) were recorded.

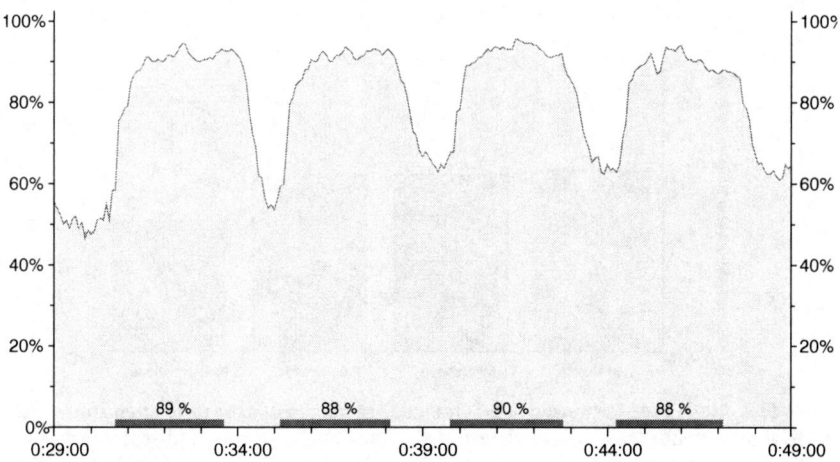

Figure 51.1. Heart rate (expressed as percentage of maximal heart rate) during one of the intermittent high-intensity training sessions

2   A 5-min submaximal version of the Yo-Yo intermittent recovery level 1 test was conducted (Krustrup *et al.*, 2003), where heart rate was recorded during and a blood sample for lactate analysis was collected after the test.

3   The Yo-Yo intermittent recovery test level 2 (Krustrup *et al.*, 2006)

4   An incremental treadmill test to exhaustion for determination of $\dot{V}O_{2\,max}$.

All tests except the $\dot{V}O_{2\,max}$ test were also carried out in the beginning and in the middle of the competitive season to provide information about the development in physical fitness prior to the intervention.

Statistical analysis

Statistical differences between pre- and post-IH-period were analysed using students paired t-tests. Differences between start of season, mid season, pre- and post-IH-period were analyzed using one-way ANOVA with repeated measurements. Statistical significance was accepted at $P<0.05$.

Results

Submaximal Yo-Yo IR1 test

At the end of the IH period the relative heart rate of the 5-min submaximal Yo-Yo IR1 test was 81.3 ± 1.2 (mean $\pm$ SEM)% which was lower ($P<0.001$) than before the IH period (87.3 ± 1.2; $n = 16$) as well as at the start and middle of the season (86.1 ± 1.5 and $86.1 \pm 1.0\%$, respectively; Figure 51.2). After the IH period blood lactate at the end of the submaximal Yo-Yo IR1 test was $2.5 \pm 0.4\,\mathrm{mmol.l^{-1}}$ and lower ($P<0.001$) than before the IH period (5.0 ± 0.5 mmol.l^1, $n = 7$).

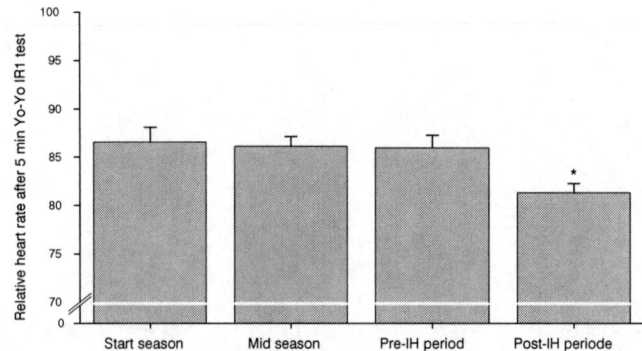

Figure 51.2 Heart rate (expressed as a percentage of maximal heart rate) after 5 min of the Yo-Yo intermittent recovery level 1 test at the start of the season, mid-season as well as before and after the IH period.

Note: * Significantly different ($P<0.05$) from before the IH period, start of season and mid-season.

Repeated sprint test

In the repeated sprint test, the fastest sprint time was 4.24 ± 0.03 and 4.22 ± 0.03 s before and after the IH-period, respectively. In the beginning of the season and at mid-season the fastest sprint time was 4.24 ± 0.04 and 4.19 ± 0.03 s. No differences were observed in the fastest sprint time during the season. On the other hand, the fatigue time after the IH period was lower ($P<0.05$) than before the IH period (0.19 ± 0.02 vs 0.24 ± 0.02 s; $n = 14$) and at the beginning of the season (0.30 ± 0.05 s), but not different from mid-season (0.21 ± 0.03 s).

Performance of the Yo-Yo IR2 test

After the IH period the performance of the Yo-Yo IR2 test was 980 ± 42 m. This value was higher ($P<0.001$) than before the IH period and at the beginning of the season (851 ± 35 and 863 ± 41 m, respectively; Figure 51.3). The performance after the post-IH period tended to be better the at mid-season (863 ± 41 m; $P = 0.094$).

Maximum oxygen uptake

The maximum oxygen uptake was 62.2 ± 1.3 ml.kg^{-1}.min^{-1} after the AH period. This value was $5.4 \pm 2.1\%$ higher ($P<0.05$) higher than before the AH period (59.0 ± 0.9 ml.kg^{-1}.min^{-1}, $n = 12$; Figure 51.4).

Discussion

The major findings of the present study was that just one 30 min session of intermittent drills per week significantly improved the elite players' ability to perform repeated high-intensity exercise as evaluated by the improved performance of the Yo-Yo IR2 test. Since the results of the test have been shown to reflect the

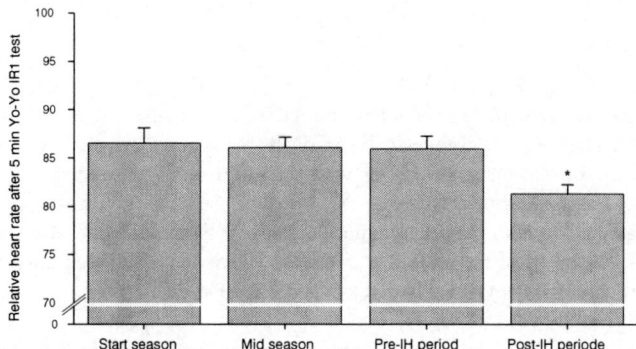

Figure 51.3 Performance of the Yo-Yo intermittent recovery level 2 test at the start of the season, mid-season as well as before and after the IH-period

Note: * Significantly different ($P<0.05$) from before the IH period and start of season.

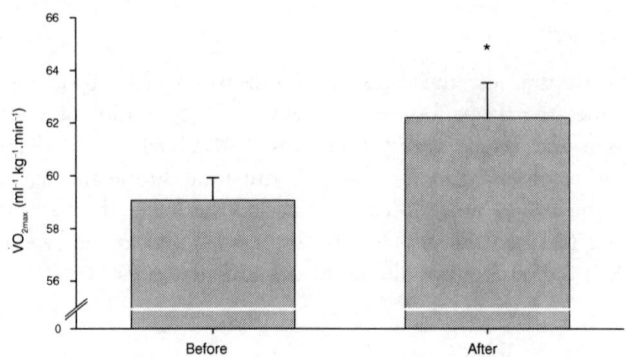

Figure 51.4 Maximum oxygen uptake before and after the IH-period

Note: *:Significantly different ($P<0.05$) from before the IH period

ability to perform high-intensity exercise during a match (Randers *et al.*, 2007), it is likely that the training also improved the performance of the players during match play. The increase in Yo-Yo IR2 test performance was accompanied by an improved $\dot{V}O_{2\,max}$ (5.4 ± 2.1%) as well as lowered heart rate and blood lactate during the submaximal Yo-Yo IR1 test, reflecting an improved endurance capacity (Bangsbo *et al.*, 2006). Thus, the aerobic capacity of the players appears to have been elevated as a result of the training. Additionally, repeated sprint ability was improved after the intervention period, whereas the best sprint time was unaltered.

Intermittent high-intensity training appears to have positive effects not only on the aerobic effect and capacity but also on the anaerobic energy system. Furthermore, the present study shows that elite soccer players can improve their performance within the competitive season by 30 min sessions of intermittent training organized as small-sided games without increasing the total training volume.

References

Bangsbo, J, Mohr, M, Poulsen, A, Perez-Gomez, J. and Krustrup, P., 2006, Training and testing the elite athlete. *Journal of Exercise Science Fitness*, 4, 1–14.

Chamari, K., Hachana, Y., Kaouech, F., Jeddi, R., Moussa-Chamari, I. and Wisloff, U., 2005, Endurance training and testing with the ball in young elite soccer players. *British Journal of Sports Medicine*, 39, 24–8.

Impellizzeri, F.M., Marcora, S.M., Castagna, C., Reilly, T., Sassi, A., Iaia, F.M. and Rampinini, E., 2006, Physiological and performance effects of generic versus specific aerobic training in soccer players. *International Journal of Sport Medicine*, 27, 483–92.

Krustrup, P., Mohr, M., Amstrup, T., Rysgaard, T., Johansen, J., Steensberg, A., Pedersen, P.K. and Bangsbo, J., 2003, The Yo-Yo intermittent recovery test: physiological response, reliability, and validity. *Medicine and Science in Sports and Exercise*, 35, 697–705.

Krustrup, P., Mohr, M., Nybo, L., Jensen, J.M., Nielsen, J.J. and Bangsbo J. 2006, The Yo-Yo IR2 Test: Physiological response, reliability, and application to elite soccer. *Medicine and Science in Sports and Exercise*, 38, 1666–73.

McMillan, K., Helgerud, J., Macdonald, R. and Hoff, J., 2005, Physiological adaptations to soccer specific endurance training in professional youth players. *British Journal of Sports Medicine*, 39, 273–7.

Randers, M.B. Rostgaard, T. Jensen, J.M. Bangsbo, J. and Krustrup, P., 2007, Match performance and Yo-Yo IR2 TEST Performance of players from successful and unsuccessful professional soccer teams. *Journal of Sport Science and Medicine*, 6, 70.

Reilly, T. and Bangsbo, J. 1998, Anaerobic and aerobic training. in training in sport. *Applying Sport Science*, edited by Elliott, B. (Chichester: John Wiley), pp. 351–409.

52 The effects of strength training and practice on soccer throw-in performance

G.M.S. de Carnys and A. Lees

Research Institute of Sport and Exercise Sciences, Liverpool John Moores University, UK

Introduction

The throw-in is increasingly becoming recognized as an important skill in the game of soccer (Chang, 1979; Kollath and Schwirtz, 1988). During the World Cup in Mexico in 1986 the number of throw-ins near the opponent's goal was similar to the number of free kicks in that area (Laux, 1986). Literature suggests that the long throw-in, when performed well, can reach a maximum horizontal range (MHR) of around 30 m. It has also been established that the long throw-in is largely a more accurate skill than the corner kick (Chang, 1979) and consequently can allow a player to pick out a team-mate for a goal scoring opportunity more easily when within range. The long-range throw-in can be performed from a stationary position or with a run-up.

Strength and practice affect the performance of most skills so the aim of this study was to investigate the influence of two training regimens (strength training and practice) on performance.

Methodology

A total of 13 male and 10 female university standard outfield football players were sampled into three groups (control group $n = 7$, strength group, $n = 9$ and practice group, $n = 7$). Each subject gave consent to participate in the study. Subjects were allowed several practice throws before testing began. Testing was conducted on a grass surface for males, and on a synthetic surface for females. Subjects wore their own regulation football boots. All subjects were familiar with both the standing and running throw-in techniques as described in the laws of the game (FIFA, 2004) and normal football warm-ups were performed before testing in all cases. Subjects were instructed to perform five standing throws and five throws with a run-up of five metres in length (run-up was marked by a ground peg). The throw-in line was the sideline of a football pitch. All trials were filmed using a digital video camera positioned eight metres from the throw-in point to provide a sagittal view. The point at which each ball landed was marked and measured using a measuring tape positioned at a right angle to the throw-in line to quantify the MHR.

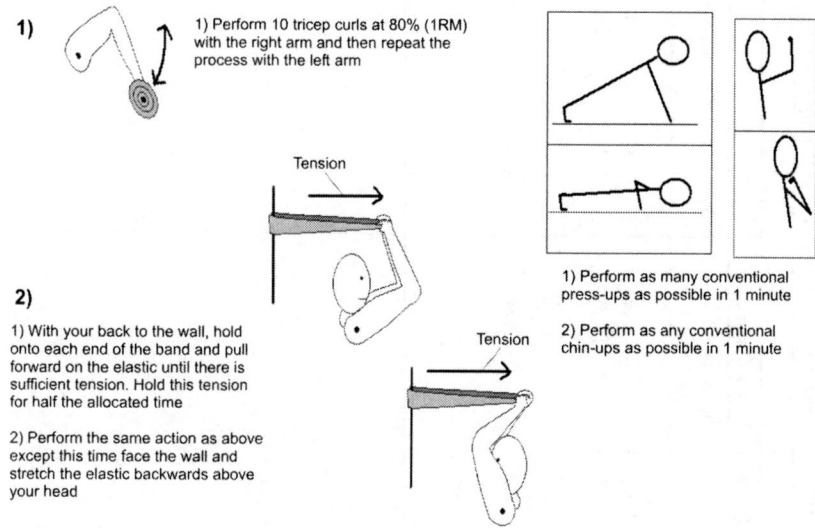

1) Perform 10 tricep curls at 80% (1RM) with the right arm and then repeat the process with the left arm

Tension →

2)

1) With your back to the wall, hold onto each end of the band and pull forward on the elastic until there is sufficient tension. Hold this tension for half the allocated time

2) Perform the same action as above except this time face the wall and stretch the elastic backwards above your head

Tension →

1) Perform as many conventional press-ups as possible in 1 minute

2) Perform as any conventional chin-ups as possible in 1 minute

Figure 52.1 Two-minute circuit training set to be repeated three times

This procedure was repeated once a week over a six-week period during which time the practice group participated in three practice sessions per week. These sessions lasted for approximately 30 minutes and involved a 5-minute warm-up prior to starting and a 5-minute cool-down at the end. For the main content of the sessions subjects were asked to perform a set of 15 maximal standing throws followed by a set of 15 maximal throws with a 5 m run up and this process was repeated for a total of 60 throws. Subjects were given no extrinsic feedback. The strength group attended a twice-weekly session, during which a set muscle strength training routine was followed. The one repetition maximum (1 RM) triceps curl value of all the subjects in the strength group was tested at the start and this formed the basis of the training programme. Figure 52.1 shows one complete set to be performed three times during a strength session. At the start of each session all subjects performed a light warm-up including stretches. Each exercise was followed by a 1-minute rest and a 3-minute rest between sets.

Finally, those subjects in the control group received no intervention. The furthest standing and running throw of each subject for each trial was digitized using the SIMI Motion Analysis program (SIMI Reality Motion Systems, Unterschleissheim, Germany) to obtain ball release parameters. Statistical analysis was conducted on the mean MHR using two-way (group × time) mixed design ANOVA (SPSS, version 13). Statistical significance was set at $P < 0.05$.

Results

All groups displayed a greater MHR in the running throw-in than that of the standing throw in both week 1 and week 6 of the experimental procedure (Table 52.1). An increase in mean MHR was apparent in all groups over the six-week

Table 52.1 The effect of a six-week strength (n = 9) and practice (n = 7) programme on mean MHR of university standard soccer players (n = 23)

	Week 1				Week 2			
	MHR (m)	Release parameters			MHR(m)	Release parameters		
		Speed of release (m/s)	Height (m)	Angle (°)		Speed of release (m/s)	Height (m)	Angle (°)
Control (n =7)								
Standing	15.33	11.35	2.14	26.03	15.46	13.06	2.09	27.86
Running	17.93	12.78	1.94	25.77	18.03	15.39	1.98	28.70
Strength (n = 9)								
Standing	14.83	11.64	2.06	32.08	14.43	10.91	2.02	29.91
Running	17.06	12.81	1.88	29.09	18.27	14.80	1.88	29.39
Practice (n = 7)								
Standing	14.31	11.79	2.07	33.34	15.24	11.33	2.09	29.91
Running	16.40	12.51	1.93	29.09	17.81	14.08	1.88	29.39

period apart from the standing throw-ins of the strength group which showed a mean decrease of 0.37 m (from 14.83 to 14.43 m). Both strength training (17.05–18.27 m) ($F_{1,14} = 6.21, P < 0.05$) and practice (16.40–17.81 m) ($F_{1,12} = 7.29$, $P < 0.05$) were found to increase running throw-in performance significantly over six weeks. The decrease in standing throw-in performance for the strength group was not found to be statistically significant (14.83–14.43 m). An increase in performance was found for the practice group which was also not significant (14.31–15.24 m).

Discussion

The most practically significant finding from this study was the influence of a six-week strength training programme on the increase in the running throw-in MHR. Since height and angle of release did not change substantially, this change in MHR was due to the increase in speed of release. Interestingly, however, the standing throw of the strength group decreased in both MHR and speed of release. Although the strength training programme used in this study was designed specifically with the aim of increasing a performer's ability to perform a maximal soccer throw-in, a number of factors may have caused it to have been unsuccessful in increasing the MHR of standing throw-ins. First, over the six-week programme, it is highly likely that any increase in repetition maximum may have been attributed to a neuromuscular functioning improvement rather than an increase in muscular strength. This increase in neuromuscular response may explain the greater velocity at ball release during the running throws, as this skill is one which the performers are, perhaps, more familiar with (since very few maximal throws would be conducted using a standing throw-in technique) and where the ability to translate the speed of the run-up into a high ball velocity at point of release is essential. Perhaps also of some significance is the type of training programme. During the strength training programme, subjects underwent a mixture of both high-intensity, low-volume exercises (1 RM triceps curls) and more dynamic strength training exercises (press-ups and sit-ups). The inclusion of these more dynamic strength training exercises may also hold an explanation for the improvement in performing the more dynamic throwing technique with a run-up. However, due to its dynamic nature, the programme may have been less suited to the improvement of the standing throw-in skill. Although there have been no studies which have looked specifically into the effect of strength training on MHR of stranding and running throw-ins, the current study may provide a useful benchmark for future research of this nature to be conducted.

The finding that a weekly practice routine improves MHR supports previous research reports. In a previous study conducted by Linthorne and Everett (2006), the usefulness of repeating the throw-in task in finding the optimum angle of release through trial and error was explained. In the current study it was found that changes in angle did occur over the six weeks in the standing throws. These values were found to become closer to the 30° which is similar to that found by Linthorne and Everett (2006) through simulation.

Conclusion

In conclusion, this study has found that a six-week throw-specific strength training programme increased the MHR of the running throw-in with a 5 m run-up. Furthermore, practice of an intrinsic nature, was shown to increase the MHR of both the standing and running throw-ins. A combination of the two practice regimens is likely to be most effective.

References

Chang, J. 1979, The biomechanical analysis of the selected soccer throw-in techniques. *Asian Journal of Physical Education*, 2(4), 254–60.

FIFA, 2004, *Laws of the Game 2004*. (Zurich: Fédération Internationale de Football Association).

Kollath, E. and Schwirtz, A., 1988, Biomechanical analysis of the soccer throw-in. In *Science and Football*, edited by Reilly, T., Lees, A., Davids, K. and Murphy, W.J. (New York: E&FN Spon), pp. 460–67.

Laux, D. 1986, Annual football meet: a kinematic analysis. German Thesis, Köln: Sporthochscule College.

Linthorne, N.P. and Everett, D.J., 2006, Release angle for attaining maximum distance in the soccer throw-in. *Sports Biomechanics*, 5, 243–60.

53 The energy cost of soloing a Gaelic football

A. Hulton, T. Ford and T. Reilly

Research Institute for Sport and Exercise Sciences, Liverpool John Moores University, Liverpool, UK.

Introduction

The scientific investigation into the game of Gaelic football has been limited even though Gaelic football has the highest participation rate in sport in Ireland. Its players include both male and female participants and it embraces schools, minor (under–18), under-21, intermediate and senior to veterans' competitions (Reilly and Doran, 2001). Its beginnings link back to the foundations of the Gaelic Athletic Association (GAA) in 1884 and served to save traditional Irish games from decline following the surge in foreign games promoted by the British army's garrisons. These Gaelic games, which included Gaelic football, hurling, camogie, court handball and athletics, became the binding force in many Irish communities.

With Gaelic football becoming the most popular of these Irish sports, sport science has become increasingly relevant, coaches are more aware of the potential role of sport science in the preparation of teams. Many of the activities of the other football codes are required in playing this game (Douge, 1988). Gaelic football is characterized by quick starts and sudden stops, interspersed with changes of speed and direction. Players need to be able to undertake multiple short-duration intermittent bouts of high-intensity exercises interspersed with short-duration recovery periods. In addition, players must possess strength and flexibility to enable them to obtain and maintain possession of the ball while also optimally executing skills and tackling opponents.

A Gaelic football match requires players to walk or jog in a light-to-moderate aerobic activity for approximately 80 per cent of the distance covered, although many of the crucial match events require anaerobic efforts that are superimposed on this aerobic activity profile. An essential skill of Gaelic football is the ability to 'solo' run, an action of dropping the ball onto the foot and kicking it back into the hand (Reilly and Doran, 2001). During the game this action may induce fatigue as more muscles are employed to carry out the skill and high levels of concentration must be maintained throughout.

The solo run is a very skilful element of the game, with concentration, balance, and correct foot strike of the ball needed to complete a solo correctly. Consistency of the solo is key for players to gain advances towards the opponent's goal. The action of soloing was classed by Lennon (1971) as one of the eight fundamental skills of the game. If a player declines the opportunity to pass or shoot at goal by kicking or 'hand-passing', a striking motion with the hand or fist, after every four steps the ball must be bounced or 'soloed'. The ball cannot be bounced twice in a row.

The physiological demands of Gaelic football are thought to be similar to soccer (Strudwick *et al.*, 2002). Studies of Gaelic football players in English based clubs have suggested no difference in maximal oxygen uptake ($\dot{V}O_{2max}$), maximal heart rate (HR_{max}) or treadmill time to exhaustion between Gaelic players and English university soccer players (Florida-James and Reilly, 1995).

McCrudden and Reilly (1993) compared kicking patterns in Gaelic football (drop and punt kick) but not on the solo kick. The comparisons between football codes were limited to the study of electromyography of different kicking actions. The extent to which energy cost is increased by the action of soloing has never been previously documented. To do so, it would be necessary to study the physiological cost of soloing a Gaelic football over different speeds in comparison to running without the ball for the same given speeds. Therefore the aim of this study was to establish the extent to which soloing increased physiological responses compared to running without the ball.

Methods

Twelve non-elite university-level Gaelic footballers (20 ± 2 years, 1.78 ± 0.6 m, 76.4 ± 8.3 kg) participated in this study after completing written informed consent. Subjects avoided vigorous exercise and refrained from alcohol the 24 hours prior to testing.

Subjects performed eight trials in a randomised order, consisting of a control and experimental condition for four different speeds (9 km.h^{-1}, 10.5 km.h^{-1}, 12 km.h^{-1} and 13.5 km.h^{-1}), each for 4 min. The control trials consisted of running 20 m shuttles back and forth at the different speeds. The experimental trials were at the same speeds but subjects were required to solo the football during this time. The subjects kept at the correct pace by running in time with a 'bleep' that was administered to indicate that the subjects should have reached the end of the shuttle.

Resting heart rate (HR) was measured prior to the exercise trials and then recorded every 5 s during the trials using short-range radio telemetry (Sports Tester PE3000, Polar Electro, Finland) to discover the maximum HR for the given trial. Blood lactate concentration was determined via finger prick blood samples and measured pre-exercise and immediately post-exercise. Blood lactate was analysed using an Analox GMX lactate analyser (Analox, UK). During the final 2 min of exercise $\dot{V}O_2$ was measured using a portable Metamax 3B online gas analyser (Cortex, Germany). Immediately following the completion of exercise, subjects rated their perceived exertion (RPE) using Borg's Scale (Borg, 1970).

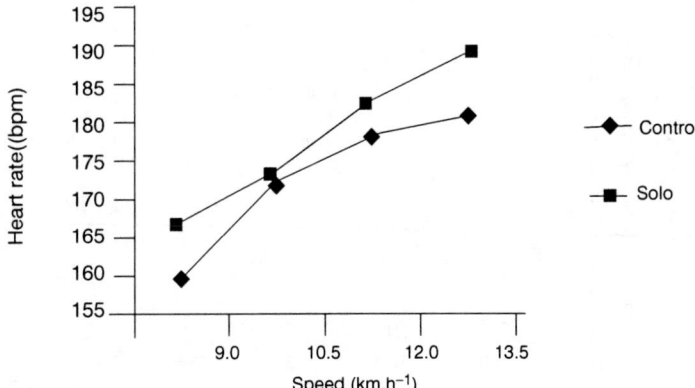

Figure 53.1 Mean heart rate (beats.min⁻¹) response to the different speeds and the two conditions

The data were analysed by two-way repeated measures ANOVA for both control and experimental conditions. The Shapiro-Wilks test of normality was used for all data. The significance value for all data was for set at $P<0.05$.

Results

There was a significant difference for HR (Figure 53.1) between soloing and running where $F_{1,11} = 14.82$, $P<0.05$. Mean values increased for normal running from 160 beats.min⁻¹ at 9 km.h⁻¹ to 181 beats.min⁻¹ at 13.5 km.h⁻¹, while further increasing from 167 to 189 beats.min⁻¹ for the same speeds whilst soloing. There was a significant difference in HR in relation to the different trials, $F_{1.47,16.2} = 26.70$, $P<0.05$. There were no significant interactions between the conditions and trials $(F_{2.7,33} = 2.04, P>0.05)$.

Soloing significantly increased subjects' ratings of perceived exertion (Figure 53.2) compared to normal running, where $(F_{1,11} = 26.45, P<0.05)$. The effect of the speed of the trial was also significant $(F_{1.99,21.94} = 226.06, P<0.05)$, although there was no significant interaction between the conditions and trials $(F_{2.25,24.73} = 2.04, P>0.05)$.

Mean blood lactate values increased from 4.7 to 18.2 for running and 6.1 to 21.3 for soloing for the four speeds $(P<0.05)$. There was a significant main effect for both conditions $(F_{1,11} = 107.27, P<0.01$ and trial $F_{1.91,20.99} = 547.04, P<0.01.)$ Both main effects were due to a significant interaction between the condition and the type of speed of motion viewed $(F_{2.16,23.75} = 7.55, P<0.05)$. Blood lactate increased more steeply at the top speed when soloing rather than running normally (Figure 53.3).

Mean values for an oxygen consumption (Figure 53.4) ranged from 52 to 63.63 ml.kg⁻¹.min⁻¹ for running and 54.77 to 65.31 ml.kg⁻¹.min⁻¹ for soloing for the four speeds. Running induced a mean $\dot{V}O_2$ value of 57.80 ± 0.32 ml.kg⁻¹.min⁻¹, and soloing induced a value of 60.38 ± 0.29 ml.kg⁻¹.min⁻¹. This comparison showed a significant main effect for between conditions (running and soloing); $F_{1,6} = 39.22$,

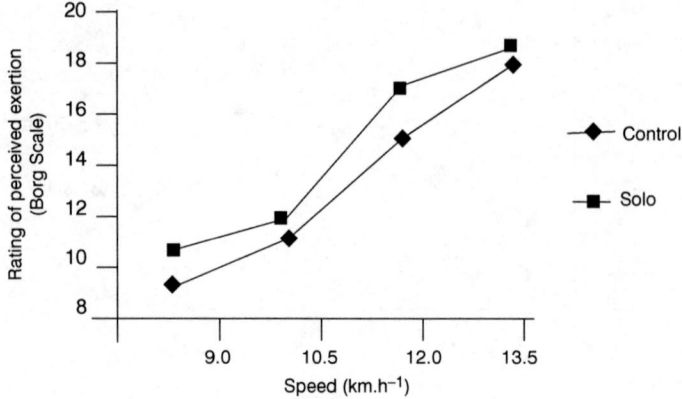

Figure 53.2 Rating of perceived exertion for the different speeds and conditions

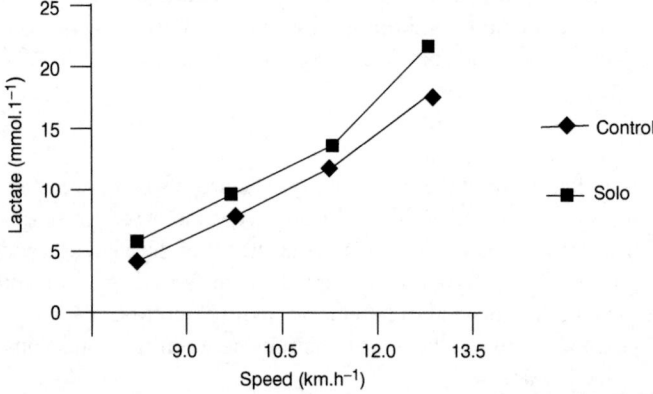

Figure 53.3 Post-exercise lactate accumulation due to the different speeds and conditions

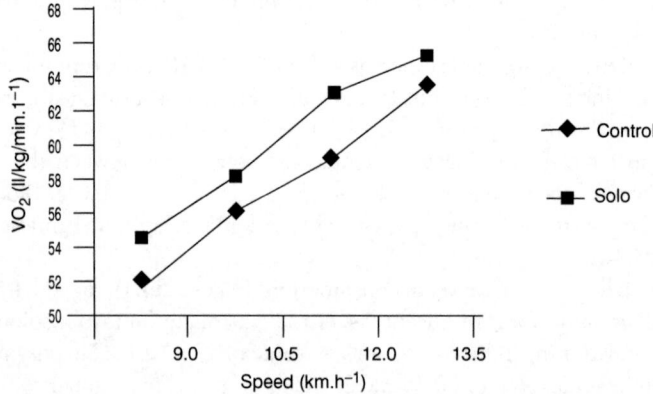

Figure 53.4 Average $\dot{V}_{O_2}$ (ml.kg^{-1}.min^{-1}) during the final 2 minutes of exercise

$P<0.05$ and trial $F_{1.71,10.28} = 9.35$, $P<0.05$. There was no significant interaction between condition and trial ($F_{1.19,7.13} = 0.62$, $P>0.05$).

Discussion

The energy cost of soloing was found to increase linearly with the speed of running. When soloing in tight control of the ball, the stride rate increases and the stride length shortens compared with normal running at the same speed, which contributes to the additional energy cost. Increasing or decreasing the stride length beyond that freely chosen by the individual causes the oxygen consumption for a given speed to increase (Reilly and Ball, 1984). The added energy cost may be further highlighted in matches as the Gaelic footballer changes stride characteristics intermittently or fakes lateral movement whilst in possession of the ball when trying to outmanoeuvre an opponent.

Significant differences were found for HR (Figure 53.1) between running and soloing, signifying that soloing induced higher exercise intensities. The rise in HR increases cardiac output for delivery of oxygen to the extra working muscles that are needed to return the ball back to the hands, while running at the same time. With additional values evident at each speed, the highest HR values were produced when subjects performed the 13.5 km.h^{-1} solo trial and responses were close to subjects' age predicted HR$_{max}$. The linear increase in HR with speed of motion showed the need for the increased energy cost of running and in particular when soloing at higher speeds. Florida-James and Reilly (1995) recorded a mean HR of 164 $\pm$ 10 and 157 $\pm$ 11 beats.min^{-1} for the first and second half involving English Gaelic football club players. These figures corresponded to 81 per cent of the HR$_{max}$ during the match and support the findings from this study in that soloing causes a significant physiological strain in players. Only when running without the ball at 9 km.h^{-1} were values lower than observed during match play.

The increases in perceived exertion, resulting from an elevation in metabolism, found in this study are similar to findings of Reilly and Ball (1984) with soccer dribbling, indicating a similar pattern with soloing (Figure 53.2). Unlike in soccer, where dribbling can be spaced out between contact with the ball, soloing has to be done every four steps. Although ball contact in soloing might be more frequent than in soccer, the effect on stride length is unknown. All-out efforts are likely to be limiting in soloing practices as all subjects failed to complete both trials at 13.5 km.h^{-1}, with soloing resulting in subjects desisting in a time shorter than in the control trial.

Blood lactate levels were also elevated as a consequence of soloing the ball, the increased concentrations being disproportionate at the high speeds. The relationship of speed to blood lactate was similar to that reported by Reilly and Ball (1984) for dribbling a soccer ball where levels increased proportionally before skewing. The 'lactate threshold' lay before the values skewed but were higher for a given speed than for dribbling a soccer ball as recorded by Reilly and Ball (1984). The soccer players retained linear motion when dribbling the ball on a treadmill test whereas the Gaelic players were required to turn around every 20 m, a manoeuvre that would raise the physiological demand. In the current study, the 4 mM 'lactate threshold' occurred at a lower running speed for soloing compared to running. Failure to complete both 13.5 km.h^{-1} trials may be attributed to the high lactate values recorded. It is evident that soloing a ball at a given speed will affect the performance sooner than running without a ball. Accumulation of lactic acid and the accompanying muscle fatigue are likely causes of this reduction in performance (Westerblad *et al.*, 2002).

The $\dot{V}O_2$ for soloing was significantly higher than the $\dot{V}O_2$ for running and showed a difference of 4 ml.kg^{-1}.min^{-1} for the 12 km.h^{-1} trials (Figure 53.4). This result indicated that approximately 7 per cent more oxygen was needed for the working muscles that had a greater demand for ATP to supply the energy to endure the pace that was set. The energy cost is far greater for soloing the ball than normal running over any speed of motion. The additional cost was constant for each speed, evident in the parallel linear relationship between the two conditions.

Gaelic footballers use significantly more energy while soloing than running without the ball. This difference was reflected in the physiological responses from the two conditions. Blood lactate concentration, HR, $\dot{V}O_2$ and rating of perceived exertion were all significantly higher for soloing. The 13.5 km.h^{-1} trials for soloing were too intense for subjects to sustain four minutes of exercise. However, activity in Gaelic football is intermittent where short sharp bursts at this speed or greater are called for. Future studies are needed to single out match-play requirements in order to improve the players' technique and prolong performance before the onset of fatigue. Training drills akin to soccer dribbling (i.e. dribbling around cones) could be applied to soloing in Gaelic football to show relevance to competitive characteristics.

References

Borg, G., 1970, Perceived exertion as an indicator of somatic stress. *Scandinavian Journal of Rehabilitation Medicine*, 2, 92–8.

Douge, B., 1988, Football: the common threads between the games. In *Science and Football*, edited by Reilly, T., Lees, A., Davids, K. and Murphy, W.J. (London: E&FN Spon), pp. 3–19.

Florida-James, G. and Reilly, T., 1995, The physiological demands of Gaelic Football. *British Journal of Sports Medicine*, 29, 41–5.

Keane, S., Reilly, T and Hughes, M., 1993, Analysis of work-rates in Gaelic Football. *Australian Journal of Science and Medicine in Sport*, 25, 100–2.

Lennon, J., 1971, Football (Gaelic). In *Encyclopeadia of Sport Science and Medicine*, edited by Larson, L.A., (New York: Macmillan), pp. 683–4.

McCrudden, M and Reilly, T., 1993, A comparison of the punt and drop kick. In *Science and Football II*, edited by Reilly, T., Clarys, J. and Stibbe, A. (London: E&FN Spon), pp. 362–6.

Reilly, T. and Ball, D., 1984, The net physiological cost of dribbling a soccer ball. *Research Quarterly for Exercise and Sport*, 55, 267–71.

Reilly, T. and Doran, D., 2001, Science and Gaelic football: a review. *Journal of Sports Sciences*, 19, 181–93.

Strudwick, A., Reilly, T. and Doran, D., 2002, Anthropometric and fitness profiles of elite players in two football codes. *Journal of Sports Medicine and Physical Fitness*, 42, 239–42.

Westerblad, H., Allen, D.G. and Lannergren, J., 2002, Muscle fatigue: lactic acid or inorganic phosphate the major cause? *News Physiology and Science*, 17, 17–21.

54 The effect of short-term intense soccer-specific exercise on technical performance in soccer

Thomas Rostgaard,[1] *Fedon Marcello Iaia*[2] *and Jens Bangsbo*[1]

[1] Institute of Exercise and Sport Sciences, Department of Human Physiology, University of Copenhagen, Denmark; [2] Faculty of Exercise Sciences, State University of Milan, Italy

Introduction

It is well established that soccer players during a game perform intermittent exercise with changes in activity every 3–5 s and that soccer is physically demanding due to multiple brief intense actions involving jumps, turns, tackles, high-speed runs and sprints (Mayhew and Wenger, 1985; Bangsbo *et al.*, 1991; Bangsbo, 1994). It has been observed that players experience fatigue both towards the end of a game and temporarily during a match (Krustrup *et al.*, 2006a; Mohr *et al.*, 2003). Soccer at high level is characterized by a significant amount of high-intensity exercise performed during a game. Thus, players at international elite level have been shown to perform 25 per cent more high-intensity running and 35 per cent more sprinting during competitive games than professional players at a moderate elite level (Mohr *et al.*, 2002). However, it is unclear to what extent intense short term intermittent exercise affects a player's technical skills.

Thus, the aims of the present study were to examine the technical performance of soccer players during soccer-specific intermittent exercise resembling intense periods of a soccer game, and relate this performance to the technical performance without prior intense exercise and to the physical capacity of the players.

Methods

Subjects and procedures

Twenty-one healthy male soccer players with an age of 22.4 (range: 16.1–33.2) years, height 1.81 (1.65–1.90) m and body mass of 76.0 (63.1–92.4) kg participated as subjects in the study. All subjects were informed of any risks and discomfort associated with the experiment before giving their written consent to participate.

In the cases where the subjects were below 18 years, written informed consent was obtained from the subject's parents.

The players performed a physical-technical test (PT-test) consisting of ten 30 m kicks separated by soccer-intense intermittent activities including high-intensity running and dribbling actions alternated with active recovery using low to moderate intensity movements as observed during soccer matches. The players also performed a control test (CON-test) with ten long kicks without prior intense exercise. In both tests each kick was evaluated in a scale from 0 (miss) to 3 (perfect). In addition, they carried out the Yo-Yo intermittent recovery test level 2 (Yo-Yo IR2; Krustrup *et al.*, 2006b). All tests were performed at least 48 hours apart.

Statistical analysis

Changes in technical performance during the CON- and PT-test as well as differences in technical performance between the CON- and PT-test were compared using a binomial test. The summed performance (kick 1 through 5 and 6 through 10) in the CON-test and the PT-test was evaluated by one-way analysis of variance (ANOVA) with repeated measures. When a significant interaction was detected, data were subsequently analysed by application of a NewmanKeuls posthoc test. Significant level was set to $P<0.05$. Values are presented as means±SEM.

Results

Technical performance during the PT-test tended ($P<0.1$) on average to decrease from on average 1.9 ± 0.3 points at the first repetition to 1.6 ± 0.3 points at the last repetition (Figure 54.1). The summed performance of the first five repetitions was higher ($P<0.05$) than for the last five repetitions (8.4 ± 0.6 vs 6.9 ± 0.5). Technical performance during the PT-test tended ($P<0.1$) to be lower compared to

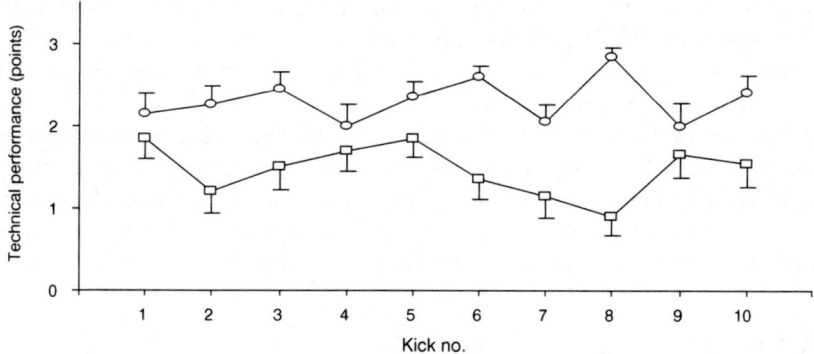

Figure 54.1 Test score at the PT-test (squares) and CON-test (circles) during each of the 10 kicks

Note: * Significant difference ($P<0.05$) between PT- and CON-test.

CON-test in each repetition, but the difference in performance was only significant ($P<0.05$) at the seventh and eighth repetition. The summed performance of the first five and the last five repetitions during the PT-test was lower ($P<0.05$) than in the CON condition. Difference in performance between the PT- and CON-test was greater ($P<0.05$) during the last five repetitions compared to the first five repetitions ($20.5 \pm 0.56\%$ vs $42.9 \pm 0.61\%$). No correlation ($n = 18$) between Yo-Yo IR2 test performance and PT-test performance was found.

Discussion

The present study showed that technical performance was reduced as the PT-test progressed, and that the performance of last five kicks in the PT-test was lower than in the first five kicks. In order to express the effect of the physical work on the technical performance, the test result was compared to the result in a control (CON) test consisting of ten long passes carried out at low physical loading. It was observed that performance in the PT-test was lower than for the CON-test. Together these findings suggest that the physical work influenced the players' ability to kick. It has been demonstrated that the activity pattern and the physiological responses during the test were similar to what have been observed during the intense periods of a soccer game (Rostgaard et al., 2007). Thus, the data suggest that the physical stress during a game influences the technical performance of the players.

For all players the performance of the PT-test was not as good as the performance of the CON-test, but a large variation in the difference between the two tests was observed, showing that the players were affected differently by the physical work. Thus, the test shows that the players technically respond differently to the same physical loading even though none of the players showed signs of fatigue, as the speed was maintained throughout the test. Apparently, the tests can reveal the effect of physical stress on a player's technical skill.

The Yo-Yo intermittent recovery test performance, which has been shown to be closely related to high-intensity exercise performance during a soccer match (Krustrup et al., 2003), was not correlated with the PT-test performance. This observation suggests that the result of the PT-test is not solely dependent on the physical performance of the player.

In conclusion, even though there may not be any objective sign of fatigue during a soccer game, the physical loading imposed on a player may affect his technical capacity. Furthermore, the test can evaluate individual differences in physical and technical performance of soccer players, and may be used to examine the effect of a fitness programme or a technical training programme.

References

Bangsbo, J., 1994, The physiology of soccer with special reference to intense intermittent exercise. *Acta Physiologica Scandinavica, Supplementum*, 619, 1–155.

Bangsbo, J., Nørregaard, L. and Thorsøe F., 1991, Activity profile of competition soccer. *Canadian Journal of Sports Sciences*, 16(2),110–16.

Krustrup, P., Mohr, M., Amstrup, T., Rysgaard, T., Johansen, J., Steensberg, A., Pedersen, P.K. and Bangsbo, J., 2003, The Yo-Yo intermittent recovery test: physiological response, reliability and validity. *Medicine and Science in Sports and Exercise*, 35, 695–705.

Krustrup, P., Mohr, M., Steensberg, A., Bencke, J., Kjær, M. and Bangsbo, J., 2006a, Muscle and blood metabolites during a soccer game: Implications for sprint performance. *Medicine and Science in Sports and Exercise*, 38, 1165–74.

Krustrup, P., Mohr, M., Nybo, L., Majgaard Jensen, J., Jung Nielsen, J. and Bangsbo, J., 2006b, The Yo-Yo IR2 Test: physiological response, reliability and application to elite soccer. *Medicine and Science in Sports and Exercise*, 38, 1666–73.

Mayhew, S.R. and Wenger, H.A., 1985, Time-motion analysis of professional soccer. *Journal of Human Movement Studies*, 11, 49–52.

Mohr, M., Krustrup, P. and Bangsbo J., 2002, Seasonal changes in physiological parameters of elite soccer players. *Medicine and Science in Sports and Exercise*, 36, 24.

Mohr, M., Krustrup, P. and Bangsbo, J., 2003, Match performance of high-standard soccer players with special reference to development of fatigue. *Journal of Sports Sciences*, 21, 439–49.

Rostgaard, T., Iaia F.M., and Bangsbo, J, 2007, A test to evaluate the physical impact on technical performance in soccer. *Journal of Strength and Conditioning Research*, 22, 283–92.

55 Physical demands and training of top-class soccer players

Jens Bangsbo and Peter Krustrup

Copenhagen Muscle Research Centre, Department of Exercise and
Sport Sciences, University of Copenhagen, Demark

Introduction

In recent years much research regarding match performance and training has been conducted, and science has been incorporated to a greater extent, in the planning and execution of training. Changes in both performance and physiological response throughout a game have been studied. Another aspect that has drawn attention in practical training is information regarding individual differences in the physical demands to which players are exposed in games and training. These differences are related to the training status of the players and the specific tactical role of the player. Thus, some top-class clubs have integrated the tactical and physical demands of the players into their fitness training. A critical factor when training elite athletes is when to do what, i.e. to plan the training. An example of the preparation of the Danish national soccer team for the European Championship 2004 is given in the text. Thus, this review deals with the present knowledge of the demands of the game at a top-class level and provides insight into training and planning of training at an elite level. The chapter will mainly deal with male players, but at relevant places information about female players is given.

Match activities

The typical distance covered by an outfield player at top level during a match is 10–13 km with that of midfield players being greater than players in the other positions (Reilly, 1997; Mohr et al., 2003; Krustrup et al., 2005). However, the majority of the distance is covered by walking and low-intensity running, and in terms of energy production mainly the high-intensity exercise periods are important. Thus, it is clear that the amount of high-intensity exercise separates the top-class players from players at a lower level. Computerized time–motion analysis has demonstrated that international top-class players performed 28 per cent more high-intensity running (2.43 vs 1.90 km) and 58 per cent more sprinting (650 vs 410 m) than professional players at a lower level (Mohr et al., 2003). It should be emphasized that the recordings of high-intensity running do not include a number of energy-demanding activities such as a short accelerations, turns, tackles and jumps. The number of tackles and jumps depends on the individual playing style and position in the team and at a top level has been shown to vary between 3–27 and 1–36, respectively (Mohr et al., 2003). Most authors have used video analysis followed by manual computer analysis to examine individual performance during a match. Development of new technology in recent years has allowed the study of all 22 players for each one-sixth of a second during the entire match and the systems are used by a considerable number of top teams in Europe. There are reasons to believe that in the future such systems will provide significant added information and they have already found their way to scientific journals (Bangsbo and Mohr, 2005; Di Salvo et al., 2007). For example, in a recent study Bangsbo and Mohr (2005) examined, with a high time resolution, fluctuation in high-intensity exercise, running speeds and recovery time from sprints during a number of top-class soccer matches. This study showed that sprinting speed in games reached peak values around $32\,km.h^{-1}$ and that sprints longer than $30\,m$ demanded markedly longer recovery than the average sprint (10–$15\,m$) during the game.

There are major individual differences in the physical demands of a player in part related to the position in the team. Mohr et al. (2003) studied top-class players and found that the central defenders covered less total distance and high-intensity running than players in the other positions, which probably is closely linked to the tactical roles of the central defenders and their lower physical capacity (Bangsbo, 1994; Krustrup et al., 2003; Mohr et al., 2003). The full-backs covered a considerable distance at a high-intensity and by sprinting, whereas they carried out fewer headers and tackles than players in the other playing positions. The attackers covered a distance at a high intensity equal to the full-backs and midfield players, but sprinted more than the midfield players and defenders. Furthermore, in the study by Mohr et al. (2003) the attackers had a more marked decline in sprinting distance than the defenders and midfield players. In addition, the performance of the attackers on the Yo-Yo intermittent recovery test was not as high as the performance of the full-backs and midfield players. Thus, it appears that the modern top-level attacker needs a high ability to perform high-intensity actions repeatedly throughout a game.

The midfield players performed as many tackles and headers as defenders and attackers. They covered a total distance and distance at a high intensity similar to the full-backs and attackers, but sprinted less. Earlier studies have shown that midfield players cover a greater distance during a game than full-backs and attackers (Reilly and Thomas, 1976; Withers et al., 1982; Ekblom, 1986; Bangsbo et al., 1991; Bangsbo, 1994). These differences may be explained by the development of the physical demands of full-backs and attackers, since, in contrast to earlier studies (Bangsbo, 1994), Mohr et al. (2003) observed that players in all team positions had a significant decline in high-intensity running towards the end of a match. This finding indicates that almost all players in elite soccer utilize their physical capacity during a game. Individual differences are not only related to position in the team. Thus, in the study by Mohr et al. (2003), within each playing position there was a significant variation in the physical demands depending on the tactical role and the physical capacity of the players. For example, in the same game, one midfield player covered a total distance of 12.3 km, with 3.5 km covered at a high intensity, whilst another midfielder covered a total distance and high-intensity distance of 10.8 and 2.0 km, respectively. The individual differences in playing style and physical performance should be taken into account when planning the training.

Energy production in soccer

Soccer entails intermittent exercise in which the aerobic energy system is highly taxed with average and peak heart rates around 85 and 98 per cent of maximal values, respectively (Reilly and Thomas, 1979; Ekblom, 1986; Ali and Farally, 1991; Bangsbo, 1994; Krustrup et al., 2005). These values can be 'converted' to oxygen uptake using the relation between heart rate and oxygen uptake obtained during treadmill running (Bangsbo, 1994; Krustrup and Bangsbo, 2001; Esposito et al., 2004; Krustrup et al., 2005). However, it is likely that the heart rate values during a match lead to an overestimation of the oxygen uptake, since a number of factors such as dehydration, hyperthermia and mental stress elevate the heart rate without affecting oxygen uptake. Taking these factors into account the heart rate measurements during a game seem to suggest that the average oxygen uptake is around 70% $\dot{V}O_{2\,max}$. This suggestion is supported by measurements of core temperature during a soccer game. The findings of core temperatures in the range of 39–40°C during a game also suggest that the average aerobic loading during a competitive game is around 70% $\dot{V}O_{2\,max}$ (Ekblom, 1986; Mohr et al., 2004a).

More important for performance than the average oxygen uptake during a game, may be the rate of rise in oxygen uptake during the many short intense actions. A player's heart rate during a game is rarely below 65 per cent of HR_{max}, suggesting that blood flow to the exercising leg muscles is continuously higher than at rest, which means that oxygen delivery is high. However, the oxygen kinetics during the changes from low- to high-intensity exercise during the game appear to be limited by local factors and depend, among other factors, on the oxidative capacity of the contracting muscles (Krustrup et al., 2004). The rate of rise of oxygen uptake can be changed by intense interval training (Krustrup et al., 2004). The observation that elite soccer players perform 150–250 brief, intense actions during a game (Mohr et al., 2003) indicates that the rate of anaerobic energy turnover is high during periods of the game. Even though not studied directly, the intense exercise during a game would lead to a high rate of CP breakdown, which to a major extent is re-synthesized in the low-intensity exercise periods that follow (Bangsbo 1994). Measurements of CP in muscle biopsies obtained after intense exercise periods during a game have shown levels around 75 per cent of the level at rest. This is, however, likely to be significantly lower during the match, because these values are obtained from biopsies taken 15–30 s after match activities in which a substantial re-synthesis of CP undoubtedly has occurred (Krustrup et al., 2006). Using proper values for re-synthesis of CP and the measured CP values, as well as the delay time in obtaining the biopsies, it can be estimated that the CP concentration during the game would have been about 60 per cent of the resting level. On the other hand, it may be expected that during parts of a game the CP levels may become low, i.e.

below 30 per cent of resting level, if a series of intense bouts are performed with only short recovery periods.

Average blood lactate concentrations of 2–10 mM have been observed during soccer games, with individual values above 12 mM (Table 55.1). These findings indicate that the rate of muscle lactate production is high during match play, but muscle lactate has been measured in only a single study. In a friendly game between non-professional teams, it was observed that muscle lactate rose fourfold (to around 15 mmol.kg^{-1} d.w.) compared with resting values after intense periods in both halves, with the highest value being 35 mmol.kg^{-1} d.w (Krustrup *et al.*, 2006). Such values are less than one-third of the concentrations observed during short-term intermittent exhaustive exercise (Krustrup *et al.*, 2003). An interesting finding in that study was a low correlation coefficient between muscle and blood lactate (Krustrup *et al.*, 2006), which can be explained by the lactate clearance rate being higher in muscle than in blood (Bangsbo *et al.*, 1993). This also means that the blood lactate level can be high even though the muscle lactate concentration is relatively low. Thus, the rather high blood lactate concentration often observed in soccer (Bangsbo, 1994; Ekblom, 1986; Krustrup *et al.*, 2006) may not represent a high lactate production in a single action during the game, but rather an accumulated or balanced response to a number of high-intensity activities. This is important to take into account when interpreting blood lactate concentrations as a measure of muscle lactate concentrations. Nevertheless, based on numerous studies using short-term maximal exercise performed in the laboratory and the finding of high blood lactate and moderate muscle lactate concentrations during match play, it can be suggested that the rate of glycolysis is high for short periods of time during a game.

Substrate utilization during a soccer match

Muscle glycogen is an important substrate for the soccer player as evident from the various studies where glycogen has been measured. Saltin (1973) observed that the muscle glycogen stores were almost depleted at half time when the pre-match levels were low (~45 mmol.kg^{-1} w.w.). In that study, some players also started the game with normal muscle glycogen levels (~100 mmol.kg^{-1} w.w.), and the values were still rather high at half-time, but below 10 mmol.kg^{-1} w.w. at the end of the game. Others have found the concentrations to be 40–65 mmol·kg^{-1} w.w. after the game (Smaros, 1980; Jacobs *et al.*, 1982), indicating that muscle glycogen stores are not always depleted in a soccer game. However, analyses of single muscle fibres after a game have revealed that a significant number of fibres are depleted or partly depleted at the end of the game (Krustrup *et al.*, 2006).

It has been observed that the free fatty acid (FFA) concentration in the blood increases during a game, and more so during the second half (Bangsbo, 1994; Krustrup *et al.*, 2006). The frequent rest and low-intensity periods of a game allow for a significant blood flow to adipose tissue, which promotes release of FFA. This effect is also illustrated by the finding of high FFA concentration at half-time and after the game. The suggestion of a high rate of lipolysis during a game is supported by the observations of elevated levels of glycerol, even though the increases are smaller than during continuous exercise, which probably reflects a high turnover of glycerol, e.g. as a gluconeogenic precursor in the liver (Bangsbo, 1994). Hormonal changes may play a major role in the progressive increase in the FFA level. The insulin concentrations are lowered and catecholamine levels are progressively elevated during a match (Bangsbo, 1994), stimulating a high rate of lipolysis, and thus release of FFA into the blood (Galbo, 1983). The effect is reinforced by lowered lactate levels towards the end of a game, leading to less suppression of mobilization of fatty acids from the adipose tissue (Bülow and Madsen, 1981; Galbo, 1983; Bangsbo, 1994; Krustrup *et al.*, 2006). The changes in FFA during a match may cause a higher uptake and oxidation of FFA by the contracting muscles especially during the recovery periods in a game (Turcotte *et al.*, 1991). In addition, a higher utilization of muscle triglycerides might occur in the second half due to elevated catecholamine concentrations (Galbo, 1992). Both processes may be compensatory mechanisms for the progressive lowering of muscle glycogen and are favourable in maintaining high blood glucose concentration.

Fatigue during a soccer game

A relevant question when planning training is whether fatigue occurs during a soccer game and what is causing the fatigue. Several studies have provided evidence that the players' ability to perform high-intensity exercise is reduced towards the end of games in both elite and sub-elite soccer players (Reilly and Thomas, 1976; Mohr *et al.*, 2003, 2004b, 2005; Krustrup *et al.*, 2006). Thus, it has been demonstrated that the amount of sprinting, high-intensity running and distance covered are lower in the second half than in the first half of a game (Reilly and Thomas, 1976; Bangsbo *et al.*, 1991; Bangsbo, 1994; Mohr *et al.*, 2003). Furthermore, it has been observed that the amount of high-intensity running is reduced in the final 15 min period of a top-class soccer game (Mohr *et al.*, 2003) and that jump, sprint and intermittent exercise performance is lowered after compared with before a soccer game (Rebelo, 1999; Mohr *et al.*, 2004a; Mohr *et al.*, 2005; Krustrup *et al.*, 2006).

Recent findings using computerized time-motion analysis of top-class professional male soccer players have indicated that the players are fatigued during a game (Mohr *et al.*, 2003). Thus, in the 5 min period following the most intense period of the match, the amount of high-intensity exercise was reduced to levels below game average. This phenomenon has also been observed in elite women's soccer (unpublished observations). These findings suggest that performance was reduced after a period of intense exercise, which could have been a result of the natural variation in the intensity in a game due to tactical or psychological factors. However, in another study players performed a repeated sprint test immediately after intense match play and also at the end of each half (Krustrup *et al.*, 2006). After intense periods in the first half, the players' sprint performance was significantly reduced, whereas at the end of the first half the ability to perform repeated sprints had recovered. Together, these results suggest that soccer players experience fatigue temporarily during the game.

Training of a top class player

Components of training

Fitness training can be divided into aerobic, anaerobic and specific muscle training. Each type of training has a number of subcategories, which allows for a precise execution of the training when the aim of the training is known. The terms aerobic and anaerobic training are based on the energy pathway that dominates during the activity periods of the training session. The exercise performed should resemble the activities during a game as closely as possible. Thus, in soccer, the exercise intensity during a drill varies continuously, and both energy systems are often stimulated even though the athletes are performing aerobic training (see Bangsbo 2007). Based on the analysis of the game it is clear that the training of elite players should focus on improving the players' ability to perform intense exercise and to recover rapidly from periods of high-intensity exercise. This aim is obtained by performing aerobic and anaerobic training in a regular manner (Bangsbo, 2007). Below the separate components within fitness training are briefly described.

Aerobic training

Aerobic training causes changes in central factors such as the heart and blood volume, which result in a higher maximum oxygen uptake. A significant number of peripheral adaptations also occur with this type of training. The training leads among other things to a proliferation of capillaries and an elevation of the content of mitochondrial enzymes, as well as the activity of lactate dehydrogenase 1–2 (LDH_{1-2}) isozymes. Furthermore, the mitochondrial volume and the capacity of one of the shuttle systems for NADH are elevated. These changes cause marked alterations in muscle metabolism (Sahlin, 1992). The overall effects are an enhanced oxidation of lipids and sparing of glycogen, as well as a lowered lactate production, both at a given and at the same relative work-rate (Reilly and Bangsbo, 1998).

Aerobic training not only improves endurance performance of an athlete, but also appears to influence an athlete's ability to recover from intense exercise and, thus, capacity to perform maximal efforts repeatedly (Reilly and Bangsbo, 1998). The overall aim of aerobic training is to increase the work-rate during competition, and also to minimise a decrease in technical performance as well as lapses in concentration induced by fatigue towards the end of a game.

Aerobic training can be divided into three overlapping components, namely aerobic low-intensity training, aerobic moderate-intensity training and aerobic high-intensity training. For specific information about each category see Bangsbo (2007). To obtain information about the load on the players, heart rate determinations can be used. It should, however, be emphasised that such measurements do not provide a clear picture about the anaerobic energy production during training. Figure 55.1 illustrates the changes in heart rate for a soccer players performing aerobic high-intensity training as a small-sided game

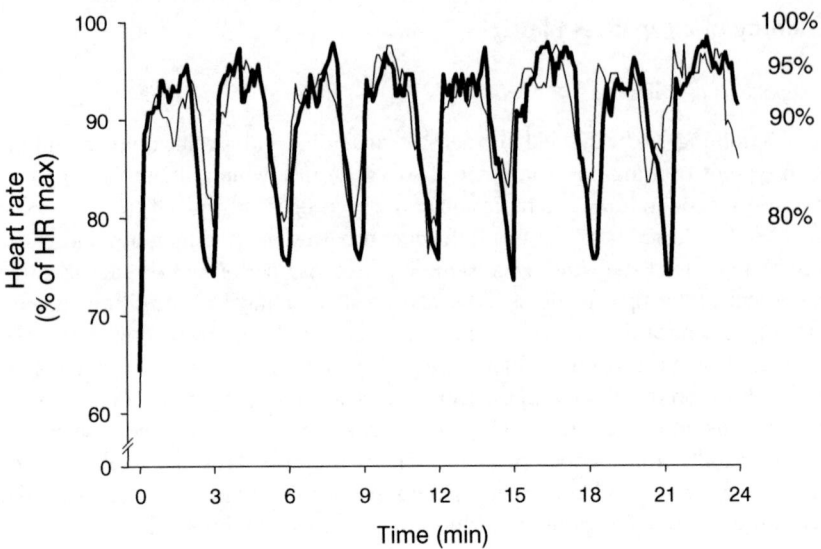

Figure 55.1 Percentage of maximal heart rate for two players during an aerobic high-intensity 'back-to-back' exercise drill

called 'back-to-back' (Bangsbo, 2007) with 2 min exercise periods and 1 min rest periods. It is clear that the heart rate in the last phase of each exercise period is in the zone fulfilling the criteria for aerobic high-intensity training.

Anaerobic training

Anaerobic training results in an increase in the activity of creatine kinase and glycolytic enzymes, as well as the muscle glycogen concentrations, which is of importance for performance during repeated high-intensity exercise (Reilly and Bangsbo, 1998). The capacity of the muscles to release and neutralise H^+ (buffer capacity) is also increased after a period of anaerobic training (Pilegaard *et al.*, 2002; Nielsen *et al.*, 2004). This will lead to a lower reduction in pH for a similar amount of lactate produced during high-intensity exercise. Therefore, the inhibitory effects of H^+ within the muscle cell are smaller, which may be one of the reasons for a better performance in high-intensity tests after a period of anaerobic training (Bangsbo *et al.*, 1995). Another important effect of anaerobic training is an increased activity of the muscle Na^+/K^+ pumps resulting in a reduced net loss of potassium from the contracting muscles during exercise, which may also lead to increased performance (Fraser *et al.*, 2002; Nielsen *et al.*, 2004). Thus, the overall aim of anaerobic training is to increase an athlete's potential to perform high-intensity exercise. Anaerobic training can be divided into speed training and speed endurance training. The aim of speed training is to improve an athlete's ability to act quickly in situations where speed is essential. Speed endurance training can be separated into two categories: these are production training and maintenance training. The purpose of production training is to improve the ability to perform maximally for a relatively short period of time, whereas the aim of maintenance training is to increase the ability to sustain exercise at a high intensity. For specific information about each category see Bangsbo (2007).

Specific muscle training

Specific muscle training involves the training of muscles in isolated movements. The aim of this type of training is to increase the performance of a muscle to a higher level than can be attained just by participating in the sport. Specific muscle training can be divided into muscle strength, muscle speed endurance and flexibility training. The effect of this form of training is specific to the muscle groups that are engaged, and the adaptation within the muscle is limited to the kind of training performed. Strength training can result in hypertrophy of the muscle, partly through an enlargement of muscle fibres. In addition, training with high resistance can change the fibre type distribution in the direction of fast twitch fibres (Bangsbo *et al.*, 1993). There is also a neuromotor effect of strength training and part of the increase in muscle strength can be attributed to changes in the nervous system. Improvements in muscular strength during isolated movements seem closely related to training speeds. However, significant increases in force development at very high speeds ($10-18$ rad.s^{-1}) have also been observed with slow-speed, high-resistance training. Strength training can be divided into functional strength training and basic strength training. Further information about strength training as well as an overview of muscle endurance and flexibility training can be found in Bangsbo (1994).

Planning of training

In a typical week for a professional soccer team with one match, the players have six training sessions in five days, i.e. one day with two sessions, keeping the day after the match free. If there is a second match in mid-week the team often trains once on the other days. However, there are great variations depending on the experience of the coach.

When planning fitness programmes the time course of adaptations in the various tissues should be taken into account. A change in heart size is rather slow, and there is a need for training over a long period of time (years) to improve the pump capacity of the heart significantly. Blood volume changes more quickly than does the heart size, but this adaptation is optimal first after a dimensional development of the cardiovascular system has occurred. The content of oxidative enzymes in a tissue and the degree of capillarization of skeletal muscle change more rapidly than the volume of a tissue, for example, the heart, but months of regular training are needed to obtain considerable increases in muscle capillaries and oxidative enzymes. On the other hand, a reduction in these parameters can occur with a time constant of weeks. The changes in glycolytic enzymes are rapid and they can be markedly elevated within a month of appropriate training (Reilly and Bangsbo, 1998).

To give an example of the priorities and the amount of training within the different aspect of training, the programme of the preparation of the Danish national soccer team for the European Championship 2004 will be described. After the season the players had one to two weeks of holiday before they started the preparation for the championship. The preparation period lasted 18 days, which was divided into two periods: 23 May to 1 June (phase I) and 2 June to 11 June (phase II). In each period the team played one match. The various elements of each training session are described in Table 55.1. The players wore heart rate monitors during every training session allowing for an evaluation of the loading of each player during both phases of the preparation. It should, however, be emphasized that the heart rate measurements do not give a clear picture of the amount of anaerobic work performed during a training session. Figure 55.2 shows the distribution of the time in the different heart zones for the whole team. It is clear that the amount of work leading to a high heart rate was the same in the two phases, and that the total amount of training was reduced in the second phase. This is in accordance with the high number of studies showing that performance can be maintained and even improved by reducing the amount of low-intensity training and keeping a sufficient amount of high-intensity training (Mujika, 1998). It should be mentioned that the team seemed to have been well prepared, since Denmark qualified for the quarter-final at the expense of Italy and Bulgaria. It should be emphasized that there were large individual differences in time when the players were in the high heart-rate zones. These variations were due to individual programmes and to large differences between players in the amount of high-intensity work performed during their tactical training. Therefore, it is essential to evaluate the physical loading of the players carefully also during training sessions where the specific aim is not fitness training.

Overview

In soccer the players perform intermittent exercise. Despite the players performing low-intensity activities for more than 70 per cent of the game, heart rate and body temperature measurements suggest that the average oxygen uptake for elite soccer players is around 70 per cent of maximum oxygen uptake ($\dot{V}_{O_{2\,max}}$). This may be partly explained by the 150–250 brief intense actions a top-class player performs during a game, which also indicate that the rates of creatine phosphate (CP) utilization and glycolysis are frequently high during a game. Muscle glycogen is probably the most important substrate for energy production, and fatigue towards the end of a game may be related to depletion of glycogen in some muscle fibres. The oxidation of fat probably increases progressively during a game, partially compensating for the progressive lowering of muscle glycogen. Fatigue appears also to occur temporarily during a game. There are major individual differences in the physical demands on players during a game related to physical capacity and

Table 55.1 Training schedule for two nine-day periods (phases 1 and 2) before Euro 2004

	Phase 1	Phase 2
Day 1	Morning: Yo-Yo IR2 test Technical/tactical training Afternoon: Aerobic HI training (6×2 min) Play – 20 min	Yo-Yo IR2 test Technical/tactical training Speed training Technical/tactical training Play – 20 min
Day 2	Morning: Free Afternoon: Technical/tactical training	Free Aerobic high intensity training (6×2 min) Technical/tactical training Play – 20 min
Day 3	Morning: Technical/tactical training Afternoon: Speed training Technical/tactical training Speed Endurance Maintenance training	Technical/tactical training Speed training Technical/tactical training
Day 4	Morning: Free Afternoon: Technical/tactical training Play – 30 min	Group C: Speed Endurance Production training Evening: Friendly game
Day 5	Morning: Free Afternoon: Speed training Aerobic high intensity training (8×2 min) Play – 20 min	Free (traveling) Free (traveling)
Day 6	Morning: Free Afternoon: Technical/tactical training Group C: Aerobic high intensity training (6×2 min)	Aerobic moderate intensity (3×5 min) Play – 30 min Free
Day 7	Morning: Free Afternoon: Friendly game	Technical/tactical training Speed training Technical/tactical training Speed Endurance Production training
Day 8	Morning: Free Afternoon: Group A: Recovery training Group B: Speed training ¨ Play – 30 min	Free Technical/tactical training
Day 9	Morning: Free Afternoon: Aerobic high intensity training (8×2 min) Play – 20 min	Yo-Yo IR2 test Technical/tactical training Speed training Technical/Tactical training Play – 20 min

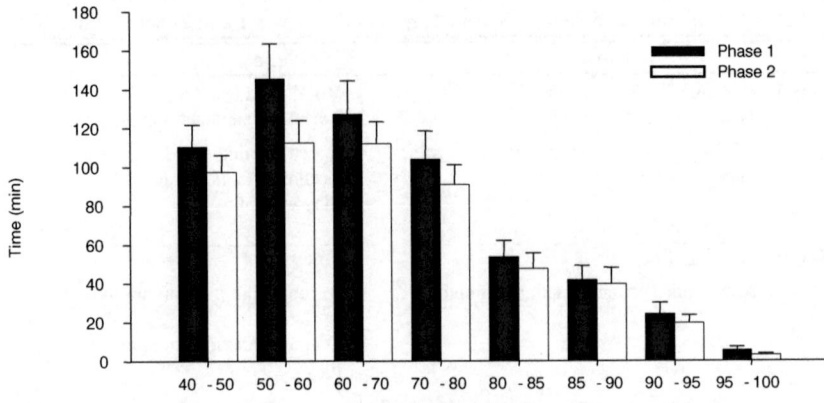

Figure 55.2 Heart rate distribution during two eight-day preparation periods (phase 1 and phase 2) for the Danish National team soccer squad before the European Championship 2004; values are expressed as means ± SEM

tactical role in the team. These differences should be taken into account in the training of a top-class player.

With appropriate training, the performance of a player can be increased and the risk of injury can be reduced. Aerobic training increases a player's ability to exercise at an overall higher intensity during the game, and minimizes a decrease in technical performance induced by fatigue. Anaerobic training elevates the player's potential to perform high-intensity exercise. Muscle strength training, combined with technical training, improves an athlete's power output during explosive activities in a match. Planning of the training is essential in order to obtain an optimal effect.

Acknowledgements

The original studies by the authors of this review were supported by Team Denmark and The Sports Research Council, Ministry of Culture, Denmark.

References

Ali, A. and Farally, M., 1991, Recording soccer players' heart rate during matches. *Journal of Sports Sciences*, 9, 183–9.

Bangsbo, J., 1994, The physiology of soccer – with special reference to intense intermittent exercise. *Acta Physiologica Scandinavica*, 151 (Suppl. 619): 1–155.

Bangsbo, J., 2007, *Aerobic and Anaerobic Training in Soccer - With Special Emphasis on Training of Youth Players*. Fitness Training in Soccer I, (Bagsvaerd: HO+Storm).

Bangsbo, J. and Mohr, M., 2005, Variations in running speed and recovery time after a sprint during top-class soccer matches. *Medicine and Science in Sports and Exercise*, 37, 87.

Bangsbo, J., Norregaard, L., and Thorsoe, F., 1991, Activity profile of competition soccer. *Canadian Journal of Sports Science*, 16 (2), 110–16.

Bangsbo, J., Johansen, L., Graham, T. and Saltin, B., 1993, Lactate and H$^+$ effluxes from human skeetal muscles during intense dynamic exercise. *Journal of Physiology* 462, 115–33.

Bangsbo, J., Aagaard, T., Olsen, M., Kiens, B., Turcotte, L.P. and Richter, E.A., 1995, Lactate and H$^+$ uptake in inactive muscles during intense exercise in man. *Journal of Physiology*, 422, 539–59.

Bülow, J., and Madsen, J., 1981, Influence of blood flow on fatty acid mobilization form lipolytically active adipose tissue. *Pflugers Archiv*, 390(2): 169–74.

Di Salvo, V., Baron, R., Tschan, H., Calderon Montero, F.J., Bachl, N. and Pigozzi, F., 2007, Performance characteristics according to playing position in elite soccer. *International Journal of Sports Medicine*, 28, 222–7.

Ekblom, B., 1986, Applied physiology of soccer. *Sports Medicine*, 3, 50–60.

Esposito, F., Impellizzeri, F. M., Margonato, V., Vanni, R., Pizzini, G. and Veicsteinas, A., 2004, Validity of heart rate as an indicator of aerobic demand during soccer activities in amateur soccer players. *European Journal of Applied Physiology*, 93(1–2): 167–72.

Fraser, S.F.L.J.L., Carey, M.F., Wang, X.N., Sangkabutra T., Sostaric S., Selig S.E., Kjeldsen, K. and Mckenna, M.J., 2002, Fatigue depresses maximal in vitro skeletal muscle Na(+)-K(+)-ATPase activity in untrained and trained individuals. *Journal of Applied Physiology*, 93, 1650–9.

Galbo, H., 1983, *Hormonal and Metabolic Adaptations to Exercise*. (New York: Theme-Stratton).

Galbo, H., 1992, Exercise physiology: humoral function. *Sport Science Reviews*, 1, 65–93.

Jacobs, I.N., Westlin, J., Karlson, M., Rasmusson, A. and Houghton, B., 1982, Muscle glycogen and diet in elite soccer players. *European Journal of Applied Physiology*, 48, 297–302.

Krustrup, P. and Bangsbo, J., 2001, Physiological demands of top-class soccer refereeing in relation to physical capacity: effect of intense intermittent exercise training. *Journal of Sports Sciences*, 19, 881–91.

Krustrup, P., Mohr, M., Amstrup, T., Rysgaard, T., Johansen, J., Steensburg, A., Pederson, P.K. and Bangsbo, J., 2003, The Yo-Yo intermittent recovery test: physiological response, reliability and validity. *Medicine and Science in Sports and Exercise*, 35, 695–705.

Krustrup, P., Hellstein, Y. and Bangsbo, J., 2004, Intense intermittent training elevates transient O$_2$ uptake in human skeletal muscle at high but not at low exercise intensities. *Journal of Physiology*, 559, 335–45.

Krustrup, P., Mohr, P., Ellingsgaard, H., and Bangsbo, J., 2005, Physical demands during an elite female soccer game: importance of training status. *Medicine and Science in Sports and Exercise*, 37, 1242–8.

Krustrup, P., Mohr, M., Steensburg, A., Bencke, J., Kjaer, M. and Bangsbo, J., 2006, Muscle and blood metabolites during a soccer game: implications for sprint performance. *Medicine and Science in Sports and Exercise*, 38, 1165–74.

Mohr, M., Krustrup, P. and Bangsbo, J., 2003, Match performance of high-standard soccer players with special reference to development of fatigue. *Journal of Sports Sciences*, 21, 439–49.

Mohr, M., Nordsborg, N., Nielsen, J.J., Pederson, L.D., Fischer, C., Krustrup, P., and Bangsbo, J. 2004a, Potassium kinetics in human interstitium during repeated intense exercise in relation to fatigue. *Pflügers Archiv*, 448, 452–6.

Mohr, M., Krustrup, P., Nybo, L., Nielsen, J.J. and Bangsbo, J., 2004b, Muscle temperature and sprint performance during soccer matches – beneficial effects of re-warm-up at half time. *Scandinavian Journal of Medicine and Science in Sports*, 14(3): 156–62.

Mohr, M., Krustrup, P. and Bangsbo, J., 2005, Fatigue in soccer: a brief review. *Journal of Sports Sciences*, 23, 593–9.

Mujika, I., 1998, The influence of training characteristics and tapering on the adaptations in highly trained individuals: a review, *International Journal of Sports Medicine*, 19, 439–46.

Nielsen, J. J., Mohr, M., Klarskov, C., Kristensen, M., Krustrup, P., Juel, C. and J. Bangsbo, 2004. Effects of high-intensity intermittent training on potassium kinetics and performance in human skeletal muscle. *Journal of Physiology*, 554, 857–70.

Pilegaard, H., Keller, C., Steensberg, A., Helge, J.W., Pedersen, B. K., Saltin, B. and Neufer, P.D., 2002, Influence of pre-exercise muscle glycogen content on exercise-induced transcriptional regulation of metabolic genes. *Journal of Physiology*, 541(1): 261–71.

Rebelo, A. N. C., 1999, Studies of fatigue in soccer. PhD thesis. University of Porto.

Reilly, T., 1997, Energetics of high-intensity exercise (soccer) with particular reference to fatigue. *Journal of Sports Sciences*, 15, 257–63.

Reilly, T., and Bangsbo, J. 1998, Anaerobic and aerobic training, in *Applied Sport Science: Training in Sport*, edited by Elliott, B. (Chichester: John Wiley).

Reilly, T. and Thomas, V., 1976, A motion analyses of work-rate in different positional roles in professional football match-play. *Journal of Human Movement Studies*, 2, 87–7.

Reilly, T. and Thomas, V., 1979, Estimated energy expenditures of professional association footballers. *Ergonomics*, 22, 541–8.

Sahlin, K., 1992, Metabolic factors in fatigue. *Sports Medicine*, 13, 99–107.

Saltin, B., 1973, Metabolic fundamentals in exercise. *Medicine and Science in Sports*, 5, 137–46.

Smaros, G., 1980, Energy usage during a football match. In *Proceedings of the 1st International Congress on Sports Medicine Applied to Football*, edited by Vecchiet, L. (Rome: D. Guanello).

Turcotte, L. P., Kiens, B. and Richter, E.A., 1991, Saturation kinetics of palmitate uptake in perfused skeletal muscle. *Federation of the European Biochemical Society*, 279, 327–9.

Withers, R.T, Maricic, Z., Wasilewski, S. and Kelly, L., 1982, The maximum aerobic power, anaerobic power, and body composition of South Australian male representatives in athletics, basketball, field hockey and soccer. *Journal of Sports Medicine and Physical Fitness*, 17, 291–400.

56 Physiological responses to playing futsal in professional players

Carlo Castagna,[1,2] *Stefano D'Ottavio*[1,2] *and José Carlos Barbero Álvarez*[3]

[1] Corso di Laurea in Scienze Motorie, Università di Roma Tor Vergata, Italy;
[2] Federazione Italiana Giuoco Calcio, Settore Giovanile e Scolastico, Italy;
[3] Departamento de Educación Física y Deportiva, Universidad de Granada, Spain

Introduction

Futsal is the indoor version of soccer that is officially sanctioned by soccer's international governing body (Fédération de Football Association, FIFA). Every four years since 1989 a World Championship has been contested by 16 national teams. Despite its popularity and competitive status, there have only been a few investigations that have examined futsal. Furthermore the reports available in the international literature only addressed game analysis or the physiological demands of small-sided versions of soccer played at recreational level (Barbero et al., 2008; Castagna et al., 2007) but not at the professional level. To date, no studies have described the $\dot{V}o_{2\,max}$ heart rate and blood lactate concentrations ($[la]_b$) of professional futsal players during the game. Therefore, the aim of this study was to examine $\dot{V}o_{2\,max}$ HR and $[la]_b$ in professional futsal players during competitive match-play. It was hypothesised that professional futsal playing induces physiological demands different from those previously reported during targeted training in professional soccer players (Hoff et al., 2002).

Methods

Subjects

Eight Second Division full-time professional futsal players (age 22.4 ± 1.8 years, body mass 75.4 ± 7.9 kg, height 1.77 ± 0.09 m) volunteered to this study. Each player had a minimum of five years playing experience in the playing division at the time of the investigation and trained nine times a week with a competition taking place during the weekend.

Game measurements

Players were observed during highly competitive friendly games in order to allow physiological variables to be assessed without restriction. The game consisted in 4×10 min periods with 5 min recovery between bouts. To assess game $\dot{V}O_2$ players in a random order wore a portable gas analyzer (K4b^2 Cosmed, Rome, Italy) during one game period (10 min each). Earlobe blood samples were taken in a random order (Krustrup et al., 2006) during the game to assess $[la]_b$ (Doctor Lange Plus LP20, Dr Lange, Germany). Heart rate (HR) monitoring was performed throughout the 4×10 min games in all players using short range telemetry (Polar Team System, Polar Oy, Kempele, Finland).

Fitness assessment

Maximum oxygen uptake ($\dot{V}O_{2\,max}$) was determined using an incremental running test on a motorized treadmill (RunRace, Technogym, Gambettola, Italy). After an individually adjusted warm-up (5 min) subjects ran for 6 min at 8 km·h^{-1}, and the velocity was increased by 1 km·h^{-1}min^{-1} until exhaustion (8–12 min). Expired gases were analysed using a breath-by-breath automated gas-analysis system (K4b^2, COSMED, Rome, Italy).

Ventilatory threshold (T_{vent}) was assessed according to Beaver et al. (1986). Running economy (RE) was considered as average $\dot{V}O_2$ during the final minute of the 6 min run at 8 km.h^{-1}. Maximal aerobic speed was calculated using the relationship between $\dot{V}O_2$ and running speeds (Billat and Koralsztein, 1996). Maximal HR (HR$_{max}$) was considered as the highest 5 s mean during the treadmill test. Heart rates were monitored by means of short-range radio telemetry.

Statistical analyses

Data are reported as mean ± standard deviation. Before using parametric tests, the assumption of normality was verified using the Shapiro-Wilk W test. ANOVA models (one-way and repeated measurements) were used to assess group differences. Significance was assumed at 5 per cent ($P \leq 0.05$) a priori.

Results

Treadmill test results are shown in Table 56.1. Game $\dot{V}O_2$ and HR values were 75.5 ± 8.6 and $89.7 \pm 3.1\%$ of maximal treadmill test values. During the game peak values for $\dot{V}O_2$ and HR were 99 ± 5.3 and $96.1 \pm 2.9\%$ of $\dot{V}O_{2\,max}$ and HR$_{max}$, respectively. Average $\dot{V}O_2$ (K4b^2) during the game was 48.6 ± 4.32 ml.kg.$^{-1}$min^{-1}. Players spent 46.4 and 38.9 per cent of the playing time at exercise intensities higher than 80 and 90 per cent of $\dot{V}O_{2\,max}$ and HR$_{max}$, respectively. Average ($[la]_b$) was 5.3 ± 2.6 mmol.l^{-1}. No significant differences were observed between periods for HR and $[la]_b$.

Table 56.1 Treadmill test responses ($n = 8$)

$\dot{V}O_{2\,max}$ (ml.kg^{-1}.min^{-1})	64.8 ± 5.6
Speed at $\dot{V}O_{2\,max}$ (ml.kg^{-1}.min^{-1})	17.7 ± 1.5
Peak treadmill speed (km.h^{-1})	18.2 ± 1.3
RE (ml.kg^{-1}.min^{-1})	33.7 ± 2.9
$\dot{V}O_2$ at T_{vent} (ml.kg^{-1}.min^{-1})	46.0 ± 5.1
% $\dot{V}O_{2\,max}$ at T_{vent}	71.0 ± 3.0
Speed at T_{vent} (km.h^{-1})	12.9 ± 1.4
HR at T_{vent} (beats.min^{-1})	162.0 ± 7.0
%HR$_{max}$ at T_{vent}	84.8 ± 2.34
VE$_{max}$ (l.min^{-1})	162.0 ± 15.0
HR$_{max}$ (beats.min^{-1})	191.0 ± 8.0
$[La]_{b\,max}$ (mmol.l^{-1})	11.9 ± 2.5

Discussion and conclusions

The main finding was that aerobic metabolism is heavily involved during the game, accounting for the 76 per cent of maximal individual values. In this study, the futsal players played at an average exercise intensity that was higher than that at their individual T_{ven}t. In fact during the game the players maintained an average $\dot{V}O_2$ and HR that was 6.3 and 5.8 per cent higher than individual T_{vent}. This exercise intensity was slightly higher than that reported for competitive soccer (Stølen *et al.*, 2005) and suggests that development or aerobic fitness is a training priority for professional futsal players. Indeed, we suggest that aerobic fitness should be properly developed with generic or specific training programmes (Impellizzeri *et al.*, 2006).

The average HR attained in this study is higher than that reported for professional soccer but similar to what was reported in professional basketball players by McInnes *et al.* (1995). A possible explanation for the higher HR in futsal compared to soccer may be that work-rate during futsal is higher (Barbero Alvarez *et al.*, 2004; Stølen *et al.*, 2005)

In this study anaerobic involvement was examined using blood lactate concentrations taken randomly during competitive match-play. The $[la]_b$ values from this study are similar to what has been previously reported in soccer (Stølen *et al.*, 2005). Moreover, mormalizing $[la]_b$ data according to maximal values obtained at the end of exhaustive treadmill tests, players attained blood lactate concentrations that at times were close to 100 per cent of values at exhaustion.

In summary, the present results show that futsal played at a professional level is a high-intensity exercise mode that heavily taxes the aerobic and anaerobic metabolic pathways. In the light of the reported average $\dot{V}O_2$ during games maximal aerobic power levels higher than 55 ml.kg^{-1}.min^{-1} are advisable to play futsal at a professional level.

References

Barbero Alvarez, J., Soto Hermoso, V. and Granda Vera, J., 2004, Effort profiling during indoor soccer competition. *Journal of Sports Sciences*, 22, 500–1.

Barbero, J.C., Soto, V.M. and Granda, J., 2008, Match analysis and heart rate of futsal players during competition. *Journal of Sports Sciences*, 28, 63–77.

Beaver, W.L., Wasserman, K. and Whipp, B.J., 1986, A new method for detecting anaerobic threshold by gas exchange. *Journal of Applied Physiology*, 60, 2020–7.

Billat, V. and Koralsztein, J.P., 1996, Significance of the velocity at $\dot{V}O_{2max}$ and time to exhaustion at this velocity. *Sports Medicine*, 22, 90–180.

Castagna, C., Belardinelli, R., Impellizzeri, F.M., Abt, G.A., Coutts, A.J., and D'Ottavio, S., 2007, Cardiovascular responses during recreational 5-a-side indoor-soccer. *Journal of Science and Medicine in Sport*, 10(2): 89–95.

Hoff, J., Wisloff, U., Engen, L.C., Kemi, O.J. and Helgerud, J., 2002, Soccer specific aerobic endurance training. *Bristol Journal on Sports Medicine*, 36, 218–21.

Impellizzeri, F.M., Marcora, S.M., Castagna, C., Reilly, T., Sassi, A., Iaia, F.M. and Rampinini, E., 2006, Physiological and performance effects of generic versus specific aerobic training in soccer players. *International Journal of Sports Medicine*, 27, 483–92.

Krustrup, P., Mohr, M., Steensberg, A., Bencke, J., Kjaer, M. and Bangsbo, J., 2006, Muscle and blood metabolites during a soccer game: implications for sprint performance. *Medicine and Science in Sports Exercise*, 38, 1165–74.

McInnes, S.E., Carlson, J.S., Jones, C.J. and McKenna, M.J., 1995, The physiological load imposed upon basketball players during competition. *Journal of Sports Sciences*, 13, 387–97.

Stølen, T., Chamari, K., Castagna, C. and Wisløff, U., 2005, Physiology of soccer: an update. *Sports Medicine*, 35, 501–36.

Part VIII

Fitness assessment

57 The reliability of a repeated sprint test during simulated team-sport running on a non-motorised treadmill

Anita C. Sirotic and Aaron J. Coutts

University of Technology, Australia

Introduction

The physical demands of the various football codes have been reported to be broadly similar (Reilly and Gilbourne, 2003). Specifically, most football codes require players to generate brief maximal sprints $(1-6\,s)$, repeatedly interspersed with short recovery periods $(<21\,s)$. The capacity to repeat these brief maximal sprints in a short period of time has been termed repeated sprint ability (RSA) and is considered an important performance characteristic (Spencer *et al.*, 2006). For these reasons, researchers have examined the reliability of RSA measures using a $5 \times 6\,s$ sprint test in a 'non-fatigued' state (Hughes *et al.*, 2006; McGawley and Bishop, 2006). However, in a typical football match (i.e of various football codes), repeated sprint efforts are often completed in a fatigued state. Therefore, while existing RSA tests may be a reliable way of assessing RSA in team sport participants, they may not reflect the physiological state of a participant when repeating sprint efforts during a match. Therefore, the purpose of this study was to determine the ecological reliability of a $5 \times 6\,s$ RSA test when completed under fatigue on a non-motorised treadmill (NMT).

Methods

To determine the reliability of a $5 \times 6\,s$ RSA test in a pre-fatigued state each subject completed a standardised 30 min team-sport running simulation on a NMT (Woodway Force 3.0 Treadmill, Wisconsin, USA). The test was undertaken prior to performing a $5 \times 6\,s$ RSA test, on three occasions, separated by six days.

Subjects

Eleven moderately trained male athletes ($\dot{V}o_{2\ max} = 52.7 \pm 4.5\,mL \cdot kg^{-1} \cdot min^{-1}$, age $= 23.6 \pm 4.5$ years, body mass $= 78.0 \pm 8.4\,kg$) of various football codes (four soccer, four Australian Rules football, and three rugby union players) participated in this study. All subjects completed familiarization with all test procedures.

Thirty minute team-sport running simulation

The 30 min team-sport running simulation was based on previous time–motion studies of various football codes (Reilly and Gilbourne, 2003). The simulation included six running speeds of different duration: standing (8 s), walking (8 s), jogging (8 s), running (6 s), fast running (4 s) and sprinting (3 s) (Figure 57.1). Instructions for the team-sport match simulation were given to the subjects using specialized software (Force Software, Innervations Joondalup, Australia) and were arranged so that the amount of time at any given speed would reflect that which occurred during a typical football match (Reilly and Gilbourne, 2003). At the end of the 30 min simulation, a 5 × 6 s RSA test was performed, consisting of five, 6 s sprints each separated by 24 s of jogging.

5 × 6 s RSA measures

Performance measures for repeated sprint ability included total sprint distance, total sprint work and mean maximal sprinting speed (MxSP). Fatigue variables for RSA included the percentage decrement in each of the performance variables. Percentage decrement scores were calculated using equation 57.1:

$$100 - ([\text{total sprint performance} / \text{ideal sprint performance} \times 5]) \times 10$$

$$(57.1)$$

Statistical analyses

A one-way ANOVA with repeated measures was used to detect any differences in RSA performance or fatigue variables between the three trials. The coefficient of variation (CV), intraclass correlation coefficient (ICC), and technical error

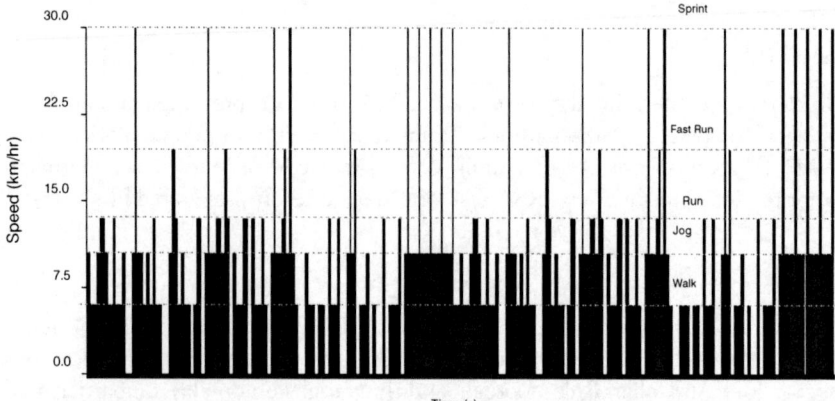

Figure 57.1 Activity profile of the 30 min team-sport running simulation for a subject with a maximal sprinting speed of 30 km.h^{-1}; a 5 × 6 s RSA test was performed at the end of the 30 min period

Table 57.1 Measures of reliability of performance and fatigue variables of a 5 ×6s RSA test completed at the end of a 30 min team-sport running simulation on a NMT (*n* = 11)

RSA variables	Grand mean (± SD)	CV (%)	Limits of agreement	TEM	ICC
Performance variables Trial 2–3					
Sprint distance (m)	155.3 ± 8.2	3.1	1.04 */÷ 1.09	4.6	0.65
Sprint work (kJ)	19.7 ± 2.1	5.4	1.00 */÷ 1.16	1.0	0.76
MxSP (m·s⁻¹)	6.2 ± 0.4	2.5	1.02 */÷ 1.07	0.2	0.85
Fatigue variables Trial 2–3					
Distance decrement (%)	9.2 ± 4.6	30.2	0.96 */÷ 2.08	2.5	0.71
Work decrement (%)	16.5 ± 7.7	38.2	1.00 */÷ 2.45	5.7	0.48
MxSP decrement (%)	8.8 ± 5.0	31.3	1.05 */÷ 2.14	2.7	0.73

Note: MxSP, mean maximal sprinting speed; CV, coefficient of variation; TEM, technical error of measurement; ICC, intraclass correlation coefficient; RSA, repeated sprint ability

of measurement (TEM) were calculated according to the methods of Hopkins (2000). Limits of agreement were calculated as recommended by Bland and Altman (1986). Analyses were performed using Microsoft Excel® (Microsoft, Redmond, USA) and SPSS (Version 14.0, Chicago, USA). Statistical significance was set at $P<0.05$.

Results

A significant difference was shown in RSA sprint distance between trial 1−2 (146.9 m vs 152.3 m $P<0.05$) and trials 1−3 (146.9 m vs 158.4 m $P<0.05$). No other significant differences were shown in any other performance or fatigue variable.

Limits of agreement for trial 2−3 were lower for MxSP (1.02 */÷ 1.07) and sprint distance (1.04 */÷ 1.09) when compared to sprint work (1.00 */÷ 1.16) performed during the pre-fatigued 5 ×6s RSA test (Table 57.1). The largest measurement error was shown in the fatigue variables such as the work decrement (CV = 38.2%) during the pre-fatigued 5 ×6s RSA test. Based on the nomogram designed by Batterham and Atkinson (2005) and using the CV for trial 2−3, it was estimated that a sample size of at least 8, 11 and 24 is required to detect a 5 per cent change in MxSP, sprint distance and sprint work, respectively (statistical power = 0.9). To detect a 5−10 per cent change in RSA fatigue variables a sample size of greater than 200 is required.

Discussion and conclusions

In agreement with previous research, the RSA fatigue variables in this study were found to be less reliable than directly measured performance variables (McGawley and Bishop, 2006; Spencer et al., 2006). This poor reliability of fatigue variables may be due to the amplification of slight variations in single sprints when calculating decrement scores. In contrast, the performance variables showed a high reliability with all measures reporting a CV of less than 10 per cent. It has been suggested that a CV of 10 per cent is a common criterion used to define the acceptable level of reliability in a test (Atkinson *et al.*, 1999). This level of reliability in directly measured performance variables is consistent with previous research showing a CV of between 2.4−5.5 per cent for total work completed during a 5 × 6 s sprint cycle test over five trials (McGawley and Bishop, 2006). In addition to the high reliability of performance variables, low sample sizes of between 8 and 24 were estimated to detect a 5 per cent change in RSA performance variables. Conversely the minimum sample size of greater than 200 to detect a 5−10 per cent change in all RSA fatigue variables would be considered unfeasible in most research study designs.

On the basis of the present results, we suggest that performance variables such as total sprint distance covered during the pre-fatigued 5 × 6 s RSA test be used as a criterion measure. We also recommend that a minimum sample size of between 8 and 24 is adequate to detect a 5 per cent change in 'pre-fatigued' RSA performance on a NMT and suggest that two familiarization sessions be completed. These results can be used to determine appropriate sample sizes required for future studies and assist researchers to interpret meaningful changes in RSA performance.

References

Atkinson, G., Nevill, A.M. and Edwards, B., 1999, What is an acceptable amount of measurement error? The application of meaningful 'analytical goals' to the reliability of sports science measurements made on a ratio scale. *Journal of Sports Sciences*, 17, 18.

Batterham, A.M. and Atkinson, G., 2005, How big does my sample need to be? A primer on the murky world of sample size estimation. *Physical Therapy in Sport*, 6, 153–63.

Bland, J.M., and Altman, D.G., 1986, Statistical method for assessing agreement between two methods of clinical measurement. *The Lancet*, 1, 307–10.

Hopkins, W.G., 2000, 10 Oct 2005, Reliability from consecutive pairs of trials (Excel spreadsheet). Online at sportsci.org/resource/stats/xrely.xls (accessed 22 June 2006)

Hughes, M.G., Doherty, M., Tong, R.J., Reilly, T. and Cable, N.T., 2006, Reliability of repeated sprint exercise in non-motorised treadmill ergometry. *International Journal of Sports Medicine*, 27, 900–4.

McGawley, K. and Bishop, D., 2006, Reliability of a 5 × 6-s maximal cycling repeated-sprint test in trained female team-sport athletes. *European Journal of Applied Physiology*, 98, 383–93.

Reilly, T. and Gilbourne, D., 2003, Science and football: A review of applied research in the football codes. *Journal of Sports Sciences*, 21, 693–705.

Spencer, M., Fitzsimons, M., Dawson, B., Bishop, D. and Goodman, C., 2006, Reliability of a repeated-sprint test for field-hockey. *Journal of Science and Medicine in Sport*, 9, 181–4.

58 Validity of a group intermittent high-intensity test for repeated sprint ability

José Carlos Barbero Álvarez[1] and Carlo Castagna[2]

[1]Departamento de Educación Física y Deportiva, Universidad de Granada, Spain; [2]Corso di Laurea in Scienze Motorie, Università di Roma Tor Vergata, Italy

Introduction

The ability to repeat maximal sprints with minimal recovery time is considered as an important performance determinant in team sports (Spencer et al., 2005). As a consequence of that, many tests have been introduced in order to assess 'repeated sprint ability' (RSA) of players in team sports (Spencer et al., 2005).

In addition to the large difference in exercise protocols, the proposed RSA tests need trained personal and expensive devices (i.e. photocell beams) that enable only single subjects to be assessed at a time. Furthermore, RSA protocols require subjects to be well familiarized with test procedures (Wragg et al., 2000) in order to avoid pacing during performance, giving full effort from the first sprint to attain a tangible sprint decrement (Fitzsimons et al., 1993). Assessment of RSA may be expensive and time consuming as team rosters are usually composed of more than 10 players.

This investigation was conducted to examine the validity of a group intermittent high intensity field-test (GRSA) for distance to estimate RSA performance in recreational soccer players. The working hypothesis was that players GRSA performance (distance covered) is related to RSA variables.

Methods

Subjects

Eighteen amateur soccer players (age 21.8 ± 4.8 years, height 1.76 ± 0.2 m, body mass 69.0 ± 7.8 kg) randomly chosen from a population of soccer players volunteered for this study. All players were actively involved in varsity championships before the commencement of the investigation and trained two/three times a week, playing a competitive match during the weekend.

Repeated sprint ability (RSA) test

The RSA test consisted of 8 bouts of 2×15 m shuttle run sprints (30 m total per bout) with 30 s of passive recovery. Sprint times were assessed using custom-made (University of Granada, Campus de Melilla, Spain) infrared light sensors (OMRON E3S-CR11), connected to a personal computer.

Infrared photocell-beam height was set at 30 cm from ground level with players starting from a line set 50 cm from the photocell beam. According to Fitzsimons *et al.* (1993) total sprint time (TT) and sprint decrement as fatigue index (FI) were considered as RSA variables. Players were well-motivated and instructed to give a maximal effort during each sprint-bout and to avoid pacing. Standard verbal feedback and encouragement were given throughout the test.

According to suggestions by Wragg *et al.* (2000) players were accurately familiarized with the RSA procedures, performing the RSA test with full effort at least twice in the six weeks before the commencement of the study. Players were submitted to RSA procedure only when a satisfactory sprinting profile was attained following the suggestions of Wragg *et al.* (2000).

Group intermittent high-intensity test (GRSA)

The GRSA protocol consisted of 2×15 m of high-intensity shuttle running bouts interspersed with 30 s of passive recovery. The GRSA test began with a familiarization phase consisting in $4 \times 2 \times 15$ m shuttle-running bouts where speed was increased by 1 km·h^{-1} per bout from an initial speed of 14 km·h^{-1}. Thereafter the speed was set at 18 km·h^{-1} and increased by 0.5 km·h^{-1} every 8×30 m until the nominal speed of 19.5 km·h^{-1} was attained. The latter speed was maintained until exhaustion. During the whole test the subjects were guided by pre-recorded audio cues broadcast by a CD played on a laptop computer (Microsoft Windows Player, Microsoft, USA). The test was considered to end when the subject twice failed to reach the control-line set 50 cm before the starting/finish line in time with the corresponding audio cues (objective evaluation) or he felt not able to cover another shuttle at the dictated speed (subjective evaluation). The total distance covered during the GRSA before exhaustion was considered as the test score.

Common test procedures

Before each test subjects performed a standardized warm-up (10 min) consisting of paced (CD pre-recorded audio cues) shuttle running (3×15 m) performed at progressive speeds and flexibility exercises (Barbero Alvaréz *et al.*, 2005). During both tests, heart rates were monitored using short-range telemetry with a 5 s sampling interval (Polar XT Training, Kempele, Finland). Fingertip blood-lactate concentration was assessed at rest and 3 minutes after the end of each test using a portable analyzer (Mini-photometer plus LP20, Dr Lange, France).

Statistical analyses

Data are reported as mean ± standard deviation (SD). Before using parametric tests, the assumption of normality was verified using the Shapiro-Wilk W test. Pearson's product-moment correlations and linear regression analysis were used to examine the relationships between GRSA performance (m) and RSA variables (i.e. TT and FI). Comparison between means of field-test variable was performed using paired t-tests. The a priori level of confidence assumed for significance was 5 per cent ($P \leq 0.05$).

Results

The results of the tests are presented in Table 58.1. Significant correlations were found between GRSA distance and TT ($r = -0.83$; $P = 0.001$) and RSA best time ($r = -0.77$; $P = 0.002$). No significant correlation was found between GRSA performance and FI ($P > 0.05$).

Maximal heart rates attained during RSA and GRSA tests were not significantly different ($P = 0.08$), corresponding to $93 \pm 2.9\%$ (88.8–98.5) and $93 \pm 3.4\%$ (86.5–99.5) of maximal HR, respectively. Mean HR during the GRSA and RSA were $88 \pm 2.83\%$ (83.1–93) and $86 \pm 2.5\%$ (81–90) respectively ($P = 0.002$). Players' mean HR during the first eight high-intensity bouts of GRSA was $86 \pm 3.1\%$ (80.6–90.5) of maximal. This result was not significantly different from average HR in the RSA test ($P = 0.5$). No significant differences were observed between maximal HR attained during the first eight GRSA high-intensity bouts ($92 \pm 3.1\%$, 86.5–97) and RSA test ($P = 0.46$). The RSAT and GRSA blood-lactate concentrations at rest ($3.4 \pm 0.95\,$mM and $3.2 \pm 1.33\,$mM, respectively, $P = 0.7$) and post-tests ($13.6 \pm 4.3\,$mM and $13.3 \pm 3.14\,$mM, respectively, $P = 0.7$) were not significantly different.

Discussion and conclusions

The results of this study showed the criterion validity of a team sport-specific high-intensity test in estimating players' repeated sprint ability. In this regard coaches and fitness trainers may use GRSA for a fast and economical evaluation of their team players' ability to maintain sprints over time. The use of GRSA may be of interest during the competitive season when due to often busy game schedules

Table 58.1 Results of GRSA and RSA tests

	Group RSA test			RSA test	
	Best time [BT] (s)	Total sprint time [TT] (s)	Fatigue index [FIX] (%)	Distance (m)	No sprints
Average	5.83	47.92	–2.75	390.00	13
SD	0.28	2.15	1.30	182.07	5.98
Range	6.27	51.07	–1.54	780	26
	5.41	44.76	–6.24	120	4

time for fitness assessment may be limited or when for various reasons photo-cell beams are not available.

According to physiological responses elicited by GRSA, this test protocol may be used to promote team-sport specific adaptations particularly in the anaerobic-lactic domain (Spencer *et al.*, 2005).

References

Barbero Alvaréz, J.C., Andrín, G. and Méndez-Villanueva, A., 2005, Futsal-specific endurance assessment of competitive players. *Journal of Sports Sciences*, 23, 1279–81.

Fitzsimons, M., Dawson, B., Ward, D. and Wilkinson, A., 1993, Cycling and running tests of repeated sprint ability. *The Australian Journal of Science and Medicine in Sport*, 25, 82–7.

Spencer, M., Bishop, D., Dawson, B. and Goodman, C., 2005, Physiological and metabolic responses of repeated-sprint activities specific to field-based team sports. *Sports Medicine*, 35, 1025–44.

Wragg, C.B., Maxwell, N.S. and Doust, J.H., 2000, Evaluation of the reliability and validity of a soccer-specific field test of repeated sprint ability. *European Journal of Applied Physiology*, 83, 77–83.

59 Match performance and Yo-Yo IR2 test performance of players from successful and unsuccessful professional soccer teams

Morten Bredsgaard Randers, Jack Majgaard Jensen, Jens Bangsbo and Peter Krustrup

Institute of Exercise and Sport Sciences, Department of Human Physiology, University of Copenhagen, Denmark

Introduction

Many factors determine the outcome of a soccer match and one of these may be the physical performance during a match and the fitness levels of the players. Thus, recent studies have shown that the physical demands in a game are related to the level of competition, e.g. Italian Serie A players ran significantly more high-intensity running than Danish Premier League players (Mohr *et al.*, 2003; Krustrup *et al.*, 2006). Also the players' ability to perform intense intermittent exercise varies according to the level of play, e.g. Yo-Yo IR2 performance was higher for Danish Premier League players than Second Division players. However, it is still unknown whether match activities differ between top, middle and bottom teams in the same league and whether any difference is related to the players' ability to perform repeated intense exercise.

Methods

Subjects

Sixty-two elite male players from the Danish Premier League took part in the study (age: 26 range: 19–34 years). Thirteen players represented two teams from the top (ranking 1–2; top-players), thirteen players represented three teams from the middle (5–8; mid-players) and another thirteen players represented three teams from the bottom (10–12; bottom-players) of the league (Part I). Players were chosen with respect to playing position.

A total of twenty top-players, twenty-two mid-players and twenty bottom-players carried out a Yo-Yo IR2 test (Part II).

Match analysis and testing

Top- ($n = 13$), mid- ($n = 13$) and bottom team players ($n = 13$) were video filmed during matches in the Danish Premier League for computerized time-motion analyses. The analysis of each group included five central defenders, five midfield players and three attackers (Part I). Each player was filmed close up during the entire match by digital video cameras (GR-D23E, JVC, Japan). The recordings were later replayed on a monitor for computerized coding of the activity pattern.

The following locomotor categories were used: standing ($0\,km\cdot h^{-1}$), walking ($6\,km\cdot h^{-1}$), jogging ($8\,km\cdot h^{-1}$), low-speed running ($12\,km\cdot h^{-1}$), moderate-speed running ($15\,km\cdot h^{-1}$), high-speed running ($18\,km\cdot h^{-1}$), sprinting ($30\,km\cdot h^{-1}$), and backward running ($10\,km\cdot h^{-1}$). Jogging, low-speed running and backward running were categorized as low-intensity running; whereas moderate-speed running, high-speed running and sprinting were categorized as high-intensity running. The locomotor categories were chosen in accordance with Mohr *et al.* (2003). The numbers of headers and tackles were also recorded. In addition, 20 top-, 22 mid- and 20 bottom-players performed the Yo-Yo IR2 test (Part II) (Krustrup *et al.*, 2006).

Statistics

Differences between top-, mid- and bottom-team players were evaluated by one-way ANOVA tests. Correlation coefficients were determined and tested for significance using the Pearson's regression test. A significance level of 0.05 was chosen. Data are presented as means ± SEM.

Results

Match analysis: successful and unsuccessful teams

Total distance during a match covered by top-, mid- and bottom-level players was not different (10.62 ± 0.15, 10.55 ± 0.35 and $10.32 \pm 0.29\,km$, respectively). Nor was the distance at high-intensity different (2.14 ± 0.13, 2.06 ± 0.15 and $1.87 \pm 0.11\,km$; Figure 59.1a). On the other hand, the top- and mid-level players sprinted 25 and 33 per cent longer ($P<0.01$) respectively than the bottom-level players (452 ± 29, 481 ± 36 and $362 \pm 26\,m$; Figure 59.1b). In the most intense 5 min period, top- and mid-level players sprinted 45–49 per cent more ($P<0.01$) and ran 28–31 per cent longer ($P<0.05$) at high intensity ($\geq 15\,km.h^{-1}$) than bottom-level players (73 ± 6, 71 ± 4 and $49 \pm 3\,m$; 216 ± 13, 211 ± 13 and $165 \pm 11\,m$ respectively).

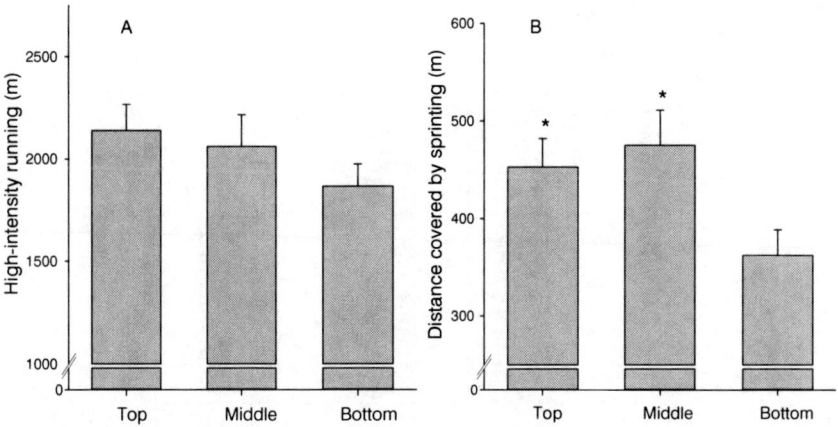

Figure 59.1 High-intensity running (a) and sprinting (b) of players in top-, middle- and bottom-level teams

Notes: * denotes significant different (P<0.05) from players from the bottom-level teams.

Yo-Yo IR2 performance: successful and unsuccessful teams

In the Yo-Yo IR2 test the top-players covered a distance of 1089 ± 47 m, which was 12 per cent and 28 per cent better (P<0.01) than for mid- and bottom-level players respectively, and the mid-players performed 14 per cent better (P<0.05) than the bottom-level players (Figure 59.2). For the midfield players the performance of the Yo-Yo IR2 test was correlated with the amount of high-intensity running during a game (r = 0.75; P<0.001; Figure 59.3).

Discussion

The major findings of the present study were that the players in successful teams performed more high-speed running and had a higher fitness level than the players in the bottom of the league. These results are in accordance with other studies (Mohr *et al.*, 2003; Krustrup *et al.*, 2006) which have shown that the higher the level of football, the more intense is the exercise that is performed. The present study shows that this is even valid between teams from the same league.

The observation that top- and mid-level players performed better on the Yo-Yo IR2 test than the bottom-level players suggests that the better physical performance in a game among these players is also related to a higher degree of fitness. This is supported by the finding that the Yo-Yo IR2 test performance was related to the amount of high-intensity running carried out by midfield players in a match. However, it appears not to be the only factor, since the mid-level players performed as much high-intensity work during a game as top-level players, despite being at lower Yo-Yo IR2 test levels.

In conclusion, successful teams performed more high-intensity running and had a higher fitness level than players in unsuccessful teams in the same league.

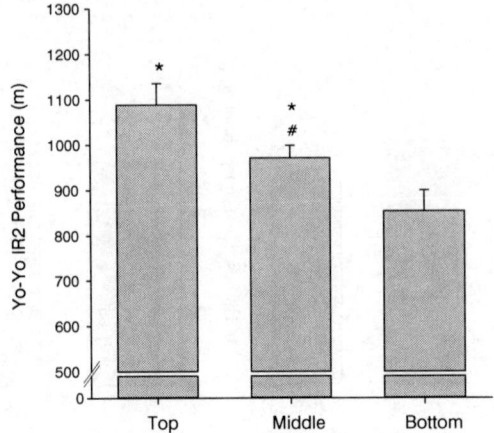

Figure 59.2 Yo-Yo intermittent recovery test level 2 performance of players in top- , middle-
and bottom-level teams

Notes: *: denotes significant different (P<0.05) from players from the bottom-level teams. # denotes
significant difference (P<0.05) from players from the top-level teams.

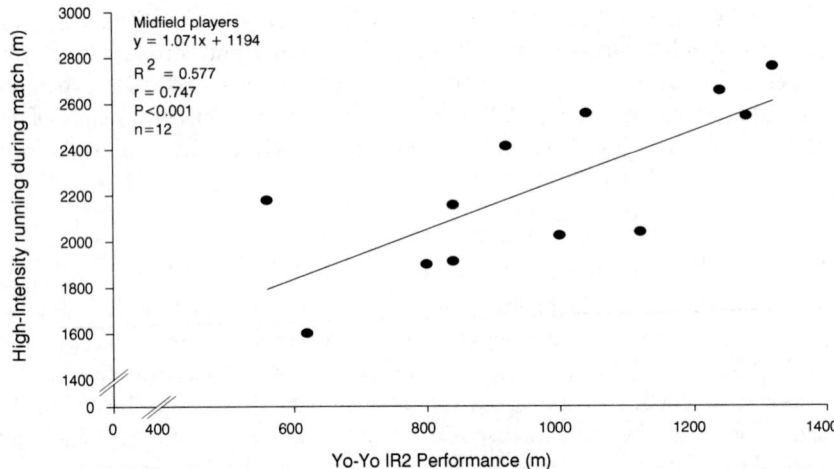

Figure 59.3 Individual relationship between performance of the Yo-Yo intermittent recovery
test level 2 and amount of high intensity running for midfield players during a soccer game

References

Krustrup, P., Mohr, M., Nybo, L., Majgaard Jensen, J., Nielsen, J.J. and Bangsbo, J., 2006, The Yo-Yo IR2 test: reliability, physiological response and application to elite soccer. *Medicine and Science in Sports and Exercise*, 38, 357–68.

Mohr, M., Krustrup, P. and Bangsbo, J., 2003, Match performance of top level soccer players with special reference to development of fatigue. *Journal of Sports Sciences*, 21, 519–28.

60 Performance on two soccer-specific high-intensity intermittent running protocols

Marcus Svensson, Paul Conway, Barry Drust and Thomas Reilly

Research Institute for Sport and Exercise Sciences, Liverpool John Moores University, UK

Introduction

Soccer match-play challenges players to recover quickly from the physiological consequences of high-intensity exercise which they must perform repeatedly over 90 minutes of play (Bangsbo, 1993). Recovery from this type of intermittent exercise is facilitated by a high level of aerobic fitness (Tomlin and Wenger, 2001). It seems logical therefore that aerobic training should be an important component of training for soccer.

Soccer coaches need to place a high priority on players' abilities to recover from high-intensity intermittent exercise. Commercially available fitness tests such as the Yo-Yo tests (Bangsbo, 1993) have been designed for this purpose. The '15–30 protocol' is a new and unique test where the ability to recover from high-intensity exercise can be examined through either sub-maximal or maximal measures (Svensson et al., 2006). The protocol may also be used in training by coaches as a conditioning drill. The aim of this study was to examine the sensitivity of the 15–30 protocol to detect changes in fitness over 1) six weeks of pre-season training and 2) six weeks of in-season aerobic interval training in young male professional soccer players.

Methods

Subjects

Ten male professional youth soccer players (age: 16.3 ± 0.4 years; stature: 1.70 ± 0.04 m; body mass: 70.2 ± 8.2 kg) from a Coca-Cola Championship club in England were used for the first part of this study (Group 1). In addition, thirteen male professional youth soccer players (age: 16.5 ± 0.5; stature: 1.79 ± 0.05 m; body mass: 71.6 ± 9.0 kg) from a Coca-Cola League Two club in England were used for the second part of this study (Group 2).

Experimental procedure

Group 1 was tested on three different occasions: these times were at the end of the 2005–2006 season, beginning of the 2006–2007 pre-season and at the end of six weeks of 2006–2007 pre-season. At each test occasion, the players performed the Yo-Yo Intermittent Recovery Test (Level 1) YIRT–1 (Bangbso, 1993) and the 15–30 protocol. Due to unforeseen circumstances, only the YIRT–1 was performed at end of the 2005–2006 season. Each test was performed on separate days.

Group 2 performed the 15–30 protocol and a laboratory treadmill test for the determination of maximal aerobic power ($\dot{V}O_{2\ max}$) on two separate occasions. These were at the beginning and at the end of a six-week aerobic interval training programme four weeks into the competitive 2006–07 season.

Training programmes

The pre-season training period for Group 1 lasted for six weeks. During the six weeks, there were 27 training days (46 training sessions), four friendly matches and 11 recovery days in total. The duration of each session was 90–120 min. Due to a change in the management at the club, heart rate responses of subjects could not be measured during the training sessions.

Group 2 performed a six-week aerobic interval training programme four weeks into the competitive season. Two training sessions per week were devoted to the training programme with 12 sessions in total. The sessions were based on 3 bouts of exercise each lasting for 3 min with a 3 min active rest period. For the final 3 weeks of the intervention, 4 exercise bouts were performed. The mode of exercise consisted of interval running without the ball as well as conditioned small-sided games. The target exercise heart rate for each bout was 90–95 per cent of HR_{peak} and the target heart rate in the recovery periods was 60–65 per cent of HR_{peak}. Pilot work had ensured that the players could achieve the target exercise intensity in all drills.

Field tests

All the field tests were performed either on a natural (Group 1) or an artificial grass surface (Group 2). The details of the YIRT–1 have been described elsewhere by Krustrup et al. (2003).

The 15–30 protocol was made up of short and long high-intensity intermittent shuttle runs. The test consisted of two parts i.e. a sub-maximal stage (Part 1) and a maximal stage (Part 2). The aim of Part 1 was to perform a set number of exercise blocks and the aim of Part 2 was to perform as many high-speed runs as possible. Performance in Part 1 was evaluated via heart rate measurements where the mean heart rate responses from each block and the rest periods were recorded. Performance in Part 2 was evaluated by means of the number of successfully completed high-speed runs. The running speed in the test was dictated via a series of pre-recorded audio signals from a CD.

In Part 1, the subjects had 6 s to run 15 m from the start line, turn and run 13 m back to the start. A 6 s passive rest period then followed after which the subjects ran 30 m in 6 s. After the long high-speed run they rested passively for 12 s. This running pattern was then completed seven times in total, which was equivalent to one exercise block. The duration of each block was 3 min 30 s and the distance covered 406 m. There was a 90 s passive rest period between each exercise block. In total, Part 1 consisted of five exercise blocks with the total distance 2030 m.

At the end of Part 1, there was a 30 s passive rest period before the start of Part 2. Part 2 consisted of the same running pattern as in Part 1 with the only difference being that the rest period after the long high-speed run was 6 s instead of 12 s. One running cycle (one short high-speed run with a turn and one long high-speed run without turn) was 58 m. This running cycle continued until the subjects could no longer maintain the running pace dictated by the audio signals.

Heart rate was measured every 5 s during the Yo-Yo Intermittent Recovery Test and the 15–30 protocol via short-range telemetry for both Group 1 and Group 2 using the Polar Team System (Polar Electro Oy, Kempele, Finland). Heart rate was also classified into six intensity zones: these were recovery ($<60\%$ of HR_{peak}), light intensity (60–75%), medium intensity (75–85%), medium-high intensity (85–90%), high intensity (90–95%) and maximal (95–100%).

Laboratory test

Group 2 performed an incremental treadmill test to determine maximal oxygen uptake ($\dot{V}O_{2\,max}$) in the physiology laboratories at the Research Institute for Sport and Exercise Sciences, Liverpool John Moores University, UK. The test was performed on a motorised treadmill (h/p Cosmos Pulsar, Nüssdorf-Traunstein, Germany). Following a warm-up, the initial running speed was 14 km.h^{-1} for 2 min and was then increased to 16 km.h^{-1} for 2 min. The running speed was then fixed at 16 km.h^{-1} while the treadmill incline was increased by 2% every 2 min until the subjects reached volitional exhaustion. Oxygen uptake was measured continuously during the test by means of an on-line gas analyser (MetaMax, Cortex Biophysik, Leipzig, Germany). Heart rate was measured every 5 s with the Polar S810 heart rate monitor (Polar Electro Oy, Kempele, Finland). A blood sample was taken at rest and immediately at the end of the treadmill test. Blood lactate concentration was determined using the Lactate Pro (Arkray, Kyoto, Japan) device.

Statistical analysis

All the data were tested for normality using the Shapiro-Wilk test. All comparisons between test conditions for parametric data were made using a Student's T-test. When the data violated the assumptions of normality, a Wilcoxon signed ranks test was used. Comparisons of Yo-Yo test performance between test conditions were made using one-way analysis of variance (ANOVA). Statistical significance was set at $P<0.05$.

Results

Training programme

During the six-week training programme, Group 2 performed ten out of the twelve training sessions. Two sessions had to be cancelled on the coach's discretion. The average intensity during the exercise bouts for the players was 171 ± 8 beats.min^{-1} which was equivalent to $88.5 \pm 3.2\%$ of HR$_{peak}$. The mean heart rate during the rest periods was 148 ± 12 beats.min^{-1} ($76.4 \pm 5.7\%$ of HR$_{peak}$).

The Yo-Yo Intermittent Recovery Test

For Group 1, there was a 19.1% improvement in distance covered in the YIRT-1 from end of season (1656 ± 344 m) to beginning of pre-season (1972 ± 299 m), and a 16.2% improvement from beginning of pre-season to end of pre-season (2292 ± 316 m). There was also a significant ($P<0.05$) 38.4% improvement in distance covered from end of season (1656 ± 344 m) to end of pre-season (2292 ± 316 m). Peak heart rate was not significantly ($P>0.05$) different between end of season (197 ± 6 beats.min^{-1}), beginning of pre-season (198 ± 8 beats.min^{-1}) and end of pre-season (195 ± 8 beats.min^{-1}).

The 15–30 protocol

Heart rate in Part 1 was significantly ($P<0.05$) lower at end of pre-season (163 ± 12 beats.min^{-1} or $81.7 \pm 5.6\%$ of HR$_{peak}$) compared to beginning of pre-season (176 ± 9 beats.min^{-1} or $88.1 \pm 4.5\%$ of HR$_{peak}$) in Group 1. The players spent a significantly ($P<0.05$) shorter time in the 95–100% zone at end of pre-season. They also spent a significantly ($P<0.05$) longer time in the <60%, 60–75% and 75–85% zones, as shown in Figure 60.1. There was no significant ($P>0.05$) difference in mean heart rate during Part 2 at beginning of pre-season (188 ± 10 beats.min^{-1} or $94.3 \pm 3.2\%$ of HR$_{peak}$) compared to end of pre-season (188 ± 8 beats.min^{-1} or $94.2 \pm 2.5\%$ of HR$_{peak}$). The players performed 6 ± 5 runs (343 ± 303 m) at the beginning of pre-season, which significantly ($P<0.05$) improved to 30 ± 13 runs (1740 ± 778 m) at end of pre-season.

The mean heart rate in Part 1 for the players in Group 2 was also lower ($P<0.05$) at end of the aerobic interval training programme (158 ± 11 beats.min^{-1} or $81.7 \pm 4.4\%$ of HRpeak) compared to the beginning of the aerobic interval training programme (165 ± 12 beats.min^{-1} or $86.0 \pm 4.6\%$ of HRpeak). The players spent a significantly ($P<0.05$) shorter time in the 90–95% and 95–100% heart rate zones after the training programme. A significantly ($P<0.05$) longer time was also spent in the <60%, 60–75% and 75–85% heart rate zones at the end of the aerobic interval training programme, as shown in Figure 60.2. No significant change was observed in heart rate during Part 2 at beginning of the training programme (181 ± 9 beats.min^{-1} or $94.3 \pm 3.1\%$ of HRpeak) or at the end of the training programme (183 ± 10 beats.min^{-1} or $94.2 \pm 1.9\%$ of HRpeak).

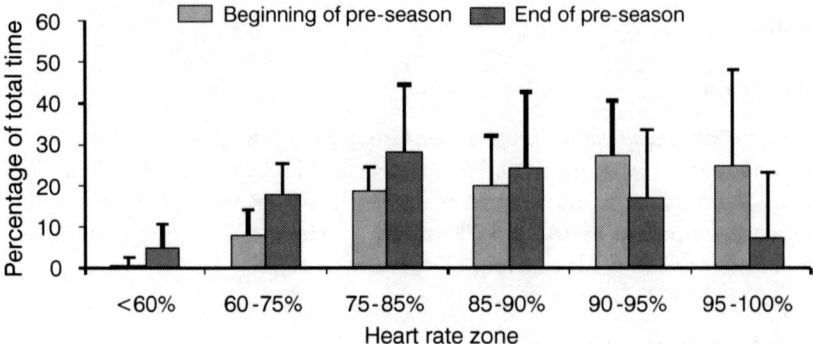

Figure 60.1 Percentage of total time spent in each heart rate zone for Group 1 at the beginning and end of six weeks of pre-season training (n = 10)

Note: † = significant (*P*<0.05) to beginning of pre-season.

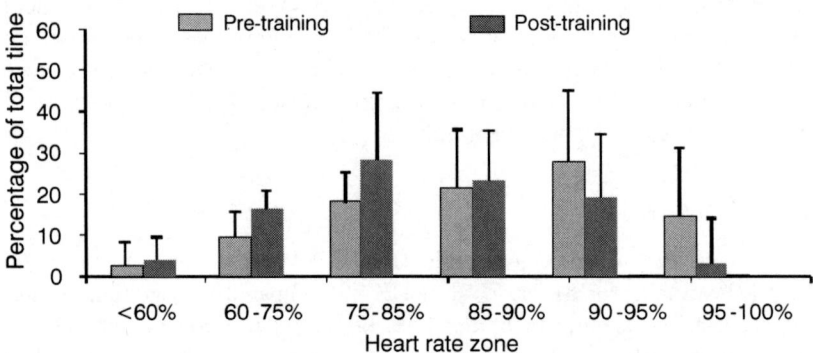

Figure 60.2 Percentage of total time spent in each heart rate zone for Group 2 at the beginning and end of the six-week aerobic training programme (n = 13)

Note: † = significant (*P*<0.05) to pre-training.

The number of runs in Part 2 significantly (P<0.05) increased by 117% from 18 ± 16 (1029 ± 949 m) at the beginning of the training programme to 39 ± 35 runs (2123 ± 2018 m) at the end of the training programme.

Laboratory test

In Group 2, relative and individual $\dot{V}O_{2\,max}$ increased by 4.3% and 4.2% respectively from beginning of the interval training (64.06 ± 5.66 ml.kg^{-1}.min^{-1}; 184.8 ± 13.4 ml.kg^{-1}.min$^{-0.75}$) to the end of the interval training (66.83 ± 4.85 ml. kg^{-1}.min^{-1}; 192.5 ± 13.2 ml.kg^{-1}.min$^{-0.75}$) but this change was not significant ($P = 0.093$ and $P = 0.070$). There was no change in peak heart rate or peak blood lactate concentration at the end of the treadmill test from beginning of the interval training programme (192 ± 9 beats.min^{-1}; 11.5 ± 1.6 mmol.l^{-1}) to the end of the interval training programme (191 ± 9 beats.min^{-1}; 11.3 ± 2.0 mmol.l^{-1}). Time to exhaustion was significantly ($P<0.05$) longer at the end of the interval training programme (431 ± 105 s) compared to at the beginning of training (414 ± 117 s).

Discussion

The main finding of this study was that performance in the 15–30 protocol improved after both the pre-season and in-season training interventions. Improvement in maximal oxygen uptake was small following the in-season training intervention, and bordered on statistical significance.

As expected, performance in both the 15–30 protocol and the YIRT-1 in Group 1 improved significantly after six weeks of pre-season training. Less time was spent in heart rate zones $>90\%$ of HR_{peak} in Part 1 and the number of runs performed in Part 2 increased by 400%. The large improvement in number of runs in proportion to YIRT-1 improvements may be due to the fixed running speed in Part 2 as opposed to a progressive increase in running speed in the YIRT-1. These findings correspond well to other reports of improvements in performance on the YIRT-1 (Krustrup *et al.*, 2003) following pre-season training.

Similar improvements in the 15–30 protocol were also found after the six weeks of aerobic interval training conducted in-season in Group 2. The relative and individual maximal aerobic power values in this study increased by 4 per cent which was lower than that reported for other similar training interventions using young professional soccer players (Helgerud *et al.*, 2001). However, Impellizeri *et al.* (2006) similarly reported that the major part of a 7 per cent increase in $\dot{V}O_{2\,max}$ of junior Italian players over 14 weeks of aerobic interval training occurred in the four weeks of pre-season training. Bangsbo (1993) found little change in aerobic power following five weeks of training but significant improvements in performance on a field test of soccer-specific endurance. Moreover, those players significantly improved their time to exhaustion on the treadmill test after six weeks of training. Findings suggest that peripheral as opposed to central physiological adaptations may have occurred following the training intervention.

In summary, the 15–30 protocol is sensitive to detect changes in training status in young soccer players. These changes were evident following a controlled programme of both pre-season and in-season aerobic interval training conducted.

References

Bangsbo, J., 1993, *The Physiology of Soccer – With Special Reference to High-Intensity Intermittent Exercise.* (Copenhagen: H+O Storm).

Helgerud, J., Engen, L.C., Wisløff, U. and Hoff, J., 2001, Aerobic endurance training improves soccer performance. *Medicine and Science in Sports and Exercise*, 33, 1925–31.

Impellizzeri, F.M., Marcora, S.M., Castagna, C., Reilly, T., Sassi, A., Iaia, F.M. and Rampinini, E., 2006, Physiological and performance effects of generic versus specific aerobic training in soccer players. *International Journal of Sports Medicine*, 27, 473–82.

Krustrup, P., Mohr, M., Amstrup, T., Rysgaard, T., Johansen, J., Steensberg, A., Pedersen, P.K. and Bangsbo, J., 2003, The Yo-Yo Intermittent Recovery Test: physiological response, reliability and validity. *Medicine and Science in Sports and Exercise*, 35, 695–705.

Svensson, M., Andersson, H. and Balsom, P., 2006, Utveckling av två högintensiva intermittenta löptest för fotboll samt idrotter med liknande arbetsprofil. *Svensk Idrottsforskning*, 3, 50–5.

Tomlin, D.L. and Wenger, H.A., 200t1, The relationship between aerobic fitness and recovery from high intensity intermittent exercise. *Sports Medicine*, 31, 1–11.

61 Seasonal changes in intermittent exercise performance of soccer players evaluated by the Yo-Yo intermittent recovery test level 2

Fedon Marcello Iaia,[2,1] Thomas Rostgaard,[1]
Peter Krustrup[1] and Jens Bangsbo[1]

[1]Institute of Exercise and Sport Sciences, Department of Human Physiology, University of Copenhagen, Denmark; [2]State University of Milan, Italy

Introduction

The ability to perform repeated high-intensity exercise is of great importance in soccer. Thus, players at an international elite level have been shown to perform 25% more high-intensity running and 35% more sprinting during competitive games than professional players at a moderate elite level (Mohr *et al.*, 2003).

Therefore, it is important that the players develop their ability to perform intense intermittent exercise and have this ability evaluated at different stages during the competitive season. Due to its specificity and practicality, the Yo-Yo intermittent recovery test 2 (YYIR2) has been extensively used in soccer to assess players' abilities to perform repeated high-intensity exercise. Studies have shown its sensitivity in discriminating players' performances at various competitive levels, between different playing positions, and after periods of different types of training.

Thus, the aim of the present study was to examine the changes in fitness level occurring during pre-season and any changes that may occur during a season for professional soccer players as well as to evaluate the effectiveness of the YYIR2 to detect such changes.

Method

Subjects and procedures

Twelve professional male soccer players belonging to a team from the Danish top division took part in the study. The mean age, mass and height of the players was 22.4 ± 3.7 (mean $\pm$ SEM) years, 73.5 ± 1.4 kg and 1.84 ± 0.07 m, respectively. The players performed the YYIR2 at the beginning of the pre-season (Start-Pre), which lasted ten weeks, and after ten days of preparation (10–Pre), as well as at

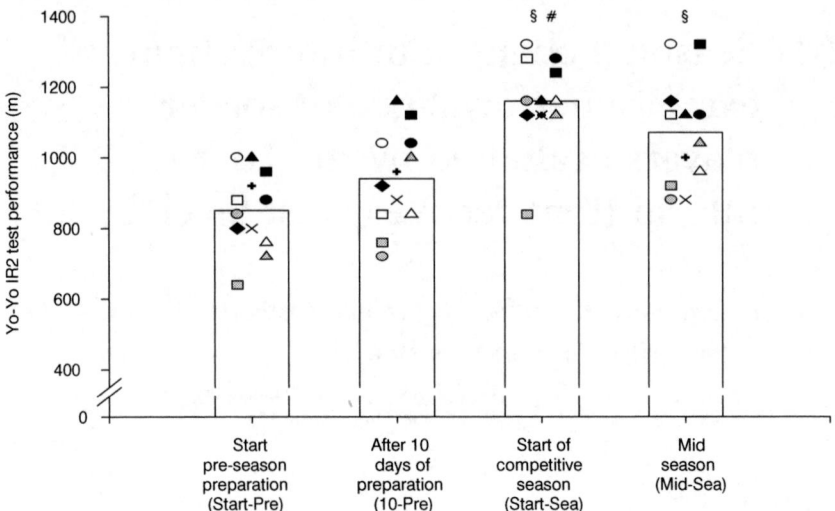

Figure 61.1 Individual and mean seasonal changes in the Yo-Yo IR2 test performance expressed in metres for 12 elite male soccer players; values are means ± SEM. §: Significant (P<0.05) different from Start-Pre (P<0.05); #: Significant (P<0.05) different from 10–Pre

the start of the competitive season (Start-Sea) and seven weeks later during the season (Mid-Sea). All YYIR2–tests were performed on the same outdoor artificial turf ground and under similar weather conditions from time to time. Evaluation of each player's performance was conducted by the same experienced test leader.

Statistical analysis

Seasonal changes in YYIR2 performances were evaluated by a one-way ANOVA with repeated measurements. When a significant interaction was detected, data were subsequently analyzed using a NewmanKeuls posthoc test. The coefficient of variation was calculated as SD of repeated measures divided by the mean and multiplied by 100. A significant level of 0.05 was chosen. Data are presented as means ± SEM (standard error of the mean).

Results

The YYIR2 performance at the start of the season was 1160 ± 39 m, which was 36 and 23% better (P<0.05) than at Start-Pre and 10–Pre, respectively (Figure 61.1). At mid-season performance (1068 ± 52 m) was still better than at Start-Pre, but it tended to be lower (-7.5 ± 3.1%) compared to the start of the season. Large individual variations were observed with three players improving performance (range: 40–80m) and eight decreasing performance (40–280m) whereas one player was at the same level (Figure 61.1).

Discussion

The present study showed that the professional soccer players had a considerable improvement in the ability to perform high-intensity intermittent exercise during the pre-season. The increase of 36% was significantly greater than changes observed in maximum oxygen uptake in other studies for the same period (2.9–7.4%; Bangsbo, 1994; Krustrup *et al.*, 2003; Impellizzeri *et al.*, 2006) indicating that the Yo-Yo performance test is a much more sensitive measure of the performance capacity of a soccer player.

During the season two-thirds of the players had a drop in performance ranging from 40 to 280 m (3–24%). The coefficient of variation between performances at the start and the end of the season was 14%. These findings show that a significant number of the professional players had difficulties in maintaining their fitness level during the season. Thus, it appears that some players at a professional level have a need for further fitness training.

At any point of formal testing, a large variability in performance within the team was found, which to some extent is related to the players' position in the team (Krustrup *et al.*, 2003, 2006). Nevertheless, at the start of the season only one player had a value below 1000 m in the Yo-Yo IR2 test, suggesting that such a basic level of fitness is needed to perform at a high level.

In conclusion, professional soccer players showed a significant improvement in their ability to perform repeated high-intensity exercise during the pre-season period; in contrast a considerable number of players had a decrease in fitness level during the season. Thus it is fundamental to monitor the players individually; the study also revealed that the Yo-Yo IR2 test is a sensitive tool to detect changes in players' performance levels during the season.

References

Bangsbo, J., 1994, The physiology of soccer – with special reference to intense intermittent exercise. *Acta Physiologica Scandinavica*, 151 (Suppl. 619), 1–155.

Impellizzeri, F.M., Marcora, S.M., Castagna, C., Reilly, T., Sassi, A., Iaia, F.M. and Rampinini, E., 2006, Physiological and performance effects of generic versus specific aerobic training in soccer players. *International Journal of Sports Medicine*, 27, 483–92.

Krustrup. P., Mohr, M., Amstrup, T., Rysgaard, T., Johansen, J., Steensberg, A., Pedersen, P.K. and Bangsbo, J., 2003, The Yo-Yo intermittent recovery test: physiological response, reliability and validity. *Medicine and Science in Sports and Exercise*, 35, 697–705.

Krustrup, P., Mohr, M., Nybo, L., Majgaard Jensen, J., Nielsen, J.J. and Bangsbo, J., 2006, The Yo-Yo IR2 test: physiological response, reliability, and application to elite soccer. *Medicine and Science in Sports and Exercise*, 38, 1666–73.

Mohr, M., Krustrup, P. and Bangsbo, J., 2003, Match performance of high-standard soccer players with special reference to development of fatigue. *Journal of Sports Sciences*, 21, 519–28.

62 Comparison of physiological profiles of soccer players in U17, U19, U21 and over-21 age groups

A.K. Emre, Ahmet Yıldırım, Şeref Çiçek
and Feza Korkusuz

Middle East Technical University, Turkey

Introduction

Physical characteristics and fitness components have been identified as crucial elements for soccer players, including flexibility, body fat, BMI (body mass index), blood lactate and heart rate responses. Characteristics of soccer players have been widely reported. Soccer players should have a fit and flexible body in order to use their energy sources economically and perform their techniques efficiently. Players should be able to continue running at a high velocity without getting tired. Therefore, the aim of this study was to examine the running velocity and heart rate responses of soccer players at 2, 2.5, 3 and 4 mM lactate levels across U17, U19, U21 and over-21 age groups. Flexibility, body fat and BMI were also compared between the age groups, as were physical characteristics.

Methods

Subjects and procedures

Ninety-seven Turkish sub-elite soccer players from soccer clubs located in Ankara with a mean (SD) age of 19.8 (3.6) years participated in this study. The players all received an explanation of protocols informing them about the risks and benefits of the study. Players over the age of 18 signed informed consent and a parental permission form was signed by the parents of players under the age of 18. The study was approved by the local ethics committee. The participants' characteristics were: height (1.76 ± 0.06) m, mass (71.1 ± 7.5) kg, BMI (22.9 ± 1.8) and body fat ($10.3 \pm 5.0\%$). The BMI was calculated from body weight and height and expressed as kg/m^2. Height was measured to the nearest 0.1 cm using a stadiometer. Body mass was measured to the nearest 0.1 kg using a digital scale.

Skinfold measurements were determined using a Tanita TBF-350 device (Tanita Corp, Tokyo, Japan). Subjects stood still, wearing only light football shorts. Skinfold thicknesses were measured using Holtain calipers (Holtain Ltd., Crymych, UK) at seven sites on the non-dominant side of the body: these were biceps, triceps, abdomen, subscapula, thigh, calf, and chest. All measurements were performed by the same experimenter. Body density was calculated as described by Durnin and Womersley (1974) using biceps, triceps, subscapula, and suprailiac values. The proportion of body fat was calculated from body density using the equation of Siri (1956).

A standard sit-and-reach box was used to assess flexibility, and the sliding ruler located on the top of the box was used to obtain the sit-and-reach test (SRT) scores. The markings on the ruler were positioned so that the 23 cm mark represented the point at which the subjects' fingertips were in line with their toes. The minimal acceptable score to pass, as determined by AAHPERD (American Alliance for Health, Physical Education, Recreation, and Dance, 1900 Association Dr, Reston, VA 22091) is 25 cm, for all ages and both genders and without consideration of anthropometric variables. Blood lactate concentrations were measured with a Lactate Pro LT-1710 instrument (Arkray KDK Co., Kyoto, Japan). The portable lactate meter is a highly accurate tool for monitoring lactate concentrations (Saunders et al., 2005). The test protocol consisted of individual 3 min exercise stages, with a 1 km.h^{-1} velocity increase in treadmill speed (Quinton Q65, Quinton Instrument Co, Seattle-USA) until termination of the test. The test was ended when the blood lactate concentration exceeded 4 mmol.l^{-1} or at the subject's own request. Blood lactate concentrations were determined from capillary samples (5 ml) obtained from the ear lobe at the beginning of the protocol and during the 30 s breaks between the work stages. The treadmill inclination was set at 1.5 % .

Heart rates were recorded using recordable Polar Vantage NV heart rate monitors (Polar Electro Oy, Kempele, Finland). The resting heart rate was established after 10 min rest. Heart rates during the test protocols were recorded every 30 s until the test was terminated. This test was terminated when the heart rate exceeded the predicted maximum heart rate value (220age).

Statistical analysis

Heart rates and running velocities at 3 and 4 mM lactate levels were determined using Originlab 7.5 software (Originlab Corporation, 2003). Means and standard deviations were calculated for each of the dependent variable. ANOVA and paired t-tests were performed to determine the differences between them. The significance level was set at 0.05.

Results

One-way ANOVA was conducted in order to examine the differences in dependent variables across age groups. The ANOVA results revealed that there were significant differences between BMI scores ($F_{3,96} = 4.34$, $P = 0.007$). Pairwise comparison analysis was conducted in order to localise the difference. The results showed that players in the over-21 age group ($M = 23.7 \pm 1.7$) had higher BMI than U17 ($M = 22.5, \pm 1.9$) and U19 ($M = 22.2, \pm 1.5$) age groups (Table 62.1).

Table 62.1 Means and standard deviations for anthropometric variables for age groups

	U17 (N = 33)	U19 (N = 20)	U21 (N = 15)	Over 21 (N = 29)	Total (N = 97)
BMI	22.5 ± 1.9*	22.2 ± 1.5**	23.3 ± 1.4	23.7 ± 1.7*	22.9 ± 1.8
Body fat (%)	9.9 ± 6.2	8.7 ± 3.1	11.3 ± 4.7	11.2 ± 4.5	10.3 ± 5.0
Flexibility	16.8 ± 5.7	18.9 ± 6.8	16.1 ± 7.1	16.3 ± 5.7	16.9 ± 6.1

Notes: (*$P<0.05$); * significant difference between U17 and over-21; ** significant difference between U19 and over-21

Table 62.2 Means and standard deviations for HR (beats.min^{-1}) of the age different groups

Heart rate	U17 (N = 33)	U19 (N = 20)	U21 (N = 15)	Over 21 (N = 29)	Total (N = 97)
(2 mM)	145.0 ± 12.9	145.2 ± 22.9	148.1 ± 11.2	143.6 ± 12.3	145.1 ± 15.0
(2.5 mM)	154.9 ± 12.3	154.6 ± 18.5	156.8 ± 8.8	153.1 ± 10.9	154.6 ± 12.9
(3 mM)	163.3 ± 12.1	162.9 ± 15.0	165.5 ± 7.6	160.5 ± 10.5	162.7 ± 11.7
(4 mM)	179.3 ± 10.6*	175.3 ± 9.2	177.0 ± 7.2	172.6 ± 9.6*	176.1 ± 9.8

Note: (*$P<0.05$)

Table 62.3 Means and standard deviations for running velocities (km.h^{-1}) of different age groups

Velocity	U17 (N = 33)	U19 (N = 20)	U21 (N = 15)	Over-21 (N = 29)	Total (N = 97)
(2 mM)	8.9 ± 2.0*	9.2 ± 3.4	11.1 ± 1.9*	10.2 ± 1.4	9.7 ± 2.3
(2.5 mM)	10.2 ± 1.9*	10.4 ± 3.0	12.1 ± 1.7*	11.3 ± 1.5	10.9 ± 2.1
(3 mM)	11.3 ± 1.8*	11.5 ± 2.6	13.0 ± 1.6*	12.1 ± 1.2	11.8 ± 1.9
(4 mM)	13.2 ± 1.7*	13.3 ± 1.6	14.5 ± 1.3*	13.5 ± 1.1	13.5 ± 1.5

Note: (*$P<0.05$)

The ANOVA results revealed that there was a significant difference between groups in HR responses ($F_{3,96} = 2.81$, $P = 0.044$) at 4 mmol.l^{-1} across age groups. Pairwise comparison analysis showed that the over-21 age group (M = 172.6, ± 9.6) had significantly lower HR values than the U-17 age group (M = 179.3, ± 10.6) (Table 62.2).

The ANOVA results revealed that there were significant differences between running velocities at 2 ($F_{3,96}$) = 4.33, $P = 0.007$), 2.5 ($F_{3,96} = 3.91$, $P = 0.011$), 3 ($F_{3,96} = 3.19$, $P = 0.027$) and 4 mM ($F_{3,96} = 2.81$, $P = 0.044$) lactate levels across age groups. Pairwise comparison analysis showed that the U21 age group had significantly higher running velocities than the U17 age group at all blood lactate levels (Table 62.3).

Discussion

The purpose of the present study was to compare the physical (BMI, body fat, flexibility) and physiological (lactate and running velocity) characteristics of soccer players across different age groups. The results demonstrated that the over-21 group had significantly higher BMI than the U17 group. All groups had

BMI values in the normal range according to WHO (World Health Organization). The skinfold results also showed that there was no significant difference between the age groups. Östenberg et al. (2000) found that older age groups had higher BMI than their younger groups. Whitney et al. (1987) and Barnekov-Begkvist et al. (1996) stated that body fat percentage increases with age but it is also possible that the members of the older group could have a larger muscle mass.

The U21 age group has higher running velocities than members of the U17 age group. Guner et al. (2005) compared the same age groups (except 21+) and found that there was no significant difference between age groups in terms of running velocities at the same lactate levels as in this study. They followed 20 players for 3 years and found that running velocities were increased and heart rates were decreased over this period.

There was a significant difference between over-21 and U17 age goups in terms of heart rate. Guner, et al. (2006) found that heart rates in the U21 and U19 age groups were significantly lower than in the U17 age group. Guner et al. (2006) reported that HR values of players aged 30+ years of age were significantly lower than those of players in their other age groups.

In conclusion, trainers and coaches should be aware of the individual characteristics of the different age groups. They should adjust the training sessions in accordance with these differences.

References

Barnekow-Bergkvist, M., Hedberg, G., Janlert, U. and Jansson, E., 1996, Development of muscular endurance and strength from adolescence to adulthood and level of physical capacity in men and women at the age of 34 years. *Scandinavian Journal of Medicine Science and Sports*, 6, 145–55.

Durnin, J.V.G.A. and Womersley J., 1974, Body fat assessed from total body density and its estimation from skinfold thickness : measurements on 481 men and women aged from 16 to 72 years. *British Journal of Nutrition*, 32, 77–97.

Guner, R., Kunduracioglu, B., Ulkar, B. and Ergen, E., 2005, Running velocities and heart rates at fixed blood lactate concentrations in elite soccer players. Advances in Therapy, Nov–Dec, 22, 613–20.

Guner, R., Kunduracioglu B. and Ulkar B., 2006, Running velocities and heart rates at fixed blood lactate concentrations in young soccer players, *Advances in Therapy*, May–Jun, 23, 395–403.

Östenberg, A., Roos, E.M., Ekdahl, C. and Roos, H., 2000, Physical capacity in female soccer players;Does age make a difference. *Advances in Physiotherapy*, 2, 39–48.

Siri, W.S., 1956, *The Gross Composition of the Body: Advances in Biological Physics.* (New York: Academic Press).

Saunders, A.C., Feldman, H.A., Correia, C.E. and Weinstein, D.A., 2005, Clinical evaluation of a portable lactate meter in type I glycogen storage disease. *Journal of Inherited Metabolic Disease*, 28, 695–701.

Whitney, E.N., Cataldo, C.B. and Rolfes, S.R., 1987, Energy balance and weight control. In *Understanding Normal and Clinical Nutrition*, edited by Whitney, E.N., Cataldo, C.B. Rolfes, S.R. (St Paul, MN: West Publishing Company), pp. 247–248.

63 A comparison of skinfold thickness measurements and dual-energy x-ray absorptiometry analysis of percent body fat in soccer players

J. Wallace,[1] M. Marfell-Jones,[2] K. George[1] and T. Reilly[1]

[1]Liverpool John Moores University, UK; [2]Universal College of Learning, New Zealand

Introduction

There is considerable interest in the evaluation of football players' body composition. It is known that body composition has a significant effect on performance, and an athlete's body composition must be specifically suited to meet the demands and needs of the particular sport. Body composition is an important factor in preparing for peak performance in soccer, since excessive adipose tissue acts as a dead weight in activities where the body mass must be repeatedly lifted against gravity during locomotion and jumping (Reilly et al., 1996).

Using skinfold thicknesses to predict percent body fat is one of the most common practices for field based assessment of body composition. The reliability and accuracy of using skinfold depend on several factors, especially the choice of equation used to estimate fatness. Although skinfold measurement is among the most frequently used techniques in the assessment of soccer players, there is not a well-validated prediction equation that is unique for professional or amateur male soccer players.

The development of dual-energy x-ray absorptiometry (DXA) has promoted a renewed interest in the field of anthropometry, as this method overcomes the population-specific nature of equations for predicting body fat from anthropometric measures. The aims of this study were to reassess the validity of skinfold measurements by callipers in predicting percent body fat (%BF), to establish which is the most valid existing formula and to formulate a new prediction equation based upon skinfold measurements to estimate %BF using DXA as the criterion method in elite English Premier League soccer players.

Materials and methods

Participants

Twenty-eight elite male subjects were recruited from a local Premier League soccer club, with an age, mass and height of 24.1 ± 5.4 years, 81.94 ± 9.16 kg and 1.82 ± 0.06 m (mean $\pm$ SD), respectively. Written informed consent was received from all players prior to testing. Ethical approval for this study was obtained from the University's Research Ethics Committee.

Anthropometry

Height (stretched stature), mass and skinfold (SF) measurements were made according to standard procedures adopted by the International Society for Advancement of Kinanthropometry (Marfell-Jones *et al.*, 2006). Measurements of whole-body mass (kg) and percent body fat (%BF) were also performed using the technique of DXA (Hologic QDR series Discovery A, Bedford, MA). Eight skinfold thicknesses (triceps, biceps, subscapular, iliac crest, supraspinale, abdominal, front thigh and medial calf) were marked and measured using Harpenden callipers. An investigator trained to ISAK level 4 performed all the measurements. Percent body fat was then predicted using several popular formulae (Durnin and Womersley, 1974; Jackson and Pollock's $\Sigma 3$ and $\Sigma 7$, 1978; Lohman, 1981; British Olympic Association's $\Sigma 5$ – Reilly *et al.*, 1996; Withers *et al.* 1998; Eston and co workers' $\Sigma 2$ and $\Sigma 6$, 2005). Where body density was calculated from a formula, the formulae of both Siri (1956) and Brozek *et al.* (1963) were used to estimate percent body fat.

Statistical analysis

Means and standard deviations (SD) of percent body fat for all methods and formulae were calculated and were tested for statistical significance using a one-way within groups ANOVA with pairwise comparisons. Correlations between the different methods and formulae were established using Pearson's product moment correlation. A new elite male soccer-specific prediction equation was determined using bivariate linear regression analysis. The relationship between body mass index (BMI) and percent body fat was also assessed using a correlation coefficient. Statistical analyses were conducted with SPSS for Windows version 12.0.2 (SPSS, Chicago, IL); an alpha-level of 0.05 was used for all significance tests unless otherwise stated.

Results

The %BF for each formula was calculated (Table 63.1). The mean total %BF from the DXA method was 11.5 ± 1.6 % or by using the subtotal DXA values (those excluding the head) 11.0 ± 1.7 %. The closest agreement between DXA values of %BF and those estimated using the various skinfold formulae occurred

Table 63.1 Percent body fat values (Mean ± SD) and correlation coefficient with DXA total and subtotal %BF

Method/formulae	%bf	r value DXA subtotal	r value DXA total
DXA (total)	11.5 ± 1.6	–	–
DXA (subtotal)	11.0 ± 1.7	–	–
Durnin and Womersley - Siri	15.4 ± 2.6	0.831 *	0.697 *
Durnin and Womersley - Brozek	15.5 ± 2.4	0.831 *	0.697 *
Jackson and Pollock Σ3 - Siri	10.3 ± 2.9	0.888 *	0.668 *
Jackson and Pollock Σ3 - Brozek	10.8 ± 2.7	0.888 *	0.668 *
Jackson and Pollock Σ7 - Siri	9.7 ± 2.8	0.882 *	0.691 *
Jackson and Pollock Σ7 - Brozek	10.2 ± 2.6	0.882 *	0.691 *
Withers	11.2 ± 2.5	0.895 *	0.700 *
Lohman - Siri	12.0 ± 2.6	0.846 *	0.665 *
Lohman - Brozek	12.3 ± 2.4	0.846 *	0.665 *
Eston Σ2	15.0 ± 3.1	0.854 *	0.680 *
Eston Σ6	12.5 ± 1.2	0.845 *	0.677*
BOA Σ5		0.859 *	0.693 *
BMI		0.220	0.082

* $P < 0.0001$

using the formula of Withers et al. (1998); it showed only a 0.2% overestimation in comparison to DXA subtotal. Jackson and Pollock's Σ3 skinfolds using the transformation of Brozek et al. (1963) was also only +0.2% different from DXA subtotal values. There was a significant difference between the various skinfold formulae for estimating %BF ($P < 0.001$). Post hoc analysis of DXA subtotal %BF and the skinfold formulae, showed no significant differences ($P > 0.05$) with Jackson and Pollock's (1978) Σ3 or Σ7 – using Brozek et al. (1963), Lohman (1980) – using Siri (1956) and Withers et al. (1998).

All skinfold formulae were highly correlated with both DXA total and subtotal %BF values (Table 63.1). All %BF relationships were stronger with DXA subtotal values rather than with DXA total values. The strongest correlations for %BF were between DXA subtotal and the formula of Withers et al. (1998) ($r = 0.895$; $P < 0.001$) and Jackson and Pollock's (1978) sum of 3 ($r = 0.888$; $P < 0.001$).

The systematic bias (mean difference – MD) and the random error (standard deviation of the difference – SDD) for the estimation of percent body fat for the various skinfold formulae demonstrated a wide range of values. Jackson and Pollock's (1978) Σ3 (MD = 0.23; SDD = 2.45) and Σ7 (MD = –0.17; SDD = 2.75) and Withers et al. (1998) (MD = –0.78; SDD = 2.67) formulae provided the lowest systematic bias and random error.

Each skinfold site's relationship with DXA %BF was determined. All the skinfold sites had a better correlation with DEXA subtotal %BF than they did with DXA total values. The abdominal skinfold site produced the best correlation with DXA subtotal values ($r = 0.758$; $P < 0.01$).

In this cohort of elite male soccer players, there was no significant correlation ($P > 0.05$; $r = 0.220$) between their %BF (DXA subtotal) and their body mass index (BMI). The sum of five skinfold measures as recommended by the British Olympic Association (Reilly *et al.*, 1996) showed a good relationship with %BF. This association was considerably stronger when using subtotal rather than total %BF DXA values ($r = 0.859$ and 0.693 respectively).

A new prediction formula (Equation 63.1) was formulated using multiple-regression stepwise analysis; the outcome was that 3–skinfold sites were best variables predictive of DXA subtotal %BF; these sites were the abdominal, thigh and calf. These variables accounted for 82.5% of the variability in %BF. Using all eight skinfold (SF in mm) measures in the multiple regression analysis (Equation 63.2) only increased the explained variance to 85.4%:

$$\%BF = 5.011 + (0.175 \times \text{abdominal SF}) + (0.182 \times \text{thigh SF}) + (0.136 \times \text{calf SF}) \quad (63.1)$$

$$\% \, BF = 5.178 + (0.134 \times \text{triceps}) - (0.095 \times \text{subscapular}) - (0.058 \times \text{biceps}) + \\ (0.074 \times \text{iliac crest}) - (0.188 \times \text{supraspinal}) + (0.195 \times \text{abdominal}) - (0.161 \times \text{thigh}) \\ + (0.144 \times \text{calf})$$

$$(63.2)$$

Discussion

The main finding of this study was that the %BF of elite male soccer players can be determined accurately within 0.2% by using skinfold callipers, either the formula of Withers *et al.* (1998) or that of Jackson and Pollock's (1978) Σ3 or Σ7, should be the preferred technique. Another key finding from this study was that when body fat is measured by means of DXA, subtotal percent body fat (whole-body minus the head data) ought be the reported value. These values demonstrate stronger correlations and reduced measurement errors for all the skinfold formulae in the prediction of %BF and also displayed improved correlation with each individual skinfold measurement site. The British Olympic Association's recommendation to use the sum of five skinfolds rather than a prediction formula is vindicated; the sum of five skinfolds did produce strong correlations with percent body fat as measured by means of DXA. The World Health Organisation's recommendation to use BMI as an index for assessing adiposity does not apply to this population of elite male soccer players and should not be used to monitor or assess the players' body composition, as there was no correlation between BMI and the percent body fat.

Estimation of %BF from skinfold thickness has been considered the most appropriate tool for use in the field setting. Selection of the most suitable skinfold equation is imperative, because percent body fat predictions are validated for specific populations and are not appropriate outside of that population. Soccer players have a physique specifically adapted for the demands of their sport. Their muscle and bone densities are generally much greater than the normal male population and their fat patterning does not always conform to the general distributions assumed by many of the skinfold formulae. Adams *et al.* (1982) and Clark *et al.* (1993) concluded that the density of the fat-free body was not constant across individuals and that these variations in body density affect the prediction of %BF, thus violating one of the major assumptions for estimating %BF from body density. The bone mineral density observed in the current sample was also higher than the equipment manufacturer's reference values, this could perhaps explain why some of the skinfold formulae that estimate percent body fat based on body density produced large measurement errors. This rationale provides further support for using the formula of Withers *et al.* (1998) when assessing adiposity in soccer players, as their formula does not estimate percent body fat by means of body density and therefore does not depend on the assumption of the body tissues having constant densities.

The present research supports use of either the formula of Withers *et al.* (1998) or Jackson and Pollock's (1978) Σ3– or Σ7–skinfolds. Clark *et al.* (1994), who conducted a similar cross-validation study, also concluded that the formula of Jackson and Pollock (1978) provided the most accurate prediction of %BF. In the present study two formulae were developed, one using all eight commonly measured skinfold sites and the other using the sites that were the best predictive variables. Both these formula now need to be validated using a different cohort of elite male soccer players, to see which of these equations provide the more accurate and valid method for predicting %BF in this specific population.

In recognition of the importance of the thigh skinfold as a predictor of percent body fat (Eston *et al.*, 2001), the British Olympic Association's Steering Group recommended using the sum of five skinfold sites including the anterior thigh (Reilly *et al.*, 1996); the report stated that these five skinfolds should be summed and the resultant value used as an index of subcutaneous adiposity. Present findings demonstrated that the thigh skinfold measure produced the third strongest relationship and was greater than those for upper body sites. Results also confirmed that the sum of five skinfolds was very strongly correlated with the percent body fat of the players. These strong correlations support the BOA's recommendation for the inclusion of the thigh skinfold.

One assumption in using the technique of DXA is that the composition of soft tissue layer overlaying the bone has the same fat to lean ratio as that for the non-bone pixels in the same scan region. The non-bone pixels are used to estimate the body's fat to lean ratio; this value is then applied to the soft tissue component in the adjacent bone pixels. The head contains an even higher proportion of bone pixels than the rest of the body, so there are even fewer pixels in which to estimate the underlying soft tissues. This assumption could be one reason why DXA subtotal values (those excluding the head) demonstrate greater correlations with each individual skinfold site measurement and also better correlations with predicted %BF values, than the DXA total values. In light of these findings, subtotal values for percent body fat should be preferred to using total percent body fat values.

Conclusions

The assessment of percent body fat in elite male soccer players can be accurately predicted from skinfold measurements using the formulae of either Withers *et al.*

(1998) or Jackson and Pollock's (1978) sum of 3– or sum of 7–skinfolds; other formulae should be avoided where possible due to the increased measurement errors. When the technique of dual-energy x-ray absorptiometry is used, the subtotal (minus the head) percent body fat values should be chosen in preference to whole-body total percent body fat values. The recommendation of the British Olympic Association to use the sum of five skinfolds is suitable to use in soccer populations; the use of BMI is inappropriate.

References

Adams, J., Mottola, M., Bagnall, K. M. and Mcfadden, K. D. 1982, Total body fat content in a group of professional soccer players. *Canadian Journal of Applied Sports Science*, 7, 36–40.

Brozek, J., Grande, F., Anderson, J. T. and Keys, A. 1963, Densitometric analysis of body composition: revision of some quantitative assumptions. *Annals of New York Academy of Sciences*, 110, 113–40.

Clark, R. R., Kuta, J. M. and Sullivan, J. C., 1993, Prediction of percent body fat in adult males using dual energy x-ray absorptiometry, skinfolds and hydrostatic weighing. *Medicine and Science in Sports and Exercise*, 25, 528–35.

Clark, R. R., Kuta, J. M. and Sullivan, J. C., 1994, Cross-validation of methods to predict body fat in African-American and Caucasian collegiate soccer players. *Research Quarterly for Exercise and Sport*, 65, 21–30.

Durnin, J. V. G. A. and Womersley, J., 1974, Body fat assessed from total body density and its estimation from skinfold thickness: measurements of 481 men and women aged from 16–72 years. *British Journal of Nutrition*, 32, 77–97.

Eston, R. G., Rosolia, S. and Rowlands, A. V., 2001, Prediction of DXA-determined whole-body fat from skinfolds: empirical evidence for including the thigh skinfolds. *Journal of Sports Sciences*, 20, 36.

Eston, R. G., Rowlands, A. V., Charlesworth, S., Davies, A. and Hoppitt, T., 2005, Prediction of DXA-determined whole body fat from skinfolds: importance of including skinfolds from the thigh and calf in young, healthy men and women. *European Journal of Clinical Nutrition*, 59, 695–702.

Jackson, A. S. and Pollock, M. L., 1978, Generalized equations for predicting body density of men. *British Journal of Nutrition*, 40, 497.

Lohman, T. G. 1981, Skinfolds and body density and their relation to body fatness – a review. *Human Biology*, 53, 181–225.

Marfell-Jones, M., Olds, T., Stewart, A. and and Carter, J.E.L., 2006, International Standards for Anthropometric Assessment. Potechefstroom: International Society for the Advancement of Kinanthropometry.

Reilly, T., Maughan, R. J. and Hardy, L. 1996, Body fat consensus statement of the steering groups of the British Olympic Association. *Sports Exercise and Injury*, 2, 46–49.

Siri, W. E. 1956, The gross composition of the body. *Advanced Biology Medicine and Physiology*, 4, 239–280.

Withers, R. T., Laforgia, J., Pillarns, R. K., Shipp, N. J., Chatterton, B. E., Schultz, G. and Leaney, F., 1998, Comparisons of two-, three-, and four-compartmental models of body composition analysis in men and women. *Journal of Applied Physiology*, 85, 238–245.

64 Physiological profiles of soccer players with respect to playing positions

Ahmet Yıldırım, A. K. Emre, Feza Korkusuz and Şeref Çiçek

Middle East Technical University, Turkey

Introduction

Soccer is the most popular sport in the world and is characterized as high intensity, intermittent, non-continuous exercise. Coaches always strive to develop physical performance and maintain a high overall work-rate during the competition season. Assessment of physical and physiological profiles in soccer players has become important in recent years, in that training load can be decided according to individual capacity.

Physical and physiological characteristics of soccer players can be promoted by modifying training programmes to help individual players prepare for matches. Soccer players are expected to have different physiological characteristics according to their playing positions (Dunbar and Power, 1995). On the other hand, some authors have reported that soccer players have similar physiological capacities in all playing positions (Capranica *et al.*, 2001; Chamari *et al.*, 2004; Guner, Kunduracioglu and Ulkar, 2006). Understanding their physiological capacities may assist coaches when preparing different training programmes for goalkeepers, defenders, midfielders and strikers, should differences between these positions be established. The aim of this study was to examine the physical and physiological differences of Turkish soccer players with respect to their playing positions.

Materials and methods

Eighty-one soccer players from three different soccer clubs participated in the study. Players were from a youth team (mean age: 17.4 ± 0.5, $n = 25$), a second division (mean age: 22.1 ± 3.0, $n = 23$) and a third division team (mean age: 22.1 ± 3.0, $n = 33$). All 81 players were assigned to one of the four groups as goalkeeper, defender, midfielder and striker according to their playing position. The physical characteristics of the players are shown in Table 64.1. Physical and physiological variables including body mass index (BMI), body fat, sit-and-reach, running velocity, heart rate and lactate measurements were recorded and

Table 64.1 Means and standard deviations (SD) for age, height, and mass of players

	N	Age (years)	Height (m)	Mass (kg)
Defenders	23	20.4 (3.3)	1.768 (0.046)	73.1 (5.8)
Midfielders	34	20.0 (2.80)	1.749 (0.049)	69.5 (5.6)
Strikers	15	21.9 (3.9)	1.755 (0.072)	71.4 (7.8)
Goalkeepers	9	21.8 (3.7)	1.828 (0.037)	81.2 (6.8)
Total	81	20.7 (3.3)	1.765 (0.056)	72.1 (7.1)

compared among goalkeepers, defenders, midfielders and strikers. All participants were informed about the nature of the study.

A portable lactate meter Lactate Pro LT-1710 (Arkray KDK Co., Kyoto, Japan) was used to analyse blood lactate responses to an incremental treadmill (Quinton Q65, Quinton Instrument Co, Seattle, USA) protocol. The test protocol required an increase in speed of $1 km.h^{-1}$ every 3 min until the termination of the test ($8-10-11-12-13-1 km.h^{-1}$). The test was ended when the blood lactate concentration exceeded $4 mmol.l^{-1}$ or on the subject's own request. Blood lactate concentrations were obtained from the ear lobe at the beginning of the protocol and during the 30 s breaks between the 3 min work stages. Treadmill inclination was set at 1.5 per cent.

Heart rates were recorded using Polar Vantage NV heart rate monitors (Polar Electro Oy, Kempele, Finland). The resting heart rate was established after a 10 min rest. Heart rates during the test protocols were recorded every 30 s until the test terminated when the heart rate exceeded the predicted maximum heart rate value (220–age). Heart rate and velocity values at 3 and 4 mM lactate levels were determined for each player.

Flexibility measures were taken by using the sit-and-reach test. All flexibility measures were taken after a 10 min warm-up period. The mean of the three trials was recorded as the score.

Skinfold measurements were taken from chest, abdomen and thigh sites by using a Holtain callipers (Holtain Ltd., Crymych, UK). Two measurements were taken from each site and the mean was used. All skinfold measurements were taken by same investigator for consistency. The BMI values were calculated as $kg.m^2$. Height was measured by using a stadiometer and body mass was measured with a digital scale.

Descriptive statistics and analysis of variances (ANOVA) were used to examine the differences among defenders, midfielders, strikers, and goalkeepers. Significance was set at a level of 0.05.

Results

Results showed that goalkeepers were significantly taller and heavier than defenders, midfielders, and strikers. A significant difference was found between playing positions in terms of BMI ($F_{3,77} = 2.792$, $P < 0.05$). Post-hoc analysis was conducted and a significant difference was found between goalkeepers and

Table 64.2 Means and standard deviations for independent variables for different playing positions

	Defender (N=27)	Midfielder (N=39)	Striker (N=20)	Goalkeeper (N=11)
BMI	23.3 ± 1.4	22.7 ± 1.6*	23.1 ± 1.6	24.3 ± 1.8*
Body Fat (%)	11.2 ± 5.7	9.9 ± 4.7	9.7 ± 3.2	11.8 ± 5.8
Sit-and-Reach (cm)	16.6 ± 6.1	17.0 ± 5.9	16.8 ± 7.2	17.7 ± 5.4
HR- 3 mM (beats.min^{-1})	164 ± 8	162 ± 13	165 ± 11	157 ± 9
Velocity - 3 mM (km.h^{-1})	12.4 ± 1.7	11.7 ± 2.1	12.7 ± 1.4	11.2 ± 0.9
HR - 4 mM (beats.min^{-1})	175 ± 8	176 ± 10	177 ± 9	170 ± 10
Velocity - 4 mM (km.h^{-1})	13.9 ± 1.4	13.5 ± 1.5	14.1 ± 1.1	12.8 ± 0.9

midfielders. No significant difference was found between playing positions with respect to body fat, sit-and-reach, HR and velocity (3 and 4 mmol^{-1}).

Discussion and conclusion

No significant differences were found in physical and physiological comparisons among defenders, midfielders, and strikers. These results were consistent with some previous studies (Capranica *et al.*, 2001; Chamari *et al.*, 2004; Guner *et al.*, 2006). However, the goalkeepers were significantly heavier and taller than outfield players. This can be taken as an indication that the taller and heavier goalkeeper has an advantage in reaching the ball. This physical characteristic is consistent with previous studies (Davis, Brewer and Atkin, 1992; Arnason *et al.*, 2004; Tahara *et al.*, 2006). In addition, the present study showed that there was a significant difference between midfielders and goalkeepers in BMI.

The very small difference observed in physical fitness between players in different playing positions may explain the competitive facet of modern football for all positions. Non-significant differences among the playing positions may be the result of the collective nature of the game for all players. It can be concluded that playing position did not have a discriminant effect on the physiological and physical profiles of these Turkish players.

References

Arnason, A., Sigurdsson, S. B., Gudmundsson, A., Holme, I., Engebretsen, L., and Bahr, R. 2004. Physical fitness, injuries, and team performance in soccer. *Medicine and Science in Sports and Exercise*, 36, 278–85.

Capranica, L., Tessitore, A., Guidetti, L., and Figura, F. 2001. Heart rate and match analysis in pre-pubescent soccer players. *Journal of Sports Sciences*, 19, 379–84.

Chamari, K., Hachana, Y., Ahmed, Y. B., Galy, O., Sghaier, F., Chatarad, J-C., Hue, O. and Wisloff, U. 2004. Field and laboratory testing in young elite soccer players. *British Journal of Sports Medicine*, 38, 191–6.

Davis, J. A., Brewer, J. and Atkin, D. 1992. Pre-season physiological characteristics of English first and second division soccer players. *Journal of Sports Sciences*, 10, 541–7.

Dunbar, G. M. J. and Power, K. 1995. Fitness profiles of English professional and semi-professional soccer players using a battery of field tests. In *Science and Football III*, edited by Reilly, T., Bangsbo, J. and Hughes, M. (London: E&FN Spon).

Guner, R., Kunduracioglu, B. and Ulkar, B. 2006. Running velocities and heart rates at fixed blood lactate concentrations in young soccer players. *Physical Therapy*, 23, 395–403.

Tahara, Y., Moji, K., Tsunawake, N., Fukuda, R., Nakayama, M., Nakagaichi, M., Komine, T., Kusano, Y. and Aoyagi, K. 2006. Physique, body composition and maximum oxygen consumption of selected soccer players of Kunimi High School, Nagasaki, Japan. *Journal of Physiological Anthropology*, 25, 291–7.

65 Criterion validity of an intermittent futsal-specific high-intensity test

Carlo Castagna,[1,2] *Stefano D'Ottavio*[1,2] *and José Carlos Barbero Álvarez*[3]

[1]Corso di Laurea in Scienze Motorie, Università di Roma Tor Vergata, Italy;
[2] Federazione Italiana Giuoco Calcio, Settore Giovanile e Scolastico, Italy;
[3]Departamento de Educación Física y Deportiva, Universidad de Granada, Spain

Introduction

Futsal is an intermittent high-intensity activity that places important demands on the aerobic and anaerobic pathways (Castagna *et al.*, 2007). As consequence of this aerobic load, endurance has been reported to affect game performance (Barbero Alvarez *et al.*, 2004; Castagna *et al.*, 2007). Recently, Barbero Alverez *et al.* (2005) developed an intermittent high-intensity field test based match-analyses of futsal (FIET) to assess specific endurance. This new test demands that players perform shuttle running bouts (3×15 m) at progressive speeds interspersed with passive rest of 10–30 s until exhaustion. Despite the growing popularity of this test, no research has addressed the criterion validity and physiological demands of FIET. Therefore, the aims of this study were to examine the physiological demands and criterion validity of FIET.

Methods

Subjects

Eighteen well-trained futsal players from the Spanish futsal league (age 20.6 ± 3.1 years, body mass 71.6 ± 8.5 kg, height 1.75 ± 0.079 m), performed the FIET and a treadmill test (TM) in random order to assess aerobic-fitness.

Fitness assessment

Maximum oxygen uptake ($\dot{V}O_{2\,max}$) was determined using an incremental running protocol on a motorized treadmill (RunRace, Technogym, Gambettola, Italy). After an individually adjusted warm-up (5 min) subjects ran for 6 min at 8 km·h⁻¹, and the velocity was increased by 1 km·h⁻¹min⁻¹ until exhaustion (8–12 min). Expired gases were analysed using a breath-by-breath automated gas-analysis system (K4b², COSMED, Rome, Italy). Ventilatory threshold (T_{vent}) was assessed according to Beaver *et al.* (1986). Running economy was considered as average

$\dot{V}O_2$ during the final minute of the 6 min run at 8 km.h^{-1}. Maximal aerobic speed was calculated using the relationship between $\dot{V}O_2$ and running speeds (Billat and Koralsztein, 1996). Maximal HR (HR$_{max}$) was considered as the highest 5 s mean during the treadmill test. Heart rates were monitored with a short-range telemetry system (Polar Team System, Polar Electro Oy, Kempele, Finland).

FIET (Futsal intermittent endurance test)

The FIET test consists of shuttle running bouts of 45 m (3×15 m) performed at progressive speeds until exhaustion. Every 45 m subjects are allowed to rest actively for 10 s. After each 8×45 m bout players passively rest for 30 s before continuing. Starting speed is set at 9 km.h^{-1} and speed increments during the first 9×45 m bouts are of 0.33 km^{-1} and successively shifting to 0.20 km.h^{-1} every 45 m until exhaustion. The test ends when subjects are unable to reach the front line in time with beeps for twice in succession.

Players' FIET performance (distance covered) was assessed on a futsal court set-up according to Figure 65.1.

During the test HR and $\dot{V}O_2$ were assessed with the same devices used for aerobic-fitness assessment. Blood lactate concentration ([la]$_b$) was assessed taking earlobe blood samples at rest and three minutes after exhaustion either during treadmill testing or FIET (Doctor Lange Plus LP20, Dr Lange, Germany).

Statistical analysis

Data are reported as mean ± standard deviation. Bland and Altman plots were used to assess measurement agreements. Pearson's correlation coefficient was used to assess association between aerobic fitness parameters and FIET variables. Significance was assumed at 5% ($P \leq 0.05$) a priori.

Results

The physiological responses to TM and FIET protocols are shown in Table 65.1. Significant correlations were detected between FIET performance and TM speeds at $\dot{V}O_{2max}$ and Tvent ($r = 0.61$ and 0.60, $P<0.01$, respectively).

Discussion and conclusions

The significant relationship found between FIET performance and speeds at selected aerobic fitness measures and the $\dot{V}O_{2peak}$ level achieved during FIET confirm the aerobic nature of this test. However, the high blood lactate concentrations found at exhaustion demonstrate an important anaerobic pathway involvement during FIET as well. In light of results of this study, FIET seems to simulate the physiological demands of futsal during the most intensive moments of the game (Castagna *et al.*, 2007). However, test specificity should be further investigated relating FIET performance to game analyses for ecological validity. We suggest

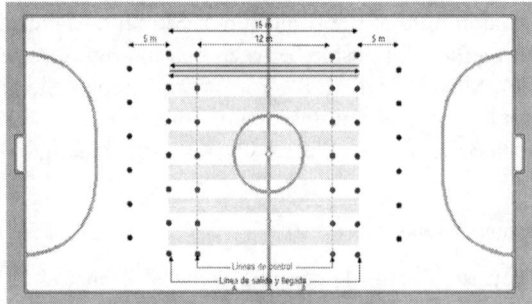

Figure 65.1 Court set-up for FIET

Table 65.1 Physiological variables for the treadmill test and FIET protocols.;** = P<0.01

Variable	Treadmill	FIET
$VO_{2\,max}$ (ml.kg^{-1} min^{-1})	65.1 ± 6.2	61.6 ± 4.6**
RE (ml.kg^{-1}.min^{-1})	35.6 ± 3.4	
Tvent (ml.kg.$^{-1}$.min^{-1})	45.2 ± 4.6	
Peak blood lactate (mmol.l^{-1})	12 ± 2.9	12.6 ± 2.3
HR_{max} (beats.min^{-1})	193 ± 8	191 ± 7
RER	1.15 ± 0.01	1.14 ± 0.01
Ventilation (l.min^{-1})	162 ± 16	177 ± 25**

that futsal coaches and fitness trainers may use FIET to assess anaerobic capacity and HR_{max} in field conditions.

References

Barbero Alvarez, J., Soto Hermoso, V. and Granda Vera, J., 2004, Effort profiling during indoor soccer competition. *Journal of Sports Sciences*, 22, 500–1.

Barbero Alvaréz, J.C., Andrín, G. and Méndez-Villanueva, A., 2005, Futsal-specific endurance assessment of competitive players. *Journal of Sports Sciences*, 23, 1279–81.

Beaver, W.L., Wasserman, K. and Whipp, B.J., 1986, A new method for detecting anaerobic threshold by gas exchange. *Journal of Applied Physiology*, 60, 2020–27.

Billat, V. and Koralsztein, J.P., 1996, Significance of the velocity at $VO_{2\,max}$ and time to exhaustion at this velocity. *Sports Medicine*, 22, 90–180.

Castagna, C., D'Ottavio, S. and Barbero Alvarez, J.C., 2007, Effect of playing Futsal in professional players. In *Abstract Book of the VI World Congress on Science and Football* (Antalya, Turkey: WCSF VI).

Part IX
Psychology

66 Sport psychology for football

Daniel Gould

Institute for the Study of Youth Sports, Michigan State University, USA

Introduction

Sport psychology has been defined as the scientific study of human behaviour in the sport and the practical application of that knowledge (Weinberg and Gould, 2007). With this general objective in mind, sport psychology researchers strive to understand why athletes, coaches, officials and spectators behave the way they do. They generally do this by examining one of two general questions: (1) What effect do psychological factors have on the athlete's and team's performance (e.g., How does a goal-keeper's confidence influence his play? What effect does a team's cohesion have on performance? Do players who use stress management perform better than their counterparts who do not?); and (2) How does participation in sport influence the player's psychological development and functioning (e.g., Do athletes develop higher self-esteem than their non-athletic counterparts? Is teamwork taught through participation in football? Does playing football build one's character?).

Not only have sport psychologists attempted to better understand the role of psychological factors in sport in general over the last 25 years but also they have begun to examine the role that psychology plays in various forms of football as it is played around the world. Given the popularity of football around the world, it is no surprise, then, that a psychology of football has begun to emerge. This review is designed to summarize this literature and in so doing outline implications for both research and practice. Characteristics of studies having the greatest impact will be identified, as well as a case report of an elite soccer team's efforts to develop mental skills for the purpose of enhancing performance.

Research on the psychology of football

Literature review

A SPORTDISCUS computer search conducted in December of 2006 using the key words of psychology, football, rugby and soccer identified over 150 research articles conducted on the psychology of football. A review of these studies revealed a wide variety of topics, ranging from motivation and stress to peer leadership and transitions out of the game. Topics receiving the most attention included: motivation; personality; stress, anxiety and burnout; aggression and moral development; team cohesion; injuries; the effectiveness of psychology-based interventions; and general perceptions of psychological characteristics of top performers. In general, the findings in each of these areas parallel the research conducted across sport, although there are certain football-specific nuances.

Unfortunately, space limitations prevent a detailed review of all the literature in these areas. However, examples of studies in four of the most popular areas will be reviewed for the purpose of providing illustrative examples of what is known about the psychology of football. These areas include: (1) perceptions of sport psychology; (2) aggression and moral development; (3) the psychology of injuries; and (4) the effectiveness of psychological skills training.

Perceptions of psychology

The topical area labeled 'perceptions of psychology' included manuscripts that identified psychological aspects of football deemed most important by participants, as well as coaches' and players' views of the role psychology plays in football, barriers to entry and topics of greatest interest. For example, Thelwell *et al.* (2005) built upon the general sport psychology research examining mental toughness and its components in elite competitors by studying elite soccer players in England. In-depth interviews and surveys were used to define mental toughness and its components in male professional soccer players. Results revealed that mental toughness was defined as "having the natural or developed edge that enables you to always cope better than your opponents with the many demands (competition, training, lifestyle) that soccer places on the performer" (p. 322). Players were found to be better than their competitors relative to their focus, confidence, determination and control under pressure.

In addition to defining mental toughness in the soccer context, Thelwell and colleagues (2005) were also able to identify its specific components (See Table 66.1). These findings could be used in several ways by sports psychology specialists and coaches. For example, they could be used as a guide to develop mental training programmes for junior players.

The player's strengths and weaknesses relative to the 10 attributes could be identified and intervention programmes developed to enhance areas needing improvement. A second way in which the findings could be used would be in talent identification efforts. Scouts might rate the players on each attribute in an effort to define their mental abilities. Finally, researchers might explore the process by which these attributes develop and what factors influence their development as Gould *et al.* (2002) have done to trace the psychological development in Olympic champions from a variety of sports.

A good example of an investigation designed to examine players' views of sport psychologists and the services they provide was conducted by Pain and Harwood (2004). In this investigation 8 national coaches, 21 soccer academy directors and 27 academy coaches were assessed using interviews and questionnaires. Survey

Table 66.1 Components of mental toughness in professional soccer (Thelwell et al., 2005)

1. Total self-belief
2. Wanting the ball at all times
3. Having ability to react to situations positively
4. Hang on and be calm under pressure
5. Know what it takes to grind self out of trouble
6. Ignore distractions and remain focused
7. Control emotions
8. Have presence that affects opponents
9. Have everything outside of game in control
10. Enjoy performance pressure

results revealed that problems fitting in with players, players' negative perceptions of sport psychology, and a lack of clarity concerning services provided by sport psychologists were some of the major barriers affecting the use of sport psychology. The highest-rated barrier identified, however, was a lack of finances to support such services. It was concluded that coaches and players must be better informed about the nature of sport psychology and that consultants develop strategies for overcoming the barriers that inhibit their work.

Aggression and moral development

Aggression and moral development have been topics of considerable interest by researchers studying football psychology. In one of the early studies in the area, for instance, Stephens and Bredemeier (1996) studied 212 youth soccer players' judgements about aggressive play and how they were influenced by moral and motivational constructs. Using multiple regression analysis, they showed that

> players who were more likely to aggress against opponents also were more likely to (a) identify a larger number of teammates who would aggress in a similar situation, (b) perceive their coach as placing greater importance on ego-oriented goals (e.g., winning), and (c) choose situations featuring preconventional rather than conventional moral motives as tempting for aggressive action. (p. 158)

It was concluded that a team's "moral atmosphere" including team norms for aggressive behaviour and coach characteristics, as well as the moral reasoning capability of the young player, influences aggressive behaviour.

More recently, Kavussanu and Spray (2006) examined the relationship between motivational climate (emphasis placed on outcome versus personal improvement goals), moral atmosphere and moral functioning in 325 British youth soccer players with a mean age of 14.6 years. Results from structural equation modelling data analyses showed that players' views of condoning aggression and cheating were associated with a perception of an outcome-oriented motivational climate in the team.

Paralleling the growing body of aggression and moral development studies in sport psychology in general, football research shows that the moral atmosphere of the team and the motivational climate created by the coach play an important role on an athlete's moral functioning. Football, then, does not automatically teach moral behaviour and character in young people; football coaches and the culture they and the parents of participants create do! This is a critical point that must be included in football-related coaching education programmes.

Psychology and injuries

The role that psychological factors play in football-related injuries has been a topic of considerable interest to sport psychology researchers. While often studied, little relationship has been found between personality measures and the onset of athletic injuries. However, the level of stress players experience (both on and off the field) has been shown to be the most important psychological factor related to the onset of athletic injuries. In one of the earliest psychology of injury studies, for example, Blackwell and McCullaugh (1990) surveyed 105 US college American football players and recorded injury rates across the season. Survey assessments included measures of player life stress, competitive anxiety and coping resources. The injured players scored high on all life stress factors and competitive anxiety and lower on coping resources. Thus, as has been the case with subsequent studies conducted in other sports, player life stress increases the chances of being injured above and beyond physical factors.

Given the life stress–athletic injury link, it is no surprise that researchers have also examined if stress reduction decreases player injuries. Davis (1991) did this by assessing injury rates in an American university football team across a season as the team practised progressive relaxation during team workouts. Specifically, during the pre-season period, relaxation was practised 10 minutes during each practice. Then during the season it occurred twice a week. Associated with implementation of the stress management programme was a corresponding 33 per cent drop of major injuries from the previous year. While the design of this study was weak, similar conclusions have been found in much better designed studies using athletes in other sports. Hence, stress management training has been shown to be associated with lower rates of athletic injuries. This certainly suggests that sport scientists should consider implementing stress management programmes in football not only for their potential benefit in facilitating performance but also in reducing injuries.

The effectiveness of psychological training interventions

A critical topic of study for those interested in helping athletes function and perform better focuses on the efficacy of psychological training in athletes. For this reason various sport psychology researchers have examined the effectiveness of mental skills training in footballers. Using a multiple baseline design across participants, Johnson *et al.* (2004) assessed the effectiveness of how players' self-talk influenced their play. Four female elite junior soccer players served as participants and were taught to say cue words (e.g., "down" and "lock") on low drive shots and their performance was assessed in both training and competition. Results demonstrated that the self-talk intervention enhanced performance for two of the three players in the treatment group and that both the players and coach felt the programme was successful.

Stress-management interventions have also been of interest to football psychology researchers. In a well-designed stress management study conducted in professional soccer, Maynard *et al.* (1995) examined the effects of a somatic anxiety intervention on performance and competitive anxiety in semi-professional soccer players. Players' cognitive and somatic anxiety was assessed and players were assigned to a control (8) or experimental (9) group. Experimental group participants took part in an eight-week stress management intervention that focused on physical anxiety coping strategies while control participants received placebo instructions to control for attentional effects. Performance was assessed in game settings. Results revealed that the stress management training participants reduced player anxiety, supporting the matching hypothesis that contends that anxiety treatments (somatic or cognitive) tied to the type of anxiety experienced (somatic or cognitive) by the athlete would be most effective. Performance did not improve but the authors contended this may have resulted from problems with the performance measure.

In summary, psychological interventions conducted in football show that players can improve their mental functioning (e.g., increase their confidence, lower their anxiety) through systematic training and instruction. Performance has also been shown to increase as a result of mental skills training. Hence, increased emphasis should be placed on training players psychologically.

Characteristics of studies having the greatest impact

The psychology of football research identified for this review contained reports of varied quality and scientific and practical impact. Looking across these studies, those that made the greatest impact to advancing knowledge had a number of characteristics. First, they were part of a systematic line of research that integrated knowledge from previous football-specific studies or the general sport psychology research. For example, the study of Maynard *et al.* (1995) which was reviewed earlier in this manuscript was part of a series of studies examining stress and stress management (Maynard and Howe, 1987; Maynard and Cotton, 1993). Conducting a series of studies allows investigators to assemble the pieces of the knowledge puzzle much more effectively than when studies are conducted in isolation. Series of studies are more effective because they build from one study to the next, both empirically and methodologically.

A second characteristic of the high impact studies is that they were theoretically guided, or tested existing theory. For example the study by Thelwell *et al.* (2005) of mental toughness was based on the recent theorizing of Jones *et al.* (2002). Not only did the results help define mental toughness in a soccer context, they also extended current general sport psychological theorizing to a new sport context, thereby, enhancing the generalizability of the theory.

Studies with the most impact also addressed practical issues that can be implemented in the field. The importance of this application cannot be forgotten as all too often well-conducted sport science research has missed the mark with practitioners because it did not address a need of real practical importance (only one the investigator mistakenly felt was important) or derived results or implications that were too difficult or costly to implement in practice. To resolve this issue some sport governing bodies like the US Olympic Committee required coaches and athletes to be involved in the design and conceptualization of sport science projects to ensure they had practical significance.

Finally, high impact football psychology studies have used varied methods and followed the long-standing dictum of having the problem being addressed determine the method choice versus using one's favourite or preferred method to answer all questions. In this review alone, structural equation modelling, qualitative interviewing, experimental and multiple baseline designs have been employed. Future investigators should continue this precedent.

Personal development through sport: a new direction for the psychology of football

A major new trend in sport psychology research and practice is the development of studies and programmes focusing on using the sport experience to develop life skills in young people. For example, the National Football Foundation in the United States has funded the Play it Smart Program, a national intervention that uses sport as a vehicle to facilitate academic achievement and life skill development in underserved urban youth by providing academic coaches to help the student athletes in their "off the field" development. Moreover, Petitpas et al. (2004) evaluated the implementation of the programme by tracking 252 high school football players (most from minority and economically disadvantaged backgrounds) who took part in it. Results from two years of programme evaluation showed an increase in grades (grade point average shift from 2.16 to 2.54 compared to 2.2 for the general school averages) with 98 per cent of the final year students graduating from high school and 83 per cent of that group going on to higher education. While it was concluded that additional data were needed, initial results showed the programme to be very effective.

Our research group at Michigan State has also begun to examine the issue of how football participation influences the way players develop as people, with particular emphasis on the development of life skills or those emotional, social and mental skills and attributes athletes acquire or refine through sports participation and have the potential to transfer to other non-sport areas of their lives (Gould et al., 2006; 2007). In particular, we studied the characteristics of high school football coaches who were recognized for developing character and positive personal characteristics in their players. In-depth phone interviews were conducted with 10 finalists for the National Football League Charities "Coach of

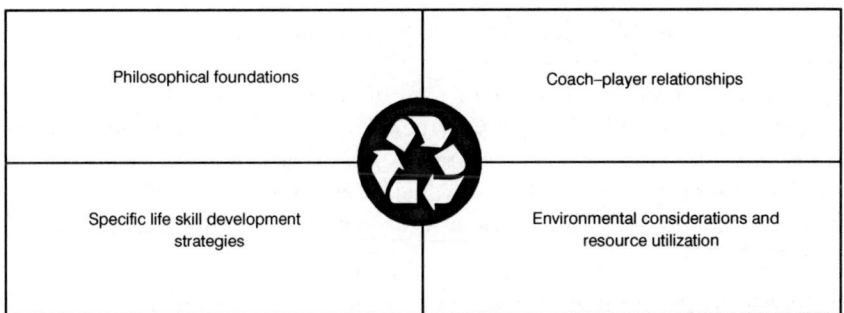

Figure 66.1 A model for coaching life skills

the Year Program" – a national award given to coaches for positively influencing players' lives. Ten of their former players were also interviewed. Coaches averaged 31 years of coaching experience and were highly successful, winning an average of 161 games (77 per cent) over their careers. While highly motivated to win, these coaches made the personal development of their players a top priority. They were also had well thought-out coaching philosophies that were characterized by clear expectations relative to rules, player behaviour, and team expectations. Several coaches emphasized what they called 'tough love' in that they 'demanded' maximum effort and discipline, but always made it clear that they cared about their players as people. While common themes and patterns were evident across coaches, each coach focused on a relatively small number of individual-specific key principles such as having discipline, working hard, being totally prepared and respecting and putting one's family before other needs. These core principles drove their coaching in general and development of life skills in particular.

While our original intent was to identify the life skill coaching strategies these individuals employed, it became clear that life skills development could not be divorced from their general coaching philosophy and strategies. In fact, the effectiveness of these coaches did not result from the fact that they implemented one or two strategies or held to one or two key philosophical principles. These coaches did not do one or two simple things that magically developed life skills in their players. Rather, coaching life skills was found to be a never-ending process guided by a strong philosophical base, involving the ability to facilitate athlete trust and form strong coach–player relationships. In addition, these coaches implemented specific strategies and follow-up procedures for helping their players develop. Finally, the coaches recognized limits to their efforts, while at the same time found ways to utilize environmental resources such as players' parents to facilitate their life skills coaching.

Based on our findings, a model for understanding the coaching of life skills was developed (see Figure 66.1). An inspection of this model reveals that there are four primary considerations in teaching life skills. These include: (1) philosophical foundations; (2) coach–player relationship skills; (3) specific strategies for developing life skills; and (4) environmental considerations and resource utilization. This model provides a useful resource for those interested in developing life skills programmes or for football association representatives responsible for coaching education.

Given the current emphasis to use football as a vehicle to help develop young people around the world (Reilly, 2008), the emerging work on developing life skills through football participation is very timely. It also places importance not only in seeking performance excellence on the field, but also to help all players become better people and world citizens through the football experience.

Apply sport psychology: the case of a championships team

Sport psychology as a field is devoted not only to enhancing the scientific understanding of human behaviour in sport, but also to applying what is learned. The example studies in this review have shown players can develop their psychological skills and attributes through systematic training. An excellent example of how this can be done results from studies my colleagues and I carried out to examine variables that influenced performance of individual athletes and teams at the Olympic Games (Gould *et al.* 1999; Greenleaf *et al.* 2001; Gould *et al.* 2002). We found, for example, that more successful athletes and teams had well-developed mental preparation routines, had better plans for dealing with distractions, and spent more time developing their mental games. As part of this research, players from the men's and women's US soccer teams were included and the case profile that follows demonstrates both how mental factors are involved in football success and how one team mentally prepared for its Olympic experience.

This team had a record of being highly successful, having won the World Cup. It did not perform well the year before the games. It did, however, have a highly successful Olympic campaign, winning the gold medal.

Based on individual and focus group interviews conducted with the players and coaches after their successful Olympic experience, numerous positive factors influencing performance were reported, while respondents only cited a few negative performance influences. Part of the reason for this pattern of findings was the athletes' and coaches' abilities to reframe and adapt to potentially negative influences (e.g., some media interactions, a less than optimal tournament seeding, roster number restrictions, time delays do to increased security). The Opening Ceremony was cited as a factor that both positively and negatively influenced performance: positively, by enhancing motivation and team spirit, negatively by being a physically tiring experience that took much special attention to ensure that it did not have negative performance repercussions.

Positive factors reported as influencing performance prior to the Games included reframing the disappointing World Cup finish in the year before the Olympics into a positive source of motivation. The coaches of the team also implemented a well-thought out performance plan that tied to a larger vision for Olympic success that was cited as having a positive influences on the athletes. This plan included having the team train in a residency programme, training at the Olympic venue prior to the games, utilizing a sport psychology consultant to teach skills such as reframing negative events into positive ones, stress management and ways to enhance team cohesion, finding an optimal blend of balancing a demanding schedule with appropriate breaks and limited travel prior to the Games.

This team embraced the pressure of being Olympic favourites by exhibiting team chemistry. Player leadership, and an attitude that there were "no insurmountable obstacles", and a "we are winning this, no doubt about it" view were cited as helping facilitate performance. Having housing away from the Olympic venue, not letting their less than desirable seeding place influence performance, positive crowd and fan support, and having a well thought out plan for handling opening ceremonies and potential distractions were also viewed as important for helping ensure a good performance. From a psychological perspective factors that helped this team to be successful included: learning how to stay focused on the positive, especially in difficult situations; making a commitment to excellence and to the team; developing consistent mental preparation routines; teaching players to adhere to their mental preparation routines, identifying and discussing potential unexpected events and developing multiple ways to cope with unexpected events/distractions; having a very organized coaching staff who placed considerable importance on mental preparation; and securing the services of a sport psychology consultant and then engaging in mental training for several years before the Olympics.

Finally, while the players and coaches felt that sport psychology was critical to their performance success, they approached performance from a holistic, well-rounded perspective. In particular, they consciously and deliberately worked on their attitude, team cohesion, fitness, mental preparation, nutrition, strength training, acclimatization and enjoyment of the experience. Thus, sport psychology was applied to football as a part of total sport science based high-performance training programme.

Summary and conclusions

This review and the larger computer search on which it was based clearly show that scientific evidence is amassing and allowing a psychology of football to develop. Researchers are focusing on better understanding both the performance enhancement and personal development through participation aspects of football in its various codes. For progress to continue, researchers must focus on conducting high-impact studies that are parts of systematic lines of research, incorporate or test theory, integrate previous football and general sport psychology literature and ask practically relevant questions. It has also been found that players' mental skills can be developed through systematic training and this training influences both performance and personal well-being. Finally, coaches and the motivational and moral climates they create have major influences on players' psychological development. Hence, it is critical that they receive training on the psychology of football.

References

Davis, J.O., 1991, Sport injuries and stress management: An opportunity for research. *The Sport Psychologist*, 5, 175–82.

Gould, D., Collins, K., Lauer, L. and Chung, Y., 2006, Coaching life skills: A working model. *Sport and Exercise Psychology Review*, 2, 10–18.

Gould, D., Collins, K., Lauer, L. and Chung, Y., 2007, Coaching life skills through football: A study of award winning high school coaches. *Journal of Applied Psychology*, 19, 16–37.

Gould, D., Dieffenbach, K. and Moffett, A., 2002, Psychological characteristics and their development in Olympic champions. *Journal of Applied Sport Psychology*, 14, 177–209.

Gould, D., Greenleaf, C., Chung, Y. and Guinan, D., 2002, A survey of U.S. Atlanta and Nagano Olympians: Factors influencing performance. *Research Quarterly for Sport and Exercise*, 73, 175–86.

Gould, D., Guinan, D., Greenleaf, C., Medbery, R. and Peterson, K., 1999, Factors affecting Olympic performance: Perceptions of athletes and coaches from more and less successful teams. *The Sport Psychologist*, 13, 371–95.

Greenleaf, C., Gould, D. and Dieffenbach, K., 2001, Factors influencing Olympic performance: Interviews with Atlanta and Nagano US Olympians. *Journal of Applied Sport Psychology*, 13, 154–84.

Johnson, J.J.M., Hrycaiko, D.W., Johnson, G.V. and Halas, J.M. 2004, Self-talk and female youth soccer performance. *The Sport Psychologist*, 18, 44–59.

Jones, G., Hanton, S. and Connaughton, D., 2002, What is this thing called mental toughness. *Journal of Applied Sport Psychology*, 14, 205–18.

Kavussanu, M. and Spray, C.M., 2006, Contextual influences on moral functioning of the male youth footballers. *The Sport Psychologist*, 20, 1–23.

Maynard, I.W. and Cotton, P.C.J., 1993, An investigation of two stress management techniques in field settings. *The Sport Psychologist*, 7, 375–87.

Maynard, I.W., Hemmings, B. and Warwick-Evans, L., 1995, The effects of a somatic intervention strategy on competitive state anxiety and performance in semiprofessional soccer players. *The Sport Psychologist*, 9, 51–64.

Maynard, I.W. and Howe, B.L. 1987, Interrelations of trait and state anxiety with game performance of rugby players. *Perceptual and Motor Skills*, 64, 599–602.

Pain, M.A. and Harwood, C.G., 2004, Knowledge and perceptions of sport psychology within English soccer. *Journal of Sports Sciences*, 22, 813–26.

Petitpas, A.J., Van Raalte, J.L., Cornelius, A.E. and Presbrey, J., 2004, A life skills development program for high school student athletes. *Journal of Primary Prevention*, 24, 325–34.

Reilly, T., 2008, Science and football: an update, In *Science and Football VI*, edited by T. Reilly and F. Korkusuz. London: Routledge.

Stephens, D.E. and Bredemeier, B.J.L., 1996. Moral atmosphere and judgements about aggression in girls' soccer: relationships among moral and motivational variables. *Journal of Sport and Exercise Psychology*, 18, 158–73.

Thelwell, R., Weston, N. and Greenlees, I., 2005, Defining and understanding mental toughness within soccer. *Journal of Applied Sport Psychology*, 17, 326–32.

Weinberg, R.S. and Gould, D., 2007, *Foundations of Sport and Exercise Psychology*, fourth edn. Champaign, IL. Human Kinetics.

67 Adaptation of 'Self' and 'Other' versions of the Revised Power in Soccer Questionnaire (RPSQ) for Turkish culture

Erkut Konter

Dokuz Eylül University, Department of Education, Turkey

Introduction

Leadership power has frequently been studied within a theoretical framework known as the bases of social power (French and Raven, 1959). Wann *et al.* (2000) were the first to adapt French and Raven's five social (interpersonal) powers construct in sport. This study involved an exploration of validity and reliability of the revised versions of Power in Sport Questionnaires (RPSQ–O and RPSQ–S) with RPSQ data collected from male soccer coaches and players, following from an easier study (Konter, 2007). Analysis of the revised forms (RPSQ–O and RPSQ–S) involved confirmatory factor analyses with respect to the hypothesized two-factor, three-factor and five-factor models. Confirmatory factor analyses (CFA) of the RPSQ forms revealed that two-, three- and five-factor models did not fit with the data collected in Turkey. It seems more research is needed regarding how interpersonal power is involved in cross-cultural sport leadership, since there is still a striking lack of research on individuals from various cultures in sport and exercise psychology (Duda and Hayashi, 1998).

People in general, and coaches, sport officials, players, and even spectators in particular, possess power to influence or change the attitudes and behaviours of others (French and Raven, 1959; Wann *et al.*, 2000). French and Raven (1959) defined five types of social power: reward, coercive, legitimate, expert and referent power. Reward power involves the ability to reward others such as verbal praise, positive body language, and more playing time. Coercive power concerns the ability to control access to one or more punishments: for example, verbal reprimands, negative gesture, giving less playing time, making players run laps or do sit-ups or push-ups. Legitimate power involves the ability to use one's position and authority within the organization, group or team, for example, being an authority figure, possessing official status, ownership of the organization, being the head coach and so on. Expert power is derived from the perception that one is knowledgeable, skilful, or talented in a specific domain: for example, being a former star in that sport, having specific education and experience, having been awarded many titles or medals. Referent power involves the ability to be liked and respected by the group members: for example, athletes like, respect and admire their coaches, and follow their decisions (French and Raven, 1959; Sage, 1975; Wann et al., 2000).

In addition to French and Raven's (1959) interpersonal power construct, two other typologies have also been proposed. Kelman (1958) put forward a three-power taxonomy including compliance, identification and internalization while a number of authors suggested a two-power typology incorporating personal and positional powers (Yukl and Fable, 1991; Wann et al., 2000; Yukl, 2002).

Hofstede (2001) indicated the importance of cultural differences and syndromes in cross-cultural psychology. There are studies supporting cultural differences in various countries for example, perception and sport leadership (Challadurai et al., 1988; Sidonio et al., 1991) and autocratic behaviour (Salminen and Lukkonen, 1994).

Wann et al. (2000) used French and Raven's five interpersonal power construct, developed the scales and labelled them 'Power in Sport Questionnaire – Self (PSQ–S)' and 'Power in Sport Questionnaire – Other (PSQ–O)'. Konter (2007) adapted the Self and Other versions of the Power in Sport Questionnaire for Turkey and found support with the elimination of some items (7 and 11 from the PSQ–S, 1, 6, 7 and 11 from the PSQ–O). Items were eliminated and revised and the data were then collected from male soccer coaches and players for this second study in Turkey.

Turkey has a unique position between European, Asian and Middle Eastern countries which makes it an interesting country for cross-cultural sport psychology research related to leadership power. For example, Göregenli (1995) found that the Turkish culture was neither predominantly collectivist nor individualist in orientation. Kagitcibasi (1970) also showed that an authoritarian orientation was stronger in Turkey than in the United States. Maykel (2002) reported that Turkish adolescents were more strongly in favour of *culture* maintenance than Dutch adolescents.

The forms of the PSQ would be of value to cross-cultural sport psychology because they could provide information about a football team's chemistry, players' and coaches' perception, cognition, behaviour, communication, leadership, satisfaction and performance. Therefore, this study involved an exploration of validity and reliability of PSQ–O and PSQ–S forms with revised items (7 and 11 from the PSQ–S, 1,6,7 and 11 from the PSQ–O) for Turkey.

Methods

Data were collected from male soccer coaches ($n = 165$) and players ($n = 870$) including amateur ($n = 697$) and professional ($n = 173$) participants. The coaches had a mean age of 40.24 (SD = 8.40) years and had been coaching for an average of 8.56 (SD = 6.75) years. The players had a mean age of 18.40 (SD = 4.00) years and had been playing soccer for an average of 6.00 (SD = 4.15) years with licence.

Head coaches for each sport were contacted and the nature of the research project was explained. The RPSQ forms with brief instructions were then administered to players (RPSQ–O) and coaches (RPSQ–S) at their soccer clubs and training locations. Completion of each RPSQ form required approximately 10–15 minutes.

Analysis of the RPSQ–O and RPSQ–S involved CFA (LISREL 8.7 for Windows) with regard to the hypothesized, two-factor (Yukl and Fable, 1991), three-factor (Kelman, 1958) and five-factor (Wann et al., 2000) models.

Results

PSQ–O results

Confirmatory factor analyses revealed that two-, three- and five-factor models did not fit with the soccer players' data (RPSQ–O), yielding poor results (Table 67.1).

Confirmatory factor analyses showed that the five-factor model [$\chi^2 = 856.10$ ($N = 870$, df $= 80$, $P = 0.001$), (χ^2 /df) $= 10.70$, GFI $= 0.88$, AGFI $= 0.83$, RMR $= 0.08$, RMSEA $= 0.11$, CFI $= 0.91$], the three-factor model [$\chi^2 = 1121.30$ ($N = 870$, df $= 87$, $P = 0.001$), (χ^2 /df) $= 12.88$, GFI $= 0.84$, AGFI $= 0.77$, RMR $= 0.08$, RMSEA $= 0.13$, CFI $= 0.81$], and the two-factor model [$\chi^2 = 1293.21$ ($N = 870$, df $= 89$, $P = 0.001$), (χ^2/df) $= 14.53$, GFI $= 0.83$, AGFI $= 0.78$, RMR $= 0.08$, RMSEA $= 0.12$, CFI $= 0.83$] are not consistent with the data collected in Turkey.

PSQ–S Results

Confirmatory factor analyses revealed that two-, three- and five-factor models were not fit with the head coaches' data (RPSQ–S) yielding poor results (Table 67.1). The analysis revealed that the five-factor model [$\chi^2 = 316.25$ ($N = 165$, df $= 80$, $P = 0.001$), (χ^2/df) $= 3.95$, GFI $= 0.80$, AGFI $= 0.69$, RMR $= 0.12$, RMSEA $= 0.13$, CFI $= 0.84$], the three-factor model [$\chi^2 = 491.13$ ($N = 165$, df $= 87$, $P = 0.001$), (χ^2/ df) $= 5.64$, GFI $= 0.71$, AGFI $= 0.61$, RMR $= 0.13$, RMSEA $= 0.17$, CFI $= 0.71$], and the two-factor model [$\chi^2 = 589.91$ ($N = 165$, df $= 89$, $P = 0.001$), (χ^2/df) $= 6.62$, GFI $= 0.69$, AGFI $= 0.56$, RMR $= 0.15$, RMSEA $= 0.19$, CFI $= 0.68$] are not consistent with the data collected in Turkey.

Discussion

The analyses described above suggest that both forms of the RPSQ with the two-, three- and five-factor models are not confirmed in Turkey (Table 67.1). The reason for this, as Hofstede (2001) stated, could be cultural differences in thinking and social action including the factors of power distance, uncertainty avoidance, individualism versus collectivism, masculinity versus femininity, and long-term versus short-term orientation in different cultures. Thus, cultural differences provide fertile ground for misunderstanding and conflict (Gauvin and Russell, 1993; Duda and Hayashi, 1998). Concepts, relationships and test results

Table 67.1 Results of CFA of the Turkish RPSQ–O and RPSQ–S

Models	χ^2	df	χ^2/df	RMSEA	RMR	GFI	AGFI	CFI	P
RPSQ–O results (soccer players form)									
5–Factor	856.10	80	10.70	0.11	0.08	0.88	0.83	0.91	0.001
3–Factor	1121.30	87	12.88	0.13	0.08	0.84	0.77	0.81	0.001
2–Factor	1293.21	89	14.53	0.12	0.08	0.83	0.78	0.87	0.001
RPSQ–S results (soccer coaches form)									
5–Factor	316.25	80	3.95	0.13	0.12	0.80	0.69	0.84	0.00
3–Factor	491.13	87	5.64	0.17	0.13	0.71	0.61	0.75	0.00
2–Factor	589.91	89	6.62	0.19	0.15	0.68	0.56	0.69	0.00

Note: Results by LISREL 8.0 for Windows.

that are valid in Asia or Africa may not apply in North America or Europe, and vice versa.

Podsakoff and Schriensheim (1985) and later Schriesheim *et al.* (1991) reported that existing literature related to French and Raven's (1959) interpersonal power should be interpreted with great caution because of theoretical and methodological shortcomings. In contrast, Frost and Stahelski (1988) used exploratory factor analysis and showed for the first time that French and Raven's (1959) five-power constructs are factorially identifiable and orthogonal with multi-item Likert scales.

It seems that item eliminations, additional new items and models may be needed for further analyses of the RPSQ forms. Although factors of leadership power certainly exist across cultures, present RPSQ forms fall short in measuring the five-factor construct without elimination of some items for Turkey. Wann *et al.* (2000) suggested that questionnaire validation should be an on-going project with subsequent attempts at validation and refinement.

References

Challadurai, P., Imamura, H., Yamaguchi, Y., Oinuma, Y. and Miyauchi, T., 1988, Sport leadership in a cross-national setting: The case of Japanese and Canadian university athletes. *Journal of Sport and Exercise Psychology*, 10, 374–89.

Duda, J.L. and Hayashi, C.T., 1998, Measurement issues in cross-cultural research within sport and exercise psychology. In *Advances in Sport and Exercise Psychology Measurement*, edited by Duda, J.L. (Morgantown, WV: Fitness Information Technology).

French, J. and Raven, B.H., 1959, The bases of social power. In *Studies in Social Power*, edited by Cartwright, D. (Ann Arbor, MI: Institute for Social Research).

Frost, D.E. and Stahelski, A.J., 1988, The systematic measurement of French and Raven's bases of social power in workgroups. *Journal of Applied Social Psychology*, 18, 375–89.

Gauvin, L. and Russell, S.J., 1993, Sport-specific and culturally adapted measures in sport and exercise psychology research: Issues and strategies. In *Handbook of Research on Sport Psychology*, edited by Singer, R.N. Murphy, M. and Tennat, L.K. (New York. Macmillan).

Göregenli, M., 1995, Individualism-collectivism orientations in the Turkish culture: A preliminary study. *Türk Psikoloji Dergisi [Turkish Journal of Psychology]*, 10, 1–14.

Hofstede, G., 2001, *Cultures, Consequences, Comparing Values, Behaviors, Institutions, and Organizations across Nations* 2nd edn, (London: Sage).

Kagitcibasi, C., 1970, Social norms and authoritarianism: Turkish-American comparison. *Journal of Personality and Social Psychology,* 16, 444–51.

Kelman, H.C., 1958, Compliance, identification, and internalization: Three process of attitude change. *Journal of Conflict Revolution,* 2, 51–60.

Konter, E., 2007, Adaptation of self and other versions of the Power in Sport Questionnaire for Turkey. 13th Annual Scientific Conference, Personality, Motivation, Sport, National Sports Academy, 11 May, Sofia, Bulgaria.

Maykel, V., 2002, Multiculturalism among minority and majority adolescents in the Netherlands. *International Journal of Intercultural Relations,* 26, 91–108.

Podsakoff, P.M. and Schriesheim, C.A., 1985, Field studies of French and Raven's bases of power: Critique, reanalysis, and suggestions for future research. *Psychological Bulletin,* 97, 387–411.

Sage, G.H., 1975, An occupational analysis of the college coach. In *Sport and SocialOrder,* edited by Ball, D.W. and Loys, J.W. (Reading, MA: Addison-Wesley).

Salminen, S. and Lukkonen, J., 1994, The convergent and discriminant validity of the coach's version of the Leadership Scale for Sport. *International Journal of Sport Psychology,* 25, 119–27.

Schriesheim, C.A., Hinkin, T.R. and Potsakoff, P.M., 1991, Can ipsative and single-item measures produce erroneous results in field studies of French and Raven's (1959) five bases of power? An empirical investigation. *Journal of Applied Psychology,* 76, 106–14.

Sidonio, S., Vitor, P. and Frederico, S., 1991, Leadership patterns in handball international competition. *International Journal of Sport Psychology,* 22, 78–89.

Wann, D. L., Metcalf, L.A., Brewer, K.R. and Whiteside, H.D., 2000, Development of the Power in Sport Questionnaires. *Journal of Sport Behavior,* 23, 423–43.

Yukl, G., 2002, *Leadership in Organizations* (5th edn) (Englewood Cliffs, N.J.: Prentice Hall).

Yukl, G. and Fable, C. M., 1991, Importance of different power sources in downward and lateral relations. *Journal of Applied Psychology,* 76, 416–23.

68 Alternatives to the penalty shoot-out

Jon Billsberry and Patrick Nelson

The Open University, UK

Introduction

Recent comments by FIFA President, Sepp Blatter, have focused attention on the use of the penalty shoot-out to determine the result of drawn games in the knock-out stages of international football tournaments. He stated,

> When it comes to the World Cup final, it is passion, and when it goes to extra time it is a drama. But when it comes to penalty kicks, it is a tragedy. ... Football is a team sport and penalties are not for a team, it is the individual.
>
> (Szczepanik, 2006)

He revealed that FIFA is considering removing penalty shoot-outs and looking at alternatives. There appears to be momentum behind replaying deadlocked finals, but this is not thought to be possible in earlier stages of tournaments due to issues of fatigue and scheduling. He stated that trials would be conducted on methods of removing players and playing for a golden goal. These are just two of the possible alternatives to the penalty shoot-out.

In this report, we explore the range of options open to FIFA and, drawing on experience in other sports, we develop a set of criteria that a replacement should satisfy in order to be effective. Following this, we evaluate the main alternatives against these criteria.

Categorising tie-breaks

Looking at the way that other sports solve the problem of drawn games is very instructive as it allows us to produce a categorisation of forms. These tie-breaks fall into three categories. The first category is to wait until the end of the game and then do something extra to separate the teams. Playing extra time and then a penalty shoot-out if the teams are still level would fall into this category. These post-game tie-breaks can be sub-categorised into three types, namely: sports that continue playing the game with the usual manner of scoring; sports that continue playing the game with a different manner of scoring and, sports that take an episode from the game and create some form of shoot-out.

The second category is to make an assessment of the game that has been played. The screens of match data put up at the end of games by television companies illustrate this approach in a football context. The third method is to eliminate the draw altogether by making the draw favour one of the two sides. Again, football uses this method in the second leg of games in competitions, such as in the knockout stages of the Champions' League, where the 'away goal counts double'. Unless the exact reverse score is achieved in both legs of the tie, a draw favours one side over the other. A range of hybrids is also possible.

Replacement criteria

Based on an analysis of tie-breaks in football and other sports, which cannot be included for reasons of space, we suggest the following ten criteria that a replacement to the penalty shoot-out should satisfy:

1   It should have face validity by being a football-centred solution.
2   It should be based on an objective assessment of something measurable.
3   It should not produce a contentious decision.
4   It should be easily understood and applied.
5   It should involve the whole team, not individuals or groups of individuals.
6   If it alters the manner in which the game is played, it should so in a manner that promotes attractive play.
7   If possible, it should promote attractive play in all games in the tournament.
8   It should not so exhaust players as to give them a disadvantage in subsequent games.
9   It should not put players at an increased risk of injury.
10 It should not offer an advantage to any nation, other than that based on the ability to play football.

Evaluation of alternatives

Post-game tie-breaks

The potential post-game tie-breaks in football fall foul of several of the proposed criteria. The penalty shoot-out is an individual event, as is a confrontation between attacker and goalkeeper or a free kick competition. Endless extra-time would risk exhausting players for future games and increase the risk of injury given the extreme conditions, as do the many variations that involve removing players until a goal is scored. Lotteries (e.g. a coin toss) and races fall foul of the face validity criterion. In addition, all post-game tie-breaks run into the 'psychological refuge' problem; they give weaker teams and players a way of progressing without taking risks.

Assessment of games

Finding a way to assess the best team during a game is, in many ways, the best way to settle the result of the game. There is a distinct advantage of finding a second tier of score to separate the teams. Many have been suggested, but most seem inevitably to lead to contention. Awarding the fixture to the team with the fewest number of cautions would not just create a terrible burden on the referee but would lead to intense scrutiny of every decision. Counting the attempts on goal, or saves, would require some form of subjective assessment on close calls and may encourage 'unrealistic' attempts from distance. Counting corners would lead to players playing for corners rather than trying to beat their opponents. Counting the number of times each goalkeeper touches the ball will alter the way the game is played and may lead to games being settled on blunders as players do risky things to avoid involving the goalkeeper. Asking a referee or an expert panel to decide the result breaks the objectivity and contentiousness criteria and may put people's personal safety at risk.

There are, however, several ways of assessing the game that might give a result that satisfies the criteria. Whereas measuring the 'time of possession' is flawed because it promotes keeping possession instead of attacking, measuring 'time of possession in the opponent's half' may be possible. The drawback is that the players and spectators cannot see the time being measured, but this may be solvable. Moreover, it would still encourage keeping hold of the ball rather than taking attacking risks. Perhaps the best secondary assessment is to count the times each team hits the opponent's woodwork. No one would deliberately do this rather than score and it does measure a positive attribute of the game. Moreover, it is easily counted by a remote official using television and the running score of woodwork hits can be relayed to players and spectators. However, its use might raise the question of why a minor score is not introduced in other competitions.

Eliminate the draw

There are many different ways of eliminating the draw. All of the following could be measured and used: goal difference in the tournament, number of goals scored, win/loss record, number of cautions, number of corners, and the number of free kicks conceded. If the Australia–Croatia 2006 World Cup game is any guide, determining the outcome of games deadlocked after 120 minutes with these methods (probably in some order of priority to counter problems associated with equal records, e.g. goal difference, number of goals scored, win/loss record, number of cautions) seems likely to improve the quality of the game as one team has to attack. Moreover, if goal difference or goals scored in prior games are the main criteria for settling the deadlock, attacking play may be encouraged in all games in the tournament.

The main objection to this approach must be that the competing teams will have played teams of different standards and that this will be unfair. However, when considering the World Cup, there are various counters to this argument.

First, the draws for the group stages of the tournament are seeded according to nations' playing strength. Second, all qualifiers have made their way through qualifying tournaments which increasingly make use of inter-continental play-offs to ensure the best teams in the world qualify. Another problem with this approach is that it does not involve any evaluation of the game played between the two sides or any post-match contest. In addition, it might be feared that it will encourage one side to defend. Although evidence from Champions' League knockout games does not appear to support this fear, it seems a valid concern.

An alternative way of eliminating the draw is to change the nature of the tournament so that there are no knockout games. There are many examples of tournaments in a wide variety of sports that adopt an all-play-all approach. The 'Swiss' system that is adopted in many chess tournaments allows for multiple participants to play in a tournament and for a winner to be found without the need for everyone to play each other. As the tournament progresses, players with similar records are paired together so that the later rounds become key games that shape the destination of the result. Draws are included as a natural part of the game and do not require resolution. The drawback with these approaches is that football has moved away from 'league' games, which are more likely to be tame affairs, to knock-out games because of the drama they offer.

Perhaps the simplest method of all is to adapt the 'away goal counts double' approach and give advantage to one of the goals. For example, if scores are level at the end of the game, the team that scored the first (or last) goal could be adjudicated the winner, i.e. a 'first (or last) goal counts double' approach. Intuitively, it might seem that the scorer of the first goal should be given preference as it rewards attacking intent from the start of the game. However, the team conceding the first goal would find itself at a tremendous disadvantage and would need to score twice before the end of the 120 minutes to win. Perhaps, therefore, a 'last goal counts double' might be preferable as a single goal difference between the two sides would still encourage both to attack. However, there seems something wrong for a team that has been leading throughout the game to be eliminated by a last minute equaliser. In addition, there might be concerns that players will begin the game with a sense of vulnerability, due to the catastrophic effect of conceding a goal, causing them to be more defensive.

Hybrids

The example of rugby union, which sometimes counts tries and, if level, awards the deadlocked fixture to the away team, illustrates that some sports use methods that involve two or more of the categories. There are several ways in which football may do something similar. One approach would be to address the concern that the pre-game assessments do not include any assessment of the game between the two sides that is being determined. A decision to a deadlocked game could be made in the following way. The teams would enter the game knowing each other's goal difference. During the game, the teams would gain one goal difference for every time they hit their opponent's woodwork. For example, Team A started with a goal difference of six and Team B started with a goal difference of four. During the game, Team A hit the opponent's woodwork once and Team B hit it four times. Team B would win the deadlocked fixture 8–7. This approach produces a dynamic solution that rewards attacking play and makes it less likely for the team ahead on the tie-break to play for the draw. A drawback is that it is slightly complex and it requires an acceptable way of counting woodwork hits.

Another hybrid is to hold the penalty shoot-out (or some other post-game assessment) before the end of the game (probably before the game or after 90 minutes; Carrillo, in press). There appear to be several advantages of this approach. First, it gives players a chance for redemption if they miss a penalty kick. Second, it reduces the blame attributed to the individual because of the chance of comeback. Third, it should produce more exciting play because the imbalance between the two teams has been established. This approach fails one of the criteria because the tie-break is based on individual performance. Moreover, the break in the continuity of play may be problematic.

Conclusion

A replacement to the penalty shoot-out is an issue that fascinates many people. In writing this report, our concern was to establish some ground rules that could be used to assess the suitability of replacements. It is too easy to say 'we have a problem, here is a solution, let's test it'. A more systematic approach is to develop a set of criteria, test all alternatives against these options and then select the best one.

Our conceptual testing of alternatives suggests that the development of a minor score (e.g. hits against the woodwork) and finding ways to eliminate the draw (e.g. using goal difference or goals scored in the tournament) may be more fruitful than post-game lotteries or extended play. Theoretically they seem to offer the possibility of stimulating more attacking and exciting play not just in the game that is being adjudicated, but also in other games in the tournament. This approach is just conceptual and we now call upon others to test these options in real football tournaments. Are they achievable? What is their impact?

References

Carrillo, J. D. (in press) Penalty shoot-outs: Before or after extra time? *Journal of Sports Economics*.

Szczepanik, N., 2006, Shoot-outs face sudden death under Blatter plan. *The Times*, 28 September 2006, p. 82.

69 Penalty kicks and stress

*Nelson Miyamoto,[1] Marco Bertolassi,[1]
Edgard Morya,[1, 2] Miguel L. Batista, Jr.,[1]
Alex S. Yamashita,[1] Carla O. Carvalho[1] and
Ronald Ranvaud[1]*

[1]Department of Physiology and Biophysics, University of Sao Paulo, Brazil;
[2]Alberto Santos Dumont Association for Science, Institute of Research and
Teaching, Brazil

Introduction

Previously we studied the point of no return (PNR) in a laboratory simulation of a soccer penalty kick (Morya *et al.*, 2003). By PNR we mean the moment beyond which the probability of the kicker being able to respond to an early dive by the goalkeeper – and wilfully put the ball to the opposite side – is < 50 per cent. The PNR for the laboratory simulation, in ideal conditions, was found to be about 250 ms before the shot (Morya *et al.*, 2003). In more realistic conditions it was later found to be about twice this value (Van Der Kamp, 2006). Stress has been considered critical in the performance of professional players in a real penalty situation, but this problem has been rarely addressed (McGarry and Franks, 2000). The present objective, therefore, was to study the effect of stress, as promoted by a noisy and participative audience, on the performance of motivated volunteers in a simulated penalty kick task.

Material and methods

Ten undergraduate students performed the simulated penalty task (Figure 69.1) as part of a practical class on motor control. This simulation of the penalty kick followed the procedure of Morya *et al.* (2003), and had been previously approved by the local ethics committee. A commercial software MEL Prof. 2.01 (Psychology Software Tools, PST Inc., Pittsburgh, PA) generated white visual stimuli on a black background on the screen, representing a goalmouth with a goalkeeper, a ball and a kicker (Figure 69.1). The MEL Prof. 2.01 software also recorded the participants' response and provided feedback on each response.

The kicker moved vertically upwards at a speed of 4.7 cm.s^{-1} towards the ball. The kicker connected with the ball 1344 ms after the beginning of the trial. This coincidence lasted for the next 17 ms, the duration of a frame on the computer screen. Randomly, the goalkeeper might move laterally, also at a speed of 4.7 cm.s^{-1}, whereas the ball was always still, at the centre of the display.

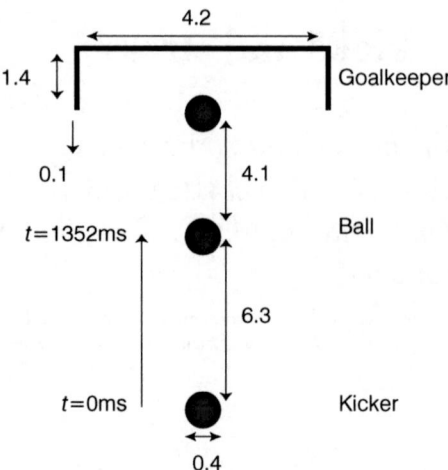

Figure 69.1 Visual stimuli of the experimental design; three disks represented the goalkeeper, ball and kicker, each 0.48° in diameter; straight vertical lines 1.48° high and a straight horizontal line 4.28° wide represented the goalposts and the crossbar; at the start of every trial, the goalkeeper was in the middle of the goalmouth, 4.18° vertically above the ball, which in turn was 6.38° vertically above the kicker

This experiment consisted of 80 trials in which the goalkeeper moved randomly sideways (right or left) on 90 per cent of trials and remained stationary on 10 per cent of trials. The goalkeeper moved randomly at one of nine possible intervals (51, 102, 153, 204, 255, 306, 357, 408, 459 ms) before kicker-ball contact – these intervals were called 'available time' (AT), since they corresponded to the interval between stimulus onset (goalkeeper movement) and the moment at which the response should occur (tilting a lever to the opposite side of the goalkeeper, exactly when kicker and ball coincided).

The performance of participants in the penalty kick simulation was measured in two situations: an acoustically isolated booth with dimmed lights (control); and in a large room in the presence of a loud participative audience that could accompany their performance on a large screen. In both situations, they sat in front of a computer and had their eyes centred 57 cm from the 17-inch screen (60 Hz) by a chin and forehead support. In the presence of an audience there was, in addition, a large 260 cm screen (1.90×2.0 m – 60 Hz), showing everybody present the stimuli of the penalty simulation, and the feedback indicating the performance of the participant.

Participants performed two sessions of about 60 min on separate days in a counterbalanced design with and without stress, in analogy with the protocol with and without fatigue, described above. At three moments, immediately before, immediately after and 45 min after task performance, samples of saliva were collected to analyse cortisol salivary level as a physiological index of stress (commercial radioimmunoassay – RIA). After 30 training trials (data discarded), participants began the experiment. In the penalty kick simulation with stress, participants were divided into two naturally competitive teams, according to the course they were enrolled in (Physical Education vs. Sport). More than 70 students loudly supported or booed participants as they performed their task. As a control, without stress (PKC), participants performed the same task but alone, with no one to disturb them.

Data analysis

The average percentage of correct responses as a function of 'available time' (AT) was fitted to a logistic curve model to find how long AT must be to saturate performance and for what value of AT (PNR) the chance of tilting the lever to the correct side is half way between pure chance performance (short ATs) and best possible performance (saturation value, long ATs). Levels of cortisol in the saliva, used as a physiological measure of the stress condition, were examined using ANOVA.

Results and discussion

Cortisol levels in the laboratory were always lower than during the practical (Figure 69.2), especially soon after task performance (>20%, vs. ~7% before, ~5% 45 min after task performance), confirming that the audience protocol had caused some stress, but that volunteers recovered well from the experiments. In laboratory conditions little or no stress was induced, at any time, according to cortisol measurements. As expected, the PNR under stress conditions backed up (from 249 to 292 ms before ball contact).

In addition, and unexpectedly, performance under stress saturated at ~80%. That is, mistakes occurred even if the goalkeeper moved a full 100 ms sooner than necessary for perfect performance in the laboratory. Participants under stress seemed unable to show 100 per cent perfect performance, putting the ball on the same side as the goalkeeper on about >20 per cent of the trials even when the time available to decide was very long, >450 ms.

Failure rates in actual penalties in official games is around 20–35 per cent, remarkably close to the result we obtained in our laboratory simulation. We speculate that, under the circumstances, there may be a link between stress and imagining failure. The former would be in part the result of the latter, in a vicious feedback circle. Imagining failure inevitably contributes to imperfect motor planning, leading to a certain error rate, which is difficult to avoid, at least without adequate preparation.

Conclusions

Looking at the aerospace industry, and the extreme stress situations to which successful pilots are submitted, it would appear that appropriate preparation (Bourne and Yaroush, 2003) and advance player selection would provide a means to overcome errors due to stress and improve performance of the kicker at the highest levels.

A

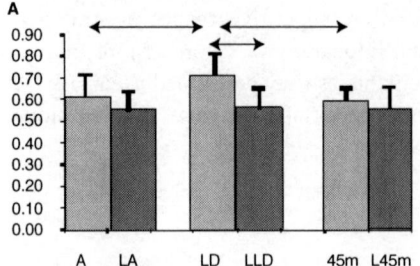

B

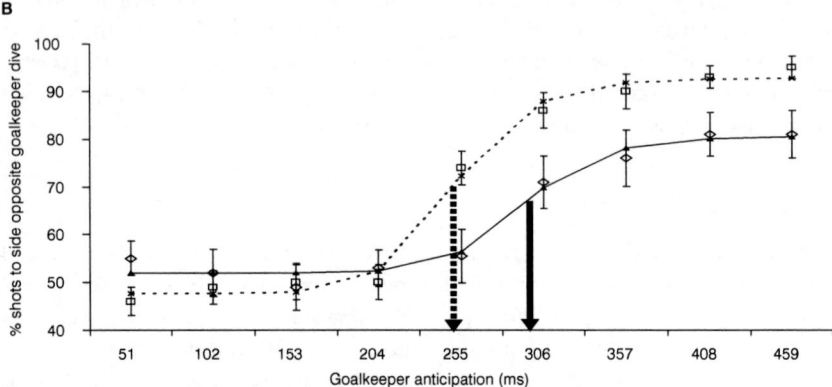

Figure 69.2 A) Salivary cortisol levels of volunteers before (A, AL), soon after (LD, LLD) and 45 min (45 m, L45 m) after task performance; light shading: under stress (with noisy audience); dark shading: no stress (quiet, laboratory conditions); arrows denote significant difference (P<0.05) between conditions; no stress bars are all different from LD, but no different from each other; B) Logistic fit to performance of volunteers in a simulated penalty situation; dotted line, in the laboratory, full line with a participative and interfering audience – notice the longer times required to improve performance above chance levels, and noticeable permanence of errors even when the goalkeeper dives very early

Acknowledgements

Financial support: CNPq, FAPESP

References

Bourne, L.E. and Yaroush, R.A., 2003, Stress and cognition: a cognitive psychological perspective. *NASA Final Report*, Grant Number NAG2-156, Bouldr, CO: Universirty of Colorado, Department of Psychology.

McGarry, T. and Franks, I.M., 2000, On winning the penalty shoot-out in soccer. *Journal of Sports Sciences*, 18, 401–09.

Morya, E., Ranvaud, R. and Machado-Pinheiro, W., 2003, Dynamics of visual feedback in a laboratory simulation of a penalty kick. *Journal of Sports Sciences*, 21, 87–95.

Van Der Kamp, J., 2006, A field simulation study of the effectiveness of penalty kick strategies in soccer: late alterations of kick direction increase errors and reduce accuracy. *Journal of Sports Sciences*, 24, 467–77.

70 Developing methods to evaluate player selection

Edgard Morya,[1] Marco Bertolassi,[2] Nelson Miyamoto,[2] Miguel L. Batista, Jr.,[2] Alex S. Yamashita,[2] Carla O. Carvalho,[2] Cinthia Itiki[3] and Ronald Ranvaud[2]

[1]Institute of Research and Teaching, Brazil; [2]Department of Physiology and Biophysics, University of Sao Paulo, Brazil; [3]Biomedical Engineering Laboratory, University of Sao Paulo, Brazil

Introduction

Technological development has produced better equipment, such as faster balls and more efficient boots. It has improved injury prevention and training methods to aid soccer players in enhancing performance. However, in specific situations, such as the penalty kick, technological advances may overwhelm the possibilities of human skills. For example, a faster ball could be kicked in such a way that no professional goalkeeper could reach it in time no matter how skilled and well trained. There is motivation, therefore, to investigate in advance individual performance limits and the variables that affect it, which is also important for player selection and training. Focusing on the penalty kick situation, developing complete enough methods to investigate all the variables involved is a complex challenge that is receiving growing attention in the scientific literature.

Since the introduction of the dramatic penalty shoot-out (FIFA, 2002), penalty kicks have played a decisive role in important championships, determining the winner of the 1994 and 2006 World Cups. Several factors have been considered as key in penalty shoot-outs, such as stress, fatigue, kicker's technique, goalkeeper's technique (Morya *et al.*, 2005; Jordet *et al.*, 2007), visuo-motor coupling (Williams and Burwitz, 1993; Franks and Harvey, 1997; Savelsbergh *et al.*, 2002; Morya *et al.*, 2003; Van Der Kamp, 2006; Panchuk and Vickers, 2006) rather than mere chance (Hughes and Wells, 2002; Whitfield, 2002). Deciding the winner after 90 or 120 min of play can be a very stressful situation, which added to the high level of fatigue that most players experience towards the end of the match (Mohr *et al.*, 2005, Rahnama *et al.*, 2006), might result in significant impairment of the kicker's performance (Kellis *et al.*, 2006).

The aim of this study was to develop a simulation method in the laboratory to probe the limits on performance imposed by fatigue and stress, in support of the improvement of training, player selection and equipment engineering in the soccer penalty kick.

Material and methods

Subjects

Twenty male university soccer players participated, aged between 18 and 31, all with experience in taking penalty kicks. They had normal or corrected-to-normal vision, were right-handed (Oldfield, 1971) and they provided informed written consent before beginning this study, which had been previously approved by the local Ethics Committee.

Experimental design of the penalty kick simulation

The simulation of the penalty kick followed the study published by Morya *et al.* (2003). A commercial software MEL Prof. 2.01 (Psychology Software Tools, PST Inc., Pittsburgh, PA) generated white visual stimuli on a black background on the screen, representing a goalmouth with a goalkeeper, a ball and a kicker (Fig. 70.1). The MEL Prof. 2.01 software also recorded the participants' response and provided feedback on each response.

The kicker moved vertically upwards at a speed of $4.7\,\mathrm{cm.s^{-1}}$ towards the ball. The kicker coincided with the ball 1344 ms after the beginning of the trial. This coincidence lasted for the next 17 ms, the duration of a frame on the computer screen. Randomly, the goalkeeper might move laterally, also at a speed of $4.7\,\mathrm{cm.s^{-1}}$, whereas the ball was always still, at the centre of the display.

This experiment consisted of 80 trials in which the goalkeeper moved randomly sideways (right or left) on 90 per cent of trials and remained stationary on 10 per

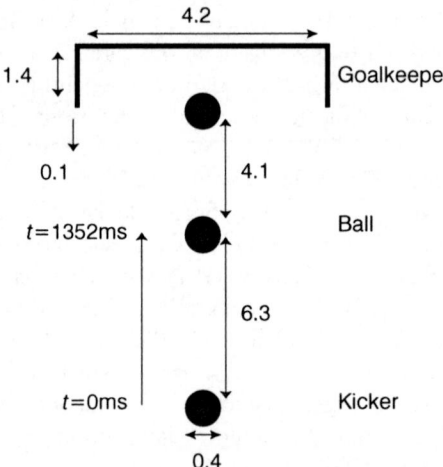

Figure 70.1 Visual stimuli of the experimental design; three disks represented the goalkeeper, ball and kicker, each 0.48° in diameter.; straight vertical lines 1.48° high and a straight horizontal line 4.28° wide represented the goalposts and the crossbar; the goalkeeper was in the middle of the goalmouth, 4.18° vertically above the ball, which in turn was 6.38° vertically above the kicker

cent of trials. The goalkeeper moved randomly at one of nine possible intervals (51, 102, 153, 204, 255, 306, 357, 408, 459 ms) before kicker-ball contact – these intervals were called 'available time' (AT), since they corresponded to the interval between stimulus onset (goalkeeper movement) and the moment at which the response should occur (tilting a lever to the opposite side of the goalkeeper, exactly when kicker and ball coincided). The manual lever allowed only movements of pronation or supination. Participants performed this task under two separate experimental conditions: peripheral fatigue and stress. In both, feedback of their performance was provided at each trial.

Induction of peripheral fatigue

Participants were tested with the penalty kick simulation in an acoustically isolated booth with dimmed lights. They sat in front of a computer and had their eyes centred 57 cm from the 17 in screen (60 Hz) by a chin and forehead support. A commercial software, MEL Prof. 2.01, generated visual stimuli on the screen and recorded when and which way participants tilted the lever, which was connected to the joystick port. The lever might (or might not) offer resistance (50 per cent of the participant's maximum load). Surface electromyography of brachioradialis and supinator was recorded with two electrodes per muscle (diameter 2 cm, inter-electrode distance 2 cm, Ag-Biopac) in a Polygraph amplifier (Grass Instrument Comp, USA), an A/D Digidata 1200 interface (Axon Instruments, USA) using Axotape 2.0 (Axon Instruments, USA) software.

Participants performed two sessions of about 60 min each, on separate days. The sequence of protocols, penalty kick simulation with and without fatigue (PKF, PKC respectively), was randomly counterbalanced. In both protocols, participants were asked to fixate their eyes on the ball (their gaze was monitored with an eye-tracker) and to tilt the lever to the side opposite to the goalkeeper movement (but priority was to act exactly at kicker-ball coincidence). After 30 training trials (data discarded), participants began the experiment. In the penalty kick simulation with fatigue (PKF), participants performed pronation and supination movements with 50 per cent of their maximum load until reaching the maximum exertion level in a subjective scale of effort (Borg, 1998). As soon as the participant graded the subjective sensation as maximum effort, the penalty kick simulation was initiated, without load. In the penalty kick simulation without fatigue (PKC), participants performed the same task without preliminary maximum exertion.

Induction of stress

The performance of participants in the penalty kick simulation was measured in two situations: while alone, in an acoustically isolated booth with dimmed lights (control); and in a large room in the presence of a loud participative audience that could accompany their performance on a large screen. In both situations, they sat in front of a computer and had their eyes centred 57 cm from the 17 in (43.2 cm) screen (60 Hz) by a chin and forehead support. In the presence of an audience there was, in addition, a large 260 cm screen (1.90 × 2.0 m 60 Hz), showing the stimuli of the penalty simulation, and the performance of the participant.

Participants performed two sessions of about 60 min on separate days in a counterbalanced design with and without stress, analogous to the protocol with and without fatigue described above. On three occasions, immediately before, immediately after and 45 min after task performance, samples of saliva were collected for analysis of salivary cortisol as a physiological index of stress (commercial radioimmunoassay (RIA)). After 30 training trials (data discarded), participants commence the experiment. In the penalty kick simulation with stress, participants were separated into two naturally competitive teams, according to the course they were enrolled in (Physical Education vs. Sport). More than 70 students loudly supported or booed participants as they performed their task. As a control, without stress (PKC), participants performed the same task but in isolation, without an audience to promote stress.

Data analysis

The mean percent of correct responses as a function of 'available time' was fitted to a logistic curve model to find the duration required for ATs to be to saturate the curve at best performance, and the AT corresponding to the half-way mark between chance performance (very short ATs: 50 per cent chance of tilting the lever to the correct side) and saturation. Larger amplitudes and loss of the high-frequency in the EMG were used to confirm the fatigue condition. The concentration of salivary cortisol was used to evaluate the stress condition.

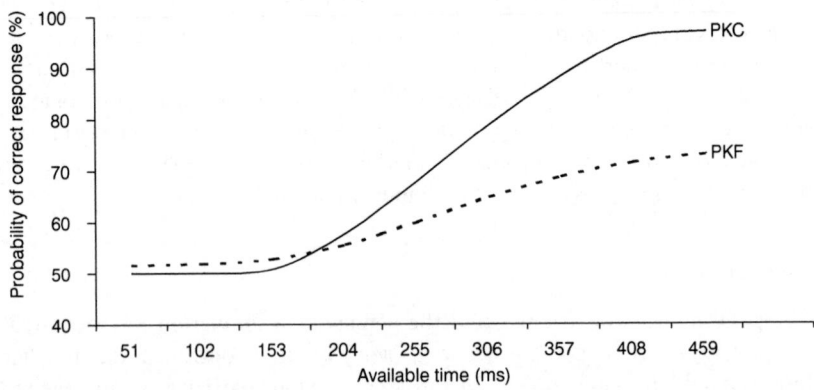

Figure 70.2 Logistic fit of the mean percentage of correct responses (tilting the lever towards the opposite side of the goalkeeper) as a function of 'available time' in control (PKC) and fatigue (PKF) conditions

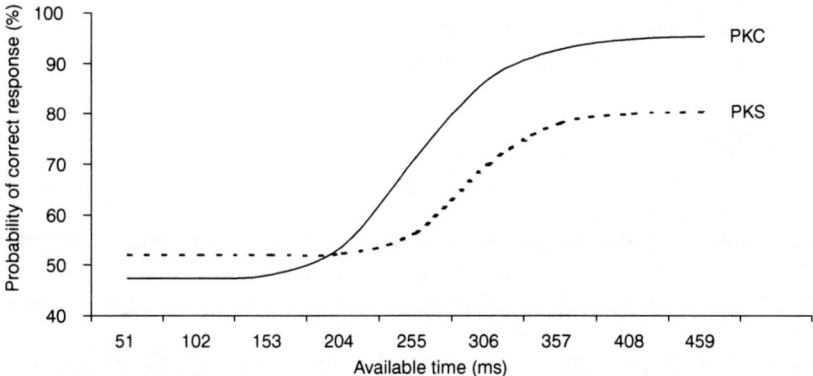

Figure 70.3 Logistic fit of the mean percentage of correct responses (tilting the lever towards the opposite side of the goalkeeper) as function of 'available time' in control (PKC) and stress (PKS) conditions

Results and discussion

In this study, participants showed an expected significant performance impairment both under stress and fatigue (Figures 70.2 and 70.3), needing in both cases longer ATs, i.e. they were able to react only to very early dives by the goalkeeper.

The effect of fatigue might be attributed to alterations of the neuromuscular system. An additional surprising effect appeared on the decision-making process, stabilizing participants' decision capabilities at about 70 per cent (fatigue – Figure 70.2) and 80 per cent (stress – Figure 70.3), even with the longest ATs (>400 ms) to decide which way to move. This is contrary to the findings of Royal *et al.* (2006) who showed an improvement of decision-making in water-polo players submitted to fatigue.

The data shown here suggest two distinct mechanisms of performance deterioration, whether it be as a result of fatigue or of stress, in a penalty kick simulation. Not only are earlier goalkeeper dives needed for kickers to be able to respond, but, significantly, decision capability saturates at 70–80 per cent correct responses even if the available time is very long. Considering the surprisingly high index of missed penalty kicks by top players (about 20–35 per cent, Kuhn, 1988; Morris and Burwitz, 1989, Franks and Harvey, 1997; Morya *et al.*, 2005), this study suggests that improving performance in penalty kicks may require dedicating engineering effort to the motor control system as well as soccer equipment. This remark is particularly relevant considering the general lack of specific training in penalty kicks at the highest levels related in the literature (Bonizzoni, 1988).

Conclusions

This study showed evidence of distinct effects of both fatigue and stress in a controlled laboratory simulation that might be impairing the performance of penalty takers, especially in important final shoot-out matches. It introduces perspectives for improved performance in the penalty situation through innovative methods for training and selection of players.

References

Bonizzoni, L., 1988, *Penalty. Calcio di punizione. Calcio d'angolo. Rimessa laterale* (Roma: Societa Stampa Sportiva).

Borg, G., 1998, *Borg's Perceived Exertion and Pain Scales* (Champaign, IL: Human Kinetics).

FIFA, 2002, The penalty kick. In: *Laws of the Game* (Zurich: FIFA).

Franks, I.M. and Harvey, T., 1997, Cues for goalkeepers: high-tech methods used to measure penalty shot response. *Soccer Journal*, May–June, 30–38.

Hughes, M., Wells, J., 2002, Analysis of penalties in shoot-outs. *International Journal of Performance Analysis in Sport*, 2, 55–72.

Jordet, G., Hartman, E., Visscher, C., and Lemmink, K.A.P.M., 2007, Kicks from the penalty mark in soccer: the roles of stress, skill, and fatigue for kick outcomes. *Journal of Sports Sciences*, 25, 121–9.

Kellis, E., Katis, A. and Vrabas, I.S., 2006, Effects of an intermittent exercise fatigue protocol on biomechanics of soccer kick performance. *Scandinavian Journal of Medicine and Science in Sports*, 16, 334–44.

Kuhn, W., 1988, Penalty-kick strategies for shooters and goalkeepers. In: *Science and Football*, edited by Reilly, T., Lees, A., Davids, K. and Murphy, W.J. (London: E&FN Spon).

Mohr, M., Krustrup, P. and Bangsbo, J., 2005, Fatigue in soccer: a brief review. *Journal of Sports Sciences*, 23, 593–9.

Morris, A. and Burwitz, L., 1989, Anticipation and movements strategies in elite soccer goalkeepers an penalty kicks. *Journal of Sports Sciences*, 7, 79–80.

Morya, E., Bigatão, H., Lees, A. and Ranvaud, R., 2005, Evolving penalty kick strategies: world cup and club matches 2000–2002. In *Science and Football V*, edited by Reilly, T., Cabri, J. and Araújo, D. (London: E&FN Spon).

Morya, E., Ranvaud, R. and Machado-Pinheiro, W., 2003, Dynamics of visual feedback in a laboratory simulation of a penalty kick. *Journal of Sports Sciences*, 21, 87–95.

Oldfield, R.C., 1971, The assessment and analysis of handedness: the Edinburg Inventory. *Neuropsychologia*, 9, 97–113.

Panchuk, D. and Vickers, J.N., 2006, Gaze behaviors of goaltenders under spatial-temporal constraints. *Human Movement Sciences*, 25, 733–52.

Rahnama, N., Lees, A. and Reilly, T., 2006, Electromyography of selected lower-limb muscles fatigued by exercise at the intensity of soccer match-play. *Journal of Electromyography and Kinesiology*, 16, 257–63.

Royal, K.A., Farrow, D., Mujika, I., Halson, S.L., Pyne, D. and Abernethy, B., 2006, The effects of fatigue on decision making and shooting skill performance in water polo players. *Journal of Sports Sciences*, 24, 807–15.

Savelsbergh, G.J.P., Williams, A.M., Van Der Kamp, J. and Ward, P., 2002, Visual search, anticipation and expertise in soccer goalkeepers. *Journal of Sports Sciences*, 20, 279–87.

Van Der Kamp, J., 2006, A field simulation study of the effectiveness of penalty kick strategies in soccer: late alterations of kick direction increase errors and reduce accuracy. *Journal of Sports Sciences*, 24, 467–77.

Whitfield, J., 2002, Penalties no lottery. *Nature Science Update*, May.

Williams, A.M. and Burwitz, L., 1993, Advance cue utilisation in soccer. In *Science and Football II*, edited by Reilly, T., Clarys, J. and Stibbe, A. (London: E&FN Spon).

71 Emotions at the penalty mark

An analysis of elite players performing in an international penalty shootout

Geir Jordet, Marije T. Elferink-Gemser,
Koen A.P.M. Lemmink and Chris Visscher

University of Groningen, Netherlands

Introduction

> So we staggered on to penalties, and here I will make a declaration: there is nothing so nerve-racking as a penalty shootout, except maybe stepping into a boxing ring, which I did twice as a boy. Fighting for your life, one on one, or taking a penalty in a big game – in both instances your body simply doesn't belong to you.
>
> (Michael Owen, 2004: 98)

The rules of soccer state that when a winner has to be declared and two teams are tied after extra time in a tournament, the 'penalty shootout' (or kicks from the penalty mark) is used to decide the winner. The penalty shootout has been used to decide almost a quarter of games in the knockout stages of major tournaments (Jordet *et al.*, 2007), including several finals (e.g., the 2006 World Cup final). Thus, the event has become a normal feature of top level international soccer and more knowledge is needed to help coaches and players prepare optimally for these kicks.

In contrast to what one could expect based on its frequent occurrence, research on the penalty shootout has been noticeably sparse in the sport science literature. Success factors in all the penalty shootouts (involving a total of 409 kicks) ever held in the World Cup, European Championships and Copa America have recently been studied (Jordet *et al.*, 2007). It was demonstrated that both goal scoring skill (derived from positional roles in the team) and competitive pressure (derived from the relative importance of each shot) were related to kick outcomes. Most noteworthy though was competitive pressure – the higher the pressure, the fewer goals were scored. Thus, coping with stress seems to be a central success factor in penalty shootouts. Unknown, however, is how important it is for players to perform well and how stressful it actually is to participate in such an event.

Competitive stress can be defined as 'an ongoing transaction between an individual and the environmental demands associated primarily with competitive performance' (Mellalieu *et al.*, 2006: 1). Some researchers have argued that stress and emotions are strongly interrelated and that emotions may provide a rich understanding of the stress process (e.g., Lazarus, 2000). Thus, one way to learn about competitive stress is to study the emotions that are experienced when athletes compete under stressful conditions.

Emotions can be described across several dimensions. Popularly measured dimensions are hedonic tone (whether an emotion is pleasant [positively toned] or unpleasant [negatively toned]), intensity (the perceived strength of the emotion), and direction (whether the emotion is experienced as facilitative or debilitative to performance) (Hanin, 2000). In a recent study, 61 athletes from various sports were asked to reflect back on a stressful event experienced in the 2000 Olympic Games and indicate the intensity and direction of their emotions (Pensgaard and Duda, 2003). The results revealed that the athletes experienced a high range of intense facilitative emotions and fewer, less intense debilitative emotions.

The current study was conducted to learn about the emotions that elite level soccer players experience during their performances in a major international tournament penalty shootout. The objective was to identify the emotions that players experience, as well as the intensity and direction of these emotions. Given that no empirical studies have been conducted on emotions in penalty shootouts, these descriptive data were expected to give researchers and practitioners some fundamental information upon which future studies and interventions can be based.

Methods

Participants

The 10 participants of the study were all involved in the penalty shootout in the quarter-final match between Sweden and Netherlands in the 2004 European Championship tournament. The sample included successful and unsuccessful shooters as well as goalkeepers. Because the data in this study are potentially sensitive and all participants are well known in the international soccer community, no further information about the participants' demographics (or the outcomes of their shots) that could reveal their identities, is disclosed.

Procedures

Personal acquaintances were used to get access to the participants. At the time of the data collection, the participants played in five different European countries. Thus, the interviewers travelled to the players' respective clubs where the interviews were conducted in the club house cafeteria or in a press room. The first and the second author conducted the interviews in Swedish and Dutch, respectively. Three pilot interviews were conducted with both interviewers present.

The interviews took place between 8 and 12 months after the shootout. To facilitate memory, at the start of the interview, the participants were shown a video of the event. This stimulated-recall method has been used successfully in other studies of competitive emotions (e.g., Eubank and Collins, 2000).

Measurements

The participants were asked to rate the personal importance of the event on a 0 to 10 point scale (0 indicating not important and 10 indicating very important). In addition, to obtain a simple measure of perceived stress, the participants were asked to think back to the series of kicks from the penalty mark and indicate the level of stress they experienced on a scale from 0 to 10 (0 indicating not stressful and 10 indicating the most stressful experience in my life so far) (question and format obtained from Pensgaard and Duda, 2003).

Following guidelines by Hanin (2000), the participants were then provided with a list of 24 emotions, which included 14 positively toned (enthusiastic, determined, certain, ready, relaxed, optimistic, happy, safe, energetic, easygoing, charged, excited, attacking, and motivated) and 10 negatively toned emotions (tired, anxious, pessimistic, tense, dissatisfied, angry, afraid, unwilling, uncertain, and nervous). These emotions were selected because they have been most commonly identified in previous studies of elite athletes (e.g., Hanin, 2000; Pensgaard and Duda, 2003). The participants were asked to think back to the kicks from the penalty mark and identify from the list the emotions that they experienced. They then indicated the intensity of each emotion, using a Borg-like scale (Hanin, 2000), with categories: 0 = nothing, 0.5 = very, very little, 1 = very little, 2 = little, 3 = moderate, 5 = much, 7 = very much, 10 = very, very much, and * (later coded as 11) = maximum. Finally, they were asked to indicate whether each emotion was experienced as helpful (facilitative) or harmful (debilitative) to performance.

Results

Perceived importance and stress

The personal importance of the event was assessed very high on a 0 to 10 point scale. All participants, except one, rated the event importance at the maximum 10 ($M = 9.8$, $SD = 0.7$). When asked to rate the level of stress experienced during the series of kicks from the penalty mark on a scale from 0 to 10, the mean score among the participants was medium high: 6.25 ($SD = 2.5$, ranking from 2 to 10).

Emotions

The participants indicated experiencing a range of emotions, both positively and negatively toned (Figure 71.1). The negatively toned emotion 'anxious' was most common, identified by all ten players. Thereafter followed a group of positively toned emotions: first 'determined', (eight players), then 'motivated', 'certain',

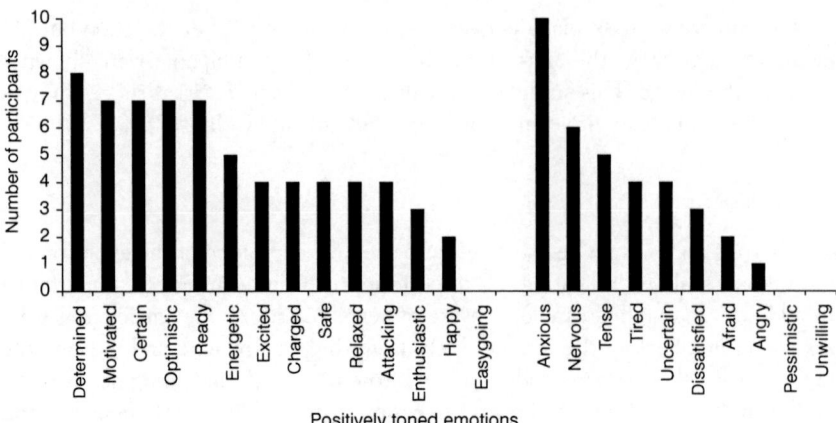

Figure 71.1 The number of participants identifying positively toned and negatively toned emotions in their experiences of participating in the penalty shootout

'optimistic' and 'ready', (seven players). Three emotions: 'easygoing', 'pessimistic' and 'unwilling' were not identified by any of the players.

The participants reported experiencing both positively and negatively toned emotions as facilitative and debilitative (Table 71.1). With regard to positively toned emotions, the most intense facilitative emotions were 'happy', 'motivated', and 'enthusiastic'. The most intense debilitative emotion was 'charged'. Regarding negatively toned emotions, the most intense facilitative emotions were 'anxious', 'tense' and 'nervous', whereas the most intense debilitative emotions were 'tense', 'angry', and 'tired'. Some emotions were either only facilitative (e.g., motivated, certain, and determined) or only debilitative (i.e., angry), while other emotions 'overlapped' and could be facilitative for some participants and debilitative for others (e.g., charged, safe, anxious, and tense).

The mean intensity of the positively toned emotions ($M = 7.5$, $SD = 2.1$) was higher than that of the negatively toned emotions ($M = 5.8$, $SD = 2.3$) (effect size $= 0.36$, $d = 0.77$). The mean intensity of the facilitative emotions ($M = 7.1$, $SD = 2.4$) was higher than that of the debilitative emotions ($M = 5.7$, $SD = 2.1$) (effect size $= 0.30$, $d = 0.62$). Cohen (1988) suggested that effect sizes around 0.20 are small, around 0.50 are moderate, and around 0.80 are large. Nonetheless, half of the participants reported experiencing four or more negatively toned emotions and eight of the ten participants rated the intensity on one or more of their negatively toned emotions to at least 'very much' (7 on the Borg-like scale). Similarly, seven of the participants reported debilitative emotions and five participants rated the intensity on one or more debilitative emotions to 'very much' or more.

Discussion

The participants in this study all took part in a penalty shootout at the highest possible level of international soccer. Importance ratings demonstrated that they

Table 71.1 The number, mean intensity and standard deviation of positively toned, negatively toned facilitative, and debilitative emotions experienced by the participants in the penalty shootout

Positively toned emotions				Negatively toned emotions			
Facilitative emotions				*Facilitative emotions*			
	N	M	SD		N	M	SD
Determined	8	7.4	1.8	Anxious	8	7.0	2.0
Motivated	7	9.6	1.3	Nervous	4	6.0	2.7
Optimistic	7	7.6	1.7	Tense	3	6.7	1.2
Certain	7	7.6	1.6	Tired	2	3.5	2.1
Ready	6	8.0	1.7	Dissatisfied	1	4.0	–
Energetic	4	7.8	2.6	Afraid	1	3.0	–
Relaxed	4	5.8	2.9	Uncertain	1	3.0	–
Attacking	4	4.2	2.4				
Enthusiastic	3	9.0	2.0				
Excited	3	7.7	2.1				
Safe	3	7.7	2.1				
Charged	3	7.0	2.6				
Happy	2	10.0	0				
Debilitative emotions				*Debilitative emotions*			
	N	M	SD		N	M	SD
Charged	1	9.0	–	Uncertain	3	5.3	3.1
Safe	1	5.0	–	Tense	2	9.0	0.0
Excited	1	4.0	–	Tired	2	7.0	0.0
Ready	1	4.0	–	Nervous	2	5.0	1.4
Energetic	1	4.0	–	Anxious	2	4.5	2.1
				Dissatisfied	2	3.8	0.4
				Angry	1	8.0	–
				Afraid	1	5.0	–

viewed the event as very important. This may precipitate 'choking' (Baumeister, 1984). Not all of the participants viewed the event as stressful though, which suggests variability in the response to the pressure of the penalty shootout.

The emotion results show that the participants experienced more positively toned than negatively toned emotions and that most emotions were interpreted as facilitative, rather than debilitative, to their performance. This finding is consistent with previous studies of elite level athletes (e.g., Jones *et al.*, 1994; Pensgaard and Duda, 2003). However, the intensities of the negatively toned emotions were rated relatively high and all emotion intensities were noticeably higher than the emotion intensities reported for athletes reflecting back on their most stressful experience in the Sydney Olympics (Pensgaard and Duda, 2003). This indicates that kicks from the penalty mark may trigger intense and potentially stressful experiences.

Despite the dominance of positively toned emotions, negatively toned and debilitative emotions were present for most of the players during the kicks and a negatively toned emotion, anxiety, was the only emotion experienced by all ten participants. Thus, although the case has been made for targeting emotions other than anxiety in sport psychology research (Hanin, 2000), our results back up the principal role of anxiety in situations with high competitive pressure. Given previously published evidence for the link between competitive pressure and penalty shootout outcomes (Jordet *et al.*, 2007), the present results highlight the importance of coping with anxiety to achieve success from the penalty mark.

In sum, performing well in the penalty shootout is very important to players and implies some degree of stress. Although the participants in this study experienced more positively than negatively toned emotions, anxiety was the only emotion experienced by all participants. This finding indicates the importance of coping with anxiety to achieve success at the penalty mark.

References

Baumeister, R.F., 1984, Choking under pressure: Self-consciousness and paradoxical effects of incentives on skilful performance. *Journal of Personality and Social Psychology*, 46, 610–20.

Cohen, J., 1988., *Statistical Power Analysis for the Behavioural Sciences*. (Hillsdale, NJ: Lawrence Erlbaum Associates).

Eubank, M. and Collins, D., 2000, Coping with pre- and in-event fluctuations in competitive state anxiety: A longitudinal approach. *Journal of Sports Sciences*, 18, 121–31.

Hanin, Y.L., 2000, Individual zones of optimal functioning (IZOF) model. In *Emotions in Sport*, edited by Hanin, Y.L. (Champaign, IL: Human Kinetics).

Jones, G., Hanton, S. and Swain, A.B.J., 1994, Intensity and interpretation of anxiety symptoms in elite and non-elite sports performers. *Personality and Individual Differences*, 17, 657–63.

Jordet, G., Hartman, E., Visscher, C. and Lemmink, K.A.P.M., 2007, Kicks from the penalty mark in soccer: The roles of stress, skill, and fatigue for kick outcomes. *Journal of Sports Sciences*, 25, 121–29.

Lazarus, R.S., 2000, How emotions influence performance in competitive sports. *The Sport Psychologist*, 14, 229–52.

Mellalieu, S. D., Hanton, S. and Fletcher, D., 2006, A competitive anxiety review: Recent directions in sport psychology research. In *Literature Reviews in Sport Psychology*, edited by Hanton, S. and Mellalieu, S.D. (Hauppauge, NY: Nova Science).

Owen, M. 2004, *Off the Record: My Autobiography*, (London: CollinsWillow).

Pensgaard, A.M., and Duda, J.L., 2003, Sydney 2000: The interplay between emotions, coping, and the performance of Olympic-level athletes. *The Sport Psychologist*, 17, 253–67.

72 System of tests used for assessing coordination abilities of soccer players

Mikhail Shestakov,[1] Andrey Talalaev,[2] Anna Zubkova,[1] Sergey Sarsania,[1] Andrey Leksakov[1]

[1]Russian State University of Physical Education, Russia; [2]Russian Football Union, Russia

Introduction

The problem of developing coordination abilities is one of the least investigated aspects of sport training and one of the most 'undervalued' tasks (Hirtz, 1995). For some time, more and more specialists in the field of sport training have recognized the existence of this problem and tried to discern proper functions of coordination training within the training of technique. Many experts emphasize the necessity to determine separate roles, tasks and content of coordination training in the systematic training of athletes in various sports (Hirtz, 1995; Ljach, 1995). In this context, assessment of coordination abilities of athletes, determination of general rules and simulation of processes underlying this phenomenon, emerge as key problems of coordination training. In recent times few research projects have been conducted to determine the main and significant coordination abilities of participants in different sports. Consensus of experts and experimental data are still lacking. More than twenty versatile complex sets of coordination abilities of general, special and specific character have been distinguished (Sadowki, 2003).

The aim of the present study was to develop and validate experimentally a system of tests used for assessing coordination abilities in soccer players.

Methods

Fifty-four soccer players of the national Russian teams in three age groups (15, 16, and 18 years) and 40 players of two Premier League club teams of the Russian Championship took part in the research. The examination of the players took place during preparatory team gatherings prior to official games of the European championship in the corresponding age group.

The assessment of coordination abilities consisted of assessing the movement control system using instrumental methods with a biomechanical unit 'Stabilan-01' – a computer stability-analyzer with biological feedback. The frequency range of oscillation of the human body's centre of pressure in sagittal and frontal planes was 0–25 Hz; measurement increments were 0.03±4 mm for the oscillation range and 0.25±32 mm for the oscillation range for the two planes.

Diagnosis of motor-coordination disturbances by means of biological feedback consists of assessing deviations from optimal execution of motor actions. The use of biological feedback improves diagnostic efficacy of testing and offers scope for professional selection of athletes in sports with high demands for motor-coordination functions.

The methods used in computer-based stabilographic studies consist of assessment of biomechanical parameters of a human performing voluntary movements and maintaining vertical posture in the standing position. Keeping balance is a dynamic phenomenon manifested by incessant motion of the body that results from interaction of vestibular and visual sensors, muscular and joint proprioceptors, and higher segments of the CNS. Evidently, the character of this motion largely depends on the psycho-emotional state of a person and the condition of his/her musculoskeletal system.

The coordination of mechanisms responsible for body equilibrium occurs at different levels of the nervous system: in the spinal cord, cerebellum, and cerebral cortex, information from visual analyzers, proprioceptors and vestibular analyzers is processed. Therefore, the use of this approach permits the study of those features of the movement control system operating in athletes, which has hardly been examined in the past. It is apparent that such data are necessary to effect improvements in athletes' technique.

The test procedure included a set of motor tasks performed by subjects one by one on a stabilographic platform in a standing position. The following indices were measured:

1   Lateral asymmetry: revealing the leading cerebral hemisphere in a person and defines a lateral type of psychic activity; in soccer it permits detection of a potential play-maker.
2   Evolvent: quality of a tracking movement: results demonstrated in this test permit estimation of the athlete's capability to make motor decisions in response to an external command signal.
3   Steps: state of the system of motor control programs: the test shows the reaction of a person to gradually increased stimulation; characteristics of the transitional phase permit prediction of probable behaviour of a person in extreme conditions.
4   Triangle: state of short-term motor memory: the test permits estimation of the ability of an individual for precise repetition of a memorized motor action.

The test procedure took 5–6 minutes. All the tests comprise an integral system used for assessment of the state of the movement control system.

We analyzed stabilographic parameters related to the deviation of the centre of pressure of a subject. The test 'Steps' assessed the precision of a single ballistic movement; the test 'Triangle' showed the precision of reproducing a spatial figure recalled from memory; the test 'Evolvent' revealed the mean error of the centre of pressure deviation from the preset model in sagittal and frontal planes.

Results and discussion

Examination of motor asymmetry revealed that every youth soccer team included 1–4 players with pronounced right-side asymmetry, who play in central positions in defence and half-back lines. These data are consistent with practical experience of coaches engaged in selection of players for the national teams. They also corroborate the hypothesis implicit in the following dichotomy according to the character of stimulus: analytical strategy of recognition of faces and complex forms – the left hemisphere; immediate perception of complex configurations using the strategy of gestalt (integral image) – the right hemisphere (Zaidel and Sperry, 1973; Nebes, 1978).

Table 72.1 displays data registered in 15-, 16-, and 18-year-old soccer players divided into three groups: forwards, backs and half-backs.

In the test 'Steps' forwards and backs/half-backs demonstrated a statistically significant difference in precision of the motor task ($142.9 \pm 23.5\%$ vs. $149.8 \pm 19.5\%/156.6 \pm 22.5\%$, $P<0.05$). Half-backs, acting mainly in the centre of the field, revealed better and faster motor adaptation to alteration of game situations, than forwards and backs. Best results in prediction of unexpectedly developing situations (test 'Evolvent') were observed in the group of backs (8.5 ± 1.9 mm, $P<0.05$). Generally speaking, these data correspond to different requirements to be met by different positional roles in the game. When counteracting forwards, backs must recognize their displacements as quickly as possible. Half-backs, who execute the greatest amount of motor work in the game, must solve the task of strategic organization of the game among their team and at the same time disrupt the strategy of the opposition. Higher precision of movements demonstrated by forwards must have been due to a greater amount of training aimed at realization of precise shots at goal and finding the most precise position in the opponents scoring-area during team attacks.

Data presented in Table 72.2 reflect the dynamics of stabiligraphic indices with age. There was a difference ($P<0.05$) between players of different ages in performance of the test 'Triangle' (15 years: 15014 ± 492 mm^2, 16 years: 14363 ± 442 mm^2, 18 years: 12321 ± 294 mm^2) that is closely connected with space orientation and quickness of motor learning. The difference is evident ($P<0.05$) between the group of 18-year-old soccer players (Steps: $150.1 \pm 30.2\%$;

Table 72.1 Stabilographic parameters registered in soccer players

	Forwards n = 13	Half-backs n = 15	Backs n = 17
Steps (SprA), %	142.9 ± 23.5*,**	149.8 ± 19.5*	156.6 ± 22.5**
Triangle (SqrAn), mm^2	13955 ± 460	11485 ± 335***	14248 ± 464***
Evolvent (MidErrX), mm	11.0 ± 3.54**	10.5 ± 2.86***	8.5 ± 1.9***,**

Statistically significant difference ($P<0.05$): * forwards vs. halfbacks, ** forwards vs. backs, *** halfbacks vs. backs.

Table 72.2 Stabiligraphic parameters registered in soccer players of different ages

	15 years n = 18	16 years n = 18	18 years n = 18	Adults n = 40
Steps (SprA), %	150.6 ± 32.8	144.9 ± 20.8	150.1 ± 30.2 ^	138.2 ± 19.1 ^
Triangle (SqrAn), mm²	15014 ± 492 ***	14363 ± 442 **	12321 ± 294 ***,**	1147 ± 2876
Evolvent (MidErrX), mm	10.2 ± 2.5 ***	10.4 ± 2.5 **	8.8 ± 2.0 ***, **, ^	6.8 ± 2.3 ^

Statistically significant difference ($P<0.05$): * 15-year-old vs. 16-year-old players, ** 16-year-old vs. 18-year-old players, *** -15-year-old vs. 18-year-old players, ^ 18-year-old vs. adult players.

Evolvent: 8.8 ± 2.0 mm) and adult members of club teams playing in the Russian Premier League (Steps: $138.2 \pm 19.1\%$; Evolvent: 6.8 ± 2.3 mm). It shows that the higher qualification of the adult players is determined by highly developed precision of movement control and the ability for quick and accurate prediction of developing situations that reflect their rich game experience.

To assess motor abilities and adroitness of an athlete, deviation is estimated from the optimal way of executing voluntary movements in standard tasks. It considerably increases the efficacy of tests used for controlling athletes' condition in game sports, including soccer, which demand a high level of coordination abilities.

Movements with complex coordination can be executed efficiently only in case of correspondence between a motor programme and functional capacities of muscles and vegetative organs providing muscular work. From this point of view, the main feature of movements performed in game sports is that quick motor actions must be done in conditions of limited time for decision-making. The most important role in such activity belongs to the integrative function of the central nervous system (CNS) and important functions of the autonomic nervous system, which maintains homeostasis and provides various forms of psychic and physical activity.

The analysis of movement control systems in an athlete helps to determine general and individual features of the factors, on which successful execution of technical elements of the game depends.

Conclusion

A system of tests has been elaborated for estimating coordination abilities of soccer players. The analysis of movement control systems and specific preparedness of athletes permits the determination of general and individual peculiarities of their condition at the moment of testing. It also provides recommendations concerning corrections to be made in technical and tactical training plans. The comparative analysis of the experimental data revealed specific characteristics of soccer players related to their age and to their roles in the game.

A new system of tests is put forward in order to assess coordination abilities of soccer players. These tests have prognostic value for selection of soccer players and determination of their roles, as well as for assessment of the current degree of coordination abilities according to their roles in the game.

References

Hirtz P., 1995, Koordinationstraining gleich Techniktraining?. In: *Sportliche Leistung und Training*, Sankt Augustin: Academia).

Ljach, W., 1995, Metrological basis of the control of coordination of athletes in team sports. *Movement Coordination in Team Sport Games and Martial Arts*, International Scientific Conference, IWFiS, Biala Podlaska, pp. 81–8.

Nebes, R.D., 1978, Direct examination of cognitive function in the right and left hemispheres. In: *Asymmetrical Function of the Brain*, edited by Kinsbourne, M. (Cambridge: Cambridge University Press).

Sadowki. J., 1999, Coordinative training of highly qualified taekwon-do athletes. In *Proceedings of the 3rd International Scientific Congress on Modern Olympic Sport*, Vol. 3, Suppl. 1.

Zaidel, D. and Sperry R.W., 1973, Performance on the Raven's colored progressive matrices test by subjects with cerebral comissurotomy. *Cortex*, 9, 34 –9.

73 Sleep, pre-game fatigue, and game performance in female college soccer players

Vanessa Martinez and Edward Coyle

Human Performance Laboratory, The University of Texas at Austin, USA

Introduction

Soccer is a demanding sport that requires both mental and physical readiness for optimal performance (Barbour, 1993; Beswick, 2000). Sleep is important for maintaining one's mental and physical well-being because it has two important functions: these are memory consolidation and learning, and body restoration and regeneration (Savis, 1994; Walters, 2002). Thus, sleep may influence players' feelings of mental and physical fatigue before a match, and indirectly affect game outcome and performance. For this reason, the purpose of this study was to investigate the relationships between sleep duration the night before a match; pre-game perceived levels of head alertness (HA, indirect and subjective measure of mental fatigue) and leg quickness (LQ, indirect and subjective measure of physical fatigue); game outcome and six game performance variables (GPV) during the competitive season of an American Division I collegiate women's soccer team.

Methods

The participants were 21 female college soccer players (age 20.3 ± 1.4 years; height 1.69 ± 0.04 m; body mass 64.32 ± 6.18 kg). Sleep duration and pre-game perceived levels of HA (mental fatigue; scale of 1: very dull to 5: very sharp) and LQ (physical fatigue; scale of 1: very slow to 5: very quick) were recorded before 21 games out of 24 total season games. Table 73.1 displays the complete HA and LQ scales used in this study.

The collection of sleep duration, HA, and LQ data before each game usually took less than 5 minutes. Players were trained to tell the investigators three numbers: sleep duration (i.e. 7 hours), HA (i.e. 4), and LQ (i.e. 4) either verbally or non-verbally (showing the numbers with their fingers) after their warm-up routine. We chose to collect these data after the warm-up to allow players to assess their mental and physical fatigue before the game more accurately. The game outcome and six GPV (goals difference (GD), assists difference (AD), points difference (PD), shots difference (SD), shots on goal difference (SGD), and corners difference (CD) between the team and each opponent) were obtained and calculated from the team's statistics archives. A Pearson correlation analysis

Table 73.1 Head alertness and leg quickness scales

Head alertness		Leg quickness	
5	Very sharp	5	Very quick
4	Sharp	4	Quick
3	OK	3	OK
2	Dull	2	Slow
1	Very dull	1	Very slow

was used to investigate the relationships among all variables. Descriptive statistics are presented as means ± SD.

Results

Descriptive statistics of the variables were as follows: sleep duration (8.99 ± 0.62 hours); HA (3.98 ± 0.22); LQ (3.79 ± 0.25); game outcome (14–5–2); and the six GPV were: GD (1.10 ± 2.40); AD (1.57 ± 2.90); PD (3.76 ± 7.56); SD (8.10 ± 11.18); SGD (3.48 ± 5.37); CD (2.38 ± 4.26).

A Pearson correlation analysis revealed a significant positive relationship between sleep duration and HA; a significant negative relationship between sleep duration and game outcome, and sleep duration and all six GPVs; and no correlation between sleep duration and LQ. Head alertness was positively related to LQ but negatively related to game outcome and five GPVs. No significant association was found between LQ and game outcome, and LQ and GPV. Specific Pearson correlation coefficients (r) and P values are shown in Table 73.2.

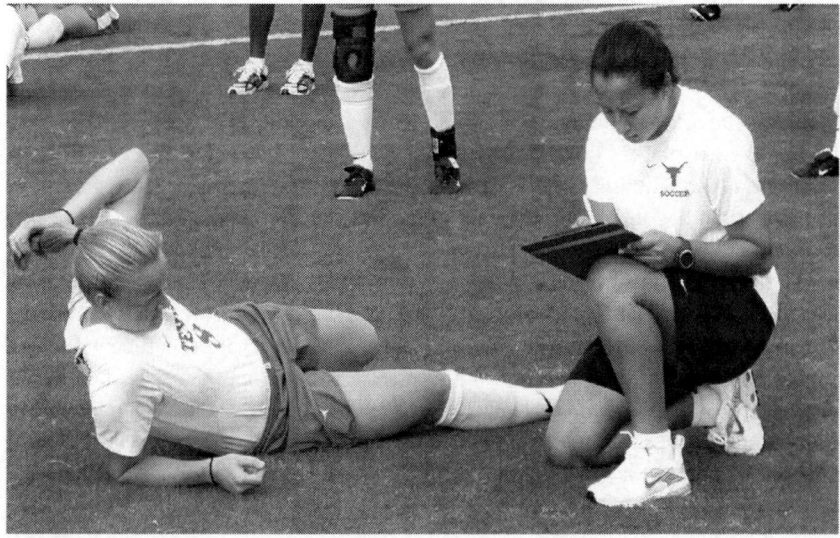

Figure 73.1 Collection of data for players' sleep duration and perceived levels of head alertness and leg quickness before a game

Table 73.2 Results of the correlation analysis

Variable	r	P
Sleep duration		
Head alertness	0.488*	0.025
Game outcome	–0.508*	0.019
Game performance variables		
Goals difference	–0.576**	0.006
Assists difference	–0.605**	0.004
Points difference	–0.599**	0.004
Shots difference	–0.500*	0.021
Shots on goal difference	–0.506*	0.019
Corners difference	–0.543*	0.011
Head alertness		
Leg quickness	0.787**	0.001
Game outcome	–0.457*	0.037
Game performance variables		
Goals difference	–0.464*	0.034
Assists difference	–0.466*	0.033
Points difference	–0.475*	0.030
Shots on goal difference	–0.434*	0.049
Corners difference	–0.504*	0.020

* Correlation significant at the 0.05 level (2–tailed); **. correlation significant at the 0.01 level (2–tailed); $N = 21$ games.

Discussion

The significant positive correlation between sleep duration and HA, and the non-significant correlation between sleep duration and LQ are in agreement with previous reports, which support the view that sleep deprivation impairs cognitive ability, whereas physical ability shows little degradation (Reilly and Deykin, 1983; Myles, 1985; VanHelder and Radomski, 1989; Savis, 1994; Youngstedt and O'Connor, 1999; Walters, 2002; Reilly, 2003). Soccer is a sport that requires constant decision making, and thus, game outcome and performance may be impaired if players have a diminished cognitive ability due to lack of sleep. Additionally, adequate sleep is one of the important recovery strategies post-exercise that become influential in preparing for the next match (Reilly and Ekblom, 2005).

The relationships between sleep duration and game outcome, sleep duration and GPV, HA and game outcome, and HA and GPV were statistically correlated but in an opposite direction to that expected. This observation can be explained by the fact that most of the team's losses were against opponents ranked in the American top 25 women's collegiate teams ($r = –0.567$, $P < 0.01$). The team lost four games out of six in which they faced a top 25 ranked opponent. Thus, facing elite teams and not lack of sleep or head alertness was the cause of these losses.

Conclusion

Sleep is not the only factor that influences game outcome and performance. Thus, it is possible to perform poorly even when players get adequate sleep. However, sleep is usually a controllable factor, and therefore players should strive to get adequate amounts of sleep (8–10 hours) before competition. Soccer coaches and trainers can easily monitor players' sleep, and perceived levels of mental and physical fatigue before a match using the scales and data collection procedure we employed in this study. This information will be useful not only to ensure that players are getting sufficient sleep but also to identify and modify other possible variables that might be affecting the mental and physical state of players before competition (i.e. overtraining, poor nutrition and hydration, travelling, anxiety, etc), and ultimately, give players a competitive edge.

Acknowledgements

The authors wish to thank the coaching staff and players of the 2004 University of Texas Women's Soccer Team for their participation. This study was supported by a student grant from the Gatorade Sports Science Institute.

References

Barbour, S. A., 1993, Developing physical and mental readiness. *Soccer Journal*, 38(2), 27–30.

Beswick, B., 2000, The complete player: mental and emotional readiness is needed along with the physical skill. *Soccer Journal*, 45(2), 33–5.

Myles, W. S., 1985, Sleep deprivation, physical fatigue, and the perception of exercise intensity. *Medicine and Science in Sports and Exercise*, 17, 580–4.

Reilly, T., 2003, Environmental stress. In *Science and Soccer*, 2nd edn, edited by Reilly, T. and Williams, A.M. (London: Routledge).

Reilly, T. and Deykin, T., 1983, Effects of partial sleep loss on subjective states, psychomotor and physical performance tests. *Journal of Human Movement Studies*, 9, 157–70.

Reilly, T. and Ekblom, B., 2005, The use of recovery methods post-exercise. *Journal of Sports Sciences*, 23, 619–27.

Savis, J. C., 1994, Sleep and athletic performance: overview and implications for sport psychology. *Sport Psychologist*, 8 (2), 111–25.

VanHelder, T. and Radomski, M. W., 1989, Sleep deprivation and the effect on exercise performance. *Sports Medicine*, 7, 235–47.

Walters, P. H., 2002, Sleep, the athlete, and performance. *Strength and Conditioning Journal*, 24, 17–24.

Youngstedt, S. D. and O'Connor, P. J., 1999, The influence of air travel on athletic performance. *Sports Medicine*, 28, 197–207.

74 Sport motivation and self-efficacy in American football players

Müge Çelik Örücü[1] and Selin Metin Camgöz[2]

[1]Middle East Technical University, Turkey; [2]Hacettepe University Department of Business Administration, Turkey

Introduction

The concept of motivation, cited as the reason for behaviour, has received much attention over the past three decades. It is difficult to imagine anything more important than motivation for success in sport. Motivation concerns energy, direction and persistence (Ryan and Deci, 2000). Perhaps more important, in the real world, motivation is highly valued because of its consequences. Without motivation even the most talented athlete is unlikely to reach his or her full potential. Therefore motivation is also pertinent to how the athlete experiences and responds to sport (Duda and Treasure, 2006).

Within an educational and sport context, researchers have also viewed motivation from a multidimensional perspective as containing intrinsic, extrinsic and amotivational factors. Motivation, especially intrinsic motivation, is the foundation of sport performance and achievement. Vallerand and Losier (1999) proposed that intrinsic motivation (IM) which refers to doing an activity for the inherent satisfaction of the activity itself, and extrinsic motivation (EM) referring to the performance of an activity in order to attain some separable outcome, have three dimensions such as: IM to know, IM toward accomplishment, IM to experience stimulation; and for EM, external regulation, introjection and identification.

In the present study, Bandura's self-efficacy which is a critical component of social cognitive theory was considered for understanding and investigating the aforementioned motivational issues. Self-efficacy is a contextual-related judgment of personal ability to organize and execute a course of action in order to attain designated levels of performance (Bandura, 1982; Bandura, 1986; Bandura, 1995). For example, if an athlete perceives or believes that he or she can influence the outcome of a contest for good, she/he will eagerly enter into the competition.

Despite the documented importance of self-efficacy in various areas, limited attention has been paid to the role of self-efficacy in a sport context. In general self-efficacy is conceived as a positive predictor of motor skill acquisition, execution, and competitive sport performance (Bandura, 1997). Moreover, research addressing sport motivation, self-determination, adherence and self-efficacy has involved North American athletes in most cases. However, psychology applied in sport has become the main focus of research for only two decades in Turkey. American football is a relatively new area for research since its arrival in Turkey can be traced back to the early 1990s. The sport has not been played nationwide, but there are 12 university teams. As it is a new sport for Turkey, not many studies have been conducted. One study of the goal orientation and motivational climate of American football players showed that American football players were more task oriented and perceived motivational climate as mastery oriented (Arıburun and Aşçı, 2005).

Due to the inadequacy of the research concerning American football in Turkey, the aim of this study was to investigate the relationship between sport motivation and generalized self-efficacy in American football players. In particular the following research questions were addressed:

1   To what extent does self-efficacy predict total intrinsic motivation for sports?
2   To what extent does self-efficacy predict total extrinsic motivation for sports?
3   What is the relation between self-efficacy and amotivation?

Methods

Participants

The sample consisted of a convenience sample of American football team players from two universities. One university sample contained 33 players out of 35 and the other university sample contained 27 players out of 44. The final sample size was 60 with a response rate of 81 per cent. The mean age of the study sample was 21.7 years.

Measurement instrument

The measurement instrument was composed of three parts. In the first part, sport motivation of the players is assessed by using the Sport Motivation Scale developed by Pelletier *et al.* (1995). The Turkish adaptation and validation of the scale were carried out by Kazak-Çetinkaya (2004). The scale contains 28 items including 6 sub-scales of sport motivation; intrinsic motivation to know, to experience stimulation, introjection, identification, external regulation and amotivation. For intrinsic motivation, the total scores of respondents were obtained by adding up the scores given to each item of intrinsic motivation to know, for accomplishment and experience stimulation subscales. For extrinsic motivation; the total scores of respondents were obtained by adding up the scores given to each of the items; introjection, identification and external regulation subscales. A Likert-type scale enables the respondents to evaluate each item by providing five alternatives, scoring from 1 (strongly disagree) to 5 (strongly agree). The higher scores were accepted as highly motivated.

The second part of the measurement instrument, the General Perceived Self-efficacy Scale was developed by Schwarzer and Jerusalem (1993), revised in 2000. This instrument has been used in numerous research projects, where it has typically yielded high internal consistencies in several languages including Turkish and English. The Turkish adaptation and validation of the same instrument were carried out by Yesilay, Schwarzer and Jerusalem (1996). It is a 10-item scale with response format ranging from not at all true (1) to exactly true (4).

In the last part of the survey, some demographic variables including age, university, position, etc. were requested.

Results

The data were analyzed utilizing the SPSS program. Prior to analysis, the data were screened for normality, linearity and homogeneity of variance assumptions. Table 74.1 illustrates the intercorrelations among study variables, the reliability coefficients and the descriptive statistics of the scales. The reliability coefficients of the scales and subscales yielded high internal reliability coefficients (in a range between 0.64 and 0.86) consistent with the original scales.

As shown in Table 74.1, American football players use mostly *intrinsic motivation to experience stimulation* ($x = 5.52$), followed by *introjection* ($x = 5.50$) and lastly *external regulation* ($x = 3.37$) for motivating themselves. Moreover, self-efficacy was positively correlated with intrinsic motivation ($r = 0.33$, $P<0.001$) as well as its subscales of intrinsic motivation to know ($r = 0.29$, $P<0.05$) and intrinsic motivation to experience stimulation ($r = 0.33$, $P<0.001$).

To test the first hypothesis identifying the role of self-efficacy in total intrinsic sport motivation, regression analysis was conducted. Linear regression analysis was carried out by taking the total intrinsic motivation as dependent variable, with self-efficacy as the independent variable (Table 74.2).

The result ($R^2 = 0.13$, $P<0.00$], indicates that self-efficacy is a significant predictor of total intrinsic sport motivation. The beta coefficient of self-efficacy was found to be significant ($\beta = 0.33$, $P<0.05$), indicating a direct and positive relationship between total intrinsic sport motivation and generalized self-efficacy of athletes.

To test the second hypothesis identifying the role of self-efficacy in total extrinsic sport motivation, regression analysis was conducted. The regression model was not significant ($F_{1,59} = 2.24$, $P = 0.139$), meaning that self-efficacy did not account for total extrinsic sport motivation variability.

To explore the relation between self-efficacy and amotivation, linear regression analysis was conducted. The result of the regression analysis was not found to be significant ($F_{1,59} = 3.26$, $P = 0.07$).

Table 74.1 Descriptive statistics and intercorrelations among study variables

	Variable	Reliability	Mean	SD	1	2	3	4	5	6	7	8	9
1	Intrinsic motivation to know	0.82	4.65	1.00	–								
2	Intrinsic motivation to experience stimulation	0.72	5.52	0.96	0.60**	–							
3	External regulation	0.72	3.37	1.20	0.53**	00.19	–						
4	Identification	0.67	4.47	1.06	0.49**	00.45**	0.56**	–					
5	Introjection	0.70	5.50	0.97	0.34**	00.30*	0.31*	0.26	–				
6	Amotivation	0.64	1.96	0.97	0.11	–00.06	0.10	–0.01	–0.08	–			
7	Generalized self-efficacy	0.84	3.03	0.47	0.29*	00.33**	0.08	0.05	0.30*	–0.21	–		
8	Total intrinsic motivation	0.86	4.94	0.90	0.96**	00.80**	.046**	0.53**	0.36**	0.06	00.33**	–	
9	Total extrinsic motivation	0.78	4.45	0.84	0.60**	00.40**	0.84**	0.79**	0.64**	0.01	00.18	000.59**	–

Table 74.2 Results of the linear regression analysis for predicting intrinsic sport motivation, extrinsic sport motivation and amotivation

Intrinsic motivation						
Predictor	R^2	*Adj* R^2	F	β	t	P
Self-efficacy	0.14	0.12	8.072**	0.332	2.84	0.001
Extrinsic motivation						
Predictor	R^2	*Adj* R^2	F	β	t	P
Self-efficacy	0.03	0.01	2.240	0.183	1.49	.139
Amotivation						
Predictor	R^2	*Adj* R^2	F	β	t	P
Self-efficacy	0.04	0.03	3.261	-0.219	3.26	0.07

**$P<0.001$

Discussion

In this study we sought to investigate to what extent does self-efficacy predict a) intrinsic sport motivation b) extrinsic sport motivation and c) amotivation.

Concerning the first research question, the results of the regression analysis provide previously unavailable information that self-efficacy made a significant contribution to the prediction of intrinsic sport motivation for American football players in Turkey. Athletes who possess higher amounts of self-efficacy are more likely to choose tasks they can accomplish, work harder, persist longer when they experience difficulties and achieve at a higher level than those with lower levels of self-efficacy (McAuley, 1992). It seems that repeated success raises the individual's efficacy appraisal and also increases motivation. Only when individuals are intrinsically motivated towards an activity is the behaviour considered to be fully self-determined and the person is high in self-efficacy.

No significant relationship was found between extrinsic motivation and self-efficacy. Extrinsic motivation comes in many forms like awards, money and fear of punishment. These kind of motivational factors do not exist for the study's sample of university teams. People, especially non-professional players, readily participate in activities that they perceive to be interesting and unthreatening (Cox, 2007). The other side of the coin is that there is no need for rewards or any sort of external control to motivate an athlete to engage in an intrinsically motivating behaviour (Cox, 2007).

Specifically, amotivation represents the lack of both intrinsic and extrinsic performance of an activity in order to attain some separable outcome motivation and is characterized by the lack of value for an activity (Ryan, 1995) or not feeling competent to do it (Bandura, 1986). When amotivated, people either do not act at all or act without intent: they just go through the motions. This statement concurs with the current finding that there was no relation between self-efficacy and amotivation.

To sum up, the results of the current study suggest that intrinsic motivation toward an activity can be developed by increasing a person's belief in his/her self-efficacy. Therefore by assessing and recognizing low intrinsic motivation in athletes, sport psychologists might be able to design interventions addressing the enhancement of self-efficacy specifically focusing on four determinants like performance accomplishment, vicarious experience, verbal persuasion and physical and emotional arousal (Duda and Treasure, 2006). The next step will be to assess how interventions affect performance outcomes.

References

Arıburun, B. and Aşçı, H. F., 2005, A study of goal orientation and motivational climate in American football, *Spormetre Beden Eğitimi ve Spor Bilimleri Dergisi*, 3 (3), 111–14.

Bandura, A., 1982, Self-efficacy mechanism in human agency. *American Psychologist*, 37, 122–47.

Bandura, A., 1986, *Social Foundations of Thought and Action: A Social Cognitive Theory* (Englewood Cliffs, NJ: Prentice-Hall).

Bandura, A.,1995, *Self-efficacy in Changing Societies.* (Cambridge and New York: Cambridge University Press).

Bandura, A.,1997, *Self-efficacy: The Exercise of Control,* (New York: W.H.Freeman).

Cox, R. H. 2007, *Sport Psychology: Concepts and Applications,* (New York: McGraw-Hill).

Duda, J. L., and Treasure, D.C. 2006, Motivational processes and the facilitation of Performance, persistence, and well-being in sport. In: *Applied Sport Psychology, Personal Growth to Peak Performance* 5th edn, edited by Williams, J.M. (New York: McGraw-Hill).

Kazak-Çetinkaya, F. Z., 2004, "Sporda Güdülenme Ölçeği – SGÖ" nin Türk sporcularıiçin güvenirlik ve geçerlik çalışması" (A study on reliability and validity of "The Sport Motivation Scale – SMS" for Turkish athletes). *Hacettepe Journal of Sport Sciences*, 15, (4), 191–206.

McAuley, E., 1992, Understanding exercise behavior: A self-efficacy perspective. In *Motivation in Sport and Exercise,* edited by Roberts, G. C. (Champaign IL: Human Kinetics).

Pelletier, L. G., Fortier, M. S., Vallerand, R. J., Tuson, K. M., Brière, N. M. and Blais, M. R..,1995, Toward a new measure of intrinsic motivation, extrinsic motivation, and amotivation in sports: The Sport Motivation Scale (SMS), *Journal of Sport and Exercise Psychology*, 17, 35–53.

Ryan, M. R., 1995, Psychological needs and the facilitation of integrative processes. *Journal of Personality*, 63, 397–427.

Ryan, M. R. and Deci, E. L., 2000, Self-determination theory and the facilitation of intrinsic motivation, social development, and well-being. *American Psychologist*, 55, 68–78.

Schwarzer, R. and Jerusalem, M., 1993, The general self-efficacy scale (GSE), available online at http://userpage.fu-berlin.de/~health/engscal.htm (ccessed 3 November 2006).

Schwarzer, R. and Jerusalem, M., 2000, Generalized self-efficacy scale, available online at http://www.fu-berlin.de/gesund/skalen/procop_engl.htm (accessed 3 November 2006).

Vallerand, R.J. and Losier, G. F., 1999, An integrative analysis of intrinsic and extrinsic motivation in sport. *Journal of Applied Sport Psychology*, 11, 142–69.

Yeşilay, A., Schwarzer, R. and Jerusalem, M., 1996, Turkish adaptation of the general perceived self-efficiacy scale, http://userpage.fu-berlin.de/~health/turk/htm

75 Cognitive styles of elite and non-elite female soccer players

Hiroyuki Horino

School of Sport Sciences, Waseda University, Japan

Introduction

The cognitive capability of soccer players to recognise situations is one of the important factors which determine performance. Using Witkin's 'field dependence–independence theory' (Witkin *et al.*, 1977), studies have investigated the cognitive styles of athletes in sports (Kane, 1972; Drouin *et al.*, 1986; Cano and Marquez, 1995; McMorris, 1997). These dealt with participants in closed- and open-skill-dominated sports. Many suggested that participants who had field dependence could be at an advantage in the open-skilled sports. On the other hand, they also argued that individuals who had field independence could be more suited to closed-skilled sports. While differences of cognitive style were found by some researchers, others indicated no differences between them (Drouin, *et al.*, 1986; Brady, 1995). Thus most researchers into the cognitive styles of athletes and field dependence–independence, argued between closed- and open-skill-dominated sports.

Suda *et al.* (1999) investigated cognitive styles of soccer players according to the level of their performance. They employed several tests to investigate cognitive styles. From the field independence–dependence perspective, they showed that elite soccer players had a tendency to field dependence compared to non-elite players. Raviv and Nable (1988) compared the cognitive styles of elite and non-elite basketball players with a similar procedure. However, there is little research on cognitive styles according to the performance level in the same kind of sport. In particular, there are few investigations into cognitive styles of female soccer players.

The purpose of this study was to investigate cognitive styles of female soccer players. A further aim was to investigate the relation between performance level and cognitive style.

Methods

Subjects

The 78 female soccer players were assigned into four groups according to their performance level and age: national team under 19 years (N-U19; $n = 18$, mean age $= 16.5 \pm 1.20$); national team from all universities (N-Univ; $n = 20$, mean age $= 20.60 \pm 1.96$); general high school team (G-U19; $n = 18$, mean age $= 16.63 \pm 1.22$); and general university team (G-Univ; $n = 22$, mean age $= 20.75 \pm 1.99$).

Materials

After adequate explanation and their agreement, subjects participated in Group Embedded-Figures Test (GEFT) to determine their cognitive styles (Suda *et al.*, 1999).

Results

Table 75.1 shows the scores of GEFT for each group. The GEFT scores were each subjected to a two groups (performance; elite and non-elite) × two groups (age category; U19 and Univ) analysis of variance (ANOVA). The ANOVA showed that the elite players (N-U19 and N-Univ) scored significantly low ($F_{1,74} = 8.88$, $P<0.005$) compared with the non-elite players (G-U19 and G-Univ). The U19 players scored significantly lower than the university players ($F_{1,74} = 6.54$, $P<0.05$). Also younger elite players significantly had the lowest score of all groups (comparison with U19s: $F_{1,74} = 13.39$, $P<0.001$; comparison with elites: ($F_{1,74} = 11.24$, $P<0.005$).

Discussion

The results of this study confirmed that the higher the performance level of female soccer players, the more they had a tendency towards field dependent cognition.

Liu (2003) reported that male wrestlers were found to be significantly more field independent than football players, even though both groups were participating in open-skill-dominated sports. He argued that this result was caused by differences

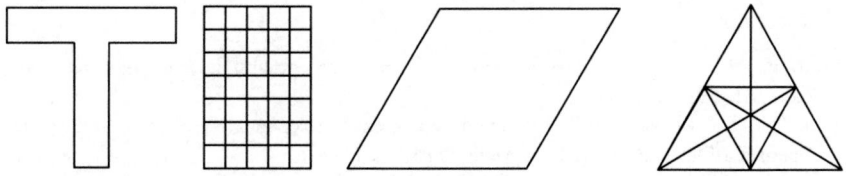

Figure 75.1 Samples of Group Embedded-Figures Test (GEFT); subjects try to find out a left-hand figure out of a right-hand complicated figure

Table 75.1 Mean score of Group Embedded-Figures Test (GEFT)

Group	Score
N-U19	14.44 ± 3.32
N-Univ	17.55 ± 2.65
G-U19	17.83 ± 2.33
G-Univ	18.32 ± 3.01

in athletic situations where the latter were involved in a more 'open' or unstable environment than the former. He also suggested that players and athletes who train and compete in more varied situations have a greater tendency to field dependence. Raviv and Nable (1988) showed that elite basketball players tended to be more field-dependent than other groups. Our data supported their results that elite participants in open-skill-dominated sports tended to be more field dependent.

The difference in the GEFT score between N-U19 and N-Univ may be related to the present situation of women's soccer in Japan. In recent years the performance of Japanese female players has improved rapidly. Therefore, it is considered that, in younger players, the slight difference in age may have induced an improvement in performance level.

Soccer players need to recognize situations that relate to other players and situations surrounding him/her. In order to play at a higher level, a footballer must develop the capability to be adapted to 'more open' situations. Therefore it is thought that the ability to adapt to various surrounding situations is improved as performance level increases.

Our results suggest that improvement in the cognitive capability for various situations enhanced the tendency to field dependence. The results of this study also support the view that GEFT is effective in evaluating the cognitive style of female soccer players.

Conclusion

In this study cognitive styles of female soccer players were investigated according to their performance level and their age category with GEFT. As a result, it was shown that the tendency to field dependence in elite players was higher, especially for players in high school. Moreover, our data suggest that game characteristics could be reflected in cognitive styles of soccer players.

References

Brady, F., 1995, Sports skill classification, gender, and perceptual style. *Perceptual and Motor Skills*, 81, 611–620.

Cano, J.E. and Marquez, S., 1995, Field dependence–independence of male and female Spanish athletes. *Perceptual and Motor Skills*, 80, 1155–61.

Drouin, D., Talbot, S., and Gvoulet, C., 1986, Cognitive styles of French Canadian athletes. *Perceptual and Motor Skills*, 63, 1139–42.

Kane, J. E., 1972, *Psychological Aspects of Physical Education and Sport*. (Oxford: Routledge & Kegan Paul).

Liu, W., 2003, Field dependence-independence and sports with a preponderance of closed or open skill. *Journal of Sport Behavior*, 26, 285–97.

McMorris, T., 1997, Performance of soccer players on tests of field dependence/independence and soccer-specific decision-making tests. *Perceptual and Motor Skills*, 85, 467–76.

Raviv, S. and Nable, N., 1988, Field dependence/independence and concentration as psychological characteristics of basketball players. *Perceptual and Motor Skills*, 66, 831836.

Suda, Y., Watada, H., Takahashi, H. and Tanaka, H., 1999, The relationship between cognitive style of soccer players. *Bulletin of the Institute of Physical Education*, Keio University, 38, 1–9.

Witkin, H.A., Moore, C.A., Goodenough, D.R., and Cox, P.W., 1977, Field-dependent and field-independent cognitive styles and their educational implications. *Review of Educational Research*, 47, 1–64.

76 The effect of memory recall on perceptual-cognitive skill in elite soccer

Development of long-term working memory

James Bell-Walker and A. Mark Williams

Research Institute for Sport and Exercise Science, Liverpool John Moores University, UK

Introduction

The ability to anticipate future action requirements is an important facet of expert performance (Baker *et al.*, 2003). Ward and Williams (2003) reported that tests of perceptual-cognitive skill could discriminate elite and sub-elite soccer players as young as nine years of age, suggesting that even from early development advanced perceptual and cognitive skills are essential requirements for expert performance. Ericsson and Kintsch (1995) proposed the 'long-term working memory' (LT-WM) theory, claiming that expert performers are able to acquire memory skills to accommodate the increased demands of working memory. Participants acquire the skills needed to perform at an advanced level due to the development of domain-specific knowledge structures held in long-term memory that allow rapid access to information via relevant retrieval cues in short-term memory.

Although several researchers have examined expert–novice differences in perceptual-cognitive skill in sport, there have been no attempts to examine recall accuracy for key match events for those with good and not so good perceptual-cognitive skills. Research in the area of recall accuracy in sport is fairly restricted. Franks and Miller (1986) investigated the reliability of eyewitness testimony by assessing the ability of novice coaches to recall key events in international soccer matches. Novice coaches had a recall accuracy of only 42 per cent. However, the low recall accuracy scores would be predicted since they are unlikely to have the domain-specific knowledge needed to develop elaborate LT-WM structures and associated retrieval structures.

The aims in this study were to examine: i) the memory recall accuracy of novice and expert soccer players; ii) the effect of perceptual-cognitive skill on memory recall in expert soccer players.

Methods

Participants

The expert group (n = 48; mean age 17.8 years) comprised of English Youth Academy players. This group was stratified into two sub-groups based on their performance on two tests of perceptual-cognitive skill:

1   Perceptually excellent (n = 12): those performing in the top quartile of all expert participants on the perceptual-cognitive tests (mean age 17.9 years);
2   Perceptually average (n = 12): those performing in the bottom quartile of all expert participants on the perceptual-cognitive tests (mean age 17.4 years).

The novice group (n = 8; mean age 24.3 years) included those who had played the sport at a recreational level only.

Procedure

Expert performers were stratified based on their performance on the perceptual-cognitive tests employed by Ward and Williams (2003). The novice group was also assessed using these tests.

Participants viewed 18 situational probability trails consisting of 11 vs. 11 offensive patterns of play each lasting 10 s. Each sequence was 'frozen' 120 ms prior to the player in possession of the ball making a pass. Participants were then required to rank players in order of their attacking importance. Performance was measured against that of four expert Academy coaches (inter-observer agreement = 94%).

Participants then viewed 24 11 vs. 11 Temporal Occlusion trials. Trials lasted approximately 10 s and consisted of offensive patterns of play from semi-professional matches, with each sequence being occluded 120 ms before the key pass. Participants were required to anticipate the final pass made by the player in possession of the ball. Response accuracy was reported as a percentage.

Altogether, three football matches each involving both the expert and novice players were recorded using a Digital Video Camera (Canon 3CCD Digital Video Camcorder XM2 PAL, 25Hz, Tokyo, Japan). Matches were analysed using Sportcode Pro 6.5.2 (Sportstec International, Sydney, Australia) on an Apple Macintosh PowerBook G4 using predetermined variables relating to individual, team and opposition performance.

Participants completed a Soccer-Specific Memory Recall Questionnaire 48 hours after each of the three matches. They were required to recall information relating to specific events that took place during each match.

Performance measure and analysis

Scores from perceptual-cognitive tests were combined and analysed using a between-participants (Novice vs. Perceptually Average vs. Perceptually Excellent) ANOVA. Memory recall was analysed using a Group (Novice vs. Perceptually Average vs. Perceptually Excellent) × Recall Category (Individual vs. Team vs. Opposition) ANOVA.

Results

A significant group effect was observed between novice, perceptually average and perceptually excellent groups on the perceptual-cognitive test scores ($F_{3,12} = 37.62$, $P<0.001$). This result confirms that participants were assigned to the correct groups for subsequent memory recall testing (Figure 76.1).

A significant difference in memory recall accuracy was observed between novice and expert groups ($F_{2,12} = 20.92$, $P<0.05$). Elite players were more accurate in recalling all aspects of match-play (individual, team and opposition events) compared to their lesser skilled counterparts (Figure 76.2). There was no

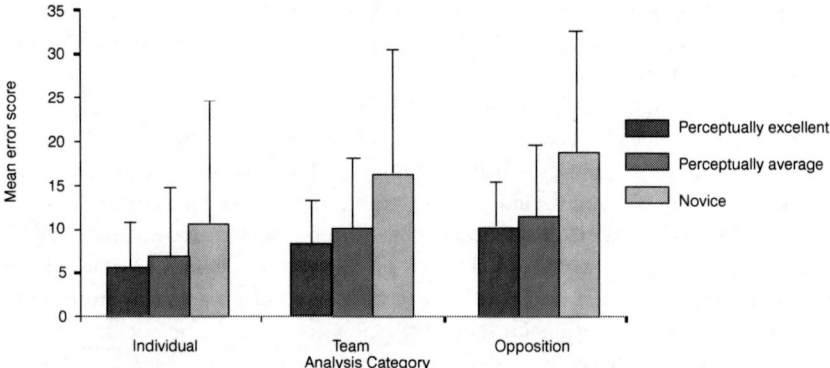

Figure 76.1 Mean group scores for accuracy (%) on perceptual-cognitive tests

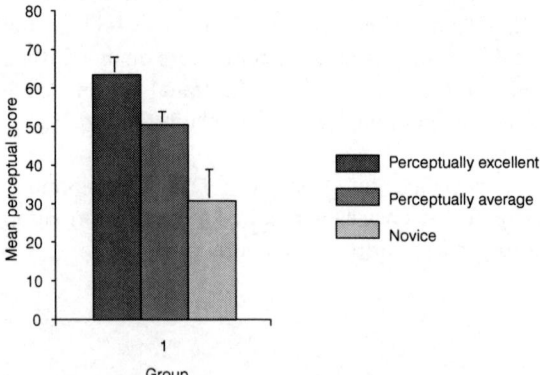

Figure 76.2 Mean memory recall error across groups for individual, team and opposition events

significant difference in recall accuracy between the two groups of expert players stratified based on their performance on the perceptual-cognitive tests.

Significant differences were found between recall categories across all groups ($F_{3,12} = 14.68$, $P < 0.05$). Players were more accurate in recalling events relating to individual performance as opposed to events relating to their team-mates or opponents.

Discussion and conclusions

The expert soccer players demonstrated superior recall accuracy compared with their novice counterparts. As predicted by Ericsson and Kitsch's (1995) LT-WM theory, expert players acquire domain-specific knowledge which positively impacts on their memory encoding and retrieval structures. It would also be logical that performers at all levels would have increased recall accuracy in individual events rather than team and opposition match actions as the LT-WM structures which were developed (or were developing) through domain-specific knowledge, would be based around individual rather than specific events.

There were no differences in memory recall between the two groups of experts, suggesting that other factors may lead to the development of perceptual-cognitive skill in elite players. Alternatively, the test of memory recall may not have been sensitive enough to discriminate between these groups. In future researchers could collect verbal reports after matches to elicit more detailed information in relation to memory retrieval and encoding processes.

References

Baker, J., Côte J. and Abernethy, B., 2003, Learning from the experts: Practice activities of expert decision makers in sport. *Research Quarterly for Exercise and Sport*, 74, 324–34.

Ericsson, K.A. and Kintsch., W., 1995, Long-term working memory. *Psychological Review*, 2, 211–45.

Franks, I.M. and Miller, G., 1986, Eyewitness testimony in sport *Journal of Sport Behaviour*, 9 (1), 38–45.

Ward, P. and Williams A.M., 2003, Perceptual and cognitive skill development in soccer: The multidimensional nature of expert performance *Journal of Sport and Exercise Psychology*, 25, 93 –111.

77 The microstructure of effective practice

The nature of the instruction process in soccer

Ian S. Yates and A. Mark Williams

Research Institute for Sport and Exercise Science, Liverpool John Moores University, UK

Introduction

Effective instruction is crucial to the pursuit of optimal sporting performance. Researchers have shown that coaches use similar behaviours when dealing with elite and sub-elite performers (Potrac*et al.*, 2002). Moreover, current coaching philosophy appears to favour a prescriptive coaching style over a more 'hands-off', constraints-led approach (Williams and Hodges, 2005).

Few researchers have examined how coaches alter their behaviour due to the learner's age and skill level or with reference to the form of the practice activity. We examined the coaching behaviours employed during effective practice activities using players of different age and skill level.

Methods

Participants

English male youth soccer coaches ($n = 54$) from three different skills levels were filmed. Teams were defined as elite (Youth Academy with The Football Association Premier League status, $n = 3$), sub-elite (Youth School of Excellence with lower level professional league status, $n = 3$) or recreational (Local Football Association Charter Standard status, $n = 3$). Within each team, three sessions from three age groups (U9, U13, U16) were covered over successive weeks ($n = 81$).

Apparatus

The instructional behaviours employed by coaches were analysed using a validated observation instrument, modified from the Arizona State University Observation Instrument (Lacy and Darst, 1984). The modifications were undertaken following consultation with elite coaches at professional soccer clubs (Table 77.1).

Table 77.1 Behaviour categories and their definitions

Activity	Definition
Pre-instruction	Initial information given to a player preceding the desired action to be executed.
Concurrent instruction	Cues or reminders given to a player(s) during the actual execution of the skill or play.
Post-instruction	Correct, re-explanation, or instructional feedback given after the execution of the skill or play.
Management	Statements related to the organisational details of practice sessions, not referring to skills or strategies.
Modelling	Provision of a demonstration of correct or incorrect performance of a skill or playing technique.
Questioning	Any question to players concerning strategies, techniques, assignments associated with the sport.
Praise	Verbal or non-verbal compliments, statements or signs of acceptance towards the players.
Scold	Verbal or non-verbal statements or signs of displeasure towards the players.
Hustle	Verbal or non-verbal statements intended to intensify the efforts of the player(s).
Un-codeable	Any behaviour that cannot be seen or heard or does not fit into above categories.
Silence	Period of time when the coach is not talking.

Procedure

Sessions were recorded using a digital video camera (Canon XM2, Holland) mounted on a stationary tripod. During the session the coach wore a head-set microphone attached to a transmitter (Sennheiser EW3, Germany). The audio footage was transmitted to a radio receiver (Sennheiser EK100, Germany) mounted to the camera. Overall session time varied from 50 to 113 (mean = 73.79) minutes.

Practice sessions were viewed on a laptop computer. Coaching behaviour data were analysed from activities identified as 'effective' forms of practice through time motion analysis (see Yates *et al.*, 2006). Behavioural data were recorded using time sampled event recording.

Data analysis

Percentages and rate per minute for each category were calculated. Each behaviour was analysed separately using a Group (elite vs. sub elite vs. recreational) × Age (U9, U13, U16) ANOVA.

Results

Coaches used praise more with elite players than with sub-elite and recreational players ($F_{2,27} = 13.59$, $P < 0.05$). Elite coaches were also less likely to be silent than coaches with sub-elite and recreational players ($F_{2, 27} = 7.56$, $P<0.05$). Decreased levels of concurrent instruction were also shown by coaches working with elite players compared to coaches working with recreational players ($F_{2, 27} = 3.58$, $P<0.05$).

Significant age differences were found at all skill levels for the use of management behaviours, pre-instruction and silence. All behaviours increased proportionally with player age ($P<0.05$).

There were no significant differences across age groups for exposure to the use of post-instruction, questioning, hustle and un-codeable behaviours, ($P>0.05$).

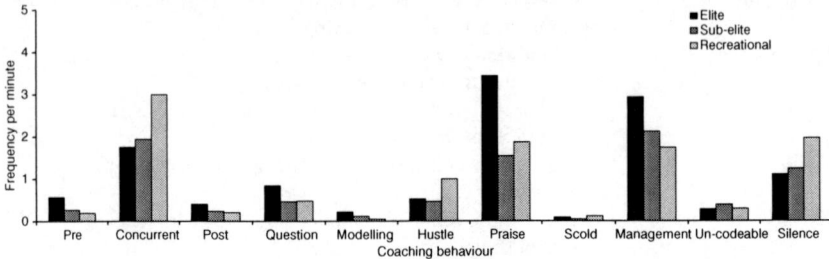

Figure 77.1 Rate per minute of behaviours exhibited by coaches working with U9s

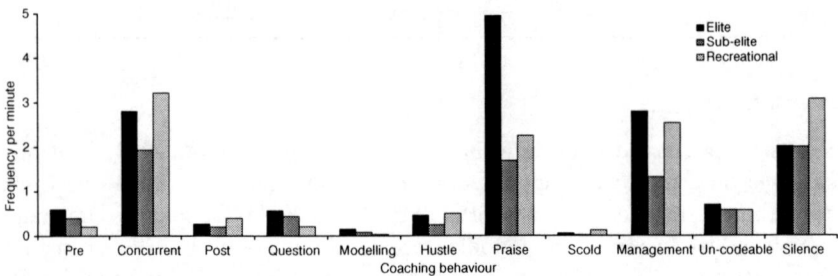

Figure 77.2 Rate per minute of behaviours exhibited by coaches working with U13s

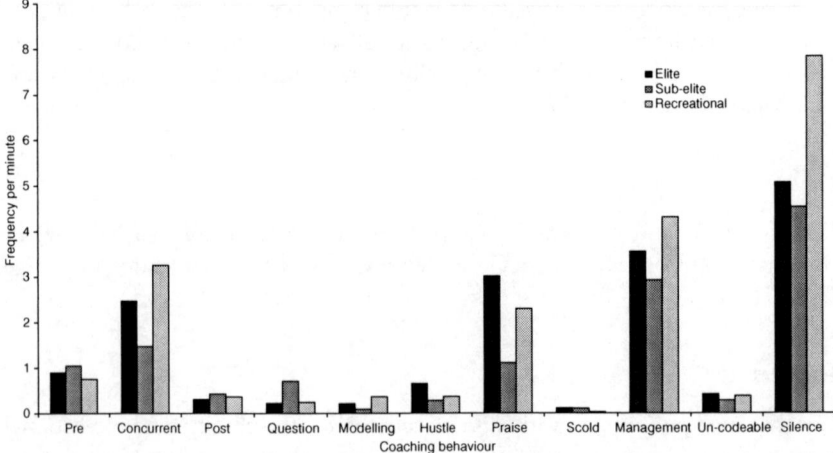

Figure 77.3 Rate per minute of behaviours exhibited by coaches working with U16s

Discussion and conclusions

Although players are provided with an increased positive environment at an elite level, less technical and tactical information is provided. This finding suggests that skilled players receive less prescriptive information during practice.

Senior players are also subject to an increase in the provision of pre-activity information, although they are provided with elongated periods of silence. This reduction in the amount of overall information supports the view that coaches should employ a more 'hands off' approach at the elite level.

Although the type of activity is important in gaining optimal performance benefits, results support the suggestion of Williams and Hodges (2005) that provision of a constraints-led approach to coaching should be employed at elite levels of the game.

References

Lacy, A.C., and Darst, P.W., 1984, Evolution of a systematic observation instrument: The ASU Observation Instrument. *Journal of Teaching in Physical Education*, 3, 59–66.

Potrac, P., Jones, R. and Armour, K., 2002, 'It's all about getting respect': The coaching behaviours of an expert English soccer coach. *Sport, Education and Society*, 7, 183–202.

Williams, A.M. and Hodges, N.J., 2005, Practice, instruction and skill acquisition: Challenging tradition. *Journal of Sports Sciences*, 23, 637–50.

Yates, I.S., Williams, A.M., and Ford, P.R., 2006, The microstructure of practice in soccer: a comparison of the duration and frequency of practice activities. *Journal of Sport and Exercise Psychology*, 28, S196.

78 The microstructure of practice in soccer

A comparison of duration and frequency of practice

Ian S. Yates and A. Mark Williams

Research Institute for Sports and Exercise Science, Liverpool John Moores University, UK

Introduction

A typical dilemma confronting coaches is how to structure training to optimise skill acquisition and prepare for competition (Cobley, 2005). Coaches must manipulate training content, frequency, volume, intensity and recovery to achieve these dual objectives ensuring both effective and efficient learning. However, despite the importance of these objectives in developing elite performers, current coaching practice is determined mainly by 'lay' opinion rather than empirical research (Williams and Hodges, 2005).

Researchers have indicated that to achieve excellence, athletes must accumulate extensive amounts of practice – the '10 year' or '10,000 hour' rule. Although the amount of exposure to a sport is an important factor in coaching, the type and structure of activities undertaken may be as or even more important. There is a need to move the experimental paradigm away from 'number crunching' to assess in greater detail what athletes actually do during practice (Starkes, 2000).

Preliminary time–motion analysis indicates that elite athletes spend a small amount of practice time on challenging activities (Deakin *et al.*, 1998), yet the nature of these activities has not been identified. The aim in this study was to examine the microstructure of practice in soccer by comparing the specific practice activities undertaken by elite, sub-elite and recreational players from different age groups using time-motion analysis.

Methods

Participants

Participants were recruited from nine English male youth soccer teams from three different skill levels. Teams were defined as elite (Youth Academy whose senior team participate in The Football Association Premier League, $n = 3$), sub-elite (Youth School of Excellence whose senior team participates in a lower level professional league, $n = 3$), or recreational (local youth soccer clubs with Football Association Charter Standard, $n = 3$). Within each club, three coaching sessions from each of three age groups (U9, U13, U16) were filmed ($n = 81$).

Apparatus

The time–motion analysis instrument included a total of eight categories of practice activities (see Table 78.1). The categories chosen and definitions employed resulted from consultation with elite coaching personnel at professional soccer clubs.

Procedure

Practice sessions were recorded using a digital video camera (Canon XM2, Amstelveen) mounted on a stationary tripod (Libec, Arizona). The camera was positioned at the furthest point from the action taking place so as to track the movements of the players and coach. The sessions were filmed at each club's training ground and all data were gathered over a 2–3 month period mid-season. Session time varied from 50 to 113 (mean = 73.79) minutes.

Practice sessions were viewed and coded using a laptop computer. The session structure was analysed using a continuous recording method with observations being coded onto a specifically designed recording sheet. Each time an identifiable pre-defined activity was exhibited during practice, including any change in activity, a record was entered on a coding form.

Performance measure and analysis

The total time spent in each activity (in seconds), the frequency that each activity occurred and the mean percentage of time spent in each activity were calculated.

Table 78.1 Categories and definitions for time–motion analysis

Activity	Form	Definition
Physiological	Training	Primary goal of physiological aspects of game (e.g., warm up, cool down, conditioning)
Technical practice	Training	Individual or with a group, covering isolated technical skills under no pressure.
Skills practice	Training	Individual or with a group covering technical elements under opposing pressure.
Functional practice	Training	Re-enacting isolated simulated game incidents without focus on particular technical skills.
Phase of play	Playing	Opposed practice using one goal to cover the cognitive team strategies used.
Possession game	Playing	No goals in which ball retention rather than scoring a goal is the primary objective.
Conditioned game	Playing	Variations to rules, goals or areas of play, but with teams scoring in the same way.
Small-sided game	Playing	Two goals, realistic to regulation rules, with teams scoring in the same way.

Each activity was analysed separately using a Group (elite, sub-elite, recreational) × Age (U9, U13, U16) ANOVA.

Results

A significant Group effect was observed for the amount of time spent in technical practice, ($F_{2, 27} = 3.737$, $P<0.05$). Recreational players spent more time in these activities than both elite and sub-elite players. In contrast, the elite players spent significantly more time in conditioned games than both sub-elite and recreational player ($F_{2, 27} = 6.873$, $P<0.05$), and also more time in possession

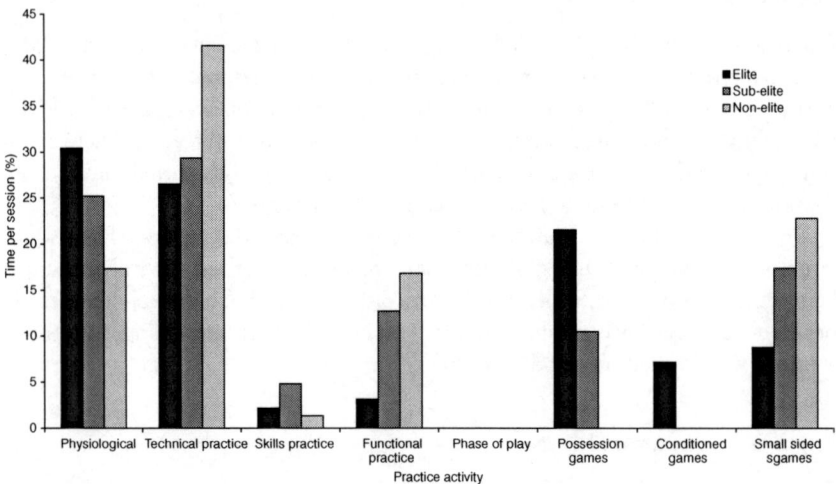

Figure 78.1 Percentage of time in varying soccer-specific training activities for U9s

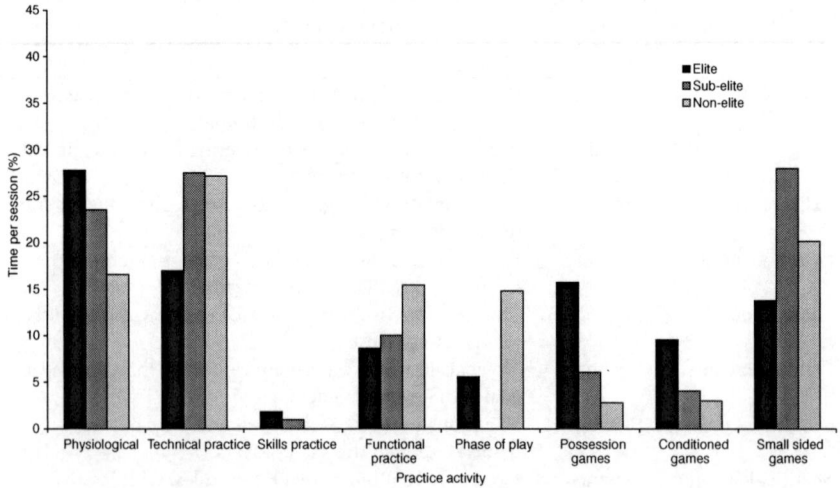

Figure 78.2 Percentage of time in varying soccer-specific training activities for U13s

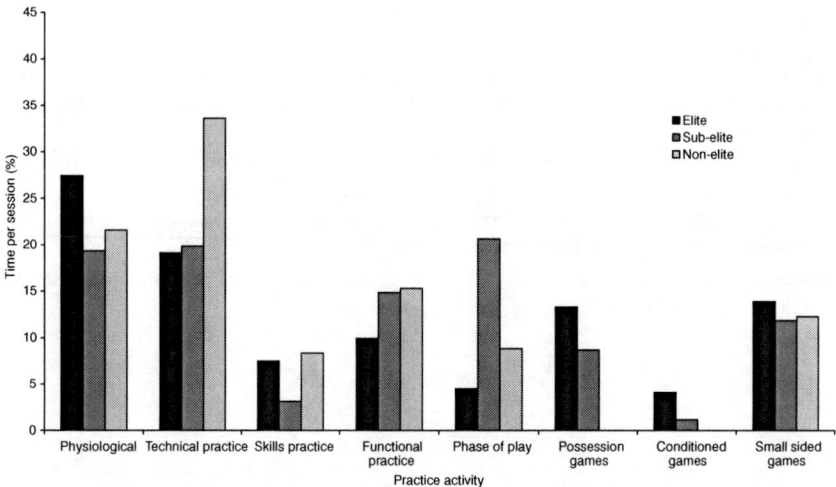

Figure 78.3 Percentage of time in varying soccer-specific training activities for U16s

games than recreational players ($F_{2, 27} = 5.451$, $P<0.05$). Both of these findings were irrespective of age.

A significant age effect was observed ($F_{2, 27} = 4.120$, $P<0.05$). The older players spent more time in phase of play compared with younger players. An increase in age was directly proportional with the time spent in this activity.

There were no significant differences across age groups for participation in physiological training, skills practices, functional practices or small sided games ($P>0.05$).

Discussion and conclusions

Elite players spent twice as much time playing in 'open' forms of practice (conditioned games and possession games) compared with their sub-elite and recreational counterparts. This finding is in contrast to the sub-elite and recreational players who spent more time in 'closed' repetitive 'drill-like' activities.

No change was seen across skill levels as a function of age: however, there was an increase in the use of tactical based activities across all skill levels. This finding may suggest that although there is a switch in the content of information delivered as a result of a player's age (i.e. technical to tactical), the structure in which the information is presented does not vary greatly. A possible implication is that there may be increased benefits by adopting game-orientated activities throughout all stages of learning.

In conclusion, although the amount of accumulated practice is an important precursor to expertise, it seems that the nature of the practice activities may be at the very least of equal importance with respect to the development of expertise in soccer.

References

Cobley, S., 2005, Attaining expertise in sport: training structure for skill improvement and competition preparation. ISSP 11th World Congress of Sport Psychology, 15–19 August, Sydney, Australia.

Deakin, J.M., Starkes, J.L. and Allard, C., 1998, *The Microstructure of Practice in Sport*. Sport Canada Technical Report. Ottowa: Sport Canada.

Starkes, J., 2000, The road to expertise: Is practice the only determinant? *International Journal of Sport Psychology*, 31, 431–51.

Williams, A.M. and Hodges, N.J., 2005, Practice, instruction and skill acquisition: Challenging tradition. *Journal of Sports Sciences*, 23, 637–50.

Part X
Social sciences

79 A critical survey of football rating systems

Raymond T. Stefani,[1] Richard Pollard[2] and Aylin Seckin[3]

[1]California State University, USA; [2]California Polytecnic State University, USA; San Luis Obispo, USA; [3]Istanbul Bilgi University, Turkey

Introduction

The creation of a fair and objective rating system for the codes of football provides a challenge, since the performance of one team affects that of the other team. A survey of football rating systems is provided in this report as a resource for those interested in that topic. Further, the various systems are compared and critiqued constructively to provide a platform for improvement of the current systems and for guidance to those who may want to create such systems.

In the early 1840s, there were two codes of football, one in which the ball was mainly advanced by dribbling, the precursor to soccer, and one in which the player could run with the ball, the rugby game. In both versions, the ball could be batted and caught. The current soccer rules of handling-only-by-goalkeeper may be traced to the Football Association Rules of 1863 while the other codes evolved from the rugby union rules of 1871. Today's eight football codes are as follows, including the date first played under a published set of rules and an abbreviation for the agency governing and/or rating each sport: American college football (1869, BCS), American professional football (1895, NFL), Canadian football (1861, CFL), Australian Rules football (1858, AFL), Gaelic football (1887, GAA), rugby union (1871, IRB), rugby league (1895, RLIF) and soccer (1863, FIFA, Elo).

Overview of rating systems

There are three basic types of sports rating system (Stefani 1998, 1999), subjective, adjustive and accumulative. Let each team have an index i and let each of team i's competitions be numbered consecutively with index m. Team i's opponent in competition m may be denoted by j. Let y_i^m be a measured outcome of the match between i and j. Finally, a rating system function f creates the ratings for team i, denoted r_i.

$$r_i = f\left(y_i^m, r_i^{m-1}, r_j^{m-1}\right) \tag{79.1}$$

For a subjective rating system, an expert facilitates the function f in Equation (79.1) and the combined expert ratings are used to rank teams.

In an accumulative system, a team gains points after a successful game or, at worst, gains zero points in a loss. An accumulative system can be represented by a summation over past games indexed by m.

$$r_i = \Sigma_m \, a(y_i^m) \tag{79.2}$$

A league standings table, ranked by total earned points, is an example of an accumulative rating system. In Equation (79.2), a is an ageing function which may be used to discount old data.

An adjustive system causes each rating to change based on the actual points gained, y_i^m, compared to an estimate, y_{ie}^m, of the points gained, usually driven by the ratings of the two opponents prior to the game. The ratings of the two opponents are adjusted by equal and opposite amounts, after game m. The new rating for team i is given by

$$r_i^m = r_i^{m-1} + K \, [\, y_i^m - y_{ie}^m\,] \tag{79.3}$$

K can be chosen to emphasize some games. Stefani (1998) provided a discussion of various choices for K. An adjustive system based on score difference is usually a better predictor of future performance than an adjustive system based only on winning, drawing, and losing. Berry (2003) evaluated 15,728 US college football games played over a 32-year period. The correct winning team was predicted in 71.9 per cent of the games using an adjustive system based on score difference but in only 63.8 per cent of the games based on winning, drawing and losing.

Survey of football rating systems

The responsible agencies for five of these eight codes do not provide a comprehensive rating system. The NFL, CFL, AFL and GAA govern domestic league competition, where the teams are rated using a simple accumulative win-tie-loss table as in Equation 79.2, followed by play-off competition. There is domestic rugby league competition employing accumulative results tables, while international competition is governed by the RLIF, which does not sponsor a comprehensive rating system. Three codes have comprehensive rating systems, worthy of further discussion.

BCS American College Football

In the absence of a national league or a play-off structure for the highest-level college football teams in the US, the Bowl Championship Series (BCS) was established prior to the 1998–99 season, to rate the approximately 120 elite teams playing unbalanced schedules so as to place top teams into what were then four single post-season 'BCS bowl games' from 1998–99 to 2005–06 and into five such games starting in 2006–07. About US\$ 13 million is distributed on behalf of each of the eight or ten teams. On a rotating basis, one of those BCS bowl games became the national championship game (see www.bcsfootball.org). Over the span of years that the BCS system has been in existence, the factors that were included can be divided into three components. First, a computer component has included from three and eight sets of computer ratings, using various means to combine those computer-generated ratings. Second, two sets of subjective human polls have been combined. Third, other factors have been included to form a somewhat miscellaneous component. For the first six years, ranking positions were added. Since then, the fraction of points earned in each component has been averaged.

There have been four seasons in which a popular BCS-bowl contender's overall placement differed from that of the subjective human polls. In each case, the BCS Committee changed the system for the following year, in such a way that the previous season would have resulted in the human poll being followed for the problematic team. Over time, the adjustive computer systems have been required to delete score difference and only use game outcome. Logically, only polls should be used to placate the typical fan and bowl organizer; however, it is unlikely that the poll organizations want to be the sole arbiter of the BCS bowl pairings. It is therefore highly likely that conflict will continue to plague the BCS process, as it attempts to combine diverse human and computer components.

IRB Rugby Union

A world rating system for rugby union football was introduced by the IRB in 2003 (www.irb.com/EN/World+Rankings), after analyzing games played since the establishment of that code in 1871. The IRB system is adjustive, using the form of Equation 79.3. For convenience, define d as $r_i^{m-1} - r_j^{m-1} + h_{ij}$. The IRB defines the home advantage h_{ij} as 3 rating points if i is the home team, -3 rating points if j is the home team and zero for a game played at a neutral site. In Equation 79.3, y_{ie}^m is defined as $.1\,d$, where the magnitude of d is limited to 10. The adjustive term becomes $K[1 - .1d]$ when i wins, $K[-.1d]$ for a tie and $K[-1 - .1d]$ for a loss. Only full international games are used, with $K = 2$ for a world cup match, $K = 1.5$ for a win of more than 15 points and $K = 1$ otherwise. The probability that i will defeat j in the next match is approximately $0.5(1 + y_{ie}^m)$, under this system. The defeat of a weaker opponent ($d \approx 10$) results in a small gain relative to the defeat of an equal opponent ($d \approx 0$) and conversely, losing to a weaker opponent has more of a negative impact on a team's rating than losing to an equal opponent. Past results diminish exponentially in importance so that recent results are emphasized. The IRB system has much to recommend it. The International Cricket Confederation employs a similar system to rank international cricket teams (see www.icc.com).

FIFA Soccer and Elo Soccer

The international governing body, FIFA, has employed three systems since rankings started in 1993. The procedures for the original 1993 system (using six years of data) and the modified 1999 system (using eight years of data) are very similar. In those systems, the result of a game, two match points, are assessed in relation to the strength of the two teams by a formula that FIFA never made public. Adjustments to these totals are then made according to the number of goals scored by the two teams (again by a secret formula), with a subsequent bonus given to the away team in recognition of the major role that home advantage plays in soccer. Further adjustments in the form of multiplicative weights are then made to the team totals according to the importance of the game, regional strength and the time period in which the game took place. When six years of past data were used, that meant that either one or two World Cup years could be used. Newer data are weighted more than older data. Teams not playing a minimum number of games are penalized. In 1999 a stabilizing mechanism was introduced to dampen large, short-term fluctuations in rankings. The methodology for this was not released. It is ironic that for a sport that prides itself on its transparency and simplicity, FIFA should have not only introduced such a complex system, but also have refused to release the precise details of its methodology.

In retrospect, it is surprising that it survived as long as 13 years considering the increasing criticism and ridicule to which the discredited system was subjected. This criticism culminated in the U.S.A. rising to fourth place in the rankings shortly before the 2006 World Cup. It was at this time that FIFA announced that a new ranking system was to be introduced in July 2006 after the World Cup. This new accumulative system is both simple and transparent, a major improvement. A team starts off with 3, 1 or 0 points depending on the result of the game, adjusted by means of three multiplicative weights representing the strength of the opponents, the importance of the match (friendly games are given less importance than previously) and the regional strength. One World Cup cycle of four years is used.

However, drawbacks are that losses are scored as zero points irrespective of both the strength of the opposing team and of other factors; home advantage is ignored, as are the number of goals scored and conceded. See Pollard (2006) for a discussion of the importance of home advantage. Continental final tournaments occur with different frequency, while World Cup qualifying competitions vary in format and hence the number of games played. Thus different countries will, through no fault of their own, have different opportunities to improve their rankings. The international soccer version of the adjustive Arpad Elo chess rating system was developed by Robert Runyan in 1997 (see www.eloratings.net). In Equation 79.3, y_{ie}^m is defined as $P(d)$, the Elo normal-distribution based approximation of the probability that team i will defeat team j. Here d is defined as for the IRB system; however, d is not limited. The Elo system produces ratings with a standard deviation of 200 rating points. The home advantage is defined as 100 rating points. K varies linearly from 20 for a friendly match to 60 for a World Cup final. K is increased multiplicatively for large goal differences (by 25 per cent for a two goal win and by 100 per cent for a five goal win). The adjustive term in Equation 79.3 becomes $K[1-P(d)]$ when i wins, $K[0.5-P(d)]$ for a tie and $K[0-P(d)]$ for a loss. As for the IRB system, a win against a weaker opponent $(P(d) \approx 1)$ produces less gain than against an equal opponent $(P(d) \approx 0.5)$. Also, more points are lost when defeated by a weaker opponent than by an equal opponent. A less desirable feature of the Elo system is the multiplicative increase in K due to score but a linear increase due to importance. A better way of incorporating goal difference would be to make the effect additive instead of multiplicative.

References

Berry, S.M., 2003, College football rankings: the BCS and the C.I.T. *Chance*, 16, (3), 46–9.

Pollard, R., 2006, Worldwide regional variations in home advantage in association football. *Journal of Sports Sciences*, 24, 231–40.

Stefani, R.T., 1998, Predicting outcomes. In *Statistics in Sport*, edited by Bennett, J. (London: Arnold).

Stefani, R.T., 1999. A taxonomy of sports rating systems, *IEEE Transactions on Systems, Man, and Cybernetics*, Part A, 29, (1), 116–20.

80 FIFA provisions on government interference in administration of national football federations

Hindrances to full compliance in Africa

Ebenezer Olatunde Morakinyo

Dept of Human Kinetics and Health Education, University of Ibadan, Nigeria

Introduction

Sports has become a phenomenon that has cut across all barriers, whether ethnic, religion or racial and it has become an edifying vehicle for the development of young people. Internationally, sports has become a factor in determining the supremacy of a country over others. The International Association of Football Federations (FIFA) was founded in 1904 to regulate and develop international football and protect the interests of its members. To achieve this aim, FIFA introduced a statute, which was reviewed in 2003 (FIFA, 2003). The statutes indicated that only the association which is responsible for organisation and supervision of football in its country may become a member of FIFA (Article 10) and members are required to comply fully with the statutes, regulations, objectives and decisions of FIFA bodies at all times (Article 13a). National football associations (FA) in Africa are members of FIFA by virtue of Article 10 and so are required to act in accordance to the demands of Article 13(a). One of the sections of the statutes that require total compliance by associations is Article 17 which requires total autonomy for FIFA members and does not permit interference from any external body. In recent developments, the provision of this section of the statutes has been facing a lot of problems, most especially in Africa.

It is in recognition of the non-compliance with the FIFA provision on government interference in the administration of national football associations, and in all sports generally, that the International Olympic Committee (IOC) organized a seminar in Lausanne on 21–22 September 2006 on the autonomy of the Olympic Movement. At the seminar, the FIFA President pointed out that:

observing the FIFA statutes is imperative for every member association...
Despite the undisputable respect that the world of football must show
national legislation, it must be extremely vigilant with regard to attempts
by governments, as well as supra-national government organisations – to
control the most popular sports on earth, and this is a trend which has
become increasingly evident in recent year.

(FIFA, 2006a)

Nigeria Football Association is a member of FIFA and like many other
African football associations (such as Cameroon, Nigeria, Kenya, Tunisia) has
experienced government interference in its administration and this has incurred
the wrath of FIFA.

There is no doubt that the circumstances that lead to government interference
in Nigeria are likely to be similar to those of other African football associations.
Therefore the issues that invariably lead to African associations violating Article
17 of FIFA statutes were examined in the study.

Political governance

This is the process by which governments or governing bodies endeavour to
control the sports system 'through moral pressures, use of financial or other
incentives' (Henry and Lee, 2004: 26). Governments today have established
structures that will address sports needs such as facilities, programmes and
international participation.

According to Acosta (2002) through the establishment of governmental
agencies, governments attempt to regulate the practice of sports. In the case
of Nigeria, the federal government through the Federal Ministry of Sports and
Social Development regulates the practice of sports at the national level, while
the constituent states establish sports councils, through which they regulate the
practice of sports. To enhance governmental control further, sports associations
are established to administer individual sports

In Nigeria today, football association membership is politically influenced,
since only those that are government approved candidates can assume the
leadership of Nigeria Football Association (NFA). This situation is confirmed
by Acosta (2002: 25) who pointed out that 'unscrupulous leaders can find
(in sports) new avenue for their selfish satisfaction and a way to nurture their
frustrated dreams of political power'. According to Article 10 of NFA's statutes,
the membership is composed of:

- state football associations
- the leagues
- the premier division clubs
- the players' association
- the Nigerian Football Coaches Association

- the Nigerian Referees Association
- the agency of the Government of Nigeria in charge of sports.

Most of the members appointed through the above listed avenues to be members of NFA are government nominees, because state governments nominate members of their state's FAs and the football clubs in Nigeria, whether playing at the league or premier divisions, are owned by governments at the state level.

The unique position of football in countries like Nigeria dictates that whoever leads the FA must be acceptable to those in the government's sport agency and should be a person who is politically acceptable to those in authority. Members of the NFA leadership who are not willing to adhere to the wishes of the government will invariably be removed, legally or illegally, and if FIFA itself is not circumspect, it becomes an unwitting tool in the hands of the power brokers. It is not surprising, therefore, that since 1945 when the NFA was founded, the chairmanship has been held by no less than 29 people (Ogunyemi, 2002), an average of two years per chairman. This means that some chairmen were not allowed to finish their term of office.

An example is the case of NFA election held in Kano in 2005 which FIFA adjudged to be 'legitimate and must stand' (FIFA 2006b and Adedipe and Okusan, 2006) but was later nullified by the same FIFA and a new election ordered for August 2006 (FIFA, 2006c).

Funding

Generally in Africa, the largest percentage of funds to administer sports comes from government. The funds are made available through direct governmental allocations. Only recently has the issue of marketing sports been emerging in some African countries, Nigeria included. According to Acosta (2002: 28) such government funding does have political price, 'such funds often influence the nominations of NF and NOC leaders, in certain countries with local regulations or in violation of them'.

In Nigeria, the government is the sole source of finance for sports and because of the unique position of football, most government funds for sport go to the NFA. In spite of the fact that the government funding policy for sports indicates that NFA should be self-financing, it has not been possible because sponsors are not forthcoming and where sponsorship *is* available, it covers only a fraction of budgetary needs.

It is not surprising, therefore, that because NFA operates only with government funds, it is always relyiant on the goodwill of third parties (Federal Minister for Sport, etc) whose mood and political persuasion cannot be predicted. Since the government holds the keys to the NFA's purse, the government has the power to interfere in the administration of football in Nigeria, as happens in other African countries. This position was confirmed by Ojo-Oba (2006) who pointed out that since NFA depends on government funding, then government has to be involved in the administration of football in the country, so as to oversee effectively the spending of government money. This is an indicator that government interference in the administration of football should be expected and accepted.

Economic environment

The economic environment of most African countries is such that it does not encourage non-governmental generation of funds. This is because viable economic enterprises are not encouraged, policy-wise, to delve into sports sponsorship. For example, the idea of legislative policy that will enable companies to enjoy tax-free benefits on funds expended on sports as a form of sponsorship has been discussed and promised for many years by the Nigerian government but has not been implemented.

According to Acosta (2002) and Arthur (2004), both sports sponsorship and marketing are two avenues through which sports organizations, like NFA, could generate funds when the government is unable or unwilling to provide adequate funds to support football. However, in an environment in which the economy is not buoyant, there is a tendency for these avenues of raising funds to be unavailable.

In Nigeria, football sponsorship and marketing are just taking root, but the money is not adequate. For instance, MTN – a telecommunications enterprise – proposed to spend 600,000,000 naira, equivalent to USD5,000,000, on the national league. According to the NFA, from this each team expected to receive 10,000,000 naira (USD $80,000) to spend in the 2007 league season. This sum is paltry when compared with the 200,000,000 naira (USD1,600,000) which an individual team requires to participate in the league (Makinde, 2006), and yet teams are not allowed to project the image of other sponsors, only that of the main sponsor.

The danger in single sponsorship, according to Acosta (2002) is that these sports sponsors, 'through political or financial pressure, become deeply involved in the affairs' of the national football association. This then may be another form of interference which FIFA frowns upon.

Club ownership

One of the strongest means for government interference in football administration in Nigeria is club ownership. As indicated in Article 10 of NFA statutes, the composition of NFA's membership is made up of, among others, the leagues and the premier division clubs. These are the football stakeholders in Nigeria. Of all the football clubs in Nigeria, 98 per cent are totally owned by state or local governments. The remainder are owned by individuals. Unfortunately, because the economic status of private owners, most of the privately owned football clubs have disappeared (Ogunyemi, 2002).

The implication of this is that the machinery for football administration in Nigeria is in the hands of government right from the lowest level (local government) to the highest level of government (federal government). This situation makes it very easy for government to interfere in the administration of football in Nigeria and indeed in Africa.

This situation is in contrast to European countries where football clubs are owned and managed by private individuals or companies and members of the club's supporters are encouraged to be partners of the clubs by buying shares just like any other company quoted on the stock exchange (Henry and Lee, 2004). By this means, the administration of football is not concentrated in the hands of a few people. As pointed out by Henry and Lee (2004) 'the adoption of the principle of systemic governance of sport especially football has created a web of interactions between stakeholders in which different groups exert power in different ways and in different contexts by drawing on alliances with other stakeholders' (p. 28). This model of football administration reduces the chances of government interference.

Sport facilities

The Nigerian football league, especially the professional league, was designed along the lines of professional leagues in Europe and it was, at the outset, intended to achieve certain goals and objectives (Salami, 1999). In the process of establishing professional football leagues in Nigeria, the NFA laid down certain conditions to be met before a professional football club could be registered. According to Ogunyemi (2002, p. 67), two of the conditions are:

1   availability of an acceptable and approved stadium to the clubs in the vicinity; and
2   construction of the clubs' own training facilities.

It is rather unfortunate that today no professional football club registered in Nigeria has its own stadium or training facilities. They all depend on government-owned stadia to host and play their matches.

This situation is in contrast to European professional football clubs who own their own facilities and so do not need to seek the permission of government to use the stadium, or lead to situations in which there will be a clash of interests. For instance, in 1991, the IICC Shooting Stars of Ibadan needed the government-owned Lekan Salami Stadium in Ibadan to play an international match. Unfortunately, the government had hired out the stadium to a private organisation to host a non-sporting event. This situation nearly created international embarrassment, but for the success of meaningful dialogue before the football club could play the match at the venue (Salami, 1999).

In addition to the convenience of use, a stadium could also serve as a source of revenue to the professional football club that owns it. This is because spectators will have to buy tickets to watch the match generate funds for the club. However, at present in Nigeria more than 50 per cent of match spectators do not pay because they are government workers or officials. Consequently football clubs are denied revenues and the dependence on government funding is increased. This further strengthens the process of government interference.

Conclusion

Government interference in the administration of football is an issue that is causing much worry to FIFA since it is now carried out in a more sophisticated manner. There is no doubt that government interference in the administration of football will inevitably jeopardize the Football Association's capacity for action and limit the possibility of it establishing successful sport programmes of its own (Acosta, 2002); this happened when the Minister for Sports in Nigeria nullified the NFA's nomination of coaches for the national teams in April 2006 and the NFA could do nothing about it.

This report has attempted to outline the problems that the Nigeria Football Association, and indeed all African FAs are confronted with, and which make it impossible for them to adhere strictly to the tenets of Article 17 of FIFA statutes.

There is a need for FIFA to understand the 'hostile' environment in which the African FAs operate and a need bring to fruition the resolution for 'total, harmonious collaboration with government bodies while showing complete mutual respect for the autonomy of structures and organizations' (FIFA, 2006a). African football associations need a sympathetic understanding of their situation, so that the 'beautiful' game can grow in Africa.

References

Acosta, R.H., 2002, *Managing Sports Organisations* (Champaign, IL: Human Kinetics).

Adedipe, A. and Okusan, L., 2006, 2006 in retrospect (January–June). *The Guardian* 26 December.

Arthur, D., 2004, Sport event and facility fanagement, In *The Business of Sports Management*, edited by Beach, J. and Chadwick, S., (Harlow: Pearson Education).

FIFA, 2003, Statutes. (Zurich: FIFA).

FIFA, 2006a, Unanimous appeal to defend the autonomy of football. http://www.fifa.com/aboutfifa/federation/releases/newsid=106799.html Accessed 7 December, 2006.

FIFA, 2006b, Association committee decides on cases in Albania and Nigeria. http://www.fifa.com/aboutfifa/federation/releases/newsid=102974.html Accessed 9 January, 2007.

FIFA, 2006c, FIFA to monitor elections in NFA on 29t August 2006. http://www.fifa.com/aboutfifa/federation/releases/newsid=105545.html Accessed 7 December 2006.

Henry, I and Lee, P.C., 2004, Governance and ethics in sports. In . *The Business of Sport Management*, edited by Beech, J. and Chadwick, S., (Harlow: Pearson Education).

Makinde, O., 2006, Author's interview with O. Makinde as Secretary, Oyo State Football Association on 10 December, 2006.

Nigerian Football Association, 2006, Statutes. Abuja: NFA.

Ogunyemi, A. O., 2002, Evaluation of selected sports management indices and the performance of Nigerian national soccer teams. Unpublished doctoral thesis, Ibadan: University of Ibadan.

Ojo-Oba, B., 2006, Author's interview with B. Ojo-Oba as a football administrator in Nigeria, 10 December, 2006.

Salami, I. A., 1999, An evaluation of resources allocation and utilization towards effective performance of professional Division 1 soccer clubs in Nigeria. Unpublished doctoral thesis, Ibadan: University of Ibadan.

81 Research informing practice

Implications of rule changes to modified rugby league

Donna O'Connor

Faculty of Education and Social Work, University of Sydney, Australia

Introduction

'Modified games' is a vital area of the Australian rugby league's (ARL) operations. It is the grassroots of the game and involves approximately 25,000 registered children in the 6–12 years age group. The programme has now been in place for over 25 years. In recent years some regions (e.g. Queensland Rugby League) have piloted several law alterations for the different age groups. This innovation has now led to different laws being used in different regions throughout Australia. Consequently there is much debate as to which laws should now be adopted universally.

Whatever action is taken must be done as a result of professional empirical research rather than anecdotal or subjective judgments. Far too often, administrators of sport may promote the introduction of changes based on what may amount to a false premise e.g., in the case of modified games 'to make administration easier' without considering what impact these changes may have on player participation levels. The initial impetus for law alterations in the modified games programme arose from a perceived confusion among officials and supporters on the value of the modified games try.

The current modified games 'pilot programme' involves changes to the following laws:

- point score system for tries (3 and 5 points for tries v 4-point tries);
- when the defensive line can move forward at 'play-the-ball';
- the mandatory number of passes performed by the attacking team in its 20 metre zone.

Although these law alterations may be well considered, they now require proper and valid evaluation by means of empirical research. Therefore the aim of this study is to determine the impact of the three law alterations on children's participation and performance levels during scheduled games.

Methods

Sample

This project involved the match analysis of 89 modified rugby league games during the 2006 season. The relevant laws determining the playing conditions administered in the Sydney metropolitan (SYD), Queensland (QRL) and NSW Country (CRL) regions and the number of games that were included in this project are depicted in Table 81.1. To reduce the impact of individual team play, teams were videotaped on no more than three occasions.

Rule alterations

The current modified games 'pilot programme' involved changes to three laws. The official point scoring system defines a 3-point try as a try that involved zero-to-two passes and a 5-point try is awarded if greater than two passes are thrown. In the pilot programme this law has been changed to 4 points being awarded for all tries, regardless of the number of passes involved.

The second law difference is when the defensive line can move forward at the 'play-the-ball'. The official law indicates that the defensive team can move once the ball reaches the first receiver whereas the pilot programme allows the defence to move forward as soon as the ball clears the ruck (play-the-ball area).

Third, the official law stipulates that a minimum of two passes must be thrown during every possession. The pilot programme reduced the mandatory number of passes performed by the attacking team in its own 20 m zone to one (CRL) or zero (QRL) passes. The mandatory two-pass law was enforced for all other areas of the field.

Match analysis

The games were coded using a standard software package by two trained analysts. The definition of 'events' to be coded was first validated by members of the Australian Rugby League Development Committee. The reliability of all 'event' codes was in the range $r = 0.93 - 0.99$ except for number of play-the-balls within own 20 m zone ($r = 0.75$).

Table 81.1 Playing conditions and sample size

Group	Laws	Age group	Region	Games
1	3/5 point try, defence moves when ball reaches the first receiver, two passes in own 20 m	12 yrs	SYD	35
2	4 point try, defence moves when ball clears the ruck, 0 passes in own 20 m	12 yrs	QLD	41
3	4 point try, defence moves when ball reaches the first receiver, 1 pass in own 20 m	12 yrs	NSW Country	13

Data analysis

All data were analysed using one-way analysis of variance (ANOVA). A Scheffe post-hoc comparison was used to distinguish between the groups. The analyses were performed using the SPSS for Windows version 12.01 software. Significance was set at $P<0.05$ and all data are presented as mean±SD.

Results

The mean and standard deviations for events are displayed in Table 81.2. This analysis is for the whole game unless a significant difference occurred in either the first or second half of play.

There was a greater number of 'sets' (possession for potentially six tackles) per QRL team (21) compared to SYD and CRL (18.4) teams. This resulted from significantly more change of possessions that occurred under the QRL playing conditions, particularly at play-the-ball 1 and 5. However, there was no difference in the number of completed sets (10.6) achieved by each team. The QRL teams also had to perform an additional 10 tackles per game compared to their counterparts. Statistical analysis revealed that the point scoring system (3/5 points v 4 points) did not influence when, where or how tries are scored. The majority of tries were scored from at least two passes from a play-ball within 20 m from the try-line. The range of tries scored from dummy-half (0–3) was low for all playing conditions. The range for number of tries scored in a game was large (0–15) and no pattern emerged for when in the tackle count the try was scored.

Other significant differences between playing conditions were a greater number of dropped balls, dummy-half runs, kicks in general play, first receiver total errors and dropped balls in the second-half by QRL players. Playing conditions had no impact on a team's ability to make ground as demonstrated by the number of times a team surpassed the 'advantage line' and was able to progress out of its 20 m zone.

Discussion

As a result of the advent of a number of law alterations the modified rugby league programme was evaluated against the philosophy of the programme 'Children play and learn in an environment that maximises participation …'. For the 12 years age division, each team has 13 players on a full-sized field (100 m × 69 m plus in-goal area) with the game generally played in two 20 min halves. The implications of the three proposed law alterations will first be discussed separately and then the collective impact on all aspects of the game.

The law alteration that has been the most contentious in the game involved the point scoring system for tries. The original, more complex, rule was instigated to encourage greater player involvement and ball movement. Teams were rewarded for executing at least two passes in the direct lead-up to a try (5 points). The law alteration to the point scoring system (4-point tries regardless of the number

Table 81.2 Mean and standard deviations for game events under different playing conditions

Events	SYD	QRL	CRL
Game sets §§	36 (6.4)	41.83 (6.1)	36.69 (3.8)
Percentage completed sets	57.43 (12.9)	52.29 (14.9)	56.9 (14.7)
Team tackles §	58.71 (18.2)	68.12 (13.7)	62.08 (12.0)
Team tackles (2nd half) §§	27.48 (10.3)	32.99 (7.9)	27.96 (8.4)
Change of possession PTB 1**	1.91 (1.22)	2.57 (1.66)	1.92 (1.94)
Change of possession PTB 2	1.50 (1.3)	2.0 (1.69)	1.35 (1.13)
Change of possession PTB 3	1.55 (1.45)	1.84 (1.64)	1.19 (0.98)
Change of possession PTB 4	1.41(1.35)	1.70 (1.22)	1.50 (1.22)
Change of possession PTB 5 §§	1.14 (1.19)	2.29 (1.77)	1.38 (1.06)
Change of possession PTB 6	3.83 (2.77)	4.85 (2.70)	4.35 (2.37)
Percentage advantage line achieved +	71.38 (16.8)	73.6 (18.3)	63.3 (15.6)
Tries	3.29 (3.3)	3.02 (2.7)	2.69 (1.9)
Tries with < 2 passes	0.89 (1.8)	0.96 (1.8)	0.96 (1.7)
Tries ≥ 2 passes	2.49 (4.3)	1.12 (3.2)	1.71 (2.6)
Team passes	120.5 (36.5)	133.4 (29.2)	125.8 (31.6)
Passes play-the-ball 1	0.98 (0.7)	0.75 (0.4)	0.84 (0.3)
Passes play-the-ball 2	2.1 (0.3)	1.82 (0.3)	2.01 (0.2)
Passes play-the-ball 3	2.24 (0.5)	2.1 (0.2)	2.12 (0.2)
Passes play-the-ball 4	2.38 (0.5)	2.35 (0.3)	2.29 (0.4)
Passes play-the-ball 5	2.39 (0.7)	2.38 (0.4)	2.32 (0.6)
Passes play-the-ball 6	1.89 (0.9)	1.76 (0.6)	1.64 (0.4)
Line-breaks	2.68 (2.6)	3.8 (3.3)	2.85 (1.8)
1st receiver tackled	3.02 (2.3)	3.30 (2.5)	3.65 (1.5)
1st receiver 'takes the line on'	2.22 (2.5)	2.68 (2.3)	2.88 (1.6)
1st receiver total errors §§	0.48 (0.8)	1.02 (1.1)	0.42 (0.6)
1st receiver dropped ball (2nd half) **	0.16 (0.42)	0.47 (0.83)	0.08 (0.28)
Dropped ball §§	2.19 (2.5)	4.86 (3.4)	2.62 (2.9)
Turn-overs in own 20 m	0.89 (0.8)	1.11 (1.2)	1.10 (0.8)
Dummy-half runs §§	0.2 (0.3)	4.7 (2.2)	0.5 (0.5)
PTBs to get beyond 20 m line	1.57 (1.2)	1.82 (0.9)	1.95 (1.1)
Kicks in general play §	4.0 (2.9)	5.6 (2.6)	5.5 (2.5)
Penalties awarded in the game	6.03 (2.9)	5.78 (2.5)	6.46 (2.7)

§ $P<0.01$ QRL significantly different to SYD; §§ $P<0.01$ QRL significantly different to SYD and CRL; + $P<0.01$ QRL significantly different to CRL; * $P<0.01$ QRL significantly different to SYD ; ** $P<0.01$ QRL significantly different to SYD and CRL

of passes executed) was introduced to reduce the stress on the referee to count the number of passes from every start of play to indicate accurately whether a 3- or 5-point try should be awarded and to reduce the 'confusion' and potential arguments for officials and supporters on the value of the try that had just been scored. While acknowledging the above reasons, the reservation to adopt this law alteration universally was the concern that there would now be an influx of dummy-half and one-pass tries at the expense of more attacking football. It was also surmised that this may reduce the overall number of passes thrown in a game, thereby reducing player participation and skill development. However, results clearly indicated that these reservations are unwarranted. The point scoring system (3/5- v 4-point try) appears to have no significant impact on the number of tries scored, the number of passes thrown in the lead-up to the try, when the try was scored or where on the field the try was initiated (in terms of first and final play-the-ball). Results indicated (Table 81.2) that regardless of whether a team was playing under SYD, QRL or CRL conditions, there was no difference in the number of tries scored from less than two passes or those scored involving at least two passes. On average, a team will score 3.1 tries a game from two to three passes with the final play-the-ball occurring in zone 1 (within 20 m of try-line) and the set commencing in either zone 2 or 3 (between the attacking and defending 20 m). There was also no significant difference in the number of passes thrown by a team under each playing condition. Interestingly, the Sydney playing conditions resulted in a greater number of passes at play-the-ball 1–3 compared to the QRL games. As the CRL demonstrated a similar number of passes to that demonstrated in the Sydney games, it can be suggested that the average number of passes thrown in a rugby league game is not influenced by the point scoring system. As there was no real difference in any of the relevant variables, it can be concluded that the point scoring system does not influence when, where or how tries are scored.

The second law alteration allowed the defensive players to move forward earlier in play, aligning the game more with the playing conditions for older age groups. The results of this study indicate that when the defensive team is allowed to move does have an impact on a number of variables within the game. Under QRL playing conditions the defensive team was allowed to move forward once the ball had cleared the ruck (play-the-ball area). The attacking players in the Sydney metropolitan and CRL regions got more time and space as the defensive team was restricted in moving forward until after the first receiver had made contact with the ball. Allowing the defence to move earlier resulted in a greater number of mistakes by the first receiver and a greater number of tackles having to be executed. This trend was particularly evident in the second half when perhaps this rule alteration took its toll and the QRL players were more fatigued. There were also more kicks in general play and dummy-half runs under the QRL conditions perhaps because this was a more effective way to advance forward up the field. Results indicate that twice as many dropped balls occurred throughout the QRL game (first and second half) that could be attributed to this law alteration. This is also supported by the greater number of change of possessions occurring on the first play-the-ball (QRL). These two factors perhaps have contributed to the greater number of sets performed in the QRL game. That is, due to errors the start of a new 'set' occurs more frequently. These results suggest that attacking players are put under additional pressure when the defensive team is allowed to move once the ball has cleared the ruck and may be more fatigued by the end of the game.

In relation to the final law alteration involving the mandatory number of passes that must be executed in a team's own 20 m zone, there were no significant differences between the three regions in terms of turn-overs (change of possession) within a team's own 20 m, and the number of 'play-the-balls' to reach the 20 m area. These results should be interpreted cautiously as differences in camera work and the various fields, made it difficult to determine accurately where the 20m lines were located. If we broaden this to consider the amount of completed sets achieved by a team, there is again no difference between playing conditions (52–57 per cent). Again care must be taken with the interpretation of these results. Having similar completion rates does not reveal what a team does with the ball throughout the game. For example, a team that plays basic football emphasising 'ball control and limited passing' may make minimum errors and record a high completion rate. On the other hand, another team may be more ambitious and pass the ball a lot increasing the risk of error but also the probability of breaking the defensive line, and record a lower completion rate for the game. It could be speculated for example, that if QRL players run from dummy-half or only throw one pass there is less likelihood of a mistake in this area of the field. This could then compensate for the greater number of errors that occurred in other areas of the field where the mandatory two-pass law was enforced with the defensive team moving forward early. The result could be similar completion rates to teams playing under the Sydney conditions where the mandatory two passes were in effect at all times but the defensive team was delayed in moving forward and putting pressure on the opponent. The rationale for reducing the number of compulsory passes within this zone was to reduce errors and the probability of a team having to defend 'the line' continually and be stuck in the defensive area of the field. Also a change of possession in this zone is more likely to result in a try to the attacking team. As there is some merit in this reasoning coupled with the lower reliability for these 'events', it may be best to accept a compromise of one pass in this area. In theory, this would reduce the chance of errors without a significant impact on player involvement.

Recommendations

In summary, the recommendations based on these findings are as follows: adopt the 4-point try law as it does not impact on participation and performance levels and will be 'easier' for the referee and administrators; retain the current defensive law – i.e. the defensive line is allowed to move once the first receiver makes contact with the ball; and adopt the policy of allowing one pass within a team's own 20m zone.

Acknowledgements

This project was funded by the Australian Rugby League.

82 Ticketing in 2002 and 2006 FIFA World Cup

Hiroko Maeda

National Institute of Fitness and Sports in Kanoya, Japan

Introduction

In recent years, many countries have sought out to hold large sporting events such as the FIFA World Cup and the Olympic Games and have been actively participating in the bidding process. Because of this, it can be considered that holding such an event can bring large benefits to the host country or host city. The positive effects are not only economic; the residents of the city are also given the opportunity to enjoy a major sports event.

Through television broadcasts, people all over the world are provided with the opportunity of watching these big sport events. However, in order to watch a game in the flesh, one has to go to the actual venue. If an event is held in a certain city, spectators from all over the world will visit and as a result, the host city can profit economically. On the other hand, residents of the city can watch the game with relatively lower cost in time and money. This can be seen as another benefit for the host city.

Accordingly, the process in which the sales of the game tickets were carried out became a prime interest in this study. In particular, attention was paid to the ticket distribution among different subjects. It was also decided to compare the ticketing methods of the 2002 and 2006 tournaments. Although the 2002 tournament was a joint co-sponsorship between Japan and Korea, only the Japanese ticket holdings were used as a part of this research.

The purpose of this research was to clarify the differences in ticketing between the 2002 and 2006 World Cup tournaments. Furthermore, an attempt was made to explain the differences through the factors surrounding the respective tournaments.

Methods

First, data regarding the subject's classification, distribution and application methods, as well as the re-distribution of the remaining tickets in the 2002 and 2006 tournaments were collected from the Tournament Organization Committee. The differences between the two tournaments are summarized from these data. Moreover, a range of factors surrounding the tournament, such as the soccer environment of the host country and the purpose of the host's tournament bidding, were also causes taken into consideration. Various references from the official website and formal news were used for data.

Results

The ticket purchase subjects were divided into the following categories: residents of the host country or the people from the rest of the world, soccer associations from outside the country, and sponsor-related or high-paying persons. Contents of the national category differed somewhat between the two tournaments. Although the category for the general public existed in the 2002 tournament, it did not exist for the 2006 tournament. The general public was classified into a world-oriented general category in 2006. In addition, a venue resident's category also existed in 2002. However, in 2006 there was a host city and a holding stadium-related category.

The distribution for each category was as follows. At a glance, the clear difference between the two tournaments was the proportion between the domestic category and the rest of the world. In the 2002 tournament 48.2 per cent, close to half of the entire number, was allocated for sale within the country. On the other hand, in the 2006 tournament the allocation for the rest of the world accounted for 36.2 per cent of available tickets, the largest proportion for that year. The distribution among sponsors and television licence holders was almost the same in the 2002 and 2006 tournaments.

The methods of applying for tickets were essentially the following: first, for the 'universally available' category, it was possible to apply through the Internet in both 2002 and 2006 tournaments. Moreover, the websites were created in several languages including English, German, French and Spanish. However, to apply for the domestic category (including venue residents, domestic soccer associations, and general domestic) in 2002, a mailing method was employed.

Redistribution of the remaining tickets differed greatly in the two tournaments. During the 2002 tournament, all the remaining tickets were redistributed for domestic use with sales by telephone, which could only be accessed domestically. On the other hand for the 2006 tournament the remaining tickets were redistributed for the whole world and an Internet application method was used.

Discussion

Taking the background of the ticketing in the 2002 and 2006 tournaments into consideration, the causes in the differences observed so far may be investigated.

The incomes for large sporting event are derived through sponsors, television-broadcasting rights contracts, and ticket sales. The revenue that goes directly to the host country is from ticket sales, which is why it is important for a host country to sell as many tickets as possible.

However, the venue of 2002 was in the Far East and very far from Europe from which many of the participating nations originated. As a result, there was uneasiness as to whether or not there would be a worldwide demand for tickets, and whether the tickets would sell out.

In Japan, which was to be one of the host countries for the 2002 tournament, the concern arose because after 1993, when a professional Japanese soccer league (J-League) was established, there was an initial rapid increase in the number of soccer spectators,. but the boom declined within a few years. This period of decline in spectators coincided with Japan being selected, in 1996, as one of the venues for the 2002 tournament. Moreover, the J-League took the European professional soccer conditions at the time into consideration and tried to cultivate soccer clubs in provincial cities. Nevertheless, it was difficult to attract many spectators in the stadium of a provincial city.

It was hoped that as a result of holding the World Cup, the interest in national soccer would be raised and the number of spectators would be increased. It is thought that the priority sale to people and venue residents of the host country during the 2002 tournament was carried out with the intention of guaranteeing tickets would be sold out, as well as giving an opportunity to residents to watch games at their local stadium.

In 2006, the residents of the host country did not have priority assignment of tickets. However, the ratio of German spectators was still high. This is because many Germans applied for tickets through the 'universally available' sale. More than 80 per cent of applicants were European residents and of those, 90 per cent were German residents. Thus it can be said that a method of giving priority to German residents was not necessary.

Conclusion

The similarities between the two tournaments were the goals of selling all the available tickets while employing a fair distribution method. Initially, the organizing committees, JAWOC and OC, had similar policies regarding ticket sales. JAWOC explained that 'the stadium should become full' and 'the ticket sale system should be fair'. In contrast, OC had stated, 'we're hoping not just to sell all the tickets, but to fill the stadiums down to the very last seat', and 'we have laid down the fairest possible guidelines which we hope will work well and be widely accepted'.

The differences resided in the distribution ratios and categories. This variation can be attributed to the soccer environment of the host country as well as the differing expectations of the outcomes from holding the two tournaments.

As a result, almost all of the tickets sold out and the goals were reached for both tournaments. Therefore, although ticketing for the World Cup must be carried out fairly, it can be said that the situation of the host country also needs to be taken into consideration when determining the methods of allocation.

References

FIFA World Cup official site, http://www.fifa.com/worldcup/index.html.

JAWOC (Japan World Cup Organizing Committee) official site, http://jawoc.or.jp/, accessed from September 2001 to July 2002. (Built for 2002 FIFA World cup)

OC2006 official site, http://fifaworldcup.yahoo.com/, accessed from November 2002 to July 2006. (Built for 2006 FIFA World Cup).

Maeda, H., 2006, Research regarding 2002 FIFA World Cup ticketing, *Proceedings of Japanese Society of Science and Football 3rd Congress*, Tokyo: JSSF.

83 Career development process for youth soccer players in the J-League Academy

Career formation and career orientation

Yoshiaki Iida,[1] Kanshi Uemukai[2] and Mayumi Yaya Yamamoto[3]

[1]School of Economics, Senshu University, Japan; [2]Faculty of Humanities, Musashi University, Japan; [3]School of Sport & Exercise Sciences, Loughborough University, UK

Introduction

Professional sport in Japan has gained social status and media attention. It is seen as giving passion and dreams to children and more children in recent years are attracted to becoming professional athletes. After the Japanese professional soccer league, J-League, was inaugurated in 1993, it went through a crisis period with decreased numbers of spectators. However, as can be seen from the 2006 league championship won by Urawa Reds, who broke the record for spectator numbers, we can argue that the professional soccer league has established a consolidated structure.

On one hand, the more soccer leagues become popular, the larger the number of children who start playing soccer endeavouring to become a professional player. On the other, while more than 100 new professional players are contracted each year, the same number of players retires annually. The average age for players leaving the players' list in J-League is 26 years and 70 per cent choose to retire around that age. Although it is not certain to what extent this situation is reflected in recent research activity on career transition, as most are focused merely on after-retirement careers.

Little research has been done with regard to the career formation of professional sportsmen and women in Japan, except for research focused on i) factors for career decisions of high school tennis and volleyball players (Iwashima *et al.*, 1993); ii) the processes of career formation of high school soccer players (Yamamoto, 1999); and iii) the examination of the role of coaches in terms of career decision of high school soccer players (Yoshida *et al.*, 1996). Moreover, previous research has focused on athletes who are in the school context and no research can be found specifically focusing on the players who are outside school and engaged in soccer. Unlike players in high school soccer clubs, players who belong to the youth academy of professional soccer clubs have gone through competitive selection processes and it can be assumed that they would have a stronger career orientation to be professional players. Therefore, this research was designed to examine the processes of their career formation and career orientation.

Methods

Participants

The participants for this research were 261 young soccer players from 11 J-League youth academy teams. All players were full-time high school students as well as engaging in a youth team (High School Year 1 = 97, Year 2 = 99, Year 3 = 65).

Measures

The questionnaire presented to young soccer players was concerned with their attributes (e.g. school year, the length of player's experience in soccer, the length of father's experience in sport, economic circumstances), factors affecting career paths as a soccer player (e.g. when did one start playing soccer, motivation), current conditions for engaging in soccer (e.g. the level of satisfaction, home and school environment, anxieties and worries), followed by 18 questions in relation to their future career orientation.

Results and discussion

Process of career formation as a soccer player

Table 83.1 shows the highest level that the participants had played at: 32 players (12.3 per cent) had experienced the Japanese national youth team and 34 players (13.0 per cent) had played at a junior youth representative team. There was a greater representation of high-level players compared to the study by Yamamoto *et al.* (1999) who had only 1 national youth player (0.3 per cent) plus 7 junior national youth players (2.5per cent).

Table 83.2 shows when participants started engaging in soccer and their motivations in the previous teams they belonged to. Altogether, 57.7 per cent of players started playing soccer in the lower grades of primary school (6–9 years) and 33.7 per cent of them had been playing soccer before entering primary school, followed by 8.4 per cent from the upper grades (9–12 years). In other words, more than 90 per cent of the players started playing soccer before the age of 9.

In terms of clubs where participants started playing soccer, 46.7 per cent were junior sports clubs and 41.8 per cent were local soccer clubs. It should be highlighted that local sport/soccer clubs have become more accessible to a wider group of children compared to the previous study that showed around 40 per cent of players had gone through school clubs, rather than local or regional clubs. The significance of club teams in becoming a professional should be emphasised

Table 83.1 Participants' competitive history

	Number	%
U-20 Japan national team	32	12.3
U-17 Japan national team	34	13.0
U-12 Japan national team	1	0.4
Selected at Japanese high school level	6	2.3
Selected at regional level	23	8.8
Selected at county level	89	34.1
Selected at city level	36	13.8
Not previously selected	40	15.3

Table 83.2 Career development process as youth soccer players

When started playing soccer	Number	%
Before primary school	88	33.7
Years 1–3 of primary school	150	57.5
Years 4–6 of primary school	22	8.4
Junior high school	1	0.4
High school	0	0.0
Clubs in pri mary school		
Local soccer clubs	109	41.8
Junior sports clubs	122	46.7
Private sports clubs	2	0.8
School clubs	19	7.3
Business/company clubs	6	2.3
Others	3	1.1
Clubs in junior high school		
Junior youth clubs	155	59.4
Other club teams	81	31.0
School clubs	25	9.6
First motivation to play soccer		
Recommendation from parents	32	12.3
Recommendation from brothers	42	16.1
Recommendation from friends	53	20.3
Recommendation from teachers	7	2.7
Recommendation from neighbours	4	1.5
Impression from TV or comics	7	2.7
Lived in area famous for soccer	4	.25
Watched soccer matches	8	3.1
Wanted to be an admired player	9	3.4
Own decision	78	29.9
Other reasons	20	7.7

as 59.4 per cent of the participants had joined the junior youth team of their current J-League club and 31.0 per cent had played for another club youth team, in contrast to 9.6 per cent who played for their junior high school team.

Participants' own decision was the strongest motivation to be engaged in playing soccer (29.9 per cent), followed by such external influence as the recommendation from friends (20.3 per cent), from brothers (16.1 per cent) and from parents

(12.3 per cent). It is worth mentioning that the popularity of professional soccer had influenced the children as experienced from the answer that eight players had begun playing football because they 'watched soccer matches' and that nine players 'wanted to be an admired player'.

Career orientation

Table 83.3 indicates the intensity of professional career orientation depending on the level of competitiveness and performance. One-way analyses of variance revealed significant difference among their performance level ($F_{2,258} = 5.83$, $P<0.01$). An average five per cent difference can also be found from the multiple comparison through Tukey's method between the players who experienced national team and municipality/prefectural representative team and between the players who had national team experience and those who hadn't. In short, the higher the level players are exposed to, the stronger the career orientation to become a professional player. It can be argued that those players who are selected for the national team gain confidence and the reality of becoming a professional player gets stronger. In particular, this tendency is strongest for the players with national team and international match experience.

   Table 83.4 indicates the intensity of professional career orientation depending on the grades in high school. One-way analyses of variance revealed significant difference among their grades ($F_{2,258} = 7.21$, $P<0.01$). Tukey's method applied to multiple comparison shows an average five per cent difference between high school Year 1 and Year 3 and between Year 2 and Year 3. As a player becomes older (or mature), he strives more strongly to be a professional player. However, a smaller number among Year 3 participants has an implication that those players who are not good enough to continue playing have to give up soccer and choose different career paths. In other words, those players still playing in their final year

Table 83.3 Mean and SD for intensity of professional career orientation on competitive level

Level of experience	N	Mean	SD
National	73	2.63	0.63
County	148	2.30	0.80
None	40	2.20	0.79
Total	261	2.38	0.77

Table 83.4 Mean and SD for intensity of professional career orientation by high school class grade

	N	Mean	SD
Year 1	97	2.23	0.80
Year 2	99	2.33	0.81
Year 3	65	2.67	0.59
Total	261	2.38	0.77

at high school should have a stronger career orientation to become professional players.

References

Iwashima, T., Hamada, K. and Suehiro, T., 1993, A study on the major factors influencing high school athletes' concept of their future and related decision-making. *The Bulletin of National Institute of Fitness and Sports in Kanoya*, 10, 35–41.

Yamamoto, N., 1999, Career developing process and career orientations of elite soccer players in Japanese high school. *Journal of Health Science, Kyushu University*, 21, 29–39.

Yoshida, T., Nakatsuka, Y. and Kurata, Y., 1996, A consideration on the coaches' participation in choosing post-graduation courses of senior high-school soccer athletes. *Kyusyu Journal of Physical Education, Health and Sport Sciences*, 10–11, 41–9.

84 Youth development structures, philosophy and working mechanisms of top-level football clubs

A pan-European perspective

H. Relvas, D. Richardson, D. Gilbourne,
and M. Littlewood

Research Institute for Sport and Exercise Sciences, Liverpool John Moores
University, UK

Introduction

Professional football clubs are now seen as service enterprises engaged in the business of performance, entertainment, and financial profit (Bourke, 2003; Vaeyens *et al.*, 2005). Maguire and Pearton (2000) stated that this entertainment and business perspective of European football is influenced by the finance flowing from media, sponsorship and marketing contracts.

It is possible to identify players in youth categories as future high-level players but frequently when they progress to the professional environment they do not perform or achieve the level expected of them. One must ask what 'things' (e.g., circumstances, experiences) does the player face in the professional environment that he doesn't face in youth development programmes that may influence his performance (Garcés, 2006: 44). Moreover, it seems appropriate to explore the structure and nature of these environments to ascertain whether certain operational conditions are more conducive to the successful progression of young players.

Purpose of youth development

Stratton *et al.* (2004: 183) stated that 'talent development is predominantly associated with the provision of a suitable environment from which potential talent can be realised'. Talent development incorporates social, intellectual, educational, welfare, physiological, physical, and psychological factors. Development itself depends on several elements including the efficiency of the sport organization; human resources; methods of coaching and training; and the application of sports medicine and sports sciences (Maguire and Pearton, 2000). When a player enters a systematic developmental process, the objective is to develop playing ability and nurture the individuals towards realizing their potential (Reilly *et al.*, 2000).

In this sense, a more structured approach to developing talent may reap both sporting and financial rewards (Stratton *et al.*, 2004). It would appear necessary to reduce the risks of the investment (i.e., financial and time intense investments) in youth training (Gonçalves, 2003).

Emerging issues from the complexity of the youth development process

Presently, it would appear that there is a preoccupation to win at all costs, and that club managers prefer to invest in experienced and recognized football players in order to increase their chances of instant success (Maguire and Pearton, 2000). The perceived need to invest in more 'finished' players suggests a lack of readiness in the preparation of the indigenous Academy players. The apparent lack of emerging young talent in the Federations of the Union of European Football Associations (UEFA) and the perceived reluctance of investment in youth development programmes by some clubs (Richardson *et al.*, 2005), have prompted some measures to change this situation. For example, in England, the implementation of the 'Charter for Quality' by the English Football Association (Football Association Technical Department, 1997), focused a concern on the young player's development (Stratton *et al.*, 2004). UEFA established that, by the 2008–09 season, each club should include in its squad four players from its own academy and four others from clubs of the same national association (UEFA, 2005). However, the EU legislation (i.e., freedom of movement) prevents UEFA from restricting player movement within the European Union. As a result, clubs may be encouraged to begin recruitment at a younger age all over the globe.

A structured and coherent development approach

The period between 17 and 21 years of age, which generally concerns the player's transition from the youth to the professional environment, can be considered as a critical development period (Richardson *et al.*, 2005; Vaeyens *et al.*, 2005). This period is not only marked by a high proportion of drop out, but also is heightened by the conflicts of adulthood, difficulties of peer group acceptance (i.e., young players start to interact with the players from the reserves and first team), and adaptability to the professional football environment (Parker, 2001). Further, such a transition is characterized by a heightened level of performance expectation alongside a reduced tolerance for failure. A successful transition in this critical period seems to depend on some external factors such as, the opportunities to play, the absence of injuries, the nature of guidance and training, and personal, social, and cultural factors (Reilly *et al.*, 2000). It has been suggested that young players would benefit from a more structured, coherent and informed development approach in order to aid a player's, practitioner's and/or club's understanding of the complexity of such a critical transition (Richardson *et al.*, 2005).

Present research

The above synopsis of the literature suggests that it is important to explore the factors that influence a young football player's development. Furthermore, it appears pertinent to explore the determinants of a suitable environment, which may facilitate the process of development and help players progress to a higher level. As stated by Durand-Bush and Salmela (2001: 285) 'we cannot change our genetic makeup, but we can change our environment to make it as conducive as possible to improving performance'.

The present study aims to outline the different organizational structures, working mechanisms and philosophy concerning youth development programmes from across Europe. According to Chick (2000), cross-cultural comparative studies in sport have immense potential for the understanding of such phenomena in human culture. This study presents similar and distinct elements of structure, philosophy and practice that exist within 19 top-level clubs across four European countries.

Methods

This research includes top-level clubs from four European countries, namely England ($n = 4$), Portugal ($n = 5$), Spain ($n = 6$), and Sweden ($n = 4$). In order to be included in the study, each club had to be a professional organization playing in the top league of its own country. From the total sample of 19 clubs, 14 have been in European competitions in the seasons 2005–06 or 2006–07. The other five clubs have previously been in European competitions. The study utilized individual semi-structured interviews ($n = 19$) (Biddle et al., 2001) with the Heads of Youth Development (HYD)/Academy Managers (or equivalent representative) from each club. The lead author also collected a range of strategic and operational policy and practice documentation from a range of secondary sources alongside the continual development of unobtrusive field notes concerning the youth development programme from each club (see McFee, 1992). This information was supplemented by informal conversations with youth development staff members, and observation of the youth development environment.

Results and discussion

It was possible to identify two distinct club structures: one where the executive board directly controls both the youth and the professional football environments; and another where a 'sports director' appears to operate as a link between the board and each of the distinct football departments (i.e., youth and professional). Neither of these distinct organizational structures could be associated with any one particular country or culture (see Structures A and B respectively in Figure 84.1).

Two distinct youth development structures were also evidenced. The majority of the clubs appeared to favour the identification of different departments (e.g.

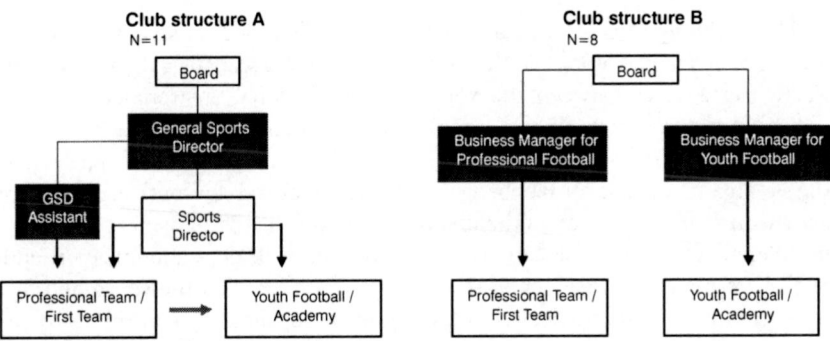

Figure 84.1 Representation of the two types of club structure evidenced within the 19 clubs across 4 European countries

technical, medical) similar to that outlined by Stratton *et al.* (2004) whereas the Swedish clubs operated with age-group personnel teams (i.e., each age group team operated with the same relevant personnel). The clubs from Portugal, Spain, and England, all identified similar departments, although sometimes there appeared to be slightly different operationalization of some designated positions. Specifically, all participant clubs seemed to have similar youth staff members, but their specific roles and responsibilities appeared to vary slightly within each club. For example, some sport psychologists develop their practices as an outside consultant, while others are employed internally by the club. However, it appeared that the role and objectives of the sports psychologist (i.e., whether internally employed or on a consultancy basis) differed across clubs. In some cases, the sports psychologist was only concerned with non-sport aspects (e.g., education, lifestyle) whilst in others they adopted a more performance-oriented approach.

It was clear that the predominant aim of each youth development programme was to develop players for the first team. However, all clubs recognized other benefits of the development process, such as the player's personal development, and financial reward. Similarly, Stratton *et al.* (2004, p.201) stated that 'academies aspire to develop players for the first team or (at least) generate income through the sale of "marketable assets"', and also develop the 'whole' individual. Only the Swedish clubs offered a sense that their purpose was to also develop players for the Swedish national side.

All clubs considered that they provided sportive (sport-related issues), medical, psychological, and social support to their players. Some of them also referred to the fact that they provide academic support (i.e., especially to those players with distinct learning needs that could be provided by the club). The HYDs all stated that they 'staff-develop' their coaches through workshops (e.g., technical, tactical, socio-psychological and lifestyle issues), but only seven clubs stated that they provide (similar) workshops for players and/or parents. Most workshops provided by the clubs did not appear to be strategically located, planned or managed. However, most HYDs recognized that this may be more necessary in the future.

Three different organizational practices were identified. First was one where the fist team trained alongside the older youth team players ($n = 8$); second, one where the contact between the youth and professional environment was co-ordinated through a sports director with no apparent 'direct' contact between the HYD and the first team manager ($n = 5$). The third perspective appeared to suggest that no regular contact between the first team and the youth environment existed ($n = 6$). In some cases the first team and youth environments also existed in different geographical locations. The perceived lack of communication and/or the apparent inconsistency of the contacts (i.e., between the youth and first team environments), particularly in scenario 3, appeared to contribute to the appearance of different 'game' cultures (e.g., attacking versus defensive strategies, a passing style versus a long ball style) within the same club, and some consequent dissatisfaction within the staff members. Strangely, this study only evidenced one circumstance where the first team manager was the direct line manager of the HYD.

The results indicated that there was no evidence of specific philosophies, structures and/or working mechanisms towards youth development that were peculiar to any one particular country. However, it was possible to identify some differences within the organizational structure, e.g., the role and responsibility of the practitioners, the presence, function and operationalization of the reserves (or 'B' teams), the pragmatics of transition from youth to the professional team, communication mechanisms (e.g., first team/youth environment), and the dominant presence of an orientation of more clubs towards the development of young players (i.e., only in Sweden did they offer orientation towards the national side).

Future directions

The perceptions of the 19 HYDs have implied that a range of different organizational structures, working practices and consequently different youth development environments exist across the European countries included in this study. It now seems pertinent that any future work explores the working practices of the youth development practitioners themselves, not only to understand the operationalization of the practitioner's working mechanisms, roles and responsibilities, but also to clarify some concepts and development practices not completely explained or articulated by the HYDs.

It is recommended that further research should attend to the specific training conditions experienced by young players (also see Helsen *et al.*, 2000; Volossovitch, 2003). This research provides further understanding of the environment in youth football development, its culture and its characteristics, which may provide the youth practitioners with tools to better prepare the players for their (difficult) transition from youth to professional football.

References

Biddle, S., Markland, D., Gilbourne, D., Chatzisarantis, N. and Sparkes, A., 2001, Research methods in sport and exercise psychology: quantitative and qualitative issues. *Journal of Sports Sciences*, 19, 777–809.

Bourke, A., 2003, The dream of being a professional soccer player: insight on career development options of young Irish players. *Journal of Sport & Social Issues*, November, 27, 399–419.

Chick, G., 2000, Editorial: opportunities for cross-cultural comparative research on leisure. *Leisure Sciences*, 22, 79–91.

Durand-Bush, N. and Salmela, J., 2001, The development of the talent in sport. In *Handbook of Sport Psychology*, 2nd edn, edited by Singer, R., Hausenblas H. and Janelle, C. (New York: John Wiley).

Football Association Technical Department, 1997, *Football Education For Young Players: "A Charter For Quality"*, (London: The Football Association).

Garcés, E., 2006, Síndrome de Peter Pan – Quando a "jovem promessa" não se torna uma certeza. *Futebolista*, Outubro, 14, 44–6.

Gonçalves, C., 2003, Fórum – Selecção e detecção de talentos. *Treino desportivo*, April, Ano V, 21, 3ª série, 32–3.

Helsen, W.F., Hodges, N.J., Van Winckel, J. and Starkes, J.L., 2000, The roles of talent, physical precocity and practice in the development of soccer expertise. *Journal of Sports Sciences*, 18, 727–36.

Maguire, J. and Pearton, R., 2000, The impact of elite labour migration on the identification, selection and development of European soccer players. *Journal of Sports Sciences*, 18, 759–69.

McFee, G., 1992, Triangulation in research: Two confusions. *Educational Research*, 34 (3), 215–19.

Parker, A., 2001, Soccer, servitude and sub-cultural identity: football traineeship and masculine construction. *Soccer and Society*, 2, (Spring), 59–80.

Reilly, T., Williams, A.M., Nevill, A. and Franks, A., 2000, A multidisciplinary approach to talent identification in soccer. *Journal of Sports Sciences*, 18, 695–702.

Richardson, D., Littlewood, M. and Gilbourne, D., 2005, Homegrown or home nationals? Some considerations on the local training debate. *Insight Live* https://ice.thefa.com/ice/livelink.exe/fetch/2000/10647/466509/477135/477257/Homegrown_or_Home_Nationals._The_Case_for_the_Local_Training_Debate.?nodeid = 675785&vernum = 0 (accessed 20 September 2005).

Stratton, G., Reilly, T., Williams, A.M. and Richardson, D., 2004, *Youth Soccer – From Science to Performance*. (London: Routledge).

UEFA, 2005, Formação recebe luz verde. http://pt.uefa.com/news/newsId = 297234 (accessed 25 April 2005).

Vaeyens, R., Coutts, A. and Philippaerts, R., 2005, Evaluation of the "under-21 rule": Do young adult soccer players benefit? *Journal of Sports Sciences*, 23, 1003–12.

Volossovitch, A., 2003, Fórum – Selecção e detecção de talentos. *Treino desportivo*. April, Ano V, 21 – 3ª série, 34–5.

Index

Lightning Source UK Ltd.
Milton Keynes UK
UKOW030353210312

189323UK00001B/10/P